The United States and the Berlin Blockade, 1948-1949

INTERNATIONAL CRISIS BEHAVIOR PROJECT

Director

MICHAEL BRECHER
Department of Political Science
McGill University

Advisory Board

A. L. GEORGE
Department of Political Science
Stanford University

G. L. GOODWIN
Department of International Relations
London School of Economics

E. HAAS
Institute of International Studies
University of California
Berkeley

C. F. HERMANN
Director
Mershon Center
Ohio State University

K. J. HOLSTI
Department of Political Science
University of British Columbia

O. R. HOLSTI
Department of Political Science
Duke University

K. KNORR
Woodrow Wilson School of Public
and International Affairs
Princeton University

C. A. MCCLELLAND
School of International Relations
University of Southern California

R. C. NORTH
Department of Political Science
Stanford University

G. D. PAIGE
Department of Political Science
University of Hawaii

P. A. REYNOLDS
Department of Political Science
University of Lancaster

T. C. SCHELLING
Kennedy School of Government
Harvard University

R. TANTER
Department of Political Science
University of Michigan

AVI SHLAIM

The United States and the Berlin Blockade, 1948-1949

A STUDY IN CRISIS DECISION-MAKING

UNIVERSITY OF CALIFORNIA PRESS
BERKELEY   LOS ANGELES   LONDON

University of California Press
Berkeley and Los Angeles, California

University of California Press, Ltd.
London, England

© 1983 by
The Regents of the University of California
First Paperback Printing 1989
Library of Congress Cataloging in Publication Data

Shlaim, Avi.
The United States and the Berlin Blockade,
1948–1949.
"International Crisis Behavior Project."
Bibliography: p.
Includes index.
1. Berlin (Germany)—Blockade, 1948–1949.
2. United States—Foreign relations—Soviet Union—
Decision making. 3. Soviet Union—Foreign relations
—United States—Decision making. I. International
Crisis Behavior Project. II. Title.
DD881.S46   943.1'550874   81-19636
ISBN 0-520-06619-7

Printed in the United States of America
1 2 3 4 5 6 7 8 9

To Aida

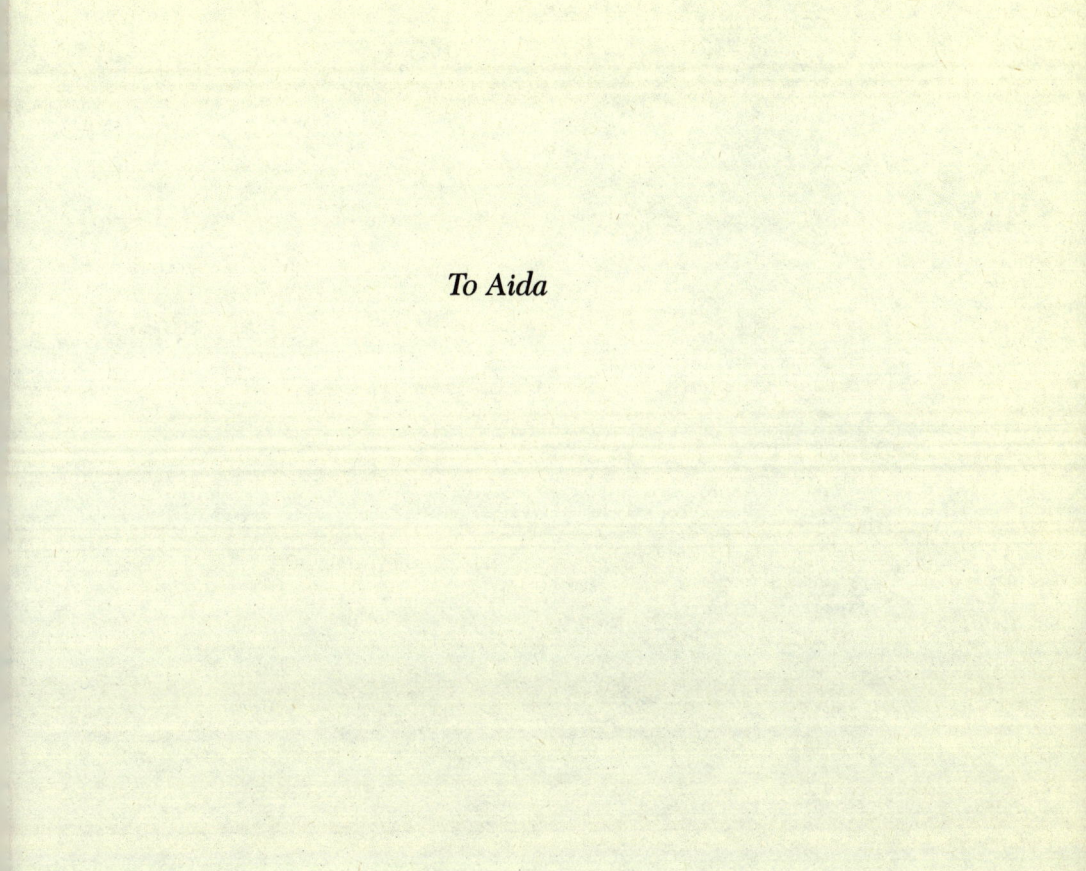

Contents

List of Maps viii
Foreword by Michael Brecher ix
Preface to the Paperback Edition xi
Acknowledgments
List of Abbreviations

PART I: INTRODUCTION

1. Crisis Decision-Making 3
2. Origins of the Berlin Crisis 11

PART II: PRE-CRISIS PERIOD

3. Psychological Environment 43
4. Decision Flow 110

PART III: CRISIS PERIOD

5. Psychological Environment 171
6. Decision Flow 195

PART IV: POST-CRISIS PERIOD

7. Psychological Environment 283
8. Decision Flow 305
9. Conclusions 402

Bibliography 425
Index 445

Maps

1. Germany: Zonal Boundaries, Air Corridors, and Airlift Bases, 1948–1949   13
2. Berlin: Sectors of Occupation   17

Foreword

THE International Crisis Behavior Project was launched in 1975 with the aim of shedding light on a pervasive phenomenon of twentieth-century world politics. Underlying the project are three assumptions: first, that the destabilizing effects of international crises are dangerous to global security; second, that understanding their causes, evolution, actor behavior, outcomes, and consequences is possible by systematic investigation; and third, that knowledge can facilitate the avoidance of crises or their effective management so as to minimize the adverse effects on world order. Our objectives are to discover and disseminate knowledge about international crises between 1930 and 1980, to analyze the effects of stress on coping and choice by decision-makers in crisis situations, and to search for crisis patterns.

In this series on international crises, each author uses the same research design. The reader is informed about the key decision-makers, the type of decisional unit, and the major decisions taken in response to their perception of threat to values, time pressure, and the likelihood that they will become involved in military hostilities before the challenge has been resolved. A detailed narrative is provided of the flow of decisions throughout the crisis, both for its intrinsic interest and to provide the necessary data to illuminate information processing, consultation, and the search for and consideration of alternatives before making critical choices.

Dr. Shlaim has made a splendid contribution to knowledge at two levels. He explores with sensitivity the abundant primary and secondary source materials on one of the turning points in the emerging cold war following the collapse of the Grand Alliance in the late 1940s. And he dissects the images of American decision-makers confronted with what they regarded as the gravest challenge to Western security and Western values by the Soviet Union under Stalin. Throughout his discussion, he displays the skills of an academic historian at their best, combined with the analytic insight of modern social science. All this has been presented with a felicity of style to which many aspire but few attain. The result is a major contribution to our understanding of the Berlin Blockade Crisis of 1948–1949, along with provocative conclusions about how statesmen behave under the stress which invariably accompanies international crises.

The outstanding quality of Dr. Shlaim's book, as well as an illustration of the many lessons to be learned, is best revealed in his concluding remarks: "With respect to the precious cognitive abilities which are so crucial in times of crisis, it has been suggested that the law of supply and demand seems to operate in a perverse manner: as crisis increases the need for these abilities, it also diminishes the supply. A small grain of comfort may be derived from the knowledge that in the intense, critical, and exceptionally protracted superpower confrontation which centered on Berlin, the law of supply and demand did not operate invariably in so perverse and invidious a manner."

Michael Brecher, Director
International Crisis Behavior Project

Preface to the Paperback Edition

THE fortieth anniversary of the lifting of the Soviet blockade of Berlin, a major Western victory in the Cold War, occurs on 5 May 1989. It is highly fitting, therefore, that the paperback edition of this book, originally published in 1983, should also appear in the spring of 1989.

This edition reprints the original text with only a few minor corrections. No major archival sources have become available on the momentous events of 1948–49 since I carried out the research for this book a decade ago. Nor have there been any full-scale studies of the Berlin crisis since the appearance of my book, with one notable exception: Ann and John Tusa's *The Berlin Blockade* (London: Hodder and Stoughton, 1988). But in essence what I had to say still stands, both at the level of diplomatic history and at the level of theories concerning the crisis behavior of states.

Indeed, at both levels recent scholarship has tended to corroborate my conclusions. Historical scholarship on the origins of the Cold War has steadily moved away from the strident polemics of the 1960s toward a more balanced view. A genuine synthesis of previously antagonistic views has been emerging. It is now generally acknowledged that a new stage has been reached, beyond orthodoxy and revisionism, in the historiography of this period. Various labels have been suggested to describe this new school of thought, "postrevisionism" being the most widely accepted. And there is an excellent review of the literature on this subject by the leading proponent of the postrevisionist school of thought—John Lewis Gaddis, "The Emerging Post-Revisionist Synthesis on the Origins of the Cold War," *Diplomatic History,* Summer 1983. My own approach to the Cold War was greatly influenced by John Gaddis and other members of this school of thought. My book deals with only one episode in the history of the Cold War, but I am now inclined, on the basis of subsequent reading and reflection, to present it more consciously as a contribution to the postrevisionist synthesis than I did when I wrote it.

Recent scholarship has also thrown additional light on some specific aspects of the Berlin crisis, such as the role of atomic weapons and the role of Britain. Harry R. Borowski's *A Hollow Threat: Strategic Air Power and Containment before Korea* (Westport, Conn., 1982) contains a discussion of the Berlin crisis and the decision of the United States to move two squadrons of B-29 bombers to Britain at the height of the crisis. The implicit threat of using atomic weapons against the Soviet Union was indeed hollow. In my book I disclosed that the B-29s dispatched to Britain did not carry any atomic bombs and, more surprisingly, the bombers themselves were not of the type that could deliver atomic bombs. But since the crisis is often taken as a rare instance in which the nuclear balance affected superpower diplomacy, the actual size and state of the American nuclear arsenal and its relationship to policy merits careful investigation. This was done by David Alan Rosenberg in "U.S. Nuclear Stockpile, 1945 to 1950," *The Bulletin of the Atomic Scientists*, May 1982. He concluded that since few foreign policy makers had access to accurate information about the strength of the U.S. nuclear arsenal, it is unlikely that the actual size of the stockpile played a significant role in shaping particular Cold War policy decisions. This is not to say that the Russians did not take the implied atomic threat seriously but merely to point out that the atomic bomb itself was less critical as an element of American diplomacy in 1948 than the assumptions and myths surrounding it.

Another aspect of the Berlin crisis on which more information has become available conerns the role played by Britain. There is a general tendency among American students of the Cold War to focus on the principal protagonists, the United States and the Soviet Union, virtually to the exclusion of all other actors. There has been no proper recognition, for example, of the vital contribution made by Britain to the airlift. My own view is that Britain played a major and even decisive part in forging the Western policy of firmness in response to the Soviet challenge. I expounded this view in "Britain, the Berlin Blockade and the Cold War," *International Affairs*, Winter 1983/4. Other scholars, using the offical British documents, have provided a great deal of additional evidence to support the view that the part played by Britain in the management of the Berlin crisis is far greater than is commonly recognized. They include Alan Bullock, *Ernest Bevin: Foreign Secretary, 1945–1951* (London: Heinemann, 1983) and Ann and John Tusa, *The Berlin Blockade*.

The second level at which significant progress has been made since the appearance of this book is that of developing theories about crisis decision-making in general. Here the prevailing orthodoxy is that high degrees of stress are invariably debilitating and undermine policymakers' ability to function effectively in crises. My own view is that this is too simplistic a view and that the impact of stress needs to be differentiated much more carefully than is usually done. During the Berlin blockade, American policymakers displayed an ability to resist or to cope with stress to a surprising degree. In many ways the stress they experienced tended to enhance rather than erode their ability to make sensible decisions. These findings call into question the widely accepted view that stress inevitably impairs performance. While recognizing that too much cannot be made of the conclusions of a single case, I hoped that my argument would be sufficiently convincing to reopen the issue and to prompt a reassessment of the conventional wisdom.

It has therefore been rather encouraging to discover that several other students of the crisis behavior of states share my doubts about the conventional wisdom and that they have independently reached similar conclusions. The greatest contribution here is that of Michael Brecher and other research associates in his International Crisis Behavior Project. Mine was the second volume to appear in the series edited by Michael Brecher, after his own introductory volume in which he set out the scope, aims, and methodology of the project as a whole as well as applying it to two Israeli case studies. Since then, a number of other case studies have been published in the series: Alan Dowty, *Middle East Crisis: U.S. Decision-Making in 1958, 1970, and 1973* (1984); Karen Dawisha, *The Kremlin and the Prague Spring: Decisions in Crisis* (1984); and Geoffrey Jukes, *Hitler's Stalingrad Decisions* (1985). The authors of all these studies, in their various ways, pointed to the need for a radical revision of previously accepted hypotheses. All put forward evidence contradicting the previous consensus on the debilitating effects of stress. None found that there was a *general* increase in cognitive rigidity during the crises, even though they encountered specific instances of such rigidity alongside contrary examples of the positive effects of stress.

Collaboration with other scholars in this international project and the opportunity to compare our findings have confirmed me in my view that the distinction between diplomatic history and international relations theory is largely meaningless and that the best way to develop the latter is through carefully planned case studies. One of the most fruitful trends in foreign policy analysis in recent years has been the growing number of case studies undertaken within an analytical framework and with a view to offering conclusions that go beyond the particular decision or policy being examined. The best exposition of the rationale for this approach known to me is an article by Alexander George, "Case Studies and Theory: The Method of Structured, Focused Comparison." And it seems to me, though I am hardly a detached observer, that the International Crisis Behavior Project is a good example of this approach in action.

Whether the lessons drawn from the experience of an earlier period are still relevant to foreign policy in the contemporary world is another question. Some take the extreme view that no lessons whatever can be derived from past experience because of the uniqueness of historical events, a view summed up in Hegel's aphorism that "the only thing that history teaches is that history teaches nothing." Others may reasonably wonder whether decisions will be made as effectively in crises where the pressure to act is measured in hours rather than in weeks.

My own view is that insights gained from the study of this early postwar confrontation are of continuing relevance to American foreign policy forty years later but that the utmost caution is called for in any attempt to apply the "lessons" of this early success to future nuclear crises because the conditions and the personalities involved could hardly be more dissimilar. Nevertheless, identifying the principal ingredients of Western success in 1948 can serve as a useful general guide to crises management today when the threat of a nuclear conflagration looms ever larger.

It was essentially through a combination of good judgment and skillful use of the limited resources at their disposal that the Truman and Attlee governments carried the day. Their good judgment manifested itself in their ability to distinguish between central and peripheral threats to the security of the Western world and to concentrate on fending off the former. It was also reflected in their measured assessment of actual Soviet intentions on the basis of all the available evidence and the avoidance of simple stereotypes as a guide to action.

As far as the instruments of crisis management were concerned, the Western leaders were fortunate in having at their disposal a range of capabilities that reinforced one another, in marked contrast to NATO's contemporary strategy of heavy reliance on the nuclear end of the spectrum, which severely limits the options available to leaders in times of crisis.

The early postwar leaders also understood the importance of diplomacy in dealing with an adversary, and their implicit threats of force were part of a coherent overall diplomatic strategy for handling the crisis that Clausewitz would have found admirable. Resisting the temptation to get quick results, the Western leaders maintained a continuous and patient dialogue with Moscow that contributed in no small measure to the peaceful resolution of the crisis.

There can, of course, be no certainty that superpower leaders would act as rationally and responsibly in a future nuclear emergency in Europe as did their predecessors in 1948. But the study of history can at least help politicians better understand crises and ways of avoiding them or of minimizing their adverse effects on world order. Politicians, like others, are, of course, free to ignore the lessons of the past and to repeat the mistakes of their predecessors, but it is not mandatory they they do so!

Oxford
December 1988

Avi Shlaim

Acknowledgments

IN THE COURSE of the long journey which led to the completion of this study, I incurred many debts which I would like to acknowledge.

To Michael Brecher, the Director of the International Crisis Behavior Project, I owe a profound debt for inviting me to participate in this challenging scholarly venture, for pointing the way by means of outstanding personal example, for offering incisive comments on successive drafts of this case study of international crisis behavior, and for maintaining just the right degree of pressure on a sometimes reluctant writer.

Alexander George of Stanford University has also had a marked impact on this study. His own work on American foreign policy and policymaking in general has been a major source of intellectual inspiration to me, and I am most grateful to him for the exceptionally detailed and constructive suggestions he made on an earlier draft of this book.

I am equally grateful to several other scholars who have read and made insightful comments on earlier drafts of this book: Peter Campbell, Benjamin Geist, Roger Morgan, Robert Pollard, Keith Sainsbury, Raymond Tanter, and Samuel Wells.

The final revision of this book was carried out while I was a Fellow at the Woodrow Wilson International Center for Scholars in Washington, D.C., and I would like to extend my thanks to the Center and its Director, James H. Billington, for their support. I found the International Security Studies Program to be a congenial and highly stimulating place in which to study American foreign and defense policy, and I am grateful to Samuel Wells, the Program's Secretary, for allowing me to draw on his profound knowledge (and excellent library!) relating to American security, and for all the wise advice and generous help he gave during the year I spent at the Center.

Research for this book was initiated with the help of a grant from the Canada Council. The International Communications Agency provided a grant which enabled me to undertake a research trip to the United States in the spring of 1980.

My thanks also go to John Oneal of Vanderbilt University for giving me useful advice in planning that trip and for letting me see the chapter from his thesis which deals with the Berlin crisis.

Librarians and archivists in the following institutions facilitated access to a large body of primary and secondary sources: the University of Reading; the Library and Press Library of the Royal Institute of International Affairs; the Public Record Office in London; Princeton University; the Harry S. Truman Library in Independence, Missouri; and the National Archives in Washington, D.C. I was particularly fortunate to have Edward Reese as my research consultant in the National Archives and benefited greatly from his remarkable knowledge of the records of its Modern Military Branch.

I wish to record my warm appreciation to Marjorie McNamara, who typed and retyped successive drafts of this book with exemplary patience, skill, and good cheer; to Matthew Sigman, who brought boundless enthusiasm and resourcefulness to the task of preparing the manuscript and bibliography for publication; to Grant Barnes and Phyllis Killen of the University of California Press for their unfailing help; and to Paul Weisser for the invaluable contribution he made in editing the manuscript.

Finally, I should like to thank my wife Gwyneth for her interest, her perceptive comments, and her encouragement throughout many seasons.

September 1981

Abbreviations

ACC	Allied Control Council
AEC	Atomic Energy Commission
CFM	Council of Foreign Ministers
CIA	Central Intelligence Agency
CM	Cabinet Minutes (British)
ERP	European Recovery Program
EUCOM	European Command, United States Army
FO	Foreign Office (British)
FRUS	*Foreign Relations of the United States*
ICB	International Crisis Behavior project
JCS	Joint Chiefs of Staff
NATO	North Atlantic Treaty Organization
NME	National Military Establishment
NSC	National Security Council
OMGUS	Office of Military Government of the United States for Germany
P&O	Plans and Operations Division of the United States Army
PPS	Policy Planning Staff
PRO	Public Record Office (London)
RAF	Royal Air Force
RG	Record Group
SED	Socialist Unity Party of Germany
SMA	Soviet Military Administration
U.K.	United Kingdom
UN	United Nations
USAFE	United States Air Force, Europe
USFET	United States Forces, European Theater
USSR	Union of Soviet Socialist Republics

PART I
Introduction

CHAPTER ONE

Crisis Decision-Making

THE STUDY of crisis is almost as old as the study of international relations, and descriptive accounts of specific crises are legion. But until relatively recently, the study of international crisis has been neither systematic, in the sense of proceeding from explicit definitions and hypotheses, nor cumulative, in the sense of utilizing a comparative approach with a view to generalizing about this class of events. Scholars who have written about particular crises have naturally tended to stress their unique and distinguishing characteristics, and this has tended to obscure the fact that, for all their undoubted differences, crises do evince some recurrent patterns and common properties.

It is only in the last two decades that a sustained effort has been made to study crisis more systematically. Charles McClelland, a leading student in this field, has noted five approaches or foci of attention: "the problem of simply providing satisfactory definitions; the search for adequate classifications of types of crises according to their observed characteristics or attributes; the study of ends, goals and objectives in crises; decision-making under conditions of crisis; and how to plan for and cope with crises."[1]

DEFINITIONS

The problem of providing a satisfactory definition of the term "crisis" is particularly acute when viewed against the general tendency to use this word indiscriminately and without explaining its precise

   1. Charles A. McClelland, "Crisis and Threat in the International Setting: Some Relational Concepts," mimeo, 1975, pp. 1–2. Raymond Tanter distinguishes between crisis anticipation, crisis decision-making, and crisis management and assesses the literature on all three aspects. See his "International Crisis

meaning. It may be reasonable and even inevitable to assume that the meaning of the word will somehow be understood when it is used in everyday discourse. For the purpose of furthering the systematic study of this class of international phenomena, however, it is essential to provide at the outset a precise and rigorous definition.

A survey of the theoretical literature on crisis reveals that two different approaches have been used by scholars to define the concept. On the one hand, there are those scholars who define crisis in terms of the decision-making process within a state, and, on the other hand, there are the scholars who define crisis in terms of the interaction process between states. We may call the former the decision-making approach and the latter the systemic approach.[2]

While researchers who employ the systemic approach are by no means agreed on all definitional details, they are united in viewing crisis as a situation which involves change in the normal interaction patterns between states or in the international system as a whole. The definition suggested by Oran Young is representative of this emphasis on change: "An international crisis, then, is a set of rapidly unfolding events which raises the impact of destabilizing forces in the general international system or any of its subsystems substantially above 'normal' (i.e., average) levels and increases the likelihood of violence occurring in the system."[3] Snyder and Diesing generally agree that crisis is a change born of severe conflict which involves the possibility of violence: "An international crisis is a sequence of interactions between the governments of two or more sovereign states in severe conflict, short of actual war, but involving the perception of a dangerously high probability of war."[4]

In sharp contrast to this definitional approach is the one used by researchers who employ the decision-making perspective. They

---

Behavior: An Appraisal of the Literature," in *Studies in Crisis Behavior*, ed. Michael Brecher (New Brunswick, N.J.: Transaction Books, 1979).

2. The distinction between the decision-making approach and the systemic approach runs like a central thread through *International Crisis: Insights from Behavioral Research*, ed. Charles F. Hermann (New York: The Free Press, 1972). See also James M. McCormick, "International Crises: A Note on Definition," *Western Political Quarterly*, Vol. 31, No. 3 (September 1978).

3. Oran R. Young, *The Intermediaries: Third Parties in International Crises* (Princeton: Princeton University Press, 1967), p. 10.

4. Glenn H. Snyder and Paul Diesing, *Conflict Among Nations: Bargaining, Decision-Making and System-Structure in International Crises* (Princeton: Princeton University Press, 1977), p. 6.

define crisis essentially in terms of the perceptions of the decision-makers of a single state. The central interest of this approach, as its name suggests, lies in the process by which decisions are made during a crisis. Various definitions of crisis have been suggested by researchers who employ the decision-making approach, but the most representative and most widely accepted is that developed by Charles Hermann: "Crisis is a situation that (1) threatens the high-priority goals of the decision-making unit; (2) restricts the amount of time available for response before the situation is transformed; and (3) surprises the members of the decision-making unit when it occurs."[5] Hermann explicitly states that his definition is formulated from the perspective of the decision-makers who are experiencing the crisis: "The situation threatens *their* goals, it surprises *them*, and it is *they* who are faced with short decision time."[6] He also indicates that underlying his definition is the hypothesis that if all three traits are present, then the decision process will be substantially different than if only one or two of the characteristics appear.[7]

The International Crisis Behavior (ICB) project clearly belongs to the decision-making approach rather than the systemic approach to the study of crisis. The case studies of the ICB project, including the present one, are guided by the following definition which was formulated by Michael Brecher:

> A crisis is a situation with three necessary and sufficient conditions, deriving from a change in a state's external or internal environment. All three conditions are perceptions held by the highest level decision-makers of the actor concerned:
> 1. *threat to basic values*, with a simultaneous or subsequent
> 2. *high probability of involvement in military hostilities*, and the awareness of
> 3. *finite time for response to the external value threat.*[8]

This definition builds upon the widely accepted definition enunciated by Hermann, but it also differs from it on a number of essential points. Foremost among these are the omission of "surprise" as

---

5. Charles F. Hermann, *Crises in Foreign Policy: A Simulation Analysis* (Indianapolis: Bobbs-Merrill, 1969), p. 29.
6. Ibid., pp. 33–34; emphasis in the original.
7. Ibid., p. 30.
8. Michael Brecher with Benjamin Geist, *Decisions in Crisis: Israel, 1967 and 1973* (Berkeley: University of California Press, 1980), p. 1.

a necessary condition; the replacement of "short" time by "finite" time for response; and the addition of perceived "high probability of involvement in military hostilities."

The proposed definition concentrates on the perceptions and behavior of the decision-makers of a single state. In this respect it reflects the underlying interest of the decision-making approach in exploring the psychological setting for choice. Crisis is analyzed from the perspective of one state, not from that of all the participants or of the international system. Interaction among states is explored in the form of reactions by the crisis actor to threatening acts by other states. In this specific way, and to this limited extent, the decision-making mode of analysis incorporates some of the elements of the systemic mode. But it does not purport to fully explain the interactions between the participants or system-level phenomena. It is the perceptions and behavior of one crisis actor that are the objects of inquiry.

MODEL

A model of state behavior in international crisis has been constructed by Brecher within a general foreign policy framework which he developed in earlier works.[9] The approach, designated as "structured empiricism," is based on three assumptions: (1) every international crisis for a state can be dissected systematically through time in terms of a foreign policy system; (2) there are universal categories to classify relevant data; and (3) comparable findings can be used to assess the utility of a model, as well as to generate and test hypotheses about the crisis behavior of different types of states. The *independent* variable is perception of crisis as derived from decision-makers' images of changes in the environment. In operational terms, there are three independent—but closely related—perceptual variables: threat, time pressure, and high probability of involvement in military hostilities. The *intervening* variable is coping, as manifested in four processes and mechanisms: information, consultation, decisional forums, and the

---

9. Michael Brecher, Blema Steinberg, and Janice Stein, "A Framework for Research on Foreign Policy Behavior," *Journal of Conflict Resolution*, Vol. 13, No. 1 (March 1969); and Michael Brecher, *The Foreign Policy System of Israel* (London: Oxford University Press, 1972). A useful summary is also provided in Michael Brecher, *Decisions in Israel's Foreign Policy* (London: Oxford University Press, 1974), pp. 3–8.

search for and evaluation of alternatives. The *dependent* variable is choice—that is, decision.[10]

The model postulates a distinct time sequence and causal links among its variables. The trigger events which start a crisis necessarily precede and stimulate perceptual changes on the part of the decision-makers, initially of threat and later of time pressure and high probability of war. These perceptions (the composite independent variable) induce a feeling of stress which leads the decision-makers to adopt one or more coping strategies. Changes in perceptions of crisis do not only affect coping mechanisms and processes. They also condition the content of choices or decisions.

The three independent variables are logically separable: threat refers to value, time to temporal constraint, and war to instrumentality or means. In real life, however, they are closely interrelated. An acute perception of threat to central values, for example, is likely to raise the perceived probability of involvement in military hostilities. Conversely, a decline in the perceived probability of war is likely to ease the time constraints experienced by the decision-makers. Throughout this volume, "stress" or the term "crisis-induced stress" will be used as code words for the perception of threat and/or time pressure and/or probability of war. It is these perceptions, resulting in stress, which set in motion the multiple coping processes and mechanisms.

The instinctive response of the decision-makers, initially, is to seek more information about the threatening event or act. Their probe for further information may be conducted through ordinary, special, or improvised channels. It will be perfunctory, modest, or thorough, depending upon the level of stress. The information may be received with an open mind—that is, objectively—or it may be distorted by bias, ideological preconceptions, past memories, and wishful thinking.

With the initial acquisition of information, decision-makers begin a process of consultation with other members of the high-policy elite, as well as with civilian and military subordinates and, possibly, other persons from competing elites and interest groups. Consultation may be frequent or infrequent, ad hoc or institutional in form, within a large or small circle, comprising one or more groups.

10. This section is based entirely on Brecher, *Decisions in Crisis*, chap. 1. Only a summary outline, however, is presented here. For the original and much fuller exposition of the model, see Brecher's book.

In addition to these things, coping involves the activation of a decisional forum, which varies in size and structure. As with information processing and consultation, the size and type of decisional unit will be influenced by crisis-induced stress.

Search refers to the process of identifying and exploring alternative options, while evaluation refers to the process of calculating the expected costs and benefits of these options with a view to selecting the most satisfactory option. The search for and evaluation of options will be affected by the intensity of crisis-induced stress, especially the amount of time perceived by decision-makers as available for making their choice.

Just as changes in crisis-induced stress will affect some or all coping mechanisms, so too, the model posits, different patterns of choice will be associated with different levels of stress. A three-period model of crisis behavior was designed in order to explore more systematically the changes that take place in the course of a crisis from its inception (the pre-crisis period), through its rising, higher, and peak phases of stress (the crisis period), to its moderating and declining phase (the post-crisis period). The *pre-crisis period* is marked off from the preceding non-crisis period by a conspicuous increase in perceived threat by the decision-makers of the actor under inquiry—an increase which is triggered by an event or cluster of events. The *crisis period* is characterized by the presence of all three necessary conditions of a crisis: a sharp increase in perceived threat to basic values, an awareness of time constraints on decisions, and a perception of the probability of involvement in military hostilities. It, too, begins with a specific event or action. The *post-crisis* period begins with an observable decline in the level of intensity of one or more of the perceptual conditions: threat, time salience, and war probability. It terminates with the reduction in the intensity of these perceptions to the preceding non-crisis level.

This three-stage model of crisis behavior includes two linkages: first, between different levels of crisis-induced stress and coping mechanisms and processes; and, second, between stress levels and choice patterns. One of the tasks of this volume will be to test the validity of this model as a guide to understanding the crisis behavior of states. Apart from illuminating U.S. behavior in the Berlin crisis, the task of a case study, this volume will also test hypotheses generated in Michael Brecher's work and the earlier literature on international crisis, thereby contributing to the search for knowledge and theory about crisis behavior, the primary objective of the ICB project. The inquiry is guided by one overarching research question and several that derive therefrom. All these questions focus on the model and its critical variables. The central question may be stated thus: What is the impact of changing stress, derived from changes in perceptions of threat, time pressure, and the probability of war, on (a) the processes and mechanisms through which decision-makers cope with crisis, and (b) their choices? Following the model, the inquiry will center on nine specific questions. What are the effects of escalating and de-escalating crisis-induced stress on:

information	1. cognitive performance;
	2. the perceived need and consequent quest for information;
	3. the receptivity and size of the information-processing group;
consultation	4. the type and size of the consultative units;
	5. group participation in the consultative process;
decisional forums	6. the size and structure of the decisional forums;
	7. authority patterns within decisional units;
alternatives	8. search for and evaluation of alternatives;
	9. the perceived range of available alternatives.

The structure of this volume is dictated by the analytical division of crisis into three periods. For each period the psychological environment of the decision-makers and the decision flow will be examined in tandem. The psychological environment will establish their predispositional response pattern to a crisis. It consists of two components, attitudinal prism and specific images, and both will be examined. The emphasis, however, will be on perception of crisis, the composite independent variable which encompasses perceptions of threat, time pressure, and the probability of war.

A reconstruction of the decision flow is another essential part of the methodology of this volume—because of the dynamic character of the model. The link between perception of crisis and choice is a continuous process of interaction. The initial set of images or definition of the situation by decision-makers—that is, their interpretation of the environment on the eve of a crisis—predisposes them to choice. These perceptions are mediated through coping mechanisms in a decision-making process which begins with a quest for information and ends with an assessment of options. Once a decision is taken, its implementation affects—and may substantially change—perceptions of the altered environment. That, in turn, leads to new choices in response to new stimuli, filtered through changed coping mechanisms, in a ceaseless flow of perception, decision-making, and choice until the crisis is resolved. Thus, a detailed narrative of the decision flow performs two important functions. First, it illuminates the responsive behavior of the crisis actor as decisions and actions through time. Second, it provides the indispensable data for an analysis of the coping and the decision-making process throughout the crisis, and of the dimensions and patterns of choice by one international crisis actor.

CHAPTER TWO

Origins of the Berlin Crisis

THAT THE IMPOSITION of the Soviet blockade on the western sectors of Berlin on June 24, 1948 constituted a "crisis" for the United States as defined in the last chapter, there can be no doubt. The element of surprise, which has been widely accepted as one of the attributes of crisis, is missing. The American decision-makers were not altogether surprised by the occurrence of the crisis, since they received ample strategic warning, consisting of long-range indicators that the opponent might be preparing to act. Although the exact timing of the blockade was not predicted, the Americans were well aware, from December 1947 onwards, of the possibility and increasing likelihood of a Russian move to oust the Western powers from Berlin. General Lucius D. Clay, the American Military Governor in Germany, and his political adviser, Robert Murphy, not only anticipated the crisis but repeatedly advised their superiors that the Russians could sever the land links from the Western zones of Germany to Berlin at any time and urged Washington to consider in advance its response to this contingency.[1] But the element of surprise is deliberately excluded from our definition of crisis. On the other hand, all the necessary conditions specified in this definition were present: the blockade constituted a change in the external environment which was perceived by the American decision-makers as involving a threat to basic values; there was a high probability of involvement in military hostilities; and there was finite time for response.

---

1. Lucius D. Clay, *Decision in Germany* (New York: Doubleday, 1950), p. 239; Robert Murphy, *Diplomat Among Warriors* (London: Collins, 1964), p. 281. On the distinction between strategic and tactical warning, see Alexander L. George and Richard Smoke, *Deterrence in American Foreign Policy: Theory and Practice* (New York: Columbia University Press, 1974), p. 568.

The basic values threatened were America's entire position vis-à-vis its Cold War adversary in the ongoing contest over Germany and over Europe, as well as the credibility of America's commitments to her allies. A Western withdrawal from Berlin under Soviet compulsion, warned the Central Intelligence Agency (CIA), would "constitute a political defeat of the first magnitude." Maintenance of the isolated position there, while recognized as manifestly difficult and even dangerous, was therefore considered necessary on account of the psychological and practical effects of the presence of an island of Western security in the heart of the Soviet zone, and the implicit assurance it provided of an eventual unification of Germany from the West. Its abandonment, concluded the CIA review, would finally relinquish Eastern Germany to Communism and imply that unification could be accomplished only from the East.[2] President Truman similarly defined the stakes in Berlin as "a struggle over Germany and, in a larger sense, over Europe."[3]

Truman's account makes it equally clear that the determination of the Americans to resist this threat to their basic values carried the danger of military hostilities breaking out either by design or by accident: "Our position in Berlin was precarious. If we wished to remain there, we would have to make a show of strength. But there was always the risk that Russian reaction might lead to war. We had to face the possibility that Russia might deliberately choose to make Berlin the pretext for war, but a more immediate danger was the risk that a trigger-happy Russian pilot or hotheaded Communist tank commander might create an incident that could ignite the powder keg."[4]

The time available to the American decision-makers for deciding on their response to the Soviet blockade was not particularly short, but neither was it unlimited. To maintain their position in Berlin, the American decision-makers had to act before the existing supplies in Berlin, sufficient for thirty days,[5] were exhausted. Apart from these logistical constraints, the symbolic and psychological importance of Berlin militated against indefinite procrastination. These logistical and political constraints, particularly the former,

2. Central Intelligence Agency, "Review of the World Situation as It Relates to the Security of the United States," April 8, 1948, President's Secretary File, Harry S. Truman Library, Independence, Missouri.
3. Harry S. Truman, *Memoirs*, Vol. 2: *Years of Trial and Hope, 1946–1953* (London: Hodder and Stoughton, 1956), p. 130.
4. Ibid., p. 149.
5. Frank Howley, *Berlin Command* (New York: Putnam's, 1950), p. 201.

GERMANY: ZONAL BOUNDARIES, AIR CORRIDORS, AND
AIRLIFT BASES, 1948–1949
Based on Kenneth W. Condit, *The History of the Joint Chiefs of Staff*

left the incumbent decision-makers a finite time for decisional response to the external threat.

Before we turn to an analysis of the psychological environment of the American decision-makers and their behavior during the pre-crisis period, it is essential to place the Berlin crisis in its historical context. Without a detailed grasp of the historical background to this crisis and of the Cold War dynamics which brought it about, it will not be possible to gain a full understanding either of American behavior during the crisis—the central focus of this inquiry—or of Soviet crisis behavior, which constituted the crucial input in shaping American decisions. A reconstruction of the historical setting in which the Berlin crisis unfolded is, accordingly, the principal task of the present chapter.

The 1948 Berlin crisis had its origins in the progressive deterioration in the relations between the Soviet Union and the West which took place in the aftermath of the Second World War and, more specifically, in the divergence of their policies with regard to Germany. At the Potsdam conference (July 17–August 2, 1945), the four victorious allies agreed that occupied Germany was to be governed on the principles of the "five d's": demilitarization, denazification, de-industrialization, decentralization, and democratization. They decided to divide defeated Germany into four zones of occupation—Russian, American, British, and French—but to treat it as a single economic unit through the Allied Control Council (ACC), composed of the commanders-in-chief with a headquarters in Berlin. The ACC, agreed to at Yalta, was charged with exercising "supreme authority in Germany" as a whole. However, each commander-in-chief was to exercise final authority in his zone, thus making the ACC capable of functioning only by unanimous agreement.[6]

Under the terms of the wartime agreements, Berlin was not included in any of the zones but was to be governed by an Allied Kommandatura which reported directly to the ACC. Each ally was to appoint a commandant to take charge of its sector of the city and to represent it on the Kommandatura. Although the city was considered a special area under joint occupation and not part of the

---

6. For the full text of the Potsdam Protocol, see U.S. Department of State, *Foreign Relations of the United States, 1945: The Conference of Berlin (Potsdam)* (Washington, D.C.: U.S. Government Printing Office, 1960), Vol. 2, pp. 1477–98. (Henceforth, this series will be referred to as *FRUS*.)

Soviet zone, no provision was made for access by the Western Allies to their Berlin sectors in the agreement for the joint occupation of Germany.[7] The question was therefore taken up by the military commanders; and in June 1945, General Clay, who was at that time Eisenhower's deputy, accepted as a "temporary arrangement" the allocation of one main road, one rail line, and two air corridors, reserving the right to reopen the question in the ACC. This understanding was not put down in writing because Clay did not want a written agreement which established anything less than the right of unrestricted access. Later he felt that he was mistaken in not making free access to Berlin a condition of withdrawal into the occupation zones, and he candidly admitted that at the time he did not fully realize that the requirement of unanimous consent would enable a Soviet veto in the ACC to block all the efforts of the Western Allies.[8]

This design for the occupation of Germany, which presupposed trust and harmony on the part of the allies, was doomed to failure from the very beginning. That it should have been seriously believed that the four victors could rule Germany through a system which permitted their representatives to proceed only by unanimous agreement can only be attributed to the lingering optimism engendered by the wartime alliance. But that alliance was formed in the first place and was held together for four grueling years by the overriding imperative of defeating Nazi Germany. It was an alliance of necessity par excellence. Once Germany was defeated, there was no longer any compelling reason to subordinate sectoral interests to the common cause. Thus, ironically, but not altogether

---

7. Protocol on Zones of Occupation and Administration of the "Greater Berlin" Area, September 12, 1944 and amendment thereto, November 14, 1944, in U.S. Senate Committee on Foreign Relations. *Documents on Germany, 1944–1959* (Washington, D.C.: U.S. Government Printing Office, 1959), pp. 1–4.

8. On the question of access to Berlin, see Clay, *Decision in Germany*, pp. 25–27; Lucius D. Clay, "Berlin," *Foreign Affairs*, Vol. 41, No. 1 (October 1962); Philip E. Mosely, "The Occupation of Germany," *Foreign Affairs*, Vol. 28, No. 4 (July 1950); Michael Balfour and John Mair, *Four-Power Control in Germany and Austria, 1945–1946* (London: Oxford University Press, 1956); Robert Spencer, "The Berlin Dilemma," in Edgar McInnis, Richard Hiscocks, and Robert Spencer, *The Shaping of Postwar Germany* (London: Dent, 1960); William M. Franklin, "Zonal Boundaries and Access to Berlin," *World Politics*, Vol. 16, No. 1 (October 1963); Tony Sharp, *The Wartime Alliance and the Zonal Division of Germany* (London: Oxford University Press, 1975); and Daniel J. Nelson, *Wartime Origins of the Berlin Dilemma* (University, Alabama: University of Alabama Press, 1978).

surprisingly, the attainment of the alliance's ultimate goal carried within it the seeds of its own disintegration.

The defeat of Nazi Germany created a power vacuum in Central Europe. The question of what and who would fill that important vacuum was of central importance to the security interests of both the Russians and the Western Powers. The task of the victorious statesmen was to find a way of dealing with this power vacuum without jeopardizing the cooperative relationship which they had developed during the war. This task was rendered even more difficult by the fact that the precarious prewar international order—propped up by an unstable balance-of-power system and an ineffectual League of Nations—was completely destroyed by the war. As a result, Roosevelt, Churchill, and Stalin had the additional task of agreeing upon and proceeding to create a new international order for the postwar era, and at the same time they had to arrange matters temporarily in Central Europe in such a way as to avoid an immediate struggle as to who and what was to fill that important power vacuum. The three leaders did address these fundamental questions during the war. Various options were available, notably a clear-cut spheres-of-influence agreement, but this was precluded largely by the constraints of American public opinion. Roosevelt's effort to reincarnate a version of the Concert of Europe system in place of a more competitive and conflict-prone balance-of-power system was tried but eventually failed, as he himself realized shortly before his death. And in the absence of a broad consensus on the nature of the postwar international order, the chances that a satisfactory solution could be found to the problem confronting the victors in Central Europe appear in retrospect to have been virtually nonexistent.

The German problem dominated inter-Allied relations in peace as it had done during the war. The difference was that after the unconditional surrender of the Third Reich in May 1945, there was no longer any positive agreement on what should be done with Germany. Germany occupied the center of Europe. Her geostrategic location and her formidable industrial potential made her a crucial factor in the European and global balance of power. Whichever side controlled this vital center could dominate the whole of Europe and tilt the global balance of power against its rival. Lenin's watchword, "Whoever has Germany has Europe," had lost nothing of its truth or relevance. And it is not necessary to assume that either Russia or the West set out deliberately to gain control over the

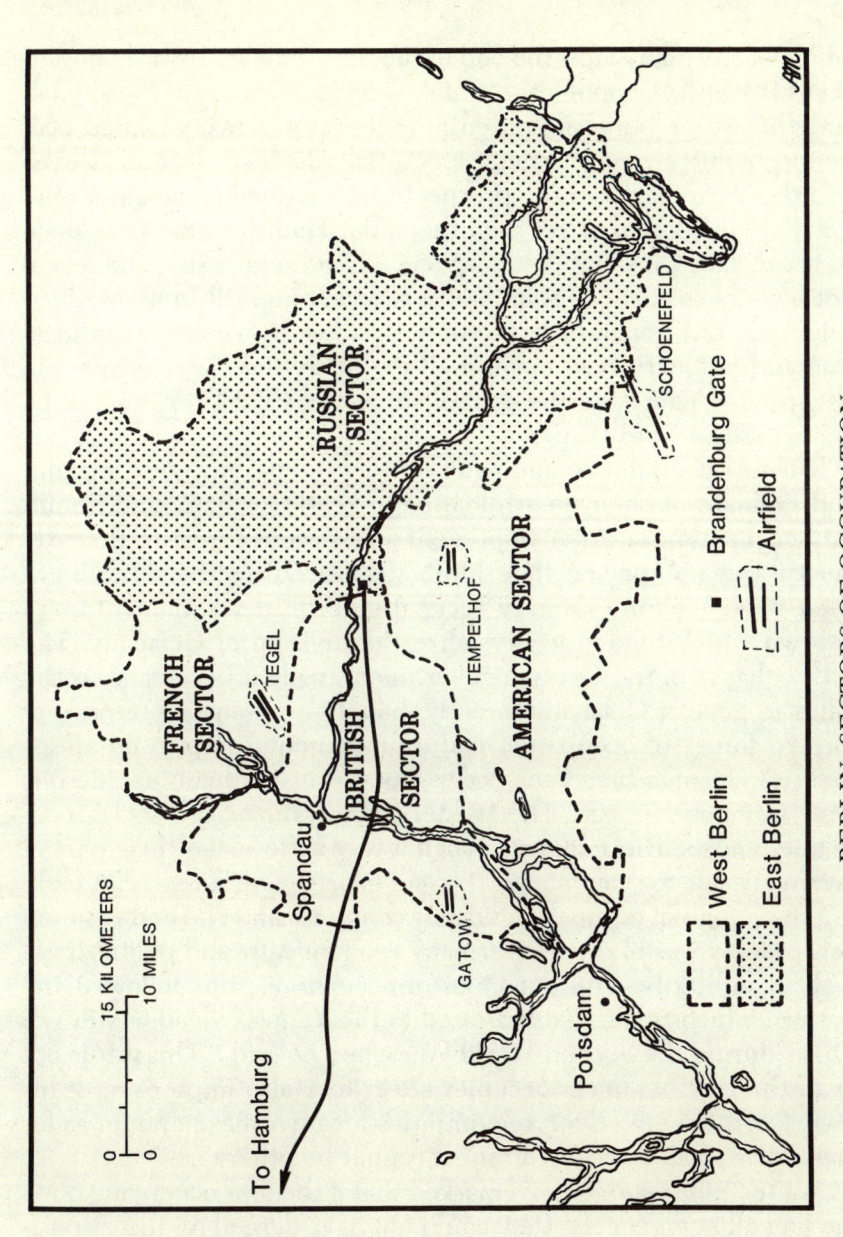

BERLIN: SECTORS OF OCCUPATION

Based on Colin Brown and Peter Mooney, *Cold War to Detente*

whole of Germany after the end of the Second World War to understand the ensuing conflict in which Germany was both the symbol and the major bone of contention. It was Germany's huge economic, political, and strategic potential which made both Russia and the West fearful of the prospect that a unified Germany would gravitate into the orbit of the other side. Had the stakes not been so great, had Germany been merely a peripheral issue, she would not have necessarily precipitated a fundamental rift in inter-Allied relations. But her importance to both sides, by virtue of her location and potentialities, made it all too likely that Germany would become the heart and the central subject of what later came to be known as the Cold War.

The one common denominator uniting Russia, America, Britain, and France was their determination to keep Germany under military occupation in order to prevent a resurgent threat to their security. But no specific time limit was placed on the duration of their presence, and military occupation acquired a momentum of its own which tended to crystalize the division of Germany. The total collapse of the German government made it necessary for the allies to govern Germany directly, but the prolonged presence of foreign forces of occupation had a fundamental impact on all aspects of German life. Each occupying power gradually molded its zone in its own image. The Western Powers managed social, economic, and political affairs in such a way as to make their part of Germany safe for capitalism. Russian efforts were directed at making their zone of occupation safe for communism. The end result of this process was to divide Germany economically and politically as well as militarily. The dynamics of occupation thus followed the pattern which Stalin had indicated to the Yugoslav leader Milovan Djilas during the Second World War when he said: "This war is not as in the past; whoever occupies a territory also imposes on it his own social system. Everyone imposes his own social system as far as his army has power to do so. It cannot be otherwise."[9]

Walter Lippmann once remarked that if the four occupying powers had all been angels, they could not have agreed on the disposition of Germany. Each was driven by hard necessity to defend perceived interests and pursue policies which, as a result of their incompatibility, produced a frustrating impasse. Britain found her-

---

9. Milovan Djilas, *Conversations with Stalin* (Harmondsworth, England: Penguin, 1962), p. 90.

self in the most acute predicament. Her zone contained the industrial Ruhr district, but this area was also the most ravaged by war and was capable of producing only about 40 percent of its food requirements. Given the parlous state of the British economy, not to mention popular feelings towards the German nation, Britain strongly resented having to expend her scarce dollar resources, at a time of food rationing at home, on feeding her populous zone in Germany. The British Government therefore insisted that means be found to make Germany pay her own way. Very soon after Potsdam, the British concluded that the division of Germany would probably be permanent, and they proposed that the United States and France cooperate with them in the three zones. America was receptive to this idea because her zone was also a deficit area, and she, too, resented having to feed an enemy that she had defeated at such a high cost. But the French Government was adamant in opposing the implementation of the Potsdam agreement to treat Germany as a single economic unit. France wanted a Carthaginian peace with massive reparations, the annexation of the coal-rich Saar, and a permanently dismembered Germany. She consistently used her veto on the Allied Control Council to block any move to create a centralized administration for Germany.

Of all the four allies, Russia had least cause for dissatisfaction with the provisions of the Potsdam agreement. The nub of the agreement was to sap Germany's war-making potential and to keep her weak and impotent, and this served to allay Soviet fears about the possible recrudescence of German militarism. The Potsdam agreement also endorsed the principle, if not the figure, of large-scale reparations. The zone allocated to Russia for occupation was more balanced than the others: it was self-supporting in food and had adequate stocks of coal to keep its light industries going. Not surprisingly, therefore, "the Kremlin regarded the decisions on Germany as a great victory for Soviet diplomacy" and set out to extract the greatest possible advantage from this victory.[10] But while placing tremendous value on Communist success in Germany, the Kremlin evidently failed to develop a clear and consistent policy towards the defeated enemy between 1945 and 1949. Moscow was pulled in two contradictory directions. On the one hand, the thirst

10. Gregory Klimov, *The Terror Machine: The Inside Story of the Soviet Administration in Germany*, translated from the German by H. C. Stevens (London: Faber and Faber, 1953), p. 147.

for revenge, the fear of a revived Germany, and the desperate plight of the war-ravaged Russian economy combined to push for a punitive policy of extracting as much as possible out of Germany in the way of material goods and services. On the other hand, the long-term hope of bringing the whole of Germany into its sphere of influence prompted the Kremlin, on some occasions, to pose as the champion of German unity.[11] This schizophrenic attitude produced some strange and striking contradictions which utterly belie the notion, popular in America during the Cold War, that Russian policy was directed by a master plan for the communization of Germany and that this single-minded and ruthless policy was alone responsible for the breakdown of Allied cooperation and the ultimate partition of Germany. Soviet policy is best seen as issuing, not from a coherent and monolithic master plan, but from various aims and considerations, some of them contradictory.[12]

The partition of Germany was not the product of a unilateral policy by one Power, still less of one clear-cut decision, but of a gradual historical process. The policies which led to it emerged from a series of pragmatic responses to changing circumstances, and the American role in this process was by no means confined to reacting to Soviet initiatives. Subsequent manifestations of Soviet

---

11. On the paradoxes and contradictions of Soviet policy towards Germany, see Isaac Deutscher, *Stalin: A Political Biography*, revised edition (Harmondsworth, England: Penguin, 1966), pp. 522–523; Adam B. Ulam, *Expansion and Coexistence: Soviet Foreign Policy 1917–1973*, 2nd edition (New York: Praeger, 1974), pp. 440–443; Djilas, *Conversations with Stalin*, p. 119; and Wolfgang Leonhard, *Child of the Revolution*, trans. C. M. Woodhouse (London: Collins, 1957), especially pp. 326–327.

12. This view is expounded at length by Hans-Peter Schwarz, *Vom Reich zur Bundesrepublik* (Berlin: Luchterhand, 1966). The revisionist historians of the Cold War are far more nearly right than the orthodox ones in their treatment of Soviet policy towards Germany. In his generally critical assessment of the revisionist literature, Stanley Hoffmann wrote: "They are right in pointing out the ambivalence of the Soviet Union towards Germany and the constant oscillation of Soviet policy between two possible lines: joint control of the whole of Germany with the Western powers, if at all possible, and—only if this is not possible—partition. Neither line entailed exclusive Soviet domination of all Germany. The revisionists are right in stating that the Soviets were concerned essentially with preventing Germany from becoming a Western, and potentially anti-Soviet, preserve, and did not set up the East German regime until after the United States and Britain began to organize a West German entity. Thus the tragedy of partition grew out of Anglo-American hostility to the idea of a neutralized Germany under four-power control." "Revisionism Revisited," in *Reflections on the Cold War*, ed. Lynn M. Miller and Ronald W. Pruessen (Philadelphia: Temple University Press, 1974), pp. 10–11.

assertiveness tend to obscure the extent to which, initially, the Soviet Union exhibited both caution and willingness to collaborate with the other victors in implementing the wartime decisions in Germany. In 1945–46, relations between American and Russian officials were in fact reasonably harmonious and cooperative.[13] The real villains in American eyes during this period were not the Russians but the French, who obstructed the creation of a central administration in their determination to dismember Germany. It was not until the spring of 1946 that Germany became a subject of real contention between America and Russia, and the first open breach occurred in May with the suspension of promised deliveries of capital goods from the Western zones to the Russian zone in Germany.[14]

The Americans were beginning to suspect that the real motive behind the Russian approach to the German problem was not legitimate and defensive but offensive and expansionist. Soviet opposition to rehabilitation measures designed to make Germany economically self-supporting was taken as evidence of Moscow's intention to move the whole of Germany into the Soviet sphere of influence. Unilateral measures carried out by the Soviets in their own zone of occupation and proposals they made within the framework of four-power discussions were seen, not as discrete actions corresponding to various strands of Soviet foreign policy, but, increasingly, as part of a carefully conceived and deliberate master plan for the communization of Germany. Robert Murphy warned Secretary of State Byrnes on February 24, 1946 that Moscow might be exploiting the delay in implementing the Potsdam call for central German administrative departments in order to consolidate its hold over its own zone as a prelude to pressing for a reunified Germany under Russian auspices.[15]

Mounting doubts over Russia's ultimate aims in Germany coincided with growing dissatisfaction in the United States Government with the nature and consequences of the Potsdam agreement. The two developments were closely related, for it was felt that the Potsdam provisions for a harsh and punitive peace paved the way for the spread of communist influence in Germany. The corollary of this line of argument was that by helping Germany

13. Clay, *Decision in Germany*, pp. 104–111.
14. Manuel Gottlieb, *The German Peace Settlement and the Berlin Crisis* (New York: Paine-Whitman, 1960), chap. 8.
15. *FRUS, 1946*, Vol. 5, pp. 505–507.

to get back on its feet economically, America would also help to check the spread of communism. Thus, the two developments—suspicion of Russia and dissatisfaction with the Potsdam agreement—converged to bring about a shift in America from the initial position of treating Germany as a single economic unit through inter-Allied collaboration, to a policy which aimed at the partition of Germany and the building up of a separate German state allied to the West.

Although the decision to set up a separate West German state was not taken until 1948, it is clear from the official American documents that the idea was already germinating in the minds of some policymakers two years earlier.[16] George Kennan, the United States chargé in Moscow, was among the first to point out that the provisions for the centralized agencies for Germany which were envisaged in the Potsdam agreement but frustrated by France were not necessarily in America's interest. On March 6, 1946, he warned against undue optimism about central agencies serving to break down exclusive Soviet control in the Soviet zone. He regarded as a major mistake the decision taken at Potsdam to "provisionally" allocate German territories east of the Oder-Neisse line to Polish and Russian administration. This, he believed, left America with only two alternatives: (1) to leave the remainder of Germany nominally united but extensively vulnerable to Soviet political penetration and influence, or (2) to endeavor to rescue the Western zones of Germany by walling them off against eastern penetration and integrating them into the international pattern of Western Europe rather than into a unified Germany. Kennan went on to say that he was sure the Russians themselves were confident that if a rump Germany west of the Oder-Neisse line were to be united under a single administration, there would be no other single political force there which could stand up against a Left-Wing bloc with Russian backing.[17] Ambassador Bedell Smith, writing from Moscow on April 2, after a visit to Germany, agreed with Kennan's estimate that it was "probably the Soviet policy to create in Eastern Germany an anti-fascist republic as a preliminary to a Soviet socialistic state, or at least a state oriented directly towards Moscow. . . . Undesirable as this is from our point of view, we may be unable to

16. For an excellent review of the documents on Germany for 1946, 1947, and 1948 published in the *FRUS* series, see Geoffrey Warner, "The Division of Germany, 1946–1948," *International Affairs*, Vol. 51, No. 1 (January 1975).

17. *FRUS, 1946*, Vol. 5, pp. 516–520.

prevent it, and we should adopt a line of action which, while proceeding in the direction of our own ideal of a central government, will on the way produce a western Germany oriented towards western democracy."[18]

The shift of American foreign policy in the direction of the second option outlined by Kennan and supported by Smith was not sudden but gradual and incremental.[19] Differences of opinion inside the Truman Administration and lingering hopes of continuing partnership with the Soviet Union slowed down the pace of change. An important attempt was made by Byrnes at the Paris meeting of the Council of Foreign Ministers, which extended over two sessions in April–May and June–July 1946, to ascertain Russian intentions concerning Germany. In April 1946, Byrnes formally presented a proposal for a four-power treaty to keep Germany disarmed for twenty-five years.[20] Stalin had welcomed the idea when it was suggested to him by Byrnes in December 1945 as a means of reassuring Russia against the danger of a renewed attack by Germany and ensuring the long-term disarmament and demilitarization of Germany. In Paris, however, the Russian Foreign Minister, Vyacheslav Molotov, reacted to the proposal with irrelevant arguments, which led Byrnes to conclude that the Russians did not want the United States involved in the maintenance of European security for fear that the pressure of American power would restrict their own freedom of action as the predominant military power in

18. Ibid., pp. 535–536.
19. Traditionalist historians of the Cold War, such as Herbert Feis and Arthur Schlesinger, seeing a consistent purpose and a clear-cut expansionist thrust behind Russia's policy in Germany, have tended to portray American policy as an unavoidable response to the Russian challenge. The revisionist historians, while providing a useful corrective to the orthodox view by emphasizing the ambivalence of Russian policy, have erred in the opposite direction by portraying American policy as emanating from a clear and consistent design for economic expansion. Denying that American policy was a response to a Russian threat, the revisionists assert that it was the product of economic imperialism which demanded free-market economies abroad in order to make the world safe for the American brand of capitalism. This line of argument, represented by William A. Williams, Joyce and Gabriel Kolko, Bruce Kuklick, and others, frequently ends up by placing exclusive responsibility for the Cold War and for the division of Germany at America's doorstep. More recently, the common denominator of these two conflicting interpretations—a governing grand design—has been persuasively challenged by a monograph based on primary sources. See John H. Backer, *The Decision to Divide Germany: American Foreign Policy in Transition* (Durham, N.C.: Duke University Press, 1978).
20. Draft Treaty, April 30, 1946, *FRUS, 1946*, Vol. 2, pp. 190–193.

Europe.[21] On July 12, the last day of the council meeting, Byrnes entreated Molotov to tell him what was really in the Russian heart and mind on the subject of Germany. "The Soviet Union," Molotov replied, "wanted what it had asked for at Yalta—10 billions of dollars of reparations and also participation with the United States, the United Kingdom and France *in a four-power control of the industries of the Ruhr.*" Byrnes stated in his memoirs that he was inclined to believe that this statement represented the real desires of the Soviet High Command,[22] but American foreign policy continued to be based on the assumption that Russia's ultimate aims in Germany went much further than reparations and participation in four-power control of the Ruhr. There is no trace of this alleged belief in Byrnes's conduct during the final phase of the Paris meeting. In fact, the Secretary appears to have shared the contrary belief, prevalent in the American delegation, that the Soviet government did not desire to reach a German settlement, because the deteriorating economy there was creating conditions favorable to the spread of communism. General Clay recorded that Byrnes agreed with him that the continued government of Germany as four separate zones could only lead to economic collapse and political deterioration and that this persuaded him of the need to move forward in consolidating the zones.[23]

The famous invitation issued by Byrnes on July 11 at the meeting of the Council of Foreign Ministers should be seen against this background of growing concern over the course of events in Germany. It was an invitation to all of the other occupying powers to merge their zones with the American zone to form an economic union. Britain accepted in principle immediately, while France demurred. Both traditionalist and revisionist historians, for different reasons, see Byrnes's initiative as an important landmark in the history of the Cold War. Typical of the traditionalists is John Lewis Gaddis, who wrote that Byrnes "became convinced that the Russians would never allow the implementation of the Potsdam Accords, and from this time on moved towards the concept of a divided Germany as the only alternative to a Russian-dominated Reich."[24] For the revisionists, Byrnes's offer is part of a preconceived

21. James F. Byrnes, *Speaking Frankly* (London: Heinemann, 1947), pp. 171–176.
22. Ibid., p. 194; emphasis in the original.
23. Clay, *Decision in Germany*, pp. 130–131.
24. John Lewis Gaddis, *The United States and the Origins of the Cold War, 1941–1947* (New York: Columbia University Press, 1972), p. 328.

plan for splitting Germany and "dishing" the Russians, and, in a larger sense, is indicative of the American thrust towards economic hegemony via the open door.[25] The relevant documents of the Paris meeting, however, do not support either of these interpretations.[26] As John Gimbel has pointed out, they show that Byrnes's offer was tactical in nature and hastily conceived, reflective of past failures rather than future plans, and responsive to a British move rather than offensive towards the Soviet Union.[27] As so often in the history of the Cold War, the conclusions suggested by the actual records are rather more mundane than those advanced by committed historians.

Byrnes's major policy speech in Stuttgart on September 6, 1946 is another "turning point," so beloved of historians, in the evolution of postwar U.S. policy towards Germany. In this speech, the Secretary publicly acknowledged that the economic provisions of the Potsdam agreement were not working; he pledged continuing American commitment to European security; and he promised American support for Germany's economic recovery and progress towards self-government.[28] Clay hailed this speech as "the first expression by a high American official of our firm intent to maintain our position in Europe," and he added elsewhere that it marked "a definite change in American policy."[29] The speech was made, in fact, following vigorous lobbying by Clay himself, and its text very closely followed a detailed memorandum summarizing United States policy and objectives in Germany which he himself had submitted on July 19.[30] Most historians, echoing Clay, view Byrnes's Stuttgart speech as representing an important reversal of America's position in Germany, which now preferred a permanent division of

25. See, for example, Bruce Kuklick, *American Policy and the Division of Germany: The Clash with Russia Over Reparations* (Ithaca: Cornell University Press, 1972), p. 220.

26. *FRUS, 1946*, Vol. 2, pp. 896–900.

27. John Gimbel, "Cold War Historians and the Occupation of Germany," in *U.S. Occupation in Europe After World War II*, ed. Hans A. Schmitt (Lawrence: Regents Press of Kansas, 1978), pp. 91–92. This article, which I followed when analyzing Byrnes's invitation to zonal union, is equally interesting for its critical treatment of the contending interpretations of Clay's reparations suspension, Byrnes's Stuttgart speech, and Marshall's Harvard speech of June 5, 1947.

28. *Department of State Bulletin*, September 15, 1946, pp. 496–501.

29. Clay, *Decision in Germany*, p. 79; and Lucius D. Clay, *Germany and the Fight for Freedom* (Cambridge, Mass.: Harvard University Press, 1950), p. 23.

30. Jean Edward Smith, ed., *The Papers of General Lucius D. Clay: Germany, 1945–1949* (Bloomington: Indiana University Press, 1974), Vol. 1, pp. 236–243.

the country, and they differ mainly on the merits of this reversal. Traditionalists see the speech as a timely and welcome response to Molotov's German policy statement of July 10 in Paris. Revisionists see it as an American initiative, in line with the broader Cold War strategy of the Truman Administration, which, in the words of Lloyd C. Gardner, "put the U.S. on the political and ideological offensive in Germany."[31] The background and text of Byrnes's speech, however, suggest that it was designed for the benefit of the Germans and America's European allies, rather than as a response to the Russians, and that it represented an acknowledgment rather than a reversal of the direction of American policy. To Clay and the occupational establishment which he headed, the speech was helpful in dispelling any doubts concerning America's intention to remain in Germany and Europe and in lending the official stamp of approval to their efforts to revive Germany. As two American officials put it, the speech "crystallized and made official the policies which the U.S. Military Government officers had been hammering out, slowly and painfully, in Berlin during the previous year."[32] To the Germans, the speech made an important overture by publicly renouncing the harsh provisions of JCS 1067 and holding out the hope of economic recovery, the reduction of occupational controls, and the gradual regaining of international acceptance under American auspices. Byrnes appealed to the French by conceding their claim to the Saar, while the intention to proceed to a formal merger of the British and American zones into Bizonia was now officially announced. The cumulative effect of all these moves amounted to an unofficial burial of the Potsdam agreement.

In 1947, mutual suspicions became more entrenched and widespread, and they served to fuel and intensify the struggle for Germany. Russian-American disagreements over the concrete issues of reparations and finance developed into a wider confrontation over the future of Germany in which each side suspected the other of wanting to dominate the whole country. The American policymakers were in fact preoccupied with the three Western zones, having long since abandoned any hope of influencing the Soviet

31. Gimbel, "Cold War Historians," pp. 93–94. The quotation is from Lloyd C. Gardner, "America and the German 'Problem,' 1945–1949," in *The Politics and Policies of the Truman Administration*, ed. Barton J. Bernstein (Chicago: Quadrangle, 1970), p. 134.

32. B. U. Ratchford and W. D. Ross, *Berlin Reparations Assignment* (Chapel Hill: University of North Carolina Press, 1947), p. 195.

zone; but in 1947, American policy towards Germany emerged more clearly. The "chief if unvoiced objectives" of the emergent American policy were described by a critical White House aide as follows: "to revive German production of all kinds as rapidly as possible; to create a West German state under a conservative government; to prevent the Soviet Union from participating in the control of the Ruhr; and to ally the West German people to the Western bloc." The same aide observed that the forces pushing for a strong Germany comprised a wide variety of men and motives. There were strategists of the Churchillian school who saw Germany as a potential part of a Western military alliance against Russia. There were industrialists and financiers who wanted to profit from a German economic revival. And there were conservative political forces in Congress and elsewhere who advocated a policy of untrammeled German revival under the slogan "Get Germany off the American taxpayer's back."[33]

When George C. Marshall succeeded Byrnes as Secretary of State in January 1947, he was subjected to strong pressure from different quarters, outside as well as inside the Truman Administration, to swiftly consolidate and strengthen Western Germany. The question of a German peace settlement dominated the agenda of the meeting of the Council of Foreign Ministers which opened in Moscow on March 10, 1947, but by this time the real options available to Marshall were severely limited, and the basic American diplomatic approach, prompted partly by fear of Soviet leverage in manipulating a German government, was to contain rather than to negotiate.[34] This was dramatically highlighted by the enunciation of the Truman Doctrine, which was tantamount to a public declaration of the Cold War, two days after the opening of the conference. On the way to Moscow, Marshall and other members of the American delegation stopped in Berlin for consultations with Clay and Murphy. They discussed a memorandum which John Foster Dulles had prepared, analyzing the European situation. It emphasized the danger from either a Germany susceptible to political penetration by the Soviet Union or a Germany independent of both East and West which would have enormous bargaining power. The memorandum concluded that "the European settlement should

33. Albert Z. Carr, *Truman, Stalin and Peace* (New York: Doubleday, 1950), pp. 191–192.
34. Backer, *The Decision to Divide Germany*, p. 167.

seek primarily to solidify and strengthen Western Europe." According to Dulles's account, there was general acceptance of the view that Germany should not be dealt with as an isolated problem; and Secretary of State Marshall, although new to this post, had an immediate grasp of the total strategy involved.[35] A vital element of this strategy, and one which Dulles continued to emphasize privately throughout the actual conference, concerned the need to gain French goodwill, without which there could be no integrated West into which Germany could be drawn.[36]

At the Moscow conference, the fundamental differences between America and Russia on all the vital questions, ranging from reparations and economic unity to the peace treaty, a German government, and borders, produced an unbreakable impasse. There was no meeting of minds, and no real negotiations took place. The inflexible positions taken up by the American delegation indicated that it saw no possibility of a settlement based on four-power agreement. Molotov's criticisms of the Western disregard for Potsdam remained relatively muted, but the precise nature of the broader settlement which he sought for Germany remained shrouded in obscurity. That Russia opposed the rebuilding and possible rearming of Germany by the West was clear enough, but what it wanted instead was far from clear. Molotov's proposals for the establishment of a central government for Germany and for ending the occupation of the country "when the Allied Powers recognize that the basic objectives of the occupation of Germany have been achieved"[37] were open to any interpretation. His more concrete and clearly defined proposals related to $10 billion in reparations, the placing of the Ruhr industrial basin under four-power control, and recognizing the permanence of the Oder-Neisse line. These demands were not unreasonable in themselves, and they made sense in terms of Russia's pressing economic needs, her fear that the industrial potential of Germany would be used against her, and her relations with Poland. But the Western negotiators viewed these demands collectively as part of a Russian "grand design" for

35. John Foster Dulles, *War or Peace* (New York: Macmillan, 1950), p. 102.
36. Ibid., p. 103; John Gimbel, *The American Occupation of Germany: Politics and the Military, 1945–1949* (Stanford: Stanford University Press, 1968), pp. 120–123.
37. V. M. Molotov, *Problems of Foreign Policy: Speeches and Statements, April 1945–November 1948* (Moscow: Foreign Publishing House, 1949), p. 441. The full texts of Molotov's statements at the Moscow conference appear on pp. 343–456.

ultimate communist mastery over Germany. The ambiguities of the Russian position and the confused manner in which it was presented accentuated these apprehensions.

Stalin tried to put the East-West differences which emerged at the conference in their proper perspective at an informal meeting with Secretary of State Marshall. "It is wrong," Stalin said, "to give so tragic an interpretation to our present disagreements." These were "only the first skirmishes and brushes of reconnaissance forces" on Germany. Differences had occurred in the past on other questions, he went on, and as a rule "when people have exhausted themselves in dispute, they recognize the necessity for compromise."[38] Marshall, however, viewed Stalin's appeal for patience as a sinister invitation to allow Germany and Europe to drift towards economic chaos, which would only pave the way for the spread of Communist power, and his determination to prevent this eventually led to the Marshall Plan.[39] More immediate was his decision to abandon the policy of trying to attain American-Soviet agreement on Germany as a unit, once he realized that no solution could be worked out in concert with the Russians. At this point, according to Murphy, the Secretary determined to amalgamate the zones of the Western powers into a single economic and political unit. On the way back from Moscow, he stopped again in Berlin and instructed General Clay to proceed vigorously with the strengthening of Bizonia and to expedite the upward revision of the level of bizonal industry to ensure the self-sufficiency of the area.[40] Another important change was Marshall's concentration, evidently following Dulles's advice, on Russian obstruction as the primary cause of the German problem, ignoring the prior role of France in preventing the creation of central agencies for Germany. The urge to accommodate France, as the State Department papers confirm, outweighed all other considerations at Moscow, and it certainly helped to bring the three Western powers into a closer partnership.[41]

38. Walter Bedell Smith, *Moscow Mission, 1946–1949* (London: Heinemann, 1950), pp. 211–212.
39. Dean Acheson, *Sketches from Life* (London: Hamish Hamilton, 1960), p. 150; Charles E. Bohlen, *The Transformation of American Foreign Policy* (New York: Norton, 1969), pp. 87–88.
40. Charles W. Sydnor, "Some Architects of U.S. Occupation Policy Respond: Summary of a Roundtable," in Schmitt, *U.S. Occupation in Europe*, p. 134; and Clay, *Decision in Germany*, p. 174.
41. Gimbel, *The American Occupation of Germany*, pp. 121–123; Dulles, *War or Peace*, pp. 103–105; and *FRUS, 1947*, Vol. 2.

In his report to the American people on the Moscow talks, Marshall referred to Germany as the "vital center."[42] The Marshall Plan, whose planning was initiated by Marshall immediately following the abortive Moscow Conference of Foreign Ministers, was directed at rescuing and rehabilitating this vital center which was considered essential to the economic stability and well-being of Western Europe as a whole. In an address at Chicago on November 18, 1947, Marshall spelled out in unmistakable terms the indissoluble link. "The restoration of Europe," he said, "involves the restoration of Germany. Without revival of Germany's economy there can be no revival of Europe's economy."[43]

The problem was how to gain American and European public acceptance for a policy based on the rehabilitation of the former enemy. "The Marshall Plan's great contribution in this respect was its focus on general European recovery rather than on Germany *per se*. It made it possible for Washington to push for German rehabilitation by arguing for Europe and without having to defend each policy change so necessary to German recovery in terms of what was being done or had been done in Germany proper."[44]

Whatever the intentions behind the Marshall Plan, its effect was to consolidate and harden the division of Germany and to intensify the Cold War between East and West.[45] Four-power cooperation having broken down, each side moved to tighten its grip over its part of Germany. The United States, after jettisoning the Potsdam agreement and merging its zone with that of its British ally, now proceeded to revive Germany's economic life and integrate it with the rest of the American sphere of influence within the framework of the European Recovery Program. The Soviets proceeded to turn their zone of occupation in East Germany into another link in their solid chain of East European satellites. Thus, 1947 was the year in which any remaining hope of four-power agreement receded into the realms of the impossible, and any ambiguity about the Powers' antagonistic policies disappeared. The lines of the Cold War were drawn clearly and firmly in the principal theater, Europe, and these lines split Germany into two halves, each of which belonged to a rival camp. The landmarks in this process were the Truman

42. *Department of State Bulletin*, May 22, 1947, pp. 919–924.
43. U.S. Department of State, *Germany 1947–1949: The Story in Documents* (Washington, D.C.: U.S. Government Printing Office, 1950), p. 12.
44. Gimbel, *The American Occupation of Germany*, p. 151.
45. Undated Morris memorandum, *FRUS, 1947*, Vol. 2, p. 889.

Doctrine, the Marshall Plan, and the formation of the Cominform. In this intensifying Cold War between East and West, Germany was both the most important battleground and its greatest prize. The German problem became merged with the Cold War, and the Cold War came to center increasingly on the German problem. From now on, questions about Germany were considered by both sides less and less on their own merits and more and more as crucial elements in the context of a gigantic global struggle for power.

The London meeting of the Council of Foreign Ministers, which took place in November–December 1947, simply registered the collapse of four-power relations over Germany. The auspices under which the Council met could have scarcely been less favorable. The basic issue before the conference, as in Moscow in the previous spring, was whether or not the Allies could agree among themselves to reunite Germany. But by now the two sides had drifted too far apart to leave any hope of reaching a mutually agreed-upon peace settlement. Ambassador Bedell Smith and General Clay, who were recalled to Washington for consultations in November, each reported independently that a break in Germany was inevitable and that it would be accompanied by an early attempt to blockade Berlin and to drive the Western powers out.[46] There was a general feeling among American officials that they would have to go ahead and set up a separate government in Western Germany. Among some officials there was a desire to prepare specific plans and to have them ready for use immediately after the anticipated failure of the CFM meeting. Secretary Marshall, however, rejected the idea, saying it was bad psychology and defeatism and that it must not even be discussed with the French and British during the course of the CFM meeting.[47] This injunction was probably inspired by concern for Allied morale and diplomatic propriety rather than by any real hope of a settlement, for the American posture remained fixed and inflexible and disclosed no sign of interest in negotiation and compromise.

The conference proceedings in London were merely a dreary repetition of what had been said and resaid at the Moscow con-

46. Clay, *Germany and the Fight for Freedom*, p. 36.
47. Memorandum for the Secretary, by Robert Plon, September 17, 1948, in the James V. Forrestal Diaries, Princeton University Library. This memorandum was a reply to the question put by Secretary of Defense Forrestal: "On what date and by whom was the decision made that the United States should support setting up a government in Western Germany?"

ference. Molotov demanded $10 billion in reparations, four-power control of the Ruhr, and the immediate creation of a government for the whole of Germany which would be entrusted with the negotiation of a peace treaty with the Allies. Marshall flatly rejected all three demands, but the real deadlock was over the issue of recreating German unity, for in the absence of agreement on this, all the other issues remained largely academic. In a "heart-to-heart" talk with the British Foreign Secretary in Bevin's flat, Molotov confirmed that the Russians, too, saw this as the crucial issue and that their objective was a unified Germany.[48]

As no progress was made at the conference on the question of recreating a unified Germany despite Molotov's relentless, almost desperate efforts, Marshall concluded that no useful purpose would be served by a debate on the other points on the agenda and moved that the session be adjourned. Molotov retorted that Marshall's proposal for the adjournment could not be considered as anything else but an attempt to untie his hands so that he could continue to act unilaterally to give the U.S. a free hand to do as it pleased in its zone of Germany.[49] In his broadcast to the American people on the failure of the London meeting, Marshall explained that Molotov's proposal for the immediate establishment of a German central government could not be accepted because "it was obvious that until the division of Germany had been healed and conditions created for German political and economic unity, any central government would be a sham and not a reality." "No real ground was lost or gained at the meeting," he said, "except that the outlines of the problems and the obstacles are much clearer. We cannot look forward to a reunified Germany at this time. We must do our best in the area where our influence can be felt."[50]

The failure of the London meeting of the Council of Foreign Ministers highlighted the irreparable rupture in inter-Allied relations over Germany and constituted another watershed in the development of the Cold War. The failure came as no surprise to the Western powers, and they coordinated their tactics well in advance.[51] "I am sure," wrote General Clay, "that all of us present in London recognized that, with the Council adjourned, we were

48. Harold Nicolson, *Diaries and Letters, 1945–1962*, ed. Nigel Nicolson (London: Fontana, 1971), p. 108.
49. *FRUS, 1947*, Vol. 2, p. 771.
50. *Department of State Bulletin*, December 28, 1947.
51. *FRUS, 1947*, Vol. 2, pp. 687–698.

now engaged in a competitive struggle, not with arms but with economic resources, with ideas and with ideals."[52] The Western powers attained unprecedented cohesion following France's shift towards the American position and maintained a remarkably united front vis-à-vis Russia throughout the conference. Immediately after the conference, British and American representatives met informally to concert their next move in what was by now a definite policy of moving towards the creation of a separate West German state. Bevin and Marshall instructed their Military Governors in Germany to develop plans for a political structure in Bizonia but avoid "unseemly haste." Secondly, it was decided to encourage French participation, and Marshall told his French colleague, Georges Bidault, that the Anglo-American fusion could be taken as a basis for discussion with the French regarding their eventual participation.[53]

These decisions were implemented with what can only be described as "unseemly haste." The Military Governors moved swiftly, and in the face of some opposition from the German representatives, to give a political character to the bizonal administrative structure. If the reason behind the cooperative attitude evinced by the Russians in the Allied Control Council following the failure of the London meeting was to get the Western powers to reconsider their policy of dividing Germany, then the Russians clearly failed to elicit the desired response. It was too late for second thoughts, and America could not be deflected from her new course by conciliatory Russian gestures. In fact, the plans for tripartite government-level discussions with France of long-range German policy assumed the shape of a full-scale international conference in London, in which not only the United States, Britain, and France participated, but also the Benelux countries.

The London conference convened on February 23, 1948 and lasted, in two separate sessions, until June. A note of urgency was introduced into its deliberations when the Communists seized full power in Czechoslovakia on February 25. George Kennan interpreted the Czech coup as a defensive reaction on the Soviet side to the initial success of the Marshall Plan initiative and to the preparations subsequently undertaken by the Western side to set

---

52. Clay, *Decision in Germany*, p. 348.
53. *FRUS, 1947*, Vol. 2, pp. 811–830; Murphy, *Diplomat Among Warriors*, p. 382; Clay, *Decision in Germany*, pp. 175–176; Oral History Interview with General Lucius D. Clay, July 16, 1974, Harry S. Truman Library, p. 30.

up a separate government in Western Germany.[54] But this was far from being the prevalent view at the time. The coup sent a shock throughout the Western world. The shock was heightened by the death on March 11 of Jan Masaryk, the Foreign Minister of Czechoslovakia, which was officially presented as a suicide but widely suspected to have been caused by foul play. In the atmosphere of crisis created by the events in Prague, the six-power delegates in London made swift progress in formulating a common policy for reconstituting Western Germany and bringing it within the framework of the European Recovery Program. As stated in their communiqué of March 6: "The participating powers had in view the necessity of ensuring the economic reconstruction of Western Europe including Germany, and of establishing a basis for the participation of a democratic Germany in the community of free peoples." Rather unconvincingly, the communiqué added that "while delay in reaching these objectives can no longer be accepted, ultimate Four Power agreement is in no way precluded."[55]

Four-power agreement was now precluded, however, not only by the West but, in all probability, by the Soviet Union as well. Early in 1948, at a meeting with visiting Bulgarian and Yugoslav delegations, Stalin stressed that Germany would remain divided. "The west will make Western Germany their own," he is reported to have said, "and we shall turn Eastern Germany into our own state."[56] If this is accepted as the true logic behind Russia's policy, then the inauguration of the attempt to force the Western allies out of Berlin, which followed close on the heels of the Czech coup, may be similarly interpreted as a defensive reaction. George Kennan, for one, viewed the two events as part of the same pattern. "They represented," he wrote, "like the Communist strike that France and Italy had just suffered in the autumn of 1947, Moscow's attempt to play, before it was too late, the various political cards it still possessed on the European continent."[57]

On March 20, 1948, Marshal Sokolovsky, the Soviet Military Governor, walked out of the Allied Control Council in Berlin. This

54. George F. Kennan, *Memoirs, 1925–1950* (Boston: Little, Brown, 1967), pp. 401–402.
55. U.S. Senate Committee on Foreign Relations, *Documents on Germany, 1944–1959* (Washington, D.C.: U.S. Government Printing Office, 1959), p. 56.
56. Djilas, *Conversations with Stalin*, p. 119.
57. Kennan, *Memoirs*, p. 401.

action signified public acknowledgment of the final parting of the ways between the Allies on the question of Germany. As President Truman observed: "For most of Germany, this act merely formalized what had been an obvious fact for some time, namely, that the four power control machinery had become unworkable. For the city of Berlin, however, this was the curtain-raiser for a major crisis."[58]

The imposition by the Soviet Union of the partial blockade, which restricted Western access to Berlin, on April 1 transformed Berlin from a problem of occupation policy into the subject of a major international crisis. Berlin was the weakest link in the American armor, and as such it was, from the Russian point of view, the ideal ground for a trial of strength. The weakness of the American position derived, in strategic terms, from the position of Berlin as a four-power enclave within the Soviet zone and, in legal terms, from the failure to secure, at the time when agreement was reached to divide the city into four sectors of occupation in 1945, written confirmation of the Western powers' rights of access by land to their respective sectors of the city. The former weakness was clearly more fundamental. Buried a hundred miles inside the Soviet zone, Berlin was largely at the mercy of the Soviet occupation forces, who could make life unbearable for the Western occupation forces at any time Moscow chose to activate this instrument for putting pressure on the West. Thus, "the four-power occupation of Berlin set up a classic conflict structure in international relations where the holding of territorial positions by one side against the displacing efforts of the other side has been the essence of the situation."[59] The vulnerability of this Western enclave as a strategic outpost in the heart of the Soviet zone raised doubts in the minds of some American policymakers about the feasibility of staying in Berlin and the wisdom of trying to do so. But the temptation to withdraw was always offset by concern over the loss of prestige which withdrawal was bound to entail. In the words of an internal Department of State Policy Statement, "Berlin has become an important symbol of the determination of the U.S. and the other Western powers to contest the Soviet claim to mastery of Germany and of Europe; with-

58. Truman, *Memoirs*, Vol. 2, p. 129.
59. Charles A. McClelland, "Access to Berlin: The Quantity and Variety of Events, 1948–1963," in *Quantitative International Politics: Insights and Evidence*, ed. J. David Singer (New York: The Free Press, 1968), p. 166.

drawal would be a great blow to Western prestige in Europe and to the strategic position of the U.S. and its associates *vis-à-vis* the USSR."[60]

The 1948 Berlin crisis was triggered by a Russian attempt (whatever the reasons and justifications behind it) to dislodge the Western powers from their position in Berlin, which encountered determined Western resistance. Berlin thus became both the instrument and the symbol of the policies of the two sides. If Germany was a microcosm of the Cold War, then Berlin was the microcosm of the German problem. And the Berlin crisis was a symbol and a watershed in both contexts. It marked the "great divide" in the postwar history of Germany. And in the wider context, it symbolized the struggle between the United States and the Soviet Union for power and influence in Europe. The great paradox was that the German problem, which in 1941 had brought the Grand Alliance into being, now shattered what remained of that alliance. By 1948, the lines of the Cold War had already been drawn. But the Berlin crisis, more than anything else, crystalized the issues and contributed to the institutionalization of the Cold War into two hostile blocs.

American behavior in the Berlin crisis was profoundly affected by the nature of the international system at the time the crisis occurred. Two features of this system are particularly relevant to the study of crisis behavior: its structure and the nature of military technology.[61]

The structure of the international system within which the crisis occurred was one of rigid bipolarity. In such a system, rivalry between the principal antagonists is almost structurally ordained, and the sensitivity of the decision-makers to external threats tends to be particularly acute. As John Spanier has noted: "Bipolarity leaves the principal adversaries feeling such a high degree of insecurity that they are virtually 'compelled' to react against one another's external threats. The reason is that in such a distribution of power the balance is constantly at stake. Each superpower, fearing that its adversary will achieve hegemony, will be extremely sensitive to

---

60. *FRUS, 1948*, Vol. 2, pp. 1314–15.
61. For a penetrating analysis of the impact of the international system on crisis interactions, see Glenn H. Snyder and Paul Diesing, *Conflict Among Nations* (Princeton: Princeton University Press, 1977), chap. 6.

the slightest shifts of power."[62] Bipolarity also creates a setting for bargaining quite different from that produced by a more fluid multipolar system.[63]

While accentuating sensitivity to threats from one's adversary, bipolarity has the effect of reducing the salience of alliance considerations. Kenneth Waltz has advanced the theorem that multipolarity is characterized by flexibility of alignment and rigidity of policy; and bipolarity by rigidity of alignment and flexibility of policy.[64] In other words, the fluidity of alliances in multipolarity imposes constraints on policy which stem from the need to discourage defections by one's allies, whereas the relative rigidity and permanence of the alliance systems in bipolarity make it less imperative to take into account the interests of one's allies in the making of policy. In the Berlin crisis, however, the ability of the United States to act independently of her allies was more circumscribed than in the majority of other bipolar crises. True, Germany was impotent as an international entity and its destiny lay in the hands of its powerful overlords, but even here the desire to secure the alignment of Western Germany in the competitive struggle against Russia constituted an influence on America's crisis decision-making. A more significant consideration was the need to retain the support of Britain and France and to coordinate policy with them, for they were not just leading members of America's alliance system but actors in their own right in the Berlin crisis by virtue of their position as occupying powers in Germany. America was unquestionably the leading actor on the Western side, but the extent of the strategic interdependence between her and her allies and the implications of this interdependence on her freedom of action should not be overlooked.

The second important attribute of the international system, in addition to its structure, is the kind of military power possessed by the actors. The definition of crisis as a situation which is perceived by the decision-makers as involving the possibility of war serves to underscore the importance of this attribute of the external setting. Clearly, crisis behavior will be affected by the military technology

62. John W. Spanier, *Games Nations Play* (London: Nelson, 1972), p. 62.
63. Oran R. Young, *The Politics of Force: Bargaining During International Crises* (Princeton: Princeton University Press, 1968), pp. 27–28.
64. Kenneth Waltz, "International Structure, National Force and the Balance of Power," *Journal of International Affairs*, Vol. 2, No. 2 (1967).

available to the adversaries and particularly by the presence or absence of nuclear weapons. Berlin was a nuclear crisis. Or, to be more precise: at the time of the crisis, Russia had not yet acquired nuclear weapons and America still enjoyed a nuclear monopoly. This marked the first time that nuclear weapons were seriously considered as a measure of last resort to check Soviet advances.[65] The possession of nuclear weapons affected both American policy during the crisis and the process by which the policy was made. In the realm of policy, it had a bearing on several key aspects, such as decision-makers' perceptions of the dangers of escalation, their calculations of deterrence, and their choice of diplomatic strategies. In the realm of process, the existence of nuclear weapons converged with the onset of the Cold War to upgrade the role of America's military leaders and to bring them nearer the center of the policymaking machine.[66]

What makes Berlin an exceptionally instructive case study is that it was the first postwar crisis in the central balance of the international system, the balance between the two new foci of power: America and Russia. Crises in the local balances in which the two superpowers were involved in one way or another had occurred before, notably over Iran, Turkey, and Greece in 1946–47. The Berlin crisis, however, marked the first open and direct confrontation between the principal Cold War antagonists themselves. In Berlin, their armies faced each other directly across the Cold War truce lines which divided East from West. No reliable rules, precedents, or conventions were available to guide their policy. But during the crisis itself, the mutually acceptable limits of behavior gradually emerged; the threshold between coercion and violence was discovered, and the pattern of mutual restraint was established which served to guide policymakers in subsequent superpower crises. In retrospect, therefore, the 1948 Berlin crisis is significant not only because it was the first open and direct superpower confrontation, but because of the skilful way it was managed and controlled.[67]

65. Hannes Adomeit, "Soviet Risk-Taking and Crisis Behaviour: From Confrontation to Coexistence?" *Adelphi Papers*, No. 101 (London: The International Institute for Strategic Studies, 1973), p. 9.

66. On this aspect of American decision-making, see Richard K. Betts, *Soldiers, Statesmen, and Cold War Crises* (Cambridge, Mass.: Harvard University Press, 1977).

67. Phil Williams, *Crisis Management: Confrontation and Diplomacy in the Nuclear Age* (London: Martin Robertson, 1976), pp. 199–203.

We have defined crisis, outlined a model, and examined the origins of the 1948 Berlin crisis and the external setting or operational environment in which it occurred. We must now introduce the American decision-makers and examine their psychological environment on the eve of the crisis.

PART II

Pre-Crisis Period

CHAPTER THREE

Psychological Environment

THE PRE-CRISIS PERIOD began when Marshal Sokolovsky walked out of the Allied Control Council on March 20, 1948. This action led to a conspicuous increase in the threat perceived by the U.S. decision-makers. It also created a sense of need for a foreign policy response. Both the perception of threat and of the need to deal with it were considerably heightened by the Soviet inauguration, on April 1, of what later came to be called the "mini-blockade." The pre-crisis period lasted until June 24, when the Soviet imposition of the full blockade marked the advent of the crisis period.

DECISION-MAKERS AND DECISIONS

The key American decision-makers during the pre-crisis period were President Harry S. Truman, Secretary of State George Marshall, and the American Military Governor in Germany, General Lucius D. Clay. Other officials also played a part in the decision-making process on Berlin, notably Under Secretary of State Robert Lovett, Secretary of Defense James Forrestal, Secretary of the Army Kenneth Royall, Army Chief of Staff Omar Bradley, and the State Department's Political Adviser in Germany, Robert Murphy. Truman, Marshall, and Clay, however, were the key decision-makers: their position within the decision-making structure was central, and the influence they exercised on U.S. policy was fundamental. Clay, despite his subordinate place in the official hierarchy, played such a crucial part both in the formulation and in the implementation of U.S. policy that he must be included in the group of key decision-makers.

Six major decisions were taken during the 1948 pre-crisis period, along with several incremental reinforcement actions at the bureaucratic and military levels. Of the six decisions, two were taken by President Truman, one was taken by the Cabinet, one was taken by Secretary Marshall, and two were taken by General Clay.

Decision Number	Date	Content
1	March 22	The President, in consultation with Royall and Marshall, decided that (a) the Army was to retain control over the nonmilitary aspects of U.S. policy concerning the American zone of occupation, instead of these being taken over by the State Department, and (b) that Clay, who had planned to retire at the end of 1948, was to retain his dual positions as American Military Governor in Germany and Commander of U.S. forces in Europe.
2	March 26	The Cabinet decided to impose a selective embargo on trade between Western and Eastern Germany by denying export licenses for items that would affect production in key segments of Soviet and satellite economies.
3	March 31	The President, in consultation with the State Department, the Department of the Army, and the Joint Chiefs of Staff, authorized Clay to send test trains through the Russian checkpoints and instruct the guards to prevent Soviet personnel from entering but not to shoot except in self-defense.
4	April 29	Secretary Marshall, after discussion in the Cabinet and after obtaining the President's approval, decided to instruct Ambassador Smith to make a statement to Molotov about America's position and policies.
5	June 1	Clay, following prolonged consultations with the Department of the Army and with the British and French Military Governors in Germany, took the decision to implement currency reform in the Western zones of Germany.
6	June 23	Clay, after consultation with the British and French Military Governors in Germany, decided to extend the currency reform to the Western sectors of Berlin.

PSYCHOLOGICAL ENVIRONMENT

The link between psychological environment and decisions is the key to the framework for analyzing foreign policy. The need to explore the psychological environment of the decision-makers who determine the crisis behavior of the state stems from the simple fact that decision-makers act in response to their perception of reality, not in response to reality itself. It is what they think the world is like, not what it is really like, that conditions their actions. A decision is a choice of one course of action from a range of perceived alternatives. Both the field of choice and the ordering of the field from which the preferred option is selected lie in the decision-makers' images of the situation.[1] The operational environment defines the setting within which the decision-makers must act. Their psychological environment predisposes them to act in a particular way. While the outcome of state behavior can be understood in terms of the decision-makers' operational environment (the capabilities and intentions of the relevant actors), the decisions themselves must be understood in terms of the decision-makers' psychological environment (their beliefs about the world and other actors).[2]

The psychological environment comprises two closely interrelated elements: attitudinal prism and images. Attitudinal prism may be defined as a belief system, a world-view or *weltanschauung*. It is shaped by political culture, historical legacy, and the personality traits of the decision-makers. It embraces all the knowledge that the individual has accumulated about himself and about the external world. These manifold influences constitute the screen or prism through which decision-makers perceive the operational environment. The content of what they perceive is the image, or rather images. The attitudinal prism is the background or long-term component which generally orients the decision-maker towards the external environment. Image is the more immediate and

---

1. Kenneth Boulding, "National Images and International Systems," *Journal of Conflict Resolution*, Vol. 3, No. 2 (1959), pp. 120–121. See also Louis J. Halle, *American Foreign Policy: Theory and Reality* (London: Allen and Unwin, 1960), p. 316.

2. Harold Sprout and Margaret Sprout, "Environmental Factors in the Study of International Politics," in *International Politics and Foreign Policy: A Reader in Research and Theory*, ed. James N. Rosenau (New York: The Free Press, 1969), pp. 41–56. See also Joseph Frankel, *The Making of Foreign Policy: An Analysis of Decision-Making* (London: Oxford University Press, 1963), p. 45.

specific component. Together they constitute the psychological environment—the framework of choice, decision, and action.[3]

The link between image and decision underlies all foreign policy decision-making, both of the crisis and non-crisis varieties. Crisis, however, as a phase in an ongoing adversary relationship, and one which involves the possibility of war, tends to focus the political actor's perceptions very sharply on the opponent. And the image of the opponent will consequently dominate all other images to an extent rarely paralleled in non-crisis situations. This is not to say that the image of the opponent is unimportant in times of comparative stability. On the contrary, as Alexander George has argued: "A political actor's belief system about the nature of politics is shaped particularly by his orientation towards other political actors. Most important of these are one's opponents. The way in which they are perceived—the characteristics a political actor attributes to his opponents—exercises a subtle influence on many other philosophical and instrumental beliefs in his operational code."[4] What is postulated here is that, in a crisis, the image of the enemy assumes an overriding importance. The actor's beliefs about the character and the ultimate aims of the opponent will strongly color his immediate image of the opponent's objectives and behavior in the crisis at hand. Perception of threat concentrates the actor's mind on the intentions and capabilities of the opponent, and the actor's interpretation of all incoming information relevant to the crisis is shaped by this image of the opponent. Once the crisis has started, the image of the opponent becomes crucial not only to the actor's definition of the situation but also to his choice of strategies for dealing with the threat.

In line with the foregoing observations, my analysis of the psychological environment of the core group of American decision-makers involved in the early phase of the Berlin crisis is divided into two parts. The first part deals with the attitudinal prism of the American decision-makers—that is, with their background beliefs and assumptions about the external environment in general and

3. See Michael Brecher, *The Foreign Policy System of Israel: Setting, Images, Process* (London: Oxford University Press, 1972), pp. 11–12 and 229.

4. Alexander L. George, "The 'Operational Code': A Neglected Approach to the Study of Political Leaders and Decision-Making," *International Studies Quarterly*, Vol. 13, No. 2 (1969), pp. 201–202. For an interesting case study of John Foster Dulles's image of the Soviet Union, see Ole R. Holsti, "Cognitive Dynamics and Images of the Enemy," in *Enemies in Politics*, by David J. Finlay et al. (Chicago: Rand McNally, 1967).

the Soviet Union in particular. My aim is not to provide an exhaustive account but to review the major components of this prism and the principal factors which shaped it. To speak of the attitudinal prism of a group necessarily involves a high degree of generalization, since the world-views of its individual members are bound to differ in some respects. But while important differences existed, the key American decision-makers who held office during the Berlin crisis were sufficiently homogeneous in terms of their outlook, belief system, values, and ideological orientation to make it meaningful to talk about a collective attitudinal prism. The second part deals with the other element of their psychological environment: images. Here I analyze the crisis images of each decision-maker separately, after giving a brief account of his role, personality traits, and distinctive qualities as a decision-maker. Once again, the emphasis is on their images of the opponent.

Attitudinal Prism

If practitioners are placed along an idealist-realist continuum in accordance with their world-view, then there is no doubt that the key American decision-makers in 1948 all occupied positions nearer the realist pole. The prism through which they viewed the outside world corresponded in all essentials to the "realist" archetype. This prism was shaped by a great variety of influences, foremost among which was the actual experience of dealing with the Soviet Union in the period after the defeat of Germany. Two other factors whose influence was significant were the transformation of the international system from multipolarity to bipolarity and the incompatibility of the ideologies to which America and Russia subscribed.

The identification of friends and enemies—a fundamental element of the prism—was partly determined, for both superpowers, by the bipolar structure of the international system which emerged clearly in the aftermath of the Second World War. America and Russia could scarcely avoid perceiving each other as rivals within this system, because for each one the other was the only state capable of posing a serious military threat to its security or to smaller states whose independence or affiliation was considered essential to that security.[5] Whether Russia intended to use its preponderant

5. Glenn H. Snyder and Paul Diesing, *Conflict Among Nations: Bargaining, Decision-Making and System-Structure in International Crises* (Princeton: Princeton University Press, 1977), p. 420. Snyder and Diesing consider the "imperatives of system structure" as the primary cause of the Cold War. They point

military power in order to pose an actual threat to America's European allies is a separate question and, of course, the subject of a fascinating debate between the traditionalist and the revisionist historians of the Cold War. What mattered, however, was that Russia had the potential to pose such a threat, and that this potential was enough to arouse American suspicions. The resulting security dilemma had the dual effect of accentuating America's own fears and blinding it to the genuine security fears of the other side. In this sense, the Cold War and the characteristically somber and stern world-view that went along with it may be said to have had some structural causes.[6]

The conflict of ideologies between capitalist America and communist Russia also affected the way in which they perceived one another. America had an anti-communist tradition whose historical roots can be traced back to the Bolshevik takeover of power in Russia in 1917, but the impact of ideology as a determinant of American foreign policy remained rather muted during the war. President Roosevelt's blueprint for a postwar order which was predicated on continuing Russo-American collaboration implied at least a hope, if not a conviction, that the different social and economic systems of the two countries would not pose an insurmountable barrier to an understanding between them. But the ideological differences became more pronounced and disruptive in the course of the unsuccessful attempt to recreate with Russia a variant of the Concert of Europe system in place of the defunct balance of power. Thus, even if ideological hostility was not a primary cause of the Cold War, once the unfolding pattern of Russian action in the context of a bipolar international system had identified Russia as America's principal rival, ideological differences served to sour their relations, exacerbate their misunderstandings, and deepen their rivalry. This was an intricate and spiraling process in which

---

out that this cause is overlooked by revisionist writers, who see the cause of the Cold War in the American capitalist system, and by the traditionalists, who find its cause in "Soviet imperialism." To conclude, however, as they do, that U.S.-Soviet rivalry was "structurally ordained" implies an excessively deterministic, reductionist explanation.

6. For other accounts which clearly recognize the structural roots of the Cold War, see Louis J. Halle, *The Cold War as History* (London: Chatto and Windus, 1971); and Robert W. Tucker, *The Radical Left and American Foreign Policy* (Baltimore: Johns Hopkins University Press, 1971). Tucker exposes the revisionists' blind spot on this point (pp. 89–90).

the clash of interests was compounded by mutual suspicion, misperception, and ideological antagonism.

Revisionist historians of the Cold War have exaggerated the suddenness with which Truman reversed his predecessor's policies after entering the White House in April 1945.[7] In fact, the perceptions underlying American foreign policy changed only gradually, and the fundamental reorientation of policy did not take place until the Spring of 1946.[8] In the early period, two schools of thought existed within the Truman Administration, based on contradictory perceptions of Moscow's intentions. One group of decision-makers, the so-called "realists," had come to believe that the totalitarian nature of the Soviet regime, allied to its Marxist-Leninist ideology, committed Moscow irrevocably to the overturn of the international system and to unlimited expansion in pursuit of world dominance. In their view, Roosevelt's confidence in the possibility of continuing Great Power collaboration was based on a set of dangerous illusions, notably the belief that Russian goodwill could be bought with Western concessions. They sought to supplant the accommodating policy of F.D.R. with a tough and uncompromising posture and the deployment of America's economic, political, and military resources to uphold the precarious postwar order and to check Russia's expansionist ambitions. The logic behind their policy was summed up by the realist precept which holds that the only effective antidote to power is power. But there was a second school of decision-makers who were still disposed to believe that Moscow's encroachment on Eastern Europe, however despotic and objectionable, was prompted not by an insatiable appetite for territorial expansion but by the defensive need to safeguard the security of the Soviet state. This group recognized that specific disagreements arising out of conflicting interests were bound to occasion some strain in the relations between America and Russia, but it felt that with goodwill and readiness to negotiate and compromise on both sides, the alliance could be preserved.

7. See, for example, D. F. Fleming, *The Cold War and Its Origins, 1917–1960* (London: Allen and Unwin, 1961), Vol. 1, pp. 165–170; Gar Alperovitz, *Atomic Diplomacy: Hiroshima and Potsdam* (New York: Vintage, 1967), pp. 12–13; Lloyd C. Gardner, *Architects of Illusion: Men and Ideas in American Foreign Policy, 1941–1949* (Chicago: Quadrangle, 1970), pp. 55–83.

8. For a detailed elaboration of this view, see John Lewis Gaddis, *The United States and the Origins of the Cold War, 1941–1947* (New York: Columbia University Press, 1972), chap. 9.

In his perceptive study of the origins of the Cold War, Daniel Yergin has labeled these two interpretations of Soviet intentions, which competed for hegemony in the American high-policy circles in 1945, the Riga axioms and the Yalta axioms. The first set is named after the Baltic port where the American mission was maintained during the interwar years, nurturing hard-line attitudes towards the Soviet Union; the second, after the Crimean conference of February 1945, which marked the high tide of American efforts to work with rather than against the Soviets:

> At the heart of the first set was an image of the Soviet Union as a world revolutionary state, denying the possibilities of coexistence, committed to unrelenting ideological warfare, powered by a messianic drive for world mastery. The second set downplayed the role of ideology and the foreign policy consequences of authoritarian domestic practices, and instead saw the Soviet Union behaving like a traditional Great Power within the international system, rather than trying to overthrow it.[9]

The Riga axioms, says Yergin, triumphed in American policy-making circles in the postwar years and provided a foundation for the anti-communist consensus. Indeed, the entire course of American foreign policy after 1945 may be viewed in terms of the gradual ascendancy of the Riga axioms. This ascendancy is evident both in the thinking and in the actual conduct of external policy by the Truman Administration. The Riga axioms received their clearest and most powerful articulation in February 1946 in a sixteen-page cable sent by George Kennan, the deputy chief of mission in Moscow, to the State Department. In this cable, which rapidly gained fame as the Long Telegram, Kennan undertook to analyze and explain Moscow's international behavior, to suggest the behavior to be expected in the future, and to spell out the practical implications for American foreign policy.

Kennan's central argument was that the Soviet party line arises mainly from internal Russian necessities and is not based on any objective analysis of the situation beyond Russia's borders. At the bottom of the Kremlin's neurotic view of world affairs, he claimed, was the traditional and instinctive Russian sense of insecurity. This insecurity drove the Russian leaders to put forward the Marxist dogma which pictured the outside world as evil, hostile, and men-

---

9. Daniel Yergin, *Shattered Peace: The Origins of the Cold War and the National Security State* (Boston: Houghton Mifflin, 1977), p. 11.

acing but bearing within itself germs of creeping disease and destined to be overwhelmed by the rising power of socialism. Experience had taught them to seek security only in the patient but deadly struggle for the total destruction of rival power, never in compacts and compromises with it.

The implications both of this neurotic drive for the expansion of Soviet power and of the basic Soviet instinct that there can be no compromise with rival power were spelled out by Kennan in dramatic fashion. "In summary," he wrote, "we have here a political force committed fanatically to the belief that with the U.S. there can be no permanent modus vivendi, that it is desirable and necessary that the internal harmony of our society be disrupted, our traditional way of life be destroyed, the international authority of our state be broken, if Soviet power is to be secure."

Kennan considered that the problem of dealing with this force was the greatest task American diplomacy ever faced or was likely to face, but he also recorded his conviction that the problem was within America's power to solve. In support of this conviction, he pointed out that the Soviet Union, unlike Hitlerite Germany, is not adventuristic and does not take unnecessary risks: "Impervious to the logic of reason, it is highly sensitive to the logic of force. For this reason it can easily withdraw—and it usually does—when strong resistance is encountered at any point. Thus, if the adversary has sufficient force and makes clear his readiness to use it, he rarely has to do so."[10]

The effect produced in Washington by this elaborate pedagogical effort was "nothing less than sensational."[11] Dean Acheson, who was Under Secretary of State at the time, described it as a "truly remarkable" dispatch which had a deep effect on thinking within the government.[12] Louis Halle, who was an official in the State Department, gave a vivid account of the impact it had on the government's world-view. "It came at a moment," he wrote, "when the Department, having been separated by circumstances from the wartime policy towards Russia, was floundering about, looking for new intellectual moorings. Now, in this communication, it was of-

10. Kennan to Byrnes, February 22, 1946, in *Foreign Relations of the United States, 1946* (Washington, D.C.: U.S. Government Printing Office, 1969), Vol. 6, pp. 696–709. (Henceforth, this series will be referred to as *FRUS*.)
11. George F. Kennan, *Memoirs, 1925–1950* (Boston: Little, Brown, 1967), p. 294.
12. Dean Acheson, *Present at the Creation* (New York: Norton, 1969), p. 151.

fered a new and realistic conception to which it might attach itself. The reaction was immediate and positive. There was a universal feeling that 'this was it,' this was the appreciation of the situation that had been needed. Mr. Kennan's communication was reproduced for distribution to all the officers of the Department. . . . We may not doubt that it made its effect on the President. It was communicated to the War and Navy Departments as well."[13]

The significance of the Long Telegram cannot be overestimated, precisely because it provided the intellectual moorings which the makers of American foreign policy felt in need of. It firmly fixed the assumptions and axioms on which American foreign policy continued to be based for the next two decades until detente began to supplant the Cold War. If any single document may be regarded as the Bible of the American policymakers during the Cold War era, Kennan's Long Telegram was it. Both parts of this Bible—the analysis of the threat posed by the Soviet Union and the prescription for dealing with it—commanded an overwhelming allegiance. This allegiance, however, owed more to the "get tough with Russia" policy towards which the Truman Administration was already moving than to the originality and persuasiveness of Kennan's analysis. As he himself recognized, the timing of his document was largely responsible for the powerful resonance it created.[14] For it preached against the dangers of concession and compromise to policymakers who had little inclination to engage in either. The Riga axioms had been steadily gaining ground inside the Administration following the fruitless and frustrating experience of negotiating with the Russians on a long list of issues. The number of officials who still viewed Moscow's international conduct as dictated by genuine security fears was small and rapidly dwindling. The great majority, including such men as Dean Acheson, Averell Harriman, James Forrestal, and Clark Clifford, shared Kennan's view that the Kremlin was propelled by internal pressures along its revolutionary and expansionist course, and that it could not be checked by conciliatory diplomacy but only by firm opposition backed by superior American military force and the display of the will to use it to safeguard America's vital interests.

The speed with which the hard-line approach advocated by Kennan was elevated to the status of a new orthodoxy by American of-

13. Halle, *The Cold War as History*, p. 105.
14. Kennan, *Memoirs*, p. 195.

ficials can be gauged from a report submitted to Truman by his special White House counsel, Clark Clifford, in September 1946. Truman had read Kennan's Long Telegram but wanted an even more comprehensive report, written by somebody close to him. So he asked Clifford in the summer of 1946 to prepare a "position paper" on U.S.-Russian relations.[15] Clifford consulted all the major agencies of the government and assembled the views of numerous experts on Russia in the course of preparing his hundred-page report. In his covering letter to the President, Clifford mentioned the remarkable agreement among officials with whom he had talked on the need to review America's relations with the Soviet Union. The content of the report, if it is taken as a reflection of this consensus, indicates the degree to which the Riga axioms permeated the inner thinking of the Administration. "The gravest problem facing the United States today," the report began, "is that of American relations with the Soviet Union. The solution of that problem may determine whether or not there will be a third World War." Soviet leaders appeared to be conducting their nation on "a course of aggrandizement designed to lead to eventual world domination by the USSR." The key to understanding current Soviet foreign policy, said Clifford, is the realization that Soviet leaders adhere to "the Marxian theory of the ultimate destruction of capitalist states by communist states." Next, in the manner of a legal brief, Clifford presented a detailed catalogue of agreements broken by Russia. So long as the Russian leaders adhere to their Marxian beliefs and continue their aggressive policy, he went on to say, it is highly dangerous to conclude that hope of international peace lies only in "accord," "mutual understanding," or "solidarity" with the Soviet Union. "The language of military power is the only language which the disciples of power politics understand." The American government must therefore use this language in order to make the Soviet leaders realize that it will uphold its interests. Compromise and concessions are considered by them as evidence of weakness, and American retreats only encourage them to make new and greater demands. The prospect of defeat is the only sure means of deterring the Soviet Union. On a note of cautious optimism, Clifford concluded his report by observing that if America's opposition to the Kremlin's expansive and proselytizing tendencies is maintained

15. Margaret Truman, *Harry S. Truman* (New York: William Morrow, 1973), p. 347.

firmly enough and long enough, the logic of it must permeate eventually into the Soviet system.[16]

Truman's reaction when he had finished reading this report was to order Clifford to round up all the copies and put them under lock and key. The reason he gave was that if the report got out, it would have exceedingly unfortunate repercussions on America's relations with Russia.[17] This was a tactical reason. As far as the substance of the report was concerned, Truman did not register any dissent. Unlike the Long Telegram, therefore, the Clifford report had only limited influence on Washington's outlook. What it does provide is a highly revealing picture of the newly developed consensus on the all-important question of relations with the Soviet Union.[18]

At this stage, it was still a consensus within the Administration on the need to get tough with Russia rather than a national consensus. One of the aims behind Truman's "all-out-speech" to Congress on March 12, 1947 was to generate public support and Congression-

16. Both the covering letter and Clifford's report are printed as Appendix A in Arthur Krock's *Memoirs* (London: Cassell, 1968), pp. 419 and 421–482, respectively. The original report is in the Clifford Papers, Box 14, Harry S. Truman Library, Independence, Missouri. The Truman Library has fourteen out of the twenty copies made by Clifford. Truman apparently retained one copy of the report, and it is likely that this was the copy which Krock obtained and published when it was still classified.

17. Margaret Truman, *Harry S. Truman*, p. 347; Richard M. Freeland, *The Truman Doctrine and the Origins of McCarthyism* (New York: Knopf, 1972), p. 67.

18. A different conclusion is suggested by Richard J. Powers in "Who Fathered Containment?" *International Studies Quarterly*, Vol. 15, No. 4 (December 1971), pp. 516–543. Powers stresses Clifford's heavy reliance on Kennan's Long Telegram, and he demonstrates, on the basis of a close textual comparison, both the uses and misuses which Clifford made of the earlier analysis. He concludes that Clifford's summary, which was soon to be embodied in the Truman Doctrine and the concomitant efforts at the containment of the Soviet Union, had the greater impact on the actual formulation of policy. The explanation for this is that "Clifford was commissioned by the President to prepare the study. By this act, Truman not only demonstrated confidence in Clifford but he also became, in an indiscernible measure, a party to the subsequent report. The Clifford memorandum was the product of consultation with the highest members of government, the men upon whom the President of necessity and, presumably, preference relied totally for guidance in foreign affairs" (p. 540). Powers, however, does not adduce any concrete evidence to support his contention that the Clifford memorandum was more influential in guiding policy. He also overlooks the fact that, whatever impact it had on Truman's own thinking, by impounding all the copies the President himself curtailed its circulation, and therefore its influence, outside the White House.

al appropriations for the policy of firm opposition to Russia, which in time would become known by the less precise but more ominous term "containment." A few months after the enunciation of the Truman Doctrine, Kennan published his widely read and highly influential article on "The Sources of Soviet Conduct," which elaborated on the themes of the Long Telegram. Originally written for the "private edification" of Secretary of the Navy James Forrestal, who received it enthusiastically and recommended it to others, the article appeared in the July 1947 issue of the prestigious journal *Foreign Affairs*, the unofficial voice of the American foreign policy establishment.[19] The article appeared under the anonymous name of Mr. X, but its real authorship soon became common knowledge, and no attempt was made to deny it. Since the author had become, by the time of publication, the Director of the newly created Policy Planning Staff of the State Department, it was widely taken to represent the official policy of the Administration and to disclose to the world at large the assumptions, calculations, and estimates on which this policy was based. Thus, by 1947, the assumptions which constituted the operative consensus among the makers of Washington's foreign policy were not only firmly entrenched inside the government, but widely recognized outside it. The effect of this inner core of beliefs and assumptions was all too evident in the foreign policy of the Truman Administration. We have already traced in the previous chapter the shift of the American approach to Germany which was part of the tough, overall containment strategy. We noticed the attitude of firmness and the marked reluctance to enter into any serious negotiations with the Soviet Union on the future of Germany that characterized the American approach in the meetings of the Council of Foreign Ministers held in the spring and winter of 1947. Similarly, American policies in other areas both proceeded from and reinforced the Riga axioms. So at the time of the outbreak of the Berlin crisis, there was in existence a distinctive prism which conditioned the Truman Administration's interpretation of the crisis and its response to it.

Four dimensions of this prism call for a more extended treatment: world-view, image of the opponent, self-image, and strategy preferences.[20] The American world-view was unmistakably "real-

19. X [George F. Kennan], "The Sources of Soviet Conduct," *Foreign Affairs*, Vol. 25, No. 4 (July 1947).

20. This fourfold typology is suggested by Snyder and Diesing in *Conflict Among Nations*, p. 298.

ist" in its emphasis on power, conflict, and interest. The world was perceived as an arena of perpetual struggle and conflict in which power politics rather than morality or idealism held sway. This perception of a harsh external environment, conflict-ridden and fraught with risks and dangers, led to a very marked preoccupation with American security and to an extreme sensitivity to threats. Finding their country thrust into a new situation of danger so soon after the protracted war which ended in the defeat of Nazi Germany, the American decision-makers became acutely concerned with the intentions and capabilities of this new opponent and with the perceived threat posed by this opponent to the stability of the precarious postwar international order. This concern with American security took the form of extreme sensitivity to power-strategic considerations and especially to the military balance between America and Russia. In consequence, American foreign policy became increasingly dominated by a national security perspective. In fact, it was the intersection of the Riga axioms with the doctrine of national security which formed the distinctive prism of the American foreign policy elite during the Cold War.[21]

The two-camps image featured very prominently in this commanding world-view. The world was perceived not simply as conflict-ridden but as sharply divided into two groups of nations, the "free world" and the Communist bloc, led by America and Russia, respectively. Rivalry between them was seen to derive not just from conflicting interests but from an ideological confrontation between freedom and totalitarianism, between capitalism and communism. Once the division between the two groups had taken on such an overt ideological form, American decision-makers increasingly saw the other camp not as a limited opponent but as an irreconcilable adversary, and the relationship between them not as ordinary political rivalry but as an all-embracing, worldwide, and

---

21. Both the national security perspective and the sensitivity to threats were epitomized in an extreme form by James Forrestal, Navy Secretary and later Defense Secretary in the Truman Administration. Forrestal was not typical. His fear of the Communist threat developed into paranoia, and his concern about American security became an extreme and irrational obsession. He committed suicide in a hospital where he was undergoing psychiatric treatment shortly after leaving office in 1949. But although Forrestal is a special case involving psychiatric disorder, he does illustrate some general tendencies which were at work in American society during the Cold War. For an interesting psychobiography, see Arnold A. Rogow, *Victim of Duty: A Study of James Forrestal* (London: Rupert Hart-Davis, 1966).

deadly contest.[22] Some of them saw the contest in even more apocalyptic terms as a struggle between the forces of Light and the forces of Darkness whose outcome would determine the fate of civilization itself. This rigid conception of the Cold War, with its moral undertones, imprisoned American foreign policy within an ideological straitjacket and impaired the ability of the American decision-makers to make subtle, but often crucial, distinctions between different kinds of communist states and the different degrees of threat they posed to America's security.

Within the context of a global contest between the free world and the Communist bloc, special place was reserved for America's major allies, Britain and France. These countries were identified as America's allies by their position on the western side of the bipolar international power structure, and the alliance was cemented by the ideological affinity which linked them to America. In addition, they were the only two countries among America's western allies who had a direct role in the occupation of Germany. Yet, the two countries were perceived very differently by the Americans. Britain was perceived as a friendly, like-minded, and generally supportive country, staunch in its opposition to the spread of communism and willing to assume burdens and run risks in containing the Soviet Union. France, on the other hand, was perceived as lacking in military strength and political determination and given to pursuing a unilateral and misguided policy, and therefore as a far less valuable or reliable ally than Britain in the conflict with the Soviet Union. The different images reflected a realistic appraisal of the positions of the two countries, which were rooted in divergent perceptions of the principal source of threat to their security. Britain,

22. In their reply of July 27, 1946 to Clifford's request for information, for example, the Joint Chiefs of Staff signaled their conviction that the Soviet Union and the United States, with their respective allies, were locked in a deadly conflict—below the level of a "shooting war," but a war nevertheless. See James F. Schnabel, *The History of the Joint Chiefs of Staff*, Vol. 1: *1945–1947* (Washington, D.C.: Historical Division, Joint Secretariat, Joint Chiefs of Staff, 1979), Record Group 218, Records of the United States Joint Chiefs of Staff, the National Archives, pp. 103–104. A later National Security Council report stated that "The ultimate objective of Soviet-directed world communism is the domination of the world," and that in the circumstances, which it went on to describe, "the USSR has engaged the United States in a struggle for power, or 'cold war' in which our national security is at stake and from which we cannot withdraw short of eventual national suicide." NSC 7, "The Position of the United States with Respect to Soviet-Directed World Communism," March 30, 1948, in *FRUS, 1948*, Vol. 1 (Part 2), p. 546.

like America, had come to regard the Soviet Union as the real adversary and Germany as a potential ally in the Cold War. The French, on the other hand, had not yet overcome their traditional hostility and deeply embedded fear of Germany and still hoped to reach agreement with Russia on the control of Germany in order to lay the foundation for European security. This was the source of the negative component in America's attitude to France. General Marshall complained that French preoccupation with Germany as a major threat was "outmoded and unrealistic."[23] Clay was convinced that their thinking "suffers from a time lag and is not synchronized with the developing pattern of Soviet policy in Germany."[24] In general, the Anglo-American alliance was seen by the Americans as the dominant and most satisfactory bilateral relationship, whereas the relationship with France was recognized to be more tense, problematic, and to some extent unpredictable.

The image of the opponent is the second dimension of the American prism and one which deserves in-depth analysis because of the profound influence it had on a wide spectrum of philosophical and instrumental beliefs. While in 1945, as has already been noted, two images competed with one another, within a year of the ending of hostilities, the image of the Soviet Union as a traditional and conservative Great Power had disappeared almost without trace, yielding unchallenged dominance to the image of a revolutionary, subversive, Marxist-inspired, and uncompromising state, striving relentlessly towards world mastery. Since the aims of the Soviet Union were unlimited, according to this image, political accommodation with it was out of the question and the Cold War was taken to be preordained in the expansionist and millenarian character of the Soviet state.

As far as its methods were concerned, the Soviet Union was perceived to be monstrously cruel, utterly unscrupulous, and uncommonly willing to use military force to achieve its political ends. The image of the courageous and loyal comrade-in-arms was replaced by that of a sinister and aggressive enemy out to conquer the world and ready to use any means, fair and foul.[25] But although Russian

23. *FRUS, 1948*, Vol. 2, p. 71.   24. Ibid., p. 155.
25. See, for example, Schnabel, *The History of the Joint Chiefs of Staff*, Vol. 1, pp. 103–107. The American Commandant for Berlin gave the following colorful account of this image change as it was experienced by those who dealt with the Russians in Germany. "We went to Berlin in 1945," he wrote, "thinking only of the Russians as big, jolly, balalaika-playing fellows, who drank prodigious

power was likened to a fluid stream which moves constantly, wherever it is permitted to move, until it has filled every nook and cranny in the basin of world power,[26] the men behind it were not seen as irrational. On the contrary, as Kennan—the author of this analogy—emphasized, if the leaders of the Kremlin find unassailable barriers on their path, they accept these philosophically and accommodate themselves to them, for they are under no compulsion to accomplish their purpose in a hurry and feel no compunction about retreating in the face of superior force.[27] Although there were some exceptions, the majority of American decision-makers shared this view of the Kremlin as a single-minded and ruthless opponent that was at the same time cool and calculating and ready to retreat when danger threatened.

This commonly held view of the adversary had a number of other facets. In the first place, a highly centralized command structure and a monolithic unity were attributed to the Moscow-led Communist bloc. This typically hard-line view of internal relations within the international Communist movement, which was implicit in Kennan's X article, became increasingly explicit and prevalent in America as the Cold War intensified.[28] Kennan himself later explained that when he used the term "Soviet power" in that article, he had in mind the system of power organized, dominated, and inspired by Joseph Stalin. "This was a monolithic power structure," he wrote, "reaching through the network of highly disciplined Communist parties into practically every country in the world. In these circumstances, any success of a local Communist party, anywhere, had to be regarded as an extension in reality of the political orbit, or at least the dominant influence, of the Kremlin. Precisely because Stalin maintained so jealous, so humiliating a control over foreign Communists, all of the latter had, at that time, to be regarded as the vehicle of his will, not their own. His was the only

---

quantities of vodka and liked to wrestle in the drawing room. We now know—or should know—that we were hopelessly naive. You can't do business with the Russians. . . . They can't be trusted. They will promise anything, sign anything, provided it benefits them, and will scrap the pledge the moment it doesn't. . . . The Russians are the world's most colossal liars, swindlers and cutthroats and there is no reason to think they will change." Frank Howley, *Berlin Command* (New York: Putnam's, 1950), pp. 11–12.

26. X [George F. Kennan], "The Sources of Soviet Conduct."
27. Ibid.
28. See, for example, NSC 7, in *FRUS, 1948*, Vol. 1 (Part 2), pp. 546–550.

center of authority in the Communist world; and it was a vigilant, exacting and imperious headquarters, prepared to brook no opposition."[29]

Secondly, Soviet and Soviet-inspired activities anywhere around the globe were considered to be the product of careful planning and coordination in Moscow.[30] This quality of Soviet foreign policy was closely related to the monolithic power structure from which it issued. The link was indicated explicitly in the Clifford memorandum: "Because the Soviet Union is a highly-centralized state, whose leaders exercise rigid discipline and control all governmental functions, its government acts with speed, consistency and boldness."[31] The documents prepared for Clifford by the State Department pictured the Kremlin as a superbly functioning mastermind. "The Soviet Union operates on a worldwide basis," said the authors of the Information Statement. "Each move in its foreign policy is care-

29. Kennan, *Memoirs*, p. 366. This perception of a monolithic international communist movement was relaxed, however, when Yugoslavia broke away from the Soviet bloc. PPS (Policy Planning Staff paper) 35, dated June 30, 1948, constituted the first explicit recognition of the possibility that a communist state might exist independent of Moscow's control. For the text of PPS 35 and commentary on its significance, see Thomas H. Etzold and John Lewis Gaddis, eds., *Containment: Documents on American Policy and Strategy, 1945–1950* (New York: Columbia University Press, 1978), pp. 169–172. The CIA's "Review of the World Situation," published on July 14, 1948, observed that "The breach between Tito and the Kremlin is the most significant development in international Communism in twenty years. It brings into the open the latent conflict between international Communist discipline and national sentiment which has been inherent in the situation since the expansion of Communist control beyond the historical frontiers of Russia and puts in question the ability of Russian-controlled Communism to retain power indefinitely beyond those frontiers." CIA 7-48, Harry S. Truman Library.

30. As Robert Jervis points out, it is a common misperception to see the behavior of others as more centralized, planned, and coordinated than it is. This is a manifestation of the drive to squeeze complex and unrelated events into a coherent pattern. Jervis also observes that perceptions of overcentralization and over-Machiavellianism are more apt to occur if the two sides are in conflict. Robert Jervis, *Perception and Misperception in International Politics* (Princeton: Princeton University Press, 1976), pp. 319 and 329. This was certainly true of America during the Cold War. By showing that the notion of a worldwide communist conspiracy was essentially a projection of America's own universalism, the revisionists advance a highly plausible explanation for this common American perception of Soviet moves not as improvisations but as the unfolding of a design. See Stanley Hoffmann, "Revisionism Revisited," in *Reflections on the Cold War*, ed. Lynn M. Miller and Ronald W. Pruessen (Philadelphia: Temple University Press, 1974), p. 11.

31. Krock, *Memoirs*, Appendix A, p. 401.

fully planned and integrated with moves on other fronts."[32] A Policy Planning Staff report, in February 1948, described the men in the Kremlin as "an able, shrewd and utterly ruthless group who operate through a political organization of unparalleled flexibility, discipline, cynicism and toughness."[33] Interestingly, Kennan himself, who wrote this report and repeatedly stressed the ruthlessness and Machiavellian cunning of the men at the Kremlin, did not slip into the common error of attributing their conduct in world affairs to an overarching plan. Rather, and with complete logical consistency on his part, he saw the men in the Kremlin as masters of improvisation. "There is no governing group anywhere in the world," he told an audience at the Air War College in April 1947, "which is less inclined to political thinking in . . . international affairs . . . than the Kremlin. . . . They play it by ear."[34] It was not Kennan's nuanced image, however, but the cruder version propogated by Clifford which lurked behind a great deal of popular and official Cold War attitudes. And those who shared the simplistic idea that the Kremlin's conduct was not only Machiavellian but centralized and guided by a long-term plan were naturally predisposed to treat the Berlin blockade not as an isolated move but as an integral part of this plan for expansion and world domination.

Taken together, these various facets of the American view of its Cold War adversary suggested a parallel with the country's earlier adversary, Nazi Germany. It was galling, so soon after defeating the Nazi dictatorship, to be confronted by another ruthless and aggressive totalitarian power leading a millenarian movement that endangered American security and the whole fabric of international order, and it was probably inevitable that the new threat would be interpreted in the light of the earlier experience. The image of Hitler was indelibly seared in the eye of all those who fought him. When America's leaders tried to comprehend the confused and threatening new world emerging from the smoke of war, they gazed at Stalin and saw in him another Hitler. They had underestimated one dictator by ignoring *Mein Kampf*, and they had paid a heavy price for their mistake. To guard against making the same

32. Dean Acheson to Clark Clifford, August 6, 1948, Box 15, Clifford Papers, Harry S. Truman Library.
33. PPS 23, February 24, 1948, in *FRUS, 1948*, Vol. 1 (Part 2), p. 528.
34. Lecture delivered at the Air War College, April 10, 1947, Box 17, George F. Kennan Papers, Seeley G. Mudd Manuscript Library, Princeton University.

mistake again, they dabbled in Marx and Lenin.[35] Once they had designated Russia as the "enemy," it became much easier for Americans to transfer their hatred for Hitler's Germany to Stalin's Russia. The analogy provided frightened Americans with the assurance that they knew what to expect from Russia by convincing them that the 1940s were simply a replay of the 1930s.[36] James Forrestal, for example, who greatly admired Kennan's analysis of the motives behind Russia's international behavior, overlooked the differences which Kennan was careful to point out between Stalin's Russia and Hitler's Germany. In a statement he made on March 24, 1948, Forrestal compared the prevailing international situation with that of 1914 and 1939 and placed the aggressive policies of the Soviet Union squarely beside those of Hitler and Mussolini. "The record," he said, "shows that despotism, whatever its form, has a remorseless compulsion to aggression."[37] But the comparison of Stalin with Hitler and of Russian communism with German fascism was often misleading because it focused attention on the superficial similarities while ignoring the differences between the erstwhile and the current opponents. The men of the Truman Administration thought about the issues before them in a frame of reference made of historical parallels, but the history employed for this purpose was narrowly selected and subjected to no deliberate scrutiny or analysis.[38]

The troubled course of postwar relations with the Soviet Union helped to generate not only intense hostility towards the former ally but also profound suspicion. And the consequent attribution of bad faith to the Soviet Union meant that its actions and statements were usually placed in the worst possible light. The opponent came to be viewed within the framework of an "inherent bad faith" model. The term "inherent bad faith" was suggested by Henry Kissinger to denote a conception of the other side as evil irrespective of the na-

---

35. Richard J. Barnet, *The Giants: Russia and America* (New York: Simon and Schuster, 1977), pp. 66–68.
36. Les K. Adler and Thomas G. Paterson, "Red Fascism: The Merger of Nazi Germany and Soviet Russia in the American Image of Totalitarianism," *American Historical Review*, Vol. 75 (April 1970), pp. 1046–47.
37. Walter Millis, ed., *The Forrestal Diaries* (New York: Viking, 1951), p. 400.
38. Ernest R. May, *"Lessons" of the Past: The Use and Misuse of History in American Foreign Policy* (New York: Oxford University Press, 1973), p. 51. On the use and misuse of historical analogies to interpret current events, see also Jervis, *Perception and Misperception in International Politics*, chap. 6.

ture of its actions.[39] In other words, the possibility of change in the direction of good faith is ruled out virtually *a priori*. It should be pointed out that within the framework of such a model, the negative image of the enemy can become self-perpetuating, since the assumption of "inherent bad faith" does not easily admit of evidence that could invalidate it. The striving for consistency certainly played a role in enabling the American decision-makers to maintain their basic image of the Soviet Union as malevolent and hostile in the face of seemingly contradictory evidence. When the Kremlin's behavior appeared reasonable and conciliatory, as it occasionally did during the Berlin crisis, the strain to render such discrepant information consistent with the preexisting negative image of this enemy activated various strategems for discounting, ignoring, or discrediting the new information.[40]

The third significant dimension of the attitudinal prism of the Truman Administration was its self-image. Here, as in the case of the great majority of actors engaged in an acute international conflict, the demonological view of the adversary had its natural corollary in a highly favorable view of oneself. The tendency to rationalize America's own behavior in terms of "good" motives was just as irresistible as the tendency to rationalize Russia's actions as springing from "bad" and sinister motives. For one thing, America was trying to preserve the status quo, whereas Russia was perceived to be trying to overthrow it, and this lent credibility to the view that America's actions were legitimate while Russia's actions were illegitimate. Moreover, America's foreign policy objectives were identified with the universal goals of international peace and justice. America was pictured not simply as defending its own national interests but as carrying the torch of liberty, upholding the rights of democratic nations everywhere, and defending the free world against communist subversion and encroachment. This self-image was partly the product of the American public's aversion to power politics, which tempts American policymakers, even when they are using the traditional instruments of statecraft and pursu-

39. Henry A. Kissinger, *The Necessity for Choice: Prospects of American Foreign Policy* (New York: Doubleday, 1962), p. 201.
40. In elaborating the idea of "inherent bad faith," I relied on Ole R. Holsti in Finlay et al., *Enemies in Politics*, pp. 26–27; and Alexander L. George, *Presidential Decisionmaking in Foreign Policy: The Effective Use of Information and Advice* (Boulder, Colorado: Westview, 1980), pp. 65–66.

ing a classical balance-of-power policy, to project their policy as the expression of selfless internationalism. This self-image was also partly the product of the congenital aversion of American politicians themselves to take specific decisions on specific problems and their persistent urge, of which the Truman Doctrine is the most striking example, to attribute universal morality to actions undertaken in pursuit of America's national and parochial interests. But whatever its sources, the consequences of this self-image were to sharpen the dichotomy between the aggressive enemy and the defensive self, and to blind Americans to the security fears and problems of the other side and to the justice that it saw in its own cause. The American self-image also obscured the fact that many actions, especially in a bipolar setting, are both defensive and potentially offensive, and that a move which may appear to its American initiators as purely defensive and perfectly legitimate may be interpreted in Moscow as detrimental to its own security and therefore warranting countermoves (which are perceived as defensive) to neutralize its effect.

This ambiguity of actions as an indicator of intentions makes it relevant to ask whether the men in Washington were aware of how their goals were interpreted by the men in the Kremlin. In general, a political actor is likely to rely on two sources in assessing how its goals are perceived by the opponent: (1) knowledge of what its own goals actually are, and (2) cues about how the adversary is actually perceiving its goals. To the extent that the actor relies on the former source, its image will be "autistic"; to the extent that it relies on the latter, its image will be "realistic."[41] To describe the American image in this respect as autistic would involve a gross exaggeration. Some of the men in Washington were capable of appreciating how their country's goals and behavior appeared from the vantage point of Moscow. Secretary of the Army Kenneth Royall, for example, came close to recognizing, in private, that the blockade of Berlin was seen by the Soviets as a response to threatening moves initiated by the West. "The Soviets have some basis for their argument," he wrote in a letter to former War Secretary Henry Stimson in April 1948, "in view of the tripartite actions we have been forced to take regarding Germany, as a result of the breakdown of the Council of Ministers last December. They can argue with

---

41. William A. Gamson and Andre Modigliani, *Untangling the Cold War: A Strategy for Testing Rival Theories* (Boston: Little, Brown, 1971), p. 27.

PSYCHOLOGICAL ENVIRONMENT 65

some logic that the Three Power talks on Germany, initiated in London in February, . . . are proof of our intention to abandon four-power control."[42] But this degree of empathy for the opponent was rare. The majority of American decision-makers tended to assume, quite uncritically, that it was as clear to the Russians as it was to them that America's actions were entirely defensive.

The strategy preferences of the American decision-makers, the fourth and final dimension of their attitudinal prism, were a natural extension of their world-view, their image of the opponent, and their self-image. The most fundamental determinant, however, was the image of the opponent. Once the image of the Soviet Union shifted from that of an estranged ally to that of an unlimited and relentlessly expansionist adversary, certain conclusions logically followed in the realm of policy. First and foremost among these was the downgrading of the role of diplomacy and conciliation as the means of promoting harmony between the two powers. American diplomacy, however accommodating and benign, was deemed incapable of establishing coexistence with an adversary bent on world domination. Kennan elaborated on the reasons for this conclusion in one of the telegrams he sent from Moscow. The belief that Soviet suspicions could be assuaged by means of direct contact, persuasion, or assurances of the good faith of American aims and policies, he noted, reflected a serious misunderstanding about Soviet realities and constituted the most insidious single error which Americans could make in their thinking about that country. If Americans wished to pursue, at all costs, the goal of disarming Soviet suspicions, "nothing short of complete disarmament, delivery of our air and naval forces to Russia, and resigning of powers of government to American Communists would dent this problem; and even then, . . . Moscow would smell a trap and would continue to harbor most baleful misgivings." In these circumstances, concluded Kennan, "there can be no more dangerous tendency in American public opinion than one which places on our Government an obligation to accomplish the impossible by gestures of goodwill and conciliation towards a political entity constitutionally incapable of being conciliated."[43]

Diplomatic concessions to the Soviet Union were seen as not

42. Royall to Stimson, April 21, 1947, Stimson Papers, quoted in Yergin, *Shattered Peace*, p. 373.
43. Kennan to Byrnes, March 20, 1946, in *FRUS, 1946*, Vol. 6, pp. 721–723.

simply futile but dangerously counterproductive. By drawing a parallel between the Soviet Union and Nazi Germany, the lessons of Munich were almost automatically invoked, and they militated against any form of appeasement.[44] These lessons were ever present in the minds of the American decision-makers and conditioned their response to the challenge presented by the Berlin blockade. As one participant observed: "This was one of those situations in which each surrender makes a stand at each successive point of retreat less convincing and more dangerous—until one's defenses are overcome or, more likely, until a desperate but belated stand brings on a catastrophe at least as great as that one tried to avoid by the first retreat. These situations have their own dynamics to which even the advancing side falls victim. In 1948 the West was able to recognize, if only instinctively, that such was the situation in Berlin, and it acted accordingly."[45]

The image of the adversary and the wider world-view of the American decision-makers not only exposed the weaknesses of some strategies but also suggested alternative ones with which to confront the problems facing them. The chief problem was that of checking Soviet expansion, and to this end the strategy deemed most appropriate was one of firmness backed by superior military power. If force was the only language which the Soviets understood, then America's best road to peace and security was via firm-

44. "It seems clear," wrote John Hickerson, of the State Department's Office of European Affairs, on February 17, 1947, "that there can be no question of 'deals or arrangements' with the Soviet Union. That method was tried once with Hitler and the lessons of that effort are fresh in our minds. One cannot appease a powerful country intent on aggression. If the lessons we learnt from dealing with Hitler mean anything, concessions to the Soviet Union would only whet their appetite for more." (Quoted here from Yergin, *Shattered Peace*, pp. 171–172.) Interestingly, although he was in many respects a leading proponent of the Riga axioms, Kennan did not only *not* succumb to the Munich analogy but explicitly repudiated it. He told a small group of American and British officials who were working on the North Atlantic Pact in July 1948 that the Kremlin was not operating on any fixed timetable and that any parallels between Stalinism and Hitlerism were dangerous. *FRUS, 1948*, Vol. 3, p. 157. For further evidence of Kennan's distress by his colleagues' inability to free themselves from the Munich analogy, see Daniel F. Harrington, "Kennan, Bohlen and the Riga Axioms," *Diplomatic History*, Vol. 2 (Fall 1978), pp. 417–428. In this important article, Harrington maintains that Yergin's presentation of Kennan as the philosopher of America's Cold War crusade is based on a misrepresentation of Kennan's ideas. Harrington finds Kennan's disclaimers about his views in the late 1940s more convincing than Yergin's explanation. On a number of specific points, of which the Munich analogy is one, Harrington's argument is well supported and illuminating.

45. Halle, *The Cold War as History*, pp. 265–266.

ness, military strength, and credible deterrence. Clifford, echoing a broad consensus, repeatedly drove the point home in his report. In Forrestal's Pentagon office, there was a prominently displayed framed card with the following inscription: "We will never have universal peace until the strongest army and the strongest navy are in the hands of the most powerful nation."[46] And the Joint Chief of Staff's major objective from 1947 to 1949 was to establish military forces adequate to support Truman's policy of resistance to Soviet expansionism.[47]

Firmness and military superiority, however, were not enough in dealing with an opponent like the Soviet Union; patience and vigilance were essential, too. As Kennan argued in his X article, because of its obduracy, inexorable drive, and steadfastness of orientation, Soviet diplomacy could not be defeated by a single victory on the part of its opponents. The remorseless persistence by which it was animated could be effectively countered not by sporadic acts but only by intelligent long-range policies on the part of its adversaries. Under these circumstances, the main element in any American policy towards the Soviet Union had to be that of "a long-term, patient but firm and vigilant containment of Russian expansive tendencies." And Kennan felt confident that "Soviet pressure against the free institutions of the western world is something that can be contained by the adroit and vigilant application of counter-force at a series of constantly shifting geographical and political points, corresponding to the shifts and maneuvers of Soviet policy."[48] The article provided the intellectual underpinnings for the Truman Administration's strategy of containment, and it helped to secure Kennan's reputation as one of the architects of postwar American foreign policy. But it also drew criticisms, notably from Walter Lippmann, who depicted Kennan's concept as a "strategic monstrosity."[49] Kennan later explained that what he was talking

46. Rogow, *Victim of Duty*, p. 138.
47. Kenneth W. Condit, *The History of the Joint Chiefs of Staff*, Vol. 2: *1947–1949* (Washington, D.C.: Historical Division, Joint Secretariat, Joint Chiefs of Staff, 1976), Record Group 218, Records of the United States Joint Chiefs of Staff, National Archives, p. 23.
48. X [George F. Kennan], "The Sources of Soviet Conduct."
49. Walter Lippmann, *The Cold War: A Study in U.S. Foreign Policy* (New York: Harper and Row, 1947). On the debate provoked by the X article, see John Lewis Gaddis, "Containment: A Reassessment," *Foreign Affairs*, Vol. 55, No. 4 (July 1977); and Charles Gati, "What Containment Meant," *Foreign Policy*, No. 7 (September 1972).

about when he mentioned the containment of Soviet power was "not the containment by military means of a military threat but the political containment of a political threat."[50] The distinction is crucial, but Kennan failed to make it at the time, and the strategy adopted by the Truman Administration for dealing with the Soviet Union was, in any case, one which pivoted on military containment.[51]

A further consequence which followed naturally from the dominant American image of a conflict-ridden and polarized world, a persistently aggressive enemy, and a defensive self related specifically to crisis management. Crises in this context were perceived not as isolated occurrences but as episodes of potentially far-reaching consequences for the positions of both actors locked in the ongoing and deadly conflict. A crisis was essentially a trial of strength whose outcome was bound to affect the long-term relationship between them. Projecting a general appearance of resolve and determination was deemed necessary for preserving and improving America's position in this relationship. Any display of weakness in handling the crisis would therefore not only play into the opponent's hands and provide him with an opportunity to expand, but would also damage, perhaps irreversibly, America's general reputation for resolve. Conversely, a firm and unyielding posture was considered the best method for defending America's specific interests in the crisis and, no less importantly, for enhancing her general reputation for firmness and strength.[52]

The image of the international system held by the men of the Truman Administration pointed in the same direction of firmness in management of crises. By the time they were faced with the Berlin blockade, they had come to believe that the international system was an increasingly unstable one in which a setback in one area could have serious destabilizing effects in other areas as well. As George and Smoke noted: "The parts of the international system were seen as tightly 'coupled' so that perturbations in one lo-

50. Kennan, *Memoirs*, p. 358.
51. Kennan's contribution to the Cold War mentality should not be minimized, for as Wright has demonstrated, the essential ambiguity and, paradoxically, rigidity of Kennan's containment thesis, as expressed in 1944–47, invited the kind of interpretations he would later deplore. See C. Ben Wright, "Mr 'X' and Containment," *Slavic Review*, Vol. 35, No. 1 (March 1976).
52. For a general discussion of this phenomenon, see Snyder and Diesing, *Conflict Among Nations*, pp. 457–458; and Thomas Halper, *Foreign Policy Crises: Appearance and Reality in Decision-Making* (Columbus, Ohio: Charles E. Merrill, 1971), pp. 200–211.

cale tended to cause strong repercussions in other areas that could throw the rest of the international system into great disequilibrium."[53] Anxiety about the repercussions elsewhere of an American political defeat in Berlin thus heightened the perceived stakes, and, like everything else in the prism through which the American decision-makers saw the world, it predisposed them against appeasement and towards making a firm stand.

Images

TRUMAN

As President of the United States, Harry Truman's role in the foreign policy and national security fields was that of "ultimate decision-maker" or "decision-maker of last resort."[54] During the pre-crisis period, presidential involvement in the decision-making process was not as active and continuous as it was to become during the crisis period, following the significant rise in the perception of threat and the probability of war. Nevertheless, throughout the crisis, Truman took some crucial decisions on his own initiative, personally participated in the formulation of others, approved lesser ones, and always retained the ultimate responsibility for the policies and conduct of his Administration.

Moreover, with an institution as personal as the American Presidency at its center, it was inevitable that the ethos and style of the entire government would be profoundly influenced by the working habits, values, and preferences of the man in charge. In Clark Clifford's words, the executive branch is a chameleon taking its color from the personality and character of the President.[55] And as all President-watchers have emphasized, the incumbent's personality will shape the formal structure of the policymaking system that he creates around himself, and, even more importantly, it will influence the ways in which he encourages and permits that system to operate in practice.[56]

Truman was modest about himself but far from modest in his

---

53. Alexander L. George and Richard Smoke, *Deterrence in American Foreign Policy: Theory and Practice* (New York: Columbia University Press, 1974), p. 117.

54. The terms are suggested by Roger Hilsman, *The Politics of Policy-Making in Defense and Foreign Affairs* (New York: Harper and Row, 1971), p. 18.

55. Clark Clifford, "The Presidency As I Have Seen It," in *The Living Presidency*, by Emmet J. Hughes (New York: Coward, McCann and Geoghegan, 1972), p. 13.

56. George, *Presidential Decisionmaking*, p. 147.

conception of the office he held. He regarded this office, in the words of his last Secretary of State, as "a sacred and temporary trust, which he was determined to pass on unimpaired by the slightest loss of power and prestige."[57] In many ways, he not only protected but actually expanded the powers and prerogatives of the Presidency in the foreign policy and national security spheres. During his tenure, the presidential office was the vortex into which the elements of national decision were powerfully drawn. To understand the American government's behavior during the Berlin crisis, it is necessary, therefore, to examine the way presidential choices were made.

Three models have been identified that characterize, at least in general terms, the approaches displayed by different American Presidents to the management of the policymaking process. These are the "formalistic," "competitive," and "collegial" models, which are best exemplified by Eisenhower, Franklin D. Roosevelt, and Kennedy, respectively.[58] Truman adopted a variant of the formalistic model, which is characterized by an orderly policymaking structure, well-defined procedures, and hierarchical lines of communication, in order to cope with the larger policy issues confronting his Administration.[59]

Truman's White House staff was in some ways the opposite of Franklin Roosevelt's. Roosevelt's had been disorganized but powerful; Truman's was better organized but possessed far less power. The task of the White House staff under Truman was not to insulate the President from the officials he appointed to run the government nor to make recommendations on fundamental national policy questions but to help him with the gathering of the information he needed in reaching decisions. The one exception was Clark Clifford, the President's special counsel, whose brilliance contrasted sharply with the mediocrity of the rest of the "Missouri gang" which Truman had brought with him into the White House. In the foreign policy sphere, Clifford had less scope for exercising his talents as an advocate than in domestic politics because of the

57. Acheson, *Present at the Creation*, p. 415.
58. These three management styles are described and evaluated by Richard T. Johnson, *Managing the White House* (New York: Harper and Row, 1974); and by George, *Presidential Decisionmaking*, chap. 8.
59. For the salient features of the formalistic model, see George, *Presidential Decisionmaking*, pp. 151–152.

presence of such towering figures as George Marshall, Dean Acheson, and James Forrestal. Nevertheless, he made his influence felt by working with these and other hard-liners in the Administration, by writing speeches for his boss, and by performing various other tasks such as the preparation of the report on relations with the Soviet Union. The consistent advice he gave Truman in regard to conflict with adversaries was to stand up and fight, and such advice usually fell on very receptive ears, particularly when the adversary was Joseph Stalin.[60]

Neither the President nor the White House staff were particularly interested in the problems of U.S. occupation in Germany. In line with his overall management style, Truman left the formulation and execution of U.S. occupation policy to the functional experts in the government departments rather than to the White House aides. He himself provided no lead in performing the task of integrating the functional inputs, and his contribution to forming occupation policy between Potsdam in 1945 and Berlin in 1948 seems to have been neither extensive nor profound. It was the challenge of the blockade that prompted him to assume the reins of power and responsibility more tightly in his own hands and to tip the balance decisively in favor of firmness. The involvement of the White House staff, on the other hand, remained minimal and of little consequence during the crisis. George Elsey, who served as Clark Clifford's assistant from 1947 to 1949, states that the "White House staff, to the best of my knowledge, had no direct role whatsoever in any decisions or in the execution of any of the carrying out of the airlift."[61]

The role of the Cabinet as a collective body in determining the Truman Administration's policy towards Germany and the American response to the Berlin crisis was also minimal. In contrast to political systems in which the Cabinet wields collective responsi-

---

60. Oral History Interview with George M. Elsey, p. 46, Harry S. Truman Library; Harry S. Truman, *Mr. Citizen* (New York: Bernard Geiss, 1960), pp. 228–229; and Patrick Anderson, *The President's Men* (New York: Doubleday, 1969), pp. 102 and 134–145.

61. Edward N. Peterson, *The American Occupation of Germany: Retreat to Victory* (Detroit: Wayne State University Press, 1977), pp. 22–23; Jerry Philip Rosenberg, *Berlin and Israel 1948: Foreign Policy Decision-Making During the Truman Administration* (Ph.D. dissertation, University of Illinois, 1977), pp. 148–149; and Oral History Interview with George M. Elsey, p. 391, Harry S. Truman Library.

bility, the American Cabinet is a council of handpicked advisers whose existence and influence depend on the will of the President. The foreign policy recommendations of this presidential organ become significant in terms of national policy only insofar as the President decides to adopt them. Truman looked on his Cabinet primarily as "a board of directors appointed by the President to help him carry out the policies of the government."[62] Preoccupied with foreign affairs and domestic politics, he left his Cabinet Secretaries considerable freedom in the running of their departments, but he was careful not to turn over the complete authority of the President nor to relinquish the President's prerogative to make the final decisions.[63] As a strong President, Truman was not averse to including in his Cabinet strong-minded individuals such as Forrestal, Marshall, Vinson, and Harriman. Nor was he reluctant to bring foreign policy issues before the Cabinet for discussion. But on such issues he declined to use the Cabinet as a voting board of directors. He welcomed advice but made it patently clear at the outset that all final policy decisions would be his, and that once such decisions had been made, he expected the Cabinet officers, whatever their personal views, to support him.[64] Forrestal's suggestion that the British Cabinet system be adopted as the model in the operation of the government was dismissed with the observation that "under the British system there is a group responsibility of the Cabinet. Under our system the responsibility rests on one man—the President."[65]

The institutional framework for managing national security was established by the National Security Act of 1947.[66] In one sense the Act was a reaction against the "free and easy" way in which Roosevelt had conducted the Second World War. In another it was a response to the new conditions of recurrent emergencies and crises spawned by the Cold War. In setting out the new framework for decision and operation, the Act dealt with three main issues:

62. Harry S. Truman, *Memoirs*, Vol. 1: *Year of Decisions, 1945* (London: Hodder and Stoughton, 1955), p. 253.
63. Richard F. Fenno, *The President's Cabinet* (Cambridge, Mass.: Harvard University Press, 1963), p. 43; and William Hillman, *Mr. President: Personal Diaries, Private Letters, Papers, and Revealing Interviews of Harry S. Truman* (London: Hutchison, 1952), p. 21.
64. Truman, *Memoirs*, Vol. 1, pp. 9–10.
65. Harry S. Truman, *Memoirs*, Vol. 2: *Years of Trial and Hope, 1946–1953* (London: Hodder and Stoughton, 1956), p. 64.
66. The National Security Act (1947), 61 Stat. 495.

coordination of political and military policy, improved intelligence capability, and rationalization of the defense community.[67]

At the apex of the new organization for national security stood the President; and to deal with the first issue, that of coordination in political and military matters, the Act established the National Security Council (NSC). The NSC's statutory duties were "to advise the President with respect to the integration of domestic, foreign and military policies relating to the national security so as to enable the military services and the other departments and agencies of the government to cooperate more effectively in matters involving national security" and "to assess and appraise the objectives, commitments and risks of the United States in relation to our actual and potential military power, in the interest of national security." Truman, however, had serious reservations about the NSC and was consequently disinclined to allow it to play a major role in policymaking.[68] Prior to the outbreak of the Korean War in June 1950, Truman presided over only eleven out of fifty-six meetings. This highly irregular attendance has sometimes been attributed to a desire on Truman's part to encourage a free exchange of views, but a far more likely explanation is that he deliberately absented himself in order to underline the Council's purely advisory role and to prevent any apparent dilution of his own role as chief executive. Fending off the claims of the Secretary of Defense, Truman designated the Secretary of State as the second-ranking member of the Council and chairman of its meetings in his absence, and he did not hesitate to deal with the Secretary of State and other members and to solicit their individual opinions directly rather than through the Council. Even when he himself chaired a meeting and expressed his agreement with a particular recommendation, Truman insisted that this did not become official policy until he had signified his

67. Thomas H. Etzold, "American Organization for National Security, 1945–1950," in Etzold and Gaddis, *Containment*, pp. 8–18.
68. Truman, *Memoirs*, Vol. 2, pp. 55–64; Millis, *The Forrestal Diaries*, pp. 320–321; and Anderson, *The President's Men*, pp. 202–207. On the NSC under Truman, see also Helen P. Kirkpatrick, "Advisers and Policy-Makers: The National Security Council," *American Perspectives*, Vol. 2 (February 1949); Charles Fairman, "The President as Commander-in-Chief," *The Journal of Politics*, Vol. 2, No. 1 (February 1949); John Fischer, "Mr. Truman's Politburo," *Harper's Magazine*, Vol. 211 (June 1951); Dillon Anderson, "The President and National Security," *Atlantic Monthly*, Vol. 197 (January 1956); and Paul Y. Hammond, *Organizing for Defense: The American Military Establishment in the Twentieth Century* (Princeton: Princeton University Press, 1961), pp. 227–232.

approval in writing, because as chief executive he and he alone had the responsibility for making the final decision.[69] Within these clearly prescribed limits, the NSC played a useful role as a forum for debate, as a place for recommendations to be worked out, and as the source of numerous reports and policy statements. Its recommendations usually received formal endorsement, but it did not play a decisive role in defense decision-making or the administration of the military establishment until the onset of the Korean War. Some of the great episodes of the Cold War were not dealt with, in their most vital aspects, through the machinery of the NSC. Truman treated it in a somewhat cavalier fashion: he used it when he needed it and ignored it when he did not.

To provide an improved intelligence capability, the National Security Act created the Central Intelligence Agency (CIA). This Agency was assigned the task of coordinating, under the supervision of the NSC, all the government's intelligence activities concerned with national security. Its other major function was to correlate and evaluate national security intelligence and to report to and advise the NSC on all matters within this field. The somewhat jaundiced view with which Truman looked upon the NSC did not extend to the CIA, because the latter was not perceived by him as an institutional rival out to encroach on presidential authority. Rather, he viewed it as a badly needed new facility by which the vast amount of information available to the different departments could be coordinated and made immediately available to the President, thereby reducing the dangers of dependence on any one single source.[70] By the time of the Berlin crisis, the CIA was not only sufficiently established to ensure that an adequate intelligence base was available to sustain the deliberations of the NSC, but Truman had formed the habit of starting the day's work early each morning with an intelligence briefing from the Director of the CIA.

Finally, in meeting the challenge of rationalizing the vast and complex American defense community, the 1947 Act established a two-tier National Military Establishment (NME) headed by a Secretary of Defense (instead of a Secretary of War), for which post James Forrestal became the first incumbent. The first tier con-

69. Stanley C. Falk, "The National Security Council Under Truman, Eisenhower and Kennedy," *Political Science Quarterly*, Vol. 79, No. 1 (1964), pp. 405–417.

70. Truman, *Mr. Citizen*, pp. 264–265.

sisted of five boards and committees, of which the most important were the War Council and the Joint Chiefs of Staff. The second tier consisted of three departments, Army, Navy, and Air Force, with a Cabinet-level civilian at the head of each. By limiting the Secretary of Defense's authority over the secretaries of the military departments, and by giving the latter direct access to the President as well as a place on the National Security Council, Congress, in effect, merely established a coordinator of the three existing departments; there was no real "Department" of Defense. Under each civilian secretary was the senior military commander of each service, who served as a member of the Joint Chiefs of Staff (JCS). The Act gave legal standing to the existing membership of the Joint Chiefs of Staff—namely, the Chief of Staff, U.S. Army; the Chief of Staff, U.S. Air Force; the Chief of Naval Operations; and the Chief of Staff to the Commander in Chief, should the President choose to fill this last post.[71] Admiral William D. Leahy had held this important post since it was created in 1942, and, on becoming President, Truman asked him to continue. Leahy presided over the meetings of the Joint Chiefs, who were designated as the principal military advisers to the President, and he provided invaluable liaison between them and the White House. An old conservative who was renowned for his staunchly anti-communist convictions, Leahy consistently used his influence with Truman in order to promote greater toughness on the American side in all dealings with the Soviets.

While presidential preeminence within the executive branch was firmly maintained, relations with the legislative branch posed a thorny problem for Truman. As a Democrat, he had to contend, after the election of 1946, with a Republican majority in Congress. This majority played havoc with his domestic legislative program. His international policy would have had little prospect of success without a broad domestic consensus to sustain it. To secure this consensus, Truman became a fervent proponent of a bipartisan foreign policy; and in Senator Arthur Vandenberg, who assiduously promoted it on the Republican side, he found an exceptionally valuable ally.[72] The device of bipartisanship—or "nonpartisanship," as

---

71. Condit, *The History of the Joint Chiefs of Staff*, Vol. 2, pp. 1–8.
72. H. Bradford Westerfield, *Foreign Policy and Party Politics: Pearl Harbor to Korea* (New Haven: Yale University Press, 1955); Susan M. Hartmann, *Truman*

Vandenberg preferred to call it—brought rich rewards in terms of broadly based and fairly consistent Congressional backing for the foreign policy of the Truman Administration. Moreover, the price which Truman had to pay for this support from his political opponents was minimal: Republican leaders had to be consulted and kept informed, but the requirements of consultation did not seriously curtail the freedom of action of the President in foreign affairs. In times of crisis, the President was even freer from Congressional oversight and control than at other times because it was generally recognized that, as the issues of war and peace became more central, the President might have to act quickly and often secretly, and there might be neither the time nor the appropriate opportunity for the open and lengthy procedures by which Congress could be brought into the decision.[73]

Public opinion, like Congressional opinion, was permissive rather than restrictive, leaving the President considerable latitude in determining American objectives, priorities, and policy during the Cold War. Truman, for his part, viewed public opinion as a force to be coaxed, educated, and led rather than as a force to be followed, and his ability to create and mobilize public support for his foreign policy was no less impressive than his skill in circumventing or manipulating Congress. Again, while presidential initiative in foreign policy was vigorously exercised at all times, crises created especially propitious conditions for a strong President who wanted to chart his own course. As Clark Clifford rightly pointed out, "in time of crisis the American citizen tends to back up his President."[74] Not surprisingly, a recent study has concluded that "public opinion and Congress proved malleable, compliant and permissive in the making of American Cold War foreign policy."[75] Another study of the impact of public opinion on Truman's foreign policy has similarly concluded that that impact was insignificant and that "the key is to be found in the minds and actions of a small number of executive policymakers whose view of history, under-

---

and the 80th Congress (Columbia: University of Missouri Press, 1971); and Arthur M. Schlesinger, Jr., *The Imperial Presidency* (London: André Deutsch, 1974), pp. 128–131.

73. Hilsman, *The Politics of Policy-Making*, pp. 26–27.

74. Quoted here from Richard J. Walton, *Henry Wallace, Harry Truman and the Cold War* (New York: Viking, 1976), p. 301.

75. Thomas G. Paterson, *On Every Front: The Making of the Cold War* (New York: Norton, 1979), p. 137.

standing of the Soviet Union, determination of the American system's requirements and evaluation of U.S. power primarily shaped the nation's foreign policy."[76]

Truman's personal credentials for conducting the nation's foreign policy were practically nonexistent when he entered the White House. Throughout his previous career, he had been a domestic politician through and through. Of foreign affairs he was woefully ignorant. As Vice President, he was firmly excluded by F.D.R. from the foreign policy arena and was not even kept informed about important matters. The last time he had left the American shores was during the First World War, when he served as a Captain in the U.S. Army in France. But he had the ability and the will to learn fast, and although he relied heavily on trusted foreign policy advisers like George Marshall and Dean Acheson, he was the leader and not merely the mouthpiece of his Administration. What Truman lacked in experience he made up through his voracious reading of history. Few other presidents were as steeped in American history as he was or as intent on learning from the lessons of the past and applying these lessons to contemporary problems. This aspect of his approach to policymaking is given prominence in his memoirs. "I had trained myself," he explains, "to look back into history for precedents, because instinctively I sought perspective in the span of history for the decisions I had to make. That is why I read and re-read history. Most of the problems a President has to face have their roots in the past."[77]

Apart from his penchant for turning to history for instruction, Truman had one other quality, surprisingly rare among decision-makers: he loved making decisions. This love and the readiness with which he shouldered personal responsibility for the decisions of his Administration were expressed in his famous motto as President: "The buck stops here." Those who worked with him had the greatest admiration for his capacity to grasp complex questions and make a decision. This capacity, as General Marshall frequently observed, is one of the rarest qualities possessed by man. Truman read tirelessly the material given him, listened intently to the arguments of his advisers, and then decided, clearly and firmly.

76. Walter LaFeber, "American Policy-Makers, Public Opinion and the Outbreak of the Cold War, 1945–50," in *The Origins of the Cold War in Asia*, ed. Yonosuke Nagai and Akira Iriye (New York: Columbia University Press, 1977), p. 62.
77. Truman, *Memoirs*, Vol. 1, p. xiii.

Once a matter was decided, it took a great deal of new evidence to reopen it. He went on to new problems and had little time or inclination to rehash old ones.[78] He was also remarkably successful at avoiding the stress usually associated with the making of difficult decisions. He prided himself on his ability to make difficult decisions without subsequent doubts and tormenting afterthoughts, for this ability was to him a mark of efficacy in a President. "If you can't stand the heat, stay out of the kitchen" was one of his favorite sayings.

Prompt and firm decisions were considered by Truman to be especially important in times of crisis. This comes out very clearly in a chapter on "Spot Decisions" in a book entitled *Mr. Citizen*, which he wrote after his retirement: "The most dangerous course a President can follow in a time of crisis is to defer making decisions until they are forced on him and thereupon become inevitable decisions. . . . In normal times, lack of Presidential leadership may be harmless, though it can hardly be considered a national asset. But in times of crisis irresolution on the part of the President can do the nation great harm. It can in fact damage the situation beyond anyone's ability to overcome it later." In a passage which is particularly revealing about his own pattern of behavior during crises, Truman adds:

> All the time I was President, one event followed another with such rapidity that I was never able to afford the time for prolonged contemplation. I had to make sure of the facts. I had to consult people. But to have hesitated when it was necessary to act might well have meant disaster in many instances.
>
> Many of the important decisions I had to make in the White House were what I described to myself as "spot decisions." By "spot decisions," I meant decisions which were almost instinctive with me—when I had to confront an emergency or serious situation. I never revealed to anyone what my "spot decision" was in advance of calling for all the facts available and consulting the experts or the departments of government involved. Once the facts were examined and the experts heard, I then made the final deci-

---

78. Dean Acheson, "Princeton Seminar," p. 47, Papers of Dean Acheson, Harry S. Truman Library. See also Oral History Interview with General William H. Draper, January 11, 1972, p. 20, Harry S. Truman Library. Richard E. Neustadt, who served for a time on Truman's staff, gives a detailed account of Truman's methods and style as a decision-maker and his relations with his staff, in *Presidential Power: The Politics of Leadership* (New York: Wiley, 1960), pp. 171–173.

sion. Looking back, I find that my final decisions usually corresponded to my first "spot decisions."[79]

The overeagerness to appear firm and decisive and to demonstrate that he was in control of the situation occasionally led Truman to act impulsively. His "spot decisions" were not always made on the basis of a careful study of the available facts. Inadequate information and uncertainty about the relevant facts did not necessarily inhibit Truman from acting. Nor was he deterred by the prospect of conflict from taking decisions he believed to be right. On the contrary, he thrived on conflict. "There are times in world history," Truman remarked on the eve of the Berlin crisis, "when it is far wiser to act than to hesitate."[80] If his record is anything to go by, he must have considered the occasions when hesitation was preferable to action extremely rare.

Truman's greatest preoccupation during his presidency was with what he called "the threat of Russian totalitarianism."[81] This was the key problem which shaped in no small measure his entire outlook on international relations. "A President has little time to meditate," he wrote in his autobiography, "but whenever such moments occurred, I was more than likely to turn my thoughts toward this key problem that confronted our nation."[82] As already noted, Truman did not launch into a tough policy toward Russia immediately after he succeeded Roosevelt as President. There was an interlude which lasted until the end of the year, during which the new President gradually made up his mind about the implications of Soviet totalitarianism for American security. His advisers during this period included proponents of the Yalta as well as of the Riga axioms. From the beginning, however, the second group carried more weight with Truman. Prominent among this second group were such men as James Forrestal, Dean Acheson, Admiral Leahy, Clark Clifford, and Averell Harriman.

An early glimpse of the new President's thinking emerged in the course of a conversation between him and Harriman in April 1945.

79. Truman, *Mr. Citizen*, p. 262.
80. "Special Message to Congress on the Threat to the Freedom of Europe," March 17, 1948, *Public Papers of the Presidents of the United States: Harry S. Truman, 1948* (Washington, D.C.: U.S. Government Printing Office, 1964), p. 184.
81. Truman, *Memoirs*, Vol. 2, pp. 106–107.
82. Ibid., p. 107.

Harriman, who had been sent as Ambassador to Moscow in 1943 and was to become Truman's Secretary of Commerce in 1946, came home to urge a reconsideration of American policy towards the Soviet Union, arguing that the Soviet Union did not share the Western commitment to world order and that certain elements around Stalin misinterpreted American generosity and American desire to cooperate as an indication of softness. Truman agreed and stated that he was not afraid of the Russians, that he intended to be firm but fair, and "anyway the Russians needed us more than we needed them." He was resolved to "make no concessions from American principles or traditions in order to win their favor."[83] Truman's personal encounter with Stalin at Potsdam reinforced his belief that verbal protests were not enough to disabuse the Russians of the notion that they could continue on their expansionist course without risking challenge from the United States. By the end of the year, after the unsatisfactory outcome of the Council of Foreign Ministers meeting in Moscow, he was fully convinced that a different approach was called for. He expressed his views in a blunt memorandum which, according to his own account, he read to Secretary of State Byrnes on January 5, 1946. "There isn't a doubt in my mind," Truman declared after listing a long series of accomplished facts created by Russia, "that Russia intends the invasion of Turkey and the seizure of the Black Sea Straits to the Mediterranean. Unless Russia is faced with an iron fist and strong language another war is in the making. Only one language do they understand—'how many divisions have you?' I do not think we should play compromise any longer. . . . I'm tired of babying the Soviets."[84]

Truman's image of the Soviet Union as the "world bully" only hardened with the passage of time. This image was not tempered by even the faintest empathy for the estranged ally. Truman did not seem capable of seeing Russian demands and Russian actions in Germany, in Eastern Europe, and in the Balkans from the perspective of Russian anxieties about their security. To him the suggestion that any of these neighboring countries, a resurgent Germany, or America could threaten Russia in any way was inconceivable. The greed, aggressiveness, and ruthless expansionism which charac-

83. Truman, *Memoirs*, Vol. 1, pp. 73–75.
84. Ibid., pp. 492–493. Byrnes, however, denied that Truman ever read this memorandum to him. See James F. Byrnes, *All in One Lifetime* (New York: Harper, 1958), pp. 400–403.

terized the Kremlin's conduct abroad was simply an extension of the despotism and brutality which it practiced at home. At any rate, Truman was quite clear in his own mind that the spread of Soviet rule was undermining the foundations of international peace and hence the security of the United States.[85]

The emphasis on the dictatorial nature of the Soviet regime and the threat it posed to American security loomed large in Truman's image of the adversary and suggested parallels with other adversaries from recent American history. "We had fought a long war," wrote Truman, "to crush the totalitarianism of Hitler, the insolence of Mussolini and the arrogance of the warlords of Japan. Yet the new menace facing us seemed every bit as grave as Nazi Germany and her allies had been."[86] In a letter to his daughter, dated March 3, 1948, Truman was much more explicit in the historical analogies he drew and more unrestrained in expressing the profound distaste he felt towards the Soviet regime. "Many agreements were made at Potsdam," he wrote, "agreements for the government of Germany—not one of which has Russia kept. . . . So that now we are faced with exactly the same situation with which Britain and France were faced in 1938–9 with Hitler. A totalitarian state is no different whether you call it Nazi, Fascist, Communist or Franco Spain. . . . A decision will have to be made. I am going to make it. . . . We may have to fight for it. The oligarchy in Russia is no different from the Czars, Louis XIV, Napoleon, Charles I and Cromwell. It is a Frankenstein dictatorship worse than any of the others, Hitler included."[87]

Truman's image of the United States was, needless to say, the exact antithesis of his image of the Soviet Union. He saw his country as a benign and decent liberal democracy, committed unreservedly to world order and peace, and upholding the highest standards of international behavior. In Truman's view, there was perfect harmony between the ideals that he thought America ought to promote and her national interest. This harmony followed naturally from his image of an interdependent world in which America's freedom, security, and prosperity were closely linked to those of other nations.[88]

85. Condit, *The History of the Joint Chiefs of Staff*, Vol. 2, p. 1.
86. Truman, *Memoirs*, Vol. 2, p. 107.
87. Margaret Truman, *Harry S. Truman*, pp. 359–360.
88. See, for example, Truman's "Annual Message to Congress on the State of the Union," January 7, 1948, *Public Papers of the Presidents: Harry S. Truman, 1948*, p. 7.

Seeing the free nations in the postwar world as closely interdependent led Truman to set his face firmly against any return to isolationism and to advocate an active interventionist policy to check the spread of communist power and doctrines. The forces of Communism would triumph unless stronger forces were mustered against them; and as the strongest country in the free world, it was incumbent on America, Truman felt, to shoulder global burdens and responsibilities commensurate with her power. The image of American power as a positive force in world affairs thus neatly complemented the image of Soviet power as fermenting mischief, revolution, and war. Truman's conviction that only a strong America could keep the forces of evil at bay stayed with him for the rest of his life. It was forcefully expressed in *Mr. Citizen*: "We must not at any time falter in maintaining our strong position, no matter what it costs, since we are the principal discouraging force to communist imperialism—and to war."[89]

Few men in the Truman Administration could have perceived the conflict between the free world and the Soviet bloc as intensely as its leader did. The two-camp image completely dominated Truman's world-view. He came to see relations between the two camps not as ordinary political rivalry but as an ideological confrontation between two ways of life. The classic example of this Cold War image of international politics as a global contest between democracy and totalitarianism was, of course, the Doctrine which bears Truman's name. The relevant passage in the President's address to the two Houses of Congress went as follows:

> At the present moment in world history nearly every nation must choose between alternative ways of life. The choice is too often not a free one.
> One way of life is based upon the will of the majority, and is distinguished by free institutions, representative government, free elections, guarantees of individual liberty, freedom of speech and religion, and freedom from political oppression. The second way of life is based upon the will of the minority forcibly imposed upon the majority. It relies on terror and oppression, a controlled press and radio, fixed elections, and the suppression of personal freedoms.[90]

---

89. Truman, *Mr. Citizen*, p. 204.
90. *Public Papers of the Presidents of the United States: Harry S. Truman, 1947* (Washington, D.C.: U.S. Government Printing Office, 1963), pp. 178–179.

Although the sweeping and emotive tone and the overt ideological coloring were dictated by domestic political considerations, Truman's statement nevertheless conveyed, in essence, his image of world politics as a deadly contest between two ideologically irreconcilable adversaries. It also reflected his conclusion, based on nearly two years' experience, that in dealing with the Kremlin, actions spoke louder than words. And it proposed a strategy which from now on would govern American policy towards the Soviet Union: containment.

On March 17, 1948, in an atmosphere of crisis engendered by the Communist coup in Czechoslovakia, rising tension in Berlin, and widespread expectation of war, Truman went before Congress with another special message. This time he minced no words and enunciated his devil's theory of the crisis, in which the Soviet Union featured as the principal source of the world's misfortunes. The critical world situation, he maintained, was not the result of natural difficulties that follow a great war. It was chiefly due to the fact that "one nation has not only refused to cooperate in the establishment of a just and honorable peace, but—even worse—has actively sought to prevent it." Truman accused Russia of persistently ignoring and violating international agreements, obstructing the work of the United Nations, and destroying the independence and democratic character of a whole series of nations in eastern and central Europe. "It is this ruthless course of action," he asserted, "and a clear design to extend it to the remaining nations of Europe, that have brought about the critical situation in Europe today." In view of this situation, he urged Congress to speed up the European Recovery Plan and to institute universal military training and a temporary draft.[91]

In a second speech that evening, Truman spelled out to the nation in even starker terms the issues and risks facing America and the need for resolution. He sought to dispel any confusion about the issue confronting the country. The issue, he said, was as old as recorded history: it was tyranny against freedom. "We will have to take risks during the coming year," he continued, "risks perhaps greater than any this country has been called upon to assume. But they are not risks of our own making, and we cannot make the dan-

91. "Special Message to Congress on the Threat to the Freedom of Europe," March 17, 1948, *Public Papers of the Presidents: Harry S. Truman, 1948*, pp. 182–186.

ger vanish by pretending that it does not exist. We must be prepared to meet that danger with sober self-restraint and calm and judicious action if we are to be successful in our leadership for peace."[92]

This was Truman's definition of the situation on the eve of the Berlin crisis. In this context, he perceived the blockade of Berlin as one more manifestation of Moscow's clear, planned, and ruthless design to extend its despotic rule to the rest of Europe. This move, however, was seen as a vital link in Moscow's strategy of encroachment on Western positions because it constituted a deliberate probe of America's determination. As Truman himself put it: "The Berlin blockade was a move to test our capacity and will to resist. This action and the previous attempts to take over Greece and Turkey were part of a Russian plan to probe for soft spots in the Western Allies' position all around their own perimeter."[93] The stakes which America was called on to defend in this crisis were considered by Truman to be of the greatest magnitude. "What was at stake in Berlin," he claimed, "was not a contest over legal rights, although our position was entirely sound in international law, but a struggle over Germany and, in a larger sense, over Europe. In the face of our launching of the Marshall Plan, the Kremlin tried to mislead the people of Europe into believing that our interest and support would not extend beyond economic matters and that we would back away from any military risks."[94]

There was nothing in Truman's view of the nature of the East-West conflict, or his image of the adversary, or his definition of what was at stake in this particular crisis which could have encouraged him to think that shirking the trial of strength was a viable option for America. In all previous crises involving Russia, notably over Turkey and Greece, he had adopted a tough and uncompromising stand. His stand appeared to be vindicated by the outcome of these confrontations, and these earlier successes as well as all of his own deeper instincts predisposed him to adopt a similar stand, despite the attendant risks, in response to the Soviet challenge in Berlin in the Spring of 1948.

92. "St. Patrick's Day Address in New York City," March 17, 1948, in ibid., pp. 186–190.
93. Truman, *Memoirs*, Vol. 2, p. 139.
94. Ibid., p. 130.

MARSHALL

The appointment in January 1947 of General George C. Marshall as Secretary of State startled Washington because the American tradition did not favor the appointment of a professional soldier for the highest foreign policy post. With General MacArthur exercising supreme authority in Japan and Korea, General Clay serving as the key figure in Germany, General Smith serving as ambassador to Moscow, and now General Marshall being appointed Secretary of State, several Washington commentators deplored what they called the "military takeover."[95]

With all the benefits conferred by hindsight, however, it is still not easy to penetrate Marshall's inner thinking or to assess the effect of his military background and images on American foreign policy. Before one can assess the influence which his images had on the policy positions he adopted, one needs to be able to ascertain the content of these images in the first place, and this in Marshall's case is an exceedingly difficult task, not least because he himself maintained a firm policy of not commenting on official matters in private or semiofficial correspondence. This attitude of strict and unswerving secrecy in all matters, private and official, also accounts for Marshall's refusal to write his memoirs, setting down the facts as he saw them so as to explain and justify his record.[96] The French saying, "Only silence is great; everything else is weakness," captures some of the qualities of the strong-willed, high-minded, and taciturn old general. As a motto it has much to recommend it, but it does not exactly ease the task of the historian.

Given the paucity of sources available for analyzing Marshall's inner thinking, it is not surprising that he remains in some ways an elusive and enigmatic figure and that historians differ significantly in their assessment of his contribution to American foreign policy and crisis management during the crucial two years (January 1947 to January 1949) when he served as Secretary of State.

One view, recently advanced by Jean Edward Smith—a Berlin specialist who switched from orthodoxy to revisionism with a vengeance—is that "the replacement of Secretary James F. Byrnes by

---

95. Robert Murphy, *Diplomat Among Warriors* (London: Collins, 1964), pp. 373–374.
96. Truman, *Mr. Citizen*, pp. 236–237.

General George C. Marshall accelerated the advent of the Cold War; channelled control of U.S. policy in Germany to those who thought cooperation with the USSR was neither feasible nor desirable; contributed to the imposition of the Berlin blockade; and plunged the United States into a posture of hostile confrontation with the Soviet Union which continued for the duration of the Truman Administration."[97] Smith acknowledges Marshall's creative sponsorship of European recovery, but draws attention to the dark side of this accomplishment, namely, "General Marshall's contribution to the Cold War; his reliance—celebrated by Dean Acheson, George Kennan and others—on State Department professionals (who viewed Europe in apocalyptic terms and subscribed to various demon theories of Soviet behavior); as well as his dedicated acceptance of the narrow, provincial outlook of the Administration which he so ably served."[98]

Another interpretation, advanced by Daniel Yergin, is that Marshall, aged sixty-seven, was an exhausted man by the time he went to the State Department and that this exhaustion rendered him a pliable Secretary of State. Having served as Chief of Staff of the U.S. Army since 1939, Marshall was preparing for his retirement at the end of 1945 when Truman asked him to go to China to advance the American effort at mediation in the civil war. The old warhorse reluctantly answered the call of duty, but the frustrations in China certainly did exhaust whatever patience he might have had left. He blamed the Nationalists as much as the Communists for the failure of his mission, and it did not escape his notice that the Chinese Communists operated somewhat independently of Moscow. Marshall carried great prestige with him into the office of the Secretary of State, which he assumed, once again at Truman's behest, upon his return from the abortive mission to China in early January 1947. Marshall also brought with him a good measure of exhaustion. Prestige and exhaustion did not necessarily make for a happy combination, remarks Yergin, who quotes Acheson telling Felix Frankfurter on one of their morning walks in November 1947: "Marshall is a four-engine bomber going only on one engine—I don't know what is the matter with him. He does not seem to bring

---

97. Jean Edward Smith, "The View from USFET: General Clay's and Washington's Interpretation of Soviet Intentions in Germany, 1945–1948," in *U.S. Occupation in Europe After World War II*, ed. Hans A. Schmitt (Lawrence: Regents Press of Kansas, 1978), p. 65.

98. Ibid., p. 66.

his full force into action." Yergin also observes that the new Secretary could hardly have been well acquainted with the range of foreign policy issues, and this made him even more dependent for information and guidance on the State Department experts.[99] Since by this time the hawks were firmly ensconced in the State Department and the Riga axioms were the order of the day, the new Secretary had little choice, Yergin implies, but to pursue the anti-Soviet course charted by his hawkish advisers. If this interpretation is correct, it would follow that it was not so much Marshall's personal images and dispositions but those of the hard-liners—images which Yergin recognizes to have been flawed in many crucial respects—which launched the United States on a collision course with the Soviet Union.

The truth would appear to lie somewhere in the middle between these two explanations. There is a case to be made for seeing Marshall as a Cold Warrior who contributed personally to the rigid American posture which helped to bring about the rift with Russia over Germany, but Smith surely spoils a good case by overstating it. After all, the struggle for Germany had some structural roots for which Marshall can hardly be held responsible, and his appointment as Secretary of State was as much an indication as it was a cause of the hardening of American policy, which found one of its clearest expressions in Truman's break with Byrnes and disavowal of the latter's conciliatory approach to the Soviets. Yergin's interpretation, on the other hand, while rightly emphasizing the powerful anti-communist consensus which pervaded the State Department and the growing power which the Riga adherents enjoyed after Byrnes's departure, goes too far in the other direction of minimizing Marshall's personal contribution to the new policy of firmness. Marshall, after all, even in his exhausted state, was hardly the kind of docile yes-man who would be content being a mere figurehead and mouthpiece of an organization which others controlled. It is true that he did not challenge the Riga adherents and that he tacitly adopted their premises as the basis for policy, but there is no evidence to suggest that he himself was predisposed to act differently. Although he was not an original Riga man himself, having apparently believed until he ceased to be Chief of Staff that a *modus vivendi* with the Russians was possible, these early hopes had evaporated by the time he became Secretary of State. In other

---

99. Yergin, *Shattered Peace*, pp. 261–262.

words, his failure to challenge the hard-liners may have been due to a genuine conversion on his part to the Riga axioms rather than to mental or physical exhaustion.

Truman could hardly have chosen Marshall in the expectation that the latter would prove to be a pliant Secretary of State. The Republican victory in the 1946 Congressional elections necessitated closer cooperation with the Republican leadership in the conduct of foreign policy. To secure such cooperation, the President needed a Secretary of State who commanded bipartisan respect and support as well as one in whom he himself could have full confidence. In Byrnes's successor he also needed, for dealing with the Russians, a man of stature and authority commensurate with the power and prestige of the United States—a heavy tank rather than a sniper. No other man fulfilled these requirements as admirably as the revered and distinguished General.

The relationship between the Secretary of State and the President was a major factor in the making of American foreign policy. Marshall viewed the relationship as that of a soldier to a commanding officer. He respected Truman, revered the Presidency, and carefully avoided conducting, or even the appearance of conducting, an independent foreign policy. From Truman's point of view, Marshall was the ideal Secretary. The President had the highest possible regard for Marshall, publicly referred to him as the greatest living American, and trusted him as he trusted no other individual in public life.[100] Although they sometimes differed on details, their relationship was not marred by any fundamental disagreement on policy or by personal rivalry. More than most Secretaries of State, Marshall directly influenced the formulating of foreign policy; and more than many Presidents, Truman relied on the judgment and advice of his Secretary.[101] This wholehearted presidential admiration and backing was one of Marshall's greatest assets as Secretary of State.

As head of the State Department, Marshall also earned the respect of his subordinates for his sterling qualities. George Kennan, who had many opportunities to observe him at close quarters, was particularly impressed by Marshall's "unshakeable integrity; his

---

100. On Truman's adulatory view of Marshall, see, for example, Merle Miller, *Plain Speaking: An Oral Biography of Harry S. Truman* (London: Coronet, 1973), pp. 249–255.

101. Alexander DeConde, *The American Secretary of State: An Intepretation* (London: Pall Mall Press, 1962), pp. 120–121.

consistent courtesy and gentlemanliness of conduct; his ironclad sense of duty; his imperturbability—the imperturbability of a good conscience—in the face of harassments, pressures and criticisms; his deliberateness and conscientiousness of decision, his serene readiness—once a decision had been taken—to abide by its consequences, whatever they might be; his lack of petty vanity or ambition; his indifference to the whims and moods of public opinion, particularly as manifested in the mass media. . . ."[102] Unlike his predecessor, Marshall was also a good administrator who insisted on orderly staff work and knew how to delegate authority to his subordinates. Above all, he was able to provide leadership and a sense of purpose and direction. The appointment of a man who enjoyed so much respect in the White House and on Capitol Hill uplifted the State Department from the doldrums. As one official recalled: "In a stroke, the authority, participation and responsibility of the President in the conduct of foreign relations was restored; and the Department of State as an institution was put into business again. The change was felt from top to bottom and called forth a great surge of ideas and constructive effort."[103]

The most distinctive contribution that Marshall made in his reorganization of the State Department was the creation of a Policy Planning Staff consisting of a small group of specialists, headed by George Kennan, who worked directly under the Secretary. Their function, apart from the immediate task of working out proposals for European economic recovery, was to coordinate all the planning activities within the Department, to develop long-term programs for the achievement of American foreign policy objectives, and to prepare reports on broad politico-military matters.[104] Whatever its limitations, the group did serve to focus the attention of the policymakers on the long-term aspects of policy. During the Berlin crisis, for example, it was charged with studying the German problem as a whole. Although its recommendations were not always adopted, several of Marshall's policy initiatives originated in this concerted planning activity.

Marshall's whole approach to foreign policy, both in his working methods and in his outlook, bore the stamp of his military back-

102. Kennan, *Memoirs*, p. 345.
103. Joseph M. Jones, *The Fifteen Weeks* (New York: Harcourt, 1955), p. 141.
104. On the origins, role, composition, and influence of the Policy Planning Staff, see Kennan, *Memoirs*, pp. 325–329; and Robert E. Elder, *The Policy Machine* (Syracuse, N.Y.: Syracuse University Press, 1960), pp. 71–89.

ground. He often betrayed this background by referring not to Europe but to "the European Theater." And in many ways, as his biographer observed, Marshall as Secretary of State did not have to act much differently from the way he acted as Chief of Staff during the war, for in 1947–48 there was a kind of war in progress against the Soviet Union.[105] Military terms and military imagery dominated his approach to the conduct of foreign policy in a Cold War setting. In a speech he made in May 1949, he emphasized the parallels between the problems that confronted him as Secretary of State and those with which he had to deal as Army Chief of Staff in the Second World War:

> I found the problems from the viewpoint of geographical location and of pressure to be almost identical in many respects with those of the war years. There was the same problem between East and West; the same limitations as to our capabilities; the same pressures at home and abroad, in regard to various areas, and there was the same necessity for a very steady and determined stand in regard to these various problems.[106]

In formulating a policy with regard to these problems, Marshall relied heavily, as both his critics and his admirers recognize, on the advice of experts. Accustomed to a military system in which delegation of authority was a central feature, Marshall allowed the Assistant Secretaries to conduct foreign policy in their areas of responsibility, reserving for himself only major issues and the overall strategy of the Department. Robert Lovett, who replaced Dean Acheson as Under Secretary in July 1947, was influential over the whole range of policy and served as Acting Secretary when Marshall was abroad. In interpreting the Soviet Union to Marshall, George Kennan played a significant role, although his views on the German question were at variance with the evolving Departmental line. Charles Bohlen, the counselor of the Department, was another leading Soviet expert on whom Marshall relied particularly heavily during the Berlin blockade. German policy in general was coordinated between Charles Saltzman, Assistant Secretary of State for Occupied Areas, and John Hickerson, Director of the Office of European Affairs. Additional channels of information

---

105. Robert H. Ferrell, *George C. Marshall* (New York: Cooper Square, 1966), p. 53.
106. *New York Times*, May 19, 1949.

and advice were the American Embassies in London and Moscow. Lewis Douglas, the Ambassador to the United Kingdom, had a detailed knowledge of German economic affairs. General Walter Bedell Smith, the Ambassador to the Soviet Union, was a tough and forceful individual, but he was completely awed by Marshall.[107] Regardless of their previous expectations, by 1947 all these officials had become highly skeptical of the possibility of maintaining the alliance with the Soviet Union, and many of them had come to regard a break with the Soviet Union in Germany as practically inevitable. Viewing the Soviet Union as an aggressive and insatiable adversary, they generally favored the consolidation of America's position in West Germany by enhancing America's military superiority and full use of her economic advantage rather than by diplomatic concessions which would only be misconstrued as a sign of American weakness.

To acquaint himself with the major problem areas, Marshall held a series of discussions with the State Department experts, beginning in January 1947. The discussion of the Soviet Union was based on a briefing paper, permeated by the Riga axioms, which the experts had prepared for the edification of their new political master. The paper described early postwar American foreign policy as an attempt to draw the Soviet Union into participation in the political, economic, and cultural life of the world, to break down by degrees the deeply rooted Soviet distrust of the world, and to demonstrate to the Soviet Union both the advantages of international cooperation and the fallacy of their theory of the inevitability of conflict. The Russians, however, did not respond to these efforts and proceeded instead to establish direct control over Eastern Europe as a prelude to further expansion. "It was at this point," said the paper, "that American policy, which had been benevolently disposed towards immediate Soviet aims in the early postwar period and had not recognized the nature of long-range Soviet objectives, began to harden." Conciliatory moves should not be allowed to obscure the nature of these objectives, for, according to the authors, there was no possibility that contradictory moves reflected contradictory pressures or even uncertainty in Moscow. The Soviet leaders were held to be wily and deceitful: "Lenin's slogan, 'One step back, two

---

107. Oral History Interview with Elbridge Durbrow, May 31, 1973, p. 81, Harry S. Truman Library.

steps forward,' is still the gospel of the men in the Kremlin. With the pressure off, the adversary is expected to lower his guard and be an easy target for the next blow. It is imperative that we not be misled by this tactic—one to which American public opinion has repeatedly shown itself to be vulnerable." The experts concluded by making two recommendations. The first was to formulate U.S. policy towards the Soviet Union "on a global, not a piecemeal basis," since the threat posed by monolithic international communism was of worldwide dimensions. The second recommendation was to increase America's military strength, because "we cannot effectively counter Soviet expansionist tendencies unless we maintain our armed forces at a level where they will command respect."[108]

Marshall himself entertained no illusions about the Soviet Union. His image of the adversary was that which was current in the Administration at the time he became Secretary of State, and he tacitly assumed the Riga axioms as a guide to relations with the Soviet Union. But his image of the Cold War was very much that of the military planner concerned with the balance of forces and the practical issues rather than that of the crusading moralist. Unlike Truman, he did not look on the Cold War as a confrontation between two ways of life and two antithetical ideologies but, much more pragmatically, as a political conflict between two great powers whose outcome would be determined by the underlying balance of military, economic, and psychological strength of the two sides. If he had any strong views about the character of the Soviet regime, he kept them to himself. Certainly, the sweeping, emotional, and moralistic Cold War rhetoric in which Truman excelled was seen by Marshall as misguided, if not actually dangerous, and he tried on occasion to moderate it. When he received the text of the Truman Doctrine, for example, he sent back a message to Truman questioning the wisdom of the presentation and saying he thought Truman was overstating the case a bit.[109] When Truman was preparing his major foreign policy address of March 17, 1948 and Clifford advised him that a very strong speech was essential for his own prestige and the prestige of the United States, Marshall pleaded for a

108. "Relations with the Soviet Union," memorandum for Secretary Marshall, January 17, 1947, European Affairs file, Department of State papers, quoted in Yergin, *Shattered Peace*, pp. 262–263.

109. Charles E. Bohlen, *The Transformation of American Foreign Policy* (New York: Norton, 1969), p. 87.

simple, businesslike statement and no inflammatory or belligerent language.[110]

On the substance of policy, and particularly on the need to strengthen America's armed forces, there was no disagreement. Marshall needed no prodding from his State Department advisers—or from anyone else, for that matter—to appreciate the importance of having a credible military posture in dealing with an opponent. The real danger lay in the opposite direction of overconcentration on this factor at the expense of all the others. In particular, Marshall greatly undervalued the role of diplomacy, and had neither the talent nor the taste for negotiations. A lifetime of soldiering had accustomed him to giving orders and imposing clearcut solutions, not to the diplomatic arts of verbal persuasion, tactical maneuvering, haggling, and compromise. It is true that he was compelled by wartime circumstances to acquire some of the skills required, and that he showed flexibility and willingness to compromise and even accept defeat in dealing with America's Allies. But by 1947 he seems to have left behind any notion that a soft-line approach might pave the way to cooperative relations with the Soviets, and he displayed neither flexibility nor patience in his direct dealings with their leaders. This was all too evident at his first encounter with the Russians in the Council of Foreign Ministers meeting which opened in Moscow very soon after he assumed his post

It is undeniable, as Robert Murphy who accompanied him confessed, that when Marshall flew to Moscow in March 1947, he was inadequately prepared for direct negotiations for the German peace treaty.[111] But neither was he in a mood to concede anything. Whatever remained of American willingness to negotiate completely disappeared when he replaced Byrnes. At the conference itself, Marshall was not in his element. The Russian case was presented in a hectoring manner, but Marshall was too ready to let Russian ill manners excuse the poverty of his own diplomatic approach. Marshall was not interested in compromise, and, since he could not force the Russians to accept cooperation on America's terms, he did not see the point of engaging in a dialogue at all. The meeting was a disappointing introduction to international diplomacy, and it confirmed Marshall's and Truman's feelings about the

---

110. Hartmann, *Truman and the 80th Congress*, pp. 167–168.
111. Murphy, *Diplomat Among Warriors*, pp. 374–375.

futility of conferences. A few years later, Marshall offered an explanation of his conduct in Moscow which only reinforces the impression that for him military power was the only basis on which relations with the Soviet Union could be effectively ordered:

> I remember [he told an audience at the Pentagon], when I was Secretary of State, I was being pressed constantly, particularly when in Moscow, by radio message after radio message, to give the Russians hell. . . . When I got back I was getting the same appeal in relation to the Far East and China. At that time, my facilities for giving them hell—and I am a soldier and know something about the ability to give hell—was 1⅓ divisions over the entire United States. That is quite a proposition when you deal with somebody with over 260 and you have 1⅓.[112]

The main conclusion which Marshall drew from his face-to-face encounter with the Russians, as we observed in the previous chapter, related to the need to take urgent measures to put Western Europe back on its feet economically in order to consolidate its resistance to Communism. In this sense, the Moscow conference was the birthplace of the Marshall Plan. Time was a vital factor, for, as Marshall put it in his radio broadcast, "the patient is sinking while the doctors deliberate."[113] This description was indicative of his images both of Europe's desperate plight and vulnerability and of the insidious danger of frittering away valuable time by deliberating with the Russians. Action was what was called for, and the day after these words were pronounced, Marshall summoned Kennan and instructed him to set up a Policy Planning Staff and formulate immediate recommendations. He had only one, characteristically terse, piece of advice: "Avoid trivia."[114]

The implementation of the European Recovery Program was successful in shifting the balance of power in favor of the West, as Marshall had anticipated. On November 7, 1947, he read a paper to the Cabinet on the international situation. The conclusion it offered was that "the advance of Communism has been stemmed and the Russians have been compelled to make a re-evaluation of their position." Marshall also stated, according to Forrestal's account, that "the objective of our policy from this point on would be the

---

112. Quoted here from John C. Sparrow, *History of Personnel Demobilization in the United States Army* (Washington, D.C.: Office of the Chief of Military History, Department of the Army, 1951), p. 380.
113. *Department of State Bulletin*, May 11, 1949, p. 924.
114. Kennan, *Memoirs*, p. 327.

restoration of the balance of power in both Europe and Asia and that all actions would be viewed in the light of this objective."[115]

This was a significant statement, for it indicates that Marshall had formulated the global strategy towards the Soviet Union which his advisers were urging. This strategy, based on restoring the balance of power, was endorsed by the Cabinet. But while the restoration of the balance of power was accepted as the guiding objective of American policy, there was no consensus on the components of such a balance. In the course of the reappraisal of American military policy which went on during late 1947 and early 1948, two major schools of thought emerged, one represented by Secretary of Defense James Forrestal and the other by Secretary of State Marshall.[116] Forrestal pressed for immediate large-scale American rearmament as the most assured way of preserving the balance of power against the Soviet Union. Marshall was the leading proponent of instituting universal military training in the United States to provide a base for mobilization should that be necessary and to signal to the Russians that the United States would not tolerate aggression in Europe and that she was ready to follow through on her policy.[117] The trouble, he said at a meeting of the National Security Council on February 12, 1947, was that "we are playing with fire while we have nothing with which to put it out."[118] On every front, America faced essentially the same grim alternatives: to withdraw, to attempt to stand on positions obviously untenable, simply to confess that the problem was "unsolvable," or to take vigorous action—for which the means and trained men did not exist. Marshall advocated universal military training as a measure of deterrence, a gesture of determination, "clear evidence to the world," as he put it on March 4, "that we did not propose to abdicate our responsibilities in Europe or anywhere else in combating the rising and spreading tide of Communism."[119]

Germany was perceived by Marshall as being of crucial importance in the attempt to stem the spread of communism. In Febru-

---

115. Millis, *The Forrestal Diaries*, pp. 340–341.
116. On the process of reappraisal, see Warner R. Schilling, "The Politics of National Defense: Fiscal 1950," in *Strategy, Politics and Defense Budgets*, by Warner R. Schilling et al. (New York: Columbia University Press, 1962); and Seyom Brown, *The Faces of Power: Constancy and Change in U.S. Foreign Policy from Truman to Johnson* (New York: Columbia University Press, 1968), pp. 46–52.
117. Millis, *The Forrestal Diaries*, p. 369.
118. Ibid., p. 373.   119. Ibid., p. 377.

ary 1948, in a cable intended for the general guidance of Lewis Douglas, the American Ambassador to London, he expressed the belief that in view of the new power configuration which had emerged as a result of the war, Germany would be unable in the foreseeable future to play the kind of independent role in international relations which it had played in the past. Germany could only play a significant role through alignment with other powers. Marshall observed that the Eastern zone of Germany under Soviet occupation was being reshaped in a totalitarian pattern, both economically and politically, along lines similar to developments in the East European satellite countries. Hence, Marshall argued, the Western powers had no alternative but to undertake to integrate both the economy and political life of Western Germany with those of Western Europe. Unless she were effectively associated with the Western European powers, first through economic arrangements and ultimately through mutual political understanding, Western Germany, too, would be in danger of being drawn into the Eastern orbit. The American government was determined, Marshall stressed, "not to permit reestablishment of German economic and political unity under conditions which are likely to bring about effective domination of all Germany by [the] Soviets. It would regard such an eventuality as the greatest threat to security of all Western nations, including [the] U.S."[120]

The blockade of Berlin startlingly confirmed Marshall's suspicions that Russia aimed to extend her domination over the whole of Germany. Since he regarded this eventuality as the greatest threat to the security of the United States and her European allies, Marshall was clearly predisposed to resist the Soviet move. To accept adverse consequences of such magnitude without a struggle would have been contrary to his understanding of what was at stake in the crisis. It is undoubtedly true, as J. E. Smith has argued, that Marshall's own policy in Germany contributed to the imposition of the Berlin blockade. But if one's aim is to understand why Marshall opted for the division of Germany and favored resistance to Soviet pressure in Berlin, rather than to assign blame for this crisis and for the escalation of the Cold War, then it is necessary to view the situation from Marshall's perspective. Policy preferences, as we have argued all along, are rooted in various images, of which the image of the opponent is the most important. The evidence we have con-

---

120. Marshall to Douglas, February 20, 1948, *FRUS, 1948*, Vol. 2, pp. 71–73.

cerning Marshall's images, incomplete as it is, does permit the conclusion that he perceived the Soviet Union as an expansionist power, the United States as a status quo power, and the relations between them in the German arena as a zero-sum game in which any Russian gain would be at Western expense. Marshall was almost certainly wrong in seeing Russian policy in Eastern Germany as indicative of a long-term plan to dominate the whole of Germany. Since his images were probably at variance with reality, it is arguable that the policy they prompted was unfortunate and misguided, in that it assumed too readily that the conflict over Germany was inevitable and that there was no room for compromise. But it should be recognized that Marshall's behavior, though it contributed to the escalation of the Cold War, did not spring from any demonic theories of Soviet behavior, let alone any conscious design for American expansion, but from a genuine conviction that the United States was faced with a serious threat to her security and the security of her allies.

CLAY

American policy in Germany was the product of individuals, not of abstract forces; and of the key individuals in the formulation and implementation of this policy, none was more influential than Lucius Dubignon Clay. Having been appointed Deputy Governor of the U.S. zone of Germany in 1945, Clay became Military Governor in March 1947 and held the post until his retirement in May 1949. Three principal factors help to explain the exceptional influence which he exercised: the office he held; his remarkable personal qualities of intellect, energy, and will power; and the policy vacuum in Washington regarding the occupation of Germany.

Clay in fact held a dual appointment as head of the European Command, United States Army (EUCOM), and head of the Office of Military Government of the United States for Germany (OMGUS). As Commander of U.S. Forces in Europe, General Clay was responsible to the Joint Chiefs of Staff through the Chief of Staff, U.S. Army, who had been designated as the Joint Chief of Staff's executive agent for the European Command. In matters relating to the occupation of Germany, Clay dealt directly with the Department of the Army.[121] Being the head of OMGUS conferred full and in some respects untrammeled power, for which there

---

121. Condit, *The History of the Joint Chiefs of Staff*, Vol. 2, pp. 117–118.

were few parallels in American government. "Military governor was a pretty heady job," recalled Clay's civilian successor, John McCloy. "It is the nearest thing to a Roman proconsulship the modern world afforded. You could turn to your secretary and say, 'Take a law.' The law was there, and you could see its effects in two or three weeks. It was a challenging job to an ambitious man. Benevolent despotism."[122] The Military Governor was not, of course, an entirely freewheeling agent: he had to implement major policy decisions formulated in Washington, and he received directives through the Department of the Army. But military decisions in Washington were made by high officials who depended to a very great extent on the reports and recommendations furnished by the man closest to the problem.[123] Moreover, there was a tradition in the Department of the Army of according commanders in the field considerable leeway in interpreting directives from Washington. This enabled the Military Governor to influence policy formation and to exercise his own discretion in implementing it to a degree which could hardly be imagined in the case of a nonmilitary representative abroad.[124] When General William Draper was appointed Under Secretary of the Army in July 1947, with special responsibility for supervising the American occupations in Germany, Austria, and Japan, Army backing for Clay was placed on a firm and ongoing basis because Draper had previously been economics adviser to Clay and only accepted Secretary Royall's offer to become Under Secretary after consulting Clay, with whom he retained a close and friendly working partnership.[125]

Clay's strong character and assertive personality ensured that he would exercise to the full the powers conferred on him by his office and would stretch to the limit the discretionary authority extended to him by the Department of the Army through a combination of tradition and high regard for him personally. His decisiveness was almost legendary, his self-assurance knew no bounds, and he fought with passionate intensity for the causes in which he believed. This self-assurance, coupled with a quick grasp of essentials

122. Quoted here from *The Papers of General Lucius D. Clay: Germany, 1945–1949*, ed. Jean Edward Smith (Bloomington: Indiana University Press, 1974), Vol. 1, pp. xxv.
123. Harold Zink, *The United States in Germany, 1945–1955* (Princeton: Van Norstad, 1957), pp. 29–32.
124. Ibid.
125. Oral History Interview with General William H. Draper, Jr., January 11, 1972, p. 3, Harry S. Truman Library.

and a penetrating intelligence, gave him an air of supreme authority, while his piercing eyes conveyed the impression of great force and iron determination. His impact on those who came into contact with him was powerful. "He wasn't a general, he was an atom bomb!" commented a Soviet Major who saw him at work in Berlin.[126] *Isvestia*'s description of Clay as "the American Viceroy in Germany" was somewhat less fanciful, but it conveyed the aura of authority which radiated from this four-star general.[127]

As Military Governor in Germany, Clay's decision-making style was highly centralized and authoritarian. There was a large number of experts and advisers on his staff, and he listened politely to what they had to say, but there is not much evidence that he relied heavily on their counsel. Even to his top subordinates, he was reluctant to delegate more than routine duties. All important matters, and many others that were not, were handled personally by him. He did not build around him a working team or encourage the kind of staff work which one would normally expect from a soldier. He preferred to do his own staff work and reached decisions quickly, irreversibly, and alone. Once his mind was made up, there was hardly any changing it.[128]

A policy vacuum in Washington provided a context in which a strategically placed and ambitious man like Clay could effectively pursue his own views and predilections in Germany. In theory, the State Department was supposed to develop American policy towards Germany, and the Army Department was supposed to carry it out.[129] In practice, Clay frequently found that it was difficult to find the source of authority in Washington because, in the sharing of responsibility between the two Departments, there were areas in which neither was willing or able to make a firm decision. It was a situation in which "the administration of Germany could not be separated from the foreign policy action of the United States. So

---

126. Gregory Klimov, *The Terror Machine: The Inside Story of the Soviet Administration in Germany*, trans. from the German by H. C. Stevens (London: Faber and Faber, 1953), p. 137.

127. *Isvestia*, November 16, 1947.

128. B. U. Ratchford and W. D. Ross, *Berlin Reparations Assignment* (Chapel Hill: University of North Carolina Press, 1947), p. 57; Zink, *The United States in Germany*, p. 69; and Peterson, *The American Occupation of Germany*, p. 57.

129. An internal State Department memorandum frankly acknowledged the existence of an interagency rivalry and the different perspectives which gave rise to it: "Serious difficulties have arisen in the determination and application of U.S. policies because of the division of major responsibility between the State and

you were involved in a multiple show. And in a multiple show there is no boss . . . other than the President, and obviously you can't draw the President into everyday administrative problems."[130]

When confronted with this situation, Clay was rarely at a loss, and rather than delay action until he could consult the civil authorities in Washington, he often made an immediate decision. Like General MacArthur, America's "proconsul" in Japan, Clay was very nearly an independent sovereign in relation to the State Department, which could negotiate with him but was never able to issue orders to him. This situation developed under Secretary Byrnes, whose admiration for Clay was such that he made no effort to bring German policy under the control of the State Department. It was thought that Marshall, being himself a general of enormous prestige, would try to assert his authority over all the other generals, but he did not succeed in making himself sole master of American policy in Germany.[131] The State Department's experts on Germany, Charles Saltzman and Jacob Beam, were certainly not influential enough to stand out against Clay.[132]

The unfortunate organizational arrangement for occupied area operations which placed the department charged with carrying out policy at loggerheads with the department making the policy, thereby leaving the initiative preponderantly in the hands of the military authorities in Berlin, did not work well; so, in January 1948, Secretary Royall agreed to transfer to the State Department the responsibility for the administration of Germany.[133] Marshall announced that the State Department takeover would occur on

---

Army Departments. The Army, through EUCOM and OMGUS, is entrusted with full control and administrative authority in Germany; the State Department seeks to discharge the duty assigned to it by Presidential directive of shaping U.S. policy with respect both to the internal evolution of Germany and its relations with other countries. OMGUS is inclined to view the occupation as a local operation and is conscious of its immediate responsibilities. It is inclined to resent the intrusion of the State Department or its representatives in military government operations within Germany to the extent that it becomes difficult for the Department to exercise its proper function of policy guidance." See "Department of State Policy Statement: Germany," August 26, 1948, *FRUS, 1948*, Vol. 2, p. 1318.

130. Clay, quoted here from Fred L. Hadsel, in Schmitt, ed., *U.S. Occupation in Europe*, pp. 150–151.

131. Walter Lippmann, *New York Herald Tribune*, July 26, 1948.

132. Arthur Krock Papers, Memoranda Box 1, Book II, p. 213, Seeley G. Mudd Manuscript Library, Princeton University.

133. Royall to Marshall, January 26, 1948, President's Secretary's File, Box 179, Harry S. Truman Library.

July 1, but the planned takeover was shelved when Marshal Sokolovsky flounced out of the Allied Control Council in March and the Berlin blockade started.[134]

The institutional link between OMGUS and the State Department was the Office of the Political Adviser in Germany. Although the Political Adviser, Robert Murphy, was a State Department representative, his office was part of OMGUS and he himself was subordinate to the Military Governor in the official hierarchy. His role was to report to the State Department and to advise the Military Governor on political matters. Clay never became fully reconciled to independent reports from Murphy to the State Department about matters which lay within his own sphere of responsibility. But the relations between the two men were sustained, as both have attested, by mutual confidence and a remarkable consensus on the fundamentals of policy.[135]

Clay and Murphy were both "realists" in their outlook on international politics. Both were fiercely anti-communist in their ideological convictions. Both regarded the economic revival of Germany and the formation of a capitalistic and pro-American West German state as an overriding objective to be pursued irrespective of Russian opposition. And both did not waver in their conviction that Berlin must be held at all costs. Having a State Department official who shared his own views greatly enhanced Clay's influence by helping to build up and sustain the kind of consensus at home which was necessary for the vigorous pursuit of his policy in Germany. But in Washington and in Germany, Clay was seen as the dominant figure and the driving force. He ran OMGUS largely as a one-man show and put his personal stamp on all its manifold activities. By the end of his term of office, his name had become synonymous with United States policy in West Germany.[136] In the eyes

---

134. Oral History Interview with Charles E. Saltzman, June 28, 1974, p. 20, Harry S. Truman Library.

135. Lucius D. Clay, *Decision in Germany* (New York: Doubleday, 1950), p. 58; and Murphy, *Diplomat Among Warriors*, pp. 357–358.

136. OMGUS and its policies were not the object of universal admiration. Kennan was one of its most savage critics. "This was an establishment," he wrote, "for which I had an almost neurotic distaste. I have been twice in Germany since the termination of hostilities. Each time I had come away with a sense of sheer horror at the spectacle of this horde of my compatriots and their dependents camping in luxury amid the ruins of a shattered national community, ignorant of the past, oblivious to the abundant evidences of present tragedy all around them, inhabiting the very same sequestrated villas that the Gestapo and the SS had just abandoned, and enjoying the same privileges, flaunting their silly supermarket

of the German people, he was the symbol of the United States' determination to resist the spread of Soviet rule in their country. It is not uncommon for military governors to turn gradually into advocates of the countries they are supposed to rule. Clay conformed to this pattern with even greater vehemence than most others.

Clay's influence extended far beyond the confines of the Office of Military Government in Berlin; it was felt in London, Paris, and Moscow. His high standing in Washington enabled him to play a prominent part not only in determining United States occupation policy in Germany but in the whole conduct by the West of the Cold War in Europe. His close relations with Byrnes had been a major source of Clay's political influence and helped to make him the most influential American in Europe in those crucial postwar years. As Murphy observed, the "Byrnes-Clay partnership not only changed the American conception of the German occupation, but affected the whole pattern of European events."[137] Under Byrnes's successor, Clay's lead in Germany was not followed so eagerly at home; but during the hectic summer of 1948, he forged a policy of firmness largely on his own initiative and made a large number of decisions with great speed and without clearance. His admirers commended him for the calm assurance, the marked absence of anxiety, the skill, and the decisiveness with which he acted.[138] His critics saw him as an imperious and impulsive figure whose overbearing self-confidence led him to make snap decisions and tended to create a climate uncongenial to negotiations. He had "a compulsion to force issues," it was said.[139] At the height of the Berlin crisis, his superiors in Washington curtailed his freedom of action, but he remained a key figure throughout. Clay's case illustrates the enormous impact of certain well-placed soldiers on

---

luxuries in the face of a veritable ocean of deprivation, hunger and wretchedness, setting an example of empty materialism and cultural poverty before a people desperately in need of spiritual and intellectual guidance, taking for granted—as though it were their natural due—a disparity in privilege and comfort between themselves and their German neighbors no smaller than those that had once divided lord and peasant in that feudal Germany which it had been our declared purpose in two world wars to destroy." Kennan, *Memoirs*, pp. 428–429.

137. Murphy, *Diplomat Among Warriors*, p. 308.

138. See, for example, Jean Edward Smith, *The Defense of Berlin* (Baltimore: Johns Hopkins University Press, 1963); and Frank Donovan, *Bridge in the Sky* (New York: David McKay, 1968), pp. 8–9.

139. Jack Schick, *The Berlin Crisis, 1958–1962* (Philadelphia: University of Pennsylvania Press, 1971), p. 273.

PSYCHOLOGICAL ENVIRONMENT   103

American foreign policy during the Cold War. He was certainly more than a tame bureaucrat carrying out the settled policy of his government. And there could hardly have been a more striking exception to the ideal-type of a cautious and apolitical professional soldier presented in Samuel Huntington's analysis of American civil-military relations.[140] While Clay's entire early career was spent in the army, where he had distinguished himself as an engineer and an administrator, he came from a political family (his father was Henry Clay, the U.S. Senator from Georgia). A highly skilled political operator, General Clay combined soldierly resolution with a subtle mind and command of the art of public explanation.[141] His remarkable record in Germany showed him to be, in John Galbraith's phrase, "one of the most skillful politicians ever to wear the uniform of the United States Army."

Although Clay is chiefly remembered as a staunch and militant Cold Warrior, his image of the opponent was not, at the beginning of his assignment to Germany, that of the Riga school. His deep antipathy towards communism was well known, but when he first went to Germany as Deputy Military Governor, he believed it possible to work with the Russians. On August 8, 1945, he wrote privately: "We are finally moving on quadripartite control, and I am still optimistic with regard to the possibility of success. I have found our Russian colleagues, while fully realistic, desirous of a co-ordinated and cooperative treatment of Germany."[142] In February 1946, he emphatically disputed the gloomy view of Moscow's long-term intentions contained in Kennan's Long Telegram on the basis of his own experience in Germany, where he regarded France rather than Russia as the main source of obstruction and the inventory of what had been accomplished as not too discouraging.[143] After a brief interlude, however, Clay appears to have concluded

140. Samuel Huntington, *The Soldier and the State: The Theory and Politics of Civil-Military Relations* (Cambridge, Mass.: Harvard University Press, 1957). For a challenging analysis of Clay as a highly political soldier, see Stephen E. Ambrose, "The Military Impact on Foreign Policy," in *The Military and American Society*, ed. Stephen E. Ambrose and James A. Barber, Jr. (New York: The Free Press, 1972).

141. Carr, *Truman, Stalin and Peace*, pp. 187–188.

142. Clay to Bernard Baruch, August 3, 1945, Bernard M. Baruch Papers, Seeley G. Mudd Manuscript Library, Princeton University.

143. Murphy to Matthews, April 3, 1946, Records of the Department of State, quoted here from Jean Edward Smith, "The View from USFET," in Schmitt, ed., *U.S. Occupation in Europe*, pp. 68–69. Smith argues that Clay continued to operate under the belief that his task was to achieve effective four-power government;

that Russian policy in Germany was directed not at four-power cooperation but at spreading Communism, and that the immediate threat to America's interest in a stable Europe came not from a resurgent Germany but from an expansionist Russia. He himself has recorded that by the Spring of 1946 much of his earlier optimism had gone.[144] Another German expert suggested that when the Powers failed to come to any agreement in the meeting of the Council of Foreign Ministers in 1947, Clay was so impressed by the uncooperative and aggressive attitude of the Russians in the German occupation and in Europe in general that he concluded that the important thing was to strengthen Germany and make it one of the elements in any defense necessary against Russian aggression.[145] Clay recognized the real apprehensions of Germany's neighbors regarding their future security from German aggression. However, he felt that "their traditional and well justified fear of German aggression sometimes blinds them to the immediate and overshadowing menace of the Red Army externally and planned revolution internally."[146]

In this changed international environment, America's interests would be best served, Clay believed, not in working with Russia to repress Germany, but in rebuilding Germany in order to contain Russia. This was the controlling assumption behind Clay's entire approach to the German problem from 1946 onwards. "We had created a political vacuum in Central Europe," he recalled, "and unless we could restore some sort of political opportunity to the German people, there was nothing we could do to prevent Communism from taking over. Therefore, we had the problem of rebuilding Germany."[147] All the main features in Clay's approach—

---

that he believed in being firm but correct with the Russians; and that he still thought such a policy would succeed long after Washington had based American foreign policy on the inevitability of a confrontation with the Soviet Union. The point of this argument is to emphasize that, insofar as Germany was concerned, the Cold War was neither inevitable nor inherent, and that it was certainly not sought by the military authorities in Berlin.

144. Clay, *Decision in Germany*, p. 72.
145. Oral History Interview with Charles E. Saltzman, June 18, 1974, p. 12, Harry S. Truman Library.
146. Clay to Baruch, March 2, 1947, in *The Papers of General Lucius D. Clay: Germany, 1945–1949*, ed. Jean Edward Smith (Bloomington: Indiana University Press, 1974), Vol. 2, p. 563 (hereinafter cited as *Clay Papers*).
147. Interview with Lucius D. Clay, Dulles Oral History Project, John Foster Dulles Papers, Princeton University.

suspending reparations to the Soviet zone, accepting the division of Germany as final, pressing for the merger of the Western zones, and promoting the political and economic reconstruction of the new entity—fitted logically into the pattern of this new Cold War foreign policy.

Clay's profound political conservatism made him suspicious of the native German socialists and even, for that matter, of British and French social-democrats. He was determined to make West Germany safe for capitalism and to prevent the creation of a socialist state on the ruins of the Third Reich. To foster the development of a vigorous capitalist economy, Clay did not press ahead with denazification, he did nothing to break up the cartel system, and he raised the level of industrial production above the ceiling set in the Potsdam agreement. By building up German capitalism in this way, Clay may have hoped not only to arrest the tide of Communism but to reverse it. "If we can produce a reasonably certain stable economy," he explained, "we can push Communism back beyond the Elbe."[148]

Clay would not have been able to proceed along this path of rebuilding Western Germany so rapidly without the active support of the Truman Administration. It was not a personal policy he was conducting but official policy, which was first announced in Byrnes's Stuttgart speech in September 1946 and later enshrined in the London Program. It was a policy based on the tacit assumption that Germany's geostrategic position and industrial potential made her essential to the effective containment of Russia, and hence that she must be integrated into the emergent anti-Soviet coalition. The drive to build a strong Germany with a prosperous capitalist economy also fit in with the Truman Administration's commitment to a free and multilateral world trading system—a commitment which existed independently of and preceded by some years the doctrine of containment.[149]

While Clay's image of Russia shifted, under the impact of the

---

148. Daily Summary, Smith-Bundt Committee, Berlin, Germany, September 23, 1947, Box 93, H. Alexander Smith Papers; quoted here from Thomas G. Paterson, *Soviet-American Confrontation: Postwar Reconstruction and the Origins of the Cold War* (Baltimore: Johns Hopkins University Press, 1973), p. 259.

149. Clay himself acknowledged the support he received from Washington. When he was asked, "Whose show was it over Germany?" he replied: "I think that it was something I had to grab and do. I couldn't have done it if I had not had the full support of Judge [Robert] Patterson and Royall in the Defense Depart-

Cold War, from that of a potential ally to a dangerous adversary, his image of Germany shifted in the opposite direction. He showed no vindictiveness in his attitude towards former Nazis and advocated the welcoming of Western Germany into the comity of Western nations with both hands. It was his "sincere conviction" that "a western Germany drawn into western Europe on reasonable terms and conditions may indeed become a friendly state."[150] And he was quoted as saying that "in the event of another war, the Germans probably would be the only people on whom we could rely."[151]

Clay did not in fact believe that there was an immediate danger of war. Throughout his stay in Germany, he had scoffed at the possibility of war with Russia, and he was one of the principal supporters of the view that war, if not impossible, was unlikely.[152] This estimate, however, was suddenly reversed in a cable he sent on March 5, 1948 to General Chamberlin, Chief of Army Intelligence, in which Clay stated in effect that the possibility of war could no longer be excluded:

> For many months, based on logical analysis, I have felt and held that war was unlikely for at least ten years. Within the last few weeks, I have felt a subtle change in Soviet attitude which I cannot define but which now gives me a feeling that it may come with dramatic suddenness. I cannot support this change in my own thinking with any data or outward evidence in relationships other than to describe it as a feeling of a new tenseness in every Soviet individual with whom we have official relations. I am unable to submit any official report in absence of supporting data but my feeling is real.[153]

What lay behind this disturbing revision of the earlier estimate that war was not likely? Clay explained that although the intelligence reports that came to his desk contained nothing to arouse suspicion, he somehow felt instinctively that a definite change in the attitude of the Russians in Berlin had occurred and that some-

---

ment, of Byrnes and General Marshall in the State Department and of the President. We were initiating the things that had to be done, but without Washington approving and supporting them, we'd not have been able to do them." Oral History Interview with General Lucius D. Clay, July 16, 1974, p. 18, Harry S. Truman Library.

150. Clay to Douglas (not sent), April 26, 1948, *Clay Papers*, Vol. 2, pp. 638–639.
151. Ambrose, "The Military Impact on Foreign Policy," p. 127.
152. Clay, *Decision in Germany*, p. 354.
153. *Clay Papers*, Vol. 2, pp. 568–569.

thing was about to happen.[154] Only two days previously, however, Clay had reiterated, in a cable to the Army's Public Information Division, his long-standing conviction that the communist threat to all of Europe was much more immediate and serious than the threat of physical war.[155] A more likely explanation, therefore, as the editor of Clay's papers has suggested, is that the cable of March 5 was dispatched in response to a visit to Berlin by General Chamberlin during the last week of February 1948: "Chamberlin cautioned Clay as to the pitiful state of readiness of U.S. armed forces, the fact that major military appropriation bills were pending before congressional committees, and the need to galvanize American public opinion to support increased defense expenditures. Clay's cable, sent directly to Chamberlin, and not through the normal command channels, was to be used as Chamberlin saw fit. Its primary purpose was to assist the military chiefs in their congressional testimony; it was not, in Clay's opinion, related to any change in Soviet strategy."[156] This alarmist report to Chamberlin, which caused a veritable war scare in Washington,[157] was later defended by Clay on the grounds that it speeded up American preparations for defense. With the benefit of hindsight, he also argued that the report anticipated the blockade of Berlin by a few weeks and that its imposition had in itself justified the report.[158] The important point to note, however, is that Clay's purported revision of his sober estimate concerning the improbability of war masked a cynical ploy to help the military chiefs to bludgeon a penurious Congress into increasing defense appropriations. As Michael Howard observed: "This was not to be the last occasion on which the American military were to try to influence congressional opinion by an inflated estimate of Soviet intentions and capabilities, but it may well have been the first and most significant."[159]

Clay interpreted Moscow's motives in imposing the Berlin blockade in the light of the Grand Design for the mastery of Europe on which he believed it had settled in the Fall of 1947, follow-

---

154. Clay, *Decision in Germany*, p. 354.
155. Clay to Parks, March 3, 1948, *Clay Papers*, Vol. 2, p. 564.
156. Ibid., p. 568. See also Smith, "The View from USFET," pp. 75–76.
157. Kennan, *Memoirs*, pp. 400–401; and Millis, *The Forrestal Diaries*, pp. 387–388.
158. Clay, *Decision in Germany*, pp. 354–355.
159. Michael Howard, "Governor General of Germany," *Times Literary Supplement*, August 19, 1974, p. 970.

ing the launching of the Marshall Plan. Soviet strategy and tactics were allegedly all worked out in advance within the framework of this long-term plan. "It was in Soviet interest," he explained, "to permit relationships to deteriorate, to wage a war of nerves recreating the fear in Europe which alone could make possible the further advance of Communism. The program of the Cominform was made public in the fall. Clearly it was directed at the domination of Europe but there were two obstacles: the thin screen of British and American troops in Germany which could not be penetrated without war and which prevented the fear engulfing Eastern Europe from spreading into Western Europe. . . . Therefore the Soviet Government decided that a break in Germany was desirable."[160]

The onset of the crisis focused Clay's attention, as it did the attention of the other American decision-makers, on Berlin. While some of his colleagues were ready to contemplate withdrawal from this exposed and vulnerable outpost, Clay never wavered in his conviction that the United States must stand fast in Berlin. The dominant image in his mind was what we would call today the domino theory. He expressed it powerfully on April 10, 1948 in response to an invitation by Secretary of the Army Kenneth Royall to restate his views on America's position in Berlin. "We have lost Czechoslovakia," he said. "Norway is threatened. We retreat from Berlin. When Berlin falls, Western Germany will be next. If we mean . . . to hold Europe against Communism, we must not budge. We can take humiliation and pressure short of war in Berlin without losing face. If we withdraw, our position in Europe is threatened. If America does not understand this now, does not know that the issue is cast, then it never will and communism will run rampant. I believe the future of democracy requires us to stay. . . . This is not a heroic pose because there will be nothing heroic in having to take humiliation without retaliation."[161]

Another strand in Clay's interpretation of the crisis was the perception that the Soviet act was a deliberate probe and a test of America's commitment to defend Europe. This strand is stressed in an article in which Clay's crisis images were recollected with clarity: "The blockade of Berlin by the Soviets was caused not by their desire to take over the city. . . . It came primarily from their desire to weaken our position in Europe." The Soviet Government was

160. Clay, *Decision in Germany*, p. 160.
161. Ibid., p. 361.

not sure whether America intended to stay in Europe or not. "It was fully aware of our traditional policy of remaining free of foreign entanglements and it determined to test our intent by a blockade of Berlin, which was obviously the most vulnerable and difficult spot for us to defend. I am sure the Soviet Government expected the Western Allies to withdraw from Berlin. The consequences would have been to destroy the confidence of a defenseless Western Europe in the determination of the United States to support and defend it until it could recover. We recognized immediately that the loss of Berlin might mean the loss of Europe, and with the support of our British and French Allies we determined to maintain our position."[162]

The foregoing analysis of the attitudinal prism and the images of the key decision-makers of the Truman Administration who took charge of the Berlin crisis makes it clear that there was no monolithic unity of outlook and that significant differences existed in style, emphasis, and detail. But it also reveals a shared hard core of fundamental beliefs and images which identified all of them as "realist" practitioners of international politics. Both the prism through which they saw the outside world and their specific crisis images may be described as typically hard-line, albeit with differences in degree. This hard-line and hawkish psychological environment constituted the framework for decision, choice, and action during the crisis.

162. Lucius D. Clay, "Berlin," *Foreign Affairs*, Vol. 41, No. 1 (October 1962).

CHAPTER FOUR

Decision Flow

PHASE I: MARCH 20–30, 1948

THE BERLIN BLOCKADE did not descend on the Truman Administration suddenly or unexpectedly. A varied and steadily growing mass of information and reports reaching Washington pointed persistently in the direction of an imminent breakdown of four-power relations in Germany. This strategic warning of the Soviets' intention to act in Germany was amplified in time by a more precise tactical warning pinpointing Berlin as the target for Soviet pressure against the Western powers.

As early as October 1947, General Lucius Clay and his political adviser, Robert Murphy, advised the National Security Council that America must be prepared for Soviet action designed to force the withdrawal of the Western powers from Berlin.[1] Many observers recognized that the decisions taken by the Western powers, following the abortive London conference of December 1947, to merge their zones and work for a provisional western German government would be strongly opposed by the Soviets and that the four-power government of Germany would break down completely in the ensuing struggle.[2] Admiral Roscoe Hillenkoetter, the Director of Central Intelligence, estimated in a memorandum to President Truman that the breakup of the Council of Ministers "may cause the USSR to undertake a program of intensified obstructionism and calculated insult in an effort to force the U.S. and the other Western powers to withdraw from Berlin." He further estimated, in connection with the Allied proposals to unify their zones in Germany, that the USSR would intensify its consolidation of

1. Lucius D. Clay, *Decision in Germany* (New York: Doubleday, 1950), p. 239.
2. Ibid., pp. 248–249.

eastern Germany and would use its strong position in Berlin as a lever to check Allied plans in the west.[3]

In January 1948, the Army General Staff completed a study entitled "U.S. Course of Action in Event Soviets Attempt to Force U.S. Out of Berlin." The study made no attempt to evaluate the strategic importance of Berlin to the U.S. and its allies, concerning itself instead with the practical measures which might be adopted to resist Soviet pressure there. It was pointed out that the Soviet Union could either resort to direct military action to drive the Western powers out of the city, in which case the American response would not be confined to this single theater; or it could create "administrative difficulties" which would disrupt communications and make life difficult for the U.S. forces stationed in Berlin. The latter course would be easy to implement because access to Berlin was limited to one road, two railroads, and one air corridor; and the Army staff stated quite plainly that if the ground access channels from the Western zones were disrupted, it would be impossible for the Western powers to feed the civilian population in their sectors by air alone. They recommended that, in the event of the Soviet Union imposing "administrative difficulties," the United States should make every effort to remain in Berlin, using all available means to supply the city, and should publicize Soviet responsibility for the situation.

Secretary of the Army Kenneth Royall forwarded this study to Secretary of Defense Forrestal for information rather than for decision. Forrestal wanted to know whether the study should be referred to the National Security Council so that a definite policy could be established, but he was informed by Royall that there was no need to do this, since the Department of State and the Air Force had concurred in the proposed courses of action.[4] Forrestal did not pursue the matter further, and, consequently, the nature of the

---

3. Memorandum for the President from Admiral R. H. Hillenkoetter, December 22, 1947, file 123, Admiral William D. Leahy files, Record Group (RG) 319, National Archives, Washington, D.C. See also John R. Oneal, *Creative Adaptation: Process and Potential for Foreign Policy Making in Times of Crisis* (Ph.D. dissertation, Stanford University, 1979), pp. 348–349.

4. Secretary of the Army to the Secretary of Defense, January 19, 1948, Office of the Secretary of the Army, 091 Germany, RG 319, National Archives, Washington, D.C.; and Kenneth W. Condit, *The History of the Joint Chiefs of Staff*, Vol. 2: *1947–1949* (Washington, D.C.: Historical Division, Joint Secretariat, Joint Chiefs of Staff, 1976), RG 218, Records of the United States Joint Chiefs of Staff, National Archives, p. 23.

U.S. commitment to remain in Berlin emerged during the crisis itself and emerged very slowly.

Awareness of the imminent crisis was not confined to people with access to official information. The Soviet-controlled press in Germany carried stories about the approaching withdrawal of the Western Allies from Berlin as part of a persistent propaganda campaign; while in the American press which reported these stories, speculation about Soviet pressure to force the Allies out of Berlin and the likely Western response was rife in the early months of 1948. The war of nerves waged through the Soviet-controlled press was accompanied, during these months, by a series of measures and maneuvers designed to weaken the authority of the Western powers, the central city government, and the Kommandatura and to strengthen communist preeminence in the political life of the city.[5]

Even more ominous and menacing from the point of view of the Western powers was the growing interference of the Soviet authorities with traffic between West Germany and Berlin. The instances of interference appeared random, arbitrary, and uncoordinated at first, but as the restrictions were extended and the incidents along the approaches became increasingly frequent and serious, they gave the impression of a "creeping blockade." When the first hints of a blockade appeared, Murphy and Clay reexamined the precise status of all the transport arrangements. Their survey reminded them that the only written agreement was the one made in September 1945 concerning air corridors and that the Russians could obstruct access to Berlin by land and water routes if they chose to ignore verbal agreements. Murphy and Clay repeatedly advised their government that the Russians could sever these links at any time, and they urged it to consider in advance its response to this contingency.[6]

Soviet propaganda rapidly confirmed the early estimates of Moscow's intentions in Berlin and provided the American decision-

---

5. For a detailed treatment of political events and developments inside Berlin before and during the crisis, see Philip Windsor, *City on Leave: A History of Berlin, 1945–1962* (London: Chatto and Windus, 1963); and W. Phillips Davison, *The Berlin Blockade: A Study in Cold War Politics* (Princeton: Princeton University Press, 1958).

6. Robert Murphy, *Diplomat Among Warriors* (London: Collins, 1964), p. 381.

makers with additional indicators of an imminent crisis. Murphy warned Marshall in early March that the change in Soviet tactics at the Allied Kommandatura in Berlin, which occurred at the end of January and took the form of violent propaganda attacks on the three other delegations, presaged a Soviet intention to break up the quadripartite administration of Berlin. These Soviet diatribes returned again and again to one of three points. First, they continually charged the Western delegations with violation of multipartite agreements, frequently mentioning specific accords such as the Potsdam agreement. Second, they continually charged the American and British delegations with the intention to disrupt quadripartite harmony and the quadripartite administration of Berlin. Third, they alleged that it was the intention of the Western Allies to use Berlin as a means of interfering in the affairs of the Soviet zone. These charges were significant, thought Murphy, because it had been demonstrated in the past that the Soviet Government, like the Nazi Government, attributed to its opponents those very plans it intended to carry out itself.[7] The CIA remained on firmer ground in its analysis of Soviet intentions. Admiral Hillenkoetter wrote to the President on March 16 that while no further reports had been received indicating that the USSR had decided to force the Western powers from Berlin, the recent discussions in London between the U.S., the U.K., France, and the Benelux nations concerning the formation of a Western German state to be included in a Western European Union invited some form of Soviet response stronger than the mere protests received so far.[8]

The tension which had been steadily building up at all levels of inter-Allied relations reached a climax on March 20, when the Soviet delegation, headed by Marshal Vassily Danilovitch Sokolovsky, walked out of the Allied Control Council meeting in Berlin. Marshal Sokolovsky, who was the current chairman, read out a prepared statement charging that the British, French, and American representatives did not consider the Control Council to be the organ of quadripartite administration of occupied Germany but

---

7. Murphy to Marshall, March 3, 1948, in *Foreign Relations of the United States, 1948* (Washington, D.C.: U.S. Government Printing Office, 1973), Vol. 2, pp. 878–879. (Henceforth, this series will be referred to as *FRUS*.)

8. Memorandum for the President from Admiral R. H. Hillenkoetter, March 16, 1948, President's Secretary File, Harry S. Truman Library, Independence, Missouri.

a screen behind which they could hide their unilateral actions. Following Clay's denials and counteraccusations, Sokolovsky demanded to be informed of all the agreements on Germany reached by the three Western powers in London in February and March. The Western representatives considered this request reasonable, but they said they could not provide him with the information he desired until they had heard from their governments. Sokolovsky evidently expected this reply, for he barely waited for its translation before reading a sharp statement accusing the Western powers of violating their obligations under the four-power agreements on the administration of Germany, disregarding and undermining the joint control machinery, and confirming by their actions that the ACC virtually ceased to exist as the supreme body of authority in Germany.[9] The British representative started to reply as the interpreter completed the translation of Sokolovsky's bitter and hectoring statement. Rudely interrupting, the Soviet delegation, following what looked like a prearranged plan, rose as one as Sokolovsky declared: "I see no sense in continuing this meeting, and I declare it adjourned." Without a further word of explanation, the Soviet delegation turned on its heels and walked out of the conference room.[10]

No chairman of the Council had ever before attempted to adjourn a meeting without the approval of his colleagues, nor had a chairman ever before adjourned a meeting without arranging the date for the next meeting. The Western representatives suspected that this was no spur-of-the-moment action but a calculated attempt to strike doubt in Western minds as to the advisability of proceeding with the program for Western Germany. When they left the conference room, they knew that quadripartite government had broken up and that the split of Germany which had seemed inevitable for some time had now taken place. Before leaving they arranged that as each of them became chairman for the month, he would circulate prior to the normal date a note stating that there was no agenda and that the meeting would be held only if it was desired by one of the members of the Council. No request was ever made, and it soon became apparent that further meetings

9. "Statements of Marshal Sokolovsky at the Meeting of the Control Council, 20 March 1948," Union of Soviet Socialist Republics, Ministry of Foreign Affairs, *The Soviet Union and the Berlin Question (Documents)* (Moscow, 1948), pp. 18–20.
10. Clay, *Decision in Germany*, pp. 355–356.

would not take place. "The stage had been set," noted Clay, "for the imposition of the Soviet blockade against Berlin."[11]

Commenting on the walkout, Murphy explained to Marshall that the Soviet threat to regard the Control Council as having been destroyed by the actions of the Western powers "behind its back" may represent a "bold Soviet effort to induce Western powers to liquidate bizonal administration and terminate further discussions looking towards eventual establishment of trizonal fusion." Secondly, the charge that the Western powers had destroyed the Control Council constituted an important element in the Soviet plan to "force all three Western powers out of Berlin, in order to liquidate this remaining 'center of reaction' east of Iron Curtain." In this connection, Murphy considered it significant that recent communist propaganda called for "proper regulation and control" of the railways and highways connecting Berlin and Western Germany which pass through the Soviet zone, following alleged invasions of the Soviet zone by organized bandits and refugee workers from the Western zones. He also recalled that in recent quadripartite discussions the Soviets raised the whole question of air corridors into Berlin. The walkout was thus seen as heralding a major Soviet drive to force the West out of Berlin, and Murphy reminded Marshall that "our Berlin position is delicate and difficult. Our withdrawal, either voluntary or involuntary, would have severe psychological repercussions which would, at this critical stage in the European situation, extend far beyond boundaries of Berlin and even Germany. Soviets realize this full well."[12] These perceptions that America's position in Berlin and her entire policy towards Germany were threatened, and that in Berlin the Soviets held most of the strong cards, conditioned the American response to the breakdown of the Allied Control Council.

The first significant decision taken by the Administration was that (a) the Army was to retain control over the nonmilitary aspects of policy regarding the American zone of occupation, instead of this being taken over by the State Department, and (b) that Clay, who had planned to retire at the end of 1948, was to retain his dual positions as Military Governor and Commander of U.S. forces in Europe (Decision 1). The arrangement for occupied area operations whereby the State Department set government policy and the

11. Ibid., pp. 356–367.
12. Murphy to Marshall, April 1, 1948, in *FRUS, 1948*, Vol. 2, pp. 885–886.

Army Department carried it out had not been working well and frequently placed the two departments at loggerheads with one another. Agreement was reached that the State Department would assume full responsibility for the occupation of Germany, and this was announced by Secretary Marshall in January 1948. But the handover was delayed when Marshal Sokolovsky walked out of the Allied Control Council.[13] The reversal of the earlier plan was communicated to the 51-year-old Clay in a teleconference on March 23 with Secretary Royall, General Omar Bradley, and Major-General Daniel Noce. Royall told Clay that the decision had been made on March 22 and was to be announced by the President after the teleconference. The text of the press release which Marshall had suggested, and on which Clay was invited to comment, ran as follows:

> On January 27 the Department of the Army announced that an agreement had been reached that the Department of State should assume the responsibility for the non-military aspects of the German occupation, looking toward a target date for the transfer of such responsibility on or about July 1, 1948. Following a review of the present situation it has been decided that it would be inadvisable to make any changes in our present administrative arrangements for Germany. This decision will not have any adverse effects on progress towards developing German responsibility for self-government and administrative initiative.[14]

In view of the recent developments in Germany, Clay believed the decision was wise and the press release fully satisfactory. Behind the decision lay the concern to ensure that the decision-making apparatus was efficient, well-coordinated, and ready to meet the coming crisis. The gravity of the situation had the effect of making the Army and the State Department see more eye to eye than they had done in the past. But the appointment of a civilian governor to take charge of the U.S. zone could result in friction between him and the officer commanding the U.S. forces. Retaining Clay in his dual capacity, on the other hand, carried the twofold advantage of a centralized command structure for all U.S. operations in Germany and the presence at its head of an experienced military leader with incomparable knowledge of this vital theater.

13. Oral History Interview with Charles E. Saltzman, June 28, 1974, Harry S. Truman Library, pp. 20–21.
14. Jean Edward Smith, ed., *The Papers of General Lucius D. Clay: Germany, 1945–1949* (Bloomington: Indiana University Press, 1974), Vol. 2, p. 596. (Hereinafter cited as *Clay Papers*.)

Furthermore, the measures which had been set in motion to reinforce the American forces in Europe and prepare them for the impending confrontation had the best chances of being pursued vigorously with a military rather than a civilian figure at the top. For all these reasons, it was considered imperative to defer the handover to the State Department and to avoid personnel changes at such a critical juncture.[15] But lest the decision to retain Army control over the nonmilitary aspects of policy regarding the American zone be taken to imply that the decisions on the future of Germany might be similarly reversed, the press release made it clear that the American Government fully intended to press ahead with the political reconstruction of Germany.

After reviewing the organizational arrangements for the occupation of Germany in the light of the threat signaled by the Soviet walkout from the Allied Control Council, the Americans began to grope for ways and means of curbing Soviet militancy in Germany. Truman told his Secretary of Commerce, Averell Harriman, to cut off shipments to Russia which would contribute to the Russian war machine. But before the proposed change in policy was carried out, all the relevant departments were asked for their opinion.[16] At the Cabinet meeting on March 26, Truman asked Commerce and State to present their views on export controls. Unfortunately, the only record available of this important Cabinet meeting consists of minutes taken by Matthew Connelly, and these, typically, are neither full nor particularly lucid.

Harriman opened the discussion by noting that the Atomic Energy Commission had its own controls, State controlled munitions and national defense weapons, and Commerce controlled the balance of commercial trade. Congress was generally opposed to restrictions on trade and had wrecked the bureaucratic agency that was supposed to control exports by failing to provide it with sufficient funds. Nevertheless, shipments to Eastern Europe and Russia were being screened very carefully at that time, and Commerce planned to ask Congress for import controls which could affect the supply of manganese, chrome, and other items the U.S. was getting from Russia. State distributed to the Cabinet some statistics on trade with Russia, but did not favor issuing to the public a list of

15. Ibid., p. 597.
16. Notes on Cabinet Meeting, June 25, 1948, Papers of Matthew J. Connelly, Harry S. Truman Library.

significant items whose shipment to Russia would be prohibited. State was endeavoring to obtain the consent of other nations for terminating the trade agreement with Czechoslovakia, but it was ready to cancel the agreement unilaterally if it could not get the consent of the other nations involved. Harriman considered it important to either let some items, such as twenty electric locomotives made by General Electric at a cost of five million dollars, go forward or have Congress appropriate money to cover the losses. The consensus was to let these items go forward but accept no new orders.[17]

The actual decision, reached either at the Cabinet meeting on March 26 or as a direct result of the consensus it produced, was to deny export licenses to items that would affect production in key segments of the Soviet and satellite economies (Decision 2). Here lie the rather undramatic origins of what was later to develop into a full-fledged economic counterblockade of Eastern Europe—a counterblockade which was ultimately to play an important role in inducing Stalin to call off the blockade of Berlin. The Department of the Army advised Clay of the Cabinet decision on April 3. Pending further instructions, he was told to apply this decision as a guide and suspend reparations deliveries to Soviet satellites which in his judgment would be of strategic or critical importance. He was also asked to avoid publicity and an overt refusal to deliver reparations, and he was cautioned not to destroy East-West trade.[18]

This less than clear-cut decision to impose a selective embargo on trade with the Soviet bloc and stop reparations deliveries of strategic items bore the marks of a compromise between conflicting policy considerations. The desire to bring economic pressure to bear on Russia and her allies was tempered by the reluctance to escalate the conflict and by the fear that the embargo would harm its initiators as well as its intended victims. The final decision was exactly the kind of muddled and halfhearted policy directive against which Clay's decisive temperament instinctively rebelled. Upon receiving the order, he asked that it be reexamined because it did not provide any practical guide to the question of reparations deliveries to the Soviet satellites. East-West trade, he pointed out, was conducted on the basis of an exchange of goods mutually de-

17. Notes on Cabinet Meeting, March 26, 1948, Papers of Matthew J. Connelly, Harry S. Truman Library.
18. *Clay Papers*, Vol. 2, p. 617.

sired by both parties, and he had no way of determining what would be significant items but thought all items would be significant. He also thought it impractical to attempt to make partial reparations deliveries and suspend deliveries in other instances, as the suspension in itself would clearly indicate America's intent. The only solution he saw to this problem was to decide to deliver or not to deliver, and he left no doubt as to where his own preferences lay. In fact, reparations deliveries to the satellite powers had already been stopped to all practical purposes, he reported, and if his government wanted him to make some deliveries, he wanted specific advice.[19] The handling of the embargo illustrates forcefully how control over the execution of policy can be used by a strong-minded official to appreciably modify the content and direction of policy.[20] In this instance there were two aspects to the government's policy: the embargo and the limitations with which it was hedged. Clay approved of the embargo, and to all intents and purposes had already applied it in practice before the government made up its mind. He did not approve of the limitations and managed to circumvent them by claiming that they were impractical.

Washington anticipated that, following the breakdown of four-power government, Soviet pressure on the Allies would be intensified, but it was still anxious to avoid any action which might escalate the crisis or be used by the Soviets to justify further coercive measures. Clay, on the other hand, and the commandant of the American sector in Berlin, Colonel Frank Howley, concluded that the Russians were set on driving the Allies out of Berlin, possibly by blockading the city. Howley was determined not to be caught asleep, and on March 25 he prepared with his experts a plan anticipating just such an emergency. They did not know precisely what form the emergency would take, but they labeled the plan "Basic Assumption," the assumption being that the Russians would split their sector from the other three. The plan not only provided for the building up of food and coal stocks, but also included the emer-

19. Clay to Noce, April 4, 1948, *Clay Papers*, Vol. 2, pp. 617–618.
20. Most of the theoretical literature on the foreign policy process concentrates on the formulation aspect and neglects the implementation aspect. One notable exception is Graham T. Allison's *Essence of Decision* (Boston: Little, Brown, 1971). For a recent analysis which stresses the importance of implementation and examines its impact on the substance of policy, see Michael Clarke, "Foreign Policy Implementation: Problems and Approaches," *British Journal of International Studies*, Vol. 5, No. 2 (July 1979).

gency use of what little power the Americans had in West Berlin, the creation of temporary administration in the Western sectors, and the use of a radio station for counterpropaganda against the Russians.[21] Thus, while no top-level decision had been reached on what should be done if the Soviets blockaded the city, lower down the chain of command energetic measures were being taken to prepare for this eventuality.

Howley was not alone among the American military leaders stationed in Germany to actively prepare for the approaching confrontation, nor were the military contingency plans confined to the supply of the American garrison in Berlin should the city be blockaded. Lieutenant-General Curtis LeMay, the commander of the United States Air Force in Europe (USAFE), began on his own initiative to prepare contingency plans for the outbreak of military hostilities between the United States and the Soviet Union. After the Soviets started interfering with surface traffic, it looked to LeMay as if he might have to fight at any moment, and that he and his forces had to consider something beyond the housekeeping duties in which they had been engaged during previous months. Officially there was no change in USAFE's mission, but LeMay's own estimates prompted him to start preparing for the next war. At a cursory glance, it looked like "USAFE would be stupid to get mixed up in anything bigger than a cat fight at a pet show." They had one fighter group, some transport planes, and some radar people. No less worrisome than the paucity of men and equipment was the vulnerability of the American supply lines in Europe. The principal supplies arrived from America at the port of Bremerhaven in the northwest, at the mouth of the Weser River, 250 miles away from Frankfurt, where the bulk of the U.S. troops were stationed. All the Russians had to do was to move forward and they could cut America's supply lines before they even made contact with her troops. This situation, in LeMay's words, was "a logical outgrowth of the God-bless-our-buddy-buddy-Russians-we-sure-can-trust-them-forever-and-ever philosophy which flowered away back in the Roosevelt Administration." Moreover, if the Russians did move, all the Americans had in their zone for stopping them was a couple of divisions, including the constabulary.[22]

To reduce the vulnerability of USAFE, LeMay came up with the

21. Frank Howley, *Berlin Command* (New York: Putnam's, 1950), p. 201.
22. Curtis E. LeMay with MacKinlay Kantor, *Mission with LeMay: My Story* (New York: Doubleday, 1965), p. 411.

ingenious idea of locating some strategic bases in the rear of American troops, well behind the Rhine. He got together with the Chiefs of Staff of the French and Belgian air forces and asked for their help in providing bases in which USAFE could stock up ammunition, bombs, petroleum, food, mechanical equipment, and any other supplies that might be needed. The presence of foreign troops on French and Belgian territory was illegal, as LeMay well knew, so he sent his men in civilian clothes. To elude enemy detection or even observation by Allied civilians, which was important in view of the illegality of the procedure, LeMay's trains were shuttled around France and Belgium. What this amounted to, according to LeMay, was that there was a private little NATO buzzing along in Germany, France, and Belgium before the North Atlantic Treaty Organization ever existed. A year later, NATO did come into being; but as far as USAFE was concerned, it had its own pocket-sized one first. LeMay maintained that he informed General Clay of what he was doing but was not sure whether Clay informed anybody else or not.[23] Clay himself, assuming he knew about the energetic preparations of his subordinate, does not appear to have brought them to the attention of the Department of the Army.

The situation in Berlin steadily deteriorated after the Soviet walkout. Disturbed by the transport incidents, by the occasional detention of American personnel by the Russians, and by other difficulties that were reported daily, the Department of the Army summoned Clay to a teleconference on March 30 to obtain his views on stopping further dependents of U.S. servicemen from going to Germany and gradually withdrawing families from Berlin. Clay replied that these were logical steps from a strictly military viewpoint, but that they were engaged in a struggle of a political nature, and these steps would have disastrous political consequences. He warned that withdrawal of dependents from Berlin would create hysteria accompanied by a rush of Germans to communism for safety, and that this condition would spread in Europe and would increase communist political strength everywhere.[24]

PHASE II: MARCH 31–APRIL 5

On March 31, the Deputy Soviet Military Governor for Germany, General Dratvin, sent a note to Clay's deputy, General George

---

23. Ibid., pp. 412–413.   24. Clay, *Decision in Germany*, p. 358.

Hays, informing him of a new and much more stringent system for controlling traffic between the Western and Soviet zones of occupation, to be instituted as of April 1. Under this system, all U.S. personnel proceeding to Berlin would be required to present documentary proof of their identity, and all freight brought into Berlin by or for the use of their occupation forces would require a permit from the Soviet commander.[25]

Clay immediately cabled General Bradley, the Army Chief of Staff, that he was in receipt of a peremptory letter from Dratvin announcing new conditions which would make travel by American personnel between Berlin and the American zone impossible except by air. There was no doubt in Clay's mind that this was "the first of a series of restrictive measures designed to drive us from Berlin." In view of the seriousness of this development, Clay proposed to have the Soviet military commander advised promptly that the Americans were prepared for their train commandant, on arrival at entry points, to furnish the Soviet representatives with a list of passengers together with their official orders, and that likewise they were prepared to present a manifest covering freight shipments in their trains. However, the right of free entry into Berlin over the established corridors was a condition that preceded their entry into Berlin and their evacuation of Saxony and Thuringia, and they did not intend to give up this right of free entry. He further proposed to advise Dratvin that they could not permit their military trains to be entered by the representatives of other powers, and that the guards on board the U.S. trains had been instructed accordingly.

If there was any doubt in the mind of anyone in Washington regarding this course of action, Clay hoped it would be brought to his attention without delay, as he felt it necessary to take action that very day. For him it was a very serious matter because it was his intent to instruct the guards to open fire if Soviet soldiers attempted to enter their trains, and he wanted the full consequences of this course of action to be understood. In support of the firm response he was advocating, Clay argued that "unless we take a strong stand now, our life in Berlin will become impossible. A retreat from Berlin at this moment would, in my opinion, have serious if not disastrous consequences in Europe. I do not believe that

---

25. For the full text of the Soviet note of March 31, see *Clay Papers*, Vol. 2, pp. 600–601.

the Soviets mean war now. However, if they do, it seems to me that we might as well find out now as later. We cannot afford to be bluffed."[26]

So as not to lose valuable time, Clay began preparations for sending the trains with armed guards on board to find out whether the Russians would actually deny them access by force or by sidetracking. Convinced that the Russians would back down if put to the test, he grew impatient when permission was not immediately granted. Bradley explained that the proposal needed to be taken up with the Joint Chiefs of Staff and others, and told him to delay the trains until he heard again. Reluctantly, Clay agreed to hold the trains in the British zone, where they would be at eight o'clock in the evening—the appointed time for the next teleconference.[27]

In Washington, the threatening move by the adversary created the need for more detailed information, and a process of search was initiated through several channels to obtain relevant facts and clarifications. Attention initially focused on the access rights, since the Russians were challenging that highly vulnerable point of the Western position in Germany. As George Elsey, who was Clark Clifford's assistant, recalled: "There was a great deal of mad scrambling through the records by State, by the Army, by just about everyone who had had anything to do with it or had any access to any documents, and there was just *no* evidence that could ever be found that anyone had had the foresight to see the implications of the placing of Berlin, and lack of written guarantees by the Russians that the British, the French and the U.S. would have unrestricted access to Berlin."[28] Some confusion was created by the inconsistent answers elicited by this search. Royall, for example, asked Clay whether he knew of any documentation guaranteeing free access to Berlin, since the State Department was unable to locate any. All Clay could suggest was that their access rights were established in oral agreement with Zhukov and were implied in almost three years of application.[29] The State Department Legal Adviser, on the other hand, concluded that although no formal agreement had been signed, the right of the U.S. to operate passenger

26. Clay to Bradley, March 31, 1948, copy in Leahy Diary, Papers of Admiral William D. Leahy, Library of Congress, Washington, D.C.
27. Clay, *Decision in Germany*, p. 359; and *Clay Papers*, Vol. 2, p. 599.
28. Oral History Interview with George M. Elsey, pp. 350–351, Harry S. Truman Library.
29. *Clay Papers*, Vol. 2, pp. 602–603.

and freight trains to and from Berlin, subject only to rules of safety and technical and operational control, had been recognized in the past by the Soviets, and that, consequently, the new order requiring permits and inspection went beyond such regulation and constituted illegal interference with the U.S. right of passage.[30]

The examination of alternative courses of action was conducted at the same time as the search for information and was an equally disjointed and almost random process. While Clay was waiting for the decision on his proposal to send test trains, other ideas were under discussion in Washington. With the realization that any incident involving shooting or other heavy violence might precipitate war, some consideration had been given there to the President sending an immediate note to Stalin informing him that Dratvin's requirements were a violation of existing agreements and stating that traffic would continue to move pending discussions about any proper regulations. In that event, traffic would start moving in the usual manner after twenty-four hours, even if no reply had been received from Stalin. Another suggestion was to move trains but instruct the commandants not to shoot under any circumstances.[31]

Royall brought these ideas to Clay's attention and asked him for his comments. Clay regarded both suggestions as unrealistic and likely to damage American prestige. He detected some apprehension on the part of Royall and his advisers that a firm American stand might provoke incidents involving force, which could lead to war; so he added that if the Soviets meant war, such responses would only defer the next provocation by a few days. For his part, he did not believe that the Soviet restrictions were intended to lead to war, but he was convinced that any failure to meet them squarely would have serious consequences. He realized that the test trains which he himself proposed to send would only be a token resistance, but he saw this as the only possible course of action. If he had to choose between the two courses proposed in Washington, Royall persisted, which one would he prefer? Clay replied that the proposed letter to Stalin would be the better of the two, but should be preceded by their own test.[32]

While Clay kept up the pressure for prompt action from the basement of his military headquarters in Berlin, Dratvin's letter

---

30. Memorandum from Ernest A. Gross to Lovett, April 9, 1948, RG 59, General Records of the Department of State, 740.0019 Control (Germany), National Archives, Washington, D.C.

31. *Clay Papers*, Vol. 2, p. 602.   32. Ibid., pp. 602–604.

was carefully studied by Forrestal, Royall, and Under Secretary of State Lovett, acting for Marshall, who was attending the International Conference of American States in Bogota. At the third teleconference, Bradley informed Clay that his proposed reply was considered satisfactory, subject to checking that it had not been the custom for a Russian official to walk through the trains. Clay replied that it had not been the custom for months, and that in any case they were faced with a realistic, not a legalistic, problem: "Our reply will not be misunderstood by 42 million Germans and perhaps 200 million Western Europeans. We must say, . . . as our letter does, 'this far you may go and no further.' There is no middle ground which is not appeasement." Bradley stressed that no action should be taken that was different from what had been in practice recently, because if their action provoked war, it had to be clear that the fault was not theirs. Clay sought to put to rest the fear that any action out of the ordinary might lead to a war for which the U.S. would be held responsible. "Please understand," he pleaded, "that we are not carrying a chip on our shoulders and will shoot only in self-protection. We do not believe we will have to do so. We feel the integrity of our trains as part of our sovereignty is a symbol of our position in Germany and Europe." With these clarifications and reassurances, Bradley approved Clay's proposed reply, with some minor modifications, for dispatch to Dratvin.[33]

The perception of threat evidently led to a widening of the consultative circle. Teleconferences with participants on both sides of the Atlantic were an important form of communication. In the three teleconferences held on March 31, no less than five generals took part (Noce, Bradley, Collins, Wedemeyer, and Clay), as well as Secretary Royall. In addition, extensive consultations were held in Washington. The Soviet demand for more intensive control of the American train service to Berlin and Clay's request for authorization to send a train to test how far the Russians would go were considered sufficiently serious by the Department of the Army to justify referring the matter to the President.[34] The Joint Chiefs of Staff, however, do not appear to have been consulted.[35]

33. Ibid., pp. 604–605.
34. With a covering letter to the President dated April 1, 1948, Royall enclosed (1) the letter from Dratvin to Hays, (2) the reply proposed by Clay, and (3) the record of the teleconference between Royall and Clay held on March 31 at 4:00 P.M. Copies of these documents were also transmitted to Forrestal. See President's Secretary File, Box 157, Harry S. Truman Library.
35. Condit, *The History of the Joint Chiefs of Staff*, p. 125.

Although Clay now considerably played down the probability of armed conflict, the war scare which followed the Czech coup and his own alarming report of March 5 had not completely subsided. The Central Intelligence Agency's estimate, handed to Truman on March 16, that war "was not probable within sixty days"[36] was hardly reassuring. Even if Russia did not plan war, the outbreak of violent incidents could not be confidently ruled out, and presidential approval was therefore necessary for any steps that might precipitate them. There was a continuous series of high-level conferences in Washington throughout the day, involving the State Department, the Department of the Army, and the President. When the text of General Dratvin's letter arrived, the wording was considered less truculent than could have been inferred from Clay's first message.[37] Nevertheless, Clay had requested permission for a specific course of action; and in response to that request, the President and his advisers examined the options open to them. The following suggestions were considered:

1. That the President send a message to Stalin pointing out that implementation of the Russian proposal might create an incident which might be provocative of war.

2. That he call into conference the majority and minority leaders of the House and Senate.

3. That instructions be sent to Clay endorsing his proposed action, with a qualification that he be told that his guards could not use their weapons except in self-defense.

4. It was also suggested that immediate communication be made with the British to see whether they had taken action identical to ours and given similar instructions to their train guards.[38]

At Lovett's suggestion, the proposal to have the President address a communication to Marshal Stalin was discarded on the grounds that it would place a disproportionate emphasis on this incident and might convince the Russians that they had secured precisely the effect they were after. Truman, on his own initiative, decided against calling in Congressional leaders, because it would become immediately known, and, secondly, because it would add unnecessarily to the creation of war hysteria. The question of con-

36. George F. Kennan, *Memoirs, 1925–1950* (Boston: Little, Brown, 1967), p. 400.
37. Walter Millis, ed., *The Forrestal Diaries* (New York: Viking, 1951), p. 408.
38. Ibid.

certed action was disposed of by a ticker announcement that the British intended to continue running their trains and that they would maintain armed guard personnel on them.[39]

Thus, by a process of elimination, Truman and his advisers ended up by adopting the third option—the one that Clay had recommended. The outcome of this intensive process of consultation and deliberation was to authorize Clay (1) to reject the Soviet measures for tighter control over America's military train service into Berlin, and (2) to send military passenger trains through the Russian checkpoints with the guards instructed to prevent Soviet military personnel from entering, but not to shoot unless first fired upon. Clay had proposed to double the number of guards on the passenger trains, but this suggestion was rejected. He was authorized to maintain only the same number of U.S. soldiers and the same weapons (carbines) as before (Decision 3).[40] The precise instructions, approved by Truman and transmitted to Clay by Bradley on March 31, were as follows:

> You are authorized to move trains as you see fit. It is considered important that the normal train guard be not increased and that they carry only the arms normally carried. Also that the Russians be not prohibited from taking actions which have been customarily followed. Furthermore, it is important that our guards not fire unless fired upon.[41]

This qualified endorsement of Clay's proposal constituted a decision to ascertain the limits of Soviet resolution and to resist changes in the status quo, but without resorting to excessively provocative measures and with every intention of containing the dangers of escalation.

The need for caution perceived by the decision-makers in Washington was evidenced by the restrictions on the autonomy of the U.S. commander in the field. Clay registered his disagreement with the decision not to increase the number of guards. He also thought that it was unfair to instruct a man whose life might be in danger not to shoot. But having stated these views, he assured Royall, Bradley, and Wedemeyer that the instructions he received would be carried out to the letter. Royall explained that they were sorry that "so much chaperonage was necessary but the war danger

---

39. Ibid.
40. *FRUS, 1948*, Vol. 2, pp. 886–887; and *Clay Papers*, Vol. 2, pp. 605–606.
41. Condit, *The History of the Joint Chiefs of Staff*, p. 125.

element made it necessary to consult many people and compare many views."[42]

Once the text of the reply to General Dratvin had been settled and Clay's authority to move trains had been confirmed, Clay proceeded immediately to implement his plan. Three U.S. military trains, the "Berliner" and two others, were ready to move from the British into the Soviet zone by the time of the third teleconference at 9:00 P.M. (German time). These trains entered the Soviet zone at midnight of March 31. The new Soviet measures were therefore experienced precisely at the moment they came into effect. One train commandant apparently lost his nerve and permitted the Soviet representatives to board the train. His train was allowed to continue on its way through the Soviet checkpoint to Berlin. The remaining two trains were stopped, and Soviet representatives insisted on boarding them. When denied access, they did not attempt to force their way in, but used electrical switching to shunt the trains off the main line and onto a siding. The trains could not have proceeded forward except by use of force; and with the traffic control in Soviet hands, they could not have proceeded very far even with force.[43] They were stuck at the siding until dawn approached, and then they withdrew rather ignominiously. Clay, who had to back down, commented ruefully: "It was clear the Russians meant business."[44]

How Washington would respond to this Soviet victory in stopping the passage of U.S. military trains that would not submit to inspection was far from clear. There were no clear plans of action—only an inclination to try to settle the problem of access by diplomatic rather than military means. Bradley indirectly conveyed this inclination to Clay by telling him: "After you have exhausted all efforts there to solve the problem, consideration will be given here to taking the matter up directly with Moscow."[45] This vague initial attitude left Clay some scope for influencing the ultimate American response, and in the next few days he bombarded Washington with suggestions for action, as well as taking some actions on his own initiative. In Washington, no attempt was made to search systematically for all the options available and to evaluate them in the light of Soviet behavior on the night of March 31. Rather, there

42. *Clay Papers*, Vol. 2, p. 606.
43. Clay to Bradley, April 1, 1948, in ibid., pp. 607–608.
44. Clay, *Decision in Germany*, p. 359.
45. *Clay Papers*, Vol. 2, p. 608.

was a tendency to sit back and wait for Clay to come up with suggestions, which would be examined on their merits as they came up.

Still smarting under the humiliation of having to back down, Clay was in no mood for compromise or for seeking a diplomatic solution. While conceding that the Russians had won the train victory, he was confident that the Allied action had stopped for the time being further interference with air and highway traffic, which would require force to implement.[46] The British and French Military Governors wanted a Control Council meeting to be called to discuss the problem. However, since the Russians had broken up the last meeting and had not called a successive one, Clay proposed to weigh this option for several days before making a decision.

Clay impressed on Royall and Bradley the idea that compromise was neither desirable nor feasible. He pointed out that the British Deputy Military Governor, Major-General N. C. D. Brownjohn, had visited General Dratvin on April 1 to find an opening and had found none. For his own part, Clay was intent on avoiding any response that might be interpreted as a sign of weakness or lack of steadfastness. The British wish to propose compromise, he said, "but I cannot agree that such an offer would serve any useful purpose except humiliating rebuff."[47] The British Military Governor, General Sir Brian Robertson, called on Clay on April 2 to report that London did not view favorably the idea of retaliating against Soviet ocean shipping and to inquire whether it might not be well to sound out the Soviet authorities for the purpose of ascertaining whether a compromise solution might be possible. Clay and Murphy took the position that the American reply to the Soviet note was only twenty-four hours old, and it would therefore be better to wait a reasonable time before indicating any willingness to make concessions. They preferred to test the Soviet intentions first. If the present Soviet actions turned out to be part of a larger and more ambitious program, they told Robertson, there would be nothing to be gained by hasty offers of concessions.[48]

46. Ibid., p. 614.   47. Ibid., p. 613.
48. Murphy to Marshall, April 2, 1948, in *FRUS, 1948*, Vol. 2, pp. 887–889. Robertson's report of his meeting with Clay sheds additional light on Clay's attitude: "I sounded him out on a proposal that we allow Russian unarmed inspectors on our trains while still in the British zone of Berlin before they reach the checkpoint as is normally done by passport inspecting officials on international fron-

Retaliation against Soviet shipping was one of Clay's earliest suggestions. Even before the test trains were dispatched, he proposed that if the Soviets opened fire on them, the U.S. and British governments might close certain world trade routes under their control until normal conditions were restored in Berlin.[49] Immediately after the Russian success in stopping Allied trains from going to Berlin without inspection, Clay returned to this idea. A careful examination revealed little, if anything, that could be done in Germany by way of retaliation. But he thought it advisable for the American government to give some consideration to retaliatory measures such as the enactment of stringent regulations which would make Soviet use of ocean canals, bunkering facilities, and other facilities under its control difficult, if not impossible.[50] The image of the international system as being tightly coupled meant not only that setbacks in one area were expected to have repercussions elsewhere, but also that pressure in one area could be relieved by exercising countervailing pressure on the adversary in other places. This image lurked behind Clay's advocacy of retaliatory measures against the Soviet Union. The search for such measures was conducted by the Army Department in cooperation with the State Department and the Department of Commerce.[51] But on April 6, General Wedemeyer advised Clay that, following a preliminary review, they had not found any retaliatory measures which would be effective in relation to the difficulty they were facing in Berlin and which would not rebound to their disadvantage.[52]

Another possibility raised by Clay was that of resorting to direct physical action by forcing a convoy of trucks through the Russian checkpoints on the highway to Berlin. Evidently, he did not consider the Allied trains which had been stopped an adequate test of Soviet intentions and thought the Russians would back down if the Allies demonstrated resolution in moving nearer the brink, for on April 1 he informed Bradley that he was giving some thought to

---

tiers. Clay was quite adamant against any form of compromise. He feels certain that other Russian moves will follow within a few days and that compromise will not help but will only encourage them. Personally, I think that an attempt to get a clear agreement would be worth trying but of course I must stand with Clay. His whole attitude is most pessimistic and bellicose, and that is the big difference between us." Robertson to Foreign Office, April 2, 1948, FO 371/70490/C2543/3/18, Public Record Office, London.

49. *Clay Papers*, Vol. 2, p. 604.   50. Ibid., p. 607.
51. Ibid., p. 614.   52. Ibid., p. 608.

sending a guarded truck convoy through to Berlin along the autobahn, since this could force the issue, whereas rail traffic could not be moved with others controlling the signal system.[53] Bradley replied that while he supported Clay's actions to date, he should not try to force a guarded convoy through without further consultation with Washington.[54] Some years later, Bradley explained why, from the start, he and the other military chiefs would not go along with Clay's proposal. Their contention was that even if the Russians did not oppose the convoy by armed force, for fear that this would lead to war, they could stop it in many other ways short of armed resistance. Roads could simply be closed for repairs, or "a bridge could go out just ahead of you and then another bridge behind, and you'd be in a hell of a fix."[55]

Without waiting for Washington to make up its mind, however, Clay began lobbying for British participation in his scheme. He broached the idea of forming an Anglo-American truck convoy and forcing it through the Russian checkpoint. General Robertson reported to his government that he did not see much future in this idea because a few tanks across the road at a defile would soon bring the convoy to a halt, quite apart from the fact that the Russians might get the better of a shooting match. Besides, Robertson thought that the Russians were on strong ground legally when they demanded to see documents for persons and goods entering and leaving their zone, and he observed that road traffic was being allowed through if it was properly documented.[56]

The policymakers in Washington were no more inclined than Robertson to allow their representatives in Germany to engage in brinkmanship that might go over the brink and land them in a war which they did not want and for whose outbreak they would be held responsible. On April 2, they received a report on the "Possibility of Direct Soviet Military Action During 1948," prepared by a joint ad hoc committee representing the CIA and the intelligence agencies of the Department of State, the Army, the Navy, and the Air Force. The report stated that the Soviet armed forces had the capability of overrunning all of Western Europe and the Near East

---

53. Clay to Bradley, April 1, 1948, in ibid., p. 607.   54. Ibid., p. 608.
55. Interview with General Omar Bradley, March 29, 1955, p. 9, Papers of Harry S. Truman, Post-Presidential Files, Box 1, "Memoirs," Harry S. Truman Library.
56. Robertson to Foreign Office, April 2, 1948, FO 371/70490/C2529/3/18, Public Record Office, London.

to Cairo within a short period of time, but it concluded, on the basis of the available evidence and the "logic of the situation," that the USSR will not resort to direct military action during 1948. This time, however, the Director of Intelligence of the Air Force did not concur in this conclusion, arguing that reliable data were not available upon which to base the extension of the CIA's earlier sixty-day "no war" estimate to the end of 1948. On account of the fluidity and momentum inherent in the current situation, he estimated that an abrupt change in the present balance could occur very quickly.[57]

Symptomatic of the prevailing apprehension about Moscow's intentions was the growing concern for the safety of American civilians in the danger zone. On April 2, Clay was invited to another teleconference with the Department of the Army, at which he was told that pressure was rising at home for the withdrawal of American families and that many responsible persons thought it unthinkable that they should stay in Berlin. Clay himself had received a number of applications from his officers and officials requesting permission for their families to be returned to the United States. But when he announced that any American who wanted his dependents sent home would have to accompany them, almost all of the applications previously received were withdrawn. In his reply to Bradley and Royall, Clay reported that the Americans in Berlin could be supported indefinitely with a very small airlift, and he reiterated his opposition to the evacuation of dependents. "I do not believe," he said, "we should evacuate now. In emergency, we can evacuate quickly. However, evacuation would play into Soviet hands and frighten rest of Europe."[58] Despite strong Congressional pressure for evacuation, Clay's views prevailed in Washington with the support of the Joint Chiefs of Staff. As always, the Military Governor was thinking of the political ramifications. Evacuation in face of the Italian elections and the European situation seemed almost unthinkable to him. He feared that such a logical move, from the point of view of reducing the logistical strain on supplying a greater number of people in Berlin, would be interpreted by America's friends and enemies alike as a

57. CIA, "Possibility of Direct Soviet Military Action During 1948," April 2, 1948, President's Secretary File, Harry S. Truman Library; and Millis, *The Forrestal Diaries*, p. 409.
58. *Clay Papers*, Vol. 2, pp. 613–614.

sign of her weakening resolve and a vindication of Soviet-inspired rumors of an imminent Western withdrawal from Berlin.

While America's basic policy on Berlin remained to be determined, Clay had the practical problem of supplying the needs of the American personnel, totaling 9,415, stationed in the capital. After the test trains were halted, he canceled all other military trains that would have to pass through the Russian zone. However, the decision against evacuating dependents meant that there was no reduction in the volume of supplies needed by the American garrison. To supply these needs and to sustain the stocks available in Berlin at levels that would be sufficient for forty-five days, Clay launched a small-scale airlift on April 2.[59] This "baby airlift" was conceived as a temporary measure, and the tonnage figures were very small. It was a puny forerunner of the great airlift that later supplied all the civilian population of West Berlin, and it lacked the dramatic appeal of the later effort. But it served its purpose, and on the day it was launched, Clay reported that highway and air conditions were normal, that civil freight for the German population was moving normally, that military freight appeared to be moving normally, free from attempted search, and that they could continue indefinitely under the prevailing conditions. He strongly recommended that this course be followed, although this would require a substantial increase in the air passenger lift.[60]

Within a few days, however, a major incident cast some doubt over the viability of the airlift. On April 5, a British transport plane approaching Gatow airfield in the British sector of Berlin was buzzed and then struck in the air by a Soviet fighter plane. Both aircraft crashed, killing the Soviet pilot and the fourteen crew members and passengers, including two American passengers, on the British aircraft. The British Military Governor went to see Marshal Sokolovsky to demand both a four-power inquiry under the rules laid down by the Air Safety Center in Berlin and assurances that British airplanes would not be molested. He also advised Sokolovsky that he had ordered fighter escort for all his unarmed planes, and that this escort would be maintained until Soviet assurances were received. According to Robertson's report,

---

59. Clay to Bradley, April 2, 1948, in ibid., pp. 611–612; and Lowell Bennett, *Berlin Bastion* (Frankfurt, Germany: Friedrich Rudl, 1951), pp. 35–39.
60. *Clay Papers*, Vol. 2, p. 613; and Lovett to Marshall, April 2, 1948, in *FRUS, 1948*, Vol. 2, pp. 889–890.

Sokolovsky, gravely disturbed and clearly on the defensive, expressed regret that the accident had occurred and assured Robertson that the Soviet high command had not directed and would not direct any molestation of British aircraft in the corridor.[61]

Clay was inclined to believe that the collision was not intended but rather the result of a fight-happy pilot out to show his defiance of the Western powers. However, he anticipated that earlier Soviet propaganda claims to the effect that there would be interference with Western air flights would make it difficult for the Soviet authorities to issue a satisfactory explanation without retreating from the press and radio propaganda which they had been disseminating inside Germany. Clay himself, acting on his own initiative, announced on April 5 that unless some assurances were obtained, he would order fighter escort for his planes the following day.[62] When General Bradley questioned the wisdom of this action, Clay pointed out that both the British and the French had already ordered fighter escort and that he must have discretionary authority to keep a united Western front.[63]

Sokolovsky's apologetic attitude was sharply reversed on April 6, when, following the Soviet inquiry, he sent Robertson a note in which he placed the blame for the accident on the British plane and threatened to take the necessary measures for the protection of traffic over the Soviet zone unless Robertson issued the necessary orders to the British planes for the strict following of air safety regulations. The British had apparently committed a minor technical violation by not informing the Berlin Air Safety Center of the departure and arrival times of the plane, and this may account for Robertson's retreat from his earlier insistence on written guarantees for the safety of British planes. Clay, however, described Sokolovsky's letter as very insulting and criticized Robertson's reply as "an indication of weakness which will expedite rather than defer further Soviet pressure. I could think of no weaker British action and I think it destroys our position."[64] This was an unduly pessimistic conclusion. The Western powers continued to make full use

61. Murphy to Marshall, April 6, 1948, in *FRUS, 1948*, Vol. 2, pp. 890–891; and Clay to Bradley, April 6, 1948, in *Clay Papers*, Vol. 2, pp. 618–619.

62. Clay to Chamberlin, April 5, 1948, copy in President's Secretary File, Harry S. Truman Library.

63. Clay to Bradley, April 5, 1948, copy in Papers of Clark M. Clifford, Harry S. Truman Library.

64. Clay to Bradley, April 9, 1948, in *Clay Papers*, Vol. 2, pp. 620–621.

of the air corridors without interference or harassment from the Soviets. Clay's own forthright statement that U.S. planes would continue to fly into Berlin under the old four-power agreement, regardless of any new unilateral Soviet measures, reinforced by the hint that fighter escorts might be used if necessary, may have had some salutary effect in discouraging any Soviet brinkmanship in the air.[65]

If the real aim of the Soviet tactics in the air had been to raise the level of shared risk in order to induce the Allies to back down rather than accept the continuation of the risk, then this aim was quickly abandoned.[66] Although the collision may have been unintentional, the likely object of the buzzing exercise was to exert pressure on the Allies, not by threatening deliberate violence, but by raising the risk that war would occur through loss of control. The Allies' response, however, signaled to the Russians that they would not be coerced by the manipulation of shared risks and the fear of an autonomous process leading to war into abandoning the use of air traffic to Berlin, and that they were prepared to use strong measures to deal with Soviet interference in the air corridors. The need for such measures did not arise, as the Russians themselves quietly dropped their earlier demand to inspect Western military trains on the way to Berlin, and this in turn rendered the baby airlift inessential. As General LeMay recalled:

> During one period of eleven days in early April, when the Soviets demanded the right to investigate military shipments by rail, we flew small quantities of food and other critical supplies into Berlin; something like three hundred tons. But, beginning about April 12th or 13th, we were able to use surface transportation once more, and the temporary airlift was discontinued.[67]

PHASE III: APRIL 6–JUNE 17

Throughout April, the question of whether America should maintain its position in Berlin was under constant discussion. The situation on the ground gave cause for anxiety because, while freight traffic was getting through and air traffic was free from interference after the air crash, the blockade of passenger traffic was extended

---

65. *New York Times*, April 25, 1948.
66. The tactic of raising the level of shared risk is analyzed by Thomas C. Schelling, *Arms and Influence* (New Haven: Yale University Press, 1966), chap. 3.
67. LeMay, *Mission with LeMay*, p. 415.

to outgoing trains, including the international train Nord Express. Viewing these restrictions as part of a planned, incremental, and escalating Soviet strategy aimed at forcing the U.S. and her allies out of Berlin, some people in Washington began to move tentatively towards the conclusion that the Western position in Berlin was indefensible in the long run.

At a teleconference with Clay on April 10, General Bradley voiced some of the fears and doubts that were developing in military as well as civilian circles. Western passenger trains, he said, were completely stopped, and the Russians had in effect won the first round. Did Clay see any likelihood of this being changed, asked the Army Chief of Staff, and if not: "Will not Russian restrictions be added one by one which eventually would make our position untenable unless we ourselves were prepared to threaten or actually start a war to remove these restrictions? Here we doubt whether our people are prepared to start a war in order to maintain our position in Berlin and Vienna." Given this pessimistic outlook, Bradley wondered whether it would not be prudent to start considering under what conditions the Western powers themselves might announce their withdrawal so as to avoid being forced out by Soviet threats and to minimize the loss of prestige. One possibility he mentioned was setting up Trizonia with a capital in Frankfurt.

Clay gave it as his firm conviction that the Western powers should not plan on leaving Berlin short of a Soviet ultimatum to drive them out by force if they did not leave. The one exception which could force them to leave without an ultimatum would be a Soviet stoppage of all food supplies to the German population in the Western sectors, but Clay doubted that the Soviets would make such a foolish move, because it would alienate the Germans completely. He himself was slowly reducing the number of American dependents and civilian employees without creating the impression that they were planning to abandon Berlin. "There can be no question," he emphasized, "but that our departure would represent a tremendous loss of prestige unless it were forced by military action. Of course, I realize that this final decision is a matter of high Government policy. Nevertheless, I cannot believe that the Soviets will apply force in Berlin unless they have determined war to be inevitable within a comparatively short period of time." Realizing that Bradley's question reflected not just personal concern but growing pessimism within the Pentagon, Clay mustered all his considerable persuasive powers to plead against planning to abandon the old capital. The crux of his message was that America's presence in Berlin was the symbol of her commitment to defend Western Europe against the march of communism, and that any faltering in this commitment would be disastrous:

> We retreat from Berlin. . . . After Berlin will come Western Germany and our strength there is no greater and our position no more tenable than in Berlin. If we mean that we are to hold Europe against communism, we must not budge. . . . If America does not know this, does not believe the issue is cast now, then it never will and communism will run rampant.[68]

Two days later, returning to an idea for which he had been unable to arouse any enthusiasm, Clay submitted to Bradley a specific plan for resolving the Berlin crisis. There was one course of action, he cabled, which would relieve the situation and leave no doubt in Europe as to the American position. It involved British and French cooperation and also a calculated risk, but it offered the Allies a means of recapturing the initiative. If the British and French would each assemble a division to join the First U.S. Division at the Helmsted entry to the highway corridor, they could advise the Soviet representatives that the Berlin situation required a reinforcement of their garrisons and that they were each bringing in a division. Clay predicted that the Soviet representatives would fold up in the face of such a move. He realized how little the U.S. would have left in its zone, but he added that when one has little, bold use of what he has is imperative. The calculated risk was the chance that Soviet forces would attempt to block entry with force, thereby bringing about war. This, however, was a remote chance in Clay's opinion. In support of his proposed course of action, he argued that continuation in Berlin was a test both of U.S. intent and of its strength; that it was worth taking considerable risk, particularly if the British and French responded; and that it constituted a better defense than could be offered in the U.S. zone if the Soviets did attack, which made it a wise use of the U.S.'s limited strength in the area.

General Bradley carefully considered the implications of the proposed course of action, and his response was deferential in tone but negative in substance. "Obviously," he cabled Clay, "in your position you are better equipped than I to evaluate all the advantages and disadvantages of such action. However, it appears to me

---

68. *Clay Papers*, Vol. 2, pp. 621–623.

that the deployment of our forces in such manner might jeopardize our longer range objectives in the Western zone and I therefore do not feel that the plan is desirable at this time. I am following the developments in your area and assure you of my continued support and confidence."[69]

Advice to stand firm in Berlin reached the Americans from another, rather unexpected source: the former British Prime Minister, Winston Churchill. Lewis Douglas, the American Ambassador to London, who had a number of conversations with Churchill, summarized the great war leader's views in a top secret cable to Lovett on April 17. According to Douglas, Churchill maintained that:

> When and if the Soviets develop the atomic bomb, war will become a certainty, even though by then Western Europe may have become again the seat of authority and a stable political part of the world. He believes that now is the time, promptly, to tell the Soviet that if they do not retire from Berlin and abandon Eastern Germany, withdrawing to the Polish frontier, we will raze their cities. It is further his view that we cannot appease, conciliate or provoke the Soviet; that the only vocabulary they understand is force; and that if, therefore, we took this position, they would yield.[70]

There was no inclination on the part of the men in responsible positions in America, however, to adopt such an overtly aggressive position. Even Clay's views, hawkish as they were, appeared prudent and circumspect in comparison with Churchill's. Douglas alluded in his report to the "practical infirmities" in Churchill's suggestion, but he shared Churchill's view that one could not appease or conciliate the Soviets; one could only arrest and deter them by a real show of resolution.[71]

The choice of an American strategy, however, had to go beyond such generalities and be based on a clear assessment of Soviet intentions in the specific context of the Berlin crisis. But here there was no consensus. Some Americans believed that the Russian restrictions, although haphazard in execution, stemmed from a clear purpose and a preconceived long-term plan to force the Western

---

69. Clay to Bradley, April 12, 1948, and Bradley to Clay, April 14, 1948, RG 319, Records of the Army Staff, P&O 381 ("Hot File"), National Archives, Washington, D.C.
70. Douglas to Lovett, April 17, 1948, in *FRUS, 1948*, Vol. 2, pp. 895–896.
71. Ibid.

powers out of Berlin, and, consequently, that the American position could only be defended ultimately by threatening war and being prepared to wage war. This was the estimate that Bradley conveyed to Clay on April 10. Other American officials, however, frankly confessed that Soviet intentions were open to various interpretations, and this greatly complicated the choice of strategy. General Walter Bedell Smith, the American Ambassador to Moscow, could not give his government any clear guidance because he himself was unsure whether the Soviet move in Berlin was prompted by a local grievance, which could be settled by compromise, or by a wider plan. Asked for his views on whether a note to the Soviet Government would serve any useful purpose, he replied on April 15 that the decision should be "based on best Berlin estimate whether current provocations Berlin and Vienna are opening gun in all-out campaign to make our position Berlin and Vienna untenable or whether they consider reasonable agreements can be reached and that firm stand already taken will deter Soviets from pushing matter further."[72] With such open-ended and to some extent discrepant estimates coming in, it was difficult for Washington to formulate concrete contingency plans. The uncertainty surrounding Moscow's intentions reinforced the tendency, apparent since the beginning of the pre-crisis period, to sit back and await the next Russian move.

The need to coordinate America's responses with those of her allies also inhibited serious contingency planning and injected an additional dose of caution. The idea of sending a joint note to the Soviet Government, making unmistakably clear the position of the Western Allies in the light of recent developments in Berlin, dominated inter-Allied discussions during the second half of April. This was the idea that Clay supported and on which Smith was asked to comment. A draft note was prepared by the State Department in consultation with the Department of the Army, and a copy was sent to Clark Clifford for the information of the President.[73]

Robert Lovett asked Douglas to elicit British and French reactions to the American draft. Lovett himself thought that a joint approach might have a useful effect, particularly since inaction would lead to a deterioration of the Allies' position in Berlin. The final

72. Smith to Marshall, April 15, 1948, in ibid., pp. 894–895.
73. Draper to Clifford, April 14, 1948, Box 15, Papers of Clark M. Clifford, Harry S. Truman Library.

paragraph of the proposed note stated that the U.S. Government expected that the Soviet Government "will not authorize or permit actions on the part of its military commanders inconsistent with the unquestioned rights which the U.S. Government is fully determined to maintain."[74] Douglas reported back that the British had no objection to a clear statement of the position and rights of the Western Allies, but that they interpreted the last sentence of the suggested note to mean that they were prepared to go to war, or at least commit organized acts of war, in the event that the Soviets did not, by their actions, recognize those asserted rights. They wondered whether, first, this was precisely what the Americans meant, and, second, whether it was a wise position to take. For their part, they would be unwilling to add the scorpion's sting to the assertion of their rights. Their position was that they would go to war in the event of a clear and organized act of war being committed against them by the Soviets, but they were not prepared to state categorically in advance that under all circumstances they would fight to maintain a position in Berlin. Douglas wondered whether their interpretation was correct.[75] On April 30, Marshall and Lovett replied that the last sentence of the draft note "means that we intend to stay in Berlin and that we will resist force with force. It does not spell out the point at which force will be used. We feel that this is neither necessary nor advisable at this time. We will not, however, initiate the application of force. We do not believe that the interpretation which the British have placed on this sentence is warranted."[76]

Even greater differences of opinion were revealed at a meeting between Sir William Strang, the Permanent Under Secretary of State at the British Foreign Office, General Robertson, and General Clay, at which the proposed note was discussed. In his report to Ernest Bevin, the British Foreign Secretary, Strang said that it was obvious from the outset that Clay took a more pessimistic and a more bellicose view of the position than London was inclined to do:

> He thinks that the Russians consider it so vital to get us out of Berlin, that they will face the prospect of war in doing so, though they

---

74. Lovett to Douglas, April 22, 1948, in *FRUS, 1948*, Vol. 2, pp. 896–897.
75. Douglas to Marshall, April 28, 1948, in ibid., pp. 899–900.
76. Marshall and Lovett to Douglas, April 30, 1948, in ibid., p. 900; and FO 371/70492/C3524, Public Record Office, London.

may try to contrive that we fire the first shot. He regards an early war with the Soviet Union as inevitable, i.e., within the next year or eighteen months, and judges that on a comparison of present and future resources on the two sides, the Soviet Government may think it advantageous not to wait too long. He believes that the Russians will progressively intensify their pressure and that a point will sooner or later be reached—and it may well be sooner— at which we shall have to face the alternatives of war or an ignominious retreat from Berlin.

Clay wanted to know, according to this account, whether the British intended to stay in Berlin "come hell or high water," even if it meant war. The reply he received was that while it might not be out of place to make a statement of their international rights in Berlin, it would be a mistake to say that they should, if necessary, go to war to maintain them. It was never wise, he was reminded, to let diplomacy outrun the forces available to support it. Clay's rejoinder to this was that a note without a sting in the tail would be worse than useless.[77]

In the end, the idea of sending a joint note was abandoned. But the episode illustrates the reluctance of the American decision-makers, with the exception of Clay, to formulate in advance a precise plan for the use of force under specified conditions and the additional difficulty of reaching an agreed-upon position on issues which touched the very core of national sovereignty. Close contact was maintained, however, between the U.S. and Britain at various levels up to the Foreign Secretaries. For example, in a memorandum dated April 30 addressed to Marshall, Bevin set forth his views on current relations with the Soviet Union and found reason for special concern over Soviet tactics in Berlin and Vienna. In his reply, Marshall expressed agreement with Bevin's analysis of the current situation, particularly the advisability of making clear to the Soviet Government the determination of the Western powers to remain in Berlin.[78]

Both Britain and America viewed the recent developments in Berlin within the context of the wider Cold War struggle for Germany, and they were united in their determination not to allow Soviet pressure in Berlin to deflect them from the movement towards a Western German government on which they had embarked fol-

77. Memorandum from Sir William Strang to the Secretary of State, 28 April 1948, FO 371/70492/C3579, Public Record Office, London.
78. *FRUS, 1948*, Vol. 2, p. 902.

lowing the abortive meeting of the Council of Foreign Ministers in December 1947. The French thought the Americans were proceeding too far and too fast along the road of reviving German capitalism and German power, and they were particularly perturbed by Clay's excessive zeal. Clay wants to continue to serve pure wine, President Vincent Auriol told Bevin only half-jokingly; "I count on you to put some water in it!"[79]

Some progress had been made in concerting the approaches of the three Western powers at the conference which met in London between February 23 and March 3 with the participation of the Benelux countries. This conference reconvened in London on April 20. During the intervening recess, the three Military Governors in Berlin were charged with continuing discussions relating to Germany on a tripartite basis, and several working parties were set up for this purpose. Further progress was made at this level, but divergent perspectives overshadowed the discussions. At a meeting of the three Military Governors on April 1, on the morning following the abortive test trains, Robertson said that "if we keep on talking indefinitely we might wake up some fine morning to find the Hammer and Sickle already on the Rhine." General Pierre Koenig, the French Military Governor, did not believe the menace was so great. Clay argued vigorously in support of permitting the Germans early progress towards elected government and emphasized the risk the Western powers ran of losing the support of approximately forty-five million Germans in the Western zones. He stressed the necessity of their orientation to the West and their inclusion in the European Recovery Program.[80] Clay wanted the London conference reconvened as soon as possible. He was somewhat apprehensive that if the talks were put off, the Russians would take action in Berlin and in their zone which would have an adverse effect on developments in the three Western zones.[81]

While pressing ahead with the new policy, the American decision-makers were troubled by a lingering dilemma, which was laid bare by Lovett. The real question facing them, wrote Lovett to Murphy on April 10, was what to do about the Control Council and

79. Vincent Auriol, *Journal du Septennat, 1947–1954*, Vol. 2: *1948* (Paris: Armond Colin, 1974), p. 188, diary entry for April 17, 1948.
80. Murphy to Marshall, April 1, 1948, in *FRUS, 1948*, Vol. 2, pp. 158–160.
81. Douglas to Marshall, April 2, 1948, in ibid., pp. 163–165; and Clay to Draper, April 1, 1948, in *Clay Papers*, Vol. 2, pp. 608–611.

about the timing of an announcement of intent to proceed with the establishment of a government for Western Germany. The American Government had declared its firm resolve to continue in the Control Council, and this was one of the best arguments for its staying in Berlin. How would their position be affected by their taking the lead in forming a Western German Government in advance of any similar Soviet step? If they took this initiative, the Soviets would surely exploit it to impute to the U.S. the responsibility for splitting Germany.[82] Murphy did not think there was any real problem, and he tried to reassure the State Department. In view of the attitude and conduct of the USSR in Berlin recently, he observed, America's position there would not be adversely affected by the establishment of a Western German Government in advance of a similar Soviet step. The Americans had made their position on German unity abundantly clear, and should they arrive at a point where an announcement regarding a Western German Government might be possible, it should undoubtedly be accompanied by the explanation that it was aimed in the direction of an eventual government for all Germany.[83]

The London conference reconvened on April 20 with the United States and Britain determined to press ahead with measures to ensure the reconstruction of Germany and the recovery of Western Europe. They were undeterred by Soviet pressure in Berlin and the knowledge that the Russians would continue to lambast them for the breach of quadripartite agreements. Regarding the rupture with Russia over Germany as inescapable, they simply sought to place the onus on the Russians, while the French still hoped to avoid the rupture. To some extent, however, the Allies drew closer in the face of Moscow's aggressive tactics in Berlin, and the French were certainly aware that the dangers of a rupture would not be reduced if they refused to associate themselves with the recommendations of experts in London. Such a course, they realized, would permit the Anglo-Saxons to take even more imprudent initiatives.[84] So, while trying to exercise a restraining influence in London, the French slowly and grudgingly moved into line with their allies. Some French officials, such as Couve de Murville,

---

82. Lovett to Murphy, April 10, 1948, in *FRUS, 1948*, Vol. 2, pp. 176–177.
83. Murphy to Marshall, April 13, 1948, in ibid., pp. 179–180.
84. Auriol, *Journal du Septennat*, Vol. 2, pp. 214 and 218.

underwent a genuine conversion, and this facilitated the progress of the London talks.[85]

News of the Western Allies' rapid progress towards agreement on the creation of a West German state—progress which the fitful restrictions on their access to Berlin manifestly failed to halt—caused consternation and alarm in Moscow. The balance of power in Europe was visibly shifting to the advantage of the United States and her Western allies, largely as a result of the success of the European Recovery Program. State Department officials believed that as a result of the Communist defeat in the Italian elections, the Kremlin was confronted with the necessity of making a fundamental decision which could set the course of future events in Europe. As these officials saw the matter, the Kremlin was faced with two alternatives. It could accept the situation created by the passage of the European Recovery Program and by the outcome of the Italian elections, adjusting itself with a minimum loss of face to the fact that, at the present juncture, Europe outside the iron curtain had in effect been denied to communist power. Or it could conclude that to accept without counteraction this blow to the prestige of the communist movement would place the Soviet Union so clearly on the defensive as to set in motion a train of events which would eventually jeopardize the security of its power in Eastern Europe and at home. In the latter case, the tendency might be to undertake some spectacular move designed to recoup the loss of prestige inherent in recent setbacks.[86]

The Kremlin's estimate of the U.S. reaction to any such move was obviously a major factor in its decision. It was important, therefore, to dispel any misunderstanding of U.S. intentions. An approach to the Soviet rulers was considered but not undertaken prior to the passage of the European Recovery Plan and the Italian elections lest it be interpreted as a sign of weakness and lack of confidence on America's part in the efficacy of her present policies.[87] But the success of the Marshall Plan was now so sweeping that George Kennan and Charles Bohlen felt the time had come for some conciliatory gesture on the part of the American Government, making it clear that its purpose was not to humiliate the Soviet Government or to press it against the door, and that it was

85. Jean Chauvel, *Commentaire: d'Alger à Berne, 1944–1952* (Paris: Fayard, 1972), pp. 199–200.
86. Lovett to Smith, April 24, 1948, in *FRUS, 1948*, Vol. 4, pp. 834–835.
87. Ibid., p. 834.

willing to talk over their problems. Kennan and Bohlen recommended to Marshall that a statement along these lines be made to the Soviet Government, and Marshall agreed. The proposal was discussed in the Cabinet on April 23 and approved by the President.[88] On April 29, Marshall instructed Ambassador Smith to make a statement to Molotov on behalf of the U.S. Government concerning the relations between the two countries (Decision 4). Marshall thought that with the exception of a possible miscalculation in Berlin or Vienna, the Kremlin did not intend to mount any action which would carry the risk of actual hostilities. The purpose of the statement, he told Smith, was twofold: to convince the Kremlin that the U.S. was resolute in the pursuit of its policies, and, at the same time, to make clear that it entertained no aggressive designs against the Soviet Union or any other country.[89] Smith had already been told that what Washington had in mind was merely a statement of U.S. position and policy and in no sense an indirect bid for agreement or even negotiation.[90]

On May 4, Smith made his statement to Molotov orally and, at the latter's request, left a written copy. The statement contained the assurance that "as far as the United States is concerned, the door is always wide open for full discussion and the composing of our differences."[91] Molotov's long and rambling reply, delivered five days later, similarly concluded with a "hope for the possibility of finding the means to eliminate present disagreements and to establish between our countries good relations."[92] The American *demarche* backfired, however, when Molotov proceeded to publish an edited version of the statements, affecting to understand Smith's note as an invitation for a high-level "parley" and announcing Soviet acceptance of the proposal.

The world press immediately picked up the story and blew it out of all proportion. *Le Monde*, for example, declared in an editorial: "The event is capital; it has provoked a profound sensation throughout the world."[93] The news that the Russians accepted a U.S. bid for bilateral peace negotiations was received enthusiastically by the

---

88. Kennan, *Memoirs*, pp. 246–247; and Millis, *The Forrestal Diaries*, pp. 424–425.

89. Marshall to Smith, April 29, 1948, in *FRUS, 1948*, Vol. 4, pp. 840–841.

90. Lovett to Smith, April 24, 1948, in ibid., pp. 834–835; and Walter Bedell Smith, *Moscow Mission, 1946–1949* (London: Heinemann, 1950), pp. 147–155.

91. *Department of State Bulletin*, May 23, 1947, pp. 679–680.

92. Ibid., pp. 680–682.   93. *Le Monde*, May 10, 1948.

American public and produced euphoric expectations of an end to the Cold War.[94] Among America's West European allies, however, the news unleashed a storm of protest. The representatives of friendly governments descended on the State Department in droves, angrily demanding explanations.[95] London and Paris, taken by surprise, sought immediate clarification from Washington.[96] The prospect of bilateral American-Russian talks from which they would be excluded was not one they could view with equanimity.

Taken aback by Molotov's bid for high-level talks, Marshall immediately alerted Truman to the danger of playing into Molotov's hands by failing to state publicly that this was not at all what they had intended. The trouble was that an official confession that the American message did not propose a meeting would have an unfortunate effect in the American press. Nevertheless, Marshall suggested a White House release to set the record straight.[97] Truman issued a statement to the press which denied that Smith's note represented a new departure in American policy. It was a reiteration, he claimed, of the American position as it had been repeatedly expressed both publicly and privately.[98] An even more emphatic denial was made by Marshall at a press conference he held on May 12. "General Smith," he said, "did not ask for any general discussion or negotiation. We have had a long and bitter experience with such efforts. The Government had no intention of entering into bilateral negotiations with the Soviet Government on matters relating to the interests of other governments."[99]

94. In May 1948, 63 percent of a national sample "thought it would be a good idea . . . for President Truman to call an international meeting with Stalin and the heads of other nations to work out more effective plans for peace." Gabriel A. Almond, *The American People and Foreign Policy* (New York: Harcourt Brace, 1950), p. 98.

95. Kennan, *Memoirs*, p. 347; and Smith, *Moscow Mission*, p. 155.

96. Auriol, *Journal du Septennat*, Vol. 2, p. 223; and "Memorandum of Conversation by Lovett," May 21, 1948, in *FRUS, 1948*, Vol. 2, pp. 270–271. In a private letter to Marshall, dated June 8, 1948, Smith observed that they should have been more open with Britain and France about the conversation with Molotov, and that while Britain accepted their subsequent explanation, French suspicions were not entirely removed. Copy in the George F. Kennan Papers, Correspondence, Box 28, Seeley G. Mudd Manuscript Library, Princeton University.

97. Memorandum for the President from Marshall, May 11, 1948, White House Central Files, Confidential File, Box 36, Harry S. Truman Library.

98. *Public Papers of the Presidents of the United States: Harry S. Truman, 1948*, p. 252. See also Robert A. Divine, *Foreign Policy and U.S. Presidential Elections: 1940, 1948* (New York: Franklin Watts, 1974), pp. 201–203.

99. *Department of State Bulletin*, May 23, 1948, pp. 683–684; and Smith, *Moscow Mission*, p. 155.

DECISION FLOW   147

By issuing these denials, the Administration succeeded in reassuring its allies, but it then fell under a crossfire of criticism from the columnists and editorial writers, some charging it with ineptness for issuing unintended invitations, others for not going through with the parley once it had invited it. Herblock in the *Washington Post* showed Harry Truman at bat, with the ball whizzing by him untouched, and the umpire calling "Strike one."[100] Public confidence in the foreign policy of the Truman Administration was further shaken when, in response to a much publicized letter from former Secretary of Commerce Henry Wallace which suggested an agenda for Soviet-American peace talks, Stalin praised the six-point agenda as a "good and fruitful" basis for negotiation and declared that "the co-existence of these systems and a peaceful settlement of differences between the USSR and the United States are not only possible but undoubtedly necessary in the interests of a general peace."[101]

The success of the Soviet peace campaign in portraying the Truman Administration as the intransigent party which rejected talks on outstanding difficulties deeply worried Truman and his advisers.[102] Truman called a high-level meeting to get ideas on how to deal with the Soviet offensive. In addition to Truman himself, the participants at the meeting, which took place on May 21, were: Marshall, Forrestal, Lovett, Bohlen, Kennan, Harriman, Clifford, and Sidney Souers, the Executive Secretary of the National Security Council. Their discussion revealed that not one of them believed that the suggestion of a meeting between heads of state was even worth considering, and that they were all united in viewing the Russian peace offensive as a propaganda exercise, pure and simple.[103]

Marshall was disturbed not only by the effect of the Russian tactics on the American public but also by its effect on the position of the French Government. On May 19, he informed Ambassador Douglas, who represented the U.S. in the London conference, that both the State Department and the Army believed that the par-

100. Kennan, *Memoirs*, p. 347.
101. *New York Times*, May 12 and 18, 1948; and Divine, *Foreign Policy and U.S. Presidential Elections*, pp. 203–205.
102. Harry S. Truman, Official File, Miscellaneous, Box 824, Harry S. Truman Library; the chargé in the Soviet Union (Durbrow) to Marshall, May 17, 1948, in *FRUS, 1948*, Vol. 4, pp. 869–870; and James V. Forrestal Diaries, Princeton University Library, entry for May 18, 1948, pp. 2260–61.
103. Millis, *The Forrestal Diaries*, pp. 442–445.

ticipating governments should hold to the agreed-upon time schedule for the establishment of a provisional government in Western Germany. The so-called softening of Soviet policy, he said, did not permit the conclusion that the Soviets would cooperate in the formulation of a German policy essential to the needs of the free countries of Western Europe. Marshall gave it as the official American estimate that the risks of proceeding with the establishment of a provisional government were less than the risks of further delay. He strongly urged that if the French insisted on reservations regarding the time schedule, the conference should nevertheless proceed with the completion of plans on the form of the provisional government and with work on other important matters, so that results might be achieved at that session on substantive questions.[104] The second point contained the key to Marshall's analysis of the situation and, indeed, to America's behavior during this phase of the pre-crisis period. The situation in Berlin was considered to have some bearing on America's overall policy in Germany, but the perception of threat was not sufficiently acute to bring about a reappraisal of that policy. Marshall recognized that an announcement concerning the setting up of a provisional government might give the Soviets an excuse to intensify pressure in Berlin, but he felt that the danger of delay in Germany was greater than the risks involved in the Russian reaction.[105]

The French accepted the principle of a provisional government for Western Germany, but they wanted to defer its implementation, not least because they regarded the current situation as less dangerous than the one they expected following its implementation. They resented being dragged by their ally along a dangerous path, especially since the American response to their request for a security guarantee against Germany was entirely negative. They could dissociate themselves from the London Program, but inherent in this course was the risk that Western Germany would be organized without them and in a manner which took no account whatever of their security needs.[106]

The Americans, however, were in no mood for compromise and subjected their ally to the most intense pressure. A final decision to go ahead with the implementation of the London agreements

104. Marshall to Douglas, May 19, 1948, in *FRUS, 1948*, Vol. 2, p. 158.
105. Marshall to Douglas, May 22, 1948, in ibid., p. 272.
106. Auriol, *Journal du Septennat*, Vol. 2, pp. 238–242.

was reached at a meeting in the State Department on May 24, at which Secretary Forrestal, General Bradley, and others were present.[107] Following the meeting, Marshall informed Douglas that with a full understanding of the risks involved, it was essential to proceed with completion of the London agreement without the French if necessary. He instructed Douglas to continue to persuade the French, impressing upon them that a German government was required for the success of the European Recovery Program, that any hesitation or rift in the Allied front would be exploited as a sign of weakness to the detriment of their position in Berlin, and that French defection was likely to provoke strong Congressional reaction. If the French did not yield, they should be informed that the U.S. would undertake no commitments regarding security against Germany or regarding a Ruhr settlement.[108]

In order to anticipate and counter in advance Soviet propaganda, Marshall authorized Douglas to discuss, initially with Bevin, the desirability of issuing a communiqué on the work of the conference, including a preamble that would explain the circumstances which impelled the Western nations to set up governmental arrangements in West Germany, the purpose of these arrangements, and their provisional character pending a final settlement on German economic and political unity. The statement, Marshall added, could mention the unsuccessful efforts to reach comprehensive decisions on Germany and could express the view that progress achieved respecting Western Germany would not only *not* preclude but should facilitate the eventual attainment of four-power agreement on Germany as a whole.[109]

The relentless pressure exerted by America eventually secured French agreement to a set of related measures, the crux of which was the establishment of a provisional government for West Germany. On June 2, a detailed communiqué was issued outlining the recommendations of the London conference to the six participating governments. The essential recommendations were that a constituent assembly be convened to work out a constitution for a

107. Memorandum for the Secretary, by Robert Plon, September 17, 1948, in the James V. Forrestal Diaries, p. 2503, Princeton University Library. This memorandum was a reply to Forrestal's question: "On what date and by whom was the decision made that the United States should support setting up a government in Western Germany?"
108. Marshall to Douglas, May 24, 1948, in *FRUS, 1948*, Vol. 2, pp. 275–276.
109. Ibid.

federal West Germany; that the new country contribute to and participate in the recovery of Western Europe; that an International Authority be set up, with German representation, to control the Ruhr, which would remain part of Germany; and that there would be no general withdrawal of American, British, and French forces from Germany until the peace of Europe was secure.[110] A letter of explanation justifying the recommendations was issued on June 7.[111] Its purpose, as envisaged in Marshall's telegram to Douglas, was to place the responsibility for the division of Germany on the Soviet Union. As could be expected, Marshall issued an official statement on June 9 announcing the U.S. Government's acceptance of the recommendations of the London conference.[112]

The French continued their rearguard battle to prevent a sharp and final break with the Soviet Union until the very end of the London conference. On June 1, they proposed that a note be delivered to the USSR through the respective embassies in Moscow immediately after the recommendations on Germany had been agreed upon, expressing the sincere hope that this would not mean an ultimate division of Germany and that they considered the agreements as open ones and would welcome Soviet association with them.[113] Bevin thought that it would be unwise to extend to the Russians an invitation, even though limited, to become associated with the political organization of Western Germany, and that they should simply be informed of the recommendations referred to in the communiqué. The State Department agreed with Bevin's views.[114] Accordingly, Sir William Strang, in his capacity as chairman of the London conference, called on the Soviet Ambassador to London on June 7 to deliver, as an act of courtesy, the conference communiqué in advance of its release to the press. Ambassador Zarubin reiterated the attitude of the Soviet Government, expressed in notes in February, March, and April, that decisions regarding Germany reached without the participation of the Soviet Union violated the existing four-power agreements.[115] The deadlock was complete.

110. For the full text of the communiqué, see U.S. Department of State, *Germany 1947–1949: The Story in Documents* (Washington, D.C.: U.S. Government Printing Office, 1950), pp. 76–80.
111. Ibid., pp. 81–83.   112. Ibid., pp. 83–84.
113. Douglas to Marshall, June 1, 1948, in *FRUS, 1948*, Vol. 2, p. 364.
114. Douglas to Marshall, June 4, 1948, in ibid., pp. 364–365.
115. Douglas to Marshall, June 7, 1948, in ibid., pp. 366–367.

PHASE IV: JUNE 18–24

With the final shutting of the door on four-power talks on Germany, events in Berlin rapidly moved towards a climax. East-West differences there came to center on the question of currency reform, which had a long and highly complex history. At the meeting of Western representatives following the adjournment of the Council of Foreign Ministers in London in December 1947, Clay and Murphy urged that German currency reform be started without delay, but Marshall and Bevin instructed them to make a final attempt to obtain acceptance of the new currency by the Allied Control Council in Berlin. If that failed, the Secretaries would approve their plans to introduce the new banknotes into Bizonia.[116] During a subsequent trip to Washington, Clay and Murphy ascertained that the Treasury Department was willing to print new paper money for Germany, and that the plan met with the approval of Secretary Marshall and President Truman. Tons of this money, printed in Washington, were transported to Germany in great secrecy, to prevent speculative profits, in a project called "Operation Bird Dog." The American Government was reluctant to issue this new money without Russian cooperation. It endeavored to obtain quadripartite agreement on currency reform up to and including the last meeting of the Allied Control Council on March 20.[117] This reform was considered essential to check inflation, to inspire confidence, to develop a sound banking system, and to promote economic recovery in Bizonia.

On April 29, the Department of the Army, following discussions with the State Department and the Treasury, advised Clay that when the time of the projected Soviet currency conversion was made known, he should try to reach immediate agreement with the Soviets on a uniform special currency for Berlin, but that if this failed, he should point out that the U.S. was ready to introduce a Western currency into the Western sectors.[118] In his reply, Clay pointed out that the establishment of two currencies in Berlin would be most difficult and probably untenable in the long run, and that when the time came to negotiate, he proposed to negotiate for a monetary union of Berlin with the Soviet zone, provided the issue

---

116. Murphy, *Diplomat Among Warriors*, p. 382.
117. Ibid., p. 383.   118. *Clay Papers*, Vol. 2, pp. 643 and 697.

of Soviet marks in Berlin was kept under Kommandatura agreement and control.[119] The timing and implementation of currency reform for Berlin and Germany as a whole was left to Clay's discretion. Following the breakup of the Allied Control Council, he had no difficulty in reaching agreement with the British representatives on the terms of a currency reform to be effective in the bizonal area on June 1. It was on that date that he took the decision to implement the currency reform immediately (Decision 5). At that time, the discussions were going on in London on the conditions of trizonal fusion; and at this juncture, the French representative stated that his zone was ready to join the bizonal area in currency reform without waiting for full agreement on the principles of trizonal fusion. This belated announcement created additional difficulties, which made it necessary to postpone the date of issue from June 1 to June 20.[120] In the intervening period, the various commands, the rationing offices, and the banks were to be briefed, and the banknotes were to be transported to the necessary destinations in the three zones. Finally, the three Military Governors agreed to inform the Soviet Military Government by letter on June 18 of the reform that was to take place on June 20.[121]

The implementation of the currency reform did not go smoothly and was greatly complicated by the problems of keeping the French in line. On June 10, Clay reported to Draper on events which he considered particularly disturbing. Clay, Robertson, and General Koenig had agreed that no action should be taken without prior consultation. They had also agreed that as each fixed date for a meeting of the Allied Control Council came up, they would publicly state that there would be no meeting, since no request for a meeting had been received by the chairman. Robertson and Clay followed this procedure. The French, on assuming the chair, addressed each member of the Council with the question of whether or not a meeting was desired. The Soviet response was to state that such a request was not necessary, since the chairman was responsible for the calling of a meeting and the fixing of the agenda. The French did not consult with either the British or the Americans in posing this question. On receiving the Soviet reply, the French

119. Ibid., pp. 903–904.
120. Clay, *Decision in Germany*, pp. 211–212; and Murphy, *Diplomat Among Warriors*, p. 383.
121. "Memorandum by the Assistant Secretary of State for Occupied Areas (Saltzman) to Lovett," June 4, 1948, in *FRUS, 1948*, Vol. 2, pp. 907–908.

specifically requested the Soviets to state whether or not they desired a meeting, and they expressed their readiness to call such a meeting immediately and without waiting for the next fixed date of the Control Council, which was on June 20.[122]

Clay saw this as an act of backsliding and an outward expression of the French desire to appease the USSR. Fear of further backsliding led him to work out, with Robertson, a plan to cover the contingency of French failure to ratify the London agreements for tripartite fusion of Western Germany and international control of the Ruhr. The two Military Governors agreed on a procedure to enable them to carry out previous instructions to proceed rapidly with the evolution of a political government in Bizonia.[123] However, on June 15, Draper cautioned Clay against precipitate action in the event of French failure to ratify the London agreements, since "we feel it very important to have the French go along with us and therefore will want to evaluate the significance of their reservations, if any. We will therefore wish in any case to take another look at situation promptly after French action, and will communicate with you immediately."[124]

Decision-makers in Washington were anxious to ensure that Clay cleared any action with them first. His contingency plans were not approved in advance, and the possibility of a reappraisal of American policy was kept open. Clay protested emphatically against this lenient attitude towards the French. He pointed out that French dissociation would be interpreted as reluctance to face the Soviet Union on this issue, and U.S. acceptance of this would be interpreted as a lack of a firm German policy. This would be particularly undesirable, since he regarded Soviet policy as "carefully planned, continuous and always strongly supported." "We cannot win this way," he warned. "I thought we had crossed the Rubicon at London but apparently we sat down in the middle of the stream." He feared that procrastination would seriously damage U.S. leadership in Germany, and concluded: "I have nothing to add to my proposals as they are the best I could offer with three years experience working with German officials. I await instructions."[125]

It is interesting to note that Clay foresaw that the Russians would not passively acquiesce in the Western currency reform, and that he

122. *Clay Papers*, Vol. 2, pp. 673–674.
123. Ibid., p. 674.   124. Ibid., pp. 677–678.
125. Ibid., p. 678.

kept up the pressure for its implementation with full awareness of the consequences. As early as April 10, he said to Bradley: "You will understand, of course, that over separate currency reform in near future followed by partial German government in Frankfurt will develop the real crisis. Present show probably designed by Soviets to scare us away from these moves."[126] On June 13, he still considered the currency issue as likely to precipitate a crisis. "It is quite possible," he wrote in a memorandum to his Chief of Staff, Brigadier General Charles Gailey, "that tightening of controls nearing the weekend resulted from Soviet apprehension that western zone currency reform might take place over the weekend. I am inclined to believe this more likely than a further tightening at the moment to force us from Berlin. That move will come when we install separate currency if it is to come at all." Clay went on to give an uncharacteristically pessimistic appraisal of the feasibility of staying in Berlin:

> There is no practicability in maintaining our position in Berlin and it must not be evaluated on that basis. We can maintain our own people in Berlin indefinitely, but not the German people if rail transport is severed. Nevertheless, we would propose to remain until the German people were threatened with starvation if the Soviets did resort to such extreme tactics. We are convinced that our remaining in Berlin is essential to our prestige in Germany and in Europe. Whether for good or bad, it has become a symbol of the American intent.[127]

In communications with Washington, however, Clay played down both the likelihood of a Soviet move to drive the West out of Berlin and the problems of maintaining the Western position there. He may have feared that the kind of frank appraisal he gave his Chief of Staff in Berlin might weaken Washington's resolve to proceed with the currency reform. For his part, Clay was determined to press ahead, whatever the consequences.

A more detached and candid appraisal of the effects of Soviet restrictions on the U.S. position in Berlin was submitted to the top decision-makers by the Central Intelligence Agency. The CIA took the view that the chief detrimental effect of the restrictive Soviet measures imposed in Berlin had not been interference with transportation and supply but curtailment of certain U.S. activities hav-

126. Ibid., p. 623.   127. Ibid., p. 677.

ing to do for the most part with intelligence, propaganda, and the operations of the Kommandatura—the quadripartite body responsible for the administration of the city. Concurrently with attempted inspection of U.S. military rail traffic, the Soviets both tightened their security measures and manifested greater intransigence in all city affairs. As a result, the general usefulness of Berlin as the center of an intelligence network had been impaired, and access to Soviet deserters and anti-communist Germans had been made more difficult. Since friendly Germans could not move freely to and from the Soviet zone or within the city, the U.S. could not, as before, support anti-communist activities within the Soviet zone. U.S. propaganda could no longer be freely disseminated except by radio. Lastly, the Allied Control Council and the Kommandatura had, at least temporarily, lost their usefulness in keeping up German hope of unity and in easing U.S.-Soviet tension below the governmental level. The CIA report made no policy recommendations, but it did emphasize that mere physical presence could not assure continuance of the strategic benefits derived from Berlin and that unpublicized Soviet actions had already seriously impaired the U.S. strategic position in Berlin.[128]

A turn for the worse in U.S.-Soviet relations occurred on June 16, when the Russians walked out of the Berlin Kommandatura following what they regarded as insulting behavior by Colonel Frank (Howlin' Mad) Howley, the fiery U.S. Commandant for Berlin. Another important channel of communication was now effectively severed. Clay was not happy about Howley's abrupt behavior, which was represented by the Russians as an American walkout, but the blunt Colonel was unrepentant. His attitude is reflected in a notation he made in his diary: "The status of the Kommandatura is now the same as the status of the Allied Control Council—no one knows whether it exists or not. When it suits the Russians, they will say it does exist, and when it does not suit them they will say it does not exist. Personally, I say it is good riddance to bad rubbish."[129] When the news of the breakup of the Kommandatura reached Clay, he was in the throes of frantic negotiations with the French, who were

128. CIA, "Effect of Soviet Restrictions on U.S. Position in Berlin," June 14, 1948, President's Secretary File, Harry S. Truman Library.
129. Murphy to Marshall, June 17, 1948, in *FRUS, 1948*, Vol. 2, pp. 908–909; and Howley, *Berlin Command*, pp. 179–184. The notation from Howley's diary appears on p. 184.

threatening not to join after all in the issue of the new currency. But he was determined not to allow the incident to slow down or change his plans. He believed that the prompt implementation of the currency reform was of paramount importance, and he was getting more and more exasperated with French recalcitrance. In a teleconference with Draper, he argued forcefully that it was too late for second thoughts because the machinery had been set in motion, it could not be stopped, and the die was cast. He and Robertson had made concession after concession only to meet further French demands, and they both feared the worst.[130]

The worst did not happen, for on June 17 the French Assembly finally ratified the London agreements. On the following day, the three Military Governors were therefore able to proceed as planned, notifying Marshal Sokolovsky of the terms of the currency reform that would go into force on June 20 for the Western zones of Germany but not be applied to Berlin.[131] The immediate Russian reaction was to suspend all railway and highway passenger traffic to and from Berlin and reduce in volume and subject to stricter regulation railway and waterway freight traffic, ostensibly to protect their zone from the influx of the devalued old currency. In a public proclamation to the German people, Sokolovsky charged that the agreements providing for the control machinery in Germany as well as the Potsdam agreement, which stipulated that Germany be treated as a single economic unit and that her currency remain uniform, had been violated. He declared the new currency invalid for the Soviet zone "and in the area of greater Berlin which comes within the Soviet zone . . . and is economically part of it."[132] In his reply to Clay on June 20, Sokolovsky took the position that the currency reform was illegal and completed the division of Germany, and he warned that if suitable arrangements

---

130. *Clay Papers*, Vol. 2, p. 682; and Clay, *Decision in Germany*, pp. 212–213.

131. For the text of Clay's letter, see U.S. Office of Military Government for Germany, *Documented Chronology of Political Developments Regarding Germany* (Berlin, 1948), pp. 108–110. For the text of General Robertson's letter, see Great Britain, Cmd. 7534, *Germany: An Account of the Events Leading Up to a Reference of the Berlin Question to the United Nations* (London: His Majesty's Stationery Office, 1948), p. 17.

132. "Proclamation to the German People on the Western Currency Reform, by Marshal Sokolovsky, 19 June 1948," in *Documents on the Status of Berlin, 1944–1959*, by O. M. van der Gablentz (Munich: Oldenbourg Verlag, 1959), pp. 53–54.

could not be made, he would be obliged to take immediate measures to install a new currency in the Soviet zone and in greater Berlin.[133] In a further letter of June 21, Clay denied the implication made by Sokolovsky that Berlin was part of the Soviet zone and invited the Soviet authorities to send their experts to a meeting with American, British, and French experts to discuss a quadripartite solution to the Berlin currency problem.[134]

Clay's conciliatory reply was part of a general effort by the American decision-makers to avoid an escalation of the currency dispute after putting their reform into motion and to gain public support for the course they had taken. Murphy told Marshall that some of the traffic control measures introduced by the Russians immediately after the announcement of the Western currency reform were not unreasonable as a defensive action to protect the Soviet zone from an influx of the old currency.[135] When General Robertson suggested a vigorous protest, Clay replied that it would be better to wait for two or three days because the new Soviet regulations were not immoderate, and he stated his opinion that were the situation reversed, they on their side would have been required to take similar precautions. Before making a protest, he wanted to wait a few days in order to gauge the Russian attitude towards the eventual continuance of the Berlin Kommandatura and towards the Berlin situation in general.[136]

The strongly perceived need for public support also militated against any action or statement that might be construed as provocative. Marshall and his advisers felt that developments in Berlin furnished an opportunity for a strong U.S. propaganda line. OMGUS was advised that the State Department and the Army considered it urgent (1) to utilize the media in an all-out effort to expose the Soviet strategy of attempting to undercut the power of the Berlin authority by a series of steps which would inevitably result in hardship to the Berlin population; (2) to stress the gross irresponsibility of a policy which resorted to cutting off supplies for more

---

133. For the text of Sokolovsky's reply, see Union of Soviet Socialist Republics, Ministry of Foreign Affairs, *The Soviet Union and the Berlin Question (Documents)* (Moscow, 1948), pp. 25–27.

134. For the text of Clay's letter, see U.S. Office of Military Government for Germany, *Documented Chronology of Political Developments Regarding Germany*, pp. 1341–43.

135. Murphy to Marshall, June 19, 1948, *FRUS, 1948*, Vol. 2, p. 910.

136. Ibid.

than two million Germans in order to achieve its expansionist aims; and (3) to make it clear that the basic position of the Western occupying powers remained unchanged.[137]

The Americans were still hoping to reach an agreement on a uniform currency for Berlin because of the special situation of the city, and the currency experts thought it feasible. In his letter of June 21, in which he suggested a meeting of experts, Clay also specified a time and place. Sokolovsky accepted the invitation, and the meeting opened on the morning of June 22 in the building of the Allied Control Council. The Western experts found that the Soviets would only discuss full acceptance of the new Soviet currency throughout Berlin and would not consider any proposal for a quadripartite supervision and control of the currency issue through the Berlin Kommandatura. The Soviets argued that since Berlin was so closely integrated into the economy of the Soviet zone, they could not accept any other currency in Berlin except that circulating in their zone, and that they could not agree to the suggestions of the Western powers that a special currency be issued for Berlin alone. The negotiations thus reached a complete impasse, and the meeting broke up late in the evening.[138] The Soviet Military Government immediately issued its orders for currency reform in the Soviet zone, including Berlin, and a letter from Sokolovsky was received by the three other Military Governors the following morning advising them of the Soviet currency reform and the issue of the new mark in Berlin.[139]

This Soviet move forced the issue of Berlin currency and necessitated a Western response. Clay was in constant communication with the Department of the Army during the period in which currency reform was being negotiated. He had been advised on April 29 that if he failed to obtain agreement for the use of a common currency in Berlin, separate from that used either in West or in East Germany, the American Government did not view the use of the Soviet currency as acceptable politically. Such acceptance would mean recognition of Soviet sovereignty in Berlin. However, the

137. Marshall to Douglas, June 21, 1948, in ibid., p. 911.
138. Murphy to Marshall, June 23, 1948, in *FRUS, 1948*, Vol. 2, pp. 912–914; Clay, *Decision in Germany*, pp. 263–264; and Jack Bennett (the American financial representative at the conference), "The German Currency Reform," *Annals of the American Academy of Political and Social Science*, Vol. 267 (January 1950).
139. For the text of Sokolovsky's letter, see Margaret Carlyle, ed., *Documents on International Affairs, 1947–1948* (issued under the auspices of the Royal Institute of International Affairs, London: Oxford University Press, 1952), pp. 580–581.

final decision was left to Clay's discretion, and he yielded to the arguments of his French and British colleagues to accept the Soviet currency in Berlin if the Western Allies could participate in its control. Since Sokolovsky offered no such participation, Clay assumed that his proposal was unacceptable to the American Government.[140]

To counter the Russian currency reform in Berlin, Clay decided on June 23, on his own initiative and without further reference to his government, to extend the new Western currency to the Western sectors of Berlin (Decision 6). Without any hesitation or delay, but after informing the British and French Military Governors, he wrote to Sokolovsky that he could not accept his proposal that the East Mark be recognized as the only legal tender throughout Berlin and that he would join with his colleagues in placing the West Mark in circulation in the Western sectors of Berlin.[141] Robertson fully supported this course of action. The French, having broken ranks with their colleagues at the quadripartite meeting of experts on June 22 by showing their willingness to accept the Soviet proposal, were now up in arms against the countermeasures chosen by Clay. They did join in extending the West Mark to Berlin, but at the last moment, with great reluctance, and only after advising the other Western powers in writing that they were obliged to dissociate themselves from all responsibility for the consequences of this ill-considered decision.[142]

It is extraordinary but perhaps not altogether surprising, given Clay's compulsion to force the issue, that a political decision of such gravity and incalculable consequences should have been taken by him without seeking the specific approval of his government. That his superiors were surprised by the manner in which he acted (without suggesting that he exceeded his authority) may be inferred from the fact that the Department of the Army asked him for a summary of the "circumstances and basis on which decision was made to introduce new Western zone currency in Berlin."[143] Clay's reply sheds some light on the circumstances and considerations which prompted him to make this decision. The decision, he

---

140. Clay, *Decision in Germany*, p. 364.
141. Ibid. For the text of Clay's letter of June 23, see U.S. Office of Military Government for Germany, *Documented Chronology of Political Developments Regarding Germany*, p. 125.
142. Clay, *Decision in Germany*, p. 364; and Auriol, *Journal du Septennat*, Vol. 2, p. 279. For the text of the French statement, see *Clay Papers*, Vol. 2, p. 692.
143. *Clay Papers*, Vol. 2, p. 697.

said, was made in view of the Soviet declaration that Soviet currency would be installed in Berlin under Soviet laws and complete Soviet control. According to Clay, this would have placed Berlin financially in Soviet hands. He was prepared to compromise on a special currency for Berlin or on Soviet currency with Kommandatura supervision in Berlin, although he made it clear that acceptance of the latter proposal would require the Western Governments' approval. However, in view of the Soviet "ultimatum" and in view of his own instructions, he did not believe that Soviet currency would be accepted as the currency for Berlin unless at least a semblance of Kommandatura control was maintained. He felt strongly, and the British shared this feeling, that the placing of currency in Berlin in Soviet hands would have been a recognition of Soviet sovereignty in Berlin and could defer the issues for only a few weeks. Moreover, he concluded, the Soviet announcement of their "ultimatum" left him with little choice.[144]

What this account does not altogether explain convincingly is why Clay did not leave it to his Government, with whom he was in constant contact through Draper, to accept or reject the proposal for a Soviet currency in Berlin. The economic consequences of acceptance were not particularly ominous, since there was a certain protection of Western interests in the proposal. This was pointed out to Clay by some of his own financial experts in OMGUS.[145] It is reasonable to assume, therefore, as one of these experts later argued, that the decision of June 23 was determined fundamentally not by economic reasoning but by much wider political considerations and by the mood in which they were embedded:

> The mood of conciliation on Berlin was unpopular among Western policy-makers who were set against accommodation of Soviet claims to special financial prerogatives in Berlin. Extravagant fears were voiced that the Soviets through control of the East mark would discriminate against or harm the West-Berlin economy. Irrespective of the merits of the East mark for the city, Western leaders felt it necessary to counteract the Soviet action to avoid making a precedent. It was important to show in action that the Western powers were to be masters in the Western sectors of Berlin. . . . If the Western powers were seriously intending to stay in Berlin, they would need to pull together their sectors of the city, wrench them from the Soviet zone hinterland and East sector, tear apart

144. Clay to Royall, June 25, 1948, in ibid., pp. 697–699.
145. Manuel Gottlieb, *The German Peace Settlement and the Berlin Crisis* (New York: Paine-Whitman, 1960), pp. 193–194 and 256–257, note 8.

the all-city government or convert it into a West-Berlin government and otherwise be able to govern and administer West-Berlin in close dependence upon Western Germany and with the least possible contact and association with the Soviets. Perhaps General Clay, who made American policy in Berlin and directed it from day to day, and on the German side the aggressive leader of the Berlin social-democrats, Ernest Reuter, sensed this most clearly. Those two determined men led the German and the Allied camps. With these policy-makers in control, the Soviet program to undermine the Western powers in Berlin by assuming unilateral prerogatives and by including the whole city within the Soviet currency area was going to be met head-on.[146]

It was. The Western powers introduced their new notes, stamped with a "B" for Berlin, into their sectors of the old capital on June 24.

As political developments in Berlin were moving to a head, the Russians appear to have made one last attempt to reach a compromise that would avert the final rupture. In a telegram he sent to Marshall from Berlin on June 23 at 8:00 P.M., Murphy reported:

> Today U.S. liaison officer delivering communication to Marshal Sokolovsky was received by Colonel Vyrianov, chief of SMA [Soviet Military Administration] liaison and protocol. Vyrianov who ordinarily limits contact to official formalities in this instance insisted on offering champagne and engaging in general conversation during course of which he asked whether U.S. did not consider that it was skating on very thin ice in respect of its recent actions in Germany. He developed this into a discussion of the danger of war and then made the suggestion which he carefully qualified as a strictly personal observation that possibly an adjustment of present zonal lines in Germany should be made with a view to eliminating the friction caused by U.S. and Soviet contact in Berlin. Our officer inquired whether he meant our departure from Berlin and return to Thuringia and Saxony originally occupied by U.S. forces. Vyrianov said he could not be that specific but that "some readjustment" might be a solution for present difficulties.

Murphy added that he attached significance to this voluntary Soviet comment because Vyrianov was close to Sokolovsky. "It may indicate desire to bargain and disinclination to force the issue," he opined.[147]

The documents do not record any reaction either positive or negative, let alone any response from Washington, to Murphy's intriguing report. One is therefore left with the impression that the

---
146. Ibid., p. 194.
147. Murphy to Marshall, June 23, 1948, in *FRUS, 1948*, Vol. 2, p. 915.

possibility of avoiding a showdown, hinted at in a sly and circumlocutory Oriental manner by a Soviet officer over a glass of champagne one day before the start of the Berlin blockade, remained unexplored.

At any rate, on June 24 the Soviet authorities suspended all rail passenger and freight traffic as well as barge traffic into Berlin. They also disrupted the electricity supplied to the Western sectors by power stations located in their sector and issued orders prohibiting the distribution of any food supplies from the Soviet zone to the Western sectors of the city. The Berlin blockade had begun.

FINDINGS

International crisis has been defined as a "breakpoint" or basic shift along a continuum of relations between a state and other global actors. It is triggered by an event or events in the external environment which generate three perceptual changes on the part of the state's decision-makers: a perception of threat to basic values; a higher anticipation of war; and an awareness of finite time for decisional response. The word "crisis," used alone, refers to the total phenomenon under inquiry, from the first trigger event until the return of the perceptions of threat, time, and probability of war to non-crisis levels. This phenomenon, however, is divided into three periods: the *pre-crisis period*, the *crisis period*, and the *post-crisis period*. The pre-crisis period is marked off from a preceding non-crisis situation by one indicator only: a conspicuous increase in the level of perceived threat. To what extent does the Berlin 1948 case fit this concept of a pre-crisis period?

CRISIS COMPONENTS
Environmental Change

The Soviet walkout from the Allied Control Council on March 20 served as the trigger mechanism or source for the onset of the pre-crisis period. It was a deliberately hostile act of a nonviolent kind. This was not an isolated event but part of a cluster of events which included Soviet interference with the traffic between the Western zones and Berlin and Soviet political pressure inside Berlin. For America's decision-makers, the Soviet walkout was the first link in a chain of events which, taken together, created a situational change triggering an increase in the perception of threat from the Soviet

Union. But there was no awareness, as yet, of stringent time constraints on decisions and no consistent or commonly held expectation of war. The climax of the crisis lay in the future.

Threat to Basic Values

The breakdown of the Allied Control Council did not in itself represent a threat to America's basic values, since effective four-power cooperation had ceased much earlier and the breakdown simply formalized what had been evident for some time. The real values threatened were much more basic ones: America's position and goals in Berlin, in Germany, and in Western Europe generally. Murphy interpreted the Soviet walkout as a deliberate and carefully planned challenge to America's position in Berlin and her objectives in respect to Western Germany. This view was prevalent among the American decision-makers. The imposition of the mini-blockade and the campaign conducted in the Soviet-controlled press calling for the withdrawal of the Western powers from Berlin led to a significant rise in American threat perception. America's entire position in Europe was perceived to be threatened. There is no better indication of this than Clay's statement on April 10.

Probability of War

The definition of crisis underlying this inquiry postulates that a perception of high probability of war is *not* present during the pre-crisis period; that image change occurs later. The evidence from 1948 conforms with this postulate predominantly but not entirely. It indicates that the possibility of war was considered carefully, but that none of the decision-makers rated it as a high probability. In their public statements, there was no reference to the probability of war. On the contrary, they deliberately sought to allay fears by minimizing the importance of the Soviet walkout. But their internal communications, which furnish a more reliable indicator of their real thinking, also support the conclusion that, on the whole, they did not perceive war as either imminent or likely. Individual estimates varied to some extent. Clay usually maintained that the probability of war was very low (hence his confidence) and that the Soviet bluff could be called by sending a test train; but on other occasions, notably at the meeting with Strang and Robertson, he talked as if war were inevitable. At the other end, Royall pointed to the danger of violent incidents leading to war, without suggesting that war was likely. The intelligence estimate of April 2 predicted that the USSR would not resort to military action before the end of the year, but the Air Force considered the situation too fluid to permit such a forecast. Thus, while differences existed and the responsible authorities were apprehensive that the Berlin situation might result in war at a time when the U.S. was definitely not ready, the possibility of war was generally considered to be fairly remote during the early period of the Berlin Crisis.

Time Pressure

According to our definition, decision-makers do not perceive time pressure—or even salience of time—in their deliberative process during the pre-crisis period. The findings for the Berlin crisis are broadly in consonance with this postulate. Clay did, on occasion, perceive time to be salient. On March 31, for example, he urged that America's reply to Dratvin's letter should be in Russian hands the same day, and the manner in which he implemented currency reforms exhibited extreme sensitivity to considerations of time. But Clay's perception of time pressure was as much the product of his own determination to push ahead as fast as possible with the reconstruction of Germany as it was of crisis-induced stress. In any case, Clay's perception of time pressure was not shared by the decision-makers in Washington. They refused to be bounced by him into any precipitate decisions which went against their better judgment, and their deliberations were carried out in a steady and unhurried fashion. There is no evidence that an awareness of time pressure seriously constrained the responses of these decision-makers.

COPING MECHANISMS

Information Processing

Throughout this volume, "stress" or the term "crisis-induced stress" is used as a code word for the perception of threat, time pressure, and probability of war. It is these perceptions, expressed in stress, which set in motion the multiple coping processes and mechanisms.

The initial reactive step by the American decision-makers was to seek information about the threatening move by the Russians which triggered off the crisis. Threat-induced stress generated a greater than normal felt need for information and a consequent quest. The probe was conducted through various channels, but the most important one was teleconferences with the theater commander. Another important source of estimates of Soviet capabilities and intentions and of reports on the changing situation in Berlin was the Central Intelligence Agency. Information about the behavior of the various actors involved in the crisis, both allies and adversaries, was also gleaned from the State Department's representative in Germany and from its ambassadors in London, Paris, and Moscow. The volume of incoming information increased appreciably during the pre-crisis period compared with the preceding non-crisis period. But the policymakers in Washington did not display much energy or skill in directing the search or in collating the various bits of information drawn from different sources. To give one example, the scramble for information relevant to America's rights of access to Berlin was frantic; but three months after the start of the crisis, it was striking to find how vague the legal position still was.[148]

Consultation

The consultative circle during the pre-crisis period was confined to the decision-makers and their official advisers. No evidence has been discovered to suggest that the decision-makers went outside the government to consult members of competing elites or interest groups. Truman actually turned down the idea that he should call into conference the majority and minority leaders of the House and Senate, because he wanted to preserve secrecy and avoid hysteria. Within the government, the consultative process was institutional rather than ad hoc, and it took place inside the State Department and the Department of the Army and between them. Interagency consultations sometimes included other departments, such as Commerce when export controls were being considered and the Treasury when currency reform was being discussed. When the perception of threat increased, there was a corresponding rise in the level at which consultation was held. Thus, following the receipt of the Soviet note on traffic restrictions on March 31, a series of high-level conferences was held involving the State Department, the Department of the Army, the Joint Chiefs of Staff, and the President. In general, since the level of threat perceived during the pre-crisis period was not very high, the involvement of the senior decision-makers, Truman and Marshall, in the consultative process was limited.

148. Millis, *The Forrestal Diaries*, p. 451.

It is one of the peculiar features of the Berlin Crisis that one of the decision-makers, General Clay, could only be present for consultations in Washington during flying visits. As Military Governor for Germany, he had to spend most of the time on the spot in Berlin. Consultation between the Department of the Army and its chief representative in Germany was therefore conducted by means of teleconferences. An intensive use was made of this device during the pre-crisis period, reaching a peak of three teleconferences on March 31. The device and its strengths and weaknesses were described by Clay:

> The teleconference was the most satisfactory medium of exchange for important matters since it permitted senior officials to confer directly with high officials in Washington. The teleconference is an adaptation of teletype in code, and incoming messages are received, decoded, and flashed on a screen in the teleconference room. They can be answered immediately and flashed on a corresponding screen in Washington. While this system is not as rapid as the telephone conference, questions can be answered as quickly as the answers can be written and transcribed on the typewriter and the teleconference avoids the always possible misunderstandings of telephone conversation.[149]

Since the position of Britain and France was also threatened by Soviet actions in Berlin, and since the American decision-makers attached great importance to maintaining a united Western front in dealing with the Soviet Union, inter-Allied consultations intensified following the breakdown of the Control Council. Throughout the pre-crisis period, there were frequent consultations with America's allies both through her Ambassadors to London and Paris and through her Military Governor in Germany, who maintained close contact with his opposite numbers even when they did not see eye to eye with him.

Decisional Forums

As with several aspects of information processing and the pattern of consultation, changes in the intensity of crisis-induced stress affect the structural setting in which decisions are made. During the Berlin pre-crisis period, the increase in stress was not sufficiently dramatic to activate new decisional forums. The existing structure was considered adequate for coping with the new situation. Indeed, it was considered important to retain the existing structure

---

149. Clay, *Decision in Germany*, p. 58.

and personnel unchanged, in the interest of maximum efficiency. Consequently, the first significant decision taken following the onset of the crisis was to postpone the plans for Clay's retirement and for a transfer of responsibility for the nonmilitary aspects of the German occupation from the Department of the Army to the State Department.

It should be emphasized, however, that the existing structure was elaborate and cumbersome, involving a variety of decisional units and procedures which were not firmly institutionalized. No clear pattern of decision-making is discernible in the pre-crisis period, and there was certainly no one decisional unit charged with overall responsibility for making the necessary choices. Some decisions were made by the President, following consultations with senior civilian and military advisers; some decisions were made by Clay, who was allowed considerable discretion on the currency issue; one decision was taken by the Cabinet as a whole; and one decision was taken by Secretary Marshall.

Alternatives: Search and Evaluation

The most noteworthy feature of the decision-making process during the pre-crisis period was the absence of a systematic search for and evaluation of alternatives. Admittedly, a number of alternatives were considered by the President and his advisers on March 31 in response to Clay's request for instructions on how to deal with the Soviet note of that day. But this was the exception rather than the norm; and even in this exceptional case, both the search for and the analysis of the alternatives were perfunctory. In general, information was collected and processed and consultations were held, but the product of this preliminary work was not presented to the top decision-makers in a structured form which indicated the available options and the likely consequences of each and called on them to make a choice. Nor did the decision-makers themselves actively promote analytic procedures for choice. They tended to deal with each issue as it arose rather than make strategic choices based on long-term considerations.

A number of factors tended to inhibit careful analytical consideration of the Berlin problem in the highest echelons of the American government. In the first place, there were other major problems, such as the recognition of Israel and the level of the military budget, which competed for the attention of the top decision-makers. Secondly, the start of the 1948 presidential campaign made fundamental political choices more difficult to reach. Thirdly, divergent estimates of Soviet intentions further complicated the problem of choice. Finally, as is so often the case, wishful thinking inclined the decision-makers against facing up to the worst contingencies.

The few decisions that were taken during the pre-crisis period were of a highly specific character. The fundamental question was what should be done in the event of a complete blockade of Berlin. This question was never far below the surface of the decision-makers' minds. But this nagging concern did not prompt them to embark on a comprehensive search of alternatives, and it certainly did not produce a firm and unequivocal commitment to stay in Berlin. This inability of the Administration to face up to the worst contingency meant that it was caught unprepared when the full blockade was imposed in late June.

PART III
Crisis Period

CHAPTER FIVE

Psychological Environment

THE SEVERANCE by the Soviet authorities of all land communications between Berlin and the Western zones on June 24 marked the beginning of the crisis period. This action triggered all three necessary conditions for crisis: a sharp rise in threat perception, an awareness of time constraints on decisions, and an image of the higher probability of war. The crisis period continued until July 22, when the proposal for an armed convoy to break the blockade was rejected and the decision was taken to expand the airlift. As a result, time pressure declined in intensity, marking the beginning of a much larger post-crisis period.

DECISIONS AND DECISION-MAKERS

The key decision-makers during the Berlin crisis period were President Truman, Secretary Marshall, and General Clay. The rise in threat perception, time constraints, and probability of war brought the President to the center of the policymaking arena. Indecision in Washington, however, left Clay ample scope, which he utilized fully, to influence the American response. As in the pre-crisis period, a number of other decision-makers participated alongside the three key figures in the decision process. Prominent in this second group were Secretary of Defense James Forrestal, Secretary of the Army Kenneth Royall, Under Secretary of the Army William Draper, Under Secretary of State Robert Lovett, and the State Department's representative in Germany, Robert Murphy.

Ten major decisions were taken by individual policymakers and various groups and forums during the crisis period:[1]

1. The decisions are numbered for the whole crisis *ad seriatim* rather than separately for each period.

Decision Number	Date	Content
7	June 25	Clay, on his own initiative, decided to launch the airlift to supply Berlin.
8	June 25	Truman, Forrestal, Royall, and Lovett decided against (1) sending a note of protest to Moscow and (2) outside retaliation.
9	June 26	The President directed that Clay's improvised airlift be put on a full-scale and organized basis.
10	June 28	Truman, at a meeting with Forrestal, Royall, and Lovett, ruled in favor of staying in Berlin. In addition, it was agreed that Clay should meet with Sokolovsky, and preliminary approval was given to dispatch B-29 bombers to Europe.
11	June 30	Truman agreed to a limited-purpose meeting between the JCS and the representatives of the British Chiefs of Staff.
12	July 3	Marshall, following the abortive meeting of the three Military Governors with Sokolovsky, decided to proceed with the preparation of a formal note of protest to the Soviet Government.
13	July 15	The National Security Council agreed to proceed with the dispatch of B-29 bombers to the British Isles.
14	July 19	A series of high-level conferences, ending with confirmation by the President, resulted in a firm resolution to maintain the American position in Berlin and to take all the measures necessary for the exercise of its rights.
15	July 21	The President turned down the request of the National Military Establishment that he should transfer to it the custody of the atomic bomb.
16	July 22	The NSC decided to increase the airlift materially by adding seventy-five C-54s and came out strongly in support of an oral approach to Stalin.

PSYCHOLOGICAL ENVIRONMENT
Attitudinal Prism

The attitudinal prism of America's decision-makers was essentially the same as that which obtained during the pre-crisis period. The main components of the prism—world-views, images of the adversary, and self-images—remained relatively constant. This absence of change should come as no surprise, since an attitudinal prism is the product of basic predispositions and cumulative experience, which are not susceptible to sudden or fundamental revision. Prism change, if it occurs at all, is a long-term process, although it may be accelerated by events during a crisis. In the short term, during the crisis, change in the prism or background images for a government usually results from a change of regime or a change in the balance of power within a regime, not from individuals changing their minds.[2] During the Berlin pre-crisis and crisis periods, however, no change took place in the composition of either the core group of decision-makers or the immediate circle of active participants. Nor was there a major shift in the balance of power within the Truman Administration. The decision taken on March 22 to defer the transfer of control of the nonmilitary aspects of policy regarding the U.S. zone meant that policy towards Germany as a whole remained largely the province of the Department of the Army and of the military occupational establishment in Germany. In short, the same men remained in the same positions, and the Riga axioms continued to dominate the making of American foreign policy at all levels.

The image of the adversary that lay at the heart of the Riga axioms remained essentially the same. If the Berlin crisis had any effect, it was in the direction of reinforcing the consensus, which was already well established, about the character of the Soviet Union as an actor on the world stage. By treating the civilian population of Berlin as a pawn in the game and using it as a hostage for ill-defined political ends, the Russians confirmed the Americans' conviction that they were confronting an expansionist, ruthless, and unscrupulous adversary. Cold War images of Communist "totalitarianism" and Soviet "aggressiveness" hardened, and the analogy of Nazi Germany was invoked with greater frequency and vehemence.

2. Glenn H. Snyder and Paul Diesing, *Conflict Among Nations* (Princeton: Princeton University Press, 1977), p. 329.

But while the background image of the Soviet Union as an aggressive, ruthless, and implacably hostile adversary was shared by all the American decision-makers, their immediate crisis images were not identical in every respect. In the first place, there were slightly different perceptions of what was at stake in Berlin, with the local decision-makers tending to define the stakes as rather higher than those suggested by a global view of America's interests as seen from Washington. Secondly, individual decision-makers held different images of the opponent's bargaining style. In assessing Soviet intentions, they were generally agreed that Moscow wanted to test the strength of U.S. determination to stay in Berlin. But they disagreed in their judgment of how far the Soviets would go in pursuing this objective. Some American leaders reacted to the Soviet move against West Berlin with the interpretation, probably incorrect, that Soviet leaders had deliberately chosen a high-risk strategy. The implications for the U.S. of this interpretation of Soviet behavior were obviously more ominous than the alternative that the Soviets were really engaged in a probing, reversible, low-risk strategy and would refrain from accepting greater risks.[3] Clay and Murphy held the second image of the Soviet Union as a blustering but risk-averse great power, and maintained that the Soviets were bluffing and would not go to the brink of war if confronted by the West with a strong show of force. Truman, Marshall, the Joint Chiefs of Staff, and the majority of the other members of the National Security Council did not share this confidence that the Soviets were bluffing. In their estimate, the Soviet Union was more risk-acceptant and unpredictable. Consequently, they were less willing to resort to bluff, intimidation, and overt coercion in response to the Soviet move, for fear of touching off a major armed conflict. Interestingly, the risks appeared much greater at headquarters than they did in the field. Those nearest the hot spot in Berlin were less apprehensive about a sudden outbreak of hostilities than those more removed from the Berlin scene.

Images

TRUMAN

Throughout the crisis period, Truman was deeply preoccupied with domestic politics. He had already entered the 1948 presiden-

---

3. Alexander L. George and Richard Smoke, *Deterrence in American Foreign Policy* (New York: Columbia University Press, 1974), pp. 132–133.

tial campaign to secure a second term in the White House. To dispel the widespread gloom and pessimism in the Democratic camp about his prospects for reelection, Truman went on an extended tour in June to address people directly in all parts of the country. Yet, almost unanimously, the polls taken before the 1948 Democratic convention showed that his popularity with the American people had hit an all-time low. Even some of his closest friends and advisers were counseling him to change his mind about going after the nomination.[4]

Truman's insecure domestic political base, coupled with his ambition to have a second term as President, weighed heavily on his conduct of foreign policy. With the Democratic convention coming up on July 12, he preferred to postpone any public action on the Berlin blockade. He refrained from making any comments on it at news conferences and instructed Clay not to make statements referring to the possibility of war over Berlin.[5] But he was far from being oblivious to the opportunity offered by the Berlin crisis for restoring his sagging electoral fortunes. The American public apparently made one primary demand of American foreign policy: that it be firm and resolute in its opposition to Soviet expansion.[6] Truman's greatest asset was his control over foreign policy, which provided opportunities for demonstrating that he could satisfy this requirement. This asset was taken into account in planning Truman's 1948 campaign strategy. "There is considerable political advantage to the Administration in its battle with the Kremlin," wrote Clark Clifford in a memorandum outlining this strategy. But only, he emphasized, "up to a certain point—the real danger of imminent war." Clifford also advised Truman to emerge more forcefully and dramatically as the architect of the containment policy, so that the American people would identify the tough line against Russia with the President personally.[7] Truman's handling of the Berlin crisis suggests that he heeded this advice and, in particular, that he appreci-

4. Harry S. Truman, *Memoirs*, Vol. 2: *Years of Trial and Hope, 1946–1953* (London: Hodder and Stoughton, 1956), pp. 207–208.
5. *Foreign Relations of the United States, 1948* (Washington, D.C.: U.S. Government Printing Office, 1973), Vol. 2, p. 928. (Henceforth, this series will be referred to as *FRUS*.)
6. Gabriel A. Almond, *The American People and Foreign Policy* (New York: Harcourt Brace, 1950), p. 106.
7. Clifford to Truman, November 19, 1947, Clifford Papers; quoted here from Robert A. Divine, "The Cold War and the Election of 1948," *Journal of American History*, Vol. 59 (June 1972), p. 93.

ated the importance of not carrying the contest with the Kremlin to the point where war became an imminent danger.

After securing the Democratic nomination for the Presidency on July 14, Truman had to contend with two rivals: on his left he had Henry Wallace, the leader of the Progressive Party, who attributed the blockade to the aggressive Cold War policies of the Truman Administration and recommended withdrawal from Berlin; on his right he had Thomas Dewey, the Republican candidate, who was appealing for a tougher stand against Russia. Truman shrewdly sensed that the American public would support a firm policy which stopped short of raising the risk of war. By following a middle course, he was able to deflect the charges of bellicosity and the charges of weakness directed at him from the left and the right, respectively. This middle course also enabled Truman, as Clifford had urged him, to consolidate his image as the real architect of containment and as a national leader who could be relied upon to stand up to the Russians abroad and defend America's vital interests without acting provocatively or recklessly.

But while Truman was as skilful as Franklin Roosevelt in using foreign policy for partisan advantage, it would be misleading to depict him as a politician who was solely concerned with partisan advantage. Images and perceptions pertaining to the external environment were no less important in conditioning Truman's conduct during the crisis period. The Berlin blockade presented the President with one of the most acute dilemmas of the Cold War era. If he resorted to force to break the blockade, he might touch off World War III. If he failed to take any action and withdrew from the city under duress, America's policy in Germany and Europe would suffer a major, possibly fatal, setback.

Division of opinion among Truman's advisers on the feasibility and wisdom of maintaining the Western position in Berlin did not make the task any easier. At the inception of the blockade, Berlin was not unequivocally accepted by all senior officials as vital to American interests. There were conflicting views as to whether the enclave could, or should, be defended. There were those, like Admiral Leahy, Truman's personal military adviser, who regarded the situation in Berlin as hopeless and America's ultimate withdrawal as unavoidable. And there were others, like Clay and Murphy, who, while fully aware of Berlin's strategic vulnerability, thought that there were overriding political reasons for staying there. The final decision had to be made at the highest level, and Truman, characteristically, made a clear-cut decision and carried it through. Having reached the decision to stay in Berlin without the benefit of a unanimous recommendation, he went out of his way to reassure the doubters that this was the right decision. And he never wavered in his own conviction that this was the right decision.

A number of distinct perceptual strands went into the making of this fundamental choice. They are recalled and elaborated upon in Truman's memoirs. First and foremost was the image of the Soviet Union as a threat to American security and world peace—a threat which could be countered effectively only from a position of strength. Among the things which, according to Truman's account, combined to convince him to seek reelection, "the threat being posed by Russian imperialist Communism" is placed at the top of the list.[8] In 1948, he writes, there was no doubt in his mind about the course he had to take:

> The world was undergoing a major readjustment, with revolution stalking most of the "have-not" nations. Communism was making the most of this opportunity, thriving on misery as it always does. The course of freedom was being challenged again—this time from a new and powerful quarter—Soviet Russia.
>
> I had learnt from my negotiations with the intransigent Russian diplomats that there was only one way to avoid a third world war, and that was to lead from strength. We had to rearm ourselves and our allies and, at the same time, deal with the Russians in a manner they could never interpret as weakness.
>
> Within our own nation I had seen many well-meaning groups who campaigned for "peace at any price" while apologizing for the aggressive acts of the Russians as merely a reflection of Russian reaction to our own tough policy. Many respectable Americans espoused such ideas without realizing the danger to which they were subjecting our national security and the freedoms for which we had fought so hard. . . .
>
> I also felt, without undue ego, that this was no time for a new and inexperienced hand to take over the government.[9]

Truman prided himself on having the correct image of the Soviet Union because it was the product of experience, in contrast to the image held by Henry Wallace, which he depicted as the product of wishful thinking. Wallace had consistently maintained that Truman was too rough in dealing with the Soviets and that peace could be obtained with a more conciliatory approach. Truman disagreed: "I knew from personal experience that the Wallace dream of ap-

---

8. Truman, *Memoirs*, Vol. 2, p. 202.   9. Ibid., p. 201.

peasement was futile and that, if allowed to materialize, it would be tragic. I had learnt that the Russians understood only force. Wallace did not think this was true, but he did not have the experience with the Soviets that had been mine."[10]

Russian interference with Western access to Berlin fit in with the pattern of action which Truman had come to expect as a result of his experience. "The Berlin blockade," he asserts, "was a move to test our capacity and will to resist. This action and the previous attempts to take over Greece and Turkey were part of a Russian plan to probe for soft spots in the Western Allies' positions all around their own perimeter."[11] He had no doubt at all about the real significance of the Russian action: "What the Russians were trying to do was to get us out of Berlin. At first they took the position that we never had a legal right to be in Berlin. Later they said that we had had the right but that we had forfeited it."[12]

America's alleged legal rights of access to Berlin were the object of attention and comment by Truman. When finalizing the American commitment to remain in Berlin in the White House meeting on June 28, he remarked that, whatever the consequences, the essential decision was "that we were in Berlin by terms of an agreement and that the Russians had no right to get us out by either direct or indirect pressure."[13] The significance of this statement lies in the fact that it was made to the President's advisers behind closed doors and not to the public. It supports the proposition that, in thinking through America's politico-strategic position, legal factors constituted one of the parameters and that these factors were not purely post-decision instruments of policy justification.[14] But it also reveals a highly subjective interpretation of America's legal rights, which stemmed from an instinctive moralism and self-righteousness rather than from a careful study of the facts. In his memoirs, Truman again conveniently glosses over the fact that only America's air corridors to Berlin were secured in 1945 by written agreement, while access by land routes was not, and hence that, technically, the Soviet Union was not infringing America's legal rights. "It is my opinion," he writes, "that it would have made very

10. Ibid., p. 216. 11. Ibid., p. 157. 12. Ibid., pp. 147–148.
13. Walter Millis, ed., *The Forrestal Diaries* (New York: Viking, 1951), p. 455.
14. Lawrence Scheinman, "The Berlin Blockade," in *International Law and Political Crisis*, edited by Lawrence Scheinman and David Wilkinson (Boston: Little, Brown, 1968), pp. 13–14.

little difference to the Russians whether or not there was an agreement in writing. What was at stake in Berlin was not a contest over legal rights, although our position was entirely sound in international law, but a struggle over Germany and, in a larger sense, over Europe."[15]

The last sentence contains the central perceptual strand which led to the decision to stay in Berlin—namely, that the Soviet challenge was not confined to America's legal rights over Berlin, but extended to her basic commitment to check the march of communism in Europe. Truman repeatedly emphasized the magnitude and the insidious nature of the Soviet challenge: "In the face of our launching of the Marshall Plan, the Kremlin tried to mislead the people of Europe into believing that our interest and support would not extend beyond economic matters and that we would back away from any military risks."[16] He realized, however, that the Kremlin was not riding the crest of a wave, but was desperately trying to score a victory after a long series of defeats: "The Russians were obviously determined to force us out of Berlin. They had suffered setbacks recently in Italy, in France, in Finland. Their strongest satellite, Yugoslavia, had suddenly developed a taste for independent action, and the European Recovery Program was beginning to succeed. The blockade of Berlin was international Communism's counterattack."[17]

That this counterattack was launched in Berlin was considered doubly significant: first, because the city was of symbolic importance, and, second, because of American vulnerability there. As Truman put it: "The Kremlin had chosen perhaps the most sensitive objective in Europe—Berlin, the old capital of Germany, which was and is a symbol to the Germans. If we failed to maintain our position there, Communism would gain great strength among the Germans. Our position in Berlin was precarious. If we wished to remain there, we would have to make a show of strength. But there was always the risk that the Russian reaction might lead to war."[18]

The risk of war weighed heavily on Truman and was one of the crucial considerations against the use of force to resolve the problem. "We had to face the possibility," he recalled, "that Russia might deliberately choose to make Berlin the pretext for war, but a

15. Truman, *Memoirs*, Vol. 2, p. 148. 16. Ibid.
17. Ibid., p. 149. 18. Ibid.

more immediate danger was the risk that a trigger-happy Russian pilot or a hotheaded Communist tank commander might create an incident that could ignite the powder keg."[19]

Initially, Truman may have hoped that the crisis would be resolved through negotiation. This, at any rate, is suggested by his description of the airlift as a temporary expedient to gain time. On June 26, he directed that Clay's improvised airlift be put on a full-scale organized basis and that every plane available to the European Command be pressed into service. "In this way," he recalls, "we hoped that we might be able to feed Berlin until the diplomatic deadlock could be broken."[20]

But he did not take long to reach the conclusion that diplomacy did not offer a way out and that the U.S. must take action to stay in Berlin despite the risks of war inherent in such action. The gnawing doubts which afflicted his advisers did not affect his own basic predisposition to see the situation in plain black and white without any shades in-between. This predisposition led him to reach a decision instinctively and without any prolonged reflection and soul-searching. On June 28, only four days after the start of the blockade, at a meeting in the White House at which the specific question was raised as to whether or not the U.S. would stay in Berlin, "the President interrupted to say that there was no decision on that point, we were going to stay, period."[21] Besides the domestic and international considerations, Truman's self-image as the leader of the Administration who must bear full responsibility and his innate preference for clear-cut choices affected the content of his decision and the style in which he enforced it. In his diary, Truman penned the following account of the meetings held on July 19:

> Have quite a day. See some politicos. A meeting with General Marshall and Jim Forrestal on Berlin and the Russian situation. Marshall states the facts and conditions with which we are faced. I made the decision ten days ago to *stay in Berlin*. Jim wants to hedge. . . . I insist we will stay in Berlin—come what may. Royall, Draper and Jim Forrestal come in later. I have to listen to a rehash of what I know already and reiterate my "Stay in Berlin" decision. I do not pass the buck, nor do I alibi out of any decision I make.[22]

19. Ibid.   20. Ibid., p. 148.
21. Millis, *The Forrestal Diaries*, p. 427.
22. William Hillman, *Mr. President: Personal Diaries, Private Letters, Papers, and Revealing Interviews of Harry S. Truman* (London: Hutchison, 1952), pp. 119–120.

But while Truman did not pass the buck and assumed full responsibility for staying in Berlin, domestic and foreign policy calculations made him reluctant to undertake measures which might escalate the crisis to the threshold of armed hostilities. It is for this reason that he ultimately rejected the idea of sending an armed convoy to break the blockade—an idea which appealed to his combative temperament—in favor of the more cautious policy of supplying Berlin with an airlift. Truman's caution stemmed in part from his image of the opponent's bargaining style. To him the Soviet Union appeared to be a shrewd and wily opponent, but also one capable of acting impetuously and even irrationally. Contrary to the view of his hard-line advisers, who believed that Moscow would not run any risks of World War III until ready for it, Truman believed that the crisis indicated that the Kremlin was willing to risk military incidents to test U.S. firmness and patience. Nor did he dismiss the possibility that Moscow was seeking a pretext for war. The reluctance to supply such a pretext and the fear of needlessly provoking the Soviets were important considerations in Truman's mind during the crisis. They served as a constraint on the means he would use to protect America's interests.[23]

MARSHALL

The images and corresponding policy preferences of Marshall during the crisis period were closer to those of Truman than to those of the advocates of force. No other crisis during Marshall's tenure as Secretary of State brought relations between the United States and the Soviet Union closer to the edge of war. "Throughout the first Berlin crisis," reports one State Department official, "the outbreak of a third world war, involving military combat on a vast scale all around the globe, seemed an imminent possibility. This produced, on both sides, a grim preoccupation with the implications of the general military situation."[24] This conspicuous increase in the probability of war placed Marshall under considerable stress throughout the crisis period, while his military background concentrated his mind on the implications of the military situation. The other components of stress were also present. Marshall perceived the Soviet move as threatening the basic values of the United States. At a meeting with the President and Forrestal, he

23. George and Smoke, *Deterrence in American Foreign Policy*, pp. 133–134.
24. Louis J. Halle, *The Cold War as History* (London: Chatto and Windus, 1971), p. 167.

said that they had the alternative of following a firm policy in Berlin or accepting the consequences of failure for the rest of their European policy. He argued that their policy had been successful in Greece, in Italy, and in France; that the Soviets had been reversed in Finland and had been severely shaken by Yugoslavia's breakaway; and that Russian activity in Berlin was the manifestation of the success of American policy.[25] He was also aware of the time constraints on America's response. "Our general estimate," he wrote to Ambassador Douglas on June 27, "is that the current supply situation in Berlin means that the zero hour will not be reached for two to three weeks. We intend to utilize this period in every way possible to reinforce our general position and to keep the initiative in dealing with the Soviets."[26]

Marshall made few utterances in public on the subject of the Berlin crisis and wrote no memoirs, and this makes it difficult to reconstruct his images. But he appears to have attributed to the Soviet leaders the potential recklessness that is bred by despair. This made their actions difficult to predict and the risks of escalation difficult to control. As Robert Lovett put it, the heads of the Soviet leaders were "full of bubbles." Therefore, firmness in defending America's vital interests had to be coupled with caution, and it is this combination which underlay Marshall's conviction, in the face of widespread pessimism in his department, that the U.S. should stay in Berlin as well as his reluctance to resort to force. Like Truman, he tended to think that the Kremlin had adopted a high-risk strategy and could not be compelled to rescind the blockade by a token show of force, and he consequently felt that it was incumbent on the U.S. to exercise restraint in the means it chose to counter the Russian move.

In contrast to Truman, Marshall attached little importance to the legal issues involved. He saw the blockade essentially as a political move in the Cold War struggle for power, and his response was based on pragmatic calculations of power and interest. When the suggestion of a protest note to Moscow was under consideration in the State Department, he felt that the note "should not over-stress legalistic approach but should be based on inhumanity of Soviet action in causing suffering to civilian population as well as threatening peace."[27] In his major official public statement of the U.S. posi-

25. Millis, *The Forrestal Diaries*, p. 459.
26. Marshall to Douglas, June 27, 1948, in *FRUS, 1948*, Vol. 2, p. 926.
27. Marshall to Douglas, June 28, 1948, in *FRUS, 1948*, Vol. 2, p. 931.

tion on June 30, Marshall similarly de-emphasized the question of legality and underlined the American intention and capability to stay in Berlin. "We are in Berlin," he told the press, "as a result of agreements between the Governments on the areas of occupation in Germany and we intend to stay."[28]

A much more important factor than the question of legality was Marshall's perception of the military balance. Sensitive to the need to deal with the Russians from a position of strength, he held out little hope for conciliatory diplomacy and feared that America's weakness in conventional military forces might make the Russians intransigent in negotiations and even encourage adventurism. For this reason, he sought to conceal from the Soviets, insofar as this was possible, the extent of America's military unpreparedness. At a Cabinet meeting on July 9, for example, Marshall expressed the hope that the military establishment would not find it necessary to be quite so explicit as it had been recently about the substantial time that would have to elapse before the recent decision to strengthen America's military position would become effective. He said that repetitions of such statements would emphasize American weakness and add to the difficulty of negotiating with the USSR. Such statements, he feared, might actually delude the Russians into a hasty action because they would not appreciate how much American mobilization could be speeded up under pressure.[29]

Marshall's perception of the blockade as directed at halting the implementation of the Allied plans for the Western zones of Germany was central to his definition of the situation. His assessment that the suspension of these plans was too high a price to pay for the lifting of the blockade was equally central to his position on the appropriate U.S. response. Both perceptual strands were firmly expressed in a report he sent to Douglas immediately following the meeting of the three Western Military Governors with Marshal Sokolovsky on July 3. "It is clear from Sokolovsky's reply," wrote Marshall, "that the Soviet Government intends to utilize the Berlin situation to reopen the entire German question and any proposal on our part which suggests meeting of the CFM [Council of Foreign Ministers] would only invite a Soviet reply bypassing the military governors, accepting the CFM and then at meeting agreeing to lift blockade on condition we suspend operation of the

---

28. *Department of State Bulletin*, July 4, 1948, p. 54.
29. Millis, *The Forrestal Diaries*, p. 457.

London recommendations. This, of course, is out of the question."[30]

As the crisis continued with no apparent deterioration in the U.S. position, there was a slight hardening in Marshall's position. Following a preliminary survey of alternatives, he affirmed that two considerations seemed important to him. The first was that there should be no negotiation under direct duress. The second was that the lifting of the blockade would go far in achieving the initial American objective. Although he appreciated the advantage of endeavoring to secure an assurance that the blockade would not be reinforced, he was doubtful whether the U.S. could make such an assurance a condition to opening talks. The hardening was indicated in his observation that even if the Soviets abandoned the blockade and then proposed a meeting to discuss the entire German problem, the U.S. decision-makers should consider very carefully whether they should refuse such a meeting.[31] In other words, Marshall now seemed to be saying that even if duress were eliminated through a prior Soviet lifting of the blockade, it did not go without saying that the U.S. would agree to reopen the German question.

Of the various perceived options, the one most favored by Marshall was an informal approach to Stalin. Marshall believed that prior to the dispatch of a formal note, which might elevate the matter further into the realm of prestige considerations, an effort should be made to approach Stalin directly.[32] A written reply, in his opinion, presented two risks. On the one hand, a note containing an outspoken refutation of the Soviet charges could, for prestige reasons, harden the Soviet position to the point of inflexibility. On the other hand, a conciliatory note which ignored these charges and obscured the issue of the illegal Soviet blockade would offer the impression of weakness.[33] Marshall greatly valued inter-Allied coordination in handling the crisis and, indeed, saw the success of an informal approach to Stalin as dependent on the British and French Governments sharing America's determination. But he was unprepared to accept a British proposal for a conciliatory note which appeared to propose negotiations under the continuing du-

30. Marshall to Douglas, July 3, 1948, in *FRUS, 1948*, Vol. 2, p. 947.
31. Marshall to Douglas, July 9, 1948, in *FRUS, 1948*, Vol. 2, pp. 955–956.
32. Marshall to Douglas, July 20, 1948, in *FRUS, 1948*, Vol. 2, p. 971.
33. Second telegram from Marshall to Douglas, July 20, 1948, in *FRUS, 1948*, Vol. 2, p. 974.

ress of blockade.[34] "In our view," he informed Douglas on July 21, "latest British draft is redolent with appeasement and we fail to see how necessary expression of determination could be conveyed in Moscow discussion in conjunction with presentation of a note of this character which, whatever outcome of such discussion, would do us great damage when published." Further arguments cited by Marshall against the proposed British note were that it failed to state categorically that interference with Western rights and responsibilities in Berlin was intolerable, and that a written note may not be answered for some time, thus prolonging delay in clarifying the situation.[35] But the basic image which accounts for Marshall's opposition was that of appeasement and its potentially disastrous consequences, as epitomized by the Munich surrender of 1938.

Instead of accepting what he regarded as appeasement, Marshall proposed a plan for escalating pressure on the Soviet Union. Like a good general, Marshall tried to anticipate the responses of the enemy and had a basic strategy in which the sequence of moves was worked out in advance. "Please impress upon Bevin," he instructed his ambassador in London, "the necessity of a co-ordinated plan of action to be worked out step by step. The difficulty with his proposal is that it does not envisage what would follow possible Soviet rejection of note. As we see it our program involves successive steps. First, the oral approach which gives needed flexibility and safeguards in present situation whereas written communication at first step may well freeze Soviet position. If this approach through diplomatic channels without publicity fails we should then have recourse to strong note rejecting Soviet arguments and placing problem before U.N. We consider it essential to utilize maximum U.N. procedure although we appreciate that it would in all likelihood involve Soviet veto and probably reference to a special session of the Assembly called for the purpose before taking necessary action to continue supply of Berlin which might have to take the form of armed food convoys."[36]

Of the three key decision-makers, Marshall was the least affected by rigid and distorting images during the Berlin crisis. His approach was pragmatic, low-key, and finely balanced. His awareness that America's entire European policy was at stake persuaded

34. Ibid.
35. Marshall to Douglas, July 21, 1948, in *FRUS, 1948*, Vol. 2, pp. 975–976.
36. Ibid., p. 976.

him that a determined attempt had to be made to defend this exposed outpost of the Western alliance. His perceptions of Soviet military superiority in the European theater and of the unpredictability of Soviet behavior, however, combined to dispose him against the adoption of coercive means to break the blockade. Instead, he preferred (1) to fall back on air power to supply the city, and (2) to exert steady economic, political, and diplomatic pressure on the USSR to lift the blockade.

CLAY

During the crisis period, General Lucius Clay emerged as unquestionably the most incisive, forthright, and hawkish American decision-maker. Against the background of considerable doubt and vacillation in Washington, the commander on the spot stood out as the stern and unbending champion of American interests in Germany and orthodox Cold War policy, and as the most determined opponent of withdrawal from Berlin and any other form of appeasement of the Russian bear. While the Joint Chiefs of Staff waited patiently for a political policy to be determined by the civilian authority and submitted to them for their military, strategic, and tactical guidance,[37] the commander on the spot in Berlin felt that time was of the essence and that the position of the Western powers would be fatally undermined unless they met the Soviet challenge with a quick, blunt, and decisive response. Impatient, authoritarian, and endowed with unbounded confidence in the soundness of his own judgment, Clay was inclined to take the lead rather than wait upon events, and he exercised unremitting pressure on Washington to support the tough position with which he was identified. The images which shaped his behavior during the crisis were sharply drawn and forcefully articulated, and they can be reconstructed in some detail from the voluminous papers and memoirs which he left behind.

In Clay's case, the change in perceptions brought about by the full blockade concerned the threat to basic values and the salience of time. The world, he believed, was facing the most critical issue since Hitler embarked on his policy of aggression. The U.S. clearly had to do something before its food stocks in Berlin, which were sufficient to last thirty-six days, and its coal stocks, which were suf-

37. *FRUS, 1948*, Vol. 2, p. 925.

ficient to last forty-five days, were exhausted.[38] Given the magnitude of the threat to America's basic values and the far-reaching political repercussions of this threat, Clay felt that the U.S. should respond promptly and resolutely, long before its stocks in Berlin were exhausted. The third component of crisis-induced stress—namely, the perception of a high probability of involvement in military hostilities—was missing from Clay's thinking. Paradoxically, the man who had caused an unwarranted war scare in early March 1948 rated the probability of war as very low at the height of the Berlin crisis.

Clay described the blockade as "one of the most ruthless efforts in modern times to use mass starvation for political coercion."[39] He perceived the action as brutal and ruthless for two reasons: first, because of the means employed to attain Soviet political objectives; and second, because it was directed against "innocent" and "helpless" German civilians caught between the two sides.[40]

The military balance in Berlin placed the U.S. at an overwhelming disadvantage vis-à-vis the Soviets. More than two million Germans lived in the three Western sectors of the city and became dependent on reserve stocks and airlift replacements. The Allied occupation forces, with an overall number of 20,000, including military personnel, civilians, and dependents, were no match for the two or three dozen divisions the Russians could dispatch to the trouble spot at short notice. As the commandant of the American sector, Colonel Frank Howley, put it, the two battalions of American troops would have gone down before the Russians "before you could say 'politburo!'"[41] Yet, there was little doubt in Clay's mind that the U.S. should remain in Berlin unless driven out either by force or by German suffering. In other words, this soldier did not regard Russia's military superiority in his theater as a sufficient reason in itself for running away from the conflict.

His initial definition of the situation and estimate of Russian intentions were expressed in a lengthy teletype conversation with the Department of the Army on June 25. Royall asked him specifi-

38. Lucius D. Clay, *Decision in Germany* (New York: Doubleday, 1950), p. 365.
39. Ibid.
40. Clay to the Department of the Army, June 25, 1948, in *FRUS, 1948*, Vol. 2, p. 917.
41. Frank Howley, *Berlin Command* (New York: Putnam's, 1950), p. 10.

cally for his evaluation of the possibility of armed conflict. Clay replied: "I do not expect armed conflict. Principal danger is from Russian-planned German Communist groups out looking for trouble. Obviously, conditions are tense. However, our troops and British are in hand and can be trusted. Robertson and I have been as cautious in our statements as is possible. We both realize the desire of our Governments to avoid armed conflict. Nevertheless, we cannot be run over and a firm position always involves some risk in this type of situation. We have no intent to start shooting."[42]

Clay thought that in view of the vulnerability of the American position in Berlin, a high-level decision should be taken immediately on how far the U.S. was prepared to go. "We here think it extremely important to stay," he reported, "and we are prepared to stay unless German suffering drives us out. However, except for our capacity to stick it out, we have few chips here to use and future actions would appear to be at governmental level." Royall assured the general that his currency decisions had been both proper and authorized, but he emphasized that the limited question of Berlin's currency was not a good question to go to war on. "If Soviets go to war," Clay replied, "it will not be because of Berlin currency issue but only because they believe this the right time. In such case, they would use currency issue as an excuse. I regard this probability as rather remote although it must not be disregarded. Certainly we are not trying to provoke war. We are taking a good many punches on the chin without a counter blow."[43] Clay was anxious to focus the attention of his colleagues on the real issue as he saw it. "We should not confuse currency as real issue," he told the Department of the Army. "It is a pretext. Accepting their view now will only gain a few weeks and then it will start again. Issue is western Germany and its part in European recovery." In a tone which reflected a measure of stress, he delivered an impassioned exhortation: "Please remember, emphasize, and never stop repeating that currency in Berlin is not the issue—the issue is our position in Europe and plans for western Germany."[44]

The image of the U.S.-German connection was vital to Clay, and he believed that action was called for to preserve it and to foil Soviet tactics. He pointed out that the amazingly courageous re-

---

42. Jean Edward Smith, ed., *The Papers of General Lucius D. Clay: Germany, 1945–1949* (Bloomington: Indiana University Press, 1974), Vol. 2, pp. 699–700. (Hereinafter cited as *Clay Papers*.)

43. Ibid., p. 702.   44. Ibid., p. 706.

sistance of the Berlin population would drive the Soviet Administration to extreme measures, and that Sokolovsky had issued a proclamation on June 24 declaring the end of four-power government. Sokolovsky's purpose was to frighten the Berlin population so that they would not exchange their old currency for Western currency. Clay added: "Every German leader except SED [Socialist Unity Party], and thousands of Germans, have courageously expressed their opposition to Communism. We should not destroy their confidence by any show of departure. Once again, we have to sweat it out, come what may."[45] If the Western powers were to leave Berlin, he warned, they would never get a real Western German government. It would expect to be next.[46]

On the precise action which the U.S. Government should take, Royall mentioned the possibility of a formal protest and expressed his personal view that this might just lead to a typewriter campaign instead of definite retaliatory action. Clay's comment on this possibility revealed his general resistance to any action which might be construed as appeasement. "I think governmental protest of no value," he stated, "except for the record unless we have a plan for definite measures to be taken if there is Soviet rejection which is almost certain. How far will we go to hold our position? Will we use other pressures short of war? Will our Allies stick in these circumstances? These questions can be answered only by Government. I can only say that our remaining in Berlin means much to our prestige in Germany, in Europe, and in keeping high the courage of Western Europe. To retreat now is to imply we are prepared to retreat further."[47]

To signal to the Russians that the U.S. was not prepared to retreat, Clay reverted to his proposal of an armed convoy, which he first made following the failure of his test trains to get through. In a telegram to the Department of the Army on June 25, he held out little hope for reaching a satisfactory solution through a conference with Sokolovsky. "I am still convinced," he wrote, "that a determined movement of convoys with troop protection would reach Berlin and that such a showing might well prevent rather than build up Soviet pressures which could lead to war. Nevertheless I realize fully the inherent dangers in this proposal since once committed we could not withdraw."[48]

45. Clay, *Decision in Germany*, p. 366.
46. *Clay Papers*, Vol. 2, p. 706.
47. Ibid., p. 703.   48. *FRUS, 1948*, Vol. 2, p. 918.

In addition to the perception of a threat to basic values, Clay's belief that the Russians were bluffing, and that they would back down if challenged, constituted an important element of his unyielding posture and his advocacy of strong action. He counted on America's air power to foil the blockade and deter the Russians from going any further. On June 27, he asked for fifty additional transport planes to arrive in Germany at the earliest practicable date. This augmentation of America's air forces in Germany was urgent, he said. In support of this request, he argued that

> we are no longer at a point where we need to fear that the bringing in of reinforcements will influence the Soviet position. They are either bluffing now or they have made up their minds and currency issue is in itself only a pretext. *It is our view that they are bluffing and that their hand can and should be called now. They are definitely afraid of our air might.* Moreover, arrival of aircraft will be deciding factor in sustaining Allied firmness.[49]

Clay's views on the likely course and pitfalls of negotiations with the Russians are contained in a telegram he sent to the Department of the Army on July 10. He fully shared the State Department's conclusion that they should not negotiate under duress—that is, during the period in which the Berlin blockade continued. If the Soviet Government believed that it had gone as far as it dared, it would probably settle for a face-saving compromise on the currency issue. This was unlikely, however, argued Clay, because the Soviet Government was not yet convinced of the determination of the Allied stand, and hence believed it could go further. It might therefore take the course of reopening traffic, subject to American agreement to a conference at the governmental level to consider the entire German problem. Clay felt that refusal to discuss the German problem as a whole if the blockade were lifted would put America in a bad light, and that this would be exploited by the Russians to show that the U.S. did not desire to reach an agreement. But at the same time, he was convinced that the London Program must not be compromised. He was therefore of the opinion that in the event of a Russian offer being made, the Americans should state their willingness to discuss the entire German problem, but that their course of action in Western Germany should not be changed or delayed pending such a conference. In short, like Marshall, Clay regarded a genuine reopening of the

---

49. *Clay Papers*, Vol. 2, p. 708 (emphasis added).

German problem as too high a price to pay for the lifting of the blockade. In his case, this position was buttressed by confidence that the Russians definitely did not want war. "However, they know that the Allies also do not want war and they will continue their pressure to the point at which they believe hostilities might occur." Once again he recommended an armed convoy in order to bring the Russian leaders to this critical point.[50]

Clay's images, perceptions, and evaluation of Soviet intentions did not undergo any significant change during the crisis period. But while remaining static, they were articulated in an increasingly clear-cut and emphatic manner. In a cable to Draper dated July 19, Clay himself provided a crisp, comprehensive, and systematic summary of the various perceptual strands which shaped his strategy preferences. This highly revealing document is therefore worth quoting extensively:

> The very violence of Soviet reaction now is proof of the success of our several programs to restore and build up democracy in Europe. Having committed ourselves to a course of action to this end and having backed it with large sums of money, can we afford now to throw it away as we encounter our first major evidence of Soviet resistance?
> Of course it would be difficult if not impossible for the three western nations to refuse to discuss the German problem with Russia. However, we should refuse to discuss the problem if it means abandonment or suspension of our program in western Germany. No solution of the German problem can be found which does not give USSR a voice in the Ruhr. A failure on our part to establish a German government now could only be interpreted as a weakness and apprehension on our part. Even if it were now possible with Soviet participation to establish a unified Germany, could we afford to include it in the ERP [European Recovery Program], and if we could afford it would not Soviet participation in such a government prevent it from attaining any success? Increased production from a western Germany oriented toward western European recovery must be conceded by all as essential to a successful program for European recovery. If we give up that opportunity, can we hope to carry the ERP to a successful conclusion? No final solution of the German problem is possible until ERP has invigorated western Europe so that it may develop a military strength which makes Soviet domination of Europe impossible. I doubt if such a military strength would be developed with Germany under quadripartite control. We have gone too far with

50. Clay to the Department of the Army, July 10, 1948, in *FRUS, 1948*, Vol. 2, pp. 956–958.

western Europe to have any hope of establishing a quadripartite control of Germany which would not retard the development of western Europe and a unified Germany can come now with safety only when the balance of power in Europe is restored.

Soviet measures now being taken must be based on one of two premises: (A) the first premise is that the Soviet Government, recognizing the rising tide of anti-communistic forces under European recovery, are determined to exert pressures to retard such recovery to the point of, but short of, war. In other words, they are still bluffing but will continue to do so until it is absolutely evident that their bluff is being called. In such case they will recede. To support this premise there is their evident lack of real readiness for war and their lack of preparation for immediate and major war in Europe.

(B) The second premise is that the Soviet Government has now made up its mind that European recovery can be stopped only by war. Having advised their population for three years now that America is getting ready to attack the USSR, it would be their intent to force us to the first overt act so that they could charge us with being the aggressor. If this premise is correct, war will come now because the USSR has determined it to be inevitable and that time is against the USSR. If war has been determined, it will not be fought to gain possession of Berlin, and the pressures now being exerted in Berlin if we withdraw will be applied elsewhere next, probably in Vienna, and will continue until we are provoked into an act of war. . . .

While I fully appreciate the importance of diplomatic procedures to include the further exchange of notes, the placing of the issue before the United Nations, the imposing of sanctions elsewhere, and any other measures which seem feasible, we must recognize that all of these measures take time under which our own situation may well deteriorate. Moreover, unless we and the western nations take far more vigorous measures for preparedness than we are taking now, we can only hope that the passage of time will make us really prepared for war. . . .

I can understand the reluctance of both England and France to run the risk of war due to their horror at the very thought as well as to their unreadiness and their knowledge that we too are unready. Unquestionably there is also the traditional reluctance of our own people to take steps which involve the risk of war. However, taking all of these factors into consideration, it does appear that we cannot do otherwise than retreat with possible fateful consequences to our role as a world leader unless we are prepared and without too long delay to risk a showing of force. It is only by a showing of force which is in the nature of an armed reconnaissance that we can determine the real intent of the Soviet Government.

Our right to move an armed force for garrison purposes into and out of Berlin, as far as I know, has not been questioned. The movement of such a force could be stopped only by attack. This attack would not occur unless the Soviet Government is determined upon a war course. If it has so determined, a retreat now will merely be followed by pressure elsewhere within a matter of weeks or months. If war is inevitable, the time that we can gain by retreat now is so relatively short that it has little value.

The choice before us is a hard choice. However, if we do decide to retreat now, this retreat will not save us from again and again having to choose between retreat and war. With each retreat we will find ourselves confronted with the same problem but with fewer and fewer allies on our side. . . .

I cannot but feel that the world today is facing the most critical issue that has arisen since Hitler placed his policy of aggression in motion. In fact, the Soviet Government has more force immediately at its disposal than did Hitler to accomplish his purpose. Only America can exert the world leadership, and only America can provide the strength to stop this policy of aggression here and now. The next time may be too late. I believe determined action will stop it short of war. It cannot be stopped without the serious risk of war.[51]

To recapitulate, Clay saw the blockade as evidence of the success of American policy in Europe; he considered that the Allies should refuse to reopen the German problem if this meant abandoning or suspending their program in Western Germany, because a prosperous West Germany was indispensable to European recovery and the containment of Russia; and he believed that the Russians were bluffing, that their bluff should be called, and the sooner the better, since time was not working to the advantage of the West, and the only way to do this was by a show of force. If the U.S. shirked this difficult choice, further retreats would become inevitable. The world faced the greatest threat since Hitler, and only America could exert world leadership and put an end to Soviet aggression before it was too late.

Here lay a complete and coherent analysis of the situation and a program of action. The other key decision-makers, President Truman and Secretary Marshall, shared some of the images and assumptions which informed this program. But they disagreed with others, notably the assumption that the Russian leaders were risk-averse, rational, and predictable, and hence would back down if confronted with a forceful show of Western determination to go to the brink of war. Clay denied interdependence between Russia's

51. *Clay Papers*, Vol. 2, pp. 743–746.

behavior and America's behavior during the crisis. Russia decided before the crisis whether or not it wanted to go to war. If, as Clay believed, Russia decided against war, America could be as coercive as she liked and even resort to violence without fear of escalation. If, on the other hand, Russia decided to go to war, then the war would occur irrespective of what America did. Marshall and Truman implicitly affirmed the interdependence between Russia's crisis behavior and that of the U.S. Hence their fear of provoking Russia and escalating the crisis. These partly convergent, partly divergent images were the critical inputs into the American decision flow during the crisis period.

CHAPTER SIX

Decision Flow

PHASE I: JUNE 24–30

THE BERLIN BLOCKADE presented the Truman Administration with the task of making one of the most difficult and agonizing foreign policy decisions that it was ever called on to make. The ample and varied forewarning it had of the approaching crisis did nothing to lessen the predicament, because no decision had been taken on how to respond to a determined Soviet move to cut off the Berlin outpost from its vital sources of supply in the Western zones of Germany. Conflict of opinion, among other factors, constrained the formulation of any definite plans to meet this contingency. Now that all the ground approaches to the city were blocked and its people seemed completely trapped in the Bear's paws, the decision could not be postponed indefinitely. The military logic pointed to withdrawal, but the political consequences of abandoning Berlin were widely perceived to be unacceptable. The inability of the decision-makers to resolve the conflict of values greatly added to the stress induced by the crisis.[1] As Kennan recalled: "No one was sure, as yet, how the Russian move could be countered or whether

---

1. Alexander George calls attention to the psychological tension generated by the cognitive complexity of the issues requiring decision. When multiple stakes are present, he points out, the decision-maker may experience conflict and stress because he finds it difficult to satisfy all the competing considerations or to choose among them. See Alexander L. George, "Adaptation and Stress in Decision-Making: The Individual, Small Group and Organizational Contexts," in *Coping and Adaptation*, ed. George V. Coelho et al. (New York: Basic Books, 1974), p. 182. On the question of cognitive complexity and stress, see also John D. Steinbruner, *The Cybernetic Theory of Decision* (Princeton: Princeton University Press, 1974), pp. 29–31; and Irving L. Janis and Leon Mann, *Decision Making* (New York: The Free Press, 1977), pp. 17–18.

it could successfully be countered at all. The situation was dark and full of danger."[2]

The basic constraint and the major source of stress in the decision process was the existence of three values or imperatives of American foreign policy which could not be easily reconciled. These values were: (1) maintaining America's position in Berlin, (2) avoiding war, and (3) proceeding with the implementation of the London Program. The first value effectively ruled out the option of withdrawal from and liquidation of this vulnerable enclave, which was favored by some American officials. The second value precluded the resort to coercive measures to compel the Soviet Union to rescind the blockade. The third value meant that the Administration could not negotiate, because the concessions it could offer (on the currency question) were of little interest to the Russians, while the kind of concessions that the Russians were after would have meant halting the unification of the three Western zones and the political reconstruction of Germany. The upshot was that the Administration had no coherent strategy for coping with the crisis, and the contradictory nature of the three basic imperatives prevented it from developing one. Consequently, it played for time in the hope that something would turn up. Something did turn up eventually: the airlift.[3]

The option of negotiating on Russia's terms was implicitly rejected at the very outset of the crisis period. President Truman was advised by the Director of Central Intelligence that although Soviet behavior in Germany, particularly in Berlin, had been far from conciliatory, it had not been so definitive or final as to preclude further negotiations and may have even been designed to force the Western powers into negotiations. Admiral Hillenkoetter added, however, that the negotiations desired by Russia, ostensibly to permit the unification of Germany, were actually designed to prevent the realization of the Allied plans for Western Germany.[4]

Russia's terms were spelled out in a declaration issued by the foreign ministers of the Communist bloc in Warsaw on June 24, fol-

2. George F. Kennan, *Memoirs, 1925–1950* (Boston: Little, Brown, 1967), p. 421.
3. Glenn H. Snyder and Paul Diesing, *Conflict Among Nations: Bargaining, Decision-Making and System-Structure in International Crises* (Princeton: Princeton University Press, 1977), p. 387.
4. Memorandum for the President from R. H. Hillenkoetter, June 24, 1948, President's Secretary File, Harry S. Truman Library, Independence, Missouri.

lowing a two-day conference which had been convened on the initiative of the Soviet and Polish governments. In this declaration, issued on the day that the Berlin blockade was imposed, the decisions of the London Conference and subsequent Western actions in Germany were roundly denounced as violations of the Potsdam agreement. The Soviet group proposed the restoration of four-power control of Germany, the formation of an all-German government, the conclusion of a peace treaty with Germany, and the withdrawal from Germany of the occupation forces of all the Powers within a year after the conclusion of the peace treaty.[5]

The Western governments ignored this communist overture, which in its offer of withdrawing occupation forces from Germany constituted a new element in Soviet policy. American officials saw the Warsaw declaration as indicative of Soviet desires (1) for participation in the distribution of the industrial wealth of Germany, (2) for receipt of further reparation deliveries, and (3) for the opportunity to gain political control over all of Germany. The American view, shared by Britain, was that the Warsaw declaration, like the Berlin blockade, was designed to render the Western powers more amenable to the idea of further discussion of the German problem and to giving up their plan for the creation of a Western German government.[6] It was also believed that the all-German government called for in the Warsaw declaration represented the means chosen by Moscow for realizing its aim of communizing the whole of Germany, since such a government would necessarily be situated in the East of Germany and would be subject to pressure from both the Soviet authorities and the communist-run organizations in the surrounding areas of Germany.[7] The deadlock on the

5. For the text of the declaration, see Union of Soviet Socialist Republics, Ministry of Foreign Affairs, *The Soviet Union and the Berlin Question (Documents)* (Moscow, 1948), pp. 32–41; or Beate Ruhm von Oppen, *Documents on Germany Under Occupation, 1945–1954* (London: Oxford University Press, 1955), pp. 300–307.

6. Memorandum for the Director of Plans and Operations: "Estimate of Berlin Situation," June 29, 1948, P&O 381, Record Group (RG) 319, Records of the Army Staff, National Archives, Washington, D.C.; Bevin to Sir Oliver Franks (Washington), June 28, 1948, FO 372/C5138, Public Record Office, London; and Douglas to Marshall, June 26, 1948, in *Foreign Relations of the United States, 1948* (Washington, D.C.: U.S. Government Printing Office, 1973), Vol. 2, p. 925 (henceforth, this series will be referred to as *FRUS*).

7. Report to Bevin, "Policy on Germany," July 8, 1948, FO 371/70502/C5611, and July 13, 1948, FO 371/70503/C5948, Public Record Office, London. The French were more inclined to agree to four-power talks to attempt to reach a com-

diplomatic front was thus complete: the Soviet Union would not lift the blockade unless the entire German question was reopened, and the Allies would not reopen the German question to four-power talks so long as the blockade of Berlin remained in force, and they gave no indication that they might agree to four-power negotiations on Germany even if the blockade were lifted.

The Allies were not agreed, however, on a positive course of action, and the Americans were unable to provide the lead because they themselves had not worked out their own position. In the first few days of the crisis, Washington seemed almost paralyzed by crisis-induced stress. During these few crucial days, London moved with greater speed and decisiveness in making its basic choice to stay in Berlin, in announcing this decision, and in asking the American Government to make a similar statement. Led by its forceful and staunchly anti-communist Foreign Secretary, Ernest Bevin, the British Cabinet quickly resolved to do everything possible to supply Berlin by air and to concert a common policy in this matter with the governments of the United States and France.[8] The volume of communications between Washington, London, and Paris, and between the three capitals and their representatives in Berlin, increased very markedly with the onset of the crisis and remained very high until the crisis ended. Unlike Britain, however, France played a relatively passive role, exercising virtually no influence over American policy and providing little support for it.[9]

During the morning of June 24, there was a long conference, presided over by Charles Bohlen, between representatives of the

---

prehensive solution to the German problem, but even among them the opposition to negotiating on the basis of the Warsaw declaration was considerable. See Douglas to Marshall, June 26, 1948, in *FRUS, 1948*, Vol. 2, pp. 921–925; and FO 371/70498/C5136, Public Record Office, London.

8. C[abinet] M[inutes] (48) 43rd Conclusions, Minute 3, June 25, 1948, and C.M. (48) 44th Conclusions, Minute 4, June 28, 1948, Public Record Office, London. See also Desmond Donnelly, *Struggle for the World: The Cold War from Its Origins in 1917* (London: Collins, 1965), pp. 260–261. For a general treatment of Bevin's foreign policy and attitude towards the Soviet Union, see Avi Shlaim, Peter Jones, and Keith Sainsbury, *British Foreign Secretaries Since 1945* (London: David and Charles, 1977), chap. 2.

9. The French were alarmed by recent events in Berlin and resentful of Clay's unilateral and ill-advised actions. "This is what we have been led to," noted President Auriol in his diary on the day the blockade was imposed, "by an authoritarian general who is in constant liaison with the big magnates of Berlin." Vincent Auriol, *Journal du Septennat, 1947–1954*, Vol. 2: *1948* (Paris: Armand Colin, 1974), pp. 282–283 and 292–293.

Army and representatives of the State Department to consider the situation in Berlin. It was agreed that, for the time being, inquiries from the press to either the State Department or the national military establishment should be answered by the words, "No comment." Under Secretary Lovett, with whom Bohlen checked by phone, confirmed this view, and the Army representatives similarly undertook to advise Secretary Royall and their public relations officials. At the same time, there was a growing feeling in the Army, and also in the Air Force, that the Berlin situation should be given emergency consideration by the National Security Council so that a conclusion might be reached regarding America's position.[10]

While Washington was pondering over the agonizing question of what should be done to preserve the Western position in Berlin, its military representatives there grasped the initiative. On June 24 at 2:00 P.M. local time, Colonel Frank Howley went on the air to explain American intentions to the German people: "We are not getting out of Berlin," he promised. "We are going to stay. I don't know the answer to the present problem—not yet—but this much I do know. The American people will not stand by and allow the German people to starve." And to give the Russians something to chew on besides black bread, the irrepressible commandant added: "We have heard a lot about your military intentions. Well, this is all I have to say on the subject. If you do try to come into our sector, you better be well prepared. We are ready for you."[11] Thus, the first official statement of American intentions in this major superpower crisis was made by an Irish colonel in the U.S. Army. In his memoirs, Howley admitted that perhaps he was speaking out of turn, presumptuously trying to read Washington's mind. But, he added in self-justification, "when you are faced with a long-planned attempt to create absolute chaos you can't wait until the issue goes all the way up to Pennsylvania Avenue for a decision. You have got to make an appraisal of the determination of the American people yourself." He felt justified when his appraisal was adopted as the national policy.[12]

Later in the day came General Clay's chance to speak out of

10. Memorandum for the Secretary of Defense from John H. Ohly, June 24, 1948, Secretary of Defense Office, CD 6-2-9, RG 330, National Archives, Washington, D.C.
11. Frank Howley, *Berlin Command* (New York: Putnam's, 1950), p. 200.
12. Ibid.

turn. On arrival at Heidelberg, to visit the U.S. Army Headquarters, Clay told reporters that the Russians were trying to put on the final pressure, but that "they cannot drive us out by an action short of war as far as we are concerned."[13] Since no decision to stay in Berlin had been made yet, and since the State Department had advised its own people and the Army to make no comment for the time being on queries from the press on the Berlin situation, officials in Washington were surprised to see press reports of what Clay had said and were particularly disturbed by his reference to the possibility of war.[14] It was not the first time that Clay committed his government to forward positions without being mandated to do so, and it was certainly not the last.

Clay's own staff advisers, whom he called to a meeting on the evening of June 24 after his return from Heidelberg, were deeply divided. Some believed that the Russians were bluffing and that they could be forced to back down; others felt that the only sensible policy for the United States was to make plans to withdraw. Robert Murphy argued passionately that the United States must not yield. He was supported by Major-General Robert Walsh, who gave his evaluation that "the Russians are putting up a tremendous front, but they're weak, they're vulnerable—if we face them out they'll capitulate." The proponents of withdrawal pointed out, however, that support from the Army and the State Department would be lukewarm for a variety of reasons: the lack of fighting men, the physical difficulty of defending Berlin, and the conviction that in their drive to communize Europe, the Soviets would resort to all-out war. The meeting ended without a consensus and without an agreed-upon staff recommendation, leaving responsibility for the local decision, if there was to be one, in the hands of the Military Governor.[15]

Clay considered three alternatives prior to reaching his decision: sending an armed convoy along the highway; offering the Russians a compromise proposal on the Berlin currency question; and launching an airlift to supply the blockaded city. To the currency proposal, Clay himself attached virtually no chance of its

---

13. *Newsweek*, July 5, 1948.
14. Jean Edward Smith, ed., *The Papers of General Lucius D. Clay: Germany, 1945–1949* (Bloomington: Indiana University Press, 1974), Vol. 2, p. 701 (hereinafter cited as *Clay Papers*).
15. Richard Collier, *Bridge Across the Sky: The Berlin Blockade and Airlift, 1948–1949* (London: Macmillan, 1978), p. 54.

being accepted. To the armed convoy option, on the other hand, he attached a far better chance of success. In a cable to Under Secretary Draper, he estimated that the German population would begin to suffer in a few days, and this suffering would become serious in two to three weeks. To deal with this problem, he suggested a strong governmental protest which would insist that in the event of Russian inability to reopen communications, America had the clear right to move in her troops to restore communications. After indicating the pressure for swift action, Clay concluded by affirming his conviction that a determined movement of convoys with troop protection would reach Berlin, and that such a display of force on the zonal frontier might well prevent rather than build up Soviet pressures that could lead to war. Nevertheless, he fully recognized the dangers inherent in this proposal, since, once committed, the American troops would not be able to withdraw.[16]

Any hope that Clay might have had for a positive response to this proposal must have been rudely shattered, at least for the time being, in the course of a teleconference with Royall on June 25. Clay's latest proposal could not be easily reconciled with one of the principal constraints on American policy—that of avoiding war. As soon as the conference opened, the anxious Secretary of the Army impressed on his risk-acceptant subordinate the need to exercise restraint and show some flexibility in order to avert the escalation of the crisis. "Until you are advised further," said the Secretary of the Army, "I would not want any action taken in Berlin which might lead to possible armed conflict. If in your opinion that course would require a few hours delay or a slowing up in issuance of our currency in Berlin, I would want it so delayed or slowed up." Signs of stress, with the fear of war as the main cause behind it, were evident in Royall's message. Clay protested that the difficulties to be expected from a separate currency had been fully reported, and that it was too late now to suspend its issue or slow it down. Clay was also opposed to the acceleration of the movement of U.S. dependents out of Berlin, because their people were calm and he had little fear of the crisis affecting them. What he did fear, as he had pointed out in many previous messages, was that the hardships inflicted upon the Germans in Berlin would become so great that the Western occupation forces would have to leave in order to relieve their suffering.

16. Clay to Draper, June 25, 1948, in *Clay Papers*, Vol. 2, pp. 696–697.

Royall invited suggestions from Clay for use in his conference with the State Department later that morning. Clay's only recommendations for the State Department conference were to suggest: (1) that a sharp protest to the Soviet Government be prepared in conjunction with the British and the French, and (2) that external pressures be developed which could be applied following the expected Soviet rejection of the protest. The idea of an airlift was not even mentioned at this conference except indirectly. Royall informed Clay that the Department of the Army was considering the desirability of asking the Air Force to provide additional air transport in the event that it was urgently needed, and he wondered whether Clay foresaw such a need either for supplying his own forces or for helping the French. Clay thought he had sufficient planes for the time being to meet American needs and possibly French needs as well. His British colleague had been splendid throughout, he said, but neither of them had any support, even moral, from the French.[17]

The British colleague arrived soon after the teleconference. During the pre-crisis period, he had opposed the idea of an armed convoy proposal as both impractical and dangerous, and he saw no reason to change his mind now. Britain, in any case, was not prepared to participate in an action of this kind. As an alternative, Robertson suggested to Clay the possibility of supplying Berlin by air. He himself had already secured the agreement of the Royal Air Force to start flying supplies in to the British garrison on June 25, and the British Cabinet was considering the possibilities of maintaining supplies to the civilian population by air.[18] But Clay could not be easily persuaded that a city of over two million inhabitants could be supplied entirely by air. The Americans had, of course, used air transport during the mini-blockade. But it was one thing to supply the Western garrisons as a measure of temporary reinforcement, and quite another to supply the food and fuel needs of the entire civilian population on an ongoing basis. Even if most of the needs of the Berliners could be secured over a prolonged period, would they be able to stand firm in the face of the intense propaganda campaign and severe physical hardships to which they were subjected by the Russians?

17. Ibid., pp. 699-704.
18. C.M. (48) 43rd Conclusions, Minute 3, June 25, 1948, Public Record Office, London.

In an effort to answer this question, Clay summoned to his office Ernst Reuter, the leader of the German Social Democratic Party and the Mayor-elect of Berlin. Reuter came in, accompanied by his young aide, Willy Brandt. Clay informed Reuter that he was going to try the experiment of feeding the city by air. Reuter smiled skeptically. He could not quite believe it. But he told Clay and Murphy, speaking without any sharpness: "We shall in any case continue on our way. Do what you are able to do; we shall do what we feel to be our duty. Berlin will make all necessary sacrifices and offer resistance—come what may."[19] Clay was visibly impressed. Reuter's frankness and his firm, unshakable attitude won the sympathy of the American southerner, who instinctively saw a "Red" in every Social Democrat.

Fortified by confidence that the West Berliners were prepared to face severe physical deprivations rather than surrender to Russian rule, Clay next sought reassurance that an expanded airlift could in fact be mounted. At this stage, all he had in mind was a humanitarian project to defeat a political purpose. Just to think of supplying a city by air was daring. No one realized the full potentialities of the airlift or thought it would last very long. Clay estimated that seven hundred tons a day was the maximum that could be expected from even "a very big operation."[20] The resources the Americans had in their theater to defeat the blockade were limited. Their transport and troop carrier planes, although more than a hundred in number, were C-47s, twin-engine planes with a cargo capacity of only about two and a half tons, and many of them had seen hard war service. The British resources were even more limited, and there were no French transport planes that could be made available. Nevertheless, Clay felt that the full use of the

19. Willy Brandt, *My Road to Berlin* (London: Peter Davies, 1960), pp. 185–186. Looking back on the Berlin crisis, Clay had this to say: "To me the most dramatic moment was when Ernst Reuter, the Mayor of Berlin, . . . came to my office and I said, 'Look, I am ready to try an airlift. I can't guarantee it will work. I am sure that even at its best, people are going to be cold and people are going to be hungry. And if the people of Berlin won't stand that, it will fail. And I don't want to go into this unless I have your assurance that the people will be heavily in approval.' And he said, 'General, don't doubt it for a moment.' And that is the way it worked out. They never weakened." Fred L. Hadsel, "Reflections of the U.S. Commanders in Germany and Austria," in *U.S. Occupation in Europe After World War II*, ed. Hans A. Schmitt (Lawrence: Regents Press of Kansas, 1978), pp. 156–157.

20. Lt. Gen. William Tunner, *Over the Hump* (New York: Duell, Sloane and Pearce, 1964), pp. 158–159.

available C-47s would prove that the job could be done, at least on a limited scale. He decided to act, and, without further reference to Washington, he immediately issued the necessary orders for mounting the airlift to the beleaguered city (Decision 7). Calling up Major-General Curtis LeMay, commander of the United States Air Force in Europe, at the latter's headquarters in Frankfurt, Clay ordered him to drop all other uses of the aircraft so that his entire fleet of C-47s could be placed on the Berlin run. At the same time, arrangements were made for the movement of food to the airports; and on the following morning (June 26), the first C-47s arrived in Berlin with food for its people.[21] Robertson closely coordinated the British part of the operation with Clay.

It is interesting to note that at this very early stage, when the American position had not yet been worked out, the seeds of the airlift were already germinating in the minds of several American policymakers. It was all too clear that the Soviets held all the trump cards in Berlin. They could suspend all overland traffic to and from the Western zones; they could interfere with air traffic to and from Berlin; they could seriously disrupt radio telecommunications to and from Berlin; and they could direct and support revolutionary action to seize control of the city administration. Unless America were to resort to bluff, air power was the only strong card which she had to play, and serious thought began to focus spontaneously on the possible uses of air power both as a means of transport to relieve the beleaguered city and as an instrument of diplomacy, to deter the Russians from playing their other cards.

Forrestal wanted to know what immediate capabilities were available for reinforcing Europe, and, after an urgent inquiry, Secretary of the Air Force Symington was able to provide fairly precise information. The Air Force had one Fighter Group, with seventy-five P-51s, and three Medium Bomber Groups, with thirty B-29s each, which could depart twelve hours after notification. Three ad-

---

21. Ibid.; and Lucius D. Clay, *Decision in Germany* (New York: Doubleday, 1950), pp. 365–366. "It was a pretty modest start," recalled LeMay. "I never dreamed how consequential this could become, and certainly never dreamed—then—how serious General Clay was about the whole thing. He kept increasing his requests, and eventually it dawned on me what he was talking about. He was going to buckle down and support the city of Berlin entirely by activity in the air. Not being in the airplane business, obviously Clay himself never realized that when he was talking in tonnages of such prodigious amounts, it was far beyond our capacity to operate." Curtis E. LeMay with MacKinlay Kantor, *Mission with LeMay: My Story* (New York: Doubleday, 1965), p. 415.

ditional Medium Bomber Groups, also with thirty B-29s each, could begin departure in ten days. These movements were based on the assumptions that maximum support would be furnished by the Military Air Transport Service and that all units would be deployed in the United Kingdom, where they could be supported with the assistance of the British.[22]

Draper only got word that the blockade had been clamped down in earnest after he set off on an inspection tour of Berlin and Vienna together with his chief planning officer, Lieutenant General Albert C. Wedemeyer. During the Second World War, Wedemeyer had been the U.S. Army's theater commander in China, where he had been supplied by air across the Himalayas from India, so he had a pretty good idea of what the different types of planes could carry and how often they could land at an airport. Draper, in his earlier capacity as Director of the Economics Division of OMGUS, had negotiated with the Russians on the feeding of the Berlin population, so he knew the tonnage of food necessary on a ration level to feed the Germans in the Western sectors of the city. Both men knew the number of planes they had in Europe, so they figured whether it was a physical possibility to feed that many people with that many planes, if they had the pilots and the airfields and the necessary organization. They came to the conclusion that it was a possibility but not a sure thing, and that it was worth trying.[23] Draper cabled Royall to recommend that the Air Force be requested to initiate the immediate move of transport units to the European Command.[24] Royall consulted Clay about this idea, but the latter, as we have seen, did not take up the offer of additional transport aircraft to carry supplies to Berlin, and he acted on his own initiative in launching the airlift.

Clay's airlift decision, despite the modest expectations which attended its birth, was perhaps the most momentous American decision of the entire Berlin crisis period. It was not the product of careful planning, and it was not made in the highest echelons of the government, but its importance can hardly be exaggerated, for it

22. Memorandum for Mr. Forrestal from W. Stuart Symington, June 25, 1948, enclosing Memorandum for Mr. Symington from Lauris Norstad (Lieutenant General, USAF, Deputy Chief of Staff, Operations), June 24, 1948, Secretary of Defense Office, CD 6-2-9, RG 330, National Archives, Washington, D.C.

23. Oral History Interview with General William H. Draper, Jr., January 11, 1972, pp. 62–65, Harry S. Truman Library.

24. Draper to Royall, June 24, 1948, RG 335, Records of the Office of the Secretary of the Army, National Archives, Washington, D.C.

set the pattern for American behavior until the end of the crisis. Superficially it may look like a tactical or logistical measure, but its political significance was paramount, for it implied an American commitment to stay in Berlin, and it signaled an American intention not to shirk the trial of strength initiated by the Cold War adversary. Clay took this momentous decision without consulting Washington, not because he assumed that Washington's support was assured, but, on the contrary, because he feared that the divided and hesitant government might recoil from the trial of strength. By launching the airlift, he forced the government's hand and deliberately committed it to a course of action for which it was not fully prepared. That this was his intention is evident from his revealing reply to a question on whether or not the report in an American newspaper was true that Washington had told him that he could have as many planes as he needed. Clay said: "I don't doubt that someone in Washington would have said something of the sort to me. But I didn't ask Washington. I acted first. I began the airlift with what I had, because I had to first prove to Washington that it was possible. Once I'd proved it, it was no longer hard to get help."[25] Thus, almost wholly on his own initiative, Clay forged a policy of firmness. Washington's indecision left him considerable latitude for improvising the airlift strategy. The inspiration for the airlift came from the British side, and the Royal Air Force delivered the first supplies to the British garrison on June 25. Draper and Wedemeyer independently thought along parallel lines, and Royall responded favorably to their suggestion that the Air Force be approached for help. But Clay provided the initiative, impetus, and drive behind the big airlift; and in doing so, he created a critical option for his government which spared it the difficult choice between resorting to force or resigning itself to an ignominious retreat.

The Berlin situation was brought up at the Cabinet meeting on June 25, and Royall reported that a serious situation was developing. A long but inconclusive discussion ensued on the merits of issuing licenses to export equipment and materials to Russia in exchange for manganese and other items which were vitally necessary for the American steel industry.[26] Forrestal, Royall, and Lovett

---

25. Curt Riess, *The Berlin Story* (New York: Dial Press, 1952), pp. 164–165.
26. Harry S. Truman, *Memoirs*, Vol. 2: *Years of Trial and Hope, 1946–1953* (London: Hodder and Stoughton, 1956), p. 130; Cabinet Minutes, June 25, 1948,

remained behind for a conference with the President after the Cabinet meeting. The discussion turned on the controlling legal rights and undertakings, and it is striking to find how vague the American position still was, although Soviet pressure against Berlin had been mounting for three months.[27] This more restricted gathering also discussed fully the record of the lengthy teletype conference between Royall and Clay which had taken place earlier that morning. It was agreed that Clay should be advised not to make statements referring to the possibility of war over Berlin. Royall emphasized that if war were inevitable, it should not come over the Berlin currency squabble. There was a discussion of Clay's proposals regarding a note of protest to Moscow and outside retaliation, and it was agreed not to adopt them because neither would be fully effective (Decision 8). Outside retaliation, such as closing the U.S. ports and the Panama Canal, would not seriously hurt the Soviet Union, which was self-sufficient. Furthermore, such measures could lead to general economic warfare, which would result in the stoppage of Soviet supplies of manganese to the United States. A unilateral U.S. note might lead to a "typewriter war" and would be futile unless the approach had the full support of the British and French. Note was taken of the informal and unofficial Soviet suggestion (which was made by Colonel Vyrianov and reported by Murphy) that a deal might be made exchanging Berlin for territory in Thuringia or Saxony.[28] In general, Truman's advisers urged caution and restraint, and the meeting was more noteworthy for its decisions on what should not be done than for any decision on positive action.

The following day, however, Truman decided to act. He was less worried than the military departments that positive measures to counter the blockade might lead to a major war. Clay had gone out on a limb in improvising the airlift strategy, and the President now

---

Papers of Matthew J. Connelly, Harry S. Truman Library; and James V. Forrestal Diaries, June 25, 1948, p. 2320, Princeton University Library.

27. Walter Millis, ed., *The Forrestal Diaries* (New York: Viking, 1951), pp. 451–452.

28. Memorandum by the Chief of the Division of Central European Affairs (Beam), June 28, 1948, in *FRUS, 1948*, Vol. 2, pp. 928–929. This memorandum does not, unfortunately, elaborate on the view expressed about the unofficial proposal which Murphy had reported on June 23 with the comment that he considered it significant because Colonel Vyrianov, who made it, was close to Marshal Sokolovsky. In France, the episode spawned various rumors and speculations. Madame Tabouis, in *France Libre*, offered the opinion that "the French have

rallied to his support with a decision to continue and expand the airlift (Decision 9). In his memoirs, Truman gives the following laconic account of the decision:

> On 26 June, the day after I discussed the Berlin crisis with the Cabinet, I directed that this improvised "air lift" be put on a full-scale organized basis and that every plane available to our European command be impressed into service. In this way we hoped that we might be able to feed Berlin until the diplomatic deadlock could be broken.[29]

Truman made this decision against the advice of some of his closest aides and Cabinet members.[30] He recognized that a time of crisis was a time for firm decision and swift action. Like General Clay in Berlin, "he was prepared to make that decision and to take the necessary action in the teeth of conflicting and, indeed, the contrary opinions of his principal advisers."[31] His decision displayed determination but avoided any appearance of recklessness or bellicosity. If he was not afflicted by the gnawing doubts and fears of his more cautious advisers, neither was he prepared to go all the way with the hawks by sanctioning an armed convoy. As long as the Russians were prepared to continue talks, he did not want any military incidents in Berlin.[32]

Nothing, however, would be more misleading than to represent Truman's airlift decision as the product of compromise between the different courses which he was urged to adopt by opposing groups of advisers. Circumstances conspired to maximize his power. The nature of the crisis called for a swift reaction at the top, while the division of the President's advisers left him relatively free to follow his own personal preferences and convictions. His ability to toler-

---

thought it preferable to negotiate withdrawal from Berlin, in order not to lose face and to obtain compensation for this enormous advantage given to the Russians." General Koenig, she wrote, tried to persuade the Americans to negotiate the withdrawal from Berlin, in exchange for Thuringia and half of Pomerania. General Clay, however, was reported to have opposed this suggestion. See Sir Oliver Harvey (Paris) to the Foreign Office, June 25, 1948, FO 371/40497/C5020, Public Record Office, London.

29. Truman, *Memoirs*, Vol. 2, p. 130.
30. Margaret Truman, *Harry S. Truman* (New York: William Morrow, 1973), p. 12.
31. Jean Edward Smith, *The Defense of Berlin* (Baltimore: Johns Hopkins University Press, 1963), p. 112.
32. Alfred Steinberg, *The Man from Missouri: The Life and Times of Harry S. Truman* (New York: Putnam's, 1962), p. 314.

ate stress exceeded that of the great majority of his subordinates, and the character of his response followed his usual pattern of assuming personal responsibility and making a clear-cut decision on the spot. He made up his mind on the basis of the information he received, without probing for additional information that might illuminate some of the more tangled and obscure facets of the problem. He did not prevaricate or show any inclination to engage in the extensive and prolonged consultations which some of his advisers sought to foist on him. And his choice of the airlift strategy was not preceded by a critical scrutiny of the challenge or a careful search and evaluation of the alternatives available at the time for dealing with this challenge. Having decided on a course of action, he did not concern himself with the details but assumed that his wishes would be carried out.

Truman's airlift decision is a prime example of the assertion of presidential leadership in crisis. The way in which this decision was made does not follow the pattern suggested by the "bureaucratic politics" paradigm developed by Graham Allison and other scholars.[33] This paradigm conceives of the process from which national security decisions emerge as dominated by intra-organizational conflict and by calculations of organizational interest and bureaucratically determined perceptions of American security. This strength and pervasiveness of bureaucratic forces on government decision-making, it is further assumed, places inescapable limitations on the capacity of the Chief Executive to set a consistent course of action and make it stick. In the Berlin case, there certainly were different groups advocating different courses rather than a policy consensus based on a uniform perception of security. But there was no interagency conflict as such, because the alignment of opinion did not correspond to specific agencies but cut across them: the State Department, the Pentagon, and other agencies all had their hawks and their doves. Secondly, and more sig-

33. Graham T. Allison, *Essence of Decision* (Boston: Little, Brown, 1971); Richard E. Neustadt, *Alliance Politics* (New York: Columbia University Press, 1970); Morton Halperin, "Why Bureaucrats Play Games," *Foreign Policy*, No. 2 (Spring 1971); Morton Halperin et al., *Bureaucratic Politics and Foreign Policy* (Washington, D.C.: Brookings Institution, 1974); Graham T. Allison and Morton Halperin, "Bureaucratic Politics: A Paradigm and Some Policy Implications," in *Theory and Policy in International Relations*, ed. Raymond Tanter and Richard H. Ullman (Princeton: Princeton University Press, 1972); and Michael J. Brenner, "Bureaucratic Politics and Foreign Policy," *Armed Forces and Society*, Vol. 2 (1977).

nificantly, the adoption of the airlift was not the result of the process of bureaucratic bargaining and compromise but of a clear-cut choice made by the Chief Executive. Crisis conditions played their part in bringing about this centralized, consistent, and purposive pattern of decision-making which elevated the airlift option to the status of national policy. So did personality factors, inasmuch as Truman's intolerance of bureaucratic politics and the importance he attached to preserving the appearance of national and presidential firmness and resolve predisposed him to act on his own initiative, bypassing the formal organs of government and the normal processes of consultation, deliberation, and search. By asserting his own preferences in this typically incisive fashion, Truman also provided a sense of presidential leadership and direction which countered the tendencies towards fragmentation of authority and policymaking by incremental adjustment which characterize the style of American government in non-crisis situations.[34]

By placing the airlift on an organized and full-scale basis, Truman communicated to the adversary his intention of taking a firm line in the dispute over America's access rights to Berlin as well as protecting America's long-term reputation for resolve. "The Berlin airlift was important," he said some years after the event, "because it proved to the Commies that we weren't fooling about preserving our rights in Central Europe."[35] The essence of the airlift strategy, however, was that it did not force the crisis issue but simply circumvented the blockade. In this way, it shifted back to the Russians the onus for initiating violence. There was thus a certain symmetry in the behavior of the two superpowers during the crisis, based on the exercise of self-restraint and the avoidance of high-risk strategies. Like the blockade, the airlift communicated firm intent while eschewing physical coercion.

By launching the airlift, America did not incur an irrevocable commitment to defend its position in Berlin at all costs; the option of withdrawal at a later stage was not foreclosed. In fact, the airlift was conceived as only a stopgap measure to gain time for resolving the crisis issue by negotiations. Truman's account makes it clear

---

34. The formulation of the airlift decision supports Destler's contention that a centrally designed national security policy is possible under the American system, provided the President has a clear idea of what he wishes to accomplish and the will to assert presidential leadership and direction. See I. M. Destler, *Presidents, Bureaucrats and Foreign Policy* (Princeton: Princeton University Press, 1972).

35. Steinberg, *The Man from Missouri*, p. 314.

that, by reinforcing the airlift, he hoped to be able to feed Berlin until the diplomatic deadlock was broken.[36] Neither he nor anyone else in authority at the time expected the airlift to be able to supply Berlin's essential needs indefinitely. The general view was that the airlift could not be counted upon to maintain the city at more than subsistence level for a limited period, and that it would be of doubtful utility in the winter, when the cold weather would increase the demand for fuel while thick clouds and fog would exacerbate flight conditions.[37] The Russians were even more skeptical about the possibility of supplying Berlin by air, and they did not take the airlift seriously at first.[38] It was not until the full airlift had been in operation for several weeks and had surpassed all the estimates about the amount of supplies that could be transported that the Americans began to recognize its potentialities for defeating the blockade.

36. Truman, *Memoirs*, Vol. 2, p. 130. See also Tunner, *Over the Hump*, p. 159.
37. The view that the airlift could only serve as an emergency measure was prevalent at the time in unofficial as well as official circles. For some press comments, see Max Charles, *Berlin Blockade* (London: Allan Wingate, 1959), p. 48. The same attitude prevailed within the ranks of the airmen who operated the airlift. According to LeMay, "Nobody regarded the enterprise very soberly at first. They kidded about it, called it LeMay's Coal and Feed Company." LeMay, *Mission with LeMay*, p. 416.
38. According to Ambassador Walter Bedell Smith: "Neither Stalin nor Molotov believed that the airlift could supply Berlin. They must have felt sure that cold and hunger, and the depressingly short, gloomy days of the Berlin winter would destroy the morale of the Berlin population and create such a completely unmanageable situation that the Western Allies would have to capitulate and evacuate the city." Walter Bedell Smith, *Moscow Mission, 1946–1949* (London: Heinemann, 1950), p. 244. A British official reported from Moscow that: "The Russians are convinced that they hold all the cards and will be able to manoeuvre us into a position where . . . we have no choice but to withdraw from Berlin. Our current air effort may have disconcerted them. But I doubt whether they believe we can keep it up indefinitely and on a sufficient scale." Harrison (Moscow) to the Foreign Office, July 10, 1948, FO 371/70501/C5521, Public Record Office, London. Howley detected similar skepticism on the part of Soviet officials in Berlin. See Howley, *Berlin Command*, pp. 194–195. Tunner suggested a general and a technical explanation for this skepticism: "Perhaps the failure of the German airlift at Stalingrad was one of the factors in the early Russian reaction to the American-British airlift into Berlin. The Russians had never had an airlift themselves, and they didn't take ours seriously until it was too late. I have another personal opinion on this. The Russians did not understand instrument flying themselves and therefore did not believe that we could maintain the Airlift during the long European winter. . . . I am convinced that the Russian unfamiliarity with instrument flying led them to take our airlift too lightly at the beginning. They did not think we could do it." Tunner, *Over the Hump*, pp. 184–185.

During the first few days of the crisis, the alternative of sending a protest note to Moscow continued to receive some support even after its initial rejection by the President and his advisers on June 25. Murphy added his voice to those who favored a fundamental decision to stay in Berlin followed by coordinated and vigorous diplomatic action by the Allies. He recommended that the French and British Governments be contacted immediately to see if they were willing to join in a protest to the Soviet Government coupled with an indication that the Western powers intended to take the necessary measures to ensure the right of passage. A number of reasons were listed by Murphy for this recommendation. First, retreat from Berlin would amount to a public confession of weakness under pressure—"It would be the Munich of 1948." Second, withdrawal would have political repercussions far beyond the political battle for Berlin itself, implying willingness to withdraw from Vienna and from Western Germany. Third, withdrawal would raise justifiable doubts in the minds of Europeans as to the firmness of America's European policy and her ability to resist the spread of communism. "If we are determined," concluded Murphy, "both in our minds and in our dealings with the U.K. and France, Soviet pressure tactics, no matter how skillful, should not force us out of Berlin."[39]

Britain was approached and her position on Berlin turned out to be staunch and resolute. Bevin told Ambassador Douglas, when they met on June 26, that their policy in Berlin should be one of firmness, for the abandonment of Berlin would have serious, if not disastrous, consequences in Western Germany and throughout Western Europe.[40] Bevin's reaction to the proposal for sending a note of protest to Moscow was that it should be studied promptly in the light of the Warsaw communiqué. His preliminary observation was that a note, if sent, might lead to four-power negotiations and consequent delay in carrying out their program in Western Germany, and that this would adversely affect their interests.[41] Anticipating a long drawn-out struggle, Bevin suggested that the American and French Ambassadors in London should, with Sir William Strang of the British Foreign Office, constitute a committee to

39. Murphy to Marshall, June 26, 1948, in *FRUS, 1948*, Vol. 2, pp. 919–921.
40. Bevin to Sir Oliver Franks (Washington, D.C.), June 26, 1948, FO 371/40497/C5032, Public Record Office, London; and Douglas to Marshall, June 26, 1948, in *FRUS, 1948*, Vol. 2, pp. 921–926.
41. Douglas to Marshall, June 26, 1948, in *FRUS, 1948*, Vol. 2, pp. 921–926.

keep the development of the situation in Berlin under review, so that decisions in Washington, London, Paris, and Berlin might be taken more expeditiously and on the basis of complete information.[42]

Bevin also suggested that the Joint Chiefs of Staff in Washington and the Chiefs of Staff in London should make a joint appreciation of the military situation in connection with the Berlin crisis; that the Military Governors should make a joint survey of the logistical problem of feeding the civilian population of Berlin by air or by other means; and that the Combined Chiefs of Staff should examine the possibility of sending more heavy U.S. bomber planes to Europe to disabuse the Russians of the view that the Allies lacked determination. Douglas discussed the situation with Draper and Wedemeyer, who stopped in London for consultations, and they were unanimous in agreeing on the four suggestions made by Bevin. But they explained to Douglas that the Chiefs of Staff of both countries would require policy guidance on the highest governmental level in order that they might determine the military implications of projected courses of action. And they urged Marshall, through Douglas and Royall by means of a separate message, to see to it that the basic political policy be determined and submitted to the Joint Chiefs of Staff for their military, strategic, and tactical appraisal and to give them appropriate policy guidance for their discussions with their British opposite numbers.[43]

Marshall replied on June 27, saying that the American leaders were in general agreement with British thinking and that they were prepared to continue to maintain their unprovocative but firm stand in Berlin. He expected the basic U.S. policy, including the decision on whether or not to send a note to Moscow, to be settled at a top-level meeting scheduled for the following day. As regards Bevin's suggestions, Marshall agreed that there should be a full and complete exchange of relevant information in London. He also stated that there was a possibility that the U.S. might wish to send two or three B-29 groups to Great Britain, and he asked Douglas to inform Bevin and ask him for clearance.[44]

General Wedemeyer was one of the many high-ranking Ameri-

---

42. Ibid.; and C.M. (48), 46th Conclusions, Minute 1, July 1, 1948, Public Record Office, London.
43. Douglas to Marshall, June 26, 1948, in *FRUS, 1948*, Vol. 2, pp. 921–926; and Draper to Royall, message no. 3, June 27, 1948, RG 335, National Archives, Washington, D.C.
44. Marshall to Douglas, June 27, 1948, in *FRUS, 1948*, Vol. 2, pp. 926–927.

can soldiers who regarded the situation in Berlin with deep apprehension. As the Director of Plans and Operations in the U.S. Army, he had the duty of scrutinizing every proposal for military action. Clay's proposal for confronting the Russians on the ground by forcing a passage to Berlin from the British zone seemed to him highly risky and without any prospect of success, given the strength of the Soviet Army in Eastern Germany and Poland. "Our forces," wrote Wedemeyer in a letter to the Commander of the Langley Air Force Base, "would have been annihilated."[45] Wedemeyer and Royall, like Army Chief of Staff Omar Bradley, had been infantry officers. Thus, central to their thinking was that Berlin could not be defended in a military showdown between 6,500 Allied troops poised against 18,000 crack Russian troops.[46] In their judgment, an airlift was America's only feasible military course in Berlin, to gain time for the politicians to resolve the crisis by means other than force.

When Draper, Wedemeyer, and the other American officials were taken by Douglas to see Bevin on June 27, the basic political policy which they wanted for guidance had not been settled by the American government. It was the forceful British Foreign Secretary who again took the initiative and gave the lead. Bevin told the American delegation that every effort must be made to build up in the shortest possible time an Anglo-American force which could lift at least 2,000 tons a day. Draper replied that the Americans hoped to be able to put in about 1,000 tons a day. Bevin said that this was not enough and that he was convinced that the Americans, with their great resources, could do better than this. Quite apart from the practical task of feeding the inhabitants of Berlin, there would be immense psychological value, he said, in showing not only the Germans but other countries of Western Europe and, of course, the Soviet Union and its satellites what air power could do. Draper

---

45. Quoted here from Mark Arnold-Forster, *The Siege of Berlin* (London: Collins, 1979), pp. 50–51. Bedell Smith, a former soldier, argued in message after message from Moscow against Clay's convoy proposal. See Oral History Interview with Elbridge Durbrow, May 31, 1973, p. 91, Harry S. Truman Library. Even Colonel Howley did not think that a convoy would have reached Berlin. After completing his tour of duty in Berlin, he was asked by Royall: "What would have happened if we had brought an armored convoy into Berlin when the blockade started last June?" Howley records that he gave a straight answer: "We would have had our *derrières* shot off—except," he adds, "I have never been known to use the word *derrière*." Howley, *Berlin Command*, pp. 235–236.

46. Collier, *Bridge Across the Sky*, p. 19.

and Wedemeyer reacted very favorably to this, and Wedemeyer said that they soon ought to be able to do at least as well as they had done in supplying China over the hump. They also said that they would go into the whole question with General Clay, and that they would do their best to meet the Foreign Secretary's recommendations.[47]

In Berlin, Clay began to appreciate the full extent and value of Britain's moral and material support. General Robertson came to see him on June 27 to inform him that his government was determined to stay in Berlin and to make every effort to prevent suffering among the civilian population as long as possible while ways and means were being considered by the governments to break the blockade. The British agreed to furnish all possible support to expand the airlift, and they further believed that, prior to negotiations at the governmental level, this increased airlift should be put into effect and be working effectively. From this heartening report, Clay concluded that the British Government shared the American view that their departure from Berlin would make difficult, if not impossible, the accomplishment of their common objectives in Western Europe. For a sustained effort to feed the city, Clay could use seventy C-47s (which the British called Dakotas). The British could probably provide another fifty. If so, Clay and Robertson reckoned that at least fifty more would be required to achieve the maximum effort capable of being handled at their two airports in Berlin. In Robertson's presence, Clay drafted an urgent message to Draper, asking for the immediate dispatch of fifty additional U.S. transport aircraft. With this aircraft, wrote Clay, they should be abe to bring in 600 or 700 tons a day, which, while falling below the normal food requirements of 2,000 tons a day, would substantially increase the morale of the German people and seriously disturb the Soviet blockade.

The two Military Governors also discussed the possibility of increasing their military resources in Western Europe. This, too, wrote Clay in the same telegram to Draper, was urgent. In Clay's view, the Russians were bluffing and their hand should be called. They were definitely afraid, he said, of America's air might. More-

---

47. Minute by Frank Roberts, June 29, 1948, FO 371/70499/C5215; Cabinet Committee of Ministers on Germany, Minutes of a meeting held on June 28, 1948, copy in FO 371/70498/C5136, Public Record Office, London. See also Oral History Interview with General William H. Draper, Jr., January 11, 1972, p. 265, Harry S. Truman Library.

over, the arrival of aircraft would be a decisive factor in sustaining Allied firmness. He therefore urged as strongly as possible that the movement of the fighter group scheduled to take place in August be made immediately; that the squadron of B-29s maintained in Germany be enlarged to a group; and that, if available, an additional group be dispatched to the British Isles for a prolonged visit. If these actions were to be effective, Clay concluded, speed in decisions and in the dispatch of aircraft was essential.[48]

Draper himself had stopped in Paris en route to Berlin and was relieved to discover there that the French Government was ready to proceed promptly with the implementation of the London Program, and that none of the top French politicians he talked to even raised the possibility of withdrawing from Berlin.[49] Following the consultations held in London and Paris, he cabled to Royall his own detailed analysis of the Berlin crisis, in which the principal strategic options available to the U.S. were examined in some depth for the first time. The British, French, and American staffs, Draper observed, were united in their estimate that the Russians did not want war, and that Soviet pressure to get them out of Berlin would probably not go to the extent of precipitating war. From this estimate it followed that a determined stand—either in the form of a strong note of protest, including the intention of opening the road by force, or other similar measures—should cause the removal or easing of the current restrictions. It was possible, however, that the Russians might consider that their prestige had become sufficiently engaged to require them to continue the restrictions and resist American forces trying to convoy supplies. Another alternative was to stay in Berlin and do everything possible to get the restrictions lifted short of using armed force to open transportation routes. This, thought Draper, would probably be unsuccess-

48. Robertson to the Foreign Office, June 27, 1948, FO 371/40496/C5010, Public Record Office, London; and *Clay Papers*, Vol. 2, pp. 707–708. A chance meeting with Sokolovsky on June 18 strengthened Clay's conviction that the Russians were only saber rattling but afraid of a confrontation and possibly looking for a way out. Sokolovsky was detained for an hour after being arrested for speeding through the American sector and after he believed he had identified himself. Clay called on him to express his personal regrets. He gained the distinct impression that Sokolovsky was set on his course but by no means happy or confident. He also gained the impression that Sokolovsky had hoped that Clay was bringing some proposal with him and was disappointed when no proposal was made. See Clay to Royall, June 28, 1948, in *Clay Papers*, Vol. 2, pp. 709–710.

49. Draper to Royall, message no. 1, June 27, 1948, RG 335, National Archives, Washington, D.C.

ful, forcing the Western powers to stay in Berlin under humiliating conditions, with the Germans in their sectors left to starve, and with light, power, water, and sewerage either short or nonexistent. The third alternative was to pack up and go. But in view of the repeated U.S. and British statements that they would stay in Berlin, their withdrawal under any circumstances short of force was bound to have a shocking effect upon the nations of Western Europe and for the prospects of a Western German government in Frankfurt. A fourth course of action consisted of gaining time by evacuating Berlin—and, if necessary, Vienna and Trieste—to consolidate the American position in Western Germany, in the hope that within a year or two a combination of economic help and Western military strength would restore the balance of power and improve the chances either of preventing war or of holding Europe in the event of war. The weakness of this course, argued Draper, was that if the Russians were to conclude that time was working against them, they could pick their own timing regardless of the Berlin outcome, and in the meantime America might lose the moral support of her potential allies. Draper's own conclusion was that the Russians were probing for a weak spot and trying to force the Western powers out of Berlin without bringing on war, and that a determined stand, even though it risked a conflict, would put them in less jeopardy than to withdraw from Berlin after telling the world they would remain. If the Russians had decided on war, which he doubted, American departure from Berlin would not prevent it. If they did not want war, a firm stand in Berlin should not bring it on. Since this analysis, which was very similar to Clay's, was offered before he reached Berlin, Draper added that he might wish to amplify or revise it after discussions there. General Wedemeyer reserved his judgment until after he had had the benefit of briefings and consultations in Berlin.[50]

The impression that Wedemeyer was disinclined to favor a determined stand on the ground in Berlin is supported by the fact that he basically agreed with a staff study prepared by the Plans and Operations Division, which he headed, although he wished to discuss it with Clay before recommending final action. This study maintained that the Western powers had a sound juridical and moral right to stay in Berlin; that they must act together but not

50. Draper to Royall, message no. 2, June 27, 1948, RG 335, National Archives, Washington, D.C.

initiate the use of force; and that unless the Soviets had already decided to resort to war for overall policy reasons, they would not attack the forces of the Western powers in Berlin. But it also noted that there were no retaliatory measures outside Germany which would be effective in that situation; that the Western powers could supply their Berlin garrisons by air but not the German civilian population with adequate food and coal; and that the Soviets had the physical capacity to make the position of the Western powers in Berlin increasingly difficult and eventually untenable because of the effects of Soviet action on the German population. The study concluded that the Western nations must remain in Berlin as long as their presence there served their interests in Germany and elsewhere in Europe. "If however the situation so develops that the sufferings imposed on the German people by Soviet action are so severe that they no longer warrant, on humanitarian grounds, the assertion of the right to remain, then the U.S. in concert with the U.K. and France should consider whether this factor overrides the major political and prestige reverse involved in withdrawal in the face of Soviet pressure." In other words, while the Army planners were against immediate withdrawal, they were reluctant to foreclose the option of withdrawal, because the long-term prospects of the Western powers in Berlin struck them as being exceedingly bleak.[51]

Washington did not directly confront the task of making a strategic choice in response to the blockade until Sunday, June 27, when an emergency meeting was convened in Royall's office at the Pentagon. The meeting was attended by Royall, Forrestal, Lovett, Navy Secretary Sullivan, Army Chief of Staff Bradley, Assistant Chief of Air Staff Norstad, and a number of other State and Defense officers. The discussion proceeded on the assumption that with existing food stocks, plus supplies which might be brought in by air, serious food shortages would not occur for approximately thirty days, and the German population could be fed for sixty or more days if dried foods were introduced. Three possible courses of action were discussed: (1) to decide to withdraw from Berlin at some appropriate time; (2) to decide to defend the U.S. position in Berlin by all possible means, including supplying Berlin by convoy or using force in some other manner; and (3) to maintain the un-

---

51. "U.S. Position Regarding the Continued Occupation of Berlin," June 26, 1948, P&O 381 ("Hot File"), RG 319, National Archives, Washington, D.C.

provocative but firm stand in Berlin by every local means and later diplomatic means while postponing the ultimate decision.[52]

Royall felt that a decision on America's ultimate position should not be deferred, since her actions in the immediate future ought to be patterned in the light of this decision. Those who favored the first course drew attention both to the difficulty of remaining in Berlin under the stress of recurring crises and frequent humiliation, and to the risk of war through efforts to supply Berlin by force. Advocates of the second course drew attention to the effect of withdrawal from Berlin on the U.S. position in Europe, on the spread of communism, and on the success of the European Recovery Program. There was also a preliminary discussion of the various steps that might be taken in the event of either the first or the second courses being chosen. Consideration was also given to the questions of whether two B-29 bomber squadrons should be sent to Germany, and whether it would be advisable to base two B-29 groups in Britain.

Although agreement on any one course of action proved impossible, the following definite conclusions were reached at the meeting: (1) the State Department should prepare a currency paper for transmittal to Clay for use by him as a basis for resuming discussions with Sokolovsky; (2) Forrestal, Royall, and Lovett should meet with the President the next morning and present the major issues involved for his decision, and the Army and the Department of State should prepare a short statement of the possible alternative courses of action and the arguments for and against each; (3) Clay's reaction should be obtained on the question of sending two additional B-29 squadrons to Germany; (4) Douglas should be informed that there was no particular merit in Combined Chiefs of Staff discussions; and (5) Douglas should be asked to explore the possibility of basing two B-29 groups in England.[53]

Forrestal's account of the Pentagon meeting strikingly illuminates the impact of crisis conditions on American decision-making. The meeting bore all the hallmarks of an ad hoc and improvised affair, ignoring established procedures and cutting across the formal lines of communication in the command system. The picture of bureaucratic muddle prompted Walter Millis, the editor of the *Forrestal Diaries*, to pose some highly pertinent questions:

52. Millis, *Forrestal Diaries*, pp. 452–454.   53. Ibid.

Where ... was all the elaborate machinery which had been set up to deal with just such situations—the CIA, which was supposed to foresee and report the approach of crisis; the National Security Council, which was supposed to establish the governing policy; the War Council, which was supposed to transmit the policy to the military so that they should have their plans set up to meet the requirements?

The Berlin crisis had been long in the making; but when finally it broke, the response was this *ad hoc* meeting at 4:00 p.m. on a Sunday afternoon in the Pentagon, which by-passed the formal machinery of the Security Act to take large (if rather vague) politico-strategic decisions—incidentally overlooking in doing so the potentialities of the airlift, which was actually to be decisive. Its findings, at all events, went direct to the President, at 12:30 next day.[54]

By the time Royall, Forrestal, and Lovett arrived for the meeting at the White House on June 28, their subordinates in the Army and State Departments had produced a comprehensive paper which carefully presented the pros and cons of the three courses of action which had served as the basis for the preliminary meeting at the Pentagon.[55] Lovett recounted the details of Sunday's discussions to the President. When he reached the question of America's future policy in Germany, namely, were they to stay in Berlin or not, Truman interrupted, according to Forrestal's account, to say that "there was no discussion on that point, we were going to stay, period." Royall was concerned that they might not have fully thought through the consequences of this course of action in the event of continued Russian pressure to the point where they would face the bald fact of having to fight their way into Berlin. He pointed out further that even if they sent a note to Moscow, clearly demonstrating their right to remain in Berlin on the basis of past promises by the Soviets, they might then be subjected to greater loss of face because the more persuasive the case they made to their own public and abroad, the greater the humiliation which a subsequent withdrawal would incur. The President's rejoinder,

---

54. Ibid., p. 454. On the bypassing of the elaborate bureaucratic machinery and the resort to small ad hoc groups, see also Raymond Tanter, *Modelling and Managing International Conflicts: The Berlin Crises* (Beverly Hills, Calif.: Sage, 1974), p. 52.

55. "State-National Defense Meeting of 27 June 1948 Held for the Purpose of Determining the U.S. Position Regarding the Continued Occupation of Berlin," P&O 381 ("Hot File"), RG 319, National Archives, Washington, D.C.

again as recorded by Forrestal, was that they "would have to deal with the situation as it developed; that he did not think there could be a black and white decision now other than that we were in Berlin by terms of an agreement and that the Russians had no right to get us out by either direct or indirect pressure."[56]

Truman's statement in the course of the meeting constituted the first authoritative ruling in favor of staying in Berlin (Decision 10). It represented a clear choice, by the Chief Executive, of one course of action from a range of perceived alternatives, and it was this strategic choice which was to guide U.S. behavior during all the subsequent phases of the Berlin crisis. Yet, Truman's decision, at the time it was made, was not as final and irreversible as it is generally supposed to have been, inasmuch as the possibility of making changes at a later stage was deliberately kept open. This tentative character of the decision, which does not detract from its importance, emerges fairly clearly from Royall's account of the meeting. "Both the State version and the Army version of the three alternatives relative to the Berlin situation discussed at the meeting in my office yesterday were presented to the President," Royall recorded for the guidance of his department. "After a general discussion the President indicated his tentative approval of staying in Berlin at all costs and of determining his actions with this in mind. However, he stated that this was not a final decision and he wished to review the two papers and discuss it further with us, probably tomorrow."[57] There was evidently some inconsistency in insisting, on the one hand, on staying in Berlin at all costs, and, on the other, reserving the right to review the position. The most likely explanation is that Truman reacted impulsively and struck a characteristically blunt posture when all eyes were turned to him for leadership, but then settled down, partly under the influence of Royall's cautionary words, to a more realistic appraisal of the options. Further reflection did not lead him to completely abandon his initial choice, the "spot decision" in his terms, but it did help him to qualify it in a manner which, without ducking the issue, left greater flexibility for future action. Another revealing aspect of Truman's conduct is that he used an ad hoc forum rather than the

56. James V. Forrestal Diaries, June 28, 1948, p. 2340, Princeton University Library.
57. Memorandum for the Chief of Staff from Kenneth C. Royall, June 28, 1948, copy in ibid., p. 2328.

institutional machinery which he himself had helped to establish under the 1947 Security Act for the purpose of formulating national policy.[58] The core of the policy which emerged out of this process owed more to Truman's basic world-view and strong instincts, which told him that there must be no surrender to a nation which flouted all the conventions of civilized international behavior, than it did to the advice of his military experts. Rather than waiting for the recommendations of his experts, he made up his own mind that Berlin must be held at all costs, and he expected the experts to come around to his way of thinking.

Apart from the pivotal decision to stay in Berlin, further discussion took place at the White House meeting on Clay's proposal for a meeting with Sokolovsky and on the deployment of U.S. bombers in Europe. Lovett approved of sending a telegram to Clay relating to his proposed offer of compromise on the Berlin currency issue, and he also approved of sending two squadrons of B-29s to Germany. He announced casually that he assumed that the other two groups of B-29s would go to England as soon as clearance was obtained from the British and would not be diverted to Germany unless there was to be a later decision to that effect. Forrestal agreed with both decisions. Truman expressed no opinion on the currency question, but approved of sending the B-29s to Germany.[59]

Royall promptly informed Clay that his currency proposal had been approved at the highest level and that he was now authorized to arrange a local meeting with Sokolovsky, in concert with Robertson and, if possible, the French, to sift out the currency question in order to reveal whether this was in any way the real issue or, as seemed more likely, just a phase in a major Soviet effort to drive the Western powers out of Berlin. Clay was also given a copy of a message from the State Department to Murphy, and was asked to bring it to the attention of Draper and Wedemeyer for their information and guidance. The message stated that, after preliminary State/National Defense discussions with the President, the following was the top-level Departmental policy that would be recommended for Cabinet approval:

58. On this aspect, see Richard F. Haynes, *The Awesome Power: Harry S. Truman as Commander in Chief* (Baton Rouge: Louisiana State University Press, 1973), pp. 140–141.
59. Memorandum for the Chief of Staff from Kenneth C. Royall, June 28, 1948, copy in James V. Forrestal Diaries, p. 2328, Princeton University Library; and Marshall to Douglas, June 28, 1948, in *FRUS, 1948*, Vol. 2, p. 930.

DECISION FLOW 223

1. We [will] stay in Berlin.
2. We will utilize to the utmost [the] present propaganda advantage [of] our position.
3. We will supply the city by air as a beleaguered garrison.
4. Subject to final checking by the Secretary and the President we will further increase U.S. strength in Europe.[60]

The decision on the deployment of the big bombers was simultaneously passed down through another military channel. One B-29 squadron of the 301st Bombardment Group was on a rotational tour of duty at Fürstenfeldbruch Air Base in Germany. The Strategic Air Command now ordered the 301st Group's other two B-29 squadrons to move to Goose Bay, Labrador, in preparation for movement to Germany. Two additional B-29 Groups, the 28th and 307th, were placed on alert and ordered to be ready to take off within three hours after notice, while the rest of the Strategic Air Command force was placed on a 24-hour alert.[61]

These energetic preparations did not still the doubts of the Army planners about the wisdom of the commitment to stay in Berlin at all costs. Doubt had already been expressed in the staff paper of June 26, but, two days later, after consultations with General Bradley, the Deputy Director of Plans and Operations submitted a new paper which went a step further in assuming that U.S. withdrawal from Berlin was ultimately inevitable. A decision had to be made, it was argued, whether the U.S. was willing to fight to stay in Berlin. If the decision was affirmative, then full-scale preparation for possible war should be undertaken at once. If the decision was negative—and this, for a variety of reasons, appeared to be the only logical choice—then it was recommended that the U.S. maintain a firm stand in the present crisis but let future developments determine whether to withdraw, and, if so, under what conditions. Having made the decision to stand firm in the present crisis but to avoid provoking a war, the Army recommended that a series of actions should be planned at once to cover the long-

60. Royall to Clay, June 28, 1948, in *FRUS, 1948*, Vol. 2, pp. 929–930; Marshall to Douglas, June 28, 1948, in *FRUS, 1948*, Vol. 2, pp. 930–931; and Bradley to Clay, June 28, 1948, RG 335, National Archives, Washington, D.C.
61. Memorandum for the Record by Lt. Col. Lemley, June 29, 1948, P&O 381 ("Hot File"), RG 319; Bradley to U.S. Military Attaché in London (for Draper and Wedemeyer), June 27, 1948, RG 335, National Archives, Washington, D.C.; and Strategic Air Command, *The Development of Strategic Air Command, 1946–1973* (Offutt Air Force Base, Nebraska: Headquarters of Strategic Air Command, 1974), p. 11.

term situation, including provision for ultimate withdrawal. Thus, while not recommending a commitment to withdrawal, the Army thought it necessary to plan for the conditions under which the U.S. could withdraw without the disastrous effects inherent in a precipitate withdrawal in the face of the current Soviet pressure.[62]

Admiral of the Fleet William D. Leahy, Truman's Chief of Staff and a renowned hard-liner on all matters concerning Russia, was also gloomy about his country's prospects in the current crisis. He regarded the airlift as both insufficient and risky because it was liable to bring about a "dangerous incident" resulting from a Soviet attack on air transports.[63] "American military situation is hopeless," he recorded in his diary, "because sufficient force is not available anywhere for us and we have no information to indicate that the U.S.S.R. is suffering from internal weakness. It would be advantageous to the United States prospects to withdraw from Berlin, but very bad for those Germans who joined us in good faith to reconstruct the economy of Western Germany." Leahy also thought that the Joint Chiefs of Staff were not being given access to the latest reports from Berlin and that the President was not being kept fully informed.[64]

The Berlin problem had not in fact been referred to the Joint Chiefs of Staff until the British renewed the request, originally made by Bevin, for joint military planning.[65] When Leahy consulted the President on June 29, he was told that there was no change in the U.S. national policy towards Berlin. Truman approved of a meeting with the British representatives at which the Joint Chiefs would inform them that the President desired to remain in Berlin as long as possible but that they themselves were not authorized to make any commitments (Decision 11).[66] Phrased in this way, Truman's instructions clearly indicated that the purpose of the meeting would be to exchange views and information rather than to make policy, but even this restricted mandate went beyond the consensus of the Pentagon meeting two days earlier,

62. Memorandum for the Chief of Staff from Major General Ray T. Maddocks: "Notes on the Berlin Blockade (Army View)," June 28, 1948, P&O 381 ("Hot File"), RG 319, National Archives, Washington, D.C.
63. William Leahy Diary, June 28, 1948, p. 39, Library of Congress.
64. Ibid., p. 40.
65. Captain R. D. Coleridge to General Gruenther, June 29, 1948, Leahy File, Folder No. 33, RG 218, Records of the Joint Chiefs of Staff, National Archives, Washington, D.C.
66. William Leahy Diary, June 29, 1948, p. 40, Library of Congress.

which saw no particular merit in reviving the Anglo-American military policy and planning institution which had served the two countries during the Second World War.

As a follow-up to Truman's decision, Secretary Forrestal consulted with the Joint Chiefs of Staff in his office in the Pentagon about the military situation created by the blockade imposed on the American sector of Berlin by Soviet action. Forrestal and Royall, according to Leahy's account, "seemed to be unnecessarily concerned about future prospects." Since Leahy himself was greatly concerned about the Berlin situation, it is difficult to see why the concern displayed by the Secretary of Defense and the Secretary of the Army seemed to him to be unwarranted. But fortunately the uncertainty which surrounds the decision does not extend to the outcome of this meeting: "It was decided that no positive action should be taken by the U.S. Military until the possibilities of relief by diplomatic action are exhausted by the State Department."[67] Truman's instructions that the Joint Chiefs of Staff should refrain from making commitments in their upcoming talks with the British were thus reinforced by Forrestal and Royall in an effort to keep the road completely clear for diplomatic action.

Fleet Admiral Leahy, General Bradley, Admiral Denfeld, General Vandenberg, and Rear Admiral Glover met with the representatives of the British Chiefs of Staff in Washington on June 30. Admiral Moore, head of the British delegation, said that his government regarded the matter of remaining in Berlin as vitally important, and that this battle was one which they could ill afford to lose. Leahy responded to this by saying that the President also felt that it was very necessary for the Western powers to remain in Berlin. An exchange of information on air transport capability revealed that the Royal Air Force and the U.S. Air Force together could deliver 2,000 tons per day at the present level of operations, and that the RAF alone could not fly more than 750 tons. In their opposition to any attempt to fight through to Berlin on the ground, the military chiefs of both countries found themselves in agreement. Leahy pointed out in this regard that the U.S., either on its own or combined with Britain, would not have sufficient strength to fight convoys through, and that the Joint Chiefs of Staff considered this proposal impracticable. Admiral Moore revealed that orders had been issued to General Robertson to reconnoiter the British zone

67. Ibid., June 30, 1948.

for additional troop locations to impress the Russians that they meant business, and he asked if a similar directive could be issued to General Clay. Admiral Leahy and General Bradley ruled out such a move on the ground that the Russians would recognize it as a bluff, since they knew that the U.S. had no more troops to send. The British Government, reported Admiral Moore, had authorized the shooting down of any balloons that might be put up by the Russians in the air corridors to Berlin, and he wanted to elicit the American view on this matter. It turned out that the Joint Chiefs of Staff had no evidence to suggest that the Russians would attempt to block the passage of their planes in the air corridors, and the balloon problem appeared to them to be exaggerated. They thought that in the event of a Russian attempt to obstruct passage with balloons, the U.S. Government would probably wish to exchange notes with the Soviet Government, and thereafter the decision might or might not be to shoot the balloons down.[68] All in all, the meeting did not add substantially to the airlift and bomber-deployment moves already in progress, but it did serve a useful purpose in apprising each side of the plans and intentions of the other. It also revealed that on practically every military measure under consideration to hold the Western position in Berlin, the attitude of the Joint Chiefs of Staff was more cautious and more circumspect than that of their British counterparts.

With the guns remaining silent, the politicians moved to the center of the stage to wage the war of words and the war of nerves that was steadily gaining momentum. In a sustained political offensive to boost morale on their side and to demoralize their opponents, leading Western politicians publicly affirmed their common resolution not to budge. On June 30, a defiant Bevin announced to a packed and cheering House of Commons the British Government's decision to maintain its position in Berlin and to place all its resources at the disposal of the common effort to supply the city. "We recognize," he said, "that as a result of these decisions a grave situation might arise. Should such a situation arise, we shall ask the House to face it. His Majesty's Government and the Western Allies

68. Memorandum for the Record: "U.S. Chiefs of Staff Meeting with Representatives of the British Chiefs of Staff, held on Wednesday afternoon, 30 June 1948," by Rear Admiral C. D. Glover, Leahy File, Folder No. 33, RG 218, National Archives, Washington, D.C.; and Kenneth W. Condit, *The History of the Joint Chiefs of Staff*, Vol. 2: *1947–1949* (Washington, D.C.: Historical Division, Joint Secretariat, Joint Chiefs of Staff, RG 218, National Archives, 1976), pp. 136–137.

can see no alternative between that and surrender, and none of us can accept surrender."[69] His Majesty's Loyal Opposition pledged its fullest support. Drawing back was unthinkable, proclaimed Sir Anthony Eden in a robust speech, for the effect of doing that on Britain's authority and on the authority of the Western Allies in Europe would be catastrophic. "If ever there was a time to stand firm," he declared, "it is now: if ever there was a cause in which to stand firm it is this."[70]

In Washington, on the very same day, and partly in response to persistent British prodding,[71] Marshall issued a firm declaration of his government's intention to remain in Berlin:

> We are in Berlin as a result of agreements between the Governments on the areas of occupation in Germany and we intend to stay. The Soviet attempt to blockade the German civilian population of Berlin raises basic questions of serious import with which we intend to deal promptly. Meanwhile, maximum use of air transport will be made to supply the civilian population. It has been found, after study, that the tonnage of foodstuffs and supplies which can be lifted by air is greater than had at first been assumed.[72]

President Truman confirmed that, after conferring with the President, Marshall had expressed the official position of the United States Government.[73]

PHASE II: JULY 1–15

The diplomatic efforts to have the siege of Berlin lifted took the form of a direct protest to Moscow at the governmental level. At a Cabinet meeting on July 2, Marshall read a copy of a message which the State Department had drawn up and proposed to send to

69. *Hansard*, House of Commons Debates (London), June 30, 1948, Vol. 452, cols. 2221–34.
70. Ibid., Vol. 452, cols. 2213–18.
71. The announcement, at the end of a week of official silence, was probably made at the request of the British Government. This is suggested by the following extract from the minutes of a Cabinet meeting held on June 28, 1948: "In view of suggestions issued by the Soviet-controlled press in Berlin, the Foreign Office had issued a statement over the weekend confirming the Government's intention to maintain their position in Berlin and the United States were being asked to make a similar statement." C.M. (48) 44th Conclusions, Minute 4, Public Record Office, London.
72. *Department of State Bulletin*, July 4, 1948, p. 54.
73. *Public Papers of the Presidents of the United States: Harry S. Truman, 1948* (Washington, D.C.: U.S. Government Printing Office, 1964), pp. 391–394.

Stalin. It recited both the legal and the moral justifications for the Western Allies to remain in Berlin and reaffirmed their determination to stay there. Because of the differing legal positions of the three Allies, it was not possible to send a joint note to Russia signed by all three, but the British and French agreed to their notes being very similar in general statement and underlying policy. The French and British also agreed that a meeting of the Council of Foreign Ministers was not desirable at that time because it would probably only lead to protracted discussions with the same sterile results as had been achieved at previous meetings of these personalities. With reference to the dispatch of the notes to the Soviet Government by the three Allies, the British had expressed a preference for delay until General Robertson had an opportunity to make a formal reply to Sokolovsky's note of June 29—a note which was conciliatory in tone but made no specific promise to lift the transport restrictions. The State Department, on the other hand, took the view that it was all right for Robertson to go and discuss Sokolovsky's message orally, but that he should put nothing in writing.

Marshall also reported the plans for increasing the B-29 strength in Germany from one squadron to one group. The British had been asked, he added, whether they would like to have two additional B-29 groups proceed to Britain, and Bevin had replied in the affirmative. Marshall himself now had to weigh the effect on the Russians of the implications and inferences to be derived from sending these groups to Britain. He said that the effect on the Russians had to be balanced against the appearance of what might be construed by the American people as a provocative action.[74]

Forrestal's diary does not further explain the "implications" that Marshall had in mind. But as the editor of the diaries points out, some of these may be readily guessed: "The B-29s were known throughout the world as the atomic bombers, and to put a strong force of them into British bases would be to bring them within striking distance of Moscow. The sudden exigency of the Berlin affair was, throughout the ensuing weeks, to compel much serious reappraisal of the bomb and of its real place in American policy and strategy."[75] The issues actually involved were many, serious, and interlocking.

74. James V. Forrestal Diaries, July 2, 1948, pp. 2345–46, Princeton University Library.
75. Millis, *The Forrestal Diaries*, p. 456.

Growing awareness of the relevance of America's air power to the Berlin problem boosted the confidence of the American decision-makers and relaxed the pressure for any exploratory or accommodating moves on the diplomatic front which could be interpreted as a sign of weakness. Clay began to have second thoughts about the planned meeting with Sokolovsky. In a teleconference with Forrestal, Royall, and Bradley on July 2, he presented his arguments against holding the meeting with Sokolovsky. Royall explained that the government was not firmly committed to the oral conference. What it had in mind was that the three Military Governors would ask Sokolovsky if his letter to Robertson meant that the blockade was to be lifted, and, if so, when. If his reply was evasive, they would immediately send a formal note of protest. If he specified that the blockade would be lifted within a day or two, then they would hold the note. The point of having it ready was to avoid delay, whatever the outcome of the face-to-face meeting. The decision-makers in Washington did not contemplate discussion of trade agreements or the currency question, although they did authorize it if Clay thought it essential. The final decision was left in Clay's hands, and with some reluctance he agreed to arrange a limited-purpose visit with Sokolovsky for the following day.[76]

The three Western Military Governors went to see Sokolovsky at his headquarters near Potsdam on July 3. Clay and then Robertson underlined the seriousness of the situation and urged the resumption of traffic. Sokolovsky stated in his opening remarks that this question was important to them and they wanted it treated alone, whereas there were other questions that were important to him. He claimed that he had never said that traffic on the railway was held up for other than technical reasons, and that these technical reasons still applied, although he could not foretell what further developments might be. He explained at length that the economic disorders created in the Soviet zone by the London conference made it impossible to provide alternative routes. This statement was of considerable significance because, for the first time, it related the Berlin question to the London conference as a whole, with no mention whatever of the currency problem. Sokolovsky made it clear that he was not prepared to answer any questions on the resumption of traffic unless the results of the London confer-

76. *Clay Papers*, Vol. 2, pp. 719–722; and Clay, *Decision in Germany*, p. 367.

ence were also discussed. Clay stated that no further discussion appeared useful and thanked Sokolovsky for the meeting.[77]

The British and French generals returned with Clay to his office, where they prepared a joint report to their governments. They thought this would be helpful because their governments were finding it difficult to agree on the next step. After recounting the abortive meeting, they gave it as their shared view that Sokolovsky was under instructions which permitted him no latitude in negotiating the transport problem unless there was a complete discussion of the German problem. They pointed out that he deliberately related the Berlin situation to the London conference. From this the three Military Governors concluded that the Soviet Government at that time had no intention of settling the Berlin problem except as part of the settlement of the German problem. They therefore advised that further negotiations by them in Berlin would serve no useful purpose.[78]

The conference confirmed the opinion of the heads of the Army and State Departments as to the real motives and purpose of the blockade.[79] It was also clear from the report of the Military Governors that the matter should be taken up at a higher level. Yet, the basic constraint of eschewing negotiations on Russia's terms remained in force and continued to govern America's diplomatic moves just as it had prompted the earlier rejection of the Warsaw offer. Following the failure to find a solution at the local level, Marshall promptly decided on July 3 to proceed with the preparation of a formal note of protest to the Soviet Government (Decision 12). A draft note had already been sent on June 30 for comment and approval by the British and French Governments.[80] It had also been agreed that the note would be sent only if satisfactory assurances could not be obtained from Sokolovsky. Now the joint report of the three Military Governors persuaded Marshall that the Allies must approach the Soviet Government without delay. He strongly urged, therefore, that the text of the note be agreed upon and presented

77. Joint report of the three Military Governors, in *Clay Papers*, Vol. 2, pp. 722–724; and "Translation of the French Verbatim Record of the Meeting between the Commanders-in-Chief of the Western Zones of Germany and the Soviet Commander-in-Chief at the Soviet Headquarters at Babelsberg on 3 July at 5 p.m.," FO 371/70506/C5593, Public Record Office, London.

78. *Clay Papers*, Vol. 2, pp. 722–724.

79. Royall to Clay, July 3, 1948, in *Clay Papers*, Vol. 2, p. 724.

80. For the text, see Marshall to Caffery (U.S. Ambassador in France), June 30, 1948, in *FRUS, 1948*, Vol. 2, pp. 933–936.

simultaneously to the Soviet representatives in London, Paris, and Washington—and as soon as possible, since any delay would only benefit the Soviets. In the light of Sokolovsky's reply, however, he agreed to Bevin's suggestion that the reference to reconvening the Council of Foreign Ministers be deleted from the note. It was clear from this reply, Marshall felt, that the Soviet Government intended to use the Berlin situation to reopen the entire German question, and any meeting of the Council of Foreign Ministers would only invite Soviet agreement to lift the blockade on condition that the Allies suspend the operation of the London Program. This, added Marshall, was out of the question.[81]

On July 6, the three Western powers delivered the almost identical notes to the Soviet ambassadors in Washington, London, and Paris. The notes emphasized that the Allies regarded the Soviet blockade measures as a clear violation of existing agreements concerning the administration of Berlin by the four occupying powers. They declared that the Allies would not be induced by threats, pressures, and other actions to abandon their rights. And they expressed their willingness to enter into four-power negotiations to resolve any disagreements over the Berlin situation, on condition that the restoration of transport facilities precede the opening of discussions.[82]

The State Department prepared a preliminary survey of possible Russian reactions to the Western notes and of the alternatives which the Soviet reply would present. The consensus was that the Allies should not negotiate under duress. But what if the Russians agreed to lift the blockade if the Council of Foreign Ministers were convened to consider the entire German question, including the actions of the Western powers determined by the London tripartite conference? This possibility troubled Marshall: acceptance would cast uncertainty on the plans for a West German Government; rejection would imply refusal to negotiate. No definite decision regarding future policy was taken at this stage, and General Clay was invited to comment on the State Department's proposed alternatives.[83]

Clay had little hope of a settlement by negotiation and some

81. Marshall to Douglas, July 3, 1948, in ibid., pp. 946–948.
82. For the texts of the three notes, see Great Britain, Cmd. 7534, *Germany: An Account of the Events Leading Up to a Reference of the Berlin Question to the United Nations* (London: His Majesty's Stationery Office, 1948), pp. 47–50.
83. Marshall to Douglas, July 9, 1948, in *FRUS, 1948*, Vol. 2, pp. 954–956.

hope that a prompt American move would break the blockade. The time available for decision was perceived by him to be limited, for if such a move were not made quickly, the U.S. would have to prepare for a long and patient political struggle which could last for months, if not years. The care with which the Russians avoided measures that would have been resisted with force had convinced him that the Soviets did not want war. However, they knew that the Allies also did not want war, and consequently they would continue to apply their pressure just short of the point at which they believed hostilities might occur. In his reply of July 10, Clay reported this conviction to his government, recommending that if the blockade continued not to be lifted for the allegedly technical reasons given by the Russians, then the U.S. should advise the Soviet Government that it proposed to move in an armed convoy on a specific date with the requisite bridge equipment to make the way into Berlin usable. Clay made it clear that he fully understood the risk and its implications and that this was a decision which could only be made by the government. No armed convoy could cross the border without the possibility of trouble. But in his view, the chances were small that such a convoy would be met by force, thus triggering off a war. War, he reasoned, could only result from a fixed Soviet plan, not from Western actions.[84]

Washington's immediate response was to probe for information. Clay was asked to furnish answers to a long list of questions concerning the logistical and operational details of his convoy plan. It was repeatedly stressed, however, that this information was required for further study in the Department of the Army, and that the request in no way signified approval of Clay's recommendation.[85] From the answers furnished by Clay's subordinates, it emerged that his general plan was to dispatch an armed motor convoy from the U.S. zone of Germany to Berlin as a "one-shot" ruse to break the Soviet blockade of the city by road. The convoy was to consist of two hundred trucks escorted by the equivalent of a constabulary regiment reinforced with a recoilless rifle troop and an engineer battalion. The engineer battalion would carry a bridge train and road repair equipment and be ready to clear physical obstacles in the way of march. Clay also suggested that the British

---

84. Clay to Bradley, July 10, 1948, in *Clay Papers*, Vol. 2, pp. 733–735; and Clay, *Decision in Germany*, p. 374.

85. *Clay Papers*, Vol. 2, pp. 735–736.

could provide one infantry battalion and the French a detachment of tank destroyers, presumably to further reinforce the escort.[86]

The Soviet reply to the Western powers, delivered on July 14, gave no encouragement for thinking that a diplomatic solution could be found to the Berlin crisis on terms which would be acceptable to the U.S. Government. It claimed that the difficulties in supplying the population in the three Western sectors had resulted from actions by the U.S., British, and French Governments which were in violation of the Potsdam decisions and the agreement on quadripartite control. Among the actions enumerated were the carrying out of a separate currency reform, the introduction of a special currency for the western sectors of Berlin, and the policy of dismembering Germany. The Soviet note stated further that the agreement concerning the four-power administration of Berlin was an inseparable component of the agreement for the four-power administration of Germany as a whole, and that after the Western powers destroyed the system of four-power administration of Germany and had begun to set up a capital for a separate government in Frankfurt, they "thereby undermined as well the legal basis which assured their right to participation in the administration of Berlin." The note went on to say that, while not objecting to negotiations, the Soviet Government could not accept any preliminary conditions (i.e., the lifting of the blockade) and that it considered that discussions could be effective only if they were not limited to the question of the administration of Berlin, since that question could not be separated from the general question of four-power control of Germany.[87]

Clay observed that the Soviet note shrewdly placed the Western Allies in a position of having to negotiate only at their specific request, and thus permitted the Soviet Government to establish conditions if such a request were made. He inferred from the heavy emphasis on the currency question that the blockade would be lifted temporarily if the Western currency were withdrawn, but he believed that the linking of the Berlin situation to the German

86. Ibid., pp. 736–738.
87. For the text of the Soviet Note to the U.S. Government, see Union of Soviet Socialist Republics, Ministry of Foreign Affairs, *The Soviet Union and the Berlin Question (Documents)*, pp. 42–46; or U.S. Department of State, *The Berlin Crisis: A Report on the Moscow Discussions* (Washington, D.C.: U.S. Government Printing Office, 1948), pp. 8–10. For the text of the identical notes to the British and French Governments, see Great Britain, Cmd. 7534, pp. 50–54.

question indicated quite clearly that the pressures would be resumed when a Western German government was formed. This and the Soviet refusal to lift the blockade before quadripartite negotiations were opened led Clay to the conclusion that America had no other recourse than to throw the matter of the blockade into the International Court of Justice or the United Nations as evidence of her desire for a peaceful settlement. This, he added, would not suffice: "The intransigent Soviet position as indicated in the note should be tested and I see no way in which it can be tested except by proceeding promptly with the movement of the armed convoy as I have recommended previously. I would, therefore, like to recommend that we be given the authority to proceed with this convoy movement as quickly as it can be arranged." Clay also thought it important that the two B-29 groups which were being considered for movement to Britain should be moved at once, since they should be there when the convoy movement was started.[88] Bradley replied that "future courses of action including possibility of using armed convoys are being carefully considered. However, we are not yet prepared to reach a final decision. Decision for such action can obviously be taken only by highest level."[89]

At the highest levels, the consensus was that Moscow was making no effort to compromise, but this did not make the choice of a future course of action any less problematical. The central question, as Admiral Leahy noted, was whether the Western powers had the will and the ability to defend their position by an appeal to arms. From a purely military point of view, it appeared to him advisable for all three Western powers to withdraw their noncombatant citizens from Berlin at once, to reinforce their military person-

---

88. Clay to Bradley, July 15, 1948, in *Clay Papers*, Vol. 2, pp. 739–740. "Clay has only one answer," reported General Robertson, "which is that we must now put things to the test by sending a convoy up the Autobahn heavily escorted. All his staff are talking freely about the same scheme." Robertson to the British Foreign Office, July 16, 1948, FO 371/70502/C5740, Public Record Office, London.

89. Bradley to Clay, July 15, 1948, in *Clay Papers*, Vol. 2, p. 740. While the convoy idea was still under consideration in Washington, preparations by Clay's military staff had reached a very advanced stage and included plans for bombing the Soviet troops manning the blockade and also Soviet airfields in East Germany. See LeMay, *Mission with LeMay*, pp. 411–412; Interview with General Curtis LeMay, pp. 9–10, Dulles Oral History Collection, Princeton University Library; and Lt. Gen. Arthur G. Trudeau, "Aborting of Task Force Trudeau," *The Washington Star*, May 12, 1978.

nel, and to increase their airborne support of the friendly German inhabitants. But he also believed that such actions would be expensive and dangerous from a political point of view and might well precipitate a third world war.[90]

The British Foreign Secretary impressed on the Americans that they should be in no hurry to negotiate, but should instead indicate their position by taking military measures such as stepping up the airlift and deploying the B-29 bombers in Britain. At a meeting with Lovett on July 14, Sir Oliver Franks, the British Ambassador to Washington, relayed Bevin's conviction that the character of the Soviet note in no way lessened the desirability of sending the bombers across the Atlantic, and he reiterated his government's willingness to receive them.[91]

Charles Bohlen, the Counselor of the State Department, went to see the President in the afternoon, at Marshall's request, to bring him up to date on the developments in the Berlin situation. Truman had a copy of the Soviet note, which he read, and said he considered it a total rejection of everything they had asked for. Bohlen told Truman that the State Department was studying the note and that there were several aspects to it, but that his conclusion regarding its substance was the same as the one they had reached. Bohlen outlined to the President the status of the B-29s and told him that the British were eager to have these planes moved to England, but that Marshall thought the matter required further consideration in view of the Soviet note, and it was therefore to be discussed the following day by the National Security Council for recommendation to the President. Truman said he was in complete agreement with this course of action and felt that the question of dispatching the planes should be most carefully considered in the light of the Soviet note.[92]

The proposed course of action had significant diplomatic as well as military aspects, so the National Security Council was the natural forum for developing policy proposals which took both into account. At its meeting on July 15, the Council "agreed, subject to reservations by the Secretary of the Army, that the Secretary

90. William Leahy Diary, July 14, 1948, p. 45, Library of Congress.
91. Memorandum of Conversation, by the Undersecretary of State (Lovett), July 14, 1948, in *FRUS, 1948*, Vol. 2, pp. 965–966.
92. Memorandum by the Counselor of the Department of State (Bohlen) to the Secretary of State, July 14, 1948, in *FRUS, 1948*, Vol. 2, pp. 966–967.

of State and the Secretary of Defense should recommend to the President that the United States proceed with the dispatch of B-29 bombers to the British Isles" (Decision 13). It was also agreed that a public statement concerning this movement would be carefully coordinated between the Department of State and the National Military Establishment. But the Council reserved decision on increasing the airlift to Berlin.[93] Forrestal summarized the considerations affecting the Council's decision to send the B-29s to England: (1) the action would underline to the American people how seriously their government viewed the current sequence of events; (2) it would give the U.S. Air Force experience in this kind of operation and also accustom the British to accommodate the forces of an allied power; and (3) once the planes were sent, they would become somewhat of an accepted fixture, whereas deterioration of the situation in Europe might lead to a condition of mind under which the British would be compelled to reverse their present attitude.[94]

Marshall and Forrestal went on to report these recommendations to the President. Marshall outlined the reasons for and against the dispatch of the B-29s to England as canvased in the National Security Council and reported the conclusion of that body that the planes should be sent. Truman said that he had come independently to the same conclusion. The decision to dispatch the B-29 bombers to England thrust the atomic bomb into the forefront of America's military policy; and Forrestal, who acutely felt the need to formulate a specific policy on the use of the bomb, informally broached the subject of the bomb's custody. Truman remarked that he wanted to go into this matter very carefully, that he proposed to keep the decision to use or not use the bomb in his own hands, and

93. Minutes of the 15th Meeting of the NSC, held on Thursday, July 15, 1948, President's Secretary File, Harry S. Truman Library. It has been suggested that Truman deliberately absented himself from some of the NSC meetings during the Berlin crisis because he recognized that if he hinted too early in the proceedings at the direction of his own thought, the weight of his authority, the loyalty of his advisers, and their desire to be on the winning side might shut off productive debate and inhibit candid discussion. See Theodore C. Sorenson, *Decision-Making in the White House* (New York: Columbia University Press, 1963). In the absence of any concrete evidence to the contrary, this suggestion cannot be dismissed. It seems much more likely, however, that Truman did not attend the meeting on July 15 because he had already been briefed about the issue on the Council's agenda, and, regarding the recommendation to dispatch the B-29s, of which he approved as a foregone conclusion, he saw no need to attend in person.

94. Millis, *The Forrestal Diaries*, p. 457.

that he did not propose "to have some dashing Lieutenant-Colonel decide when would be the proper time to drop one."[95]

That evening, Washington announced that the B-29s would leave the following day for Royal Air Force bases in Britain.[96] Although the flight was officially described as a routine training mission, it was accompanied by a lower-level publicity disclosure that the bombers were atomic-capable, and hints were dropped that they carried nuclear warheads. The sixty bombers sent to East Anglia on this highly publicized flight from Florida and Kansas belonged to the U.S. Strategic Air Command, which had, in 1946, been given delivery responsibility for nuclear weapons. Their arrival led to the establishment of the first U.S. Strategic Air Command base in Great Britain. A comment in a Soviet publication, repeatedly quoted by Churchill with approval, that "the British Isles had now become an aircraft carrier" increased public awareness that Britain had put herself at the forefront of Western defense.[97] But the British Cabinet remained firm and unwavering. Even its most fiery left-winger, Aneurin Bevan, had favored the boldest retort, once the Soviet challenge had been delivered. Believing that no risk of war was involved, he had argued powerfully in the Cabinet in favor of sending a force by land, covered by tanks, as the swiftest way of ending the crisis.[98] When the airlift was chosen instead, the Cabinet was determined to make it a success and agreed to the stationing of the B-29s on British territory without any formalities, conditions, or reservations.

This forward deployment of American air power was doubly significant. In the first place, it furnished America's European allies with a concrete token of her commitment to the defense of Europe. In the second place, and much more importantly, it signaled to the Russians that an attempt to seize West Berlin might provoke bomber raids into the Soviet Union. It was a display of military

95. James V. Forrestal Diaries, July 15, 1948, pp. 2362–63, Princeton University Library. Margaret Truman confirms that her father "had to fend off demands from Secretary of Defense Forrestal to authorize the use of the atomic bomb." *Harry S. Truman*, pp. 34–35.

96. *New York Times*, June 16, 1948.

97. Andrew J. Pierre, *Nuclear Politics: The British Experience with an Independent Strategic Force, 1939–1970* (London: Oxford University Press, 1972), p. 79.

98. Michael Foot, *Aneurin Bevan: A Biography*, Vol. 2: *1945–1960* (London: Davis Poynter, 1973), pp. 229–230. See also D. C. Watt, *Britain Looks to Germany: A Study of British Opinion and Policy Towards Germany Since 1945* (London: Oswald Wolff, 1965), pp. 63–67.

capability which indirectly implied intent. The hitherto implicit threat of nuclear retaliation as an alternative open to America in the event of a Russian attack was now made more conspicuous, if not explicit. Moreover, while the deployment of the bombers, first in Germany and then in England, was conceived as a temporary crisis measure, the crisis itself provided an opportunity for extending the "atomic perimeter" around the borders of the USSR. The ramifications of the decision therefore extended far beyond the particular crisis which occasioned it. In the words of Walter Millis, as they roared off across the Atlantic, the B-29s "were bringing the nuclear weapons for the first time directly into the system of diplomacy and violence by which the affairs of people were henceforth to be regulated."[99]

What Millis and many others did not know was whether the B-29s dispatched to Britain actually carried any atomic bombs, and this uncertainty spawned a good deal of speculation. Air power rattling was a familiar Cold War phenomenon, which took the form of (1) B-29 flights over various European cities as part of air shows or courtesy visits, and (2) stationing B-29s in Germany, some of which had flown into and out of West Berlin before the blockade.[100] But these B-29s were not capable of delivering atomic bombs. Those which could were not deployed outside the continental United States. The dispatch of the two groups of B-29s to Britain in mid-July 1948 was regarded as such a momentous event in the history of the Cold War because it was generally assumed, by contemporary observers as well as later historians, that these were of the modified type and hence constituted the forward movement of an American nuclear striking force. The only question which puzzled historians was whether these nuclear-capable bombers actually carried atomic weapons in their bomb bays or not. Recently, however, it was casually disclosed by official British and American historians that no atomic bombs accompanied the B-29s, and, what is much more surprising, that the bombers themselves were not of the type which could deliver atomic bombs. B-29s of the modified type did not arrive in Britain until the summer of 1949.[101]

99. Walter Millis, *Armies and Men: A Study in American Military History* (London: Jonathan Cape, 1957), p. 323.
100. George H. Quester, *Nuclear Diplomacy: The First Twenty-Five Years* (New York: Dunellen, 1970), pp. 49–50.
101. Margaret Gowing, *Independence and Deterrence: Britain and Atomic Energy, 1945–1952* (London: Macmillan, 1974), Vol. 1, p. 311; and Condit, *The History of the Joint Chiefs of Staff*, p. 139.

The American stockpile of nuclear weapons, consisting of less than fifty bombs, some of which were later discovered to be unusable, was itself in a state of considerable disarray and far from ready for instant use. Actual delivery of these unwieldy A-bombs would have taken the best part of a month, since both the unassembled bombs and the aircraft capable of delivering them would first have to be moved from the United States to bases in England, Okinawa, or North Africa. Nor did the United States have an agreed-upon strategic plan, ready for implementation in an emergency. In an atmosphere of rising international tension, the Joint Chiefs of Staff had been moved to approve, on May 19, the first emergency plan for the postwar world. Code-named "Halfmoon," this plan assumed that war with the Soviet Union was a distinct possibility; that the Soviet Union could initiate the war with concurrent offensives in Europe, the Middle East, and Asia; and that the United States would use atomic weapons in counteroffensive operations against a target list of some twenty Russian cities. The Joint Chiefs of Staff approved "Halfmoon" for planning purposes only. This was done on the advice of Admiral Leahy, who questioned the wisdom of relying so heavily on the atomic bombs at a time when there was no assurance that their use would be authorized.[102]

The decision to transfer the B-29 bombers to England was taken by the Truman Administration before the operational plan for "Halfmoon" had been completed and in advance of formulating a coherent strategy of deterrence. Caught unprepared by a crisis for which its conventional options were severely limited, the Administration was forced to improvise by bringing its nuclear monopoly into the overall military balance, and the bombers-to-England move was the result. There is no evidence to suggest that the intention behind this move was to coerce the Russians into calling off the blockade. Not coercion but deterrence was the vaguely conceived objective of the move: deterring the Russians from escalating in response to the airlift. Part of the difficulty in analyzing this aspect of the Administration's behavior is that at this time it did not operate

---

102. Samuel F. Wells, Jr., "America and the 'Mad' World," *The Wilson Quarterly*, Vol. 1, No. 5 (Autumn 1977), pp. 60–61; David MacIsaac, "The Air Force and Strategic Thought, 1945–1951," Working Paper No. 8, International Security Studies Program (Washington, D.C.: The Wilson Center, 1979); Thomas H. Etzold and John Lewis Gaddis, eds., *Containment: Documents on American Foreign Policy and Strategy, 1945–1950* (New York: Columbia University Press, 1978), pp. 315–323; and Condit, *History of the Joint Chiefs of Staff*, pp. 288–293.

with a clear conceptualization of either deterrence strategy or coercive diplomacy. Its notions of the use of force and threats of force as instruments of diplomacy were undeveloped and opaque.[103]

But notwithstanding all these operational and conceptual problems, the political impact of the forward deployment in the summer of 1948 should not be underestimated, for it is appearances and images rather than reality which constitute deterrence. America's allies certainly perceived the basing of the B-29s within striking range of Russian cities as an indication that she considered her nuclear arsenal as an appropriate instrument of policy.[104] Her adversary, too, may have shared this perception, in which case the move would have had the intended psychological effect. The fact that the Russians refrained from escalating the conflict in Berlin through the adoption of stronger measures such as interference in the air corridors appears to support this conclusion.[105]

PHASE III: JULY 16–19

The tension generated by the Berlin crisis reached a new peak in mid-July. With the Russian rejection of the Western protest, the international situation took a sharp turn for the worse. The Russians raised the stakes by questioning the Western right to be in Berlin at all. By brandishing their strategic air superiority to signal that these rights would not be lightly abandoned, the Americans accentuated public awareness of the danger of a head-on collision. The press freely discussed the danger of war and carried accurate reports of Clay's assessment of the situation and his call for a showdown.

Strong support for Clay's view was given by William ("Wild Bill") Donovan, the wartime head of the Office of Strategic Services, who spoke at a press conference in Berlin on July 17, after

103. I am indebted to Professor Alexander L. George for this point.
104. See, for example, Francis Williams, *A Prime Minister Remembers: The War and Post-War Memoirs of the Rt. Hon. Earl Attlee* (London: Heinemann, 1961), pp. 171–172.
105. On Russian military caution during the crisis and the distinct pattern of waiting to observe Western reaction to an action of theirs before proceeding to take further measures, see, for example, Philip Windsor, *City on Leave: A History of Berlin, 1945–1962* (London: Chatto and Windus, 1963), pp. 98–126; Bernard Brodie, *Escalation and the Nuclear Option* (Princeton: Princeton University Press, 1966), pp. 44–46; and Alexander L. George and Richard Smoke, *Deterrence in American Foreign Policy: Theory and Practice* (New York: Columbia University Press, 1974), pp. 117–125.

talking to senior American officials there. "The place to make a stand against the Russians," he said, "is right here in Berlin. This is not a Cold War. It is hot as hell. The Russian action in Berlin defines the issue." Clay, he declared, had seized the initiative and surprised the Russians by instituting the airlift. But supply by air was not enough, even if it could go on indefinitely. The American Government should support Clay by keeping the initiative and broadening the field of action by applying pressure on the Russians in the Far East and Middle East, "even if it means war."[106] Donovan was not at that time a government official, but his statement was immediately broadcast by radio stations in Berlin and given prominent coverage at home, where public opinion was overwhelmingly on the side of the hawks. During the first few weeks of the blockade, the mood of the American public remained militant and unyielding. When asked whether Americans should force their way through the blockade if that was necessary to carry food and coal to Berlin, 8 percent thought not, 86 percent said yes.[107]

There was a growing feeling that the Allies faced a critical decision. "Of all the crises that have racked the nerves of the world and boiled up the war clouds since V-J Day," observed the *New York Herald Tribune*, "only the showdown at Berlin has produced in official Washington so obvious an attitude that this is an hour of the gravest decision. On all sides it seems generally agreed that the Western powers stand today in Berlin at essentially the same crossroads that intersected in Munich just ten years ago. One road means retreat and appeasement; the other leads to a showdown."[108]

The choice was not in fact uniformly perceived in so stark and polarized a fashion, and some influential writers, such as Walter Lippmann and Sumner Welles, helped to focus attention on the middle ground between these two extremes which remained to be explored. Lippmann came out strongly against the views of "our military authorities in Berlin that we should cross the Rubicon and use force." "If there is to be another world war," he cautioned, "let it not be begun lightly. For it will not be concluded easily. Let it not be begun on the advice of exasperated men in Berlin, nor decided on the frivolous speculation that the Russians will not fight if we act

106. *New York Herald Tribune*, July 18, 1948.
107. Walter LaFeber, "American Policy-Makers, Public Opinion and the Outbreak of the Cold War," in *The Origins of the Cold War in Asia*, ed. Yanosuke Nagai and Akira Iriye (New York: Columbia University Press, 1977), p. 58.
108. *New York Herald Tribune*, July 18, 1948.

violently. Above all, let it never be said of the United States that it resorted to war before it had exhausted the possibilities of negotiation and peaceful settlement." The question at issue, according to Lippmann, was not whether the Western powers should retire from Berlin, but whether, while staying in Berlin, they were willing to try again to conclude a general settlement about and with Germany. Recent developments in Western Germany persuaded Lippmann that their reply to the Russians should go beyond the blockade to the wider issues of a German settlement. The attitude of the German Minister-Presidents in the British and American zones was particularly significant, for they had just made it clear that they did not want to form a Western German government, did not want to draft a constitution, and did not want to be identified with the purposes of the whole policy which Clay was pushing through. "A German policy," argued Lippmann, "which the Germans do not want, which the Russians, of course, do not want, which, in fact, the civilians in the State Department do not want, cannot be such a masterpiece of statesmanship that Europe must take it or else."[109]

A major reassessment of America's position in Berlin and of the options available in the face of the blockade was going on simultaneously in different branches and at different levels of the Truman Administration. Some officials, outside as well as inside the State Department, believed that an intermediate route between a retreat from Berlin and a resort to force should be explored in direct talks with the Russians. Inclined towards the estimate that Russia did not want war, they feared that provocative actions on America's part might touch off a chain of events which would push both sides over the precipice.

This cautious position was supported, either implicitly or explicitly, by a succession of memoranda on the military aspects of the Berlin crisis written by different Army officers. One of these memoranda, dealing with the capacity of the airlift, estimated that it would not be possible to meet even Berlin's minimum needs by air, assuming the increased requirements of the winter months. Diplomatic negotiations to lift the blockade, it concluded, must be completed before the onset of winter to avoid extreme hardships and

109. Ibid., July 20, 1948.
110. Memorandum for the Chief of Staff, U.S. Army, from Major General Ray T. Maddocks, July 13, 1948, P&O 381, RG 319, National Archives, Washington, D.C.

probable civil disorders in Berlin.[110] Another memorandum, concluding that Clay's plan for surface convoys to Berlin depended on an important psychological factor for success and risked an embarrassing failure, recommended that the plan not be approved unless there were definite evidence that the action involved would prove effective as a "one-shot" ruse to force the Soviet hand in a direction acceptable to U.S. national policy.[111] A third memorandum saw the airlift as, at best, a temporary expedient which would seriously compromise the effort required to implement emergency war plans. It recommended: (1) that no additional C-54 aircraft be dispatched to Germany; (2) that neither force nor the threat of force be employed; (3) that plans be made immediately to evacuate Berlin, and that a gradual reduction of personnel and equipment in Berlin be initiated; and (4) that if the decision were taken to resort to force or the threat of force, the evacuation of noncombatants from Germany and Austria be initiated as a matter of urgency.[112]

Air Force officers were equally skeptical about the potential and durability of the airlift under the severe conditions of the German winter. There was a tendency to regard the airlift as a costly and potentially disastrous diversion from the critical task of preparing to meet the contingency of all-out war. An early example of the conflict of priorities had occurred when General Clay told General LeMay that he would like to have B-29s drop coal in the Berlin area. LeMay opposed such a prior commitment of their combat force on the ground that the bombers would not then be ready for a striking mission if needed, and he was supported in this stand by the Air Force chiefs.[113]

Colonel R. B. Landry, Truman's Air Aide, submitted an uncommonly alarmist report to Admiral Leahy on the day that the first group of B-29s left for England, predicting a war with the Soviet Union as total as any war ever fought. He decried the tendency, prevalent in America at that time, to state that the atomic bomb

111. Study by Lt. Gen. Osmanski, July 13, 1948, P&O 381, RG 319, National Archives, Washington, D.C.
112. Study, July 13, 1948, P&O 381, RG 319, National Archives, Washington, D.C. On these and subsequent Army studies, see also Jerry Philip Rosenberg, *Berlin and Israel 1948: Foreign Policy Decision-Making During the Truman Administration* (Ph.D. dissertation, University of Illinois, Urbana-Champaign, 1977), pp. 141–144.
113. Memorandum for General Maddocks from Major General S. E. Anderson (USAF Director of Plans and Operations), June 30, 1948, P&O 381, RG 319, National Archives, Washington, D.C.

would not necessarily win a war, because such thinking was liable to encourage the Russians to take a calculated risk. It was only the atomic bomb, in his view, that had acted as a deterrent to wholehearted Russian aggression. He thought that serious thought should be given to the possibility that the Russians might well seize Allied forces in the Western sectors of Berlin as hostages to forestall any use of the atomic bomb against them. To prepare for the war, which Landry considered inevitable and imminent because the Russians would not yield and the Americans could not afford to yield, he suggested that a War Room be set up in the White House, from which the world situation could be monitored by the President from day to day as long as the Berlin crisis continued.[114]

Without succumbing to such pessimistic forecasts, General Hoyt Vandenberg, the recently appointed Air Force Chief of Staff, had to plan for the contingency of full-scale war and was consequently reluctant to commit the lion's share of the available air transport capacity to the supply of Berlin. His position was that the airlift was possible only by stripping the Strategic Air Command of all the transport aircraft required to implement the emergency war plans. These were the aircraft assigned to carry the unassembled atomic weapons and the assembly teams to bases overseas. To divert them from this primary mission in order to supply operations in Germany would deny any atomic capability should the crisis in Berlin flare up into war.[115]

The Joint Chiefs of Staff began to participate actively in the process of evaluating alternative courses of action only after receiving, on July 17, a memorandum from the Army Chief of Staff which addressed itself to the interrelated problems involved in the airlift, the convoy, and strategic warfare. General Bradley estimated that the airlift capacity would decline and fall progressively short of the 3,000 tons of supplies required daily by Berlin. Bradley accorded only a limited chance of success to Clay's proposal for opening ground access by armed convoys, but he thought it might be necessary to try it if political considerations dictated a long-term support for the present policy of staying in Berlin. The British, he reported, reserved their position on this question, and the French were opposed. Bradley's recommendations were that General Vandenberg

114. Memorandum for Admiral Leahy from Colonel R. B. Landry, July 16, 1948, Leahy File, Folder No. 33, RG 218, National Archives, Washington, D.C.
115. MacIsaac, "The Air Force and Strategic Thought," pp. 36–37.

provide as many C-54s to the airlift as the Berlin airfield could handle; that the Department of the Army request additional funds to cover the costs; that the Joint Strategic Plans Committee revise its war plans to allow for the possible loss of aircraft employed in the airlift; that the Secretary of Defense arrange with the Secretary of State to ask the British and French to give maximum support to the airlift and to join the United States in contingency planning for combined armed ground convoys; and that Clay be directed to prepare unilateral plans for the same purpose.[116]

While the Joint Chiefs of Staff were considering this memorandum with a view to making their recommendations to the Secretary of Defense and, through him, to the National Security Council, the Secretary of the Army committed to paper what he modestly described as his "tentative ideas" on the Berlin situation. In fact, his memorandum to Forrestal, dated July 19, which he showed in addition only to Bradley and Draper, contained a complete plan of action for escalating by stages all the way from diplomatic protest to unleashing nuclear attack on Russia's head. The first suggestion was to refer the problem of the German blockade to the United Nations with a statement requesting an early decision. Second, the U.S. should send a note to Russia reasserting its rights to stay in Berlin and to supply Berlin by any means necessary, while at the same time advising the Russians that the issue had been referred to the United Nations. Third, the note should be delivered personally to Stalin by a special representative of the U.S. Government with ambassadorial authority. Fourth, the U.S. should gradually increase the airlift and provide the necessary depots and airstrips for it. Fifth, the U.S. might resort to armed convoy, but only if the Russians vetoed action by the United Nations or failed to honor the decision of the United Nations. And sixth, if and when it becomes apparent that a convoy is necessary, the U.S. should "make preparations for fighter and bomber support, and at the same time have A-bombs available (in England or elsewhere) for immediate use, and . . . such use [should] be left entirely to the military."[117]

The last suggestion, the top rung along this ladder of escalation, was all the more stunning in its boldness and macabre implica-

116. Condit, *The History of the Joint Chiefs of Staff*, pp. 141–143.
117. Memorandum for the Secretary of Defense from Kenneth C. Royall, July 19, 1948, RG 335, National Archives, Washington, D.C.

tions, given the fact that, when making it, Royall knew full well that the President himself was still playing the ostrich on nuclear weapons. In contrast to the Joint Chiefs of Staff, whose private references to the A-bomb were somewhat coy, the civilian leaders, or at least some of them, were forthright and insistent about integrating the bomb as an element in America's overall strategy for managing the Berlin crisis. Averell Harriman, one of the original proponents of the "get-tough" policy towards Russia, met Draper in Paris and asked him to call on the President to express his views on the Berlin situation. Last in a long list of points which Harriman wanted impressed on the President was that the U.S., in concert with the British and perhaps the French, should determine promptly whether, if war comes, they will employ "all of the weapons at our disposal," and, on the basis of this decision, make sure their plans were ready for immediate execution.[118]

Parallel to the energetic process of collecting data and evaluating options which was going on in the different branches of the defense establishment, the diplomatic aspects of the Berlin crisis were being subjected to intensive study in the State Department. Some temporary organizational changes had been instituted by Marshall to cope with the various decisional tasks and the vastly increased work load of the Department. He set up an ad hoc committee to process the information with which the Department was being inundated from various sources and to keep the Berlin situation under constant review. Called the Berlin Group, it was composed of various State Department officials connected with the crisis. As head of the Group, which operated rather informally, Charles Bohlen was responsible for instructing the State Department's officers at home and its ambassadors abroad on the execution of policy. Because of his coordinating responsibilities, he saw all the cables coming in and all those going out, and he reported to Lovett and Marshall.[119]

Another manifestation of the stress induced by the crisis was the extension of the consultative process to include representatives of the competing political elite. Given the magnitude of the threat to national security, it was not unnatural that the Administration

---

118. Memorandum of Conversation with Mr. Harriman, July 19, 1948, RG 335, National Archives, Washington, D.C.; and President's Secretary File, Cabinet—Box 157, Harry S. Truman Library.

119. Charles E. Bohlen, *Witness to History, 1929–1969* (London: Weidenfeld and Nicolson, 1973), p. 280.

would wish to bring Republican leaders into its confidence and thereby encourage them to share support for major decisions. In addition, Truman's campaign strategy required the maintenance of a broad national consensus behind his external policy. He both preached and practiced bipartisanship, which became a pronounced feature of American foreign policy in the second half of 1948. Resisting pressure to lay the Berlin problem formally before Congress, thereby risking a public display of discord, Truman preferred to work behind the scenes, using Marshall and Lovett to drum up Republican support on Capitol Hill and to seek an understanding with Governor Thomas Dewey, the Republican candidate for the Presidency, to remove Berlin from partisan politics.[120] Lovett, who was himself a Republican serving in a Democratic Administration, worked with Senator Vandenberg, the chairman of the Senate Foreign Relations Committee, towards this goal. Throughout the summer months, while Truman and Dewey were trading verbal potshots across the country, Vandenberg kept in close touch with the State Department, and the handling of the Berlin problem proceeded with close bipartisan collaboration.[121]

As part of the same effort to prevent the Berlin crisis from becoming an issue in the presidential campaign, John Foster Dulles, who was Dewey's spokesman on foreign affairs, was invited to confidential conferences in the State Department. He called on Marshall at his office on July 19 at 9:00 A.M., and they were joined by Lovett shortly afterwards. Marshall told Dulles that they wanted his views as an intelligent observer on the Berlin situation, as they had to make important decisions that day in preparation for discussions with the British and French. He explained that it was definite policy not to evacuate Berlin voluntarily, but that the question of what step should be taken next was difficult. Lovett added that weakness at Berlin would invite pressure at Vienna and so on throughout Western Europe. Marshall said he wanted Dulles to sit down at once with their working group and give him his opinion afterwards. The pressure of time became evident when Dulles asked how much time was available and Marshall replied that they would like his views by about noon, as a position had to be taken that day.

120. Robert A. Divine, "The Cold War and the Election of 1948," *Journal of American History*, Vol. 59 (June 1972); and George W. Ball, *Diplomacy for a Crowded World* (London: Bodley Head, 1976), p. 206.
121. Arthur H. Vandenberg, Jr., ed., *The Private Papers of Senator Vandenberg* (London: Gollancz, 1952), pp. 452–454.

Lovett then took Dulles into the conference with the members of the Berlin Group: Bohlen, Kennan, Saltzman, Samuel Reber, Dean Rusk, and Jacob Beam. They said that the joint U.S.-British airlift would be good until about October, when it would decline rapidly on account of weather, thus creating food privation, lack of heating, and unemployment; that this airlift could not be much increased without drawing on Air Transport Service planes, to which the Army would not agree; and that there must be some solution by October, or their position would become untenable and drive them to try large-scale force under time pressures which might lead to war. They also said that they were considering referring the dispute to the Security Council of the United Nations.

Dulles expressed his view that the Soviet leaders did not want war, and, repeating what he had told Marshall earlier, he added that their prestige was so engaged that they could not retreat unless the U.S. facilitated such a retreat. He mentioned that in Soviet circles it was not merely a question of national prestige but of the individual standing of members of the Politburo, for whom failure of the policy they espoused was almost literally fatal. His reaction to what he had heard was to recommend that the U.S. notify the Russians (1) that it was prepared, through the Council of Foreign Ministers, to negotiate about Berlin and any other phases of the German problem, and (2) that it was sending through to Berlin supply trucks which would be stopped only by superior force. Prior to any formal diplomatic note, however, Dulles thought the U.S. should convey its intentions informally, if possible to Stalin rather than Molotov, so that the Russians would react soberly rather than hastily, and, if they wanted, have the opportunity to announce that the "repairs" had been effected, thus making it possible to resume traffic. If the sending in of trucks resulted in an incident, that would be the time to refer the matter to the Security Council. This program had three merits in Dulles's view: first, it would let the Russians realize quickly the seriousness of U.S. intentions; second, it would do so before their prestige was further committed by legal positions formulated at a high level and publicly announced; and third, it would leave time for negotiating *after* an incident—if there was to be one—instead of exhausting the negotiating time and opportunities *before* either side had made its determination clear by acts.

There was an unstructured discussion which showed that it was the opinion of the State Department that the Soviet leadership did not want war and did not plan for a war. Bohlen seemed to feel that the U.S. should not agree to negotiate about the German problem generally until the Soviets had agreed to lift the blockade, but Dulles considered such a concession to be unobtainable. Rusk, Director of the Office of United Nations Affairs, pointed out that the U.S. had not yet exhausted the possibility of trying to send through unarmored trucks. There was a general agreement that Molotov would probably garble, to the Politburo, any representation made to him.

Lovett, who had left the meeting earlier, returned to say that Marshall had had to go to the White House for a conference with Truman and could only get Dulles's views secondhand, which he greatly regretted. Dulles summarized his views to Lovett for Marshall.[122] Thus informed of the facts, including the military estimates of the situation, Dulles was able, for his part, to advise Governor Dewey and also to keep Senator Vandenberg informed.[123] As for the program espoused by this outsider, it could hardly have been adopted in its entirety even had it not bumped against tight schedules, but some of its elements, particularly those which called for sensitivity to the adversary's position and predicament, do appear to have influenced the State Department's subsequent conduct. Certainly, it is ironic to watch this man, whose name became a byword for intransigence, lecture to the State Department's leading experts on the Soviet Union on the need for flexibility and empathy in dealing with the Politburo.

On that same hectic day, July 19, Truman summoned the nation's top military and diplomatic officials to the White House for a special meeting on the Berlin situation. His principal advisers, Marshall and Forrestal, went in to see him shortly before noon. Marshall outlined for him the situation in Berlin and the various courses open to the United States and the Allies. He said that the U.S. had the alternative of following a firm policy in Berlin or accepting the consequences of failure for the rest of their European policy. Russia's activity, he suggested, was a manifestation of the success of America's policy in Greece, Italy, and France and of Soviet setbacks in Finland and Yugoslavia. He felt that there was

122. Memorandum of John Foster Dulles's Washington Conference, July 19, 1948, Papers of John Foster Dulles, Princeton University Library. See also Michael A. Guhin, *John Foster Dulles: A Statesman and His Times* (New York: Columbia University Press, 1972), pp. 153–155 and 325–326.
123. John Foster Dulles, *War or Peace* (New York: Macmillan, 1950), p. 130.

some chance of containing the Russians in Western Europe. This prompted Forrestal to point out that there would be a definite limitation on their ability in the event of Russian military aggression. He reminded Marshall that their total reserves were about two and one-third divisions, of which they could commit probably only one division with any speed. The army buildup would not get under way until the following spring or summer. Marshall responded by saying that they were much better off than in 1940, and that they could encourage the French and other Europeans by token supplies of weapons. At the conclusion of the discussion, the President said that their policy would remain fixed; namely, that they would stay in Berlin until all diplomatic means had been exhausted in order to come to some kind of an accommodation to avoid war.

Marshall outlined certain measures which were under consideration in the State Department, chief of which was to have the American Ambassador to Moscow speak on behalf of the three nations to Stalin to emphasize the fact that the Allies did not desire war but that this aversion to war would not induce them to recede from their Berlin position.[124]

Later, a full-scale meeting, lasting about thirty-five minutes, brought together the other top officials involved directly in the Berlin situation. Attending this meeting were Forrestal, Royall, Draper, Bradley, Lovett, and other State Department advisers. Marshall, who was attending General Pershing's funeral, was not present at this second meeting. Draper, who had just returned by air from Berlin, brought the latest estimate of the situation, including Harriman's views. One of Harriman's suggestions was that the President should avail himself of the recall of Congress by laying before it the significance of the Berlin crisis ahead of all other considerations. Truman considered that a statement about Berlin at the opening of Congress might unnecessarily disturb the delicate international situation, but said he would cover the present crisis with Congress at the appropriate time. None of those present spoke in support of direct military action, as advocated by Clay, to test Soviet intentions. The prevailing counsel was in favor of pursuing diplomatic efforts to deal with the Berlin crisis, and Truman agreed that any future approach to the USSR must be made directly to Stalin and not through Molotov. Truman also made it emphatically

---

124. James V. Forrestal Diaries, July 19, 1948, p. 2369, Princeton University Library.

clear that the decision to remain in Berlin even at the risk of war had already been taken.[125] Thus, the outcome of the intensive round of consultations and deliberations which went on from July 17 to 19 was a consensus, endorsed by Truman, that the U.S. would maintain its position in Berlin and take all the measures necessary for the exercise of its rights (Decision 14).

The conclusion of the first of the two White House meetings amounted to a reaffirmation of existing policy rather than a new departure. But the manner in which it was reached supports the hypothesis that a crisis situation leads to a substantial reduction in the number of participants in the decisional process.[126] In marked contrast to routine decision-making, the threat to basic values, the heightened probability of war, and the need for speed ensured that the ultimate handling of crisis decisions was centralized and elevated within the policymaking establishment. Moreover, because a crisis brings an issue for decision to a relatively small number of politicians occupying the highest positions, they can afford to bypass many customary procedures in making decisions.[127] The task of appraising the objectives, commitments, and risks of the United States in relation to its actual and potential military power had been assigned by statute to the National Security Council. Under crisis conditions, however, Truman preferred to conduct the major reappraisal at an ad hoc meeting with a small group of senior officials.[128] The second White House meeting was similarly improvised and cut across normal procedures and institutions. The lack of or-

125. Memorandum for the Record by W. H. Draper, July 19, 1948, RG 335, National Archives, Washington, D.C.; Harry S. Truman, *Off the Record* (New York: Harper and Row, 1980), p. 145; and *New York Herald Tribune*, July 20, 1948.

126. Alistair Buchan, *Crisis Management: The New Diplomacy*, The Atlantic Papers, NATO Series II (Boulogne-sur-Seine, France: Atlantic Institute, 1966); Phil Williams, *Crisis Management: Confrontation and Diplomacy in the Nuclear Age* (London: Martin Robertson, 1976), pp. 66–67; Avner Yaniv, "Domestic Structure and External Flexibility: A Systemic Restatement of a Neglected Theme," *Millennium*, Vol. 8, No. 1 (Spring 1979), p. 31; and Michael Brecher, ed., *Studies in Crisis Behavior* (New Brunswick, N.J.: Transaction Books, 1979).

127. James A. Robinson, "Crisis Decision-Making: An Inventory and Appraisal of Concepts, Theories, Hypotheses and Techniques of Analysis," *Political Science Annual*, Vol. 2 (1969).

128. Truman's handling of the NSC during the pre-crisis and most of the crisis periods supports the contention of his critics who argue that he used the Council infrequently and inadequately. See, for example, Alfred D. Sander, "Truman and the National Security Council: 1945–1947," *Journal of American History*, Vol. 49, No. 2 (September 1972).

der and logical sequence between the two meetings was particularly striking. Royall, Draper, and Forrestal, for example, came to a meeting with the President *after* he had already reached a decision at the earlier meeting with Forrestal and Marshall. The President's patience was evidently strained by having to listen to a rehash of what he already knew, and he bluntly repeated his *stay in Berlin* decision.[129]

The Administration's fundamental decision to stand fast was made public by Marshall at a press conference on July 21 in reply to a question about the possibility of war in Berlin. He said:

> I can merely say at this time that our position I think is well understood. We will not be coerced or intimidated in any way in our procedures under the rights and responsibilities that we have in Berlin and generally in Germany. At the same time we will proceed to invoke every possible resource of negotiation and diplomatic procedure to reach an acceptable solution to avoid the tragedy of war for the world. But, I repeat again, we are not going to be coerced.[130]

The order of precedence given to these two points of American policy was not accidental. Taken together, they meant that the U.S. had no intention of yielding even if the Russians pushed matters to extremes.

In a telegram to Douglas, Marshall elaborated on the nature of this decision, the reasoning behind it, and the process by which it was reached:

> High-level conferences over the weekend and today, including discussions with Foster Dulles and ending with confirmation by the President himself, have resulted in a firm determination of U.S. policy in the Berlin matter. It is that the United States is resolved to maintain its position in Berlin and to take all measures necessary for the exercise of its rights, including the fulfilment of supply of the population of its sector.
>
> In pursuit of the foregoing policy, this Government is prepared to use any means that may be necessary. However, careful analysis of the Soviet note does not support the view that the Politburo is definitely determined upon a course of action leading to war. We do not feel, up to the present, that the Soviet Government has

---

129. Truman, *Off the Record*, p. 145.
130. *Public Papers of the Presidents of the United States: Harry S. Truman, 1948*, p. 413, note 1.

committed itself so irretrievably to maintain the blockade to preclude the possibility of some face-saving retreat on their part. In these circumstances, precisely because we are firm in our determination to carry this matter through to the end, we feel we should explore every possibility which might lead to an agreed solution.

We therefore believe that prior to the dispatch of a formal note, which might elevate the matter further into the realms of prestige considerations, an effort should be made to approach Stalin directly. This, however, could only be done on an agreed three-power basis with the senior Ambassador in Moscow speaking for the three Governments, and on the understanding that the French and British Governments share our determination in this matter.[131]

Marshall described with great precision the instructions which in the Administration's view the three Ambassadors should be given in the event of British and French acceptance of the idea of a joint approach to Stalin. Among the long list of points, these instructions required that Stalin be told that the Western powers would not negotiate under duress, and that if the real but undisclosed purpose of the blockade was either an attempt to force them to withdraw from Berlin or an attempt to compel them to abandon the measures they were forced to take in the administration of the western zones in the absence of a general German settlement, he must understand that these efforts could not and would not succeed.[132]

What should be done in the event of Stalin's failing to be impressed by such brave words was not settled in Washington. The first order of business was to get the views of the British and French Governments on the idea of a joint approach.

131. Marshall to Douglas, July 20, 1948, in *FRUS, 1948*, Vol. 2, p. 971. Lovett's briefing of the British Ambassador confirmed and elaborated on Marshall's message to Douglas. Lovett told the Ambassador that they had been having talks with Dulles and experts on Russia and considered a reply to the Russian note of July 14, but had tentatively come to think that a direct approach to Stalin might be a better move at that stage than a further note. Their thinking proceeded on two assumptions. First, that the Russian blockade was violence directed at former allies, and that no yielding on this issue was possible, even though this might lead to war (which they did not think was likely). Second, given this unyielding determination, it was possible to be quite flexible in deciding what steps to take. The appeal of a direct approach to Stalin lay in the fact that apparently he alone could vary or shift the emphasis of Russian policy, and it also offered an opportunity of negotiating prestige issues in private, which could help the Russians to give way. Washington to British Foreign Office, July 19, 1948, FO 371/70502/C5875, Public Record Office, London.

132. Marshall to Douglas, July 20, 1948, in *FRUS, 1948*, Vol. 2, pp. 971–973.

PHASE IV: JULY 20-22

The expectation that Stalin might modify Soviet policy if approached informally was related, at least in part, to the growing confidence in the value of America's strategic air power as an instrument of diplomacy. Dispatching the B-29s to Britain, despite the element of bluff involved, both enhanced and outwardly demonstrated this confidence. The increasingly overt reliance on America's strategic air power as part of an evolving strategy of deterrence imparted some urgency to the task of formulating a comprehensive policy on the use or nonuse of America's nuclear weapons. A separate but closely related issue was that of the physical custody of these lethal weapons. The possibility of war over Berlin spurred the National Military Establishment, consisting of the three services with Cabinet-level civilian heads, to try to gain control over the bomb. Forrestal, who as Secretary of Defense presided over this Establishment, was particularly anxious to obtain a clear definition of the role which the bomb should play in strategic planning. On July 15, after the National Security Council session, he informed Truman that he would ask for a meeting to discuss this issue of custody. The meeting was duly convened in the White House six days later. It was attended by the President, by David Lilienthal, the chairman of the Atomic Energy Commission (AEC), by four of Lilienthal's associates, by Forrestal, Royall, and Stuart Symington, the Secretary of the Air Force, and by a few others. The subject of the meeting was the presentation of a formal request by the National Military Establishment for an executive order from the President transferring custody of the atomic bomb from the AEC to the Military Establishment. "It was an important session," recorded Lilienthal in his diary, "and a kind of seriousness hung over it that was not relieved a bit, needless to say, by the nature of the subject or the fact that even at that moment some terrible thing might be happening in Berlin that would put this group into the hands of forces that might sweep our desires and wishes away, while the tides of force took over."[133] The large number of participants, quite apart from the gravity of the subject, made this a rather formal session. Its procedure was akin to that of a court of law, with represen-

---

133. David E. Lilienthal, *The Journals of David E. Lilienthal*, Vol. 2: *The Atomic Energy Years, 1945-1950* (New York: Harper and Row, 1964), pp. 388-389.

tatives of the National Military Establishment submitting their case for the transfer of custody, with the AEC representatives presenting the case against, and with Truman acting as the arbiter and judge.

The main reasons given for the transfer were: first, that the user of the bomb, who would ultimately be responsible for its delivery, should have custody of it with the accompanying advantages of familiarity which this would bring; and second, that the concentration of authority would yield a unified command. Lilienthal based his objection to the transfer, first, on the general theory that the atomic bomb was not simply another weapon but an instrument of destruction which carried the widest kind of diplomatic and international implications; second, on the need to safeguard the constitutional principle of civilian control; and third, on the argument that actually greater efficiency in terms of surveillance, readiness, and further development could be had by leaving custody with the AEC.[134]

Truman was completely unmoved by the arguments advanced for the transfer, and on one occasion interrupted Symington to emphasize that the atomic bomb would only be used as a weapon of last resort. "I don't think we ought to use this thing unless we absolutely have to," he said.

> It is a terrible thing to order the use of something that is so terribly destructive, destructive beyond anything we have ever had. You have got to understand that this isn't a military weapon. It is used to wipe out women and children and unarmed people, and not for military uses. So we have got to treat this differently from rifles and cannon and ordinary things like that.

Royall commented that they had been spending 98 percent of all the money for atomic energy for weapons, and that if they were not going to use them, that did not make any sense. To Lilienthal it appeared that if what worried the President, in part, was whether he could trust these weapons in the hands of the military establishment, then the performance these men gave certainly could not have been reassuring on that score. "You have got to understand," said the President solemnly, "that I have got to think about the effect of such a thing on international relations. This is no time to be juggling an atom bomb around." Declining to make up his mind

---

134. Ibid., pp. 389–390; and Millis, *The Forrestal Diaries*, pp. 460–461.

right off on a question as important as this, Truman brought the meeting to a close by saying that he would read the position papers and let them know.[135] His decision, as could only have been expected from his consistently cautious attitude on the role of the bomb and from his comments at the meeting, was to turn down the request of the National Military Establishment for custody of the atomic bomb (Decision 15).

At a Cabinet meeting two days later, which was devoted to the Administration's domestic program, Truman announced that he had decided the custody matter and planned to issue a statement. Forrestal took the decision fairly well but objected strongly to the idea of a public statement, questioning why it should be announced that he had been overruled.[136] After the meeting, Truman told Forrestal that "he would make a negative decision on the question of the transfer of custody of atomic bombs and said that political considerations, at the immediate moment, had influenced his decision. He indicated that after election it would be possible to take another look at the picture."[137] In the course of the public statement made on the following day, Truman declared that he regarded "the continued control of all aspects of the atomic energy program, including research, development, and the custody of atomic weapons, as the proper function of the civil authorities."[138] So that ended, for the time being, the question of custody, with civilian control reasserted and the AEC retaining control of the bomb.

There is no reason to doubt Forrestal's contention that Truman's decision was influenced by electoral considerations. The decision, in any case, furnishes a telling example of the impact of domestic politics on the management of American national security. Political considerations were probably not the dominant influence on Truman's decision, but neither were they an irrelevant element in his calculations. The view that the essentially political character of national security policymaking is moderated, if not eliminated, dur-

---

135. Lilienthal, *Journals*, Vol. 2, pp. 389–392.
136. Ibid., p. 392. See also Richard G. Hewlett and Francis Duncan, *Atomic Shield: A History of the United States Atomic Energy Commission*, Vol. 2: *1947–1952* (Washington, D.C.: U.S. Atomic Energy Commission, 1972), pp. 169–171.
137. Millis, *The Forrestal Diaries*, p. 461.
138. Statement by the President Reviewing Two Years of Experience With the Atomic Energy Act, July 24, 1948, *Public Papers of the Presidents of the United States: Harry S. Truman, 1948*, p. 415.

ing crisis[139] is not supported by the handling of the custody question during the Berlin crisis. Truman did not act as the objective custodian of "the national interest" judging the proposal purely on its merits. He was conscious of how particular alternatives would benefit certain agencies and individuals within the government, he was wary of institutional competitors for his power, and he was aware that his own personal interests in terms of electoral appeal would be best served by maintaining the principle of civilian supremacy. It should be noted, however, that the question of which agency should have physical custody of the bomb is a technical one, and, as such, of only secondary importance. For even if the bomb were entrusted to the Military Establishment, the decision on its use would still have remained in the hands of the commander-in-chief, who was a civilian. The really vital question was that of formulating a clear policy which specified under what conditions the bomb would be used, thereby providing a basis for all military contingency planning. But this Truman was reluctant to do because he did not want to limit his freedom of choice in advance and preferred to keep all his options open.

Electoral considerations may have also encouraged Truman to leave the broader questions of nuclear strategy deliberately unsettled. His advisers felt that in order to retain bipartisan support for their policy, they had to maintain a thoroughly firm attitude towards the USSR.[140] After the official statement was made of the intention to remain in Berlin despite the Soviet blockade, 80 percent of a national sample were ready to support this policy even if it were to result in war.[141] American public opinion, while not eager for war, was permissive of actions which involved the risk of war. The prospect of war with Russia was not a sufficient deterrent to dispel popular support for American policy in those areas in which commitments had been assumed.[142] Yet, while the American public and Congress seemed determined and very air-power minded, it was by no means certain, in the psychological aftermath of Hiroshima and Nagasaki, that they would sanction a cold-blooded deci-

139. See, for example, Williams, *Crisis Management*, p. 69.
140. Report of a conversation between Lovett and the Minister at the British Embassy, Washington to the British Foreign Office, July 21, 1946, FO 371/70503/C5887, Public Record Office, London.
141. Gabriel A. Almond, *The American People and Foreign Policy* (New York: Harcourt Brace, 1950), p. 92.
142. Ibid., p. 99.

sion to use the ultimate weapon in defense of the Berlin enclave. Consequently, the adoption of an explicit nuclear strategy in advance of a Russian attack carried no domestic political advantage, and this factor could have only reinforced Truman's strong disinclination to engage in nuclear saber rattling.

One option that was risky but not morally repugnant was that of sending an armed convoy to force access to the besieged city. This option was still under active consideration by the Joint Chiefs of Staff. At Clay's headquarters in Berlin, the planning had been completed and actual preparations for the convoy were well in hand, making it possible to put the plan into motion as soon as it received the go-ahead.[143] On July 19, Clay repeated with renewed vigor his advocacy of a show of force in a cable which was quoted at length in the previous chapter and which he concluded with the exhortation that America should stop the Soviet policy of aggression there and then because the next time might be too late.[144] Clay's comprehensive analysis of the situation, his persuasive definition of the stakes involved, and his forceful advocacy of direct action stood out all the more sharply against the background of continuing doubts and hesitation in Washington. The doubling of the airlift's capacity in its first fortnight of service enhanced his confidence. Truman felt the need for a face-to-face meeting with the energetic and resourceful Military Governor, and he issued instructions to have Clay and Murphy called to Washington to present their views in person. An additional motive for recalling Clay was Truman's desire to demonstrate his personal support for a firm stand in Berlin. Until this time, Clay had been carrying the ball alone, and many in Berlin and West Germany were beginning to wonder to what extent Washington was behind him. Clay reported his concern to Bradley, and the message was relayed to Truman through Congressional channels. Truman's invitation to Clay was the result.[145]

Forrestal, who dined with Clay on the evening of his arrival (July 21), was struck by his optimistic and carefree outlook. Clay told him that he was confident he could put through an armed convoy with little difficulty and without creating a crisis. The chances, however, would grow slimmer with the passage of time because the press coverage and diplomatic activity which brought the Ber-

---

143. See note 89, above.
144. *Clay Papers*, Vol. 2, pp. 743–746.
145. Smith, *The Defense of Berlin*, p. 110.

lin impasse to the attention of world opinion would make it more difficult for the Russians to withdraw from a position so publicly taken. Clay estimated the chances of war at one in four. He believed that the French would fight and that twenty good divisions could hold the Russians at the Rhine. And he stressed that the German people were unequivocally on the side of the U.S. and would do all in their power to help.[146]

Robert Murphy has stated plainly that when he and Clay arrived in Washington, they had hoped to get permission to break the blockade, but the National Security Council did not share their confidence that the Russians were bluffing. On their arrival, they discovered immediately that:

> several extraneous factors were influencing the momentous decision. For one thing, Truman was up for election in November and all polls showed he was far behind Thomas Dewey. If the President were to approve action in Berlin which the voters considered reckless, his election chances would diminish still further. In spite of his personal predicament, Truman was more disposed than his military advisers to take chances. The Joint Chiefs of Staff were extremely conscious of how inadequate our Armed Forces were due to headlong demobilization, and they considered our defense establishment too weak to enter into any contest against the Red Army.[147]

Marshall, who was himself strongly opposed to the use of force, told Murphy that the Joint Chiefs of Staff estimated that they would need eighteen months to prepare for what might happen in Berlin if the Russians were challenged there.[148] Truman, who reluctantly approved this opinion, is reported to have said that if the Joint Chiefs of Staff put a paper before him ordering what Clay and Mur-

---

146. Millis, *The Forrestal Diaries*, pp. 459–460.
147. Robert Murphy, *Diplomat Among Warriors* (London: Collins, 1964), pp. 386–388.
148. Ibid., p. 387; and Robert H. Ferrell, *George C. Marshall* (New York: Cooper Square, 1966), p. 158. Interestingly, some State Department officials supported military action. Howard Trivers recalls that in July 1948: "Clay twice requested permission to attempt to break the surface blockade by sending an armored convoy from West Germany to Berlin. While we at the working level in the State Department supported him, the Joint Chiefs of Staff turned him down on the grounds that the United States did not then possess an adequate military posture to meet the consequences if hostilities with the Soviets were to ensue, even though the likelihood of such consequences were not regarded as great." Howard Trivers, *Three Crises in American Foreign Affairs and a Continuing Revolution* (Carbondale: Southern Illinois University Press, 1972), p. 6.

phy proposed, he would sign it. Strangely enough, comments Murphy, nobody, either military or civilian, mentioned that the United States Government in 1948 possessed a growing stockpile of atomic bombs, while Russia had none yet.[149] This fact had not, of course, gone unnoticed, and the civilian defense planners, with the support of the military, had been pressing for the integration of the bomb into America's overall strategy vis-à-vis the Soviet Union. But Truman himself prevented this with the admonition that this was no time to be juggling an atom bomb around; and without the bomb to fall back on, the Joint Chiefs were decidedly afraid to force a showdown in Berlin. So these two options, sending in an armed convoy or threatening to use A-bombs, were effectively foreclosed even before the formal discussions began.

As a matter of fact, when the moment of decision was reached on July 22, Truman did not have before him any formal recommendation from the Joint Chiefs of Staff. General Bradley's memorandum of July 17 had been referred by the Chiefs to the Joint Strategic Survey Committee, whose report was submitted on July 21. The Joint Chiefs of Staff acted on this report the following day by sending their views to the Secretary of Defense. These views, however, were not forwarded by Forrestal to the National Security Council until July 26—four days after its meeting.[150] But although the formal views of the Joint Chiefs of Staff were still in the pipeline, informally their opposition to the use of force or even the threat to use force became widely known and played a crucial role in defeating the proposal of sending an armed convoy along the highway to Berlin.

The last and most critical decision of the crisis period was made at the meeting of the National Security Council on July 22, presided over by President Truman personally. The other members of the Council who attended this meeting were Marshall, Forrestal, Royall, John L. Sullivan (Secretary of the Navy), W. Stuart Symington (Secretary of the Air Force), and Arthur N. Hull (Chairman of the National Security Resources Board). An unusually high number of invitees were also present: Clay, Murphy, Lovett, Bohlen, Admiral Leahy, General Bradley, Vice Admiral Arthur W. Radford (Vice Chief of Naval Operations), General Vandenberg, Rear Ad-

149. Murphy, *Diplomat Among Warriors*, p. 387.
150. Condit, *The Joint Chiefs of Staff*, pp. 141–143; and John R. Oneal, *Creative Adaptation: Process and Potential for Foreign Policy Making in Times of Crisis* (Ph.D. dissertation, Stanford University, 1979), pp. 378–380.

miral R. H. Hillenkoetter (Director of Central Intelligence), and General Wedemeyer.[151]

Truman opened the meeting by asking Clay to report on the situation in Germany. In reply, Clay told the Council that the abandonment of Berlin would have a disastrous effect on their plans for Western Germany, and that it would slow down European recovery, the success of which depended upon more production, particularly from Western Germany. The Allies, Clay believed, should be prepared to go to any lengths to find a peaceful solution to the situation, but they had to remain in Berlin. The attitude of the German people, Clay added, was in some respects unbelievable. The party leaders in Berlin who made up the City Magistrat with headquarters in the Soviet zone had absolutely refused to accept Soviet control. The people of Berlin were determined to stand firm even if it required undergoing additional hardship.

Clay also reported, and this was a major input into the final decision, that the airlift was no longer a makeshift experiment but a successful and viable operation which could be continued indefinitely. The airlift had been averaging about 2,500 tons per day, which was more than enough to handle food requirements but inadequate to include the necessary amount of coal. The minimum required to sustain Berlin without extreme hardship was estimated to be 4,500 tons per day. For the summer, 3,500 tons per day might suffice, but additional tonnage would be required during the winter. At the time, the airlift operation involved fifty-two C54s and eighty C-47s. Two round trips were made each day, involving more than two hundred and fifty landings. Seventy-five additional C-47 planes, in Clay's estimate, would enable him to bring in 3,500 tons daily.

However, General Hoyt Vandenberg, the Air Force Chief of Staff, had three reservations about the advisability of making these additional planes available. In the first place, he felt that if they put more planes on the Berlin run, the Military Air Transport Service would become disrupted and they would find that they needed at least one more major airfield inside Berlin to handle the traffic and at least one major maintenance depot at the other end. Secondly, Vandenberg pointed out, the maximum airlift would involve using planes which were intended for emergency use elsewhere. In the

151. Minutes of the 16th Meeting of the National Security Council, held on Thursday, July 22, 1948, President's Secretary File, Harry S. Truman Library.

event of hostilities, many of these might be destroyed and this would adversely affect the nation's capability to wage strategic warfare, since it would then be difficult to supply U.S. forces and hold outlying bases. Thirdly, Vandenberg pointed out that the air lanes to Berlin belonged to the Russians as well as the Americans, and if the Americans increased their air traffic to the point where the Russians could claim that they were forced out, international incidents might result.

This prompted Truman to ask Clay what risks would be involved if the U.S. tried to supply Berlin by means of armed convoys. Clay said he thought the initial reaction of the Russians would be to set up roadblocks. American engineers would be able to clear such obstacles, provided there was no Russian interference, but the Russians' next step, Clay thought, would be to meet the convoys with armed force.

Robert Lovett, who was in attendance with Marshall, asked Clay if he thought the Russians might try to block America's airplanes with fighter patrols or by other methods. Clay said he felt that the Russians would not attack American planes unless they had made the decision to go to war. This statement prompted Truman to ask Clay whether there were any indications known to him that the Russians would go to war. The general said he did not think so. What the Russians seemed to be aiming at, he thought, was to score a major victory—without, however, extending the conflict—by forcing the Allies out of Berlin, either then or after the fall and winter weather forced a curtailment of the airlift. Truman stated his judgment that if the Allies moved out of Berlin, they would lose everything they were fighting for. The question then was: how to remain in Berlin without risking all-out war?

General Vandenberg said again that he felt the concentration of aircraft necessary to provide Berlin with all its supplies would mean reducing American air strength elsewhere, both in planes and in personnel, and that an emergency would find the U.S. dangerously exposed. Truman did not agree with the Air Force Chief of Staff. He asked him, rhetorically, whether he would prefer an attempt to supply Berlin by ground convoy. Then, if the Russians resisted that effort and plunged the world into war, would not the Air Force have to contribute its share to the defense of the nation? Truman answered his own question. "The airlift," he affirmed, "involved less risks than armed road convoys." Therefore, he directed the Air Force to furnish the fullest support possible to the problem of supplying Berlin.

General Vandenberg interjected that this would not be possible unless additional airfield facilities were constructed. Clay pointed out that he had already selected a site for an additional field, and that construction, using German manpower, could begin at once. General Vandenberg then assured Truman that the Air Force would devote its entire energy to carrying out his order.[152]

At the conclusion of this meeting, the National Security Council formally reiterated the American determination to stay in Berlin "in any event," and to this end it approved both the construction of a new airfield in Berlin and Clay's recommendation that approximately seventy-five additional C-54s be made available for the airlift. The Council also approved Clay's current plan to reduce the number of dependents in Berlin to approximately 1,000 by the end of August, and agreed that 800 to 1,000 dependents could remain in Berlin ready for immediate evacuation by him when and if he deemed it necessary. With regard to the B-29 bombers based in the British Isles, it was agreed that they should not conduct mass maneuvers over Germany or the Mediterranean area but could engage in normal training flights over the Mediterranean and in the normal rotation of planes to replace those based in Germany. In addition, it was the strong feeling of the Council that an oral approach should be made to Stalin along the lines described by Lovett.[153] What all these various measures and guidelines amounted to was a fundamental decision to remain in Berlin, supplying the city entirely by air, and to use the breathing space provided by the expanded airlift to seek a diplomatic solution by means of a direct approach to Moscow (Decision 16).

After the Council adjourned, Truman honored Clay by asking him to remain with him for a further discussion. At this private

152. The foregoing account of the Council's discussion is based entirely on and follows very closely the account given by Truman in his *Memoirs*, Vol. 2, pp. 131–133. The quotation is from this source. Unfortunately, no official transcript or summary of the discussion is available. Truman's account, however, is supported in all essentials by other firsthand accounts, including Bohlen, *Witness to History*, pp. 277–278; Clay, *Decision in Germany*, p. 368; and William Leahy Diary, July 22, 1948, pp. 47–48, Library of Congress.

153. Minutes of the 16th Meeting of the National Security Council, held on Thursday, July 22, 1948, President's Secretary File, Harry S. Truman Library; and *FRUS, 1948*, Vol. 2, p. 977.

meeting, Truman told Clay that he was not the one who had not approved the armed convoy plan. All the military chiefs were against it, said Truman, adding: "I didn't want to go against my military chiefs. If they had been for it, you would have had it," or words to that effect.[154] Clay left Truman's office inspired by the understanding and confidence that he had received.[155] His satisfaction with the outcome of the Council meeting was not unduly marred by the veto of the convoy idea. This is not particularly surprising in view of the fact that all his other plans and recommendations were approved, whereas the Air Force objections had been brushed aside. Later he was to write in another context that when his government turned down his suggestion, he understood its desire to avoid the risk of armed conflict until the issue had been placed before the United Nations, but he himself would always believe that the convoy would have reached Berlin.[156] At the actual meeting, however, he was bound to admit, modifying his earlier views, that an armed convoy would probably provoke an armed confrontation, whereas the airlift would not. Nor does he appear to have pressed very hard at the meeting for permission to test out the Russian position.

Unlike Clay, Robert Murphy was greatly dissatisfied with the

154. Oral History Interview with General Lucius D. Clay, July 16, 1974, p. 38, Harry S. Truman Library.

155. Clay, *Decision in Germany*, p. 368. According to some speculative press reports, Marshall, too, was present at this meeting, which was intended to curtail Clay's freedom of action and tough talk and to assert civilian supremacy in the management of the crisis. The *Christian Science Monitor* of September 22, 1948, for example, contained the following report: "One outcome of the Truman-Marshall-Clay conference is expected to be less off-the-cuff comments by army spokesmen and officers in Germany. The dispatches based primarily on these sources have blown up the Berlin crisis, not out of proportion to its importance, but into a much more combustible affair, Washington feels. One other outcome of this White House 'headquarters talk' on Berlin is expected to be much closer liaison between Washington and Berlin, between Secretary Marshall and General Clay, on day-by-day, hour-by-hour developments in Germany. General Clay, of course, works through the Department of the Army. But as Secretary Marshall in the State Department still is responsible for the political and diplomatic policy and program in Germany, his voice and hand are expected to be increasingly visible in the resolving of a still tense and acute situation." This report cannot be reconciled with Clay's accounts of the conference with the President after the NSC meeting, and Clay's are the only firsthand accounts available. One possibility is that his accounts are deliberately selective. A more likely explanation, however, is that the press reports were inspired by tendentious leaks from Clay's numerous critics in the State Department.

156. Clay, *Decision in Germany*, p. 374.

outcome of the visit to Washington. While Clay's commitment to direct action to break the blockade was moderated, after his arrival in Washington, by political realism, that of his political adviser was not. Murphy arrived in Washington intent on getting permission to try to break the blockade, and, to judge from his own account, he never wavered in his conviction that this was the right course. But the opposition to this course of action, as he discovered very quickly, was formidable. From what he heard from Marshall and from his friends in the Pentagon, it was a foregone conclusion that no decision would be taken affirming military action at Helmstedt, because of determined opposition by the Joint Chiefs of Staff. Whatever persuasive powers Murphy possessed proved insufficient; the military prevailed. Before the Council's discussion closed, Marshall gave him a fair chance by asking whether he wanted to add anything to his previous arguments, but in his discouragement he declined.[157]

Murphy's conviction that the National Security Council's decision constituted a grave and costly error did not diminish with the passage of time. Looking back on his long career, he felt that the Berlin blockade was the one occasion on which he should have resigned in public protest. "My resignation," he wrote in 1964,

> almost certainly would not have affected events, but if I had resigned I would feel better today about my own part in that episode. I suffered anguish over that decision of our government not to challenge the Russians when they blockaded Berlin, and I still deeply regret that I was associated with an action which caused Soviet leaders to downgrade United States determination and capability, and led, I believe, to the subsequent Communist provocation in Korea.[158]

"Few observers," he moaned, "seemed to realize that our decision to depend exclusively upon the Airlift was a surrender of our hardwon rights in Berlin, a surrender which has plagued us ever since."[159]

In late July 1948, Murphy was one of those very few men in responsible positions to hold this view. To the overwhelming majority, the choice of the airlift seemed the right one. It seemed to demonstrate just the right degree of tenacity and unwillingness to retreat under pressure without incurring the unacceptable risks of war. It was hailed as the product of courageous and sagacious

157. Murphy, *Diplomat Among Warriors*, pp. 387–388.
158. Ibid., p. 388.   159. Ibid., pp. 392–393.

statesmanship which enabled the nation to tread a middle path between outright and reckless bellicosity, on the one hand, and weak and pusillanimous appeasement, on the other. Dean Acheson, who was a mere observer in 1948, reflected the predominant view in government circles when he wrote, in reply to Murphy's criticisms, that the airlift showed "a firm intention to insist upon a right, plain beyond question, and gave the Russians the choice of either not interfering or of initiating an air attack, which might have brought upon them a devastating response." Murphy's contention that the decision to use the airlift was a surrender of America's hard-won rights in Berlin struck Acheson as silly: "One can as well say that to put one's hands up at the command of an armed bandit is to surrender one's hard-won right to keep them down. One regains it, and we have regained and are now enjoying our hard-won rights to Berlin."[160]

The National Security Council session in which this major and controversial decision was hammered out illustrates various facets of crisis decision-making and particularly those concerned with the role of the military. The most obvious lesson to be drawn is that military participation and influence in decision-making tends to vary with the imminence of the use of force or the extent of its actual involvement in the crisis.[161] When the action contemplated was entirely diplomatic, military participation tended to be limited, although by no means insignificant. The participation and influence of the military increased following the resort to a military instrument—air power—first to supply Berlin, and later as an instrument of deterrence. When the focus of attention shifted to the use of a land force with the obvious risk of an armed clash, the military moved into the very center of the policymaking arena. The negative attitude of the Joint Chiefs of Staff was decisive in defeating this proposal, and, indeed, made it a foregone conclusion that the National Security Council would not take a different line. Even the President, who apparently looked with some favor on Clay's proposal, was bound, in the final analysis, to defer to the opinion of the top experts in the use of force on this vital question.

160. Dean Acheson, *Present at the Creation: My Years in the State Department* (New York: Norton, 1969), pp. 262–263.
161. In this respect, there is no difference between crises in a conventional setting and the crises of the Cold War era. See Snyder and Diesing, *Conflict Among Nations*, p. 360; and Richard K. Betts, *Soldiers, Statesmen, and Cold War Crises* (Cambridge, Mass.: Harvard University Press, 1977).

A second conclusion which emerges from the decision process is that the influence of the military was exercised wholly and consistently on the side of caution. This is all the more striking in light of the popular belief that in crisis situations it is the military who urge the resort to force and are anxious to prove their mettle, whereas the politicians prefer to exhaust all other means first and have to restrain the military. On July 22, when the Administration was pondering which course to adopt, the hawks were practically all civilians—Murphy, some officials in the State Department, and possibly Truman—while the Chiefs of Staff were unanimous in their preference for a moderate stand. This alignment of opinion is not unique to the Berlin crisis. A similar alignment between soldiers and politicians existed, for example, in Europe on the eve of the Second World War, notably in Germany. Nor does the caution of the Joint Chiefs of Staff in July 1948 represent a departure from an otherwise permissive attitude on their part towards the use of force during the Cold War era. On the contrary, it conforms to a relatively consistent pattern. In this respect, their behavior during the Berlin crisis supports Samuel Huntington's thesis that the true professional soldier is inclined, by the very nature of his profession, towards caution. Because the soldier's ultimate responsibility is the security of his nation, and because few situations endanger that security more than the hazards of war, the professional American soldier fears and attempts to avoid war.[162] This kind of caution, which was exhibited in the higher echelons of the services in July 1948 (but not by Clay or LeMay among their representatives in Germany), stemmed from estimates of military preparedness rather than from political preferences. Because they considered the resources available to them for fighting to be inadequate at the time, the military chiefs opposed going to the brink. Their tendency to underestimate their own strength and overestimate Russia's and their preoccupation with "worst case analysis" were further manifestations of the conservatism inherent in the military profession.

In general, the attitude of the Joint Chiefs of Staff during the Berlin crisis belies both the premises and the predictions of the bureaucratic politics paradigm, which is summed up by the adage, "where you stand depends on where you sit." The basic premise is that for most participants organizational interest is a dominant fac-

---

162. Samuel Huntington, *The Soldier and the State: The Theory and Politics of Civil-Military Relations* (Cambridge, Mass.: Harvard University Press, 1957).

tor in determining the face of the issue which they see and the stand which they take in pursuit of the nation's security interests.[163] On the basis of this premise, one would have predicted that the Chiefs of Staff would endeavor to expand the role of the military services in the management of the crisis and to press for a military solution to the challenge to the nation's security. Conversely, the civilians could be expected to treat Berlin as a diplomatic, not a military, problem and to confine themselves to diplomatic means in their quest for a resolution of the crisis. In fact, as we have seen, the stand that the various participants took in the decision process bore little relation, and in some cases was diametrically opposed, to where they sat.

One final lesson which emerges most clearly from the National Security Council's session concerns the importance of presidential leadership in a crisis. Such leadership is indispensable for bringing a divided and fragmented policy machine to the point of decision within the time constraints imposed by the crisis. A real danger is that a machine geared to gradual consensus-building, free from the imminent risk of war and intense time pressure, will not respond effectively to the challenge of an international crisis, and that the wishes of the ultimate decision-maker will be frustrated by bureaucratic conservatism and myopia. General Vandenberg exemplified the natural reluctance of military organizations to depart from their existing plans and to improvise strategies which would widen the range of options available to the top decision-maker. Truman, on the other hand, while understandably unwilling to overrule his top military advisers on the use of force, demonstrated how strong and imaginative leadership could overcome bureaucratic resistance in bringing the meeting towards the decision on the airlift. He probed military estimates and advice in order to evaluate their possible implications for diplomacy, and in a way which exposed biases and omissions in the presentation of alternatives. From Clay he elicited information which enabled him to challenge Vandenberg's estimate of what was feasible, and in this way he succeeded in relaxing organizational constraints on policymaking. Once he had made up his mind that an expanded and long-term airlift was the most appropriate strategy for coping with the crisis, he overrode all objections and dismissed the reserva-

---

163. Morton H. Halperin, *National Security Policy-Making* (Lexington, Mass.: D.C. Heath, 1975), pp. 5–6.

tions voiced by Vandenberg as irrelevant. In steering the meeting towards the airlift choice, Truman ensured that the knowledge that Air Force plans were not geared to this particular task was not allowed to deflect support for a course which he considered necessary and appropriate. Presidential leadership thus served as an indispensable input into the decision-making process which produced the airlift choice. The outcome suggests that the desire for flexibility on the part of policymakers need not be thwarted by the organizations under their command, and that although policymakers are dependent upon their subordinates for information, advice, and implementation, they are not doomed to be their prisoners.[164]

The decision of the National Security Council on July 22 to eschew a ground convoy and rely on an expanded airlift and a diplomatic approach to Stalin to cope with the threat to America's security marked the end of the crisis period. Crucial to this transition from the period of peak stress to the period of less intense stress was the emergent perception that the airlift would become sufficiently effective to buy enough time for a diplomatic approach to Stalin. The airlift strategy maximized the chances of preserving intact the three basic values underlying American foreign policy: maintaining the Western position in Berlin, avoiding war, and continuing with the political reconstruction of Germany. The belief that the expanded airlift would work obviated the need to sacrifice any of these values and thereby contributed to a reduction of the motivational stress under which the American decision-makers had been laboring. Although the choice itself was complex and difficult, once the decision had been reached it led to a general relaxation of tension and to an observable decline in the American decision-makers' perception of time pressure and the probability of war. Asked at a press conference on July 22 for his estimate of the chances of world peace, Truman replied: "I think they are good. In fact, I think they are excellent."[165] The next day, on his return to Germany, Clay told reporters that he was confident that the airlift could supply Berlin indefinitely and that he saw "an excellent chance" for a peaceful settlement of the Berlin crisis.[166] The

164. Williams, *Crisis Management*, pp. 125–127.
165. *Public Papers of the Presidents of the United States: Harry S. Truman, 1948*, p. 163.
166. *New York Times*, July 24, 1948.

Berlin crisis was to continue for many months, but after July 22 a new phase began, characterized by a lower intensity in all the perceptual indicators of crisis and a corresponding decline in the stress experienced by the American decision-makers.

FINDINGS

The Berlin crisis period will be examined here, as in Chapter 4, on two levels: first, in terms of the four crisis components; and second, with a focus on the effects of escalating stress on the American coping mechanisms.

CRISIS COMPONENTS
Environmental Change

The transition from the pre-crisis to the crisis period was triggered by the severance of all road, rail, and barge traffic to and from Berlin on June 24, 1948. For the American decision-makers, this environmental change catalyzed a sharp change in all three perceptual components of crisis: threat, time pressure, and the probability of war.

Threat to Basic Values

The basic values which were perceived to be threatened by the Soviet action were America's policy in Germany, its entire policy in Europe, and, more broadly, its global position vis-à-vis the principal Cold War adversary, particularly its reputation for firmness and resolve. Evidence of a sharp increase in threat perception is pervasive at the verbal level. Murphy regarded the Western presence in Berlin as a symbol of resistance to Eastern expansionism, and the blockade as a test of the U.S. commitment to hold Europe (June 26). Marshall rejected the official Russian explanation that the blockade was a defensive response to the Western currency reform, and saw it as a phase in a major Soviet effort to drive the Western powers from Berlin (June 28). He stated that the U.S. had the alternative of following a firm policy in Berlin or accepting the consequences of failure for the rest of its European policy (July 19). Truman defined the U.S. presence in Berlin as one which should be defended at all costs because it derived from an agreement which the Russians had no right to nullify by either direct or indirect pressure (July 19). But the most forceful articulation of the perceived threat to basic American values is contained in Clay's cable of July 19, in which he (1) argued that the Soviet challenge presented the U.S. with the most critical issue that had arisen since Hitler placed his policy of aggression in motion, and (2) warned against the display of any weakness or appeasement in the face of this challenge.

Probability of War

The blockade triggered a sharp increase in the perceived likelihood of war. Estimates of the probability of war were neither uniform nor constant for each individual; they varied from individual to individual and for each individual over time. The dominant view, shared by both the State Department experts and the military staffs, was that the Soviets did not deliberately plan or want war, but that war could nonetheless come about as a result of the exercise in brinkmanship on which they had embarked. The decision-makers were seriously preoccupied throughout the crisis period with the possibility of a war caused either by Soviet design, which seemed unlikely, or through inadvertent escalation, which seemed much more likely. Clay considered war to be exceedingly unlikely because he thought that war could only result from a conscious decision by the Kremlin to go to war and that such a decision had not been taken. Truman, Marshall, and the Joint Chiefs of Staff, on the other hand, regarded the probability of war as appreciably higher. These divergent estimates largely derived from different images of the adversary. Clay perceived the Kremlin as a cool, calculating, and controlled actor in world politics, whereas the others were not convinced that the Kremlin was so predictable or that it would react to challenge and loss of prestige in a mood of calm resignation.

The desire to avert a slide towards war exercised a profound influence on American behavior during the crisis period. Clay and Murphy, who rated the probability of war as relatively low, were also more risk-acceptant, as is evidenced by their advocacy of an armed convoy. The decision-makers in Washington, who rated the probability of war as relatively high, were more risk-averse, as is evidenced by their objection to the idea of an armed convoy and by their preference for the less provocative option of an airlift. But when it came to the crunch, even Clay had to admit that a ground convoy might provoke an armed clash; and in the end, he settled for an airlift, which, as Truman pointed out, involved less risk.

Time Pressure

Another consequence of events at the outset of the Berlin crisis period was an emerging awareness of the time dimension. Some decisional response was regarded by America's decision-makers as necessary for defending her material interests as well as for maintaining her credibility as a Great Power, and this decision could not be delayed indefinitely. Clay, who was particularly sensitive to considerations of timing, also experienced much more acutely than the others the need for speed in adopting countermeasures to foil the blockade. Time salience is evident in his decision on June 25 to mount the airlift and in his repeated warnings to Washington about the need to do something before German suffering compelled the Allies to leave Berlin in order to relieve it. The broader considerations which led him to favor an armed convoy were also governed by time considerations, for, as he told Forrestal, its chances of success would grow slimmer with the passage of time because the buildup of world opinion would make it more difficult for the Russians to back down. The other decision-makers regarded the time for response as finite but not brief. The Pentagon meeting on June 27 proceeded on the assumption that with existing food stocks, supplemented by such deliveries as could be brought in by air, serious food shortages would not occur for approximately thirty days. Once the airlift got under way, the initiative swung partially to the Allies, and the time constraints were partially, but only partially, relaxed. The series of measures agreed to on July 22 reflected a new appreciation that the airlift would buy enough time for diplomatic action.

COPING MECHANISMS

Information Processing

As the Berlin crisis became more intense, America's decision-makers felt a growing need for more information. The principal source of information was the office of the American Military Governor in Germany. Much of the information concerning developments in Berlin was conveyed personally by Clay to the Department of the Army by telegrams and by means of lengthy and frequent teletype conversations. On June 25, for example, Royall questioned Clay very closely about various aspects of the Berlin situation. On July 12, OMGUS was requested to furnish detailed replies to a set of six questions concerning the technical aspects of Clay's convoy idea. One innovation consisted of a joint report about their meeting with Sokolovsky by the three Military Governors to their respective governments. American ambassadors in Allied capitals, especially Douglas, began to supply exceptionally detailed reports on the views and actions of the governments to which they were accredited. To facilitate the exchange and processing of information at the inter-Allied level, the American and French ambassadors in London, along with Sir William Strang of the British Foreign Office, constituted a committee. Conventional cable media between Washington and London were utilized to a much greater extent than in non-crisis situations. This was supplemented by firsthand reports by Draper on high-level talks held in London, Paris, and Berlin, and by direct correspondence between Bevin and Marshall.

In Washington, Marshall instituted the Berlin Group to deal with the flood of incoming information. Charles Bohlen, who headed it, points out that task forces and committees were not as institutionalized in those days as they are now, and the Group operated rather informally. Bohlen worked with General Gerhardt, who had been appointed the coordinator in the Pentagon, and he went there frequently in the evenings for teletype exchanges with Berlin. In those working days and nights, the irrepressible Lovett provided them with welcome breaks in tension. One night, recalls Bohlen, when the subject of Berlin's sewers came up, Lovett said with a grin, "I hope General Clay would realize that our policy is open sewers, openly arrived at."[167] Information and requests on a host of administrative matters continued to receive attention all the time. This was partly the result of the complexity of the crisis, which straddled a number of issue areas: political-diplomatic, military-security, and socio-economic.

Consultation

Our discussion of the relationship between consultation and the magnitude of stress can usefully begin by taking account of the fact that consultation may be undertaken by a President or other top-level officials for a variety of reasons. Alexander George has identified at least four purposes or objectives that may be served by consulting: (1) obtaining information and advice—i.e., the execu-

---

167. Bohlen, *Witness to History*, p. 280.

tive's cognitive needs; (2) obtaining reassurance and moral support to alleviate stress—i.e., the executive's emotional needs, usually enhanced by having to make important decisions involving value complexity under conditions of inadequate information and knowledge; (3) getting others to "participate" in the decision-making process in the hope of thereby increasing their support for the decision finally taken—i.e., the executive's need for decisions that enjoy consensus; and (4) offering others in the policymaking system an opportunity to express their opinions in order to meet the public's expectations that a wide range of views from all responsible senior officials and advisers will be obtained before a decision is made—i.e., the executive's need for legitimizing his decisions.[168]

It is not always possible to discover which particular purpose is served by consulting, and it should be noted that consulting can be used not just for one but for a number of purposes simultaneously. Part of the difficulty in determining purpose is that executives are rarely clear in their own minds about the precise purpose or purposes of consulting, and one has to draw on imprecise data in any attempt to probe their motives. What is clear beyond doubt from the Berlin case is that escalating stress was accompanied by a major increase in the size of the consultative circle and in the intensity of the consultative process.

Most of the individuals drawn into policy discussions were government officials rather than politicians, and this fact may be taken to suggest that the cognitive need for information and advice was the principal reason for the change in the pattern of consultation. This change was quantitative rather than qualitative, inasmuch as senior officials from the State Department and the defense establishment had, of course, been involved in policy deliberations during the pre-crisis period. Rising stress during the crisis period, however, enlarged the group of officials whose advice was sought and markedly increased the intensity of the consultative process.

As for the two groups of civilian and military advisers, Truman turned more frequently to the latter for advice. This was no doubt the result of the increase in the perceived threat and in the probability of war. The effect was to upgrade the relative weight of the military and to downgrade the relative weight of the civilian

---

168. Alexander L. George, *Presidential Decisionmaking in Foreign Policy: The Effective Use of Information and Advice* (Boulder, Colorado: Westview, 1980), chap. 4.

branch in the consultative process. For example, the first major consultation to survey America's options, held in the Pentagon on June 27, included a preponderance of military officials. The Joint Chiefs of Staff entered the picture rather belatedly, but their position, once it was formulated, served to establish the parameters of choice for the civilian leadership. The Chiefs' advice against any course of action which involved a serious risk of an armed clash, for which they were not prepared, was decisive in the defeat of the armed convoy proposal. Military advice did not always prevail, as can be seen, for example, from Truman's dismissal of General Vandenberg's argument against an overconcentration of aircraft in the Berlin theater; but the military as a group came to play a more important role in the consultative process than did their civilian counterparts.

During the crisis period, there are only faint signs of consultation for the purpose of obtaining reassurance and moral support to alleviate stress. Temperamentally, Truman was well able to cope with stress, and, rather than seeking relief through prolonged discussions, his instinctive reaction was to do something in order to appear decisive. His airlift decision of June 26, for example, was taken not only in the absence of supportive advice but in the face of actual opposition from inside his Cabinet. On the other hand, when the critical decision had to be made, Truman ordered that General Clay be recalled to Washington to present his views in person, and afterwards he initiated a private meeting with the confident and tough-minded theater commander. To what extent Truman's move was inspired by a conscious desire for reassurance and moral support is difficult to say, because this particular example of consultation may be equally interpreted with reference to the other three purposes commonly served by consulting.

The third purpose—getting others to participate in the decision-making process in the hope of thereby increasing their support for the decision finally taken—is best illustrated by the invitation to Senator Vandenberg and John Foster Dulles to take part in some confidential conferences on Berlin held at the State Department. In contrast to the pre-crisis period, when the consultation process was confined to government circles, rising stress and the magnitude of the issues facing the nation prompted a Democratic President to seek the involvement of the rival political elite. Truman's general commitment to the pursuit of a bipartisan foreign policy received concrete expression during the Berlin crisis in the effort, strongly supported by Marshall and Lovett, to project abroad the appearance of a united people. Domestically, of course, Truman derived considerable advantage from the participation of the Republican foreign policy spokesman in the determination of the final U.S. position on Berlin, because it muted Republican criticism of his foreign policy and provided decisions which rested on a broad consensus cutting across party lines.

Finally, some of the meetings held during the crisis period were intended to offer others in the policymaking system an opportunity to express their opinions in order to meet the public's expectations that a wide range of views from senior officials were obtained before major decisions were taken. The extensive media coverage of Clay and Murphy's arrival in Washington helped to focus public attention on the fact that firsthand reports were being made available to the National Security Council. Earlier, the two meetings held at the White House on July 19 also helped to give the impression that a large number of advisers were given a chance to present their views before a major decision was taken. The fact that the decision to stay in Berlin had already been reaffirmed by Truman at the noon meeting with Marshall and Forrestal could not detract from the public-relations value of the second meeting, because this fact was not generally known.

One major conclusion suggested by these findings is that it is not sufficient to regard the relationship between stress and consultation as involving only the decision-maker's interest in and need for information and advice. The utility of a more refined, disaggregated concept of consultation, such as that suggested by George, is that it calls attention to the fact that a decision-maker who experiences stress may consult more to obtain emotional support, consensus, and legitimacy than to satisfy his cognitive needs for information and advice.

Decisional Forums

America's decisional unit during the Berlin crisis period ranged from one participant to a very full National Security Council with twenty participants. The Council made important decisions at its meetings on July 15 and 22. But the great majority of the decisions were taken by small and ad hoc groups of decision-makers. In this respect, there is a marked contrast between the consultative and the decisional patterns of behavior which emerged in the course of the crisis period. Whereas the consultative circle expanded under the impact of stress, the size of the decision-making unit moved in the opposite direction. Decision-making became more centralized, and decisional authority was monopolized to a considerable degree by a small group of powerful individuals.

No one single forum dominated the decision-making. The National Security Council made some important decisions on aircraft deployment and the expansion of the airlift, but it was bypassed on many other and no less weighty matters, such as the basic decision on whether the U.S. should stay in Berlin or abandon it. The role of the Cabinet was entirely marginal and insignificant. Evidence about its proceedings is incomplete, but the available evidence suggests that it did not take any of the crisis decisions.

The setting in which decisions were made was dominated not by any institutional body but by one individual—Harry S. Truman. Presidential involvement in and control of the decision-making on Berlin increased markedly with the transition from the pre-crisis to the crisis period. It was during the latter period, with its simultaneous increase in threat, war probability, and time salience, that Truman came into his own as the "ultimate decision-maker" or "decision-maker of last resort."[169] The initiative and direction did not always come from him. Much of this was provided by General Clay, who played a pivotal role, especially in the initial phase of the crisis period, and who took the decision to supply Berlin by air on his own initiative. Marshall, too, took some initiatives on the diplomatic front. But it was Truman who made the strategic decision to stay in Berlin, and he either made or endorsed all the fateful decisions bearing on war and peace. It was in this sense that he acted as the "ultimate decision-maker" during the crisis period.

The role of the military in the decision-making process remained clearly circumscribed. This was the direct result of the assertion of presidential authority. Clay was instructed not to make any statements referring to the possibility of war and to get clearance for any actions which might lead to escalation. The Joint Chiefs of Staff exercised some influence over the formulation of high policy, but this influence was more noteworthy in its negative aspect, in foreclosing some options, than in its positive aspect, in deciding what should be done. And it was subjected throughout to clear civilian supremacy. Truman regarded the stakes as far too

---

169. The terms are suggested by Roger Hilsman, *The Politics of Policy-Making in Defense and Foreign Affairs* (New York: Harper and Row, 1971), p. 18.

great to allow even his senior military advisers to call the bids. This was particularly evident in his rejection of the request that he should turn over to the Military Establishment the custody of the atomic bomb. It was also manifested in the restrictive mandate issued to the Joint Chiefs of Staff for the meeting with their British colleagues.

Another major feature of the institutional setting in which crisis decisions were made was the overwhelming reliance on ad hoc forums. Large and institutionalized forums such as the National Security Council were bypassed in favor of small working groups which better suited Truman's personal style. The meeting on June 26 of Truman, Forrestal, Royall, and Lovett, which decided against sending a note of protest to Moscow and against outside retaliation, did not constitute any constitutionally recognized forum. Nor did the larger meeting held in the Pentagon on June 27, or the restricted one held in the White House the following day. In acting in this highly informal manner through ad hoc forums, Truman was circumventing the elaborate institutional machinery which he himself had established.

In terms of coping with crisis, these findings indicate that crisis-induced stress led to a highly centralized pattern of decision-making and to a pronounced shift in favor of ad hoc organs of decision. The role of the President was pivotal and in no small measure contributed both to the centralization of decisional authority in a few hands and to the departure from established forums and procedures.

Alternatives: Search and Evaluation

Since no strategic decision concerning the U.S. commitment to Berlin had been made prior to the imposition of the blockade, the process of search during the crisis period covered an exceptionally broad spectrum of options, ranging from planned withdrawal to the use of nuclear weapons, and much of it was conducted at a frantic pace. But while the range of the alternative courses of action that were considered at one time or another between late June and late July was impressively broad, the process by which these alternatives were evaluated in the higher echelons of the Truman Administration was marked by poor coordination and occasional confusion.

Under the impact of stress, the responses of the American decision-makers tended to become less analytical and more intuitive, and little attempt was made to systematically calculate the likely costs and benefits of the various courses of action under consideration. This tendency is well illustrated by the changing attitude toward negotiation with the Russians at successive stages during the crisis period. At the outset of the crisis period, the possibility of negotiation implied by the Warsaw declaration was instinctively dismissed without any attempt to informally explore the Russian intentions that lay behind it. When Clay began to question the wisdom of holding talks with Sokolovsky, the other American decision-makers all too readily agreed to leave the decision to him and did not engage in any evaluation of this alternative in relation to other alternatives. It is possible that negotiation with the Russians could not have resolved the crisis on acceptable terms, but on the American side this alternative was approached not with an open mind but in a deeply suspicious fashion in which images of the communist opponent, memories of the 1930s, and the specter of appeasement played a larger part than the detached calculation of present realities and likely future outcomes.

Increasing stress led to a growing attention being given to options concerned with immediate rather than long-term objectives. The immediate objective was to ensure the flow of essential supplies to the Western sectors of Berlin, pending decision on America's long-term plans. Routine procedures could not cope with the environmental change, which involved mounting threat as well as time pressure. So Clay, acting swiftly and on his own initiative, decided to launch the airlift. Truman's decision on June 26 was primarily an extension of this earlier decision. In reaching this decision, Truman, like Clay, acted without the benefit of a comprehensive evaluation of the available options or an agreed-upon recommendation from his advisers.

The first major step in the effort to formulate a basic political response to the Soviet challenge was taken on June 27 at the emergency meeting convened at the Pentagon. Forrestal's report gives the impression that a systematic search and evaluation of alternatives was conducted at this meeting: three possible courses of action were discussed, and the pros and cons of each were weighed. But the forum in which this discussion took place was an improvised one, and the list of alternatives around which the discussion revolved was by no means exhaustive. One omission was the airlift, which is all the more surprising since the airlift had already been set in motion.

If the Pentagon meeting had at least the semblance of an orderly and careful consideration of alternatives, the White House meeting held on the following day was entirely deficient in this respect. This was the meeting which produced the first authoritative choice between the competing alternatives of holding the line or retreating from Berlin. Yet, Truman's ruling in favor of staying was not made after a careful evaluation of all the known data or with a clear recognition of the implications involved. Rather, it was an affective response in which moral indignation at what was seen as a violation of America's legal rights figured no less prominently than cold political calculation.

This pattern of affective responses is not consistently supported by all the evidence of the crisis period. The range of alternatives considered over time included various forms of legal, diplomatic, economic, and military action. Some of the alternatives were only accepted or rejected after careful scrutiny by the relevant experts in the State Department, the Army, or the Air Force. The decisions against the sending of an armed convoy and in favor of a forward deployment of American aircraft, for example, were not taken lightly but only after wide-ranging consultations and detailed study. The National Security Council examined the expanded airlift alternative on June 22 from several different angles and did not allow purely military considerations to dominate policy. But, in general, the search for and evaluation of alternatives were not carried out systematically by one organ specifically charged with this responsibility, nor were the alternatives compared to each other in terms of a single criterion of utility. The institutionalized procedures envisaged in the 1947 National Security Act precisely for such contingencies were honored more in the breach than in the observance. The process of evaluation which preceded decision was piecemeal and haphazard, and therefore more susceptible to the intrusion of extraneous influences than a structured process is likely to be. All this does not mean that the decisions taken on the basis of this largely random, if highly energetic, process of search and evaluation were unwise. Sound decisions frequently issue from faulty processes, and orderly processes are no guarantee of wise decisions. But in terms of coping with crisis, these findings suggest that mounting stress is accompanied by a shift towards unsystematic and improvised procedures in the search for and evaluation of alternatives.

PART IV

Post-Crisis Period

CHAPTER SEVEN

Psychological Environment

THE DECISION reached by the National Security Council on July 22 to refrain from sharp escalatory measures and settle for a long-haul strategy involving an expanded airlift, coupled with a diplomatic initiative, marked the end of the intense crisis period. Not all the crisis conditions declined immediately, but the perceived time pressure was relaxed and the prospects for a peaceful solution to the crisis were enhanced. The long post-crisis period, which spanned considerable fluctuations in the level of tension, continued until May 5, 1949, when agreement was reached with the Soviet Union on the lifting of the blockade and the subsequent convening of a meeting of the Council of Foreign Ministers to discuss the Berlin situation and the future of Germany.

DECISIONS AND DECISION-MAKERS

The key decision-makers during the Berlin post-crisis period were President Truman, Secretary Marshall, General Clay, and, for a brief period at the end, Dean Acheson. Truman's role was considerably less central and directive compared to the role he had played during the crisis period. Not only were there fewer supreme war-and-peace issues meriting presidential attention than before, but Truman's preoccupation with the election campaign during the late summer and autumn of 1948 precluded him from directing American policy in this external crisis personally and on an ongoing basis. As a "lame duck" President whose imminent defeat at the hands of his Republican rival was widely expected, he lacked the moral authority to effect major changes in policy. But he remained the Chief Executive throughout the period, and in this capacity he was kept informed about developments connected with Berlin, he was consulted on the more important issues, he participated in some decisions, and his approval was necessary to translate NSC recommendations into action. Moreover, he bounced back with his prestige enormously enhanced after his resounding victory in November, and assumed a more direct and active role in the final phase of the crisis.

General Clay's role was also downgraded during the post-crisis period, but for very different reasons. As the possibility of war receded, the diplomats once again took the lead in the management of the crisis. Clay remained at his post until the crisis was finally resolved, but although he continued to be the chief executor of American policy in Germany, a major source of information and advice to the policymakers in Washington, and a frequent participant in high-level policy discussions, the role he played was not as pivotal as it had been when the crisis was at its height and Washington was paralyzed by indecision. Perhaps there was no longer the need for Clay to be so assertive and dominant because, after all, it was his policy of staying in Berlin which had triumphed, and he could turn his formidable energy to the twin tasks of building up the airlift and pressing ahead with the creation of a West German government. In addition, he played a prominent and conspicuous role in the conduct of American crisis bargaining during the first week in September, when the abortive talks between the four Military Governors took place.

Secretary Marshall, despite failing health, played a more central and continuous part in the management of the crisis from July 22 onwards than any other American decision-maker. This was due to situational factors rather than to any drive on his part to encroach on presidential prerogatives and centralize decision power in his own hands. Most of the initiatives and decisions that had to be taken after the U.S. government had made its strategic choice were of a diplomatic character, and it was only natural that the Secretary of State should occupy the center of the stage. This was particularly so when the Berlin dispute was being considered by the Security Council of the United Nations, and Marshall and many of his top advisers were in Paris while Truman was waging his political campaign at home.

When Dean Acheson succeeded Marshall as Secretary of State in January 1949, he played the same leading role in the decision-making process on Berlin as his predecessor, if only for a short period. Other officials who had some influence in the formulation and execution of American policy during the post-crisis period include James Forrestal, until his retirement in March 1949; Kenneth Royall; Robert Lovett, until his resignation in January 1949; Charles Bohlen; and Philip Jessup. George Kennan's actual influence on the Berlin and German policies of the Truman Administration was very limited under Marshall and virtually nonexistent under Acheson, but he also deserves to be mentioned in this context for the major part he played, in his capacity as head of the Policy Planning Staff (PPS), in the search for and evaluation of long-term options.

The expansion of the role of the Secretary of State relative to that of the President and the military in the decision-making process during the post-crisis period is reflected in the following list of decisions:

Decision Number	Date	Content
17	August 3	Marshall decided to accept the Soviet currency as the sole currency for Berlin, provided it would be subject to quadripartite control.
18	August 10	Marshall rejected the Soviet draft agreement.
19	September 7	The NSC agreed to present an *aide-mémoire* to Molotov and to increase the number of C-54s taking part in the airlift from 125 to 200.
20	September 16	The NSC agreed that the National Military Establishment must be ready to use nuclear weapons in the event of hostilities and must plan accordingly, but the decision concerning the actual employment of nuclear weapons was left in the hands of the Chief Executive.
21	September 21	Marshall, Bevin, and Schuman reached agreement in Paris to proceed with the dispatch of identical notes to the Soviet Union and to take the Berlin question to the UN if the Russian reply turned out to be unsatisfactory.

22	September 26	Marshall, Bevin, and Schuman, following receipt of the Soviet reply, reached agreement concerning: (1) a final confirmation of the decision to refer the Berlin question to the UN Security Council; (2) the sending of a final note to the Soviet Government; and (3) the issuing of a communiqué.
23	October 4	Marshall and Bevin agreed in Paris to oppose the Soviet proposal for a meeting of the Council of Foreign Ministers so long as the blockade of Berlin remained in force.
24	October 5	Truman, as a direct result of Marshall's protest, decided to abandon the plan to send Chief Justice Vinson on a peace mission to Moscow.
25	October 22	Truman, on the recommendation of Clay and the NSC, authorized the allocation of additional aircraft and the expansion of the maintenance facilities for the airlift.
26	October 26	Marshall, on the recommendation of his advisers, decided to support the setting up of a neutral UN Commission which would study the currency problem in Berlin and propose a solution.
27	December 24	Lovett, Royall, and Draper resolved, with the President's concurrence, to reject the UN Technical Committee's preliminary proposals and to proceed immediately with the introduction of the "B" mark as the sole legal tender in the Western sectors.
28	February 1, 1949	Truman and Acheson agreed to indicate to the Russians, through a press conference, that Stalin's signal had been received and to follow this up with a secret probing operation.
29	March 29	Truman approved (1) the procedure proposed by the State Department for pursuing the Jessup-Malik talks, and (2) the text of the statement to be read to Malik.

PSYCHOLOGICAL ENVIRONMENT
Attitudinal Prism

As was only to be expected, the attitudinal prism of the American decision-makers remained essentially unchanged from the beginning until the end of the Berlin crisis. Prisms, as noted earlier, are on the whole remarkably stable and resistant to change. Prism change is a long-term process which can be marginally accelerated during a crisis. A significant change of prism in the short term, if it occurs at all, is usually brought about by a change of government or a shift in the balance of power inside a government. In the Berlin case, the same government under the same leader remained in power from the beginning until the end of the crisis. The one major change in the composition of the high-policy elite, brought about by Marshall's retirement, did not entail any radical change in the world-view of this elite, because Acheson, who succeeded Marshall, fully shared the "realist" outlook and hard-line convictions prevalent among its other members. The Riga axioms were in no way shaken or revised by Acheson's appointment. On the contrary, they found in him an ardent supporter and articulate proponent.

The blockade had an important impact in confirming the worldview of the American leaders. More particularly, it appeared to vindicate the Riga axioms as the framework for assessing Soviet intentions. The perception of the Soviet Union as an aggressive, perfidious, and expansionist power which posed a threat to international peace and stability was reinforced. A document prepared by the Policy Planning Staff in response to Forrestal's request for a comprehensive statement of national policy observed that "our difficulty with the present Soviet Government lies basically in the fact that its leaders are animated by concepts of the theory and practice of international relations which are not only radically opposed to our own, but are incompatible with any peaceful and mutually profitable development of relations between that government and other members of the international community, individually and collectively."[1] The final product of the review ini-

---

1. NSC 20/1, August 18, 1948, "U.S. Objectives with Respect to Russia," Records of the National Security Council, Modern Military Branch, National Archives, Washington, D.C.

tiated by Forrestal was an NSC paper which was approved by Truman on November 24 and served as a definitive statement of United States policy towards the Soviet Union until April 1950. It stated much more bluntly that

> Communist ideology and Soviet behavior clearly demonstrate that the ultimate objective of the leaders of the USSR is the domination of the world. Soviet leaders hold that the Soviet communist party is the militant vanguard of the world proletariat in its rise to political power, and that the USSR, base of the world communist movement, will not be safe until the non-communist nations have been so reduced in strength and numbers that communist influence is dominant throughout the world. The immediate goal of top priority since the recent war has been the political conquest of western Europe. The resistance of the United States is recognized by the USSR as a major obstacle to the attainment of these goals.[2]

While the blockade reinforced the American leaders' view of Moscow's expansionist long-term aims, the great caution and restraint which the men in the Kremlin exercised in the face of the airlift caused some American leaders to revise their earlier belief about Russian recklessness. The latent differences between those who believed that the Kremlin had embarked on a high-risk strategy and those who believed that it was deliberately pursuing a low-risk strategy were gradually transformed into a consensus which favored the latter hypothesis. The fact that the Russians made no attempt to reduce the effectiveness of the airlift, although they could have done this by a variety of means such as flying their own unarmed planes in the air corridors, jamming the Western air traffic control broadcasts, and floating barrage balloons in the air lanes, indicated that there was a fairly low ceiling of risk beyond which they were unwilling to venture.[3]

The obvious Soviet reluctance to escalate the crisis by adopting even low-risk tactics or by manipulating shared risks (e.g., through buzzing) tended to confirm the estimate of those Americans who

---

2. NSC 20/4, November 23, 1948, "U.S. Objectives with Respect to the U.S.S.R. to Counter Soviet Threats to U.S. Security," in *Foreign Relations of the United States, 1948*, Vol. 1: *General; The United Nations*, Part 2 (Washington, D.C.: U.S. Government Printing Office, 1976), pp. 663–669. (Henceforth, this series will be referred to as *FRUS*.)

3. John R. Oneal, *Creative Adaptation: Process and Potential for Foreign Policy Making in Times of Crisis* (Ph.D. dissertation, Stanford University, 1979), pp. 416–417.

believed that the adversary had not embarked on a war course. The possibility that unplanned war might arise out of Soviet actions continued to concern the American military planners, but the consensus was that the Soviet Union did not want to precipitate war and would pursue its expansionist policies by all means short of war. "The evidence points to the conclusion," said a PPS paper of August 25, "that the Soviet Government is not now planning any deliberate armed action of this nature and is still seeking to achieve its aims predominantly by political means, accompanied—of course—by the factor of military intimidation. The tactics which it is employing, however, themselves heighten the danger that military complications may arise from fortuitous causes or from miscalculation. War must therefore be regarded, if not as a probability, at least as a possibility, and one serious enough to be taken account of fully in our military and political planning."[4]

The confidence that the Soviet Government would not resort to war was shaken temporarily by the breakdown of the talks between the Military Governors during the first week of September, following the Moscow talks. But the sudden rise in the apprehension of war was reversed equally quickly. For example, on September 16, in a postmortem of all the Berlin talks to date, Ambassador Smith stated his opinion that the "Kremlin discounted completely the possibility that we might actually force the issue to point of hostilities, just as we estimated no similar intention on their part, and that their belief has been reinforced during protracted course of Moscow talks."[5] From September onwards, the fear that war would break out either by Soviet design or as a result of Soviet miscalculation steadily declined. The perceived time scale for resolving the crisis lengthened, and the emphasis shifted from the danger of being catapulted in the short term into a global war to viewing the crisis as involving a controlled contest of capabilities and resolution.

As the contest intensified, the attendant dangers persisted and possibly even increased, but new evidence was forthcoming in support of the image of the Soviet Union as a cool, calculating, and rational actor rather than a blustering and impulsive one. The

4. NSC 20/2, August 25, 1948, "Factors Affecting the Nature of the U.S. Defense Arrangements, in the Light of Soviet Policies," in *FRUS, 1948*, Vol. 1, p. 619.
5. Smith to Marshall, September 16, 1948, in *FRUS, 1948*, Vol. 2, pp. 1160–62.

view, never widely held, that the blockade was a prelude to a Soviet invasion of Western Europe disappeared without trace, making way for a generally agreed-upon assessment that the Soviet Union was not planning to resort to armed force to further its objectives. George Kennan, whose earlier analysis of the Soviet threat had exercised such a profound influence on the foreign policy ideas of the Truman Administration, now consistently argued against the view that the Soviet leaders wished to invade or were planning to invade Western Europe. In a formal PPS paper submitted to the Secretary of State on November 24, 1948, at a moment of particular tension in Berlin, he wrote:

> A military danger, arising from possible incidents or from the prestige engagement of the Russians and the western powers in the Berlin situation, does exist, and is probably increasing rather than otherwise. But basic Russian intent still runs to the conquest of western Europe by political means. In this program, military force plays a major role only as a means of intimidation.
>
> The danger of political conquest is still greater than the military danger. If a war comes in the foreseeable future, it will probably be one which Moscow did not desire but did not know how to avoid. The political war, on the other hand, is now in progress; and, if there should not be a shooting war, it is this political war which will be decisive.[6]

With this assessment there was apparently no disagreement anywhere within the State Department, and Marshall orally indicated his agreement with it.[7] Such differences as did exist within the Administration related to the implications to be drawn from this assessment for America's foreign policy and military posture. Here the military planners, who habitually attached much more importance to capabilities than to intentions, were driven by the acknowledged Soviet preponderance in conventional military forces on the continent to urge caution in the conduct of American policy and a large increase in the defense budget for the purpose of expanding American capabilities. The State Department officials, on the other hand, provided little support for the Defense Department's struggle against the ceiling which Truman sought to impose on the defense budget, and they tended to favor a tougher stand in Berlin, stemming from their reading of Moscow's intentions, to

---

6. Memorandum by the Director of the Policy Planning Staff (Kennan), November 24, 1948, in *FRUS, 1948*, Vol. 3, pp. 283–289.

7. Ibid., p. 284, note 2.

which they attached greater weight than to the military balance of forces in Europe.[8]

However, these were differences of degree rather than of substance. Although Soviet behavior during the crisis led to a revision of the image of the Soviet Union as reckless and belligerent in the means it would employ, no corresponding revision took place in the long-term objectives attributed to the adversary. Vigilance and military preparedness were therefore generally considered essential ingredients of successful containment by the U.S. of Soviet expansionist tendencies. As the paper drafted by the PPS in response to Forrestal's request exhorted: "In dealing with a government so highly centralized, so incorrigibly conspiratorial in its methods, so hostile traditionally towards its world environment, so despotic at home, so unpredictable in foreign affairs, it is necessary that we keep ourselves in a state of unvacillating mental preparedness. Without military preparedness, this would be a sham."[9]

Neither the military nor the political planners were opposed to negotiations with the Soviet Union to explore avenues for a peaceful solution to the Berlin problem, but they did not entertain undue hopes that the Soviet leaders could be moved by words alone. It was firmly believed that, in the long run, "Soviet leaders are prepared to recognize *situations*, if not arguments."[10] This belief—an integral part of the Riga axioms—underlined the dangers of displaying any weakness and predisposed the American policymakers towards creating situations of strength which the Soviet leaders would be compelled to recognize. The images of Munich and appeasement of a decade earlier returned to haunt American policy during the intense Cold War conflict with the Soviet adversary. "In addition to the risk of war, a danger equally to be guarded against," warned the authoritative NSC paper of November 1948, "is the possibility that Soviet political warfare might seriously weaken the relative position of the United States, enhance Soviet strength and either lead to our ultimate defeat short of war, or force us into war under dangerously unfavorable conditions. Such a result would be

---

8. Walter Millis, ed., *The Forrestal Diaries* (New York: Viking, 1951), chap. 13; and Oneal, *Creative Adaptation*, pp. 390–394 and 420–421.

9. NSC 20/2, August 25, 1948, "Factors Affecting the Nature of the U.S. Defense Arrangements in the Light of Soviet Policies," in *FRUS, 1948*, Vol. 1, p. 621.

10. NSC 20/1, August 18, 1948, "U.S. Objectives with Respect to Russia," Records of the National Security Council, Modern Military Branch, National Archives, Washington, D.C. (emphasis in the original).

facilitated by vacillation, appeasement or isolationist concepts in our foreign policy, leading to loss of our allies and influence. . . ."[11] Parallels from the past were thus a significant element in the prism through which the American high-policy elite continued to view their country's principal adversary during the final period of the Berlin crisis.

Images

TRUMAN

Two closely related perceptual strands dominated Truman's approach to the conduct of relations with the Soviet Union during the Berlin post-crisis period: fear of appeasement and the desire to project the appearance of strength. These perceptual strands underlie the account in his memoirs of the principal events and developments in the Berlin crisis from late July onwards.[12] A much more explicit and contemporary account of the thinking that lay behind his foreign policy, however, may be found in an address he made at the American Legion Convention on October 18, 1948.

Truman reminded his listeners that while the President of the United States can delegate authority, he has the responsibility under the Constitution for the conduct of the nation's foreign affairs. In that capacity, he wanted to stress that so long as he was President, "the United States will not carry a chip on its shoulder." But he also carefully distinguished between firmness and aggressiveness. In recent months, the trend of events had caused him deep concern, but he wanted it clearly understood that his government rejected the concept of war as a means of solving international differences. He went out of his way to dispel rumors which were circulating in Europe and at home to the effect that the United States was deliberately following a course that would lead to war:

> We have taken, and we will continue to take, a firm position, where our rights are threatened. But our firmness should not be mistaken for a warlike spirit. The world has learned that it is weakness and appeasement that invite aggression. A firm position on reasonable grounds offers the best hope of peace, and we have been open to reason at every point.

11. NSC 20/4, November 23, 1948, "U.S. Objectives with Respect to the U.S.S.R. to Counter Soviet Threats to U.S. Security," in *FRUS, 1948*, Vol. 1, pp. 663–669.
12. Harry S. Truman, *Memoirs*, Vol. 2: *Years of Trial and Hope, 1946–1953* (London: Hodder and Stoughton, 1956), pp. 133–139.

We recognize the principle of mutual conciliation as a basis for peaceful negotiation, but this is very different from appeasement. While we will always strive for peace, this country will never consent to any compromise of the principles of freedom and human rights. We will never be a party to the kind of compromise which the world sums up in the disgraced name of Munich.[13]

The timing and tone of this address suggest a link with the imminent election, but the images and corresponding policy prescriptions it discloses are entirely consistent with the ones encountered earlier. The abhorrence of appeasement and the preference for realistic and measured firmness that had predisposed Truman to take the decision to stay in Berlin and mobilize American air power to that end continued to condition his actions until the Soviet Union agreed to lift the blockade and beyond.

MARSHALL

The change which occurred in Marshall's image of the Soviet Union during the second half of 1948 illustrated the more general trend within the Administration. Having been inclined to perceive the Soviet Union as an unpredictable, risk-acceptant, and possibly adventuristic power, and having treated the imposition of the blockade as a vindication of this perception, Marshall moved towards the view, long propagated by Clay, that the Kremlin calculated its moves coldly and rationally and was unlikely to be swept along by the current of events. Only with regard to the likelihood of war breaking out inadvertently, however, was this image adjustment reassuring. The possibility that the Soviet leaders might deliberately choose to go to war still had to be reckoned with.

Both the revised image and the caveat were conveyed by Marshall at a meeting with Halvard Lange, the Norwegian Foreign Minister, on November 22. Marshall told Lange, who had come to discuss regional defense arrangements, that the most critical point, as far as possible overt Soviet aggression was concerned, would probably be reached when American arms supplies started flowing into Western Europe. He added, however, that he did not think that this by itself, or incidents arising out of the situation in Berlin, or any other incidents, with the exception of planned ones, would be the determining factor. The determining factor, in his judg-

---

13. *Public Papers of the Presidents of the United States: Harry S. Truman, 1948* (Washington, D.C.: U.S. Government Printing Office, 1964), pp. 815–818.

ment, would be a general decision, for or against, made by the Soviet leaders. When Lange asked whether impending doom was approaching, Marshall replied that he could not answer the question, that no one knew what was in the minds of the Soviet leaders or what they might have already decided, but that he thought that the decision, one way or the other, would be a coldly calculated one and not the result of any particular events taking place.[14]

While he was reluctant to commit himself to a definite estimate of the likelihood of a Soviet-provoked war, Marshall did consider American deterrence to be more credible than it had been when the crisis erupted. Until fairly recently, he had thought, as he told Lange, that the Soviet leaders probably felt that the American people would not permit the use of the atomic bomb. But in light of the developments of recent months, including Soviet provocations in Berlin, the American public would support and even demand the use of the bomb. And Marshall felt that the Soviet leaders now realized that the use of this weapon would be possible, and this enhanced its deterrent effect.[15]

Just as overall deterrence was being enhanced, the success of the airlift relaxed the time constraints which were perceived to govern American policy. At various meetings with his European partners in September, Marshall expressed himself optimistically about the possibility of indefinitely continuing to support the Western forces of occupation and the German population in Berlin by air transport.[16] This confidence made Marshall less willing to make major concessions in order to obtain an agreement with the Soviet Union on the Berlin problem. From the very start of the Moscow talks, he had been determined to avoid compromise on the London Program.[17] But as the Western capability to supply Berlin became more secure, Marshall's bargaining posture became progressively less conciliatory. The central issue underlying the dispute, as he perceived it, was the Soviet contention that the Western powers had lost their coequal rights in Berlin. The principal aim of the diplomatic campaign he orchestrated was to assert

14. "Memorandum of Conversation, by the Secretary of State," Paris, November 20, 1948, in *FRUS, 1948*, Vol. 3, pp. 279–281.
15. Ibid.
16. "Minutes of the Meeting of the Secretary of State with the Foreign Ministers of the United Kingdom and France," Paris, September 21, 1948, in *FRUS, 1948*, Vol. 2, pp. 1177–80; and British Embassy (Washington) to the Foreign Office, September 25, 1948, FO 371/70517/C8062, Public Record Office, London.
17. Marshall to Smith, August 4, 1948, in *FRUS, 1948*, Vol. 2, pp. 1014–16.

these rights effectively rather than to search for a face-saving formula. Until his retirement, Marshall himself held firmly to previous positions, impressing on his subordinates and his European partners the importance of firmness and the dangers of appeasement in dealing with the Russians.[18]

CLAY

In the case of General Clay, the long and eventful post-crisis period served essentially to confirm his previous definition of the stakes in the conflict over Berlin, his assessment of Soviet intentions, and his strategic preferences. If greater convergence between his perceptions and those of the decision-makers in Washington can be detected, it is because they moved into line with him rather than the other way round.

Clay remained acutely sensitive to the symbolic value of Berlin, and he noted that this value only increased as a result of the well-publicized and dramatic battle in which it represented both the battleground and, for the Soviet Union, a much coveted prize. In the context of the Cold War, Berlin had become a symbol of American resolution to retreat no further in the face of communist pressure. The point was made by Clay on numerous occasions, including a memorandum of May 25, 1949 in which he summarized his views of possible courses of action in the event of reimposition of the Berlin blockade. "I would repeat once again," wrote Clay soon after the long-awaited release from his post in Germany, "that Berlin has become throughout Europe, and particularly in the satellite countries, the symbol of our determination to resist Communist expansion. Abandonment of Berlin would lose us many, if not all, of the gains of the past two years; and these gains have been made as a result of substantial investment by the United States. We cannot afford to throw away that investment."[19] To define the concrete interests which necessitated continuing Western presence in Berlin, Clay on some occasions implicitly invoked the image of Western Europe as a row of dominoes with Berlin at the head of the row. At a dinner on November 13, for example, Forrestal re-

18. Marshall to Smith, September 8, 1948, in *FRUS, 1948*, Vol. 2, pp. 1140–42; and Philip C. Jessup, "The Berlin Blockade and the Use of the United Nations," *Foreign Affairs*, Vol. 50, No. 1 (October 1972), p. 169.
19. Jean Edward Smith, ed., *The Papers of General Lucius D. Clay: Germany, 1945–1949* (Bloomington: Indiana University Press, 1974), Vol. 2, p. 1170 (hereinafter cited as *Clay Papers*).

corded Clay as saying that if the U.S. got out of Berlin under duress, the Russians would walk through Europe and at least gain such power and prestige in France that France would crumble.[20]

The time factor in the Berlin crisis was perceived by Clay as much less salient as the airlift grew from the makeshift operation of a few outmoded planes into a carefully planned split-second operation of a fleet of giant transports capable of sustaining a reasonable standard of living in the Western sectors of Berlin. By September, Clay reached the conclusion that Berlin could be supplied indefinitely by airlift alone, but other considerations made this undesirable. As he pointed out in a letter to his friend, former Secretary Byrnes, the airlift had been a magnificent success and could keep the Western powers in Berlin through the winter. As long as they pursued diplomatic means to gain a settlement, the airlift would add to their prestige. If, however, they were to exhaust all peaceful means, and then rely only on the airlift to remain in Berlin, it would begin to lose them prestige.[21] That point was never reached, of course, and with the passage of time Clay attached to the airlift deeper and deeper meaning. "Mechanically," he writes, "it proved the efficiency of the Western Powers in the air in a way that the Soviet Government could understand. Morally and spiritually, it was the reply of Western civilization to the challenge of totalitarianism which was willing to destroy through starvation thousands of men, women and children in the effort to control their souls and minds."[22]

Clay discounted the likelihood of physical aggression by Soviet forces. In discussions with American defense chiefs and diplomats, he gave it as his view that they were unduly apprehensive about the Russians and conceded them a power which they did not possess, while underestimating their own capabilities for defense and deterrence. For his own part, Clay was convinced that the Russians did not want a military showdown and would back down before a determined front. He was certain that communism had lost any opportunity it might have had to capture Germany, and that the military balance was shifting in favor of the West. He believed that even the limited forces available to him in Germany could give a good account of themselves, and that with an increase in French

20. Millis, *The Forrestal Diaries*, p. 527.
21. *Clay Papers*, Vol. 2, p. 860.
22. Lucius D. Clay, *Decision in Germany* (New York: Doubleday, 1950), p. 386.

forces, tactical air support, and British willingness to commit their forces in France, the Russians could be held at the Rhine. In the event of war, Clay said he would not hesitate to use the atomic bomb.[23]

Clay's perceptions of the large stakes involved in the Berlin dispute, of the improbability that it would lead to war, and of the extended time available to America for finding a solution converged to reinforce his preference for a tough stance in negotiations with the Russians. He was quick to detect and denounce any move which could be interpreted as a sign of weakness and appeasement. He was critical of Smith's handling of the oral approach to Stalin on the ground that Smith's presentation of the American case was too much of a plea and not enough of a demand.[24] When his turn came to negotiate with the Russians in Berlin, his posture was thoroughly rigid and unyielding, and he was greatly disturbed by what he considered to be signs of Washington's willingness to deviate from its original position in order to gain agreement. He felt that the American government had sacrificed pride and prestige beyond measure in failing to insist on its juridical right to participate in a four-power government of Berlin and in negotiating under duress. Royall reassured him that in no sense had the government abandoned its original position, and that it had no intention of making any agreement with the Russians that would be incompatible with national prestige. The failure of the talks was greeted by Clay with a sigh of relief because all along he maintained that no agreement would be preferable to an agreement which did not adequately safeguard America's juridical rights and prestige.[25]

Above all others, Clay was opposed to concessions which would compromise the London Program. The Russians implied on various occasions that the blockade would be lifted if the London Program were abandoned or suspended, but Clay vigorously resisted the temptation to buy relief in Berlin by modifying the Western plans for Germany.[26] All German politicians who met Clay in those years report that only the blockade finally changed his attitude towards Germany.[27] The image of the U.S.-German connection as-

23. Ibid., p. 376; *Clay Papers*, Vol. 2, pp. 846 and 875; and Millis, *The Forrestal Diaries*, p. 527, entry for November 13, 1948.
24. *Clay Papers*, Vol. 2, pp. 846–847.   25. Ibid., pp. 814–815.
26. Ibid., pp. 760 and 859–860.
27. Hans-Peter Schwarz, *Vom Reich zur Bundesrepublik* (Berlin: Luchterhand, 1966), p. 122.

sumed a preeminent place in his thinking about the American strategy in the Cold War conflict. He conceived of a self-sufficient, self-governing, and democratic West Germany oriented to the West as indispensable to the defense of Europe against pressure from the East. If the London Program, whose goal was to translate this image of a new Germany into reality, were to be postponed, Clay predicted that the Germans themselves would be frightened by Western weakness, and, secondly, that the Western powers themselves, having once given up to win a Soviet concession, would never have the chance to proceed with the program again.[28]

During the final phase of the Berlin crisis, when the meeting of Foreign Ministers was in the offing, the London Program was rushed to completion, and its numerous authors, according to Kennan (who was not exactly an impartial observer), "clung to it like a mother to a child. Now that so much effort had gone into it, and now that its final realization was at hand, it seemed to them doubly unthinkable that anyone should contemplate jeopardizing it by pursuing other possible solutions in talks with the Russians, particularly since it was evident that the latter were disposed to remove the blockade anyway. General Lucius Clay . . . prized the London Program particularly and regarded its final adoption, in the face of formidable difficulties, as a signal part of his achievement in Germany."[29] There is nothing in Clay's memoirs or papers to suggest that he ever at any time considered the London Program as expendable in favor of any sort of agreement with the Russians, and Kennan had strong reasons for believing that Clay's veto alone, had it been necessary, would have sufficed to rule out any proposals by the American government on the four-power level that envisaged the departure of Allied forces from most of Germany and the general abandonment of occupational controls.[30]

Just before his retirement, on May 5, Clay was utterly dismayed to learn of a plan whose author was none other than Kennan, and whose central feature was the withdrawal of all the occupation forces to enclaves located on the periphery of Germany, leaving the German people to form a government for the whole country. This would have meant abandoning the efforts to set up a West German government, and Clay's predictably angry and explosive

28. *Clay Papers*, Vol. 2, p. 764.
29. George F. Kennan, *Memoirs, 1925–1950* (Boston: Little, Brown, 1967), pp. 442–443.
30. Ibid., p. 443.

reaction was that the whole approach was suicidal to American objectives and would offset all the gains of the past two years. "We cannot lose Germany now," he warned, "except by throwing it away and this withdrawal would do just that." His specific objections were twofold: first, the plan would break faith completely with the Germans by going back on assurances given to the political leaders in Bonn; second, the withdrawal of the security screen would destroy Western Europe's confidence in America. Because the security provided by the American troop screen in Germany was not, according to Clay, only military security but security against fear, if the troops marched out, fear would march in, and communism, which thrives on fear, would triumph. Clay confessed that he was shocked by what he termed a combination of appeasement and faith in Soviet intent to carry out an agreement, and he emphatically urged abandoning the idea unless the U.S. wanted to turn over Germany to the Soviets, in which case this was the way to do it.[31] Murphy quickly cabled Clay that this plan was not in accord with the official State Department view, and that Secretary of State Acheson was convinced that the West German government must go ahead and that American troops must remain until European stability was assured.[32] Clay's vision of a West Germany allied to America and integrated into the framework of European economic recovery and European defense continued to inspire and guide American policy throughout the entire era of the Cold War.[33]

ACHESON

Dean Acheson was uniquely well qualified, by virtue of his long and varied experience of government and his immense knowledge of international affairs, to assume the top foreign policy post in the Truman Administration. As Under Secretary of State from August 1945 to June 1947, he emerged as a powerful and influential figure in the making of American foreign policy and as a formidable Cold Warrior. It was he who won over wavering Congressmen to the Truman Doctrine by likening the bipolar confrontation to the historic struggles which pitted Athens against Sparta and Rome against Carthage.[34] Viewing the Soviet Union as an aggressively

31. *Clay Papers*, Vol. 2, pp. 1148–49.
32. Clay, *Decision in Germany*, pp. 438–439.
33. Edward N. Peterson, *The American Occupation of Germany: Retreat to Victory* (Detroit: Wayne State University Press, 1977), p. 80.
34. Joseph M. Jones, *The Fifteen Weeks* (New York: Harcourt, 1955), p. 141.

imperialist and implacably hostile state, he worked consistently and effectively to sharpen and harden American foreign policy and to build up "situations of strength" in order to move the recalcitrant opponent to limited agreements.

When Acheson became Secretary of State in January 1949, the same ideas, assumptions, axioms, and power strategy which he had been instrumental in developing at the beginning of the Cold War continued to govern American foreign policy. His appointment did not represent, as some observers thought at the time, a shift on Truman's part towards a more flexible and accommodating attitude in the conduct of relations with the Soviets.[35] This was not the intention behind the appointment, and it was certainly not the result. Truman chose Acheson because of his impeccably conservative credentials, which ensured that he would not knuckle under to the Soviets, and because he expected, on the basis of past experience, that Acheson, like Marshall, would give him personal loyalty as well as service. The two men in fact immediately established a close and harmonious working relationship in which Truman relied on Acheson heavily for information, advice, and the execution of foreign policy, while Acheson spared no effort to keep the President fully informed at all times so that he could perform his constitutional duty of conducting the nation's foreign relations with all the freedom of decision which each situation permitted. This unremitting concern for the President's needs and for presidential sanction for all major foreign policy decisions was one of the distinctive features of Acheson's Secretaryship that was convincingly illustrated by their joint and closely coordinated management of the final phase of the Berlin crisis. Similar images of the starkly bipolar and conflict-ridden international environment and similar images of the enemy produced a consensus on policy and helped to cement the partnership between Truman and his new Secretary of State.[36]

35. See, for example, the *New Republic*, January 17, 1949.
36. On the relationship between Truman and Acheson, see Truman, *Memoirs*, Vol. 2, pp. 454–455; Dean Acheson, *Present at the Creation: My Years in the State Department* (New York: Norton, 1969), pp. 729–737; Dean Acheson, "The President and the Secretary of State," in *The Secretary of State*, ed. Don K. Price (Englewood Cliffs, N.J.: Prentice-Hall, 1960); Alexander DeConde, *The American Secretary of State: An Interpretation* (London: Pall Mall Press, 1962), pp. 121–123; and Norman A. Graebner, "Dean G. Acheson," in *An Uncertain Tradition: American Secretaries of State in the Twentieth Century*, ed. Norman A. Graebner (New York: McGraw-Hill, 1961), p. 276.

The blockade of Berlin was one of the most serious immediate problems awaiting Acheson when he took office. The decision to hold Berlin had been made while he was a private citizen, but he identified with it completely and constantly referred to it, after he became Secretary of State, as an example of the method and the advantage of a policy of building "situations of strength."[37] As far as the appropriate method for holding Berlin was concerned, it seemed to him that the airlift was the right choice; and he did not support Clay's idea of a convoy because he did not share the premise on which it was based—namely, that the Russians were bluffing. It never seemed wise to him to base America's own actions on bluff or to assume that the Russians were doing so: "Neither side wishes to be driven by miscalculation to general hostilities or humiliation. Therefore initial moves should not, if it is possible to avoid it, be equivocal—as a small ground probe would be—or reckless—as a massive one would be."[38]

The paramount importance which Acheson attached to securing a favorable outcome to the Berlin crisis derived not from any perception of Berlin's intrinsic value to the United States but from the inevitable impact of the outcome on America's long-term reputation for resolve. In other words, it was the perception of the crisis as a trial of strength between the two superpowers, with potentially far-reaching consequences for the general relations between them, rather than concern for the material consequences that would be incurred as a result of losing the Western foothold in Berlin which was uppermost in his mind. In this respect, he displayed the traditional Cold Warrior's penchant for thinking that the opponent is always on the lookout for signs of weakness and opportunities to expand which must be countered by projecting a general appearance of toughness and determination to resist on all issues. Only steadfastness and resolution, in his view, could see America through the crisis to a satisfactory ending.

Acheson perceived American interests in Berlin, in Germany, and in Europe as so tightly interrelated that a setback in one locale would have negative effects in the others. Conversely, an American success in Berlin would have positive effects elsewhere. By overplaying its hand with the blockade, Moscow had already inadver-

37. McGeorge Bundy, ed., *The Pattern of Responsibility* (Boston: Houghton Mifflin, 1952), p. 105.
38. Acheson, *Present at the Creation*, p. 262.

tently helped to create a climate conducive to the emergence of a West German state and to the conclusion of the North Atlantic pact. Under Marshall's leadership, the premise of American policy had been that the loss of Germany would represent an unacceptable defeat. Acheson's view of Germany's role in the European balance of power went beyond that. He believed, in the words of his biographer, that "the future of Europe and, therefore, the outcome of the contest between the United States and the Soviet Union would be closely related to events in Germany. If the economic resources and population of all Germany fell under the control of the Soviet Union, the balance of power would tip irrevocably against the Atlantic nations. The United States might have to fight a third world war, and might lose it. But if the resources of the western zones of Germany could be built up and permanently added to the power of the Atlantic alliance, there would be sufficient strength to block Soviet expansion without war. . . . Stated baldly, the policy of the United States under Acheson's direction was to press for the maximum development of German power as a counterpoise to the Soviet Union and as an essential foundation for European recovery."[39]

Given this set of beliefs which was central to Acheson's whole outlook on international affairs, it is not difficult to see why he threw his weight on the side of General Clay and against the State Department's own chief planner in the review of long-term options vis-à-vis Germany which occupied the Truman Administration in the early months of 1949. As Kennan recalled, where he and Acheson really differed was over such things as the need to retain greater negotiating flexibility in America's relations with Russia; the need to permit a new West German government to become an end in itself, and thus an enduring impediment to any agreement with Russia; the need for a more searching exploration with America's French and British allies of the future of the European continent; and the weight to be given to the views of a military occupation establishment which Kennan regarded as both politically illiterate and corrupted by the misleading discipline of its own experience. For Acheson the possibility of agreement with the Russians on the retirement of Russian forces from the Eastern zone of

---

39. Gaddis Smith, *Dean Acheson* (New York: Cooper Square, 1972), p. 78. For a comprehensive policy statement by Acheson on the question of Germany, see his address before the American Society of Newspaper Publishers in New York on April 28, 1948, in the *Department of State Bulletin*, May 8, 1949.

Germany was of relatively small importance and thus expendable, whereas the Western occupational establishment and the unity it symbolized was definitely not. Kennan, on the other hand, considered his country's occupational establishment in Germany as decidedly expendable, but he clung desperately to the hope of getting the Russians to retire some day from the heart of the continent, and he fought to prevent the adoption of a stance which threatened to destroy every possibility of such a retirement for an indefinite number of years to come.[40]

Acheson's images of the Soviet Union and of the importance of Berlin and Germany to the balance of power in Europe all converged to predispose him to adopt a very tough stance in the negotiations which culminated in the removal of the blockade. He saw the signs coming from Moscow indicating readiness to lift the blockade as the fruit of the Western policy of firmness and not as a reason for relaxing Western vigilance. Convinced that the USSR had changed neither its attitude towards the West nor the basic objectives of its foreign policy, he pleaded for alertness in the talks and a steadfast refusal to make concessions.[41] The Soviet Union's eventual agreement to lift the blockade in exchange for nominal Western concessions only reinforced Acheson's prior image of this adversary and of its bargaining style. The lesson he drew from this experience is that "the Soviet authorities are not moved to agreement by negotiation—that is, by a series of mutual concessions calculated to move parties desiring agreement closer to an acceptable one. Theirs is a more primitive form of political method. They cling stubbornly to a position, hoping to force an opponent to accept it. When and if action by the opponent demonstrates the Soviet position to be untenable, they hastily abandon it—after asking and having been refused an unwarranted price—and hastily take up a new position which may or may not represent a move towards greater mutual stability."[42]

To sum up, there was a remarkable homogeneity both in the general outlook and in the immediate images of the key American decision-makers who handled the third and final phase of the

---

40. Kennan, *Memoirs*, pp. 446–447. On Acheson's attitude to Germany and the important controversy with Kennan, see also David S. McLellan, *Dean Acheson: The State Department Years* (New York: Dodd, Mead, 1976), chap. 9.

41. Memorandum of Conversation by the Secretary of State, May 2, 1949, in *FRUS, 1949*, Vol. 3, pp. 748–749.

42. Acheson, *Present at the Creation*, pp. 274–275.

Berlin crisis. This homogeneity effortlessly survived the change brought about by the advent of a new Secretary of State. Basically, Truman, Marshall, Clay, and Acheson believed that the blockade posed a threat to central American values, that the Soviet Union would pursue its objectives by political rather than military means, and that the expanded airlift substantially lengthened the time scale governing the American response; and they were united in their conviction that any display of weakness or appeasement would seriously damage the American position in what amounted to a test of strength, firmness, and resolution. Such was the psychological framework which shaped American behavior during the eventful, tortuous, and inordinately long post-crisis period.

CHAPTER EIGHT

Decision Flow

PHASE I: JULY 23–AUGUST 30

THE National Security Council's decision of July 22, 1948 laid the foundation for U.S. policy during the final and prolonged Berlin post-crisis period. The two closely related objectives of this policy were: first, to stay in Berlin and supply the city entirely by air; and second, to use the breathing space provided by the expanded airlift to seek a negotiated settlement with the Soviets. While the stress generated by the crisis declined perceptibly following the rejection of Clay's convoy idea and the adoption of this two-pronged strategy, considerations of domestic politics became increasingly prominent as the presidential election in November came nearer. As Under Secretary Lovett confided to the British Minister in Washington, the Truman Administration felt that if they were to retain bipartisan support for their policy, they had to maintain a thoroughly firm attitude towards the USSR. At the same time, however, they were most anxious that a peaceful solution should be found to the current impasse.[1]

The Administration seized every opportunity to encourage the Republicans to keep foreign policy out of the election campaign, with Lovett taking the lead by keeping Dulles informed of developments on Berlin and seeking his advice.[2] Truman was susceptible to the charge that his careless diplomacy at the Potsdam conference and his failure to negotiate secure access rights to Berlin had contributed directly to the blockade of the city, and Dewey

---

1. Washington Embassy to the British Foreign Office, July 21, 1948, FO 371/70503, Public Record Office, London.
2. Memorandum of conversation with Robert Lovett on the Berlin Blockade, July 22, 1948, the John Foster Dulles Papers, Box 35, Princeton University Library.

was tempted to launch a frontal attack on the Democrats' foreign policy. Such a course, however, was liable to have grave international implications by encouraging the Russians to think that a divided nation would be unable to stand firm in the crisis; so, on July 24, Dewey finally set aside any idea of using Berlin as a stick with which to beat his domestic opponents.[3] Following a meeting with Dulles and Vandenberg, he issued a statement which publicly committed the Republicans to a bipartisan foreign policy. "The present duty of Americans," declared Dewey, "is not to be divided by past lapses, but to unite to surmount present dangers. We shall not allow domestic partisan irritations to divert us from this indispensable unity. . . . In Berlin we must not surrender our rights under duress."[4]

Secure in the knowledge that the Republicans would back him, Truman settled down to the pursuit of a firm but nonaggressive policy over Berlin—a policy which played a greater part than is commonly recognized in bringing about his astonishing electoral victory of November 1948.[5] The State Department, far from being oblivious to domestic political considerations, actually helped the President by furnishing reports on the state of public opinion. On July 30, Marshall passed to Truman a State Department report which showed that public opinion was overwhelmingly against America's being "coerced" out of Berlin, but also in favor of negotiations so long as "a solution does not violate our principles and national interests."[6] Neither the constraints nor the opportunities implicit in this domestic consensus were lost on Truman and his

3. John Foster Dulles, *War or Peace* (New York: Macmillan, 1950), pp. 130–131.

4. *New York Times*, July 25, 1948.

5. Robert Divine has persuasively argued that by excluding foreign policy from the campaign, Dewey deprived himself of his most promising electoral issue: the Administration's conduct of the Cold War. "In retrospect it is apparent that the Berlin crisis was Truman's greatest asset in the 1948 election. Just as the Soviet move in Czechoslovakia in February had enabled him to repudiate Wallace, so the Soviet blockade of Berlin helped Truman block Dewey from waging an all-out attack on the containment policy. There can be little doubt that such an assault would have been effective. Public opinion polls taken in the summer of 1948 showed massive discontent with Truman's handling of the Cold War. . . . Instead of suffering from a Republican attack on foreign policy, Truman was able to gain public confidence by his careful handling of the Berlin blockade. He rightly sensed the desire of the American people for a tough foreign policy that stopped short of actual war." Robert A. Divine, "The Cold War and the Election of 1948," *Journal of American History*, Vol. 59 (June 1972), p. 109.

6. President's Secretary File, Box 171, Truman Papers, Harry S. Truman Library, Independence, Missouri.

subordinates when they embarked on the search for a negotiated settlement. The guiding principle was to keep the Administration's international posture in line with the domestic consensus.

The Joint Chiefs of Staff faced an even more onerous task in trying to prevent the Administration's international posture from outstripping the military resources available to support it. Their collective view was presented to the Secretary of Defense in a memorandum dated July 22 dealing with "U.S. Military Courses of Action with Respect to the Situation in Berlin." Forrestal forwarded this memorandum to the National Security Council on July 26, and two days later it was distributed to the Council's members as NSC 24.[7]

Careful study indicated that Berlin's minimum requirements could be met for a considerable, though not indefinite, period by augmenting the airlift; but this, the Chiefs pointed out, would seriously reduce their capabilities for implementing emergency war plans. Careful consideration had also been given to the alternative of attempting to supply Berlin by armed convoy if the air transport method proved inadequate or was hampered by Soviet interference in the air corridors. But, in the opinion of the Joint Chiefs, the possibility of success for this alternative was remote. Passive Soviet interference, such as road or bridge obstruction, could make the convoy method abortive, while Soviet military action could shift the stage from that of local friction to that of major war involvement.

Nevertheless, the Joint Chiefs of Staff recommended that plans should be made for attempting to supply Berlin by armed convoy so that they might be ready for such an attempt if and when the developing situation and a decision by higher authorities necessitated this course of action. But they emphasized that, from the military point of view, to attempt to supply Berlin by force would be justifiable only if: (1) every other solution had been tried first; (2) current evaluations indicated that the effort was likely to succeed; (3) the United States had first determined that the risk of war in the near future and for the Berlin cause was acceptable; and (4) all possible time had been gained to prepare for war.

In view of the limitations and heavy cost of the airlift and the hazards inherent in a convoy, the Joint Chiefs of Staff raised, in a

---

7. Kenneth W. Condit, *The History of the Joint Chiefs of Staff*, Vol. 2: *1947–1949* (Washington, D.C.: Historical Division, Joint Secretariat, Joint Chiefs of Staff, 1976), Record Group (RG) 218, Records of the United States Joint Chiefs of Staff, National Archives, pp. 142–143.

tentative and gingerly fashion, a third alternative: withdrawal from Berlin. They assumed that diplomatic efforts together with all practicable countermeasures would continue to be used to arrive at a peaceful solution of the Berlin problem. In this connection, they wrote, it might not be altogether out of the question to consider, during the time gained by the airlift, the possibility that some justification might be found for "withdrawal of our occupation forces from Berlin without undue loss of prestige." Although this course was contrary to official policy, the possibility remained that reasonable justification, such as humanitarian concern for the people of Berlin, might develop. "Therefore," wrote the Joint Chiefs, "subject to unalterable decision that withdrawal in no circumstances will be undertaken unless forced by war action, the withdrawal possibility should at least be borne in mind. The development of plans for such a solution appears desirable, as neither air transport nor armed convoy in themselves offer a long-range solution to the problem."

In conclusion, the Joint Chiefs of Staff urged a prompt decision on their future military course of action regarding Berlin. If the decision was that their occupation troops were to remain in Berlin until forced to withdraw by war action, and that an attempt would be made to supply Berlin by force if supply could be maintained in no other way, then the Joint Chiefs of Staff recommended that: (1) all possible time be gained by augmenting the airlift for preparation for the event of war; and (2) all-out preparations for war be inaugurated immediately.[8]

For the most part, although not entirely, events, in terms of firm decisions, had already outrun the recommendations contained in NSC 24. Yet, the document is of considerable interest, not simply because it was the first formal expression of the collective view of the Joint Chiefs of Staff, but also because it revealed so unequivocally their preference for withdrawal from Berlin in the long run. Since the National Security Council had already reached a decision on July 22, it simply noted the views of the Joint Chiefs of Staff at its next meeting, held on August 5, over which Marshall presided in Truman's absence.[9]

8. NSC 24, a report to the National Security Council by the Secretary of Defense on "U.S. Military Courses of Action with Respect to the Situation in Berlin," July 28, 1948, President's Secretary File, Harry S. Truman Library.

9. Minutes of the 17th Meeting of the National Security Council, held on Thursday, August 5, 1948, President's Secretary File, Harry S. Truman Library.

In accordance with the specific recommendation of the Joint Chiefs, Forrestal asked Marshall to initiate discussions with the British and French governments with a view to developing preliminary plans for an Allied convoy to supply Berlin. Forrestal stressed that the Joint Chiefs of Staff did not recommend the supply of Berlin by armed convoys at the time, in view of the risk of war involved and the inadequacy of the American preparations for global conflict. All he envisaged was a contingency plan for such an operation in the event that it became necessary or desirable.[10] In response to this request, Marshall advised Forrestal that the question of planning armed convoys should not be raised at the governmental level, in view of the reconstitution of the French Cabinet, and recommended that the matter be taken up with the British through the Combined Chiefs of Staff.[11] Forrestal accepted the Secretary of State's recommendation and instructed the Joint Chiefs of Staff to initiate preliminary planning for armed convoys in the Combined Chiefs of Staff.[12]

The British Chiefs of Staff responded on August 27 that they were still of the opinion that any attempt to force armed convoys into Berlin would be militarily unsound and politically undesirable. Nothing could be gained from attempts by rail, road, or water, since the Soviet authorities, without resort to force, could interpose effective technical obstacles. The British Chiefs were also convinced that, whatever conditions might become in the future, the fundamental impracticality of the proposal would remain. They could not, therefore, agree to the initiation of joint plans.[13]

In view of the strong position taken by their British colleagues, the Joint Chiefs of Staff saw no point in pursuing this matter further. The Commander in Chief, European Command, had already been instructed to develop unilateral plans for the use of a convoy.

---

10. Forrestal to Marshall, July 28, 1948, in *Foreign Relations of the United States, 1948*, Vol. 2: *Germany and Austria* (Washington, D.C.: U.S. Government Printing Office, 1973), pp. 994–995. (Henceforth, this series will be referred to as *FRUS*.)

11. Ibid., p. 995, note 4; and Memorandum for the Chief of Staff from Lieutenant General A. C. Wedemeyer, September 9, 1948, Plans and Operations Division (P&O) 381, RG 319, Records of the Army Staff, National Archives, Washington, D.C.

12. Memorandum for the Joint Chiefs of Staff from the Secretary of Defense, July 30, 1948, P&O 381, RG 319, National Archives, Washington, D.C.

13. Memorandum by the Representatives of the British Chiefs of Staff, August 27, 1948, P&O 381, RG 319, National Archives, Washington, D.C.

In response to this directive, General Clay submitted his plan—"Task Force Truculent"—on September 8.[14]

While all this military planning was going on, the primary subject of consultation with the Allies was the question of an approach to Stalin to see if the blockade could be removed by agreement. Truman was all in favor of a direct appeal to Stalin. Charles Bohlen, the head of the Berlin Group in the State Department, advised Marshall that while he doubted that Stalin would respond, he saw no harm in the approach: it would help reassure the British and French, who were getting nervous about Truman's vigorous reaction, that the United States was not hell-bent for war. Marshall sent Bohlen to Europe to discuss the coordination of a tripartite approach.[15] The Secretary of State feared that much confusion and delay would be caused if the Western powers continued to try to deal with the question of Berlin both in Washington and in London, and he reaffirmed the earlier decision that everything should be centralized in London.[16] Bohlen flew to Berlin with Clay, who suffered from such a painful attack of lumbago on the return trip that he had to be carried from the plane in a chair. Initially, there was some apprehension that the Soviets might try to jam the radio-guidance system, which would have made flying at night and in bad weather virtually impossible. But it soon became clear that the Soviets did not intend any overt interference with air access to Berlin. Had the Soviets interfered with any of the planes, Bohlen, for one, believed that war might easily have broken out. But all the experts believed that the Soviets did not want war and would not put themselves in the position of provoking one through an overt act of escalation.[17]

Ambassador Smith flew in from Moscow, Ambassador Douglas flew in from London, and the first meeting took place in Berlin on

14. Condit, *The History of the Joint Chiefs of Staff*, Vol. 2, p. 146; and, for details of the plan, Memorandum to the Chief of Staff from Lt. Gen. A. C. Wedemeyer, September 22, 1948, P&O 381, RG 319, National Archives, Washington, D.C.

15. Charles E. Bohlen, *Witness to History, 1929–1969* (London: Weidenfeld and Nicolson, 1973), pp. 178–179.

16. Washington Embassy to British Foreign Office, July 21, 1948, FO 371/70503, Public Record Office, London.

17. Bohlen, *Witness to History*, p. 179. General LeMay, the commander of USAFE, commented in his memoirs on Russia's evident caution; "You'd think that we might have been driven to drink by the Russians constantly buzzing our airplanes. Actually they didn't bother very much. Once they discovered that we were firmly intentioned, and going to haul that stuff up there regardless, they left

Sunday, July 25. Bohlen briefed them on Washington's strategy, and a preliminary discussion of tactics took place. The three of them then proceeded to London, where they talked with Bevin and René Massigli, the French Ambassador there. At one meeting, Bevin said to Bohlen, only half-jokingly, "I know all you Americans want a war, but I am not going to let you 'ave it." The French Ambassador also expressed fear that hasty American action would precipitate a war. Bohlen's efforts to persuade them that their fears had no basis in fact were not entirely successful.[18]

Bohlen, Douglas, and Smith spent two hours on July 26 discussing with Sir William Strang and Massigli whether the approach should be made to Molotov or Stalin, who should make the approach, and what its precise substance and purpose should be. Later in the afternoon, they met with Bevin, Strang, and other British officials. Bevin agreed only reluctantly and grudgingly to a personal appeal to Stalin, after arguing that this method had not been helpful in the past and that it would build up the Soviet ruler's prestige throughout Europe. The procedure finally worked out was for a simultaneous protest to be presented to the Soviet Government in Moscow by the three Western Ambassadors, coupled with a request for a meeting with Stalin. Detailed instructions were worked out at this meeting and subsequently confirmed by the three governments, charging the Ambassadors with the mission of probing Soviet intentions and testing Soviet willingness to find a peaceful solution. No one was particularly optimistic, however, about the results.[19]

Ambassador Smith established a very close working relationship with the new French Ambassador in Moscow, Yves Chataigneau, and with the British envoy Frank Roberts, Bevin's private secretary, who was sent to Moscow to conduct the talks because the British Ambassador, Sir Maurice Petersen, was absent on account

---

us pretty much alone." Curtis E. LeMay with MacKinlay Kantor, *Mission with LeMay: My Story* (New York: Doubleday, 1965), p. 416. See also Memorandum for the President from Colonel Robert B. Landry (Air Aide to the President), September 28, 1948, Leahy File No. 33—1948 Berlin Airlift, RG 218, National Archives, Washington, D.C.

18. Bohlen, *Witness to History*, p. 174.

19. Douglas to Marshall, July 26, 1948, in *FRUS, 1948*, Vol. 2, pp. 986–988; Record of Teletype Conference Between the Department of State and the Embassy in London, July 26, 1948, in *FRUS, 1948*, Vol. 2, pp. 989–993; and Record of Meeting Held in the Foreign Office, July 26, 1948, FO 371/70505/C6250, Public Record Office, London.

of illness. The three men agreed at the outset that they should compare and coordinate the instructions they received as well as their reports to their governments. During the discussions that followed, they had frequent and lengthy meetings at which complete frankness and understanding prevailed.[20]

Their first step was to telephone for an appointment with Molotov. Informed that the Soviet Foreign Minister was on vacation, they agreed to see his Deputy, Valerian Zorin. They called on Zorin early in the evening of July 30, and each of them presented him with an identical *aide-mémoire* in which it was stated that the Russian note of July 14 had offered no constructive suggestion, and that a request was now made for a conference with Stalin and Molotov in order to discuss the situation in Berlin in its wider implications.[21] Zorin was cool and uncompromising. He said that there was no indication in the *aide-mémoire* of any change in the position of the U.S. on any subject which would make profitable a discussion with Generalissimo Stalin and Mr. Molotov. However, he would transmit the request to his government for their consideration.[22]

On the day following the Zorin interview, the representatives of the Western powers were informed that separate appointments with Molotov had been arranged for the same evening. At the meeting with Ambassador Smith, Molotov came to the point at once by asking what kind of discussion and negotiations the Western governments had in mind both for the present and for the future. Reluctant to use his ammunition on Molotov alone, Smith replied that the *aide-mémoire* had been intentionally brief and lacking in detail, since it was the purpose of the proposed conversations to develop the necessary details. Molotov emphasized that conversations regarding Berlin were not practical except within the framework of conversations regarding all of Germany. In reply, Smith stated that the formal position of the two governments had been made clear in two notes which had been exchanged, but that the formal written word is very rigid and much more could be accomplished by informal exploration.[23]

20. Walter Bedell Smith, *Moscow Mission, 1946–1949* (London: Heinemann, 1950), pp. 229–232.
21. For the text of the *aide-mémoire*, see U.S. Department of State, *The Berlin Crisis: A Report on the Moscow Discussions* (Washington, D.C.: U.S. Government Printing Office, 1948), pp. 15–16.
22. Smith to Marshall, July 30, 1948, in *FRUS, 1948*, Vol. 2, pp. 995–996.
23. Smith to Marshall, July 31, 1948, in *FRUS, 1948*, Vol. 2, pp. 996–998.

The requested interview between the Western envoys on the one side and Stalin and Molotov on the other took place on August 2 at nine in the evening. At the time, the situation did not look very hopeful to Smith. He had previously given Marshall his estimate that the Russians felt sure of winning the battle for Berlin, saw no need to rush into overall discussions, and would demand a good deal before terminating the siege.[24] He also doubted whether a huge city could be fed and supplied by air for a prolonged period. Nor was he sure that the morale of the German people would stand the strain. He knew, however, that Clay was confident and determined. Clay had told him that he was sure he could build up the airlift to ten thousand tons per day, if necessary, and Smith felt confident that if it lay within the scope of human capability to supply Berlin and defeat the blockade, Clay could do it. So far, also, the morale of the Germans in the blockaded sectors of Berlin had remained high, and they had flatly rejected all blandishments from the Soviet side. Thus, the Western representatives, too, held some good cards when they faced Stalin and Molotov across the conference table in the Kremlin. Smith believed that they might draw even better ones as this "poker game" progressed.[25]

Speaking for the three Western governments and addressing Stalin, Smith opened the meeting with a statement which emphasized that their right to be in Berlin was unquestionable and absolute, and that they would not be coerced by any means whatsoever into abandoning it. Stalin was in an extraordinarily amiable and cooperative mood, which helped to create a relaxed atmosphere. It was evident that he wanted the conversation to produce a solution from the moment when, instead of replying to the introductory statement with an equally strong statement of the Soviet position, he simply asked whether they were there to open negotiations. He announced emphatically that it was not the purpose of the Soviet Government to oust the Western troops from Berlin. "After all, we are still allies," he said. But he added that by the decision to set up a West German government in Frankfurt, the three governments forfeited their juridical right to occupy Berlin. In his mind, he explained, the only real issue was the formation in the Western zones of a German government. He did not mind unification of the three zones and even considered it progress. Stalin refrained from easy

24. Smith to Marshall, July 24, 1948, in *FRUS, 1948*, Vol. 2, pp. 984–985.
25. Smith, *Moscow Mission*, p. 233.

optimism and showed clearly that he realized the difficulties, but he responded very readily to Smith's appeal that they make an effort to get together again instead of drifting further and further apart. As a way out of the present impasse, Stalin proposed the temporary suspension of the London decisions as well as the abolition of the special currency for Berlin, simultaneously with the abolition of the Soviet transport restrictions. The remainder of the two-hour meeting was taken up with a discussion which developed from these points. Stalin and Molotov raised frequent technical questions regarding currency. The Western envoys replied that these were issues with which they were not competent to deal but which could be settled by technical experts. Finally, when they seemed to have progressed as far as possible, Stalin threw himself back in his chair, lit a cigarette, and, smiling as he looked directly at Smith, asked: "Would you like to settle the matter tonight?" If so, Stalin could make the following proposals: (1) there should be a simultaneous introduction in Berlin of the Soviet zone Deutsche mark in place of the western mark, together with the removal of all transport restrictions; and (2) he would no longer ask, as a condition, for the deferment of the implementation of the London decisions, although he wished this to be recorded as the "insistent wish" of the Soviet Government. The three Western representatives agreed to present these proposals to their governments with a joint recommendation that they be accepted, and they promised to inform Molotov as soon as possible of the decision of their governments. The meeting then broke up in a very friendly atmosphere.[26]

Smith and his colleagues felt decidedly encouraged. It seemed to them that the atmosphere of the discussion and Stalin's proposals were such that a settlement of the Berlin crisis could be effected immediately.[27] In a private summary for Marshall, Smith confided: "Doubt if I have ever seen Molotov so cordial and if one did not know real Soviet objectives in Germany would have been completely deceived by their attitude as both literally dripping with sweet reasonableness and desire not to embarrass." If it were possible to suspend any part of the implementation of the London decisions "without undue complications or loss of prestige," he

26. Smith to Marshall, August 3, 1948, in *FRUS, 1948*, Vol. 2, pp. 999–1006; Smith, *Moscow Mission*, pp. 233–237; U.S. State Department, *The Berlin Crisis*, pp. 17–20; and Roberts to Strang, August 3, 1948, FO 371/70506/C6546, Public Record Office, London.
27. Smith, *Moscow Mission*, p. 237.

continued, "it will give us a good club as with finalization of west German government we will have fired one of the last shots in our political locker."[28] A draft statement proposed by Smith read as follows:

1. Removal of all transport restrictions. . . .
2. Cancellation of mark B in Berlin and introduction of Soviet zone deutschmark in Berlin, and
3. An anouncement of resumption of negotiations on Berlin and Four-Power meeting to consider other outstanding problems affecting Germany.[29]

Before responding to the report and proposal of his ambassador to Moscow, Marshall elicited Clay's views, through the Department of the Army, on the point in the draft relating to Berlin's currency. Clay felt that the withdrawal of the Western currency could be disastrous to their position in Berlin unless effected under agreements which gave the Western powers some voice in the issue of the currency and in the extension of credits in Berlin. He also thought that the surest way of dealing with the Soviets from a position of strength lay in pressing ahead with the setting up of a West German government, and he feared that a Council of Foreign Ministers meeting would bring strong pressures, at home and in Germany, for delay. Accepting the Soviet proposal would bring the lifting of the blockade, remove the risk of war, and gain valuable time, but these gains, cautioned Clay, could only be bought at a price: the creation of an unsettled political atmosphere for the formation of a West German government and the economic recovery of Western Germany.[30] Bohlen, who was acting as Marshall's chief adviser on the Berlin crisis, concurred entirely in this evaluation. In reading Smith's dispatches on the meeting, he concluded that Stalin was really saying that the blockade would be lifted if the Western powers abandoned the idea of forming a West German government; and this price, in his opinion, was too high.[31]

---

28. Smith to Marshall, August 3, 1948, in *FRUS, 1948*, Vol. 2, pp. 1006–07.
29. Ibid., p. 1008, note 2.
30. Jean Edward Smith, ed., *The Papers of General Lucius D. Clay: Germany, 1945–1949* (Bloomington: Indiana University Press, 1974), Vol. 2, pp. 748–753 (hereinafter cited as *Clay Papers*).
31. Bohlen, *Witness to History*, pp. 280–281; and "Memorandum by the Counselor of the State Department (Bohlen)," August 4, 1948, in *FRUS, 1948*, Vol. 2, pp. 1013–14. See also James V. Forrestal Diaries, August 3, 1948, p. 2400, Princeton University Library.

Marshall was largely guided by Clay and Bohlen's advice in issuing his specific instructions to Smith for finalizing the currency proposals that had been developed at the meeting with Stalin. "Our acceptance of Soviet zone currency in Berlin," wrote Marshall, "cannot be unconditional and its use must be subject to some form of quadripartite control. . . . The substitution of the Soviet zone mark for the B mark in Berlin can now be accepted in principle but our agreement must be supplemented by a satisfactory agreement providing for the availability and use of the Soviet currency in Berlin. In our opinion, confirmed by General Clay, such agreement should include control of credit, uniform application of credit rules and currency issue within Berlin, availability of sufficient funds for occupation powers, and some arrangements to cover trade between the Western zones and Berlin." Marshall noted with gratification that Smith had succeeded in eliminating the abandonment of a West German government as a Soviet condition. In this matter, he stressed, they had to retain a free hand, and Smith was asked to continue to safeguard the American position in this matter, should it be brought up again by the Soviets.[32] Although the tone of Marshall's message suggested that he was going along with Smith's advice, in substance it leaned heavily in the opposite direction. Smith and his colleagues had recommended an unconditional acceptance of Stalin's proposal to make the East mark the sole currency in all Berlin, whereas Marshall laid down a number of far-reaching demands as the price for America's agreement. Marshall also chose to ignore Stalin's "insistent wish" that the implementation of the London decision be suspended temporarily pending a four-power meeting on the German question. His decision thus amounted to a conditional acceptance of Stalin's proposal for resolving the Berlin crisis (Decision 17).

Because Stalin's proposal held out the best prospect of a diplomatic solution since the crisis had begun, this decision was particularly important in establishing the parameters of the subsequent bargaining. If these parameters were rather narrow, it should be noted that in fixing them Marshall was concerned to safeguard America's long-term interests as he perceived them. Like his advisers in Berlin and Washington, Marshall was unwilling to obtain relief for the short-range problem of the blockade by compromis-

---

32. Marshall to Smith, August 3, 1948, in *FRUS, 1948*, Vol. 2, pp. 1008–09.

ing what he saw as America's overriding long-range interest in the rebuilding of West Germany.[33]

The next order of business was for the Western envoys to engage in more detailed discussions with Molotov to see if the general ideas raised by Stalin could be translated into a formal agreement which would lead to a lifting of the blockade. During the subsequent discussions, close contact was maintained between the State Department, the Army Department, and American representatives in Berlin, London, and Moscow; and the Berlin Group assisted Marshall with the tasks of consultation, coordination, and supervision of the execution of policy. In addition, it was essential that the three Western representatives in Moscow speak with one voice; to this end, Marshall designated Moscow instead of London as the coordinating center for the purposes of the talks and instructed the State Department to address Ambassador Smith directly, repeating all messages to London, Berlin, and Paris.[34]

What was envisaged as a drafting session with Molotov developed into a long drawn-out series of meetings with him on August 6, 9, 12, and 16, some of them over three hours long, ending in a failure to arrive at any satisfactory agreement. While Stalin had given assent to general principles and had held out the prospect of a settlement in friendly phrases, Molotov proved again to be a stubborn, intransigent, and difficult bargainer when it came to the concrete details. Time and again, it seemed to the Western negotiators, he reneged on statements that Stalin had made.[35] The Russians, for their part, contended that the negotiations failed because

33. The CIA also approached the problem essentially as one of weighing short-term benefits against likely long-term costs, but it reached a different conclusion. As its Director put it: by accepting the minimum Soviet terms, the U.S. would in effect be gambling that the cumulative effects of the European Recovery Program and other measures that the Western powers may take will soon more than outweigh the consequences of the renewed opportunities that will accrue to the USSR for disturbing western European recovery and gaining economic benefits. "Weighed against a continuation of our present dilemma, however, the gamble would appear to be worthwhile." Memorandum for the President from Rear Admiral R. H. Hillenkoetter, August 6, 1948, President's Secretary File, Harry S. Truman Library.

34. Marshall to Smith, August 3, 1948, in *FRUS, 1948*, Vol. 2, pp. 1008–09. To his Cabinet colleagues, Marshall appealed for caution in word and deed lest they upset the delicate negotiations with Russia. Minutes of Cabinet Meetings, August 6, 1948, Papers of Matthew J. Connelly, Harry S. Truman Library.

35. Smith, *Moscow Mission*, p. 237; and Roberts to British Foreign Office, August 8, 1948, FO 371/70506/C6441, Public Record Office, London.

the Western powers shifted their ground on the currency question.[36] As a matter of fact, the Western representatives did not accept the principle of an unconditional withdrawal of their currency from Berlin, but only agreed to recommend this solution to their governments. The subsequent insistence of quadripartite control over the issue and use of the Soviet currency in Berlin, however, amounted to withdrawing the carrot with which the Russians were to be enticed to lift the blockade, and the hardening of the Russian position may have been a response to their disappointment with the terms subsequently offered by the West.

The gulf between the Western and the Soviet positions was reflected in the differences between the initial draft proposed by the Western negotiators and the counterdraft proposed by Moscow. Molotov rejected the Western draft on August 6, and at the second meeting, on August 9, presented his own counterdraft.[37] Molotov's draft challenged by implication the juridical basis for Western presence in Berlin; it made no reference to four-power control over the Berlin currency; and the only transport restrictions which it envisaged lifting were those imposed after the Western currency reform of June 18. Moreover, contrary to the understanding with Stalin, Molotov sought a definite promise that the West would suspend the London Program pending the outcome of a four-power conference. Smith stated that the Soviet draft appeared to depart materially from the formula discussed with Stalin, and that, although he would submit it to his government, in his judgment it would not prove acceptable.[38]

Smith accurately predicted the reaction of the Truman Administration. Bohlen told Forrestal that the talks in Moscow had taken a turn for the worse, and that acceptance of the Russian language would, in effect, mean that the U.S. was a vassal staying in Berlin by sufferance rather than by right.[39] Royall, Draper, and Clay were unanimous in opposing compromise on the London program.[40] Clay remarked that acceptance of Molotov's request for stopping the move towards a West German government would prove disas-

---

36. "Attitude of Three Western Powers to Control of Currency Reform in Berlin," August 22, 1948, FO 371/70510/C6915, Public Record Office, London.
37. For the texts of these drafts, see U.S. Department of State, *The Berlin Crisis*, pp. 22–23.
38. Smith to Marshall, August 9, 1948, in *FRUS, 1948*, Vol. 2, pp. 1024–27.
39. Walter Millis, ed., *The Forrestal Diaries* (New York: Viking, 1951), p. 470.
40. *Clay Papers*, Vol. 2, p. 760.

trous to America's objectives in Germany and Europe and was the one thing which would be even worse than abandoning Berlin.[41] In view of this unanimous chorus of objections, Marshall's decision was practically a foregone conclusion. On August 10, he instructed Smith to reject the Soviet draft agreement (Decision 18).[42]

The Department of the Army strongly believed that no concession must be made to the Soviets which would interfere with West European recovery and thus preclude the establishment of a balance of power between Western and Eastern Europe.[43] If the current negotiations proved fruitless, Royall thought that the U.S. should consider as a reply to the Soviet blockade a counterblockade in which the U.S. would close the Baltic and the Dardanelles by mines, after having given the USSR full warning that this was being done, and also close the Suez and Panama Canals to all Soviet ships and all Soviet goods. Royall thought that at that time the Americans might also warn the Soviets that they intended to stay in Berlin, that their rights included ground transportation, and that they would, when they felt it necessary or appropriate, send convoys through to Berlin, armed to the extent necessary.[44] It was at this juncture that General Clay was instructed to prepare a plan for armed convoys without divulging its existence to the British and French commanders.[45]

A more immediate task, and one which called for open cooperation with Britain, was the consolidation of the airlift. The U.S. Secretary of the Air Force, Stuart Symington, and General Hoyt Vandenberg, Chief of Staff of the U.S. Air Force, arrived in London on August 9, and at a meeting with Bevin, the British Foreign Secretary, impressed on the British that if the Moscow negotiations broke down, the maintenance of a substantial supply of food and fuel to Berlin was their best way to hold their position there and to avoid war.[46] The Americans emphasized that their government was

41. Murphy to Marshall, August 11, 1948, in *FRUS, 1948*, Vol. 2, pp. 1031–32.
42. Marshall to Smith, August 10, 1948, in *FRUS, 1948*, Vol. 2, pp. 1028–31.
43. Memorandum for General Draper from T. N. Dupuy, "Brief Analysis of Current U.S.-Soviet Relations," August 9, 1948, Under Secretary of the Army (Draper/Voorhees), Folder "Lock Up" SAOUS 000.1 Germany, RG 335, Records of the Office of the Secretary of the Army, National Archives, Washington, D.C.
44. Memorandum for the Record: "Secretary Royall's Views with Regard to Molotov's Proposal," August 10, 1948, by T. N. Dupuy, Project Decimal File: "Berlin Crisis," RG 335, National Archives, Washington, D.C.
45. *Clay Papers*, Vol. 2, 763.
46. Bevin to Sir Oliver Franks (Washington), August 10, 1948, FO 371/70506/ C558/3/G, Public Record Office, London. The day after this meeting, Bevin re-

determined to build up the airlift to the size necessary to meet the requirements in Berlin.[47] From London, Symington and Vandenberg flew to Frankfurt for a meeting with Clay to discuss plans for increasing the flow of food and other supplies to Berlin. Symington told reporters that many more Skymasters (C-54 aircraft) would be brought from the United States to strengthen the "air bridge." He reaffirmed that the service would be maintained through the winter, and that there would be no reduction in deliveries. The supplies to Berlin by air could not be said to have touched the figures reached in the deliveries to China from India over the "hump" during the war, but the indications were that they were now nearing that tonnage.[48]

While the talks were faltering in Moscow and the operational levels of the U.S. Government were taking energetic reinforcement measures in Berlin in anticipation of the breakdown of these talks, the Policy Planning Staff, under George Kennan's direction, were studying the options that would be open to America in Germany as a whole in preparation for a future Council of Foreign Ministers meeting, should one take place. The study had been initiated in the early days of July, following the imposition of the full blockade. As arranged with Lovett and Bohlen, the PPS, assisted by other officers of the State Department and by officers detailed from the Department of Defense, struggled with the task through the hot days of Washington's midsummer. To some of the PPS members, the possibilities for resolving the conflict in any satisfactory way by arrangements that only affected Berlin itself appeared to be small. The best prospects for resolving the problem seemed to lie

---

ceived a very pessimistic appraisal of the situation from the British Military Governor in Berlin. In Robertson's opinion, it was impossible to keep Berlin supplied by air through the winter. His conclusion was that if a halfway house could be found, it would be better to accept it than to admit the breakdown of the Moscow talks. Bevin disagreed with this appraisal and ordered that it should not be circulated. Robertson to British Foreign Office, August 10, 1948, FO 371/7056/C6531, Public Record Office, London.

47. Bevin to Sir Oliver Franks (Washington), August 12, 1948, FO 371/C6625/3/G, Public Record Office, London.

48. *The Times* (London), August 12, 1948. Although Symington was careful not to disclose any anxiety in his public pronouncements, the situation was in fact critical. As Draper subsequently revealed, one of the low points in the history of the airlift occurred in August because the original reserves were seriously depleted while the capacity of the airlift was still too limited to make up the shortfall. Oral History Interview of William H. Draper, Jr., January 11, 1972, pp. 67–68, Harry S. Truman Library.

along the lines of a new arrangement for Germany as a whole. But here an important question of principle was involved, for to make a new attack on the problem of an all-German four-power settlement would imply a readiness to suspend the London Program during negotiations and to abandon it if the negotiations succeeded. If, on the other hand, the government was content with the implementation of the London Program, the Russians would set up a rival government in their zone, the division of Germany and Europe would harden, and a real and permanent solution to the Berlin problem would become impossible to reach.[49]

Before proceeding too far along the first tack, Kennan brought this fundamental question of policy to the attention of his governmental superiors and pointed out that the PPS ought to have an indication of their preferences before planning for another Council of Foreign Ministers meeting. In a paper dated August 12, he lucidly outlined the two broad policy options and summarized the pros and cons of each. On the basis of his preliminary study, it seemed to him that there was no acceptable middle ground between the two solutions, and that, on balance, it would be better to seek the general settlement of the German problem. The important point, however, was not to think statically, in terms of the situation before them, but dynamically, in terms of the trends and developments in Germany and elsewhere, and to make a clear political choice.[50] No indication of the government's preferences was forthcoming, however. To judge from Kennan's own account, the query evoked, as far as its substance was concerned, a troubled and thoughtful silence.[51] Comments from other State Department officials to whom Kennan's paper had been circulated registered disagreement. John Hickerson summarized the views of the Office of European Affairs in a memorandum to Kennan, stating that "the dangers of the proposed approach outweigh its advantages and . . . it would not be in the interests of the United States to make this proposal." Others elaborated on the economic uncertainties and political risks involved in Kennan's proposal. The policymakers, however, to whom the paper was principally directed, evaded the

---

49. George F. Kennan, *Memoirs, 1925–1950* (Boston: Little, Brown, 1967), pp. 420–422.

50. "Memorandum by the Director of the Policy Planning Staff (Kennan) to the Secretary of State and the Under Secretary of State," August 12, 1948, in *FRUS, 1948*, Vol. 2, pp. 1187–97.

51. Kennan, *Memoirs*, p. 422.

question. On the cover of the copy of this paper in the PPS files, Lovett had written: "This needs much more discussion with the Secretary."[52] If such discussions actually took place, the PPS was certainly not informed of their outcome. "We were encouraged," Kennan observed, "or permitted, at least—to continue our exploration of what, hypothetically, another American proposal for an all-German solution might look like, in the event we should wish to press for a settlement of this nature."[53]

There was certainly no evidence of any rethinking of basic purposes or any elements of a new strategy in the American approach to the Moscow talks. At the remaining meetings with Molotov, on August 12 and 16, Smith continued to strongly press the point that the entire discussions hinged on one basic point: the Western right to be in Berlin and to participate in quadripartite regulation and control of the flow and use of the new currency when introduced. Although Molotov did not directly challenge this contention, the question of currency control proved to be the greatest ostensible stumbling block.[54] Gradually, a position of stalemate was reached, and Smith surmised that, having pursued the maximum objective of suspending the London Program and the minimum objective of sole Soviet control in Berlin, Molotov concluded that there was little prospect of significant Western concessions on either to warrant abandoning the tactics of physical pressure.[55] The only way out seemed to lie in another talk with Stalin. After reviewing the fruitless series of drafting meetings with Molotov, the three Western governments decided to try this course. On August 17, Marshall wrote to Smith: "We agree with your analysis of yesterday's conversation with Molotov and feel strongly that there is nothing to be gained and much to be lost by any further attempt to negotiate with him. We feel the time has come for an interview with Stalin in order to deal with the basic issue which has deadlocked the talks with Molotov."[56] A request for a second meeting with Stalin was made and granted, and the meeting took place on August 23.

52. *FRUS, 1948*, Vol. 2, pp. 1287–88, note 1.
53. Kennan, *Memoirs*, pp. 422–423.
54. Smith to Marshall, August 12, 1948, in *FRUS, 1948*, Vol. 2, pp. 1035–38; and Smith, *Moscow Mission*, pp. 237–239.
55. Smith to Marshall, August 17, 1948, in *FRUS, 1948*, Vol. 2, pp. 1042–47.
56. Marshall to Smith, August 17, 1948, in *FRUS, 1948*, Vol. 2, pp. 1053–56. Two days later, the Berlin situation was placed on the agenda of the National Security Council, but the official minutes of this meeting are tantalizing rather than informative. The Minutes of the 18th Meeting of the National Security Council,

In preparation for it, the three Western governments had agreed upon a new draft to put before Stalin. This took the form of a directive to the Military Governors in Berlin to work out the concrete means for implementing the principles concerning transport restrictions and currency, together with a communiqué to be issued by the Moscow conferees on behalf of the four governments, finalizing the arrangements worked out by the Military Governors.[57] Once again Stalin looked jovial, and after greeting the Western trio in a friendly fashion, declared: "Gentlemen, I have a new plan." This rather took the wind out of their sails, and Smith replied that they had a new plan, too. "Good," Stalin rejoined, "we can compare them." They handed him their draft, he handed them his, discussion proceeded on the basis of both, and it was encouraging to discover that the two drafts were in many respects close to each other. Stalin also gave definite answers to two specific questions posed by Smith. On the question of how far back the lifting of the restrictions would extend, Molotov answered that the Soviet Government would only lift the restrictions imposed after June 18. Stalin, however, suggested that it might be better to say that "the restrictions lately imposed" would be lifted, and to have it understood that all restrictions would be lifted. On the currency question, Stalin agreed to make the Soviet zone bank that printed and issued the money subject to four-power control in the form of a financial commission under the four commanders of Berlin. Having satisfied Smith on these vital points, Stalin requested that something also be said in the communiqué about the plan to establish a West German government. He suggested a text: "The question of the London decisions and the formation of a West German Government was also discussed in an atmosphere of mutual understanding. The adoption of any decision on this subject was, however, deferred until the next meeting of the Council of Foreign Ministers." Smith said that he would inform his government of Stalin's desire, but he did not anticipate that his government would

---

held on Thursday, August 19, 1948, simply record, under item 1, that the Council: "(a) Noted and discussed the remarks of the Secretary of State outlining the status of negotiations with respect to Berlin. (b) Noted and discussed comments of the Secretary of the Army relative to the situation in Berlin." President's Secretary File, Harry S. Truman Library. One can only speculate that Royall presented his ideas (recorded earlier in this chapter) on what should be done in the event that the negotiations failed, but that no decision was taken on this matter.

57. U.S. Department of State, *The Berlin Crisis*, p. 38.

accede to any such wording unless the proposed paragraph also contained the definite statement that "no agreement was reached on this subject." The ensuing drafting meeting with Molotov elaborated a joint draft directive and communiqué which was then submitted to the governments for consideration.[58]

While the French and British governments were ready to accept the joint drafts on the ground that they offered a chance of a reasonable settlement, the American government now set its face against any compromise.[59] Clay, whose views were elicited by the Department of the Army, expressed serious misgivings about the Moscow texts and did not think that any agreement could be negotiated on the basis of the proposed directive. The fundamental issue, he stated, of Western right to participate equally in the quadripartite administration of Berlin was not covered in the texts.[60]

Echoing Clay's criticisms, Marshall informed Smith of his concern that the drafts did not contain any confirmation of the principle of quadripartite administration of the city. "We recognize," he wrote, "that the present drafts represent a considerable Soviet concession on many points, but they do not satisfactorily meet the issue which we have from the beginning regarded as fundamental and controlling. As long as the Soviet representatives maintain their thesis that we have no rights in Berlin but are there, in effect, on Soviet sufferance, there is obviously no basis for a satisfactory arrangement with them on the Berlin question."[61] Stalin's proposed statement about the discussion of plans for a Western German government was also unacceptable to Marshall, because it was open to misinterpretation. The statement seemed harmless enough, but the Constituent Assembly was about to meet in Bonn to begin the drafting of the West German constitution. Marshall suspected that Stalin's proposal was subtly designed to undermine the confidence of the Germans and perhaps to encourage French

58. Ibid., pp. 35–38; Smith to Marshall, August 24, 1948, in *FRUS, 1948*, Vol. 2, pp. 1065–69; Smith, *Moscow Mission*, pp. 239–242; and Roberts to British Foreign Office, August 24, 1948, FO 371/70510/C6936, Public Record Office, London.

59. Bevin to Attlee, August 24, 1948, FO 371/70510/C6936, Public Record Office, London.

60. Teleconference, August 24, 1948, in *Clay Papers*, Vol. 2, pp. 778–785; "Memorandum by the Chief of the Division of Central European Affairs (Beam)," in *FRUS, 1948*, Vol. 2, pp. 1071–72; and Millis, *The Forrestal Diaries*, p. 479.

61. Marshall to Smith, August 24, 1948, in *FRUS, 1948*, Vol. 2, pp. 1072–74.

backsliding, too. The point of the hook was cleverly concealed, but the barb was there nonetheless. Smith was accordingly instructed to make it clear that while his government did not refuse to discuss this point at some subsequent time, it was not prepared to make any commitment whatsoever for the postponement of the London decisions in connection with the Moscow talks.[62]

Smith did not expect his government to go any further and had indeed forewarned Stalin of its likely response. But he thought that Marshall was laboring under illusions if he thought that Soviet confirmation of the principle of quadripartite administration of Berlin could have been included in the draft communiqué. The fact was that quadripartite control had ceased to exist, and the Russians had no intention of permitting its revival so long as they were unable to achieve quadripartite control of Germany. The proposed redraft sent to him by the State Department was regarded by Smith as unrealistic, and he urged his government to decide whether to stay in Berlin despite the blockade or if it would be better to have communications resumed under circumstances in which they would not have complete control over the life of their own sectors.[63]

Marshall, however, was not moved by Smith's plea for showing flexibility and realism in an effort to avert the breakdown of the Moscow negotiations; in framing further instructions for his ambassador, the Secretary spelled out in unmistakable terms "our basic requirements for agreement":

1. Insistence on co-equal rights to be in Berlin.
2. No abandonment of our position with respect to Western Germany.
3. Unequivocal lifting of the blockade on communications, transport and commerce for goods and persons.
4. Adequate quadripartite control of issue and continued use in Berlin of the Soviet mark.[64]

In a second telegram to Smith on the same day, Marshall frankly acknowledged the domestic considerations that lay behind the Administration's tough stand:

> We are disturbed by impression that British and French are prepared to go too far in order to get quick agreement on directive.

62. Ibid., p. 1077; and Smith, *Moscow Mission*, pp. 241–242.
63. Smith to Marshall, August 25, 1948, in *FRUS, 1948*, Vol. 2, pp. 1078–83.
64. Marshall to Smith, August 26, 1948, in *FRUS, 1948*, Vol. 2, pp. 1083–84.

We see no reason for haste in view of the very vital issues concerned. There has been a definite crystallization of American public and Congressional opinion over the Berlin issue and any agreement we make which appears to have sold out any of our basic rights in Berlin or Western Germany in exchange for lifting the blockade will be received with violent indignation here. From all reports the country is more unified in its determination not to weaken in the face of the pressure of an illegal blockade than on any other issue we can recall in time of peace.[65]

Soviet disappointment at the American refusal to ratify the Moscow texts was made abundantly clear by Molotov during his meeting with the Western envoys on August 27. Whereas before he had been restrained and courteous, now he became truculent and argumentative. Nevertheless, new drafts were worked out for an interim communiqué and directive, and Marshall was willing to accept the new drafts—but not the renewed Soviet request for a reference to the London decisions. Eventually, the Western envoys and Molotov reached agreement on August 30 to issue the directive to the Military Governors in Berlin that very evening, but they were unable to agree on the interim communiqué because Molotov still insisted on a final paragraph concerning the London decisions.[66] The directive required the Military Governors to work out, within seven days, detailed arrangements for the simultaneous lifting of the blockade and the introduction of the Soviet currency into Berlin under four-power supervision.[67]

PHASE II: AUGUST 31–SEPTEMBER 7

News of the Moscow agreement greatly disturbed Clay, and he was extremely reluctant to play the part assigned to him by the four governments in their directive. Paradoxically, it was the success of

---

65. Marshall to Smith, August 26, 1948, in *FRUS, 1948*, Vol. 2, p. 1085.
66. Smith to Marshall, August 17, 1948; Marshall to Smith, August 18, 1948; and Smith to Marshall, August 30, 1948, all in *FRUS, 1948*, Vol. 2, pp. 1085–97; and Smith, *Moscow Mission*, pp. 241–243.
67. For the text of the directive, see U.S. Department of State, *Germany 1947–1949: The Story in Documents* (Washington, D.C.: U.S. Government Printing Office, 1950), pp. 211–212. The time constraints imposed on the Military Governors troubled Smith. "I am sure," he wrote privately, "the talks in Berlin cannot possibly produce a solution in the time we have allowed them and if there seems to be a prospect of an agreement, this time will have to be extended." Smith to Kennan, August 31, 1948, George F. Kennan Papers, Correspondence,

the Moscow talks, such as it was, rather than their failure that led to a marked increase in the stress which the Military Governor experienced. So fierce and bellicose was Clay's attitude that his superiors became worried that he might abort the Military Governors' talks. "Lovett called me up after lunch," recorded Forrestal in his diary on August 27, "to express great concern about Clay's ability to preserve his calm and poise in these negotiations. He said that he had the impression that Clay was now drawn as tight as a steel spring." Forrestal suggested that Royall go over to help Clay, but Lovett thought this would be impractical because it would indicate a lack of confidence in Clay to send over his superior to monitor and guide him. Forrestal later talked about this to Royall, who shared Lovett's point of view.[68]

General Robertson, too, was dismayed by Clay's truculence. At Robertson's suggestion, the three Western Military Governors met on August 28 to coordinate their ideas concerning the line they should take should the proposed directive be received. Clay, who had showed some reluctance to attend the meeting, started the proceedings by saying that in his opinion there was no possibility of reaching agreement within the framework of the instructions likely to reach them from Moscow, except such an agreement as would result in turning the city over to the Soviets. He recognized that Robertson and Noiret believed that an attempt to get an agreement should be made, and he was prepared to go along with them, but he intended to refer at every stage to his government so that the responsibility for the results should not fall on his head.[69]

Draper, who learned about this preliminary meeting from Murphy's report to the State Department, impressed on Clay the importance of keeping the Army Department as well informed as the State Department during the period of negotiations that lay ahead. Stung by the implied admonition, Clay replied that he would enter

---

Box 28, Seeley G. Mudd Manuscript Library, Princeton University. To Admiral Leahy, on the other hand, the very fact that agreement was reached seemed to augur well for the prospects of keeping the peace. The information received from Moscow, he noted, "indicates today that the differences between the Soviet and Western Governments in Berlin give promise of being adjudicated without a resort to arms." William Leahy Diary, August 31, 1948, p. 55, Papers of Admiral William D. Leahy, Library of Congress.

68. Millis, *The Forrestal Diaries*, p. 480.

69. Robertson to Strang, August 28, 1948, FO 371/70511/C7136, Public Record Office, London.

no agreements nor take positions contrary to his French and British colleagues without referring each specific item to Washington for approval. "I am not going to be the warmonger," he exclaimed, "which plunges defenseless France and U.K. as well as U.S. into war. On the other hand, I have no hope of reaching a solid agreement which protects our position. . . . It is not Soviet custom to give more in the field than in Moscow." Draper relented somewhat and sought to reassure Clay by telling him that if anyone could pull the acorns out of the fire, he could, and that Secretary Royall intended to give him considerable latitude to exercise his own judgment in the negotiations and wanted him to simply keep them informed and let them know before an actual breakdown was threatened. But Clay, who was chastened by the criticism that he had exceeded his authority in pushing the Western currency reform through, refused to be mollified: "Thanks but not this time. I am cured and will ask for instructions."[70]

The final directive, when it was received, confirmed Clay in his view about the inevitability of failure in the Military Governors' negotiations. He was particularly critical of the Governors' failure to incorporate in the written directive Stalin's comment that he did not object to four-power control of the German Bank of Emission. Clay felt certain that the Soviet Foreign Office had no intention of really permitting quadripartite control of this bank for any purpose, and that the American acceptance of ambiguous wording just to obtain an agreed-upon directive would lead nowhere. He also proudly observed that his own insistence in Berlin that the final agreement reflect Stalin's comment led in large part to the breakdown of the negotiations.[71]

The four Military Governors and their staffs met in Berlin on August 31 to work out the procedure for implementing the Moscow directive. Clay arrived late, did not shake hands with Marshal Sokolovsky, and remained frosty and taciturn at first. But his forceful and efficient mind could not bear things to go untidily, and he played a greater part than he had probably intended in steering the meeting towards agreement on a procedure that involved the setting up of three committees (communications, finance, and trade) and daily meetings of both the Military Governors and the

70. Teleconference, August 30, 1948, in *Clay Papers*, Vol. 2, pp. 793–794.
71. Lucius D. Clay, *Decision in Germany* (New York: Doubleday, 1950), pp. 369–370.

committees.[72] Clay also took the lead, following this procedural meeting, in proposing to his British and French counterparts arrangements for coordination and negotiation. Under these arrangements, their political advisers would, after every meeting, agree to a common report which would be sent to their three governments. Each of the Military Governors would be free to comment on the report and to make separate recommendations, but the actual report going to the three governments would be the same. It was further agreed that the three Military Governors would meet in Clay's office one hour prior to the meeting with Sokolovsky to receive the reports of their subcommittees and to coordinate their actions as far as possible.[73] On the American side, Murphy and Clay sent both the common reports and their separate comments to the State and Army Departments, respectively, while Marshall had the responsibility of keeping Truman informed of major developments.

At the very first substantive meeting, held on September 1, it became apparent that Sokolovsky was not ready to honor the informal understanding reached with Stalin in Moscow. Adopting a very legalistic interpretation of the directive, he sought to exclude any meaningful measure of quadripartite control over the German Bank of Emission. Clay viewed this as a potential breaking point in the negotiations and reported to Washington that the acceptance of the Soviet proposal for limited control by the four-power financial commission would place the financial and economic destiny of Berlin in Moscow's hands.[74]

Marshall informed the President of the disagreement in the Berlin talks on the powers of the commission. "The matter is of central importance," he explained on September 2, "and may prove to be the breaking point of the discussions. We have, however, instructed Clay, with his full agreement, to leave this point aside and to continue discussions with the other Military Governors in an attempt to reach agreement on the other parts of the communiqué. If agreement is reached on the other points and the Military Governors are still unable to agree on the relationship of the financial commission and the German bank, the matter will then be referred back to

72. Robertson to British Foreign Office, August 31, 1948, FO 371/70512/C7198, Public Record Office, London; and Murphy to Marshall, August 31, 1948, in *FRUS, 1948*, Vol. 2, pp. 1099–1100.
73. Clay to Draper, September 1, 1948, in *Clay Papers*, Vol. 2, pp. 798–801.
74. Ibid.

Moscow for discussion with Molotov or Stalin. We feel that these negotiations should not break down in Berlin on what would appear to be a technical point but rather in Moscow on the basic issue reflected in this technical point."[75]

With respect to the transport restrictions, Sokolovsky's position was also unyielding and contrary to Stalin's explicit assurances. He began by declaring on September 3 that he would agree to the removal of only those restrictions imposed after June 18, and he even tried to discuss the introduction of new restrictions on the existing air traffic. Clay replied that they were there to discuss the lifting of all the restrictions imposed since March, not to introduce new restrictions, and he vetoed the referral of Sokolovsky's proposal to the transport committee.[76] Royall expressed complete agreement and satisfaction with the stand that Clay had taken. "The unequivocal lifting of blockade restrictions," he said, "is a vital issue and matter of principle. . . . Retention of complete freedom of airlift is equally important as a matter of principle. . . . Failure to reach agreement in Berlin giving us full satisfaction on these essential points would indicate Soviets not prepared to carry out Moscow commitments. . . . If necessary, we are fully prepared to take this issue back to Moscow and make it a breaking point."[77]

After the meeting of September 4 concluded its business, Sokolovsky announced that Soviet air maneuvers on an extensive scale would be held for several days beginning September 6, and that it would be necessary for these maneuvers to extend into the air corridors and over Berlin. Clay pointed out that the air corridors to Berlin and in Berlin were crowded with nonmilitary planes bringing essential supplies to its people, and that he had to remind Sokolovsky that maneuvers in the corridors were prohibited by the existing safety regulations. Sokolovsky denied that such regulations existed and insisted that they must use the corridors.[78] In the end, this implied threat of physical interference with the airlift did not materialize, but the hopes pinned by Washington on a negotiated settlement in Berlin also sank without a trace.

75. Brief for the President: "Difficulties Encountered in Technical Discussions by the Military Governors in Berlin," September 2, 1948, President's Secretary File, Foreign Affairs—Germany, Box 178, Harry S. Truman Library.
76. Clay to Draper, September 4, 1948, in *Clay Papers*, Vol. 2, pp. 816–821.
77. Ibid., p. 821.
78. Clay to Draper, September 11, 1948, in ibid., pp. 821–826; and Millis, *The Forrestal Diaries*, pp. 480–481.

Lovett and Bradley went to Forrestal's office on Labor Day, September 6, to review the position. To judge from Forrestal's diary notation, what took place was not a discussion but a monologue by Lovett, who took advantage of the relaxed atmosphere of the holiday to expound his views at great length. It was quite clear, stated Lovett, that an important Russian objective was the domination of Germany, the first step of which was the control of Berlin. The sheer duplicity of the Soviets during the negotiations was beyond the experience of the experts in the State Department, and, consequently, any future promise made by the Soviets should be evaluated with great caution. It appeared that they did not mind lying, so long as it was for the benefit of the state. In the Moscow talks, recalled Lovett, they had arrived at certain arrangements with Stalin and Molotov, only to find that, in the final meeting, Molotov and Vishinsky were extremely sour and disagreeable. Lovett's estimate was that when they reported the results of their negotiations with the Western envoys to the Politburo, they were informed that they "had lost their shirts." The directive issued to the four Military Governors had been completely disregarded by Sokolovsky. It was Lovett's hunch—and he reiterated that it was only a hunch—that the Soviets did not want an agreement and were ready to break off negotiations unless they could get an agreement on their terms. There was no intelligence estimate to support this conclusion, but the Under Secretary felt that there was no other explanation for the extraordinary behavior of the Soviets. He stressed the difficulty of dealing with someone "whose head is full of bubbles."[79]

On the following day, there was a special meeting of the National Security Council called by the President for the purpose of considering the Berlin situation. All the other members were also present at this special meeting, which was the first to be devoted wholly to the Berlin situation since General Clay personally reported to the Council on July 22. Marshall and Lovett reviewed the diplomatic events of the previous month and reported on the deterioration of the negotiations, which were likely to blow up shortly both in Moscow and in Berlin. Lovett called attention to the fact that the Soviets had announced their intention to hold maneuvers in the Berlin area, that they had been put on notice that the airlift would proceed, and that any interference would be

79. Millis, *The Forrestal Diaries*, pp. 481–483.

at their own responsibility. Marshall pointed out that time was on the side of the Soviets. The airlift could be continued and even stepped up, but the Russians could put pressure on the Western powers by ever new methods. Just recently, for instance, there had been communist-led riots in the Western zones of Berlin, and the situation was so dangerous that the slightest additional element could be the fuse to spark a general conflagration.

The Council, with the President presiding, adopted Marshall's proposal "to bring the disagreed issues to a definitive conclusion in Moscow and, if no satisfactory solution is reached, then to refer the Berlin situation to the United Nations Security Council under Chapter VII of the Charter." The Secretary of the Air Force made a report on the Berlin airlift, and the Council agreed that unless the Joint Chiefs of Staff saw some military objection, the number of C-54s taking part in the airlift would be increased from 125 to 200 (Decision 19). Royall reported that General Bradley was in communication with General Clay in order to plan protective measures against Russian interference. And a meeting was arranged for the following day at which Marshall and the Joint Chiefs of Staff would be present in order to discuss emergency plans.[80]

The seventh and last session of the Military Governors' meeting adjourned late in the evening of September 7, with the week of discussions in Berlin having failed to advance the prospects for a final agreement being reached. The Military Governors were unable to submit an agreed-upon four-power report. The American, British, and French Military Governors therefore submitted a three-power report to their governments, which said in part: "We feel that we can sum up the overall position by reporting that after some days of little progress Marshal Sokolovsky has given ground on most of the subsidiary issues as well as making a reasonable proposal in regard to road and rail traffic. There remain three main points of disagreement, namely, (A) the functions of the Finance Commission and in particular its relation to the German Bank of

80. Ibid., pp. 483–485; James V. Forrestal Diaries, September 7 and 8, 1948, pp. 2474–80, Princeton University Library; Harry S. Truman, *Memoirs*, Vol. 2: *Years of Trial and Hope, 1946–1953* (London: Hodder and Stoughton, 1956), p. 135; and NSC Action 109, Record of Action by the National Security Council at its Twentieth Meeting, September 7, 1948, President's Secretary File, Harry S. Truman Library. The Joint Chiefs of Staff subsequently authorized that fifty, not seventy-five, additional C-54s be made available to Clay. Memorandum for the Secretary of the Army from Lt. Gen. A. C. Wedemeyer, October 5, 1948, RG 335, National Archives, Washington, D.C.

Emission; (B) the Soviet insistence on the Soviet control of trade in Berlin; (C) the Soviet proposal to introduce restrictions on air transport." The Military Governors added that they observed no sign in Marshal Sokolovsky of an intention to yield on these three points, and that they saw no chance of progress in Berlin until action had been taken on the governmental level to resolve them.[81]

PHASE III: SEPTEMBER 8-19

The meeting with the Joint Chiefs of Staff in Washington was held, as arranged, on September 8 at 10:30 A.M. It was preceded by a two-hour teleconference with Berlin, with Royall, Draper, Bradley, Wedemeyer, and (for the last half hour) Forrestal sitting at the Washington end. Clay was in broad agreement with the proposal to confront Molotov in Moscow, but it did seem to him that their last approach to Moscow had been "too much of a plea and not enough of a demand." He realized that Smith had been under pressure from his French and British colleagues, but he stressed that the method of approach was very important with the Soviets. If no satisfaction could be gotten from Molotov, Clay agreed that then the Western powers must go to the UN. He expected no result from referral to the UN except publicity for their desire for a peaceful solution. On the other hand, he was convinced that Moscow did not want a showdown and would back down before a determined front. Bradley raised the question of Clay's actions during the recent mob violence in Berlin and asked Clay whether he intended to enter the Soviet sector with Military Police in order to protect American lives and property there—an action which would be in violation of existing agreements and make the Americans look like the aggressors. Clay replied that he did not intend such action, which would legitimize Soviet entry into the American sector, although conditions could arise that would lead him to recommend it. "You need not fear any precipitate action on our part," he added. "We have taken much without it. However, you cannot live surrounded by force and bluff without showing that you have no fear of the first and only contempt for the latter."[82]

81. For the full text of the joint report, see Great Britain, Cmd. 7534, *Germany: An Account of the Events Leading Up to a Reference of the Berlin Question to the United Nations* (London: His Majesty's Stationery Office, 1948), Annex VII, pp. 56-57.
82. *Clay Papers*, Vol. 2, p. 848.

Forrestal left no diary note on the 10:30 meeting with the Joint Chiefs, but the tangled situation did cause him to reflect on the powers and responsibility of the Secretary of Defense. He said to Royall, at the end of the teleconference with Clay, that this whole negotiation process provided food for thought on the question of the concentration of power in the Office of the Secretary of Defense:

> I pointed out that these negotiations were of a nature that requires almost continuous attendance in order to follow the threads between State and Defense Departments. That if it were all concentrated in my office, I would have had to assign some particular person to do it, but that with all the minutiae of detail in connection with the Bank of Emission, with trade arrangements, etc., I would have had to maintain daily and almost hourly familiarity. Furthermore, all discussions with State would have had to have been carried on by me.[83]

Close cooperation between the Army and State Departments was in fact maintained throughout the period of the Berlin talks and was greatly facilitated by the common assessment of Soviet objectives and tactics. Communist-inspired attacks on the Magistrat, which was located in the Soviet sector of Berlin, were followed anxiously in both departments, with the Army intent on preventing military incidents that might lead to war, and the State Department intent on minimizing the adverse effects on the morale of the West Berliners and their allies. At his press conference on September 8, Marshall condemned the recent activities of the Socialist Unity Party in Berlin as typical of the methods used by Communists to disrupt democratic processes in order to develop a Communist-dominated form of government. Such efforts must be firmly resisted, he said. Marshall did not comment on whether the Western powers were planning military countermeasures, nor upon the possibility of further talks in Moscow. He believed that the disturbances were designed to upset the conference of the Military Governors, but that they did not succeed in doing so.[84]

In a telegram to Smith on the same day, however, Marshall ad-

---

83. Millis, *The Forrestal Diaries*, p. 485.
84. *New York Times*, September 9, 1948. The following day, at a press conference, Truman gave his unqualified backing to Marshall's assertion that the United States was determined to stand up for its rights in Berlin. *Public Papers of the Presidents of the United States: Harry S. Truman, 1948* (Washington, D.C.: U.S. Government Printing Office, 1964), pp. 481–482.

mitted that he and his advisers took a more serious view of the political pressure applied by the Soviet authorities in Berlin. The choice, he said, was between accepting Soviet delaying tactics by starting a new round of fruitless talks while the Soviets proceeded to take over the city government, or facing squarely up to the fundamental question of rights. All the specific disagreements, he added, derived from the Soviet contention that the Western powers had lost their judicial rights in Berlin: "We do not accept this view and have consistently asserted our co-equal rights as victors and by agreements among Four Powers. The time has come, therefore, to recognize that all the troubles stem from this wide open difference and we are convinced that we must now insist that the Soviets recognize this right."[85] Smith was understandably surprised by this statement, for in all the talks with Molotov and Stalin both sides had tacitly recognized the irreconcilability of their positions on the fundamental question and sought a *modus vivendi* for Berlin which would permit high-level discussions on this and the other outstanding questions regarding Berlin and Germany. The real choice, according to Smith, was between preparedness to deal indefinitely with the situation existing in Berlin in the event of a breakdown in the four-power conversations, and willingness to make concessions in order to relieve the situation. Smith saw no indication that this basic strategic question had been considered and a definite line of action, beyond immediate reference to the UN, decided upon.[86]

Marshall's reply revealed an uncustomary lapse into legalism on his part and an inability to grasp that no amount of legal argumentation could bridge the fundamental conflict with the Soviets. The State Department's Legal Adviser had been asked to consider the matter carefully and gave it as his view that in the light of the three major assaults on their rights (i.e., the blockade, the refusal to implement quadripartite currency control, and the attack on the Magistrat), the Western powers had to refrain from actions or words which might be construed as acquiescence on their part in the waiving of their rights. This, Marshall thought, put them on completely solid ground, and he believed that in any further discussions in Moscow they should treat these three facts as part of a general Soviet plan to nullify their juridical rights in Berlin. He also

85. Marshall to Smith, September 8, 1948, in *FRUS, 1948*, Vol. 2, pp. 1140–42.
86. Smith to Marshall, September 9, 1948, in *FRUS, 1948*, Vol. 2, pp. 1142–44.

felt that they should either require the Soviets to expressly recognize the equal rights of the Western powers or to refrain from taking action inconsistent with those rights, the latter being a minimum demand. As to the more fundamental questions, Marshall assured Smith that the major consideration of America's future course of action was under constant study in the State Department, in the Defense establishment, and in the National Security Council.[87]

The acerbity and impatience evident in Marshall's message was symptomatic of Washington's frustration following the failure of the Berlin talks. The sheer physical strain of involvement in protracted and totally unproductive negotiations was beginning to take its toll. In his report to the Cabinet on September 10 about the Berlin-Moscow situation, Marshall observed that this was the seventy-ninth day of negotiations and all persons concerned with it were close to a state of exhaustion. Officials in Washington had been conferring by teleconference with Ambassador Douglas in London until 2:00 A.M. the night before and had resumed their talks at 8:30 A.M. the following morning. The French governmental crisis only magnified the problem of negotiation.

To judge from Forrestal's account, the Cabinet was simply being informed of recent developments: it was not called upon to take any decisions or even to discuss the Berlin situation. This passivity of the Cabinet is all the more striking given the urgency which Marshall attached to positive American action. His apprehension about a further spin of "the Berlin Merry-Go-Round" was that it would give Russia a chance to preempt America in taking the matter to the United Nations and to squeeze every political gain out of the initiative. The current plan, Marshall told the Cabinet, was to present an *aide-mémoire* to Molotov, reciting the failure of Sokolovsky to effect the agreements arrived at in Moscow and stating that unless a directive went to Sokolovsky instructing him to negotiate within the terms of reference established in Moscow, the Western ambassadors would report the fact back to their governments. This plan required British and French consent, but the British wanted to go back to Stalin, and the French were likely to support them. Marshall's objection to the British proposal was based on his expectation of getting from Stalin merely a bland statement of generalities, which would be followed by a continuation of

---

87. Marshall to Smith, September 10, 1948, in *FRUS, 1948*, Vol. 2, pp. 1145–47.

the same old delaying tactics—tactics which worked entirely in Russia's favor.[88]

The situation was tense, worrisome, and uncertain, and the danger of war once again loomed ominously on the horizon. It was nearly six weeks since Forrestal had declared that, in view of the crisis caused by the Berlin blockade, he wished a "resolution of the question whether or not we are to use the A-bomb in war." At that meeting on July 28 with Marshall, Royall, and Bradley, Forrestal also observed that it seemed to him that the Secretary of State had a deep interest in the matter, because if there were any question about the use of this weapon, "he was automatically denied one of the most potent cards in his pack in negotiation."[89] Now that tension was beginning to rise again and the hope of a negotiated settlement was being replaced by the fear of war, Forrestal returned to the subject. As the Cabinet broke up on September 10, he raised the question with Marshall, who suggested a meeting with the President.[90]

At the White House meeting on September 13, Forrestal received an answer which, while falling short of an unequivocal policy, satisfied him about the President's intent to use the bomb in the event of war. Secretary Royall and Generals Bradley and Vandenberg were invited to make the same presentation to the President that Vandenberg had made to Marshall the previous week. The question was brought up of raising with the British government the possibility of constructing huts for housing the components of the bomb on two British airfields, which would mean a net gain of ten days in the event of a decision to use the bomb in an emergency. After the briefing, the President said that "he prayed that he would never have to make such a decision, but that if it became necessary, no one need have a misgiving but what he would do so."[91] The briefing by the Pentagon leaders left Truman gloomy and dispirited. In a private memo dated September 13, he

---

88. Millis, *The Forrestal Diaries*, pp. 485–486; and Minutes of Cabinet Meetings, September 10, 1948, Papers of Matthew J. Connelly, Harry S. Truman Library.

89. James V. Forrestal Diaries, p. 2993, Princeton University Library.

90. Millis, *The Forrestal Diaries*, p. 486.

91. James V. Forrestal Diaries, September 13, 1948, p. 2494, Princeton University Library. Reassured about Truman's intent, Forrestal still had some doubts about the mechanics by which the bomb would be delivered, and he raised the matter with the Secretary of the Air Force. On October 5, 1948, Forrestal re-

wrote: "Forrestal, Bradley, Vandenberg, Symington brief me on bases, bombs, Moscow, Leningrad, etc. I have a terrible feeling afterwards that we are very close to war. I hope not. Discuss situation with Marshall at lunch. Berlin is a mess."[92]

The feeling of being close to war raised the general level of tension and subjected America's leaders, especially Truman, to acute stress, which is poignantly described in a diary entry made by David Lilienthal after a meeting with the Director of the Budget:

> Jim Webb came to see me today. The situation in Berlin is bad, he reports. The Russians seem prepared to kick us in the teeth on every issue. Their planes are in the air corridor today, and anything could happen. "Anything—they might walk in tomorrow and shoot Gen. Clay." The President is being pushed hard by Forrestal to decide that atomic bombs will be used, but the National Security Council, Jim has reason to believe, will advise the President that there is no occasion to decide that question right now. The President has always been optimistic about peace. But he is blue now, mighty blue. It is very hard on him, coming right now particularly.[93]

At the Cabinet meeting on Monday, September 13, the Secretary of State reported on the weekend developments in the Moscow-Berlin negotiations, but the discussions on the use of the bomb which had taken place earlier in the day in the White House were apparently not brought to the Cabinet's attention. The U.S. was faced, said Marshall, with continuing difficulties with both the British and the French, neither being ready to go as far in firmness of language as the Americans desired. He looked with great apprehension to the meeting of the United Nations. Lovett had suggested that both James Byrnes, the former Secretary of State, and Senator Vandenberg should accompany Marshall to give counsel and possibly to speak in some of the debates. Dulles, Marshall said, only wanted to speak from a lawyer's brief, whereas the de-

---

ceived the following memorandum from Symington: "Re our conversation last night, I talked to General Vandenberg this morning about his certainty as to whether or not the bomb could be dropped where, how and when it was wanted, and he told me again what he had already told me; namely, he was absolutely certain it could be dropped on the above basis." Copy in James V. Forrestal Diaries, p. 2539, Princeton University Library.

92. Harry S. Truman, *Off the Record* (New York: Harper and Row, 1980), pp. 148–149.

93. David E. Lilienthal, *The Journals of David E. Lilienthal*, Vol. 2: *The Atomic Energy Years, 1945–1950* (New York: Harper and Row, 1964), p. 406, diary entry for September 13, 1948.

bates in the Security Council sessions might call for a swift give-and-take and rough-and-tumble tactics. Marshall reported that Bevin had sent him a personal cable over the weekend saying that he wished, if possible, to avoid a break in the negotiations, which would send the issue to the UN. Stafford Cripps, the British Chancellor of the Exchequer who was then on an official visit to Washington, participated with Marshall in some of the weekend conversations and supported Bevin's position. Forrestal opined that this position was the result of Britain's war-weariness and extreme reluctance to face the grim prospect of another war.[94]

The next evening, at the home of Philip L. Graham, the publisher of the *Washington Post*, Forrestal, Marshall, and other high-ranking officers met with a large gathering of newspaper publishers and editors in order to brief them on the Berlin crisis. Marshall, Lovett, and Bohlen made a presentation of the sequence of events in Moscow and Berlin in the previous six weeks. Forrestal used the opportunity to pose the question of the bomb. His record of the discussion shows that there was unanimous agreement on the part of the publishers and editors that, in the event of war, the American public would not only have no question about the propriety of using the atomic bomb, but would in fact expect it to be used. There were many statements to the effect that public opinion was well ahead of the Administration in its impatience with the Soviet government. No one present expressed any desire for war, but there was strong evidence of the growing distaste for Russia's actions.[95]

The NSC had initiated discussions within the executive branch on the advisability of formulating policies regarding the use of atomic weapons. The result was NSC 30, prepared in consultation with the Departments of State, Army, Navy, and Air Force, the National Security Resources Board, and the Central Intelligence Agency. Two major arguments featured in this analysis. In the first place, it was pointed out that the Soviets should never be given reason to believe that the U.S. would even consider renouncing the use of such weapons, because this might encourage exactly the kind of Soviet aggression which U.S. policy was designed to deter. Secondly, a decision against the use of the bomb would enfeeble the security of America's European allies, because for them the

94. Millis, *The Forrestal Diaries*, pp. 489–490.
95. Ibid., pp. 487–489.

atomic bomb, under American trusteeship, offered the main counterbalance to the everpresent threat of Soviet military power. On the other hand, it was not deemed necessary to obtain a decision about the time and circumstances under which atomic weapons might or might not be employed prior to the evident imminence of hostilities. In conclusion, NSC 30 stated: "It is recognized that, in the event of hostilities, the National Military Establishment must be ready to utilize promptly and effectively all appropriate means available, including atomic weapons, in the interest of national security and must therefore plan accordingly," and "the decision as to the employment of atomic weapons in the event of war is to be made by the Chief Executive when he considers such decision to be required."[96] On September 16, the National Security Council adopted this conclusion, which signaled the military to plan for the use of atomic weapons while leaving the ultimate decision on their deployment to the President (Decision 20). To all intents and purposes, this recommendation of the National Security Council settled the question in favor of using the bomb, because military planning on the assumption of its use would leave the Chief Executive virtually no alternative in the event of a direct threat to American security.[97]

Although the final decision regarding the use or nonuse of the atomic bomb remained a presidential prerogative, Forrestal must have regarded the NSC's directive to plan on the assumption of use, taken in conjunction with Truman's earlier assurance that if it became necessary he would order its use, as a satisfactory resolution of this vital policy question. At any rate, he did not feel it necessary to raise the subject with the President again. The question of the bomb's custody, however, remained unresolved. Marshall mentioned the custody question at an informal meeting with Truman and Forrestal, following the NSC session. The President said he was most anxious to withhold this decision until after the election campaign. Forrestal said he was still convinced that physical custody of the weapon should be in the hands of the military. He added that he did not think that the six weeks until the election would make a crucial difference in their planning for the use of the bomb, but that he would like to reserve the right to come back to the President if those responsible thought the question should be

---

96. NSC 30, "United States Policy on Atomic Weapons," September 10, 1948, in *FRUS, 1948*, Vol. 1, pp. 624–628.

97. Ibid., pp. 630–631.

reopened.[98] Although national security policy almost invariably looks inwardly as well as outwardly, this conversation provides extraordinarily clear evidence of the direct impact of domestic electoral calculations on the handling by the American high-policy elite of one of the most acute and dangerous Cold War crises.

Forrestal kept a watchful eye on the state of public opinion and continually solicited, through the next two months, the views of American and European public figures about likely reactions to an American use of the bomb in the event of war with Russia. He never recorded dissent from the unanimous agreement which he had detected at the meeting with the newspaper men. Marshall was to quote to him the remark of John Foster Dulles that "the American people would execute you if you did not use the bomb in the event of war." Clay replied that he "would not hesitate to use the atomic bomb and would hit Moscow and Leningrad first." Winston Churchill, forthright as ever, told him that the United States erred in underrating the destructive power of the weapon, and that this could only lend dangerous encouragement to the Russians.[99]

Washington's fear of possible British weakness also proved unfounded. When Sir Stafford Cripps visited Washington in early October, he told Forrestal that "Britain is placing its main reliance on the development of fighter aircraft to ensure the security of Britain. Britain must be regarded as the main base for the deployment of American power and the chief offensive against Russia must be by air." On November 12, when Forrestal visited London, Prime Minister Attlee told him that "there is no division in the British public mind about the use of the atomic bomb—they were for its use. Even the Church in recent days had publicly taken this position."[100]

While Forrestal took comfort in the knowledge that the American and British people would stand firm and that moral sentiment would not inhibit a resort to the ultimate weapon in the event of war, he was not himself inclined to favor a preventive war against the Soviet Union. In the autumn of 1948, a growing number of voices, particularly among civilians, lent their support to the thesis that the United States should seize the initiative and launch a war against its adversary while it still possessed a monopoly on nuclear power. In Forrestal's view, this was an irresponsible and dangerous

98. Millis, *The Forrestal Diaries*, p. 490.
99. Ibid., pp. 488–489.   100. Ibid. pp. 490–491.

trend and one which needed to be countered. He himself insisted on a strong military posture and believed that Soviet expansionism might have to be contained by force, but the idea that the United States should launch a surprise attack unprovoked by Soviet aggression was totally unacceptable as far as he was concerned.[101]

While the broad outlines of American military policy were assuming a clearer shape under the impact of the Berlin crisis, American diplomacy was brought to a temporary standstill by inter-Allied conflicts of opinion. American diplomats spent several days trying to resolve the differences with the British and the French. Bevin made it clear that the British government would not agree to accept the line of approach set forth in the American *aide-mémoire*. Washington's line, supported by Clay, Murphy, and Smith, was that the next approach to Stalin should be planned to bring the matter to a head in such a way as to permit the Western governments to decide whether or not it would be worthwhile to continue the discussions. This, in Washington's view, could only be done by giving the Russians clear evidence of Western willingness to break the talks if they persisted in their attitude. The British and the French, on the other hand, were inclined to offer the Russians an opportunity to prolong the talks. The Americans were consequently pulled in opposite directions by the requirements of crisis management, on the one hand, and the requirements of alliance maintenance, on the other. Marshall and his advisers felt that the differences with their allies were so deep as to confront them with the following alternatives: (1) to put the importance of three-power unity above everything else and go along for one more round with the British and the French; or (2) to follow what they genuinely believed to be the correct policy in regard to the Soviets and the Berlin situation and insist on their views even at the expense of different approaches in Moscow. Marshall consulted Senator Vandenberg on these alternatives and debated them with Royall and Draper on September 11. He concluded that, on balance, the maintenance of tripartite unity was the overriding factor, and that America should therefore go along with the Franco-British approach despite the dangers inherent in it.[102]

101. Arnold A. Rogow, *Victim of Duty: A Study of James Forrestal* (London: Rupert Hart-Davis, 1966), pp. 184–186.
102. Marshall to Murphy, September 11, 1948, in *FRUS, 1948*, Vol. 2, pp. 1147–48.

Smith was instructed to immediately seek, together with his British and French colleagues, an interview with Stalin and Molotov at which they would present the agreed-upon *aide-mémoire*. Smith was also advised to avoid discussion of technical details and to confine himself simply to ascertaining whether or not the Soviets were willing to give satisfaction on the three basic issues which had to be settled before the discussions could be resumed in Berlin. The *aide-mémoire* itself charged that the Soviet Military Governor departed from the understandings reached in Moscow on: (1) transport; (2) the authority and functions of the financial commission; and (3) the control of trade in Berlin.[103]

The original request of the three Western envoys for an interview with Stalin was denied on the grounds that the Generalissimo was on vacation. They therefore had to settle for a meeting with Molotov on September 14, at which they presented the *aide-mémoire* with a brief explanation of their governments' position. Molotov's attitude at the meeting convinced Smith that the Soviet government was playing for time, that it was prepared to prolong the discussions indefinitely, and that it wanted to place on the Western powers the onus for the final break.[104]

On September 18, Molotov invited the Western envoys to the Kremlin and handed them the Soviet government's reply, which was also in the form of an *aide-mémoire*. The Soviet reply denied the allegation that Sokolovsky had deviated in the Berlin talks from the understanding reached in Moscow, and it went on to assert that the reason for the differences that arose in Berlin lay in the desire of the Western governments to give a new interpretation to the Moscow directive which had not been implied when it was being drawn up. After setting forth its own interpretation of the understanding reached at Moscow, the Soviet government suggested that the Military Governors be given more detailed instructions on the three basic issues in dispute.[105] In the discussion which ensued, Molotov's lengthy expositions frequently obfuscated rather than clarified the Soviet position, and the meeting ended with the West-

103. Marshall to Smith, September 12, 1948, in *FRUS, 1948*, Vol. 2, pp. 1151–55.

104. Smith to Marshall, September 14, 1948, in *FRUS, 1948*, Vol. 2, pp. 1157–60.

105. For the full texts of the Western and the Soviet *aides-mémoire*, see U.S. State Department, *The Berlin Crisis*, pp. 44–50.

ern envoys stating that they would refer the *aide-mémoire* to their governments.[106]

The evident hardening of the Soviet position did not altogether surprise Western diplomats. Confident in the effectiveness of the blockade, Stalin had asked the Western powers to postpone their plans for a West German government. On September 1, however, a German Constituent Assembly began its work in Bonn under the chairmanship of Konrad Adenauer. The hope of Western concessions disappeared, and Stalin lost interest in the negotiations, which produced nothing of benefit for his country. The British chargé in Moscow reported that in informal conversations a senior Soviet official told an Egyptian diplomat that the one thing his government could not allow was the consolidation of the Western zones of Germany into a springboard for an eventual attack on the Soviet domain. If the Western powers persisted in ignoring Soviet interests in Germany, then the Soviet Union would have no option but to "liquidate" the Western position in Berlin. The Soviet Union did not want war and still hoped for an agreement, but the Western powers could not have it both ways by continuing their presence in Berlin while ignoring Soviet wishes and interests in regard to Western Germany.[107]

The three Western heads of mission believed, on the basis of the last meeting with Molotov, that the Russians were no longer attempting to reach an agreement but were instead thinking in tactical terms and merely trying to spin out the talks. All they seemed willing to concede was the shadow, but not the substance, of four-power control of Berlin. Behind Molotov's relative cordiality, the three men sensed that he also suspected that this might well be the last meeting, and so he was playing his hand for the record. Smith conveyed this evaluation to his governmental superiors.[108]

Forrestal, Royall, and Draper met to discuss the Soviet note on Sunday, September 19. The Soviet claim that Sokolovsky had acted in perfect accord with the Moscow agreements did not surprise them. They did not consider the note satisfactory, but observed that at the very end of the conversation, Molotov indicated his

106. Smith to Marshall, September 18, 1948, in *FRUS, 1948*, Vol. 2, pp. 1166–73.
107. Harrison to British Foreign Office, September 19, 1948, FO 371/70515/C7704, Public Record Office, London.
108. Smith to Marshall, September 18, 1948, in *FRUS, 1948*, Vol. 2, p. 1173, note 4; and *Clay Papers*, Vol. 2, p. 876.

willingness to hold further conversations in an effort to reach an agreement. Royall made the point that it would not be good for the record to have broken on such a note—that is, with Molotov still apparently willing to work for an accommodation. Forrestal called Marshall just before the latter took off for Paris, and made the suggestion that insofar as technical matters in the Berlin area (such as trade and finance) were concerned, the Western powers might find it advantageous to suggest the creation of a neutral commission—composed of members from Holland, Sweden, Norway, Switzerland, etc.—to deal with these matters. Marshall did not pursue this bizarre and totally impractical idea, and, from that point on, the Defense Secretary's preoccupation with the Berlin crisis declined. With the steadily lessening chances that the crisis would explode into war, it was the diplomats who henceforth carried the principal responsibility.[109]

If the receding of the perceived probability of war relaxed the stress which the American decision-makers experienced, the success of their German policy and of the airlift began to reverse their perception that time was on the side of the Russians. In this respect, the rapid progress in the economic and political revival of West Germany reduced the American as well as the Soviet interest in a compromise on Berlin, at least for the immediate future. "As you know," wrote Clay in a private letter to former Secretary Byrnes, "an agreement with the Soviet Government at this time will prove impossible except under terms which would lead to our departure from Europe and I am convinced that a strong western German government reoriented towards Western Europe would do much to restore the political and economic balances in Europe in our favor. If this does happen it would of course put us in better shape for the final negotiations."[110]

Taking the dispute over Berlin to the United Nations offered maximum flexibility for pursuing this long-term strategy. Without the United Nations option, the U.S. would have been forced to choose between four alternatives, none of which was perceived to be readily acceptable: (1) indefinite continuation of the airlift under duress, with no action looking toward lifting the blockade; (2) negotiation under duress while the Soviets proceeded to wreck the

109. Millis, *The Forrestal Diaries*, pp. 490–491.
110. Clay to Byrnes, September 18, 1948, in *Clay Papers*, Vol. 2, pp. 858–860.

government of Berlin and to terrify the population of the city; (3) Western withdrawal from Berlin under duress, with an inestimable blow to their prestige and to the morale of their allies; and (4) action to relieve the blockade, which might lead to war. United Nations action appeared to Marshall and his advisers to be the only way to get more time without paying for it by appeasement.[111]

PHASE IV: SEPTEMBER 20–OCTOBER 2

Secretary Marshall flew to Paris on September 19 to attend the UN General Assembly session, taking his chief advisers on the Berlin crisis with him. John Foster Dulles also responded to his invitation to go to Paris as a member of the American delegation to the UN. For the next two months, until Marshall returned to Washington, U.S. policy in the Berlin crisis was conducted from Paris. The French capital was the convenient meeting point for all the American officials involved in the Berlin-Moscow talks. And the presence of Bevin and his advisers in Paris enabled Marshall to hold face-to-face meetings with his French and British colleagues. The purpose of the initial meetings was to discuss the entire situation with all those who had been involved in the negotiations with Russia over Berlin and also to present the appearance of a strong and united front for the three nations.[112]

President Truman could not play a very active part in American policymaking on Berlin during this phase, not simply because the entire Berlin team was abroad, but because he himself was constantly on the move, waging up and down the country the most crucial electoral campaign of his entire political career. But he kept in touch with international developments through messages and documents that were forwarded to him for approval. Robert Lovett, the Acting Secretary of State, was as meticulous as General Marshall in making sure that the President was constantly advised of developments and his approval obtained before any major step was taken or important statements issued.[113]

The part played by Dulles in Paris was as useful to Truman's electoral prospects as it was to America's international position.

---

111. Marshall to Douglas, September 15, 1948, Under Secretary of the Army (Draper/Voorhees), Folder: "Berlin Crisis," RG 335, National Archives, Washington, D.C.
112. *Clay Papers*, Vol. 2, p. 877.
113. Truman, *Memoirs*, Vol. 2, p. 136.

The great question in the minds of friendly governments—and no doubt also in the minds of the Russians—was whether the U.S. would be able to continue to act strongly abroad during the rest of the election period and the ensuing transition period which would follow the anticipated Republican victory. Marshall and Dulles cooperated closely to dispel the mounting tide of doubt and fear.[114] On weekends, Dulles traveled to Berlin, Vienna, Copenhagen, or Stockholm to reaffirm at those exposed points his confidence in the continuity of a strong European policy. During his trip to Germany, to which he attached particular importance, he sought to scotch rumors about his unfriendly relations with General Clay and to make it perfectly plain to the people of Germany and to the Soviet leaders that a Republican electoral victory would not involve any repudiation of General Clay or of the policy to hold fast in Berlin.[115]

Marshall summoned Clay and Murphy to Paris as well as Ambassadors Douglas and Smith to exchange views and provide him with the latest information. During this visit, two long discussions were held, one of which was attended by Assistant Secretary Willard Thorp, Ambassador to France Jefferson Caffery, Dr. Philip Jessup, Bohlen, Clay, and Murphy; and the other by the last three plus Douglas and Smith. The purpose of these discussions was not to provide answers to specific questions but to have a full and frank exchange of views among the officials who, under Marshall's leadership, were directly concerned in the conduct of relations with the Soviet government.[116]

Marshall directed the discussions so as to allow the participants to develop their viewpoints fully. All of them were convinced that the Western powers must remain in Berlin to preserve the courage and faith of all of their friends and to offer hope to the peoples of Eastern Europe who lived under communist domination. Clay reported his conviction that they could stay in Berlin indefinitely, and that the airlift could be built up to maintain a reasonable stan-

114. Dulles, *War or Peace*, pp. 130–135.
115. Ibid., p. 135; "Introduction of Mr. John Foster Dulles," October 15, 1948, Frankfurt, Germany, and "Statement made by John Foster Dulles in Berlin on October 17, 1948," John Foster Dulles Papers, Box 35, Princeton University Library; Interview with General Lucius Clay, p. 5, and Interview with Robert D. Murphy, pp. 5–6, in the John Foster Dulles Oral History Collection, Princeton University Library; and JBR to Krock, September 28, 1948, p. 5, in the Arthur Krock Papers, Princeton University Library.
116. Clay, *Decision in Germany*, p. 375.

dard of living. He also expressed the view that the initial progress of the European Recovery Program offered hope that they could have an economically healthy Western Europe and Western Germany which would be able to assert rather than absorb pressure, and that this power, when it developed, would bring the Berlin blockade to an end. During this period, which could take many months, they had to be prepared to indefinitely maintain and even increase the airlift. Clay had no fear of physical aggression by Soviet forces, and he was certain that Communism had lost any opportunity it might have had to capture Germany, so long as the Western powers held their ground.

Smith agreed with these views in large measure, and he, too, discounted any likelihood of immediate physical aggression by Soviet forces. On the other hand, while he recognized the need to remain in Berlin as a temporary measure, he considered it a liability to be disposed of at the first opportunity.[117] Douglas felt strongly that the Western powers had to remain in Berlin up to the point of war if they were to accomplish their objectives in Europe, but also that war must be avoided at all costs. To Clay it did not seem feasible to determine the point at which only their departure from Berlin would avert war, and he was less apprehensive of a Soviet holocaust than his associates, who seemed to him to underesti-

---

117. Ibid., pp. 375–376. Smith expounded these "personal views" again a week later in Washington at a meeting of the Policy Planning Staff in which he was asked to comment on the outline for an NSC paper on Berlin. The following extracts are not a quotation but the gist of his remarks as recorded in the minutes: "I preface these personal views with the remark that I regret very much that we are in Berlin at all. I know that some of our people in Berlin do not agree with me, but for what it is worth I have always felt that we should never have let ourselves get into an exposed salient like Berlin under such conditions. From the military point of view it makes no sense whatever to have U.S. forces in an enclave that could be chopped off with ease. From the political point of view Berlin has become the important symbol it is now largely because we ourselves have made it so. However, that is all water over the dam; my hope for the future is that the U.N. will offer a chance for us to get out of Berlin. . . . Our present outburst of humanitarian feelings about the latter [the Germans] keeps reminding me that 3½ years ago I would have been considered a hero if I had succeeded in exterminating those same Germans with bombs. I do not expect the Russians to take any direct military action which would precipitate a conflict. They will harass the airlift; we would occasionally lose a pilot or a plane. Summing up I would say, therefore, that we can, if we wish to, stay in Berlin, at great cost, at some hazard, and with diminishing effectiveness except for the business of supplying ourselves, mainly to maintain our symbolic presence there." Minutes of the 186th Policy Planning Staff Meeting, Washington, D.C., September 28, 1948, in *FRUS, 1948*, Vol. 2, pp. 1194–97.

mate America's real strength. Once again, he pointed out that he did not anticipate war, that a "cold war" always involved the risk that it might become "hot," and that the risk had to be assumed.

While these discussions were directed to long-range aspects of the situation, unanimous agreement was reached on the need to stay in Berlin for the time being and to augment the airlift. Marshall was in full accord with this position and communicated it to the National Security Council with a recommendation for the dispatch of additional aircraft.[118]

At the first meeting of the French, British, and American foreign ministers in Paris, on September 20, all three were accompanied by their senior diplomatic advisers. At this meeting, Bevin called for a comprehensive review of all the facts of the Berlin problem to determine the methods for their action, in order not to improvise in the future as they had done in the past. Marshall agreed that all the factors should be studied, but he came out strongly in favor of sending a note to the Soviet Union and agreeing on a procedure for referring the matter to the United Nations. It was decided to appoint a drafting committee which would work on the note in the light of the exchange of views that had just taken place and in consultation with the Military Governors.[119] Thus, the alternative of another round of talks with the Russians, which Bevin had mentioned at the start of the meeting, simply fell by the wayside.

The meeting on the following day was an even larger gathering with twenty-three participants, including the three foreign ministers, an increased number of diplomatic advisers, the three Military Governors, and an interpreter. Schuman opened the meeting by stating its purpose: to draft a note to the Soviet government. Several drafts had been submitted to the foreign ministers; in particular, a British draft (by General Robertson) and an American draft (by Ambassador Douglas). Bevin pointed out that it was neither timely nor tactful to describe the blockade as "illegal" and "unlawful," and Marshall agreed to omit the offending words from the American draft. On the other hand, he believed that the note

---

118. Clay, *Decision in Germany*, pp. 376–377; and Clay to Bradley, September 23, 1948, in *Clay Papers*, Vol. 2, pp. 878–879.
119. Schuman brought Chauvel, Couve de Murville, Alphand, Clappier, and de Bourbon-Busset; Bevin brought McNeil, Harvey, Strang, and Tomkins; and Marshall brought Douglas, Caffery, Dulles, and Bohlen. Minutes of a Meeting of the Secretary of State with the Foreign Ministers of France and the United Kingdom, Paris, September 20, 1948, in *FRUS, 1948*, Vol. 2, pp. 1173–76.

should remain on the level of principles by referring to the blockade and to Russian activity in the rest of Germany as violations of the rights of the Western powers. To counter any wavering by his partners, Marshall sought to communicate to them the new sense of confidence with which he himself now looked to the future. They had already broken the blockade by "air ferry," he said, which could take care of the needs of the Western sectors of Berlin for as long as they wished. Nor was it as expensive as one might expect. "In every field," continued Marshall, "the Russians are retreating. From now on, Berlin is the only foothold which they have against us; everywhere else, and particularly in Germany, they are losing ground. We have put Western Germany on its feet and we are engaged in bringing about its recovery in such a way that we can really say that we are on the road to victory."

It was in this climate of growing confidence that the three foreign ministers finally agreed to proceed with the dispatch of identical notes to the Soviet Union, and to take the matter to the UN if the Russian reply turned out to be unsatisfactory (Decision 21). Marshall stated that if he agreed to send this further note to the Soviets and make a concession to the point of view of the French and the British governments, it was because he believed that it was now clearly understood between them that if the Russian reply turned out to be unsatisfactory, they were absolutely decided to bring the matter before the United Nations. It was agreed that the note should pose a definite question to which the Russians should reply Yes or No, and that no mention should be made of recourse to the UN, so as not to deprive the note of its character as a final notice and summons. For the benefit of the experts who were set to work on the final text, Marshall made it clear that they should take care not to word it in such a way as to make it an invitation to further discussions.[120]

The final agreed-upon text of the note was completed on the morning of September 22, and it was delivered simultaneously to the Soviet embassies in Washington, London, and Paris on that same day. In these identical notes, the three governments asserted that Soviet unwillingness to accept previous agreements was still preventing a settlement. After stating their final position on the

---

120. Minutes of a Meeting of the Secretary of State with the Foreign Ministers of the United Kingdom and France, Paris, September 21, 1948, in *FRUS, 1948*, Vol. 2, pp. 1177–80; and C[abinet] M[inutes] (48) 61st Conclusions, Minute 3, September 22, 1948, Public Record Office, London.

three points at issue, they asked the Soviet government bluntly whether or not it was prepared to remove the blockade measures it had imposed, so that conditions could be established which would permit a continuance of discussions.[121]

Informal discussions, mainly on tactics, continued at all levels in Paris, following the dispatch of the note. On September 24, Bevin called on Marshall, at the latter's request, to discuss whether the Berlin question should go to the Security Council or to the General Assembly. Marshall said that he, too, favored the Security Council. His first and decisive reason was that it was only in the Security Council that a quick and clear-cut debate could take place. The General Assembly was preoccupied with other difficult problems, such as Palestine, and the atmosphere there was already so disturbed that a clear debate would be impossible. His second reason was that the normal approach under the Charter was first to the Security Council. He had been assured that there was a good chance of getting a satisfactory vote in the Security Council, whereas this was more doubtful in the General Assembly. He also thought that it would be undesirable for the foreign ministers to engage in polemical speeches before the Assembly and embarrassing to them to have to constantly chip in to reply to Vishinsky's attacks.[122]

The Soviet reply was delivered in Washington, London, and Paris on September 25, and, as expected, the Soviet government declined to lift the blockade.[123] A statement was also issued through the official Soviet news agency, Tass, giving the Soviet version of the Moscow-Berlin talks and the reasons for their failure. The foreign ministers and their aides met shortly before one o'clock at the Quai D'Orsay on Sunday, September 26, to consider the situation produced by the Soviet breach of the agreement to keep the conversations confidential. The ministers had an opportunity to study the Soviet note and were unanimously of the opinion that, in the light of the Soviet refusal, no useful purpose would be served by continuing the discussions with the Soviet government. There was no suggestion to the contrary, direct or indirect, from any official

---

121. For the full text of the American note, see U.S. Department of State, *The Berlin Crisis*, pp. 50–51.

122. Bevin to Sir Oliver Franks (Washington), September 24, 1948, FO 371/7916/C7912/3/G, Public Record Office, London.

123. For the full text of the Soviet note of September 25, see Union of Soviet Socialist Republics, Ministry of Foreign Affairs, *The Soviet Union and the Berlin Question* (Moscow, 1948), pp. 54–57.

present. Schuman said that the French government was prepared to agree with the United States that the matter should now be referred to the United Nations and specifically to the Security Council.

The discussion then turned to the question of the desirability of immediately issuing a communiqué on the part of the ministers announcing their decision. Marshall pointed out that so far nothing had come from the Western governments, while the Soviet version of the breakdown was being spread throughout the world by radio and press without opposition. He therefore urged that the ministers immediately issue a communiqué to the world in order to counteract the Soviet propaganda and to inform their publics of their true position. Bevin questioned the wisdom of issuing a communiqué in advance of the reply to the Soviet government, but Marshall's arguments in favor of immediate action prevailed. The ministers were therefore able to reach agreement at this meeting concerning: (1) a final confirmation of the decision to refer the Berlin matter to the Security Council; (2) the sending of a final note to the Soviet government; and (3) the issuing of a communiqué (Decision 22).[124]

The communiqué, which was issued in the afternoon of September 26, briefly summarized the background to these decisions. The text of the note to the Soviet Union was prepared by a drafting committee in the course of the afternoon, and was approved, with minor amendments, by the foreign ministers when they resumed their meeting at 9:30 P.M. In essence, the note charged that the "illegal" blockade of Berlin made further negotiations impossible; that this and other coercive measures taken by the Soviet government constituted a threat to international peace and security; and that the three Western governments therefore felt obliged to refer the matter to the Security Council of the United Nations.[125]

124. Record of Meetings of the Secretary of State with the Foreign Ministers of the United Kingdom and France, Paris, September 26, 1948, in *FRUS, 1948*, Vol. 2, pp. 1184–86.

125. For the texts of the communiqué and the final note of September 26, see U.S. Department of State, *The Berlin Crisis*, pp. 35–61. In addition to these texts, the State Department released to the press the so-called "White Paper" on the negotiations with the Soviet Union: *The Berlin Crisis: A Report on the Moscow Discussions*. Acting Secretary of State Lovett sent an advance copy with an explanation to the White House. Memorandum for the President from Eben Ayers, September 26, 1948, President's Secretary File, Box 171, Harry S. Truman Library.

The American complaint against Russia was formally submitted to the United Nations in a note which Ambassador Warren Austin handed to Trygve Lie, the Secretary General of the United Nations, on September 29. Dr. Philip Jessup, the American deputy representative to the UN, was put in charge of the Security Council operation, and Bohlen, as head of the State Department's Berlin Group, was assigned to work with him. Jessup was a man of considerable judicial eminence as well as a skilful diplomat who could always be counted on to carry out with intelligence and precision the instructions he received from his government. After Bohlen and Jessup planned the strategy for the Security Council debates, they went to see Marshall, who told Jessup that he would back up any action he took, provided it was not appeasement.

The objectives which the U.S. sought to achieve by taking the Berlin case to the United Nations were not defined with adequate precision. Recourse to the world organization was first suggested as early as April 1948 and figured repeatedly in inter-Allied exchanges throughout the summer. At the outset, the idea was probably endorsed by some decision-makers *faute de mieux*, since they were determined not to withdraw, not to fight, and not to negotiate under duress. Bringing the Allies into line, however, proved to be a difficult task, not least because they suspected the U.S. of harboring bellicose intentions. To dispel the suspicions of the French, they were told that the United Nations was the only machinery by which they could avoid for a time the possibility of "a brutal choice between war and submission." The British were told by Bohlen that the Soviets might be planning to go to the General Assembly with a propaganda campaign for "peace," and that it was therefore necessary to move swiftly to preempt them.[126]

But even after the tripartite decision to resort to the UN was taken, Marshall's thinking remained either deliberately obscure or plainly muddled. His advisers were not unanimously in favor of the decision. Dulles, while outwardly supporting the Administration, privately confided to Senator Vandenberg his fears of likely consequences. If the UN failed to find a solution, said Dulles, some isolationists at home would call for a U.S. withdrawal, while other extremists might go even further by calling for a preventive war

---

126. Philip C. Jessup, "The Berlin Blockade and the Use of the United Nations," *Foreign Affairs*, Vol. 50, No. 1 (October 1972), pp. 165–167.

following the use of the Russian veto.[127] Douglas, Jessup, and Dean Rusk, the director of the Office of United Nations Affairs, went to see Marshall on September 26 at the embassy residence where he met with the American delegation every morning and often summoned individual members to conferences. Douglas said that he had detected some uncertainty among members of the delegation about whether their appeal to the UN was designed merely to give them strong moral backing for actions which might ultimately become necessary, including the use of force, or whether they were genuinely seeking help towards a solution. He thought it was important for Jessup to have some guidance on this point in his preparation and handling of the case. Jessup concurred, noting that the Allies would be in a much stronger position if they could say that in going to the Security Council they sincerely desired a solution, were referring the matter in good faith, and were prepared to abide by a UN resolution. Marshall's cryptic reply was that they had to recognize the implications of the step they had taken and had to be prepared to carry it through. By the end of the discussion, the aides felt that Marshall had given a sufficient indication of general American policy, and that the matter did not need to be pursued further.[128] One is left with a strong impression, however, that considerable ambiguity still surrounded the aims and tactics of the Americans as—with Britain and France uneasily in their train—they entered the spider's parlor.

PHASE V: OCTOBER 3, 1948–JANUARY 15, 1949

American behavior in the later months of 1948 tends to support the view that the overriding reason for going to the UN was to gain time rather than to work for a negotiated solution to the Berlin crisis. The Soviet government, in its note of October 3, denied the competence of the Security Council to deal with this matter and proposed to call a meeting of the Council of Foreign Ministers in order to review the Berlin situation and also the question of Germany as a whole in accordance with the Potsdam Agreement and the directive of August 30 to the Military Governors.[129]

127. Dulles to Vandenberg, September 28, 1948, the John Foster Dulles Papers, Princeton University Library.
128. Memorandum of Conversation by Philip C. Jessup, September 27, 1948, in *FRUS, 1948*, Vol. 2, pp. 1193–94.
129. For the full text of the Russian note of October 3, see USSR, Ministry of Foreign Affairs, *The Soviet Union and the Berlin Question*, pp. 73–84.

Marshall and Bevin met briefly on October 4 and agreed that there should not be any meeting of the Council of Foreign Ministers while the blockade was on, but that they should state in the Security Council that they would be willing to have such a meeting as soon as the blockade was lifted (Decision 23).[130] To General Robertson it appeared that the Americans simply did not want an agreement with the Russians over Berlin. He was mindful of the remarks made by Marshall on October 4 that their objective at present was to gain time.[131] Bevin agreed with this assessment but felt that he could not go outside the Security Council to elicit Russian views about whether agreement was still possible.[132] Bohlen was concerned that during the Security Council debate an American hothead in Germany might do something rash. He telegraphed Murphy in Berlin, cautioning against any move that might aggravate the situation and urging that only in a grave emergency should anything be done without first obtaining Marshall's approval.[133]

On October 4, the Berlin question was placed on the provisional agenda of the Security Council. The Soviet representative objected to its inclusion on the grounds that it did not fall within the competence of the Security Council and should be settled by the governments responsible. The United States, on the other hand, supported by Britain and France, maintained that the Soviet blockade of Berlin constituted a threat to international peace and therefore fell within the competence of the Security Council. For the first time in the Council's history, three of its permanent members were accusing another of endangering the peace of the world. On October 5, by a vote of 9 to 2, the Council decided to place the Berlin question on its agenda. Since this was a procedural matter it could not be vetoed, but the Soviet and Ukrainian representatives immediately announced that their countries would not take part in the discussion.[134]

At this juncture, Truman's electoral strategy collided head-on

130. Memorandum of Conversation by the Counselor of the Department of State (Bohlen), Paris, October 4, 1948, in *FRUS, 1948*, Vol. 2, pp. 1211–12.
131. Robertson to Sir Patrick Dean, October 6, 1948, FO 371/70518/C8205, Public Record Office, London.
132. Sir Patrick Dean to Robertson, October 7, 1948, FO 371/70518/C8205, Public Record Office, London.
133. Bohlen, *Witness to History*, pp. 281–282.
134. For the records of the discussions concerning the inclusion of the Berlin question on the agenda of the Security Council, see United Nations, *Official Records of the Security Council*, Third Year, Nos. 113 and 114.

with Marshall's diplomatic strategy. Against the background of mounting and increasingly effective criticism from the Wallace camp of the Cold War policies of his Administration, Truman took up the suggestion of two of his speechwriters, David Noyes and Alfred Z. Carr, that he should send his friend Chief Justice Fred Vinson as a personal emissary to Moscow to "talk peace" with Stalin. In his account of the affair, Carr claims that the campaign and the test of attitude it imposed on high Washington officials tended to shake the President's faith in some of his war-minded officials, made him aware that the theme of peace, which had been systematically woven into his speeches, was invariably popular, and forced him to reexamine America's relations with the Soviet Union in the light of public opinion—not as that was represented by the press, but as it was tested at first hand. Truman, according to Carr, was also concerned about the impression which the idea of a "preventive war," advocated more or less openly by influential publicists, was having on ordinary Americans, and he hoped to reduce tensions by sending Vinson to Moscow. As envisaged by Truman and his White House aides, no conflict arose between the Vinson mission and the normal processes of diplomacy. Vinson's brief was to convey the seriousness and sincerity of the American people's desire for peace and to ask for Stalin's cooperation in dispelling the poisonous atmosphere of distrust which surrounded the negotiations between the Western powers and the Soviet Union.[135]

But while Carr himself may have genuinely hoped that the Vinson mission would help to check the war fever which was building up in America and restore sanity to Russo-American relations, Truman and his other political advisers appear to have been more interested in the electoral advantage which such a bold gesture could be expected to yield. After securing, on Sunday, October 3, Vinson's reluctant agreement to undertake the mission, Truman ordered his press secretary to request free radio time for a presidential statement of major public importance. When Truman belatedly informed Marshall on Tuesday, October 5, however, he found the Secretary more than a little unsettled to discover that the President was making such a major departure in foreign policy without consulting him, and relentlessly opposed to the Vinson mission be-

135. Albert Z. Carr, *Truman, Stalin and Peace* (New York: Doubleday, 1950), pp. 111–120; Truman, *Memoirs*, Vol. 2, pp. 212 ff.; and text for Truman's broadcast announcing the Vinson mission, in Papers of Clark M. Clifford, Box 15, Harry S. Truman Library.

cause it would cut the ground out from under his feet at the UN over the Berlin blockade and be interpreted by the other Western delegations as a move to bypass them in unilateral negotiations. Truman emerged from the communication room crestfallen, having promised Marshall not to send Vinson, and having asked Marshal to come back to Washington from Paris over the weekend so that he, the President, could explore the international situation directly with him. Some of the White House staff pleaded with Truman to go ahead with the plan, but he just listened and then said quietly, "I have heard enough. We won't do it."[136]

The embattled President's decision to abandon the idea of sending Chief Justice Vinson on a peace mission to Moscow was thus taken on October 5 as a direct consequence of the vigorous opposition of his Secretary of State (Decision 24). Truman's subsequent handling of the affair was marked by wavering and indecision. Before his conversation with Marshall, he had invited Senator Tom Connally, chairman of the Foreign Relations Committee, and Senator Arthur Vandenberg to a private chat in the White House in order to break the news to them about the proposed mission. Connally, who arrived first, had the impression that Truman was still trying to work up his courage to send Vinson to Moscow, but he himself opposed it strongly. In Vandenberg's presence, the dejected President did not even mention the subject. Instead, he casually sounded out the two Republican leaders about the idea that he might personally "call Stalin on the phone" to see what he could do with him. They pointed out politely that a bilingual telephone conversation would be rather difficult, and that there would be no witnesses and no documents of any agreement reached between the two leaders. Truman looked disappointed. The way in which he was groping for some substitute to the Vinson mission to spectacularly associate himself with the peace crisis abroad left Vandenberg with the impression that he was at least not "overlooking" the fact that he was coming down the home stretch in a political campaign which badly needed a "shot in the arm."[137]

---

136. Jonathan Daniels, *The Man of Independence* (Philadelphia: Lippincott, 1950), p. 361; Robert H. Ferrell, *George C. Marshall* (New York: Cooper Square, 1966), pp. 250–258; Carr, *Truman, Stalin and Peace*, pp. 317–319; and "Précis of Conversation Between Secretary of State George C. Marshall, President of the Council of Ministers De Gasperi, Foreign Minister Sforza, and Ambassador Dunn," October 18, 1948, in *FRUS, 1948*, Vol. 3, pp. 883–887.

137. Tom Connally, *My Name is Tom Connally* (New York: Crowell, 1954),

Truman's account misleadingly states that the premature publication of the planned Vinson mission compelled him to reconsider its advisability.[138] In fact, news of the plan only reached the press three days after he had made his decision to abort it. But as a result of the leak, the whole affair misfired disastrously, and the reports of the President's ineptitude and indecision must have been as humiliating to Truman personally as they were damaging to America's standing abroad. When Marshall arrived from Paris on Saturday, October 9, the political uproar was working its way up to a veritable crescendo. In an effort to repair some of the damage, Truman issued a statement, after his meeting with Marshall, explaining the circumstances in which the ill-starred mission was first conceived and later abandoned.[139]

The incident illustrated the adverse effects of a concatenation of domestic and international crises on presidential decision-making in foreign affairs. Truman was more oriented to gaining political power at home than to intelligently using diplomatic power in Europe. His mental and physical stamina were severely tested by the presidential campaign. As the election date approached, he stepped up his whistle-stops on the long train journey which everyone thought would take him nowhere. In all, he campaigned for thirty-five days, traveled 31,700 miles, and delivered 356 speeches, averaging ten speeches a day. This highly stressful schedule inevitably impaired his attentiveness to the problems his Administration faced abroad. Having to cope with these problems, on the other hand, placed Marshall, along with the rest of the American delegation in Paris, under enormous stress. The ground had to be prepared before bringing the Berlin case to the United Nations. Answers to possible arguments of opponents had to be drafted in advance; friends had to be informed, persuaded, or encouraged. A workweek of eighty or ninety hours was normal.[140] The prospect of seeing all this work brought to nought and his own "no-appeasement" policy over Berlin reduced to a shambles by a sud-

---

p. 331; and Arthur H. Vandenberg, Jr., ed., *The Private Papers of Senator Vandenberg* (London: Gollancz, 1952), pp. 456–458.

138. Truman, *Memoirs*, Vol. 2, pp. 215–219.

139. "Statement by the President following General Marshall's return from Paris," October 9, 1948, *Public Papers of the Presidents of the United States: Harry S. Truman, 1948*, pp. 724–725.

140. Jessup, "The Berlin Blockade and the Use of the United Nations."

den political move designed primarily to win votes was enough to ruffle even the cold-blooded Secretary of State.

During Marshall's brief stay in Washington, an attempt was made by Forrestal to enlist his support for an increase in the defense budget. The continuing Soviet threat in Berlin was seized on by the military establishment to try to break through the $14.4 billion ceiling imposed by the President. On Sunday, October 10, Forrestal and the Chiefs of Staff of the three armed services went to a meeting with Marshall at the State Department. Marshall stated that he considered the present situation as one involving an attempt to purchase time. Two methods were involved: (1) the airlift and (2) the U.S. monopoly of the atomic bomb. In the Security Council, said Marshall, there was a danger arising out of the strong desire of the so-called neutral members to find a solution by way of mediation, whereas the Western powers wanted to settle the issue itself and to determine who was wrong and who was right. On the other hand, Marshall believed that the Soviets themselves were beginning to realize for the first time that the United States would really use the atomic bomb against them in the event of war. In this connection, he was interested to learn that Dulles accepted the use of the bomb as a foregone conclusion, stating that "the American people would execute you if you did not use the bomb in the event of war."[141] The discussion ranged over many other matters, but Marshall remained unresponsive to Forrestal's repeated references to the need for building up the armed forces as a prerequisite for a strong foreign policy. The most plausible explanation for Marshall's relative lack of concern over the size of the defense budget is to be found in his growing belief in the effectiveness of the bomb as a deterrent against Soviet aggression.

While Truman was fumbling in search of grand gestures to Moscow, and while Marshall was struggling to maintain a united allied front and to gain time at the United Nations, General Clay concentrated on building up the airlift as the centerpiece of American strategy. By cables dated September 10 and September 13, Clay requested that 116 additional C-54 aircraft be made available to "Operation Vittles" in order to provide an average lift of 4,500 tons daily, which was the minimum required to maintain the Western sectors of Berlin during the winter months. Of the 116 aircraft

141. James V. Forrestal Diaries, October 10, 1948, pp. 2555–62, Princeton University Library.

requested, 50 were provided by the Air Force in early September by order of the Joint Chiefs of Staff. On October 4, Clay cabled that he was seriously disturbed over the delay in the decision to send the remaining 66 aircraft, because bad weather was rapidly approaching and the present airlift was not sufficient to meet minimum requirements under bad weather conditions.[142]

As a result of Clay's urgent requests, a staff study on the augmentation of the airlift was prepared by the Army's Plans and Operations Division and submitted informally by General Bradley to the Joint Chiefs of Staff at their luncheon on September 29. This study recommended that Clay's request be approved and that the National Security Council urgently review the established American policy in the Berlin crisis.[143] The National Security Council was fully aware of the need for a major reappraisal of U.S. policy and had already requested the State Department to prepare a report on what should be done following the anticipated failure of the four-power talks on Berlin. In this connection, the Joint Chiefs of Staff were asked, through the Secretary of Defense, to supply an appraisal of the military implications of continuing the airlift through the ensuing winter. A subsequent request asked the Joint Chiefs of Staff to comment on the courses of action that would be open to the U.S. in the event of partial or complete interruption of the airlift by the Soviets.[144]

The task of evaluating the American position on Germany following the anticipated failure of the Moscow talks had been assigned by the State Department to its Policy Planning Staff. Upon completion of this task, on October 4, George Kennan sent one copy of his penetrating paper to Paris for comments by Bohlen and Marshall. The Berlin deadlock, argued the Director of the Policy Planning Staff, had created an extremely awkward situation for the Russians as well as for the Western powers. If the continuation of the deadlock threatened the latter with the loss of Berlin, it threatened the Russians with the loss of Germany itself. The Russians

---

142. Clay to Bradley, September 23 and October 4, 1948, in *Clay Papers*, Vol. 2, pp. 878–879 and 890–891; and Memorandum for the Under Secretary of the Army from Lt. Gen. A. C. Wedemeyer, October 5, 1948, Under Secretary of the Army (Draper/Voorhees), RG 335, National Archives, Washington, D.C.

143. Memorandum by the Chief of Staff, U.S. Army, n.d., P&O 381, RG 319, National Archives, Washington, D.C.

144. Condit, *The History of the Joint Chiefs of Staff*, pp. 150–151; and Record of Actions by the National Security Council at Its Twenty-Third Meeting, October 7, 1948, President's Secretary File, Harry S. Truman Library.

had made it evident that they were not going to settle in good faith for a solution which permitted the Western powers both to remain in Berlin in the full enjoyment of their quadripartite rights and at the same time to proceed with the creation and development of a Western German state. This being the case, there was little chance of success for a policy which aimed to maneuver the Russians, either through direct negotiation or through UN pressures, into acceptance of the four-power status of Berlin without relation to the German problem as a whole. All this led Kennan to conclude that there could hardly be a satisfactory solution to the Berlin problem within the limits of the Berlin situation itself, and that the problem could only be made soluble, if at all, in the context of a larger framework.

Kennan outlined a number of solutions that involved the German situation as a whole, but he did not think they could be discussed with the Soviet government directly while duress was maintained. On the other hand, he felt that if the United Nations could make the direct discussion of the German problem possible by persuading the Russians to lift the traffic restrictions, the U.S. government should accept the proposal.[145] Marshall, however, did not approve the line of action indicated in PPS 42.[146] He preferred not to take the initiative in paving the way for direct negotiations on the German problem as a whole or to work through the UN to this end, but instead to use the debate in the world organization to gain time for improving America's position on the ground in Germany. Thus, while the search for long-term options was carried out by the Policy Planning Staff with considerable thoroughness and perspicacity, the key decision-maker chose to disregard its conclusions and recommendations, which were in conflict with his own strategic and tactical preferences.

If Kennan's views were quietly ignored, the view of the Joint Chiefs of Staff, contained in two separate memoranda to Forrestal dated October 13, were sufficiently alarming to ensure an immediate and unexpectedly hostile reaction. "It is the considered opinion of the Joint Chiefs of Staff," they wrote, "that our present military power cannot effectively support the supply of Berlin by air lift on an indefinite basis without such a diversion of military effort as has affected and will continue progressively to affect seriously and

145. PPS 42, November 2, 1948, in *FRUS, 1948*, Vol. 2, pp. 1240–47.
146. Ibid., p. 1240, note 1.

adversely the ability of the National Military Establishment to meet its primary national security responsibilities." Disregarding cost, both in terms of money and of readiness for war emergency, air supply to Berlin could "theoretically be continued indefinitely." In view of this fact and the July 22 decision "to remain in Berlin in any event," the Joint Chiefs recommended that the airlift be augmented by 66 aircraft to give General Clay the 116 he had requested.

The Joint Chiefs' sharpest criticism, however, was reserved for this very policy of remaining in Berlin "in any event." These words, they said, implied U.S. determination to stay in Berlin even if this course resulted in war, although this might not have been the intention behind them. If the official policy could not be modified, they insisted that at least the ambiguity surrounding it should be removed and its military implications recognized. Going well beyond their restrained comments of July 22, the Joint Chiefs urged:

> That decision be reached now as to whether or not the added risk of war inherent in the Berlin airlift is acceptable.
> That, if decision is in the affirmative full-out preparations for the early eventuality of war be inaugurated immediately.
> That, if decision is in the negative, plans logically now be made and action taken leading to our withdrawal from Berlin.

More fundamentally, the Joint Chiefs of Staff implied criticism of the Administration for allowing its foreign policy to outrun the country's military capabilities. Therefore, regardless of what the Administration decided with respect to Berlin, the Joint Chiefs recommended that efforts be continued to "strengthen our military capabilities in order that military support for our foreign policies may be available without undue weakening of our readiness for war emergency."[147]

The second memorandum, which dealt with measures to counter Soviet interference with air transport, was as pessimistic in tone as the one devoted to the broad issues of policy and strategy. As an initial measure, the Joint Chiefs of Staff mentioned policing the air corridor with combat planes. But they were certain that this could not be effective against a determined Russian air effort because of the extensive nature of the patrolling task and the limited number of American fighter planes available for the task. Another possible

---

147. Condit, *The History of the Joint Chiefs of Staff*, pp. 151–153.

measure would be to employ antiaircraft fire against Soviet planes violating air traffic rules, but this could open the way for retaliation in kind. Neither of these measures was recommended, since each would be not only ineffective but interpretable as a warlike act. A third approach consisted of warning announcements, such as an announcement that the Americans would provide fighter protection for the airlift if any serious incident took place, or an announcement that any interference would be regarded by the United States as an act of war. The Joint Chiefs of Staff recommended against issuing such a warning unless the government had first decided that war "in the near future and for the Berlin cause was acceptable," and they left no room for doubt that a war "in our present state of readiness and for the Berlin issue is neither militarily prudent nor strategically sound."[148]

The criticism of the Administration's policy met with an indignant and firm rebuttal at a special session of the National Security Council convened on October 14. In the absence of the President and the Secretary of State, the Secretary of Defense presided over the meeting, and Royall and Lovett led the counterattack. Lovett reminded the Council that its decision of July 22 to remain in Berlin "in any event" had been made with full knowledge of the facts and was intended to stress that the United States would not be forced out of Berlin. The Joint Chiefs of Staff, he remarked, seemed to have a "case of the jitters," and their recommendations served no useful purpose except as a justification for additional military appropriations. Royall charged the Joint Chiefs of Staff with trying to "pass the buck" and observed that the tone underlying their papers was unfortunate.[149]

While Lovett and Royall bluntly reaffirmed the determination of the Truman Administration not to be forced out of Berlin, neither provided an answer to the central question posed by the Chiefs of Staff: would the United States go to war to remain in Berlin? To the official historian of the JCS, this evasion suggests a policy of postponing decision until faced with the necessity to fight or get out; and he adds that to the Joint Chiefs of Staff, who were responsible for planning operations should war come, such a postponement was understandably unsettling.[150]

The Joint Chiefs of Staff agreed to withdraw their papers and to

148. Ibid., pp. 153–154.   149. Ibid., pp. 154–155.
150. Ibid., p. 155.

resubmit them, after revision, in time for the next regular meeting of the National Security Council, scheduled for October 21. All their detailed recommendations for the reinforcement of the airlift, however, were endorsed by the Council and referred to the President for decision.[151]

After further study, on October 21 the Joint Chiefs of Staff submitted a revised set of papers to the Secretary of Defense, who passed them on to the National Security Council. Having been severely reprimanded for daring to question the wisdom of the Administration's policy, the Joint Chiefs of Staff mustered all the tact of which they were capable to smooth ruffled feathers. "The Joint Chiefs of Staff," declared their first revised paper, "fully appreciate the responsibility of the National Military Establishment to support United States foreign policy and they recognize the very great importance to that policy of maintaining the Berlin air lift. Their statements regarding military implications are, therefore, intended only to be informative and to comprise only one factor of those needed for overall consideration, on a higher level than the military, of the problem as a whole." Gone was the peremptory demand for a decision to either mobilize for war or withdraw from Berlin. In its place there was a reasoned appeal that there be a full recognition of the facts that the Berlin airlift could not be a permanent solution, that it could be drastically reduced by direct Soviet action, and that such action in turn could easily bring forth the necessity for the United States to decide whether or not the Berlin situation constituted a war issue. Having made all these points, the Joint Chiefs of Staff recommended the augmentation of the airlift by 66 additional planes.[152]

Clay and Murphy made another trip to the United States on October 21 to take part in high-level deliberations which would determine, as they were well aware, the fate of the airlift. On arrival in Washington, they had breakfast with Forrestal, Royall, Draper, and Saltzman. News had just come that the Russians had agreed to a proposal by the neutral members of the Security Council for the lifting of the blockade and a meeting of the Council of Foreign Min-

---

151. Minutes of the 24th Meeting of the National Security Council, held on Thursday, October 14, 1948, and Memorandum for the President from Sidney W. Souers (Executive Secretary of the National Security Council), October 15, 1948, President's Secretary File, Harry S. Truman Library.

152. Memorandum for the Secretary of Defense (Enclosures "A" and "B"), October 20, 1948, P&O 381, RG 319, National Archives, Washington, D.C.

isters. Clay voiced his suspicion that this concession by the Russians might be the first step in a maneuver that would propose that all hands get out of Germany. American agreement to such a proposal would be tantamount to abandoning the fight to prevent the takeover of Western Europe by communism. The Russians already had an army of 200,000 people either trained or training in their zone. There was no comparable armed strength in the Western zones because the French had consistently objected to the arming of the Germans. The only thing that kept Europe stable was the presence of the American Army and the airlift. Withdraw that, said Clay, and you practically turn the show over to Russia. Forrestal told Royall that it was most important that they try to convince the President not to attribute too much significance to neutrals' suggestions, and that Clay should say to him, as bluntly as he had said to them, that any policy which contemplated withdrawal from Germany meant withdrawal from Europe and the beginning of the Third World War.[153]

At the National Security Council later that day, Clay presented a report on the technical achievements of the airlift and on the salutary effect which the American action in Berlin was having on the people of Germany. They had turned sharply against communism, closed ranks, and applied themselves vigorously to the tasks of reconstruction. After waiting to see which way it should cast its lot, Germany was veering towards the cause of the Western nations. With so much at stake, Clay made an impassioned plea for the assignment of the 66 C-54s which were urgently needed to cope with the adverse weather.[154] The Council noted and discussed Clay's oral report on the possible Soviet interruption of the airlift and on the general situation in Germany. But since it had already made recommendations to the President at its special meeting a week earlier, no further action appeared necessary.[155]

What was said in the discussion remains classified information to this very day. Clay was later to claim that the Joint Chiefs of Staff

153. James V. Forrestal Diaries, October 21, 1948, pp. 2588–89, Princeton University Library.

154. Truman, *Memoirs*, Vol. 2, p. 137; Clay, *Decision in Germany*, pp. 384–85; and Memorandum for the President, October 22, 1948, summarizing the discussion at the 25th meeting of the National Security Council, President's Secretary File, Harry S. Truman Library. Unfortunately, three pages of this four-page summary have been sanitized.

155. Minutes of the 25th Meeting of the National Security Council, held on Thursday, October 21, 1948, President's Secretary File, Harry S. Truman Library.

and everybody else were opposed to giving him the aircraft, which were made available to him only thanks to Truman's personal intervention.[156] But while it is likely that the Chiefs of Staff voiced their well-known reservations about the airlift, Clay's version cannot be easily reconciled with the recommendations, given in writing, of the National Security Council and the Joint Chiefs of Staff in favor of assigning the additional aircraft.

After the Council adjourned, Clay and Murphy were accompanied by Forrestal, Royall, and Leahy to a conference in the President's office. Clay went over much of the same ground because Truman had not been present at the Council meeting. It was at this smaller gathering with his defense advisers that Truman assured Clay and Murphy that the additional aircraft would be forthcoming.[157] Truman's decision was conveyed by means of a memorandum for the Executive Secretary of the National Security Council, signed on October 22, which approved and authorized: (1) that the Berlin airlift be augmented by up to 66 additional C-54s; (2) that action be taken to assure the availability of aviation petroleum to support the airlift and to stockpile for emergency purposes; and (3) that steps be taken to ensure that there be adequate personnel and financial support for the airlift (Decision 25).[158]

Once again it was Truman who, at the critical moment, tipped the balance in favor of a large and well-supported airlift. From then on, Clay reports that he encountered no problem in making the airlift a success. He thought that Truman deserved credit for realizing that "the Berlin crisis was a political war, not a military war." Clay was not being critical of the Joint Chiefs of Staff for visualizing the crisis as a military operation, for in the strict sense of the word they were correct. But Truman impressed him as a man of great courage and one who did not hesitate to make his own decisions.[159]

In the Security Council, activity continued behind the scenes after the Western powers presented their case on October 6. As a result of the consultations held with the parties to the dispute, the

156. Oral History Interview with General Lucius D. Clay, July 16, 1974, pp. 38–40, Harry S. Truman Library.
157. Ibid., pp. 39–40; and William Leahy Diary, October 21, 1948, p. 67, in Papers of Admiral William D. Leahy, Library of Congress.
158. Memorandum for the Executive Secretary, National Security Council, from Harry S. Truman, October 22, 1948, President's Secretary File, Harry S. Truman Library.
159. Oral History Interview with General Lucius D. Clay, July 16, 1974, Harry S. Truman Library.

Council's six neutral members presented a resolution calling for the lifting of all restrictions on traffic and commerce, the resumption of quadripartite talks on the currency problem, and a reconvening of the Council of Foreign Ministers to consider the entire German question.[160] The vote on the neutrals' resolution took place on October 25, with the three Western powers accepting and the Soviet Union cutting it down with its veto. For the time being, the Security Council was stymied.

The U.S. consultative group in Paris discussed the situation, and, on October 26, Jessup submitted to Marshall a memorandum relating to future courses of action in the Berlin case. The memorandum was based on the assumption that the case would remain on the Security Council's agenda and that any program would be fully coordinated with the British and the French. Jessup and his colleagues now felt that the earlier idea of turning to the UN General Assembly was not desirable because, even if they obtained an overwhelmingly favorable vote, that would not influence the Soviets, lift the blockade, or strengthen the UN. They also recommended against the immediate introduction of the Western "B" mark as the sole currency in the Western sectors of Berlin. A third course involved an attempt to carry out the Security Council's resolution despite the Soviet veto. This program could be put into effect by a letter informing the Security Council President that the Western powers would present rail, road, and barge traffic at the border of the Soviet zone on a stated date, that such traffic would be subject to safeguards against currency abuse, that a meeting of the Military Governors would be called, that restrictions imposed by the Western powers would be lifted, and that thereafter a meeting of the Council of Foreign Ministers would be held. If traffic were permitted to move through the Soviet zone, the Military Governors would meet immediately. But since there was no indication that the Soviets would acquiesce, and since the effect would have been to exclude the six neutral members of the Security Council from participating in the search for a solution, the group recommended against following this procedure. Clay agreed that the attempt would be futile, and Bohlen added that to have a train turned back at the checkpoint would be humiliating. The fourth and only positive recommendation was to adopt some form of the

---

160. For the text of the resolution, see U.S. Department of State, *Germany 1947–1949*, pp. 224–225.

plan for setting up a UN commission of experts to study the currency problem and propose a solution.[161]

Secretary Marshall approved this last recommendation on October 26 (Decision 26). He also informed Lovett by cable of the four alternatives which had been developed by his advisers in Paris and of the choice he had made among these alternatives. Lovett, in his capacity as Acting Secretary of State, forwarded a copy of Marshall's cable to the National Security Council for its information. No action was requested of the Council.[162]

A complete understanding was reached at the meeting of the foreign ministers of the Western powers on October 27 that their joint policy in regard to the Berlin question was to leave it on the agenda of the Security Council and to concert their actions closely in all future developments. They agreed not to take any initiative in proposing a plan of their own at that stage, but to develop their ideas in relation to possible contingencies, including the suggestion of a neutral commission, so that they would be prepared in case the six neutral members of the Council came forward with any proposals. In a joint statement to the press, the three powers reiterated that they had accepted the resolution of the Six and that they were ready to continue to fulfil their obligations as members of the Security Council.[163]

But the efforts of Marshall and his aides to convince the diplomats gathered in Paris that the United States genuinely wanted to find a solution to the Berlin problem were unavailing.[164] Suspicion of U.S. motives, even on the part of friendly countries, was widespread and did not seem to slacken. As Trygve Lie, the UN Secretary General, records in his memoirs, the success of the airlift gave rise to the theory that Washington would just as soon wait the

161. Jessup, "The Berlin Blockade and the Use of the United Nations"; Bohlen, *Witness to History*, pp. 282–283; and Marshall to Lovett, October 27, 1948, in *FRUS, 1948*, Vol. 2, pp. 1236–37.

162. NSC 24/1, "A Report to the National Security Council by the Secretary of State on Future Courses of Action with Respect to Berlin," November 17, 1948, President's Secretary File, Harry S. Truman Library.

163. The Ambassador to France (Caffery) to Lovett, October 27, 1948, in *FRUS, 1948*, Vol. 2, p. 1238; Jessup, "The Berlin Blockade and the Use of the United Nations"; and C.M. (48) 73rd Conclusions, Minute 2, November 15, 1948, Public Record Office, London.

164. On French suspicions and reservations concerning American behavior, see Vincent Auriol, *Journal du Septennat, 1947–1954*, Vol. 2: *1948* (Paris: Armand Colin, 1974), pp. 501, 526, 527, 539, 540, 551, 553, and 560.

blockade out, exploiting Soviet discomfiture and the effects of the West's counterblockade against the Soviet zone. American officials in Berlin, led by Clay and Murphy, were reportedly inclined to carry the "show" through to a successful ending; and Lie, for one, believed that the lack of anxiety for an immediate solution displayed by the American delegation to the UN was at least partly related to this growing confidence.[165] In truth, while trying to project the appearance of flexibility and reasonableness, the Truman Administration was unprepared to make any substantive concessions in the interests of a compromise solution. It regarded the reconvening of the Council of Foreign Ministers as dangerous and undesirable, and preferred to keep away from any discussion of a German settlement until it had progressed further with its plans. Truman's surprising victory in the election of November 2, which returned to the Democrats control of both Houses of Congress, effectively silenced domestic criticism and reinforced the Administration's determination and ability to proceed with the existing policy course.

The search for alternative long-term options continued within the framework of the Policy Planning Staff, but the Administration's policy in the Berlin crisis and towards Germany as a whole remained unaffected by this process. On November 15, the PPS submitted to the policymakers the result of its work in the form of a detailed report. The problem, as the PPS saw it, was whether the U.S. should come forward at an eventual meeting of the Council of Foreign Ministers with a positive program making clear the terms on which it would be prepared to consider the establishment of a German government for all of Germany and the withdrawal of forces from the major part of Germany, or rest on a basically negative position, leaving it to the Russians and others to come forward with proposals which the U.S. would then presumably decline on an ad hoc basis. The PPS presented a detailed package of proposals, entitled "Plan A," to be put forward in the event that the government wished to push for a general German settlement either at a meeting of the Council of Foreign Ministers or in any other way. Members of the PPS, as well as the qualified experts they consulted inside and outside the government, were inclined

---

165. Trygve Lie, *In the Cause of Peace: Seven Years with the United Nations* (New York: Macmillan, 1954), pp. 203 and 210.

to think that the government ought to go forward with a positive proposal of this kind. But the final decision, as Kennan observed in his covering letter to Marshall, lay with the Secretary, unless the Secretary wished to get a decision from the National Security Council.[166]

The Policy Planning Staff's report was circulated within the State Department, and a copy was sent to Berlin for comments from Clay and Murphy. From within the Department, the responses were critical and reminiscent of the responses to Kennan's earlier memorandum of August 12. Murphy reported his own and Clay's views. He found the program for Germany "a very worthwhile document and as blueprints go should be valuable. The trouble with our good blueprints often seems to be that they get bloody noses bumping into Russian, French and at times British stone walls." No explicit high-level decision was reached on the Policy Planning Staff's recommendations, although nondecision in that context could only be construed as amounting to a negative decision. Lovett penciled his opinion on a memorandum which transmitted the departmental comments to the Under Secretary. He wrote: "Mr. Kennan—I think this should be reconsidered in the light of non-concurrences."[167]

These nonconcurrences highlighted the growing divergence between Kennan's views and those of other senior officials in the State Department. Ironically, it was Kennan himself who had educated a whole generation of American officials in the need for patience, vigilance, and, above all, firmness in dealing with the Russians, but for him firmness was a technique of negotiation, not a substitute for it. In the minds of the inflexible men who set the tone in the State Department, however, this subtle but important distinction was frequently blurred, and firmness increasingly occupied the place of what should have been a positive policy vis-à-vis the Soviet Union. "Plan A" withered under the criticism of men fearful of any compromise in central Europe and was finally put out of its misery on the eve of the meeting of the Council of Foreign Ministers in Paris in May 1949. Paradoxical as it may sound, it is at least arguable that Kennan's disenchantment and waning influence over American foreign policy was related to the growing power of

166. PPS 37/1, November 15, 1948, in *FRUS, 1948*, Vol. 2, pp. 1320–38; and Kennan, *Memoirs*, pp. 422–426.
167. *FRUS, 1948*, Vol. 2, p. 1320, note 1.

the Riga axioms, and that it was not he who abandoned previously taken positions, but his colleagues who abandoned him.[168]

At the United Nations, pressure was kept on the contending parties to engage in direct negotiations. On November 13, Secretary General Lie and Herbert Evatt, the Australian President of the General Assembly, addressed a joint letter to the Heads of State of the U.S., the U.K., France, and the USSR, appealing for four-power talks to end the Berlin dispute.[169] Three days later Moscow answered, substantially accepting the call for immediate conversations. Marshall and his aides considered the Lie-Evatt initiative to be ill-advised and disturbing in its implication that the fault was not exclusively on the Russian side. Marshall asked Lovett to transmit to the President the text of the reply which he proposed to make after coordination with the British and the French. To scotch left-wing propaganda in Europe, to which Evatt was allegedly contributing, and which was putting it about that the President and the Secretary differed on relations with Russia, Marshall, Dulles, and Bohlen considered it important that the reply be approved by the President prior to its dispatch in Paris.[170]

Truman approved the text, and, on November 17, Marshall replied reaffirming U.S. readiness to engage in conversations, but only after the Soviet Union had lifted the blockade so that the conversations could take place under conditions free from duress.[171] The condition was underlined by Truman at his first post-election press conference, at which he emphasized that he would not go to Moscow to see Stalin and that the U.S. would not negotiate with Russia over the German situation until the blockade of Berlin was lifted.[172]

Marshall had been unwell and had to return home for an operation, so Truman designated Dulles as Acting Chairman of the U.S.

---

168. Daniel F. Harrington, "Kennan, Bohlen and the Riga Axioms," *Diplomatic History*, Vol. 2 (Fall 1978), pp. 430–433.

169. On the background to this initiative, see Lie, *In the Cause of Peace*, pp. 214–216. For the texts of the Lie-Evatt letter, see the *Department of State Bulletin*, November 28, 1948.

170. Acting Secretary of State Lovett to Clark Clifford for the President, October 14, 1948, in Papers of Clark M. Clifford, Box 15, Harry S. Truman Library.

171. For the text of Marshall's letter, see *Department of State Bulletin*, December 12, 1948.

172. *Public Papers of the Presidents of the United States: Harry S. Truman, 1948*, p. 944; and *New York Herald Tribune*, November 17, 1948.

Delegation during Marshall's absence, in a move calculated to demonstrate continuity and bipartisanship in American foreign policy. Dulles, however, doubted Truman's ability to provide the direction needed to keep American diplomacy on a steady course. He feared that Marshall might not return to the Assembly in Paris, and that his health might be such that he would not even be able to watch the situation from Washington. "If so," Dulles confided in a letter to Vandenberg, "we may be in here for some hard times as even with good will it would be extremely difficult for the President and his White House advisers to give direction which would not inadvertently be very confusing and prejudicial to our prestige and consistency of policy."[173]

Marshall did not in fact return to Paris, but on November 22 he reported to the Cabinet in Washington on the activities of the United Nations, and from this report it appeared that the U.S. situation vis-à-vis Berlin and with the Russians in general was rapidly deteriorating. Evatt, said Marshall, was an active source of both irritation and uncertainty. The result of his activities and, to a lesser extent, the activities of Juan Bramuglia, the Argentinian Chairman of the Security Council, had been to severely undermine the American position among the neutral nations. Bramuglia had succeeded in giving the impression that, after all, the Russian demands were not so extreme and unmeetable.[174]

Towards the end of November, Dr. Bramuglia succeeded in obtaining the agreement of the four disputants to the setting up of a United Nations committee of experts from the six neutrals to work out a formula for trade and circulation, under four-power control, of the Soviet mark in Berlin. The three Western powers stated in a note of November 30 that they welcomed Dr. Bramuglia's proposal but reserved their position as regards any resolution that might subsequently be submitted to the Security Council.[175]

In private, however, American diplomats seriously doubted the possibility that a viable solution could be worked out by the committee. Just as it began its deliberations, the Soviet-sponsored groups split Berlin by setting up a "Magistrat" in the Eastern sec-

173. Dulles to Vandenberg, Paris, November 19, 1948, in the John Foster Dulles Papers, Box 35, Princeton University Library.
174. Millis, *The Forrestal Diaries*, p. 532.
175. For the texts of Bramuglia's proposal and the Western reply, see the *Department of State Bulletin*, December 12, 1948.

tor which claimed to be the provisional government for the entire city. To Clay it seemed that the deliberations of the neutral committee had no reality from the day it was established, because the broken parts of the city could not be cemented by a technical solution.[176] The events instigated by the Soviet Command increased Western apprehensions; and in a communiqué delivered by the three governments to the committee of experts, it was pointed out that the de facto political division of the city rendered the establishment of a single currency extremely difficult.[177] Following the election held in the Western sector on December 5, the city of Berlin became divided not only economically but to a large extent administratively and politically.[178]

Actions by the Soviet military authorities in Berlin followed a basic change of policy in Moscow, and this change was detected and analyzed by the Central Intelligence Agency. In a memorandum for the President dated December 10, Admiral Hillenkoetter explained that recent action by the USSR in recognizing an east Berlin government was representative of a shift which had taken place in the Kremlin's estimate concerning its capabilities in the Berlin dispute. Originally, it appeared that the Soviet blockade of Berlin had been designed primarily to gain Western concessions regarding western Germany and secondarily to force the U.S., U.K., and France to evacuate Berlin. The refusal of these powers to negotiate under duress, however, had apparently convinced the Kremlin that its chance of gaining its primary objective was remote. Soviet strategy began accordingly to concentrate upon the secondary objective of forcing the West either to evacuate the city or to negotiate on terms which would make the Western position ineffective and eventually untenable.[179]

The perception that Western firmness was slowly but surely

176. Clay, *Decision in Germany*, p. 379; and *Clay Papers*, Vol. 2, pp. 928 and 942–946.
177. "Tripartite Communiqué to Committee of Experts," *Department of State Bulletin*, December 12, 1948.
178. Elmer Plischke, *Berlin: The Development of Its Government and Administration* (Westport, Conn.: Greenwood Press, 1970). On the shift in Soviet aims and tactics regarding Berlin, see Eric Morris, *Blockade: Berlin and the Cold War* (London: Hamish Hamilton, 1973), pp. 90–91.
179. Memorandum for the President from the Director of Central Intelligence, December 10, 1948, President's Secretary File, Box 249, Harry S. Truman Library.

modifying Soviet aims had the effect of deepening the American policymakers' commitment to this posture.[180] At its meeting on December 16, the National Security Council concurred in the suggestion of the Secretary of the Air Force that it would be desirable for morale purposes if the President issued a statement around Christmas time commending the personnel of the Berlin airlift on their outstanding accomplishments during six months of operations, and agreed that Symington should prepare such a statement for the President's consideration. The Council also endorsed the remarks of the Acting Secretary of State regarding the vital importance to U.S. foreign policy of wholeheartedly continuing governmental support to the Berln airlift, since it had become a symbol of American determination and ingenuity.[181]

A major test of America's declared willingness to cooperate with the United Nations in finding a solution occurred on December 22, when the committee of experts presented to the four occupying powers a preliminary draft of the arrangements it proposed for making the Soviet mark the sole currency for Berlin and for withdrawing the Western "B" mark from circulation.[182] Clay hastened to point out to his superiors that while it was possible to utilize a single currency even with a split city, it could not be done under the conditions outlined in the experts' report. Royall reported this view to Lovett and added his own conclusion, which was that "we have reached the point where we must, in justice to the American position and the continuing responsibility of the American Com-

180. It was recognized, however, that the blockade was not likely to be lifted in the near future, and this prompted Royall to suggest that the Armed Services be asked to determine the tangible requirements for support of Berlin over a long period. Memorandum for the Secretary of Defense from Kenneth C. Royall, December 7, 1948. The suggestion was referred to the War Council, and, at the meeting on December 7: "It was the consensus of opinion of the War Council that a study covering the support of Berlin on the assumption of an extended blockade should be undertaken as a matter of priority and that the Secretary of the Army should take the lead, and work with the Secretary of the Air Force, in carrying out this project." Memorandum for the Secretary of the Army and the Secretary of the Air Force from John H. Ohly (Special Assistant to the Secretary of Defense), December 9, 1948, RG 330, Records of the Office of the Secretary of Defense, National Archives, Washington, D.C.

181. Minutes of the 30th Meeting of the National Security Council, held on Thursday, December 16, 1948, President's Secretary File, Harry S. Truman Library; and Lovett to Douglas, December 18, 1948, in *FRUS, 1948*, Vol. 2, p. 1281.

182. The text of this document and various related papers are printed in U.S. Department of State, *Germany 1947–1949*, pp. 230–271.

mander, state in all frankness . . . the basic facts of the situation. This should include a statement that the Soviets have split the city and made any reasonable agreement impossible; that technical discussions with the neutrals, although entered into by us with the hope of success before the city was actually split, are no longer realistic or useful; and that in fact they now are serving to obscure the main issue which is, first, the illegal blockade by the Soviet, and second, the illegal splitting of the city by the Soviet. I see no alternative."[183]

Lovett was in basic agreement with this conclusion, and at a meeting with Royall and Draper it was decided to reject the Technical Committee's proposals (Decision 27).[184] American representatives abroad were informed of the official view, which was that the report was unworkable since its fundamental premise, a unified Berlin, no longer existed, and that the Western powers, after replying to the Committee, should proceed immediately to introduce the "B" mark as the sole legal tender in the Western sectors.[185] This decision to reject the Committee's preliminary proposals appears to have been taken without any dissent from within the Administration and with the President's approval. Truman's highly critical attitude towards the Committee's proposals amounted to an admission that any arrangement involving Soviet participation was inherently suspect and unacceptable from the American point of view:

> Our reaction to these proposals was that our experience with the Russians impelled us to reject any plan which provided for a four-power operation. We had learned that the Russians would usually agree in principle but rarely perform in practice. We wanted a settlement, but we could not accept a settlement that would put the people of Berlin at the mercy of the Soviets and their German Communist hirelings.[186]

The State Department delayed sending its reply to the Committee in the hope, soon to be dashed, that the Russians would reject it first, and in order to coordinate its own policy and tactics with those of its Allies. Agreement between the Allies, however, could

183. Memorandum for Mr. Lovett from Kenneth C. Royall, n.d., RG 335, National Archives, Washington, D.C.
184. Draper to Clay, December 24, 1948, Under Secretary of the Army (Draper/Voorhees), RG 335, National Archives, Washington, D.C.
185. *FRUS, 1949*, Vol. 3, p. 643.
186. Truman, *Memoirs*, Vol. 2, p. 137.

not be reached, because Britain and France, like the Soviet Union, were prepared to accept the Committee's proposals as a basis for discussion and, indeed, regarded them as workable with appropriate amendment. The proposal which turned out to be unacceptable to them at this stage was the American one, urging the introduction of the "B" mark as the sole legal tender for the Western sectors of Berlin.[187] The British and French feared that a currency switchover would slam the door on a settlement, whereas the Americans felt that it would be viewed as proof of the Western governments' determination to remain in Berlin, which might in turn make the Soviets more willing to reassess the value of the blockade.[188] With the common front temporarily broken, the U.S. proceeded, on January 15, 1949, to submit its reply to the Committee's report. The U.S. reply was embodied in three papers. The first contained general criticism of the Committee's work, concluding that it did not provide the basis for settlement of the Berlin currency and trade questions; the second paper was a detailed technical analysis of the Committee's report; while the third paper outlined a U.S. counterproposal which the Committee was asked to consider. The UN experts continued their work in Geneva, but finally reported to the Security Council, on February 11, that they were unable to recommend a plan acceptable to all four powers.[189]

As 1948 turned into 1949, there was thus a progressive hardening in the American approach to the Berlin crisis, which was partly, but not entirely, a response to the Soviet measures which completed the division of the city. Referring the crisis to the UN had not only failed to produce the expected moral condemnation of the Soviet Union, but had ended up by placing the chief complainant in a minority of one before the court of world opinion. The rejection of the proposals of the UN experts was tantamount to a public repudiation of the Moscow Agreement of August 30. Having implied that this Agreement had been overtaken by events, the U.S. now made its opposition to any proposals based on it plain for all to see. The U.S. demanded that the West mark continue to circulate

187. *FRUS, 1949*, Vol. 3, pp. 643–662; and Vincent Auriol, *Journal du Septennat, 1947–1954*, Vol. 3: *1949* (Paris: Armand Colin, 1977), pp. 100, 108, and 114–115.

188. *FRUS, 1949*, Vol. 3, p. 652; and C.M. (48), 79th Conclusions, Minute 2, December 9, 1948, Public Record Office, London.

189. The texts of the American reply and the Technical Committee's final report are printed in U.S. Department of State, *Germany 1947–1949*, pp. 257–270 and 230–232, respectively.

in the Western sectors until a unified city administration could be restored, and it was backed in this stand by Britain and France. This decision represented a major victory for Clay as well as for those in Washington who had advocated a strong line from the beginning.[190]

PHASE VI: JANUARY 16–MAY 5

Around the turn of the year 1948–49, important changes took place within the Administration. Truman inaugurated his second term as President on January 20, 1949. At the head of the State Department, Dean Acheson succeeded General Marshall, who was forced into retirement by illness and advanced age. James Webb, the Director of the Bureau of the Budget, replaced Robert Lovett as Under Secretary.

But these personnel changes did not usher in any discernible change in the direction or emphasis of the Administration's policy towards the Berlin crisis. That policy was based on two main pillars: the airlift and the counterblockade. By maintaining its position in Berlin through the airlift, the United States greatly enhanced its own standing and prestige in Germany and helped to forge, for the first time, a genuine bond of solidarity between Germany and the Western world. A technical achievement of the highest possible order, the airlift surmounted all the barriers thrown up by an exceptionally severe German winter.[191] As the airlift demonstrated its tremendous potential as a substitute for force, there was a corresponding decline in America's interest in compromise and willingness to make concessions. The conviction that Russia could be forced to yield without any significant concession on America's part steadily gained ground.

190. Auriol, *Journal du Septennat*, Vol. 3, pp. 64–66 and 69–70; W. Phillips Davison, *The Berlin Blockade: A Study in Cold War Politics* (Princeton: Princeton University Press, 1958), p. 248; and Jean Edward Smith, *The Defense of Berlin* (Baltimore: Johns Hopkins University Press, 1963), p. 127.

191. Draper later revealed that stockpiles ran down to a dangerously low point in late December as a result of the fog, and "it looked like curtains. If that fog had stayed another three weeks we probably would have had to run up the white flag. We probably couldn't have gone on. You can't have people starving, and keep on with the occupation. But the weather lifted about the fifth of January . . . and immediately we restored the situation. The Russians knew they were licked right away, but it was May before they finally gave up." Oral History Interview with General William H. Draper, Jr., January 11, 1972, pp. 68–69, Harry S. Truman Library.

This conviction was greatly strengthened by the serious consequences which the Allied counterblockade was clearly seen to be having on the economic welfare of the Soviet zone. After its introduction in March 1948, the counterblockade was expanded in scope and tightened in application. This counterblockade cut off essential steel, chemicals, manufactured goods, and other supplies from West Germany, and also reduced the trade between East Germany and Western Europe. Economically, the counterblockade was more effective than the blockade, and it could not be broken by airlift.[192]

Moreover, the blockade and the Allied rescue operation, in their different ways, radically altered the psychological and political climate in Western Germany in a direction which was favorable to the speedy implementation of the London Program and to the formation of defensive alliances against Russia. "Russia's toughness and truculence in the Berlin matter," observed Truman, "had led many Europeans to realize the need for closer military assistance ties among the western nations, and this led to discussions which eventually resulted in the establishment of N.A.T.O."[193]

Since the balance of power was perceived to be shifting, under the impact of the Berlin crisis, in favor of the West, there was little pressure on the Truman Administration at the start of its second term to revise or even reappraise its policy in the Berlin crisis or towards Germany as a whole. As Kennan recalled:

> Over the ensuing winter of 1948–1949 the operational levels of our government were fully occupied with the mounting and main-

---

192. Lucius D. Clay, *Germany and the Fight for Freedom* (Cambridge, Mass.: Harvard University Press, 1950), p. 57. Although there is reason to believe that the economic countermeasures adopted by the United States were particularly effective and played an important role in inducing the Soviets to call off the blockade, information about this aspect of U.S. policy is not readily available, partly because of the conscious effort made at the time to avoid publicity. One scholar discovered that, apart from restrictions on trade, the U.S. also convinced its allies to stop their reparations payments to the Eastern European countries as the U.S. had done much earlier. "The net result of these measures was a reduction in exports to the East in 1948 of 45%. The eastern zone of Germany was particularly hard hit because of the loss of imports from the Ruhr industries, upon which the eastern agricultural region of Germany had traditionally been dependent, and because of the inability of the Soviet Union to replace these losses fully due to its own economic needs and priorities." John R. Oneal, *Creative Adaptation: Process and Potential for Foreign Policy Making in Times of Crisis* (Ph.D. dissertation, Stanford University, 1979), pp. 403–404.

193. Truman, *Memoirs*, Vol. 2, pp. 137–138.

taining of the airlift as a means of frustrating the blockade, and with the implementation of the London Program. In this last, their efforts were of course merged with those of the French and British and the Germans themselves. The West German political leaders were busy, over the winter, with the drawing up of a constitution for the new West German state. The three Allied powers were busy working out a new occupation statute, to come into effect when the West German government was established. These procedures were elaborate; the attendant negotiations were difficult and full of anguish. As the process went forward, it gained steadily in momentum and in the aura of legitimacy. People's *amour propre* as well as their enthusiasms became engaged. There was growing personal commitment to what was being accomplished. Increasingly, as the months and weeks went by, the undertaking assumed in many minds an irrevocable character; and the idea of suspending or jeopardizing it for the sake of wider international agreement became for these people less and less acceptable. Once again, as is so often the case in American diplomacy, what was conceived as an instrument became, little by little, an end in itself. What was supposed to have been the servant of policy became its determinant instead.

In view of this preoccupation of our senior figures with the airlift and the London Program, and in the absence, as yet, of any agreement with the Russians on the convening of a new meeting of the CFM, the question raised by the Planning Staff concerning our position at an eventual meeting of this nature was placed, over the winter, on the "back burner." No formal decision was taken as to which course we would follow. Actually, of course, our position was being determined for us, from day to day, by the steady growth in the degree and solemnity of our commitment to the London Program.[194]

Acheson's commitment to the London Program was based on political conviction rather than simple convenience. Following his appointment, the division between Kennan and the rest of the State Department became more acute. The new Secretary was convinced that the London Program represented not only a solemn but a wise and necessary policy line for the United States, and he was unwilling to jeopardize it, along with Western unity, by any attempt to reach agreement with the Soviet Union on an all-German settlement. Acheson regarded Kennan's Plan A, to judge from Kennan's own account, as no more than a curious, though not uncharacteristic, aberration on the part of one whose thoughts, while sometimes stimulating and amusing, lacked foundation in

---

194. Kennan, *Memoirs*, pp. 427–428.

the daily grind of operational routine and were not generally to be taken seriously. Plan A occasionally popped up and figured as a curiosity of sorts among the various alternatives. At no time did it have any serious chance of adoption.[195]

Less than a week after Acheson took office, a signal was issued by Moscow of a change of attitude towards Berlin. On January 31, 1949, Stalin chose to reply to a question posed by Kinsbury Smith, European Manager of the International News Service. Kinsbury Smith had asked whether the Soviet Union would be prepared to remove the restrictions on access to Berlin if the Western powers agreed to postpone the establishment of a separate West German state pending a meeting of the Council of Foreign Ministers. Stalin answered that Soviet restrictions could be removed, provided that the transport and trade restrictions introduced by the Western powers were removed simultaneously. He made no reference to the currency question.[196] Bohlen, who was on the lookout for such a signal because of the success of the counterblockade, was first to detect the significant omission of any reference to the monetary dispute, previously cited as the main reason for imposing the blockade, and to point it out to Acheson.[197]

On the day Stalin's answers were published, a small group of senior State Department officials discussed them with Acheson. Bohlen, who still headed the Berlin Group which had been set up by General Marshall, cautioned that they could not be sure that Stalin was sending a signal, and urged that soundings be made. The general view was that the episode represented a cautious signal indicating that Moscow was ready to lift the blockade at a price. The price would be too high if it required abandonment of the tripartite plans for the Allied zones of Germany, in which case the Russian maneuver could be changed into a propaganda offensive against hard-won Allied unity on German policy. Cautiously, therefore, the group agreed to embark on a probing operation.[198]

Acheson presented these conclusions to the President during his regular call at the White House. They went over the answers of

---

195. Ibid., pp. 442–443.
196. The texts of the questions and answers are printed in Union of Soviet Socialist Republics, Ministry of Foreign Affairs, *The Soviet Union and the Berlin Question (Documents)*, 2nd series (Moscow, 1949), pp. 8–9.
197. Bohlen, *Witness to History*, p. 283.
198. Ibid., pp. 283–284; and Dean Acheson, *Present at the Creation: My Years in the State Department* (New York: Norton, 1969), p. 267.

the Soviet premier with great care. Acheson asked permission to signal back through a bland press conference that they had received the message and then to follow this with a secret inquiry into just what Moscow was prepared to do. Truman approved these suggestions and further agreed that their purpose and the probing operation should be kept a close secret (Decision 28). Detailed tactics were also worked out carefully in advance at this meeting. Truman approved the idea that the White House would say it had received no message from Stalin and would refer questions to the State Department, that Acheson would deal with the matter at his press conference on February 2 along the lines of a draft which he read to Truman, and that at the President's press conference on February 3, Truman would state, in answer to any question, that the Secretary of State had dealt with the matter and that he had no further comment.[199]

Acheson's press conference took place on February 2, on its regular day of the week, to deprive it of any appearance of unusual significance. His remarks were intended to serve two purposes: to play down Stalin's initiative in order to avoid premature hardening of the Russian position; and to signal to the Russians that if they wanted serious discussion, they should use a more private channel.[200]

The second step was to open a private channel. Philip Jessup, who was at the time deputy chief of the U.S. mission to the United Nations, was summoned from New York to Washington for talks with Acheson and Bohlen. They concluded that a highly secret, casual approach to the Russians could be better made by Jessup at the United Nations than through the Embassy in Moscow or by the State Department to the Russian Embassy in Washington. Fewer persons would be involved, and those who were—Jessup and the Soviet representative to the United Nations, Jacob Malik—could act in a personal capacity. So it was agreed that Jessup should try to discreetly open a private channel by talking to Malik. On February 15, the opportunity for a conversation arose and Jessup asked

199. Memorandum by Acheson on Meeting with the President, January 31, 1949, Papers of Dean Acheson, Box 64, Harry S. Truman Library; Acheson, *Present at the Creation*, p. 267; Truman, *Memoirs*, Vol. 2, p. 138; and *FRUS, 1949*, Vol. 3, pp. 666–667.

200. Acheson, *Present at the Creation*, pp. 267–268. For the full text of Acheson's remarks, see *Department of State Bulletin*, February 13, 1949, pp. 192–194.

Malik, as a matter of personal curiosity, whether the omission of any reference to the currency question in Stalin's answers was significant. Malik said that he had no information on that point. Jessup remarked that if Malik learned anything about the matter, he would be interested to know. A month later, Malik asked Jessup to call at his office on Park Avenue and told him that the omission was "not accidental." The currency question, he said, could be discussed at a meeting of the Council of Foreign Ministers together with the whole German question. Jessup inquired whether Moscow meant that the blockade would continue during the meeting of the foreign ministers. Malik replied that he did not know but would find out. Six days later, on March 21, the answer came back that if a definite date for the foreign ministers' meeting could be set, there could be a reciprocal lifting of restrictions on traffic and trade to Berlin before the meeting. Moscow, for its part, wanted to know whether the preparations for a West German government could be suspended until after the meeting. As instructed, Jessup replied that it was not necessary to urge the postponement of these steps as a precondition to a meeting if one were held soon, since no West German government was actually in existence.[201]

Jessup pursued his confidential exchanges with Malik in the utmost secrecy and with considerable skill. It took months of careful work to reach an accord. The State Department group planning the talks was now composed of Bohlen, Llewellyn Thompson, Robert Murphy, and, for part of the time, General Bedell Smith. At times, Under Secretary Webb joined them, but Bohlen continued to play the leading part. Following intensive discussions of the procedure to be adopted for further talks with Malik, Jessup presented a comprehensive memorandum to Acheson on March 28. The memorandum suggested that Jessup ask the Russians to agree that the President of the Security Council should suggest to the four powers the reciprocal lifting of the blockade and an ensuing meeting of the CFM; the four would then notify him that they accepted. However, this procedure would not be pressed if the Russians objected. The memorandum also suggested that Secretary Acheson ask the President not to tell the military about the Jessup-Malik talks until after the conversations with Bevin and Schuman and the

---

201. Acheson, *Present at the Creation*, pp. 269–270; Bohlen, *Witness to History*, pp. 284–285; and Philip C. Jessup, "Park Avenue Diplomacy—Ending the Berlin Blockade," *Political Science Quarterly*, Vol. 87, No. 3 (September 1972).

next talk with Malik. On March 29, President Truman approved the suggested procedure and the text of the statement to be read to Malik (Decision 29).[202] Truman was kept closely informed by Acheson, took great pride in his Administration's ability to conduct a professional diplomatic crisis maneuver, and had already authorized Jessup to inform his British and French colleagues at the United Nations of his private talks with Malik.

With the continuing stalemate in Berlin, as yet unaffected by the secret and frustratingly inconclusive talks, an impatient Secretary of the Army was driven to bring up again the more drastic and previously rejected remedies of withdrawal or implementation of the armed convoys plan. In a memorandum to Acheson sent through the Secretary of Defense, Royall called for a decision to be made on Berlin "one way or the other" and announced at the same time that the German government came into existence. The expense of the airlift, its adverse effect on the transport reserve of the Air Force, and the danger of incidents were all arguments, he claimed, in favor of withdrawing from Berlin with an announcement that, with a Western German government having been established in a new capital, Berlin had no other significance to Western Germany. On the other hand, there was the familiar argument that withdrawal from Berlin might affect America's international prestige and create uncertainty and fear among European nations. "If we are to remain in Berlin," Royall concluded, "consideration should be given to establishing a land route thereto even at the risk of an untoward incident."[203]

American policy by this time, however, was too firmly entrenched to permit such a drastic turn in one direction or the other. Even the architect of "Task Force Truculent" had his doubts about the timing. Asked in a teletype conversation about the chances of forcing the blockade with an armed convoy, General Clay replied that if the Soviet authorities were advised forty-eight hours in advance, such a convoy would get through and perhaps reestablish the highway route to Berlin. This, however, would not meet America's full needs in Berlin, as the rail route would probably be badly damaged. He was sure that neither the French nor the British would join the Americans in such a venture, but that if

---

202. Jessup, "Park Avenue Diplomacy."
203. Memorandum for the Secretary of State from Kenneth C. Royall, March 23, 1949, RG 330, National Archives, Washington, D.C.

they did, the odds would probably be 3 to 1 in favor of its success. Clay did not believe that the blockade would be lifted until a West German government had been established, and only then if that government could negotiate a settlement with East Germany in which the Soviets would acquiesce. In view of this and the probability that the West German government would either exist or fail within the next few months, Clay concluded that the U.S. would be justified in a further short wait before making a final decision on the use of an armed convoy. He felt that it did involve some risk of war and that the U.S. had carried on too long already, particularly with its airlift, to precipitate the issue before knowing the results and effects of the West German government.[204]

The British and French foreign ministers arrived in Washington for important talks on Germany and the signing of the North Atlantic Treaty. At a meeting on April 1, Acheson surveyed with them the Jessup-Malik talks. Bevin warned that the proposed step might imperil the London Program and the Atlantic Pact and enable the Soviets to drive a wedge between the Western allies.[205] Acheson, however, was not so pessimistic. As he recorded in his memoirs: "We all three saw the danger in allowing Stalin to edge his way into the incomplete and delicate negotiations among us regarding our relations among ourselves and with the Germans in our zones, which could lead to disunity among us and to no progress in lifting the blockade. The greatest danger of disunity lay in any postponement of our tripartite preparations together with the Germans. If the blockade was lifted and the Council of Ministers promptly convened, it would soon be apparent whether the Russians were serious about any plans for Germany as a whole acceptable to the three. My own view was that if the council failed the blockade would not be reimposed. Stalin was lifting it because as a means to his end—Allied withdrawal from Berlin—it had failed and was hurting him. He would not walk back into the trap."[206]

The three ministers agreed that the Jessup-Malik exploration was the best method to pursue and that their support should now be thrown behind Jessup's position by authorizing him to speak for

204. Memorandum for the Secretary of Defense from Kenneth C. Royall, March 31, 1949, RG 330, National Archives, Washington, D.C. For the transcript of the teleconference, see *Clay Papers*, Vol. 2, pp. 1063–66.
205. Memorandum of Conversation by the Secretary of State, April 1, 1949, in *FRUS, 1949*, Vol. 3, pp. 709–712.
206. Acheson, *Present at the Creation*, p. 272.

the three governments. He was given a short statement, which he read to Malik on April 5, to the effect that the three governments understood that only two points were under discussion: simultaneously lifting the blockade and the counterblockade, and fixing a date for a meeting of the Council of Foreign Ministers. As far as the question of the West German government was concerned, it was stated that preparations for its establishment would continue, but if the CFM were held in the near future, it would be held before this government came into existence.[207] In other words, the Western governments wanted it clearly understood that they would not accede to any Soviet condition that required them to suspend or postpone their preparations pending a meeting of the Council of Foreign Ministers.

While Malik was awaiting instructions from Moscow, the three ministers reached full agreement on a whole range of issues connected with Germany, and this was announced in a communiqué on April 8. There was no reference to Berlin in the communiqué, but Acheson also issued a statement to the press reporting the final success of many long negotiations with the British, the French, and the Germans, which he felt would impress the Soviets that Western Europe was getting along well without them. Before Bevin and Schuman left Washington, they arranged with Acheson that liaison among them on the blockade would be maintained through their representatives at the United Nations.[208]

The Russians continued to maneuver for a cessation of the preparations for the establishment of the West German government. On April 10, Malik informed Jessup of Vishinsky's understanding that no such government would be established either before or during a meeting of the Council of Foreign Ministers. Since no such understanding had been reached, Jessup immediately played his side of the record, to remove any ambiguity on this crucial point. On April 11, Acheson showed Truman Jessup's report of his last talk with Malik. Acheson suggested that the President might now wish to inform the Defense Department as well as Generals Bradley and Clay about these talks, while Acheson informed their diplomatic representatives in Berlin and Moscow. The President

207. Ibid.; Memorandum of Conversation by Jessup, April 5, 1949, in *FRUS, 1949*, Vol. 3, pp. 712–716; and Jessup, "Park Avenue Diplomacy."
208. Acheson, *Present at the Creation*, pp. 272–273; and *Department of State Bulletin*, April 17, 1949, pp. 499–500.

was intent on maintaining strict secrecy, and it was not until a week later that he informed Acheson that he had told the new Secretary of Defense Louis Johnson and authorized him to inform Clay through Bradley.[209] Meanwhile, Clay had learned about these secret conversations from the newspapers and subsequently from General Robertson, and he was understandably annoyed at having been kept in the dark.[210]

Truman also approved a strong message to Malik backing Jessup's position, but at this point the problems of multilateral diplomacy returned with a vengeance. London refused to give clearance to the message on the grounds that nothing should be given to the Russians in writing before they had committed themselves, and Bevin wanted to hold up any further talks with Malik until the Bonn constitution had been approved. Acheson cabled Ambassador Douglas to see Bevin at once and impress on him that Acheson and Truman were disturbed by the Allies' failure to reach agreement on tactics and were convinced that it was necessary to continue the informal talks with Malik in order to stave off a premature public offer from the Russians.[211]

A leak from London about the secret talks was followed first by a Tass allegation that the Western press was circulating false rumors and then by a factual Russian communiqué on April 26 summarizing the Jessup-Malik talks and stating that if a date were agreed upon for the convocation of the Council of Foreign Ministers, the mutual restrictions in Berlin could be lifted in advance. Jessup had drafted a full statement which had been approved by the President and then released by the State Department on the same day as the Tass communiqué. The American press release concluded that if the position of the Soviet government was as stated in the Tass release, the way appeared to be clear for the lifting of the blockade, but no final conclusion on this could be reached until there had been further talks with Malik.[212]

---

209. Memorandum of Conversation with the President, April 11, 1948, Papers of Dean Acheson, Box 64, Harry S. Truman Library; Jessup, "Park Avenue Diplomacy"; Memorandum (from Truman to Johnson), n.d., President's Secretary File, Box 187, Harry S. Truman Library; and Memorandum for the Secretary of State from L. D. Battle, April 19, 1949, Papers of Dean Acheson, Box 64, Harry S. Truman Library.

210. Clay, *Decision in Germany*, p. 390.

211. *FRUS, 1949*, Vol. 3, pp. 720–731.

212. Jessup, "Park Avenue Diplomacy"; and *Department of State Bulletin*, May 8, 1949, pp. 590–591.

Two further talks were held with Malik on April 27 and 29, in the course of which Jessup went to great lengths to make sure the Soviets understood that the preparations for the establishment of the West German government would continue. While the Allies waited for Moscow's unconditional agreement, the debate between Washington and London continued. Bevin maintained that working out in detail the description of the restrictions to be removed could not be done in New York but only by the Military Governors in Berlin. He cited the formula of the Moscow directive of August 30 as a precedent. The Americans, however, recalling with a shudder the fate of that directive when it was discussed by the Military Governors, preferred a broad reference to lifting restrictions, with a sufficient interval before the CFM meeting to test the sincerity of Russian intentions. Clay and Bradley strongly supported this simple procedure for lifting the blockade, as did the French, and Bevin relented.[213]

Jessup met in New York on May 2 with the British and French representatives to the UN, Alexander Cadogan and Jean Chauvel, and they agreed on the text of the letter to be sent to Malik embodying the definitive Western position. Along with the letter to Malik, they sent the draft of a four-power communiqué. Unconditional agreement on all the points in question was reached on May 4 at the meeting between Jessup, Cadogan, Chauvel, and Malik, and this was announced the next day in a four-power communiqué. All restrictions imposed by the Soviet government and by the governments of France, the United Kingdom, and the United States since March 1, 1948 would be removed on May 12, 1949. Eleven days afterwards, on May 23, a meeting of the Council of Ministers would be convened in Paris to "consider questions relating to Germany, and problems arising out of the situation in Berlin, including also the question of currency in Berlin."[214]

The accord of May 5, although not conclusive, marked the end of the Berlin crisis. At midnight on May 11, the barriers between West Berlin and the Soviet zone fell as trains, trucks, passengers, and reporters flocked into the city. The following day, which was declared a city holiday, witnessed scenes of general rejoicing and jubilation. Also on May 12, the three Western Military Governors

213. Jessup, "Park Avenue Diplomacy"; and *FRUS, 1949*, Vol. 3, pp. 732–750.

214. Jessup, "Park Avenue Diplomacy"; and *Department of State Bulletin*, May 15, 1949, p. 631.

communicated to Konrad Adenauer, the President of the Parliamentary Council, their approval of the Basic Law which was to form the constitutional basis for the emergence of the Federal Republic of Germany.

The struggle for Germany was by no means over, and the details of the Berlin situation, including the currency problem, figured prominently on the agenda of the Council of Foreign Ministers. Still, the four-power accord of May 5 was widely regarded as a major Western victory and was accompanied by a general relaxation in the crisis perceptions of the American decision-makers. Their perceptions of threat, of the probability of war, and of time pressure returned broadly to their pre-crisis level. Acheson noted that great as the airlift achievement was, it had not solved the Berlin problem. But it did put the Allies "again in the situation in which we were before the blockade was imposed."[215] To Truman the Soviet agreement to lift the blockade without a Western commitment to call off their actions to create a West German government signified that the Russians were ready to retreat.[216] That he agreed to release Clay following the agreement to lift the Berlin blockade was significant, for, as he revealed in a public statement, it had been thought several times before that the Military Governor's request for retirement could be granted, but in recurring emergencies the President had felt that Clay could not be spared.[217] Clay himself requested and obtained the Department of the Army's approval for continuing the airlift until the foreign ministers had completed their deliberations. But he also thought that there had been a complete change in Russian tactics to win Germany and that this change made the reimposition of the blockade unlikely. In fact, he was quite sure that a simple lifting of the blockade and counterblockade and a return to the pre-crisis conditions of March 1948 would better serve the interests of the Western powers than any attempt to secure a formal recognition of their rights of access at that time.[218]

Thus, while the key American decision-makers did not underestimate the problems that still lay ahead, they judged the outcome of the Berlin crisis to be highly favorable from the Ameri-

---

215. *Department of State Bulletin*, May 11, 1949, p. 662.
216. Truman, *Memoirs*, Vol. 2, p. 138.
217. *Public Papers of the Presidents of the United States: Harry S. Truman, 1949* (Washington, D.C.: U.S. Government Printing Office, 1964), p. 240.
218. *Clay Papers*, Vol. 2, pp. 1137–39.

can point of view: Berlin had been successfully defended despite the precariousness of the Western position there; war had been averted; the airlift had not only been an outstanding technical and military achievement but a great boost to American prestige in Europe; the formation of a West German state had proceeded vigorously and uninterruptedly in the face of Soviet threats and blandishments; the situation in Europe had been stabilized; and Western unity had emerged from the ordeal considerably enhanced. Above all, America had emerged triumphant from the trial of strength with its principal adversary, while the Soviet Union had been forced to concede defeat following one of the most prolonged and intense confrontations of the entire Cold War era.

FINDINGS

The Berlin post-crisis period will be examined here, as in Chapters 4 and 6, on two levels: first, in terms of the four crisis components; and second, with a focus on the effects of declining stress on the American coping mechanisms.

CRISIS COMPONENTS

Environmental Change

The transition from the crisis to the post-crisis period was triggered by the National Security Council's decision, taken on July 22, 1948, to eschew an attempt to break the blockade by force, and to rely on an expanded airlift and the resources of diplomacy to resolve the Berlin crisis. No environmental change occurred to reduce the threat perceived by the American decision-makers. The perceived probability of war was reduced through the avoidance of provocative actions by America, but the possibility of general hostilities being touched off by Soviet interference with the airlift remained. What the launching of the large airlift unquestionably did was to reduce the time pressure on the American decision-makers: it gave them a breathing spell for exploring ways of ending the crisis which incurred neither an unacceptable risk of war nor a sacrifice of basic values.

Threat to Basic Values

The most immediate value threatened by the blockade was the continuation of the American presence in Berlin. Although this presence was militarily unsound and constituted a strategic liability rather than an asset, it was of enormous symbolic importance. From the political point of view, the former German capital had become such an important symbol partly because the Americans themselves had made it so. But once the crisis broke out in the Spring of 1948, it was difficult to divest Berlin of this symbolic value. With every month that passed, the symbolic importance of Berlin only grew and American prestige became more closely bound up with maintaining the Western position there. As the effort and treasures expended to hold Berlin mounted, it became increasingly difficult, if not impossible, to disengage.

Moreover, the Soviet blockade was perceived as threatening not only the Western presence in Berlin but also the Western plans for the formation of a West German government. Progress towards this goal was perceived as a basic American value, and here, too, the American commitment became stronger rather than weaker in the face of the Soviet challenge. Thirdly, the Americans were committed to checking the spread of communism and to helping Western Europe to recover economically, to regain its political confidence, and to build up its military defenses. A retreat in Berlin was considered potentially disastrous to the attainment of this basic objective, and, once again, the transition from the crisis to the post-crisis period was not accompanied by any reduction in the perceived threat. It was not until the Soviets indicated that they would be willing to lift the blockade on terms which would not involve America in sacrificing any of these basic values that threat perception declined to its pre-crisis level.

Probability of War

The probability of war, as perceived by the American decision-makers, oscillated within a very wide margin during the long post-crisis period. It was implicitly recognized, at least by Truman and Marshall, that the probability of war was affected not exclusively by Soviet intentions and actions but by American decisions, too. Basing American strategy on the airlift rather than on an armed convoy was designed to reduce the war risk by transferring back to the Soviets the onus for choosing between risky escalation and acceptance of defeat. But the situation remained tense and uncertain because, had the Soviets responded by disrupting air supplies, war would have become virtually inevitable. As it turned out, the Soviets refrained from escalation through interference in the air corridors, and this had the effect of stabilizing the conflict.

Subsequently, however, the failure of the Military Governors' talks and Marshal Sokolovsky's announcement of the Russian intention to hold air maneuvers in the Berlin area, which carried a veiled threat of disrupting the air ferry, produced a sudden war scare in Washington. Even the coolheaded Secretary Marshall told the National Security Council on September 7 that the situation was so dangerous that the slightest element added could be the fuse to spark a general conflagration. The President, who according to Lilienthal's account had been optimistic about peace, was "blue now, mighty blue." Truman himself recorded in a private memo on September 13 that he had a terrible feeling that the world was very close to war. It was in this atmosphere, darkened by war clouds, that Truman felt impelled to reassure Forrestal that he would order the use of the bomb in an emergency, and the National Security Council directed that military planning should proceed on the assumption that nuclear weapons would be used in the event of war.

The threat of Soviet air maneuvers did not materialize, however, and in succeeding months the possibility of war looked increasingly remote. In late November, Marshall expressed the view that overt Soviet aggression would be coldly calculated and not the result of unplanned incidents arising out of the Berlin situation. This, of course, had always been Clay's view. During the post-crisis period, Clay's estimate of the likelihood of war was consequently not subject to the same sudden and dramatic changes that were common in Washington. He was also consistently less troubled by the fear of Soviet aggression than the majority of his colleagues, who were guilty in his eyes of underestimating America's real strength. Soon after Acheson took office, Stalin's signal indicated that Moscow wanted a peaceful resolution of the crisis, and this produced a general downward revision of the estimated probability of war, which brought the Washington decision-makers more into line with the commander in the field.

Time Pressure

The principal and direct consequence of the airlift decision of July 22 was a marked decline in the time constraints governing American behavior. The airlift gained valuable time for America to try to solve the Berlin crisis by negotiation, first in Moscow and then in

Berlin. The Moscow-Berlin talks failed, but their failure did not entail a reintensification of the time pressure because, in the meantime, due to the steady increase in its volume and efficiency, the airlift itself had been transformed into a powerful instrument for defeating the blockade.

America's success in pushing forward its policy in Germany reinforced the effect of the airlift in reversing the perception that time was on the side of the Russians. Soviet strategy was directed at exploiting American weakness in Berlin to compel America to reconsider its policy towards Germany as a whole. But the simultaneous reinforcement of the American position on both fronts made her leaders more reluctant to buy relief in Berlin by halting the drive towards a West German government. As Clay told Byrnes on September 19, a strong West German government oriented towards the West would restore the economic and political balance in Europe in the Allies' favor and put them in a better position for the final negotiations.

Referring the Berlin problem to the United Nations revealed a lack of concern about time, since the world organization could hardly be expected to produce a speedy solution. Clearly, the prospect that discussions at the UN would drag on inconclusively did not greatly worry either Marshall or Clay, because by then they were both convinced that time was on their side. Following the predictable failure of the Security Council to bridge the gulf between the two sides, the American decision-makers recognized even more clearly that the crisis had become a test of resolution and capabilities and that they need be in no hurry to make concessions, because the wind was now blowing their way. Once the counterblockade began to bite, it was the Soviet Union which came under pressure to end the crisis without achieving any of its original objectives.

The Berlin post-crisis period was thus characterized by an observable decline in the intensity of at least one of the perceptual conditions, as set out in our definition. The perceived threat to basic values continued until the agreement on the lifting of the blockade was reached nine months later. The perceived likelihood of war declined initially but rose to a new peak in early September before reassuming its downward trend. Only the third component, time pressure, declined conspicuously at the outset of the post-crisis period and continued to decline steadily until it virtually disappeared altogether at the beginning of 1949. The crisis terminated on May 5, 1949, when the intensity of the perceived threat, war probability, and time pressure returned, broadly speaking, to the preceding non-crisis level.

COPING MECHANISMS
Information Processing

As the Berlin crisis became gradually less intense, the American decision-makers paid less attention to the collection and processing of information. There was no evident decline in the volume of information about the crisis reaching Washington from its representatives abroad, but the task of processing this information was left increasingly to subordinates. The task of maintaining personal familiarity with all the minutiae connected with the Bank of Emission, trade arrangements, and the like was proving, as Forrestal confessed to Royall on September 8, onerous and irksome. Truman settled into a distinctly passive role during the election period and simply noted the information placed before him by his advisers. Marshall kept Truman in the picture about the major developments; and during the Secretary's prolonged stay in Paris, which coincided with Truman's whistle-stop electioneering tour around the country, Robert Lovett, the Acting Secretary of State, attended dutifully to the task of keeping the peripatetic President posted about the Berlin crisis.

Marshall himself relied very heavily on the Berlin Group, and especially on Charles Bohlen who headed the group, for the processing of the messages with which the State Department continued to be inundated. At the very outset of the post-crisis period, Marshall sent Bohlen to Europe to coordinate the tripartite approach to Stalin. Fearing that much confusion and delay would be caused if the Allies continued to try to deal with the Berlin question both in Washington and in London, the Secretary reaffirmed the earlier decision that everything should be centralized in London.

Information processing for the purpose of conducting international negotiation remained a highly complex and difficult task, despite the decline in stress, because America had to coordinate every move with its British and French allies. With the opening of the Moscow talks, these difficulties were compounded because, in addition to all the previously agreed-upon procedures, new procedures had to be worked out for the exchange of information between the three Western envoys. Ambassador Douglas would discuss the important issues with the British and French representatives in London and then with Ambassador Smith in Moscow, Clay in Germany, and the State Department in Washington. London thus served as a clearinghouse, and any differences in viewpoints had to be resolved in London so that the American, British, and French envoys in Moscow could proceed under common instructions. When differences resulted among the three Western powers in the course of the Moscow talks, they had to be referred to London, where the same process was followed in their resolution. As Clay observed, this elaborate procedure was time-consuming and made the lot of the American representatives dealing with the Soviet government, whose representatives were sure of their position, most difficult.[219]

The Americans had to cope with similar problems of exchanging information and coordinating their policy with their Allies in connection with the Military Governors' talks which opened in Berlin on the last day of August. Under the procedure proposed by Clay, after every meeting of the Military Governors, the Western Political advisers would agree to a common report which would be sent to their three governments. Clay himself would receive his British and French counterparts in his office an hour prior to their meeting with Marshal Sokolovsky in order to review the reports of their subcommittees and to coordinate their actions as far as possible. After each meeting with Sokolovsky, Murphy would send the agreed-upon report to the State Department, while Clay would send his additional comments and recommendations to the Department of the Army. Thus, in this instance, as at all other times during the post-crisis period, information processing involved not only liaison between the State Department and American representatives abroad but also liaison with the Army Department and the White House.

Consultation

As stress declined for the American decision-makers, there was a slow and barely perceptible move from the highly intensive and extended patterns of consultation which prevailed at the peak of the crisis towards the preceding pre-crisis patterns. Consultation with allies, however, constituted a partial exception to this broad generalization. Britain and France continued to be consulted at

219. Clay, *Germany and the Fight for Freedom*, pp. 44–45.

every stage until the crisis was resolved. The elaborate procedures described in the last section served a dual purpose: the joint processing of information, and consulting about policy with a view to preserving a common front vis-à-vis the Soviet Union. Consultations were held in London through Ambassador Douglas, in Moscow between Ambassador Smith and the British and French envoys, and in Germany at the level of the Military Governors. With Britain (but not with France), military consultations were held through the medium of the Combined Chiefs of Staff. Marshall's trip to Paris for the General Assembly session provided him with almost unlimited opportunities for both formal and informal consultations with his partners. Formal meetings were held on September 20 and 21 between Marshall and the British and French foreign ministers, all of them accompanied by their senior advisers, with the number of participants reaching twenty-three on the second occasion. The meeting on September 24 between Marshall and Bevin to discuss tactics is an example of the frequent informal consultations which took place in Paris. After Marshall's return to Washington, contact was maintained between the Western representatives to the Security Council, and consultations at this level were intensified during the final phase of the Jessup-Malik talks. Acheson, too, held an important series of talks with Bevin and Schuman in Washington in early April 1949, which dealt, among other topics, with Allied policy towards Berlin. So, in general, the inter-Allied consultative circle remained extensive during the post-crisis period, involving foreign ministers, foreign policy advisers, diplomats, Military Governors, Chiefs of Staff, and UN representatives. But the consultative process was not subject to the same time pressure as it had been during June–July 1948, and it dealt with less critical issues. The persistence of this elaborate consultative machinery was probably more of a reflection of the nature of the crisis, and especially of the multilateral negotiations which it necessitated, than a direct product of changes in the level of stress.

On the domestic front, the pattern of consultation with competing elites which was established during the crisis period also continued, with minor changes, for most of the post-crisis period. Marshall, for example, consulted Senator Vandenberg on the alternatives facing the United States following the breakdown of the Berlin talks. John Foster Dulles, Governor Dewey's spokesman on foreign affairs, was included in the American delegation to the United Nations as an earnest of the Democratic Administration and its Republican rival's commitment to a bipartisan foreign policy. The task of involving the Republican leaders in the formulation of the official American position over Berlin was carried out by Marshall, but Truman made a personal intervention when he invited Senators Vandenberg and Connally over for a private chat in the White House, at which the Vinson mission and the idea of a telephone call to Stalin were discussed. Truman's muddled approach to the senators may well have been prompted, as Connally suspected, by concern for his prospects in the ongoing domestic campaign. But neither consultations with the Republican leadership over the Berlin crisis nor the practice of bipartisanship in foreign policy ended with Truman's decisive political victory. On November 18, following Marshall's return to Washington, Truman designated Dulles as Acting Chairman of the United States delegation to the United Nations.

It is only within the executive branch that a direct link between the level of stress and the pattern of consultation can be discerned. With the decline in stress, the consultative circle gradually contracted and presidential involvement became less frequent. Many of the questions which had to be decided were of a diplomatic and sometimes purely tactical nature, and the consultative process surrounding them did not necessarily extend beyond the State Department. One feature which is particularly striking is the limited role played by the military in the consultative process. Just as the escalation of the perceived probability of involvement in armed hostilities had brought the Joint Chiefs of Staff to the forefront, so, with the waning of the war danger, they receded once more into the background. The voices of the civilian chiefs of the military departments, Forrestal, Royall, and Draper, were also heard somewhat less frequently within the inner councils of the Administration as attention shifted from the high-risk solutions towards a long, drawn-out campaign of diplomatic attrition. Significantly, when the no-war estimates were temporarily shattered in early September, it was the military chiefs who went to the White House to brief the President.

The consultative process became more institutional and less ad hoc as stress declined. The earlier tendency to work with informal and hastily convened groups of advisers, which suited Truman's personal style, was gradually reversed. Marshall, who directed the bulk of the policy discussions during the post-crisis period, was inclined by temperament to work methodically through the regular channels. In sounding out opinion both inside and outside the State Department, he—and Acheson after him—preferred to follow institutionalized procedures. Neither was a slave to routine. Marshall took the initiative, upon his arrival in Paris, in convening a series of meetings with American officials from various posts in Europe, and directed the discussion at these meetings towards the long-term aspects of policy. Acheson departed from departmental routine by setting up a very small committee in order to protect the secrecy of the Jessup-Malik talks. But the general trend which continued under both men was to seek the advice of the relevant governmental experts and to utilize the existing machinery to this end.

In terms of coping with crisis, these findings indicate that the decline in crisis-induced stress did not significantly reduce the intensity of the Administration's consultations with either its foreign allies or its competing domestic elites. But the decline in stress *did* bring about a reduction in presidential involvement and in the involvement of the group skilled in the use of violence; and it *did* herald a gradual return to more institutional forums and procedures for consultation.

Decisional Forums

Decision-making became less hierarchical and less centralized under the impact of declining stress. The size of the decisional unit during the post-crisis period varied from one individual to the full National Security Council, and no one forum dominated the process. But as with consultation, there was a gradual shift away from improvised forums and procedures and toward a return to working through the usual machinery.

Presidential involvement in the decision-making process declined very markedly and virtually disappeared altogether during the UN phase of the Berlin crisis. As one would expect, the further the crisis moved from the critical area of decisions affecting American national security, the more limited was the role played by the President. The role of the Secretary of State, on the other hand, was steadily enhanced as the number of questions calling for responses of an essentially diplomatic character multiplied. The wide range of decisions taken by the Secretary of State, either on his own authority or in conjunction with others, is striking. So is the fact that some of Marshall's decisions were taken in an institutional setting which brought him face to face with non-American participants with whom he could not simply rubber-stamp decisions that had already been reached by the American government. On September 21 and again on September 26, Marshall hammered out important tripartite decisions through a process of bargaining and compromise with his British and French opposite numbers.

The National Security Council continued to play a major part in two separate areas: the airlift, and military planning for the possibility of war. Having been established only two years previously, and having emerged as a vital instrument of government policy during the Berlin crisis period, it continued thereafter to debate and resolve critical questions bearing on American national security. Matters brought before the Council were worthy of the personal attention of the highest officers, its discussions proceeded on the basis of comprehensive information and previously filed memoranda, and its recommendations were quickly implemented by presidential order. Acheson considered the Council an important forum of policy innovation which operated with optimal efficiency under Truman's direction.[220] The role it played in the Berlin crisis tends to support this judgment.

The Cabinet, by contrast, was and remained to the end an insignificant forum for coping with the crisis. Not one of the thirteen post-crisis decisions were taken by this forum. The Berlin problem cropped up periodically at Cabinet meetings—on September 10, September 13, and November 22, for example. But on all these occasions, of which Forrestal left a record, the Cabinet was simply being informed of recent developments: it was not asked for its opinion, let alone for a decision. Observation under four Presidents led Acheson to the belief that Cabinet meetings can become an unorganized and discursive waste of time. President Truman, in his view, organized his Cabinet meetings into useful weekly instruction of its members on the outstanding crises of the week; and, since foreign affairs were very much to the fore, the Secretary of State, at Truman's invitation, usually opened the meetings with a review of the current situation and a recommendation of the public line to be taken.[221] The fragmentary evidence on the Cabinet's treatment of the Berlin crisis between July 1948 and May 1949 is entirely consistent with this estimate of the Cabinet's lack of influence on government policy.

220. Acheson, *Present at the Creation*, p. 733.
221. Ibid., p. 736.

Alternatives: Search and Evaluation

Although for most of the post-crisis period the American decision-makers regarded war as unlikely and were not subject to severe time constraints, their own search for alternatives became less energetic and their evaluation of the alternatives placed before them by their subordinates became less open-minded. The obvious explanation for this paradox is that success in the management of the crisis curtailed their interest in alternative courses of action. Once the airlift had demonstrated its potentiality for defeating the blockade, the urgency and incentives for finding other solutions decreased. Moreover, as George Kennan observed, what had been a mere instrument of policy became an end in itself.

Kennan himself and the Policy Planning Staff he directed did not commit the error of thinking that growing momentum behind a policy is evidence of its wisdom. They used the respite provided by the airlift to explore the broader aspects of the Berlin problem and to formulate alternative plans for solving it. Central to their thinking was the recognition that the Berlin problem should be treated not in isolation but in the context of the German question as a whole. But they could not elicit even a general indication from their governmental superiors as to whether a plan involving new arrangements for Germany should be considered. The paper completed by the Policy Planning Staff in early October and the comprehensive report it submitted in mid-November, outlining Plan A, demonstrated conclusively that the search for diplomatic alternatives was conducted with considerable thoroughness, skill, and foresight by the governmental organ specifically charged with this function. But time and again it proved impossible to obtain serious consideration for new ideas from decision-makers who were firmly committed to the existing policy line. With Acheson at the head of the State Department, the gulf separating policy planning from policy making became even wider than under his predecessor, and the work of the Policy Planning Staff ceased to be credited with even a limited margin of confidence.

In the defense establishment, contingency planning of various kinds went on continuously during the post-crisis period, and the results of this activity by experts were on the whole brought to bear more effectively on policy considerations at the higher echelons. The Joint Chiefs of Staff had been largely ignored as a corporate body, although not as individuals, during the early stages of the blockade. It was not until late July that they themselves took the initiative in formally presenting their collective view concerning the principal courses of action which were under consideration at that time. Some of their recommendations had already been overtaken by events, so they had to wait until the next reappraisal of American military policy, in October 1948, before they were able to present their revised analysis and recommendations to the policymakers. Their stark presentation of the alternatives on this second occasion—withdraw or mobilize for war—and their basic criticism of the Administration for failing to keep its foreign policy objectives in consonance with its defense capabilities met with a very sharp rebuttal, but the debate did serve a useful purpose in clarifying what could and what could not be achieved on the military plane in support of Administration policy.

The careful and responsible manner in which the evaluation of military options proceeded is best illustrated with reference to the convoy plan. Even after the idea was turned down on July 22, the Joint Chiefs of Staff instructed Clay to prepare a detailed plan of action and have it ready in case a decision from above called for its implementation at short notice. The Joint Chiefs also worked through the Combined Chiefs of Staff to secure coordination with their British opposite numbers, but the latter turned out to be unalterably opposed to the whole idea. Clay's plan, prepared after the British rebuff, was subjected to close and ongoing scrutiny within the Army's Plans and Operations Division. The synthesized product of all this staff work was funneled by the Joint Chiefs to the National Security Council with a clear indication of the practical difficulties and war risks involved. The military implications of continuing and augmenting the airlift were likewise studied and reported to the National Security Council.

With all this information relating to military options, supplemented by periodic reports from the State Department on developments concerning Berlin, the National Security Council was able, during the later stages of the Berlin crisis, to take a broad view and to start performing its statutory duties of assessing the objectives, commitments, and risks of the United States in relation to its actual and potential military power, and to advise the President on the integration of domestic, foreign, and military policies relating to national security.

The evidence from the Berlin post-crisis period thus tends to suggest that the decline in crisis-induced stress was accompanied by a continuing and even intensified search for alternatives at the level of experts, both civilian and military. At the level of policymakers, on the other hand, declining stress was accompanied, especially on the diplomatic side, by a less open-minded and less analytical approach to the tasks of policy reappraisal and long-term planning. It would therefore appear that it is one thing to allow experts to conduct the search for and evaluation of alternatives; it is quite another thing to ensure that this crucial function is taken seriously by the policymakers and integrated with the rest of the government's strategy for coping with the crisis.

CHAPTER NINE

Conclusions

THE PERCEPTIONS and behavior of a single actor, the United States, have been analyzed here in terms of the model and related research questions set out in Chapter 1. Findings for each of the periods of the crisis were indicated in the final sections of Chapters 4, 6, and 8. Overall findings from this case study will now be presented, and an attempt will also be made to indicate whether these case-specific findings are consistent with hypotheses (generated by historical and experimental research) regarding the relationship between stress and the performance of selected decision-making tasks.

Certain difficult problems complicate this effort, and they should be identified and discussed at the outset in order to indicate the limitations they impose on some of the findings. In the first place, it should be acknowledged that although the study employs an individual stress model, it does not directly measure the level of stress experienced by policymakers. While the historical record occasionally provides evidence of stress, this is fragmentary rather than comprehensive or systematic. It does not permit a precise measurement of the magnitude of stress experienced by each individual policymaker at each successive phase of the crisis.

Secondly, it must be acknowledged that although considerable progress has been made in recent years, especially by political scientists and psychologists, in refining theories of crisis decision-making, there is not in existence a coherent or generally accepted body of theoretical propositions from which definitive guidelines might be derived to direct historical research or to test its findings. As one leading student of crisis has observed, the diplomatic historian who ventures into neighboring disciplines with the expectation of finding broad agreement on key concepts that are linked together in well-established theories, and solidly buttressed by empirical evidence, is likely to be somewhat disappointed.[1]

The present study consciously proceeds from one specific theoretical perspective which seeks to explore the impact of crisis-induced stress on the performance of foreign policy decision-makers. Other and no less valid approaches to the study of crisis have only been touched in passing. Both the theoretical perspective and the actual structure of this volume are inspired by the overarching framework for research on the crisis behavior of states which was developed by Michael Brecher.[2] Brecher's definition of crisis, the dynamic three-stage model he elaborated, and the related research questions he raised were all briefly summarized in Chapter 1.

In trying to determine whether and to what extent the findings from this case study support the existing general theoretical propositions concerning the impact of stress on the performance of the makers of foreign policy, we shall use the admirable summary of the relevant literature provided by Ole R. Holsti and Alexander L. George.[3] But one has to ask, first of all, whether those general propositions are formulated precisely enough to permit this kind of testing and assessment. The Holsti-George article does not address this important question.[4] It would appear, however, that one class of general propositions summarized by Holsti and George is more easily assessed than another class. Thus, it is somewhat easier to use the case-specific findings to assess theoretical propositions that concern the impact of rising (or declining) stress on various coping patterns. On the other hand, it is quite difficult to use the case-specific findings to assess general theoretical propositions that are tied to the inverted U-curve model, for here it is a matter of whether, for the individual or the group, the rising level of stress experienced has reached or passed the threshold or crossover point

---

1. Ole R. Holsti, "Theories of Crisis Decision-Making," in *Diplomacy: New Approaches in History, Theory, and Policy*, ed. Paul Gordon Lauren (New York: The Free Press, 1979), p. 104.
2. Michael Brecher with Benjamin Geist, *Decisions in Crisis: Israel, 1967 and 1973* (Berkeley: University of California Press, 1980).
3. Ole R. Holsti and Alexander L. George, "The Effects of Stress on the Performance of Foreign Policy-Makers," *Political Science Annual*, Vol. 6 (1975), pp. 255–319.
4. For the clarifications which follow, I am indebted to Alexander George.

on the curve. As the inverted U-curve tells us: up to a point, increasing stress usually improves performance; but after that point, performance deteriorates.

What this means for the present study (and for other studies in the International Crisis Behavior series) is that the data requirements and methodology for assessing the first class of theoretical propositions ("as stress increases . . .") are much simpler and easier to meet than those for the second class of propositions ("if stress remains moderate . . ."; "if extreme stress is experienced . . ."). Because the data and methodological requirements for the second class of propositions are not fully met, great caution is needed both in stating the case-specific findings that are associated with the U-curve model and, particularly, in attempting to assess whether these findings are consistent with the corresponding theoretical propositions.

The fragmentary data gleaned from the historical record are useful in that they generally support the study assumption that stress rises as one moves from the pre-crisis to the crisis phase, and declines again in the post-crisis phase. But these fragments of data are not always adequate for making the more difficult, more refined scoring judgment whether the increased stress in the crisis phase is "moderate" or "extreme." Nor do they permit, except very occasionally, a confident judgment as to whether an individual decision-maker experiences only "moderate" stress or whether it has become "extreme," rising to and over his threshold on the curve.

One way around this problem would be to *infer* whether an individual's level of stress has remained moderate or crossed his threshold. How can such an inference be made? If one assumes that the general theoretical propositions have a reasonable validity, then one can use evidence of improved or degraded performance as an *indicator* of the level of stress. The underlying reasoning supporting such inferences would be of the following order: "stress must have been extreme and dysfunctional because there is evidence of poor performance of these decision-making tasks"; or "stress was moderate and functional because there is no evidence of deterioration in, or poor performance of, certain decision-making tasks."

However, if the existing theoretical propositions are used in this way to generate the case-specific findings regarding the phenomenon of the inverted U-curve, then the case-specific findings in question cannot be used to assess those very same theoretical propositions, since that would constitute circularity.

To avoid, as far as possible, the circularity trap, we shall rely primarily on the actual historical evidence, incomplete as it undoubtedly is, rather than on inference from performance, to assess the level of stress. What this means for the rest of this chapter is that while the first class of propositions can be assessed with a reasonable degree of confidence, propositions related to the U-curve model can be assessed only in a rough and tentative manner.

PSYCHOLOGICAL ENVIRONMENT FOR CRISIS BEHAVIOR

One of the research questions posed at the beginning of this volume concerned the impact of changing crisis-induced stress on cognitive performance. Holsti and George, in their review of the literature, found that "the overwhelming preponderance of historical and experimental evidence indicates that intense stress . . . impairs cognitive performance." Studies of U.S. foreign policy decision-making, they add, support the inverted U or curvilinear relationship between stress and cognitive performance: low to moderate stress may facilitate better performance, but high and protracted stress degrades it. Three variables, they note, are affected significantly, and adversely, by high stress: span of attention, cognitive rigidity, and time perspective. Under high stress, the first variable induces a lower cue awareness and greater reliance on past experience, the misapplication or overgeneralization of which is a primary source of low-quality decisions. Under high stress, the second variable tends to erode general cognitive abilities, including creativity and the ability to cope with complexity. Tolerance of ambiguity is likely to suffer, with the result that conclusions will be drawn more quickly than is warranted by the evidence, and increasing use will be made of stereotypes. And finally, under high stress, the third variable affects the high discount rate which foreign policy officials are said to have—that is, the tendency to assign high value to immediate achievements, and to heavily discount the value of those achievements that might be realized in the more distant future.[5]

5. Holsti and George, "The Effects of Stress on the Performance of Foreign Policy-Makers," pp. 277–280.

In the Berlin crisis, stress increased sharply after the Russians severed all land communications with the Western sectors of the city on June 24, and, after gradually declining towards the end of July, reached a new but temporary peak in the second week of September. All the key American decision-makers were robust, confident, and stable individuals who had considerable experience dealing with difficult situations and could be expected to stand up well to pressure, however intense. The crisis led them to narrow their span of attention to a few aspects of the Berlin situation, and this proved functional in enabling them to eliminate trivial distractions, to filter out irrelevant information, and to concentrate on fending off the perceived threat to basic American values. Other preoccupations continued to compete for the attention of the key policy-makers: Truman, for example, was deeply absorbed in his electoral contest with Governor Dewey; Marshall had to contend with the exceptionally volatile situation in Palestine and with the highly sensitive negotiations which eventually led to the formation of NATO; and Clay personally directed the entire occupation of Germany on a day-to-day basis. But the acute crisis in Berlin, like the proverbial hanging, concentrated their minds wonderfully. Lower cue awareness was helpful in this case because it was not accompanied, as it frequently is, by indiscriminate filtering and the consequent overlooking of important dimensions of the situation. Central questions such as the value of Berlin to the West, the nature of Soviet aims in resorting to the blockade, the implications of the military balance of power, and the importance of maintaining a united diplomatic front with America's allies in dealing with the Soviet Union were all given serious and continuous attention.

Truman, who had a tendency to be insensitive to cues which did not bear a direct relationship to the immediate task at hand, was also psychologically prone to rely on past experience as a guide to coping with current threats to basic values. He viewed the threat posed by the Soviet Union as a straightforward manifestation of the inherent aggressiveness of totalitarian regimes, and he drew the parallel with Nazi Germany repeatedly and emphatically. The precept that all totalitarian regimes are the same, whether they be Nazi, Fascist, or Communist, led him to conclude that America was facing exactly the same situation as Britain and France had faced in 1938–39 with Hitler. Clay, too, observed, in his cable of July 19, that the world was facing the most critical issue that had arisen since Hitler had embarked on his policy of aggression. But the parallel in this case was implied rather than explicitly stated. By drawing lessons from previous events, whether explicitly or inferentially, Truman and Clay illuminated some aspects of the Berlin situation, but they also obscured or distorted others. It is fascinating, for example, to watch how in Clay's mind a decision not to launch on a new and provocative course by challenging Soviet troops inside the Soviet zone of occupation in Germany becomes a "retreat" which can only lead to further retreats. Despite some superficial similarities, the situation in 1948 differed fundamentally from the situation in 1938, not least inasmuch as the Soviet blockade actions did not violate any legal agreements and were reactive rather than part of a long-term master plan of aggression. By providing a dramatic and important lesson about the dangers of appeasement, the earlier experience with Hitler constituted an analogy which in the tense situation of 1948 was applied too rigidly and uncritically.

Despite mounting stress and the concomitant propensity to supplement information about the objective state of affairs with information and "lessons" drawn from past experience, the American decision-makers retained, in varying degrees, awareness of their complex environment. Marshall, although not particularly creative in devising solutions, recognized the complexity of the challenge and the value trade-offs it necessitated between, for example, effective crisis management and alliance maintenance. He carefully refrained from resorting to stereotypes to explain Soviet behavior, tolerated ambiguity, and formed evaluations cautiously and in close contact with the available evidence. To the studied reluctance to assume unnecessary risks which had characterized Marshall's long and distinguished military career was added a diplomatic concern to leave options open for the Russians. Even at the height of the crisis, he refused to take chances with a convoy because it was liable to lead to a precipitate Russian response at a time when America had so little conventional military strength to back up an abortive probe. On the other hand, the heavy and relentless tension generated by the crisis strained the patience and may have exacerbated the health problems of the 69-year-old general. His observation to the Cabinet on September 10 that all the persons involved in the Berlin negotiations were close to a state of exhaustion applied not only to his subordinates but to himself as well. The sheer physical strain of involvement in protracted and totally unproductive negotiations was beginning to take its toll. This was reflected in Marshall's impatience with Ambassador Smith and in the uncharacteristically legalistic posture he adopted following the failure of the Berlin talks.

Clay manifested greater cognitive rigidity under pressure, but his analysis of the situation was by no means simplistic, and he was creative and resourceful in devising the airlift strategy and in finding solutions to the manifold problems associated with it. On the other hand, he was closed to information, opinions, and suggestions which did not accord with his reading of the situation and with his preferences for dealing with it. Fatigue and strain resulting from prolonged and intensive interactions also impaired Clay's cognitive performance. In particular, his ability to conduct negotiations with the Soviets in Berlin in early September 1948 was doubted even by his own colleagues, one of whom described Clay as drawn tight as a steel spring.

With Truman, cognitive rigidity was a basic personality trait, but its effects were compounded by crisis-induced stress. His ability to stand the "heat in the kitchen" was proverbial, and with it went the capacity to make difficult decisions without too much agonizing and torment. But this ability usually rested on a simplistic definition of the situation and a tendency to focus on just a few of its aspects, and it was this tendency that was accentuated under pressure. Truman's observation that there are times in history when it is wiser to act than to hesitate is highly revealing in this respect, for it made a virtue out of what for him was a basic psychological predisposition. This predisposition was vividly illustrated at the outset of the Berlin crisis period when Lovett discussed whether the Americans should stay in Berlin or not and Truman interrupted to say that there was no question on that point: they were going to stay, period. Cognitive rigidity and particularly intolerance of ambiguity and uncertainty were also evident in Truman's snappy rejoinder to Lovett, who argued for a thorough study of the problem and of the possible consequences of the proposed decision to stay. The essential decision, said Truman, was that they were in Berlin by the terms of an agreement, and the Russians had no right to get them out. His images of the adversary as systematically aggressive and expansionist and of the United States as entirely defensive became more rigid under the impact of stress and precluded any attempt to find out how Moscow perceived the dispute, let alone any genuine empathy with the opponent.

The third variable of cognitive performance—time perspective—was not significantly changed by crisis-induced stress. All the key American decision-makers assigned a very high value to the establishment of a separate West German state oriented toward the West. This was a medium-term goal. In the longer term, it was expected that this reconstructed western half of Germany would become a major ally in the Cold War struggle between East and West. During the crisis, the American decision-makers came under powerful and unremitting pressure to sacrifice this long-term value for the sake of a solution to the Berlin problem. A suspension of the London Program in exchange for the removal of the blockade was the basic package deal offered by Moscow. But no shift in the time perspective of the American decision-makers took place. They were all determined to proceed energetically with the implementation of the London Program and to steer away from any compromise that would place it in jeopardy for the sake of achieving an immediate solution to the Berlin problem.

In summary, evidence about stress and cognitive performance from America's 1948 crisis is somewhat mixed. High stress led to a reduced span of attention and, with it, to a lower cue awareness, but this was functional inasmuch as it helped to concentrate the decision-makers' minds on the critical issues involved. Truman and (to a lesser extent) Clay also began to rely more heavily on past experience and historical parallels to guide them through the crisis, but they failed to strip away from these past events, and especially from the Munich analogy, those facets that depended on the ephemeral context. High stress was also accompanied by manifestations of greater cognitive rigidity on the part of these decision-makers, but this did not render them completely oblivious to the complex reality they were facing. In Marshall's case, far from promoting cognitive rigidity, crisis-induced stress was associated with a judicious attempt to elicit Soviet motives and assess Soviet risk-taking on the basis of actual Soviet behavior. Only the hypothesis concerning time perspective is unequivocally contradicted by the experience of the American decision-makers in the Berlin crisis: they did not exhibit a high discount rate at any stage. On balance, then, intense and prolonged stress only marginally impaired the cognitive performance of the American decision-makers. There were some notable examples of impaired performance, cognitive as well as behavioral. But the adverse effects of stress did not impair cognitive performance fundamentally or drastically, nor were they incompatible with a pattern of behavior that was essentially rational and purposive.

Most of these findings, apart from being interesting in and of themselves, are sufficiently unexpected and important to suggest the need for a reexamination of the existing general theory concerning the effect of stress on cognitive performance. The findings are only partially consistent with some of the propositions suggested by the U-curve model and flatly contradict others. In the absence of direct measurement of the magnitude of stress experienced by individual decision-makers, one would not be justified in offering a reformulation of the general theory. But it should at least be noted that the widely-held assumption that high stress is necessarily dysfunctional finds little support in the Berlin case study.

COPING: PROCESSES AND MECHANISMS

Information

Our second and third research questions, relating to information, were: what is the impact of changing crisis-induced stress on (2) the perceived need and consequent probe for information; and (3) the receptivity and size of the information processing group? A major consequence of high stress, according to the Holsti-George summary of findings from other crises and the literature, is a more active search for information but one which may also become more random and less productive.[6]

What does the evidence reveal about the stress-information nexus in the 1948 Berlin crisis? In this crisis, threat perception was followed, first, by more detailed and more frequent reporting to the Secretary of State from his representatives in Berlin, London, Paris, and Moscow, and, second, by direct and fuller reports to the President from senior foreign policy and defense officials and from the Director of the Central Intelligence Agency. The principal channel through which the probe for additional information was conducted was teleconferences between the Department of the Army and the American Military Governor for Germany. These teleconferences amplified and elaborated on the regular cables which Clay sent to the Department of the Army, dealing with the various facets of the blockade. The escalation of threat prompted Truman

---

6. Ibid., p. 280.

to seek face-to-face contact with the men on the spot, and he accordingly instructed that Clay and Murphy be recalled to Washington to present their impressions and recommendations in person. Thus, a correspondence is evident between rising stress and a more active probe for information about the situation and about alternative courses of action. As threat perception escalated, the decision-makers in Washington moved beyond passive acceptance of the information which came in and began to actively probe for pieces of information needed to complete the picture about the situation in Berlin, Soviet intentions and behavior, and the position of the Allies. The reverse relationship also obtained: the felt need for information declined during the post-crisis period, and with it the active search for supplementary information.

Information during the Berlin crisis was processed by Clay in Berlin, by the committee consisting of Douglas, Sir William Strang, and the French Ambassador in London, and by the "Berlin Group" in Washington. The difficulty in generalizing about information processing arises out of the diversity of the individuals and groups involved. What is evident is that as stress increased, information was elevated to the top of the decisional pyramid. Truman, Marshall, and Forrestal began to review a growing body of information before making the required crucial choices. The National Security Council collectively played an increasingly important role in collating information from various sources and advising the President on the national security aspects of the crisis.

The task of collecting information and exchanging it between the different American posts involved in the management of the crisis was carried out with exemplary efficiency. In this respect, crisis-induced stress turned out to be functional rather than debilitating. The creativity with which the resultant data were interpreted, however, did not exhibit the same positive effects. Receptivity to new information varied enormously from one individual to another. But on the whole, bureaucrats processed new information more objectively and assessed existing information more thoroughly and critically than their political masters. Successive Soviet notes, for example, were subjected to the most detailed and searching scrutiny in an attempt to uncover every nuance and hint of change in the adversary's position. The political masters, however, and General Clay, who was a highly political animal, tended, especially during the phases of peak stress, to interpret new information in a way which conformed with their preexisting beliefs and images. The cognitive rigidity noted earlier was not conducive to unbiased, sophisticated, and integrative information processing.

Consultation

Two more research questions were posed about consultation by actors during international crises: what are the effects of changing stress on (4) the types and size of consultative units; and (5) group participation in the consultative process? The relevant findings from experimental work on groups suggests that "as stress increases, both the frequency and intensity of interaction tend to rise," and this, in turn, may give rise to standardized patterns of behavior.[7]

What does America's experience during the Berlin crisis indicate about the stress-consultation nexus? Basically, as stress rose, the number of persons and groups consulted increased and the frequency of interaction between them intensified, while declining stress was accompanied only by a slow and partial contraction of the consultative circle.

During the pre-crisis period, the persons consulted were mainly experts from within the government; the consultative process was predominantly institutional rather than ad hoc, and the involvement of the top decision-makers remained limited. America's allies, however, were consulted with increasing frequency both through the American Ambassadors to London and Paris and through the Military Governors in Germany.

Rising stress during the crisis period was accompanied by a deeper involvement of the top decision-makers in the consultative process and by an intensification of inter-Allied consultation at all levels. The American decision-makers also expanded the consultative circle by turning to Republican leaders, especially Vandenberg and Dulles, for advice and support and by seeking the views of a greater number of foreign policy and defense officials. The influence of the defense officials and military chiefs increased markedly, reflecting the growing preoccupation with the danger of war. The forums for consultation were both institutional and ad hoc; but as the crisis intensified, they became increasingly ad hoc.

During the post-crisis period, there was a slow and barely perceptible move from the frequent, highly intensive, and highly extensive patterns of consultation which prevailed at the height of

---

7. Ibid., p. 289.

the crisis towards the preceding pre-crisis patterns. The Allies continued to be consulted fully at every stage until the crisis was resolved, although these interactions were not subject to the same time pressure as during the crisis period and for the most part dealt with less critical issues. Consultations with representatives of the competing domestic political elite were also continued until the crisis was resolved and formed an important feature of the bipartisan foreign policy to which the leaders of both parties were committed. It is only within the executive branch that a direct link between the level of stress and the size and type of the consultative unit can be discerned. With the decline in stress, the consultative circle gradually contracted and presidential involvement became less frequent. The tendency to work through informal and ad hoc groups of advisers, which suited Truman's personal style, was reversed in favor of more regular forums and systematic procedures of consultation.

In the final section of Chapter 6, we noted the advantage of employing the refined, disaggregated concept of "consultation" suggested by Alexander George in his study of presidential decision-making in foreign policy. With the aid of this concept, we sifted the voluminous evidence concerning increased consultation during the high-stress period and argued that while much of this could be attributed to the chief executive's growing interest in obtaining information and advice, consulting also served his emotional need for reassurance and moral support and his need for decisions that enjoy consensus and legitimacy. One of the paradoxical findings for the crisis period as a whole is that the increase in the volume of consultation was accompanied by some deterioration in the quality of information processing. The paradox disappears if we interpret this in the light of the chief executive's resort to increased consultation for purposes other than satisfying his needs for information and analysis. Such an interpretation also explains a paradox pertaining to the post-crisis period: the persistence of close contacts with Republican leaders, ending with the nomination of John Foster Dulles as Acting Chairman of the U.S. Delegation to the United Nations, notwithstanding the decrease in the level of stress experienced by the chief executive. The explanation is eminently simple: these contacts served the domestic political need for decisions resting on a broad consensus—a need that was connected only partially to the level of international tension.

Decisional Forums

Our analysis of settings for crisis decisions focuses on two other research questions: what are the effects of changing crisis-induced stress on (6) the size and structure of decisional forums; and (7) authority patterns within decisional units? Holsti and George have noted that both experimental and historical studies have consistently shown that "in high stress situations decision groups tend to become smaller."[8]

The 1948 Berlin crisis conforms with this well-supported proposition. The seriousness of the threat and the need for speed conspired to secure the involvement of a relatively small number of top officials and politicians. While opinion was canvased at the lower levels of the bureaucratic hierarchy and outside the government, decisional authority was concentrated in the hands of a small group. This centralization and elevation of the handling of the crisis within the policymaking establishment was indeed one of the most striking features of this superpower confrontation.

Another especially important point to note is that the crisis decisional forums were of an overwhelmingly ad hoc nature. Only two decisions (13 and 16) were taken by a large and formal body—the National Security Council—and even these were, strictly speaking, recommendations rather than decisions. All of the other eight decisions of the crisis period were taken either by individual policymakers or by improvised meetings of policymakers and high-ranking officials. Bypassing the elaborate institutional machinery of the 1947 National Security Act, Truman acted swiftly and informally through a small group of people who held high positions in areas relating to national security. The critical decision to stay in Berlin, for example, was made at an ad hoc meeting in the White House on June 28 at which the Chief Executive was surrounded by a select group of advisers who constituted an elite within an elite.

Threat perception, war danger, and time pressure also increased the felt need for effective leadership. This gave rise, in turn, to a more centralized and hierarchical pattern of decision-making. Presidential involvement in and control over decision-making on Berlin increased markedly with the transition from the pre-crisis to the crisis period. Having left the handling of the Berlin problem at the level of the bureaucrats, Truman now asserted his personal au-

---

8. Ibid., p. 288.

thority; and with the airlift decision of June 26, he tipped the scales decisively in favor of firmness. His more explicit ruling of June 28 was another notable example of the assertion of presidential leadership in crisis. Truman continued to play an active and pivotal role and to provide resolute leadership within the decisional units, both institutional and ad hoc, until the end of the crisis period.

Decision-making became less centralized and less hierarchical under the impact of declining stress. There was also a shift away from improvised forums and procedures and a gradual return to working through the usual machinery. As the issues confronting the United States moved away from the critical area of war and peace, personal involvement and leadership from the President became less pronounced, while the Secretary of State and the senior foreign policy officials became more influential, and the National Security Council established itself as a major instrument of governmental policymaking. A clear link is thus discernible between the level of stress and the size and structure of decisional forums and the patterns of authority within them.

Alternatives: Search and Evaluation

This aspect of our inquiry focused on two other research questions derived from the model: what are the effects of changing stress on (8) the search for and evaluation of alternatives; and (9) the perceived range of available alternatives? A major finding of other empirical studies is that stress is liable to reduce the breadth and quality of the search for alternative courses of action. Another is that the evaluation of alternatives and their consequences tends to be less constructive, the costs and benefits receive less critical scrutiny, and the analysis is curtailed by the pressure for rapid closure.[9]

The search for and subsequent evaluation of alternatives are a crucial aspect of coping, but they are also an aspect that is highly vulnerable to the effects of stress in general and to time pressure in particular. During the Berlin pre-crisis period, search and evaluation activities were limited in scope and superficial in quality. A number of suggestions were considered by the President and his advisers on March 31 in response to Clay's request for instructions for dealing with the Soviet note announcing traffic restrictions. Given the low level of the perceived threat and the very low likeli-

9. Ibid., pp. 290–291.

hood of war, only routine procedures were used to cope with the immediate problem. The need to react quickly, which Clay heavily underlined, left little scope for seeking innovative solutions or for carefully considering the long-term implications of the proposed courses of action. By a rapid process of elimination, it was decided to authorize Clay to send test trains through the Russian checkpoints (Decision 3). The fundamental question of the American commitment to staying in Berlin was not thought through, and, as a result, the Administration had no clear policy with which to confront the full-scale crisis that had been long in the making.

This failure in policymaking constituted an important element in the development of the Berlin crisis. Despite the ample strategic warning of possible Soviet pressure against West Berlin, and despite the mini-blockade during April, U.S. policymakers did not make effective use of the time available either to formulate their commitment to West Berlin and to convey that commitment in a credible way to the Soviets in an effort to deter them from mounting the blockade, or to reduce the commitment to Berlin in an effort to limit the political and diplomatic costs of eventual withdrawal. Not the least of the reasons for the Truman Administration's failure to take advantage of the strategic warning available to it was the existence inside the Administration of deep differences of opinion regarding the wisdom of trying to remain in Berlin in the face of Soviet pressure. To take the warning seriously would have involved the Administration in making some extremely difficult and unpleasant choices; and under the circumstances, it was tempting to slip into the dangerous practice of waiting for the next Soviet move instead of clarifying in advance the nature of the American commitment or lack of commitment to the defense of Berlin.

Substantive search and evaluation activities were initiated only after the Soviets severed all land routes to Berlin on June 24. Despite the high level of stress which this action produced, the American decision-makers considered a great variety of responses, including a diplomatic protest to Moscow, retaliatory measures, and military action. The initial responses, however, were the product of individual rather than group decisions. Both Clay, who launched the airlift (Decision 7), and Truman, who placed the airlift on a full-scale and organized basis (Decision 9), acted on their own initiative and in the face of strong disagreements among their advisers. As far as America's long-term policy in relation to Berlin was concerned, three alternatives were considered at the Pentagon meeting on June 27, and a clear-cut choice was made at the highest level the following day. But the evaluation of the alternatives was somewhat hurried and lacking in depth, and Truman's decision did not reflect a careful weighing of the costs, benefits, and risks likely to be incurred through the defense of Berlin.

It would be wrong to conclude, however, that evidence from the Berlin crisis reveals an inverse relationship between stress and the quality of evaluation. The evaluation of alternatives was not carried out systematically by one governmental organ specifically charged with that responsibility. But the challenge was a complex one and required responses at the economic, diplomatic, propaganda, and military levels as well as a single strategic choice. A very large part of decision-making time in the high-stress period was devoted to assessing alternatives, and some decisions were preceded by a thorough examination of their implications and possible consequences. This was particularly true of proposals for military action, such as the forward deployment of the B-29s (Decision 13). Clay's proposal for sending through an armed convoy was scrutinized from different angles by different groups and over a long period before it was finally rejected as too risky. The pressure for premature closure of the evaluative process was effectively resisted; and at the National Security Council meeting of June 22, the task of evaluating alternatives was carried out with great skill and discrimination. The expanded airlift option was not chosen, as happens so often, simply because it was favored by the leader, but only after a searching and critical examination of its merits and shortcomings in relation to other options.

Moreover, the choice of the expanded airlift (Decision 16) did not terminate the process of searching for and evaluating alternatives. The Policy Planning Staff under Kennan's direction were charged with analyzing the broader aspects of the Berlin problem and formulating plans for consideration by their governmental superiors. In their search for new options, the Policy Planning Staff combined penetrating analysis with innovative and forward thinking, and the result was a series of imaginative plans which placed the Berlin problem firmly in the context of the struggle for Germany as a whole. On the military side, the Joint Chiefs of Staff also injected some controversial, if rather different, proposals to the policy review undertaken by the National Security Council in October 1948. But the success of the airlift was so great that the decision-makers became wedded to it ever more closely as a means of defeating the blockade without halting or modifying their policy towards Germany. In short, while search activity was stepped up under the impact of declining stress, generating a number of unforeseen options, the quality of evaluation at the top did not display the same benign effects.

The effects of changing stress on the perceived range of alternatives can be studied from different perspectives, but since crisis alternatives are often considered by small groups, the study of group dynamics provides a highly relevant perspective. It has been persuasively argued that in stressful situations, a group may discourage individual members from questioning its dominant premises, perceptions, and preferred ways of responding.[10] Irving Janis, the author of the "groupthink" hypothesis, has described groupthink as "a mode of thinking that people engage in when they are deeply involved in a cohesive in-group, when its members' striving for unanimity override their motivation to realistically appraise alternative courses of action."[11] One result of this suppression of disagreements and criticisms is "a tendency for the collective judgements arising out of group discussion to shift towards riskier courses of action than individual members would otherwise be prepared to take."[12]

In 1948, however, the makers of American foreign policy did not become "victims of groupthink" under the impact of crisis-induced stress, and groupthink certainly did not narrow the perceived range of alternatives in the interest of maintaining group cohesion. As we have seen, a very wide range of alternatives was considered, and, with some exceptions, the selection of the preferred choice was preceded by full and sometimes vigorous debates. Initially, there was even disagreement on the wisdom of trying to defend Berlin, with Royall expressing anxiety that a firm commitment might lead to a situation where the United States might have to fight its way in. After this important policy question was settled, further disagreement developed concerning the relative merits of a land convoy and an airlift. Robert Murphy reported later that at the meeting of July 22 he was discouraged from pressing for a con-

10. Ibid., pp. 266–267.
11. Irving L. Janis, *Victims of Groupthink: A Psychological Study of Foreign Policy Decisions and Fiascoes* (Boston: Houghton Mifflin, 1972), p. 9.
12. Ibid., p. 6.

voy, although he was given a fair chance to do so, by the evident strength of the opposition. But the overall picture at this meeting, and at others which involved fewer participants, is that of frank and open discussion of several alternatives rather than that of a stifling conformity and "concurrence-seeking."

Nor is there any trace of a shift toward riskier courses of action in response to the blockade as a result of groupthink. The crisis which locked the two superpowers in a direct confrontation also fostered an acute awareness of the risks and dangers of an outbreak of armed hostilities. Such striving towards unanimity as may have existed in this stressful situation was definitely insufficient to nullify the critical judgment of the individual participants.[13] A vigilant appraisal of alternatives in order to avert a slide to war, rather than a collective misjudgment of risks arising out of group dynamics, was one of the key features of the American handling of the Berlin crisis, and one which contributed in no small measure to the peaceful resolution of this dangerous Cold War crisis.

What emerges only gradually from our detailed reconstruction of the course of the crisis is that the hesitant and improvised response that U.S. policymakers undertook in an effort to cope with the dilemmas and avoid the unpleasant choices that were created by the ground blockade acquired the elements of a novel strategy that promised to be, and later proved to be, adaptive. Alexander George, labeling this strategy the "test of capabilities within very restrictive ground rules," articulated its rationale and suggested some of the conditions under which it may be preferable to other, more familiar strategies:

> The leaders of a country may resort to another strategy when they are confronted with a low-level challenge to which they cannot or do not wish to respond by means of either the quick, decisive or the coercive strategy. Caught in this predicament the defending power may decide, however reluctantly, to accept a test of capabilities within the narrow framework of limitations and ground rules implied by the carefully chosen opening action of its opponent. Even though these initial rules are clearly disadvantageous, the defending power accepts the challenge without, for the time being, escalating the conflict. . . .
>
> This strategy is clearly more conservative than either the quick,

---

13. For a perceptive discussion of "groupthink" on which I have drawn in the preceding paragraph, see Phil Williams, *Crisis Management: Confrontation and Diplomacy in the Nuclear Age* (London: Martin Robertson, 1976), pp. 78–83.

decisive military option or coercive diplomacy. However, accepting a test of capabilities under the invidious ground rules defined by the opponent does not exclude resort to one of the other two strategies later on, should it become necessary to do so in order to avoid defeat.[14]

In the Berlin crisis, it proved unnecessary to resort to other strategies because the United States, as the defending power, succeeded in reversing the expected outcome of the test of capabilities within the ground rules chosen by the opponent and thereby transferred back to the opponent the onus for deciding whether to engage in risky escalation or to accept defeat. Essentially the same strategy was employed by the United States, again successfully, in the Quemoy crisis of 1958, which was provoked by a Chinese Communist artillery blockade. Indirect and limited American naval assistance enabled the Chinese Nationalists to resupply the garrison on Quemoy. The next move was up to the initiators, who chose to discontinue the artillery shelling rather than escalate the crisis. Neither in Berlin nor in Quemoy was it necessary to embark on a policy of limited escalation backed by threats of additional escalation in order to force the opponent to abandon its blockade actions. To have done so would have been tantamount to adopting the strategy of coercive diplomacy, which involves a test of resolution rather than a test of capabilities within well-defined and stable ground rules.[15] Both historical precedents help to identify and legitimize the "test of capabilities within very restrictive ground rules" as a strategy which is not only unconventional from the military standpoint but which, if kept in mind, adds to the options available for coping with certain kinds of crises.

Whether this strategy was the best one in 1948 from America's standpoint is a question which cannot be answered with any certainty. Merely to raise it leads one step further away from the impact of crisis-induced stress on the processes of decision-making—the central theme of this concluding chapter—and into the much more subjective realm of evaluating the content of policy. To attempt to answer it, however guardedly, calls for a comparison between the actual outcome of the crisis and what might have hap-

14. Alexander L. George, David K. Hall, and William E. Simons, *The Limits of Coercive Diplomacy: Laos, Cuba, Vietnam* (Boston: Little, Brown, 1971), pp. 20–21.
15. Ibid.

CONCLUSIONS 421

pened had another course of action been adopted. History, alas, does not disclose its alternatives, so a comparison of this kind must perforce be speculative.

At one end of the spectrum, there was the option of resorting to quick and decisive military action. As we have seen, General Clay was not only a forceful advocate of this option during the crisis, but he remained convinced afterwards that an armed convoy, if authorized, would have reached Berlin. More recently, it has been suggested that the general's proposal to break the ground blockade may have had more validity than his superiors in Washington were willing to concede. "The historian cannot avoid the conclusion," writes Daniel Yergin in his *Shattered Peace*, "that the Russians would either have backed down or been at a disadvantage in a larger confrontation."[16] The first part of the conclusion, however, is not only avoidable but quite unwarranted in the absence of any direct evidence concerning the intentions of the Soviet leaders. In the second scenario of a larger confrontation, the Russians would have enjoyed a decisive advantage in conventional forces and would have only been placed at a disadvantage in the highly unlikely event that the Americans cold-bloodedly decided to use the atomic bomb in defense of a position which was not in itself of vital interest to the country's security. Most probably, the Russians would have reacted to an armed convoy neither by backing down nor by provoking a larger confrontation but by interposing passive and nonviolent obstacles along the highly vulnerable Helmstedt-Berlin highway. It was precisely the knowledge that a convoy could be frustrated and its initiators humiliated in this way, without a single shot being fired, that led the Joint Chiefs of Staff to turn so resolutely against Clay's proposal.

At the other end of the spectrum, there was the option, favored by the Joint Chiefs of Staff and other American officials, of withdrawing from Berlin. In view of the anomaly involved in basing America's European policy, if only at the symbolic level, on a city in which it enjoyed little power and whose possession was not in the long run vital to its European policy, this option was not without its attractions. The form in which it was usually presented was not one of an abrupt and naked retreat under Soviet threats but of

16. Daniel Yergin, *Shattered Peace: The Origins of the Cold War and the National Security State* (Boston: Houghton Mifflin, 1977), p. 380.

creating in the shortest possible time a West German government and a security system in Western Europe, backed by U.S. political and military guarantees, which would have enabled the United States to eventually disengage from Berlin with the minimum amount of damage to its power and prestige. Exaggerated notions of Berlin's importance as the symbol of American resistance to the spread of communism, of which Clay was the primary purveyor, worked to curtail the support for this option. But the decisive reason against its adoption was that Truman, Marshall, and other American leaders shared this perception of a retreat from Berlin as potentially disastrous to their entire policy of building an anti-communist Western Europe. Thus, if the convoy idea was rejected as militarily unsound, the planned withdrawal idea was rejected as unsound from the long-term political standpoint, and there is no compelling reason for thinking that either of these alternatives would have better served America's interests than the intermediate strategy of the airlift.

But whatever one may think of the relative merits of these three principal courses of action, it is reasonably clear from the actual historical record explored in this study that stress, as the central concomitant of crisis, can have positive effects which outweigh the negative effects on the performance of selected cognitive and decision-making tasks. A single case study on its own cannot, of course, conclusively invalidate or substantiate theoretical propositions on the crisis behavior of states. But there is sufficient evidence here to at least call into question the universal validity of the premise that high and protracted stress seriously and adversely affects decision processes and outcomes. On the whole, the American policymakers stood up to stress well and coped fairly effectively and even creatively with the acute dilemmas posed by the Soviet ground blockade. Unquestionably, there were instances of impaired cognitive performance, especially manifestations of greater rigidity, which could be traced directly to the intense stress they were experiencing, but these were not sufficiently pervasive to disrupt what was in essence a rational and calculated process of decision-making. Moreover, the performance of various decisional tasks was actually helped and improved by escalating stress. Thus, the transition from the pre-crisis to the crisis period was marked by a shift towards more efficient processing of information, more extensive consultation, more systematic and comprehensive consideration of alternatives, and more centralized and effective decision-making. To say all this is not to claim that high stress is not a potentially dangerous ingredient in crisis decision-making but merely to suggest that its beneficial effects can be greater than is commonly believed. With respect to the precious cognitive abilities which are so crucial in times of crisis, it has been suggested that the law of supply and demand seems to operate in a perverse manner: as crisis increases the need for these abilities, it also diminishes the supply.[17] A small grain of comfort may be derived from the knowledge that in the intense, critical, and exceptionally protracted superpower confrontation which centered on Berlin, the law of supply and demand did not operate invariably in so perverse and invidious a manner.

17. Holsti, "Theories of Crisis Decision-Making," p. 110.

Bibliography

ARCHIVES

Harry S. Truman Library, Independence, Missouri

Dean Acheson Papers
Clark M. Clifford Papers
Matthew J. Connelly Papers
Harry S. Truman Papers
   Central Files
   Confidential Files
   Official File
   President's Secretary File
   Post-Presidential Files

National Archives, Washington, D.C.

Diplomatic Branch
   RG 59: General Records of the Department of State
Modern Military Branch
   RG 218: Records of the Joint Chiefs of Staff
   RG 260: Records of the Office of Military Government for Germany
   RG 319: Records of the Army Staff
   RG 330: Records of the Office of the Secretary of Defense
   RG 335: Records of the Office of the Secretary of the Army

Princeton University Library, Princeton, New Jersey

Bernard M. Baruch Papers
John Foster Dulles Papers
George F. Kennan Papers
Arthur Krock Papers

Public Record Office, London

Foreign Office Papers
Cabinet Minutes and Papers

UNPUBLISHED DIARIES

James V. Forrestal Diaries, Princeton University Library
William Leahy Diary, Library of Congress

ORAL HISTORIES

Dulles Oral History Collection, Princeton University Library
- General Lucius D. Clay
- General Curtis LeMay
- Robert Murphy

Truman Oral History Collection, Harry S. Truman Library
- Lucius D. Clay
- William H. Draper
- Elbridge Durbrow
- George M. Elsey
- John D. Hickerson
- Charles E. Saltzman

NEWSPAPERS

The Christian Science Monitor
Le Monde (Paris)
The New York Herald Tribune
The New York Times
The Times (London)

DOCUMENTS AND OFFICIAL PUBLICATIONS

Berlin (West) Senate. Berlin: *Quellen und Documente, 1945–1951.* 2 vols. Berlin: Heinz Spitzing Verlag, 1964.

Dennett, Raymond, and Turner, Robert K. *Documents on American Foreign Relations.* Vols. 10 (1948) and 11 (1949). Princeton: Princeton University Press, 1950.

Etzold, Thomas H., and Gaddis, John Lewis, eds. *Containment: Documents on American Foreign Policy and Strategy, 1945–1950.* New York: Columbia University Press, 1978.

Gablentz, O. M. van der. *Documents on the Status of Berlin, 1944–1959.* Munich: Oldenbourg Verlag, 1959.

Great Britain, Cmd. 7534. *Germany: An Account of the Events Leading Up to a Reference of the Berlin Question to the United Nations.* London: His Majesty's Stationery Office, 1948.

Great Britain, Cmnd. 1552. *Selected Documents on Germany and the Question of Berlin.* London: His Majesty's Stationery Office, 1961.

Great Britain, Control Commission for Germany. *Notes on the Blockade of Berlin.* London, 1948.

Hansard. House of Commons Debates. (London).

Hildermeyer, Wolfgang, and Hindrichs, Guenter, eds. *Documents on Berlin, 1943–1963*. Munich: Oldenbourg Verlag, 1963.

Molter, A. *Berlin, 1944–1964*. Paris: Western European Union, 1964.

Oppen, Beate Ruhm von. *Documents on Germany under Occupation, 1945–1954*. London: Oxford University Press, 1955.

Public Papers of the Presidents of the United States: Harry S. Truman. Vols. for 1947, 1948, and 1949. Washington, D.C.: U.S. Government Printing Office, 1963–1964.

Royal Institute of International Affairs. *Documents on International Affairs, 1947–1948*. Edited by Margaret Carlyle. London: Oxford University Press, 1952.

———. *Documents on International Affairs, 1949–1950*. Edited by Margaret Carlyle. London: Oxford University Press, 1953.

Union of Soviet Socialist Republics, Ministry of Foreign Affairs. *The Soviet Union and the Berlin Question (Documents)*. Moscow, 1948.

———. *The Soviet Union and the Berlin Question (Documents)*. 2nd series. Moscow, 1949.

United Nations. *Official Records of the Security Council*. 1948–1949.

U.S. Department of State. *The Berlin Crisis: A Report on the Moscow Discussions*. Washington, D.C.: U.S. Government Printing Office, 1948.

———. *Department of State Bulletin*. 1946–1949.

———. *Foreign Relations of the United States, 1945: The Conference of Berlin (Potsdam)*. 2 vols. Washington, D.C.: U.S. Government Printing Office, 1960.

———. *Foreign Relations of the United States, 1946*. Vol. 2: *Council of Foreign Ministers*. Washington, D.C.: U.S. Government Printing Office, 1970.

———. *Foreign Relations of the United States, 1946*. Vol. 5: *The British Commonwealth: Western and Central Europe*. Washington, D.C.: U.S. Government Printing Office, 1969.

———. *Foreign Relations of the United States, 1946*. Vol. 6: *Eastern Europe; the Soviet Union*. Washington, D.C.: U.S. Government Printing Office, 1969.

———. *Foreign Relations of the United States, 1947*. Vol. 2: *Council of Foreign Ministers; Germany and Austria*. Washington, D.C.: U.S. Government Printing Office, 1972.

———. *Foreign Relations of the United States, 1948*. Vol. 1: *General; The United Nations* (Part 2). Washington, D.C.: U.S. Government Printing Office, 1976.

———. *Foreign Relations of the United States, 1948*. Vol. 2: *Germany and Austria*. Washington, D.C.: U.S. Government Printing Office, 1973.

———. *Foreign Relations of the United States, 1948*. Vol. 3: *Western Europe*. Washington, D.C.: U.S. Government Printing Office, 1974.

———. *Foreign Relations of the United States, 1948*. Vol. 4: *Eastern Europe; the Soviet Union*. Washington, D.C.: U.S. Government Printing Office, 1974.

―――. *Foreign Relations of the United States, 1949.* Vol. 3: *Council of Foreign Ministers; Germany and Austria.* Washington, D.C.: U.S. Government Printing Office, 1974.

―――. *Germany 1947–1949: The Story in Documents.* Washington, D.C.: U.S. Government Printing Office, 1950.

U.S. Office of Military Government for Germany. *Documented Chronology of Political Developments Regarding Germany.* Berlin, 1948.

U.S. Senate Committee on Foreign Relations. *Documents on Germany, 1944–1959.* Washington, D.C.: U.S. Government Printing Office, 1959.

BOOKS AND ARTICLES

Acheson, Dean. *A Democrat Looks at His Party.* New York: Harper and Row, 1955.

―――. *Power and Diplomacy.* Cambridge, Mass.: Harvard University Press, 1958.

―――. *Present at the Creation: My Years in the State Department.* New York: Norton, 1969.

―――. *Sketches from Life.* London: Hamish Hamilton, 1960.

Adenauer, Konrad. *Memoirs, 1945–1953.* London: Weidenfeld and Nicolson, 1966.

Adler, Les K., and Paterson, Thomas G. "Red Fascism: The Merger of Nazi Germany and Soviet Russia in the American Image of Totalitarianism." *American Historical Review*, Vol. 75 (April 1970).

Adomeit, Hannes. "Soviet Risk-Taking and Crisis Behaviour: From Confrontation to Coexistence?" *Adelphi Papers*, No. 101. London: The International Institute for Strategic Studies, 1973.

Allison, Graham T. *Essence of Decision.* Boston: Little, Brown, 1971.

Almond, Gabriel A. *The American People and Foreign Policy.* New York: Harcourt Brace, 1950.

Alperovitz, Gar. *Atomic Diplomacy: Hiroshima and Potsdam.* New York: Vintage, 1967.

―――. *Cold War Essays.* New York: Anchor, 1970.

Ambrose, Stephen E. *Rise to Globalism: American Foreign Policy Since 1938.* Harmondsworth, England: Penguin, 1971.

―――, and Barber, James A., Jr., eds. *The Military and American Society.* New York: The Free Press, 1972.

Anderson, Dillon. "The President and National Security." *Atlantic Monthly*, No. 197 (January 1956).

Anderson, Patrick. *The President's Men.* New York: Doubleday, 1969.

Armacost, Michael A. *The Foreign Relations of the United States.* Belmont, California: Dickenson, 1969.

Arnold-Forster, Mark. *The Siege of Berlin.* London: Collins, 1979.

Auriol, Vincent. *Journal du Septennat, 1947–1954.* Vol. 2: *1948.* Paris: Armand Colin, 1974.

―――. *Journal du Septennat, 1947–1954.* Vol. 3: *1949.* Paris: Armand Colin, 1977.

Axelrod, Robert, ed. *Structure of Decision.* Princeton: Princeton University Press, 1976.
Backer, John H. *The Decision to Divide Germany: American Foreign Policy in Transition.* Durham, N.C.: Duke University Press, 1978.
———. *Priming the German Economy: American Occupational Policies, 1945–1948.* Durham, N.C.: Duke University Press, 1971.
Balabkins, Nicholas. *Germany Under Direct Controls: Economic Aspects of Industrial Disarmament, 1945–1948.* New Brunswick, N.J.: Rutgers University Press, 1964.
Balfour, Michael, and Mair, John. *Four-Power Control in Germany and Austria, 1945–1946.* London: Oxford University Press, 1956.
Ball, George W. *Diplomacy for a Crowded World.* London: Bodley Head, 1976.
Barnet, Richard J. *The Giants: Russia and America.* New York: Simon and Schuster, 1977.
Bell, Coral. *The Conventions of Crisis.* London: Oxford University Press, 1971.
———. *Negotiations from Strength.* New York: Knopf, 1963.
Bennett, Jack. "The German Currency Reform." *Annals of the American Academy of Political and Social Science,* Vol. 267 (January 1950).
Bennett, Lowell. *Berlin Bastion.* Frankfurt, Germany: Friedrich Rudl, 1951.
Betts, Richard K. *Soldiers, Statesmen, and Cold War Crises.* Cambridge, Mass.: Harvard University Press, 1977.
Bobrow, Davis B., et al. "Understanding How Others Treat Crisis: A Multimethod Approach." *International Studies Quarterly,* Vol. 21, No. 1 (March 1977).
Bohlen, Charles E. *The Transformation of American Foreign Policy.* New York: Norton, 1969.
———. *Witness to History, 1929–1969.* London: Weidenfeld and Nicolson, 1973.
Boulding, Kenneth. "National Images and International Systems." *Journal of Conflict Resolution,* Vol. 3, No. 2 (1959).
Brandt, Willy. *My Road to Berlin* (as told to Leo Lania). London: Peter Davies, 1960.
Brecher, Michael. *Decisions in Israel's Foreign Policy.* London: Oxford University Press, 1974.
———. *The Foreign Policy System of Israel: Setting, Images, Process.* London: Oxford University Press, 1972.
———. "State Behavior in International Crisis: A Model." *Journal of Conflict Resolution,* Vol. 23, No. 3 (September 1979).
———, ed. *Studies in Crisis Behavior.* New Brunswick, N.J.: Transaction Books, 1979.
———, with Geist, Benjamin. *Decisions in Crisis: Israel, 1967 and 1973.* Berkeley and Los Angeles: University of California Press, 1980.
———; Steinberg, Blema; and Stein, Janice. "A Framework for Research on Foreign Policy Behavior." *Journal of Conflict Resolution,* Vol. 13, No. 1 (March 1969).

Brenner, Michael J. "Bureaucratic Politics and Foreign Policy." *Armed Forces and Society*, Vol. 2 (1977).

Brodie, Bernard. *Escalation and the Nuclear Option*. Princeton: Princeton University Press, 1966.

Brown, Colin, and Mooney, Peter. *Cold War to Detente*. London: Heinemann, 1976.

Brown, Seyom. *The Faces of Power: Constancy and Change in U.S. Foreign Policy from Truman to Johnson*. New York: Columbia University Press, 1968.

Buchan, Alistair. *Crisis Management: The New Diplomacy*. The Atlantic Papers. NATO Series II. Boulogne-sur-Seine, France: Atlantic Institute, 1966.

Bundy, McGeorge, ed. *The Pattern of Responsibility*. Boston: Houghton Mifflin, 1952.

Byrnes, James F. *All in One Lifetime*. New York: Harper, 1958.

———. *Speaking Frankly*. London: Heinemann, 1947.

Calvocoressi, Peter. *Survey of International Affairs, 1947–1948*. London: Oxford University Press, 1952.

———. *Survey of International Affairs, 1949–1950*. London: Oxford University Press, 1953.

Campbell, John C. *The United States in World Affairs, 1948–1949*. New York: Harper and Row, 1949.

Carr, Albert Z. *Truman, Stalin and Peace*. New York: Doubleday, 1950.

Charles, Max. *Berlin Blockade*. London: Allan Wingate, 1959.

Chauvel, Jean. *Commentaire: d'Alger à Berne, 1944–1952*. Paris: Fayard, 1972.

Clarke, Michael. "Foreign Policy Implementation: Problems and Approaches." *British Journal of International Studies*, Vol. 5, No. 2 (July 1979).

Clay, Lucius D. "Berlin." *Foreign Affairs*, Vol. 41, No. 1 (October 1962).

———. *Decision in Germany*. New York: Doubleday, 1950.

———. *Germany and the Fight for Freedom*. Cambridge, Mass.: Harvard University Press, 1950.

Cochran, Bert. *Harry Truman and the Crisis Presidency*. New York: Funk and Wagnalls, 1973.

Coelho, George V.; Hamburg, David A.; and Adams, John E., eds. *Coping and Adaptation*. New York: Basic Books, 1974.

Cohen, Bernard C. *The Public's Impact on Foreign Policy*. Boston: Little, Brown, 1973.

Collier, Richard. *Bridge Across the Sky: The Berlin Blockade and Airlift, 1948–1949*. London: Macmillan, 1978.

Condit, Kenneth W. *The History of the Joint Chiefs of Staff*. Vol. 2: *1947–1949*. (Washington, D.C.: Historical Division, Joint Secretariat, Joint Chiefs of Staff, 1976). Record Group 218, Records of the United States Joint Chiefs of Staff, The National Archives.

Connally, Tom. *My Name Is Tom Connally*. New York: Crowell, 1954.

Crabb, Cecil V., Jr. *Policy-Makers and Critics: Conflicting Theories of American Foreign Policy*. New York: Praeger, 1976.

Cutler, Robert. "The Development of the National Security Council." *Foreign Affairs*, Vol. 34, No. 3 (April 1956).
Daniels, Jonathan. *The Man of Independence*. Philadelphia: Lippincott, 1950.
Davidson, Eugene. *The Death and Life of Germany: An Account of the American Occupation*. London: Jonathan Cape, 1959.
Davison, W. Phillips. *The Berlin Blockade: A Study in Cold War Politics*. Princeton: Princeton University Press, 1958.
DeConde, Alexander. *The American Secretary of State: An Interpretation*. London: Pall Mall Press, 1962.
Dennet, Raymond, and Johnson, Joseph E., eds. *Negotiating with the Russians*. Boston: World Peace Foundation, 1951.
De Rivera, Joseph. *The Psychological Dimension of Foreign Policy*. Columbus, Ohio: Charles E. Merrill, 1968.
Destler, I. M. *Presidents, Bureaucrats and Foreign Policy*. Princeton: Princeton University Press, 1972.
Deutscher, Isaac. *Stalin: A Political Biography*. Revised edition. Harmondsworth, England: Penguin, 1966.
Divine, Robert A. "The Cold War and the Election of 1948." *Journal of American History*, Vol. 59 (June 1972).
———. *Foreign Policy and U.S. Presidential Elections: 1940, 1948*. New York: Franklin Watts, 1974.
Djilas, Milovan. *Conversations with Stalin*. Harmondsworth, England: Penguin, 1962.
Donnelly, Desmond. *Struggle for the World: The Cold War from Its Origins in 1917*. London: Collins, 1965.
Donovan, Frank. *Bridge in the Sky*. New York: David McKay, 1968.
Donovan, John C. *The Cold Warriors: A Policy-Making Elite*. Lexington, Mass.: D. C. Heath, 1974.
Donovan, Robert. *Conflict and Crisis: The Presidency of Harry S. Truman, 1945–1948*. New York: Norton, 1977.
Druks, Herbert. *Harry S. Truman and the Russians, 1945–1953*. New York: Robert Speller, 1966.
Dulles, Eleanor Lancing. *American Foreign Policy in the Making*. New York: Harper and Row, 1968.
Dulles, John Foster. *War or Peace*. New York: Macmillan, 1950.
Elder, Robert E. *The Policy Machine*. Syracuse, N.Y.: Syracuse University Press, 1960.
Epstein, Leon D. *Britain—Uneasy Ally*. Chicago: University of Chicago Press, 1954.
Fairman, Charles. "The President as Commander-in-Chief." *Journal of Politics*, Vol. 2, No. 1 (February 1949).
Falk, Stanley C. "The National Security Council Under Truman, Eisenhower and Kennedy." *Political Science Quarterly*, Vol. 79, No. 1 (1964).
Falkowski, Lawrence S. *Presidents, Secretaries of State and Crises in U.S. Foreign Relations: A Model and Predictive Analysis*. Boulder, Colorado: Westview, 1978.

———, ed. *Psychological Models in International Politics*. Boulder, Colorado: Westview, 1979.

Feis, Herbert. *From Trust to Terror*. New York: Norton, 1970.

Fenno, Richard F. *The President's Cabinet*. Cambridge, Mass.: Harvard University Press, 1963.

Ferrell, Robert H. *George C. Marshall*. New York: Cooper Square, 1966.

Finlay, David J.; Holsti, Ole R.; and Fagan, Richard R. *Enemies in Politics*. Chicago: Rand McNally, 1967.

Fischer, John. "Mr. Truman's Politburo." *Harper's Magazine*, No. 211 (June 1951).

Fleming, D. F. *The Cold War and Its Origins, 1917–1960*. 2 vols. London: Allen and Unwin, 1961.

Fontaine, Andre. *History of the Cold War*. 2 vols. New York: Pantheon, 1968.

Foot, Michael. *Aneurin Bevan: A Biography*. Vol. 2: *1945–1960*. London: Davis Poynter, 1973.

Frankel, Joseph. *The Making of Foreign Policy: An Analysis of Decision-Making*. London: Oxford University Press, 1963.

Franklin, William M. "Zonal Boundaries and Access to Berlin." *World Politics*, Vol. 16, No. 1 (October 1963).

Freeland, Richard M. *The Truman Doctrine and the Origins of McCarthyism*. New York: Knopf, 1972.

Frei, Daniel, ed. *International Crisis and Crisis Management*. Westmead, England: Saxon House, 1978.

Freund, Michael. *From Cold War to Ostpolitik: Germany and the New Europe*. London: Oswald Wolff, 1972.

Gablentz, O. M. von der. *The Berlin Question and Its Relations to World Politics, 1944–1963*. Munich: Oldenbourg Verlag, 1964.

Gaddis, John Lewis. "Containment: A Reassessment." *Foreign Affairs*, Vol. 55, No. 4 (July 1977).

———. *The United States and the Origins of the Cold War, 1941–1947*. New York: Columbia University Press, 1972.

Gamson, William A., and Modigliani, Andre. *Untangling the Cold War: A Strategy for Testing Rival Theories*. Boston: Little, Brown, 1971.

Gardner, Lloyd C. "America and the German 'Problem,' 1945–1949." In *The Politics and Policies of the Truman Administration*, edited by Barton J. Bernstein. Chicago: Quadrangle, 1970.

———. *Architects of Illusion: Men and Ideas in American Foreign Policy, 1941–1949*. Chicago: Quadrangle, 1970.

Gati, Charles. "What Containment Meant." *Foreign Policy*, No. 7 (September 1972).

———, ed. *Caging the Bear: Containment and the Cold War*. Indianapolis: Bobbs-Merrill, 1974.

Geist, Benjamin. *The Six Day War: A Study in the Setting and the Process of Foreign Policy Decision-Making Under Crisis Conditions*. Ph.D. dissertation, The Hebrew University of Jerusalem, 1974.

George, Alexander L. "Case Studies and Theory: The Method of Structured, Focused Comparison." In *Diplomatic History: New Approaches*, edited by Gordon Paul Lauren. New York: The Free Press, 1979.

―――. "The 'Operational Code': A Neglected Approach to the Study of Political Leaders and Decision-Making." *International Studies Quarterly*, Vol. 13, No. 2 (June 1969).

―――. *Presidential Decisionmaking in Foreign Policy: The Effective Use of Information and Advice*. Boulder, Colorado: Westview, 1980.

―――; Hall, David K.; and Simons, William E. *The Limits of Coercive Diplomacy: Laos, Duba, Vietnam*. Boston: Little, Brown, 1971.

―――, and Smoke, Richard. *Deterrence in American Foreign Policy: Theory and Practice*. New York: Columbia University Press, 1974.

Gimbel, John. *The American Occupation of Germany: Politics and the Military, 1945–1949*. Stanford: Stanford University Press, 1968.

―――. "On the Implementation of the Potsdam Agreement: An Essay on U.S. Postwar German Policy." *Political Science Quarterly*, Vol. 87, No. 2 (June 1972).

Golay, Ford. *The Founding of the Federal Republic of Germany*. Chicago: University of Chicago Press, 1958.

Goldman, Eric F. *The Crucial Decade: America, 1945–1955*. New York: Knopf, 1956.

Gottlieb, Manuel. *The German Peace Settlement and the Berlin Crisis*. New York: Paine-Whitman, 1960.

Gowing, Margaret. *Independence and Deterrence: Britain and Atomic Energy, 1945–1952*. 2 vols. London: Macmillan, 1974.

Graebner, Norman A. *Cold War Diplomacy, 1945–1960*. Princeton: Van Norstad, 1962.

―――, ed. *An Uncertain Tradition: American Secretaries of State in the Twentieth Century*. New York: McGraw-Hill, 1961.

Grosser, Alfred. *Western Germany: From Defeat to Rearmament*. London: Allen and Unwin, 1955.

Guhin, Michael A. *John Foster Dulles: A Statesman and His Times*. New York: Columbia University Press, 1972.

Halle, Louis J. *American Foreign Policy: Theory and Reality*. London: Allen and Unwin, 1960.

―――. *The Cold War as History*. London: Chatto and Windus, 1971.

Halper, Thomas. *Foreign Policy Crises: Appearance and Reality in Decision-Making*. Columbus, Ohio: Charles E. Merrill, 1971.

Halperin, Morton H. *National Security Policy-Making*. Lexington, Mass.: D. C. Heath, 1975.

―――. "Why Bureaucrats Play Games." *Foreign Policy*, No. 2 (Spring 1971).

―――, with Priscilla Clapp and Arnold Kanter. *Bureaucratic Politics and Foreign Policy*. Washington, D.C.: Brookings Institution, 1974.

Hammond, Paul Y. *Organizing for Defense: The American Military Establishment in the Twentieth Century*. Princeton: Princeton University Press, 1961.

Hanrieder, Wolfram. *West German Foreign Policy, 1949–1963: Interna-

tional Pressure and Domestic Response. Stanford: Stanford University Press, 1967.

Harriman, W. Averell. *America and Russia in a Changing World.* London: Allen and Unwin, 1971.

Harrington, Daniel F. "Kennan, Bohlen and the Riga Axioms." *Diplomatic History,* Vol. 2 (Fall 1978).

Hartmann, Frederic H. *Germany Between East and West: The Reunification Problem.* Englewood Cliffs, N.J.: Prentice-Hall, 1965.

Hartmann, Susan M. *Truman and the 80th Congress.* Columbia: University of Missouri Press, 1971.

Haynes, Richard F. *The Awesome Power: Harry S. Truman as Commander in Chief.* Baton Rouge: Louisiana State University Press, 1973.

Heller, Deane, and Heller, David. *The Berlin Crisis.* Derby, Conn.: Monarch, 1961.

Henkin, Louis. *The Berlin Crisis and the United Nations.* New York: Carnegie Endowment for International Peace, 1959.

Herbert, Major-General E. O. "The Cold War in Berlin." *Journal of the United Service Institute,* Vol. 574 (May 1949).

Herken, Gregg. *The Winning Weapon: The Atomic Bomb and the Cold War, 1945–1950.* New York: Knopf, 1981.

Hermann, Charles F. *Crises in Foreign Policy: A Simulation Analysis.* Indianapolis: Bobbs-Merrill, 1969.

———, ed. *International Crises: Insights from Behavioral Research.* New York: The Free Press, 1972.

Hess, Gary R., ed. *America and Russia: From Cold War Confrontation to Coexistence.* New York: Thomas Crowell, 1973.

Hewlett, Richard G., and Duncan, Francis. *Atomic Shield: A History of the United States Atomic Energy Commission.* Vol. 2: 1947–1952. Washington, D.C.: U.S. Atomic Energy Commission, 1972.

Hillman, William. *Mr. President: Personal Diaries, Private Letters, Papers, and Revealing Interviews of Harry S. Truman.* London: Hutchinson, 1952.

Hilsman, Roger. *The Politics of Policy-Making in Defense and Foreign Affairs.* New York: Harper and Row, 1971.

———. *Strategic Intelligence and National Decisions.* Glencoe, Ill.: The Free Press, 1956.

Hoffmann, Erik P., and Fleron, Fredric J., Jr., eds. *The Conduct of Soviet Foreign Policy.* Chicago: Aldine, 1971.

Holsti, Ole R. *Crisis, Escalation, War.* Montreal: McGill-Queen's University Press, 1972.

———, and George, Alexander L. "The Effects of Stress on the Performance of Foreign Policy-Makers." *Political Science Annual,* Vol. 6 (1975).

Howard, Michael. "Governor General of Germany." *Times Literary Supplement,* August 19, 1974.

Howley, Frank. *Berlin Command.* New York: Putnam's, 1950.

Hoxie, R. Gordon. *Command Decisions and the Presidency.* New York: Reader's Digest Press, 1977.

Hughes, Emmet John. *The Living Presidency*. New York: Coward, McCann and Geoghegan, 1972.
Huntington, Samuel. *The Common Defense*. New York: Columbia University Press, 1961.
———. *The Soldier and the State: The Theory and Politics of Civil-Military Relations*. Cambridge, Mass.: Harvard University Press, 1957.
Hurley, Alfred F., and Ehrart, Robert C., eds. *Air Power and Warfare, The Proceedings of the Eighth Military History Symposium, United States Air Force Academy, 18–20 October 1978*. Washington, D.C.: Office of Air Force History, Headquarters United States Air Force and United States Air Force Academy, 1979.
Jackson, Henry, ed. *The National Security Council*. New York: Praeger, 1965.
Janis, Irving L. *Victims of Groupthink: A Psychological Study of Foreign Policy Decisions and Fiascoes*. Boston: Houghton Mifflin, 1972.
———, and Mann, Leon. *Decision Making*. New York: The Free Press, 1977.
Jervis, Robert. *Perception and Misperception in International Politics*. Princeton: Princeton University Press, 1976.
Jessup, Philip C. "The Berlin Blockade and the Use of the United Nations." *Foreign Affairs*, Vol. 50, No. 1 (October 1972).
———. "Park Avenue Diplomacy—Ending the Berlin Blockade." *Political Science Quarterly*, Vol. 87, No. 3 (September 1972).
Johnson, Richard T. *Managing the White House*. New York: Harper and Row, 1974.
Jones, Joseph M. *The Fifteen Weeks*. New York: Harcourt, 1955.
Kahn, Herman. *On Escalation: Metaphors and Scenarios*. New York: Praeger, 1965.
Kaiser, Karl, and Morgan, Roger, eds. *Britain and West Germany: Changing Societies and the Future of Foreign Policy*. London: Oxford University Press, 1971.
Kaufman, William, ed. *Military Policy and National Security*. Princeton: Princeton University Press, 1956.
Kelman, Herbert, ed. *International Behavior*. New York: Holt, Rinehart, and Winston, 1965.
Kennan, George F. *American Diplomacy, 1900–1950*. Chicago: University of Chicago Press, 1951.
———. *Memoirs, 1925–1950*. Boston: Little, Brown, 1967.
——— ("X"). "The Sources of Soviet Conduct." *Foreign Affairs*, Vol. 25, No. 4 (July 1947).
Kirkendall, Robert S., ed. *The Truman Period as a Research Field*. Columbia: University of Missouri Press, 1967.
Kirkpatrick, Helen P. "Advisers and Policy-Makers: The National Security Council." *American Perspectives*, No. 2 (February 1949).
Kissinger, Henry A. "Domestic Structure and Foreign Policy." *Daedalus*, Vol. 95, No. 2 (Spring 1966).

———. *The Necessity for Choice: Prospects of American Foreign Policy.* New York: Doubleday, 1962.

Klimov, Gregory. *The Terror Machine: The Inside Story of the Soviet Administration in Germany.* Translated from the German by H. C. Stevens. London: Faber and Faber, 1953.

Kolko, Joyce, and Kolko, Gabriel. *The Limits of Power: The World and United States Foreign Policy, 1945–1954.* New York: Harper and Row, 1972.

Korb, Lawrence J. *The Joint Chiefs of Staff: The First Twenty-Five Years.* Bloomington: Indiana University Press, 1976.

Krisch, Henry. *German Politics Under Soviet Occupation.* New York: Columbia University Press, 1974.

Krock, Arthur. *Memoirs.* London: Cassell, 1968.

Kuklick, Bruce. *American Policy and the Division of Germany: The Clash with Russia over Reparations.* Ithaca: Cornell University Press, 1972.

———. "The Division of Germany and the American Policy on Reparations." *Western Political Quarterly*, Vol. 22, No. 2 (June 1970).

LaFeber, Walter. *America, Russia and the Cold War, 1945–1975.* 3rd edition. New York: Wiley, 1976.

Lauren, Paul Gordon. *Diplomacy: New Approaches in History, Theory, and Policy.* New York: The Free Press, 1979.

LeMay, Curtis E., with Kantor, MacKinlay. *Mission with LeMay: My Story.* New York: Doubleday, 1965.

Leonhard, Wolfgang. *Child of the Revolution.* Translated by C. M. Woodhouse. London: Collins, 1957.

Lie, Trygve. *In the Cause of Peace: Seven Years with the United Nations.* New York: Macmillan, 1954.

Lilienthal, David E. *The Journals of David E. Lilienthal.* Vol. 2: *The Atomic Energy Years, 1945–1950.* New York: Harper and Row, 1964.

Lippmann, Walter. *The Cold War: A Study in U.S. Foreign Policy.* New York: Harper and Row, 1947.

Lowenthal, Fritz. *News from the Soviet Zone.* London: Gollancz, 1950.

McClelland, Charles A. "Access to Berlin: The Quantity and Variety of Events, 1948–1963." In *Quantitative International Politics: Insights and Evidence*, edited by J. David Singer. New York: The Free Press, 1968.

———. "The Acute International Crisis." *World Politics*, Vol. 14, No. 3 (October 1961).

———. "Crisis and Threat in the International Setting: Some Relational Concepts." Mimeographed, 1975.

McCormick, James M. "International Crises: A Note on Definition." *Western Political Quarterly*, Vol. 31, No. 3 (September 1978).

McInnis, Edgar; Hiscocks, Richard; and Spencer, Robert. *The Shaping of Postwar Germany.* London: Dent, 1960.

MacIsaac, David. "The Air Force and Strategic Thought, 1945–1951." Working Paper No. 8, International Security Studies Program. Washington, D.C.: The Woodrow Wilson International Center for Scholars, 1979.

Mackintosh, J. M. *Strategy and the Tactics of Soviet Foreign Policy*. London: Oxford University Press, 1962.

McLellan, David S. *Dean Acheson: The State Department Years*. New York: Dodd, Mead, 1976.

Mander, John. *Berlin: Hostage to the West*. Harmondsworth, England: Penguin, 1962.

May, Ernest R. *"Lessons" of the Past: The Use and Misuse of History in American Foreign Policy*. New York: Oxford University Press, 1973.

———, ed. *The Ultimate Decision: The President as Commander in Chief*. New York: George Braziller, 1960.

Merkl, Peter. *The Origins of the West German Republic*. London: Oxford University Press, 1963.

Middleton, Drew. *The Struggle for Germany*. London: Allan Wingate, 1950.

Miller, Lynn M., and Pruessen, Ronald W., eds. *Reflections on the Cold War*. Philadelphia: Temple University Press, 1974.

Miller, Merle. *Plain Speaking: An Oral Biography of Harry S. Truman*. London: Coronet, 1973.

Millis, Walter. *Armies and Men: A Study in American Military History*. London: Jonathan Cape, 1957.

———. *Arms and the State*. New York: The Twentieth Century Fund, 1958.

———, ed. *The Forrestal Diaries*. New York: Viking, 1951.

Molotov, V. M. *Problems of Foreign Policy: Speeches and Statements, April 1945–November 1948*. Moscow: Foreign Publishing House, 1949.

Morgan, Roger. *The United States and West Germany, 1945–1973: A Study in Alliance Politics*. London: Oxford University Press, 1974.

Morris, Eric. *Blockade: Berlin and the Cold War*. London: Hamish Hamilton, 1973.

Mosely, Philip E. "The Occupation of Germany." *Foreign Affairs*, Vol. 28, No. 4 (July 1950).

Murphy, Robert. *Diplomat Among Warriors*. London: Collins, 1964.

Nagai, Yonosuke, and Iriye, Akira, eds. *The Origins of the Cold War in Asia*. New York: Columbia University Press, 1977.

Nash, Henry T. *American Foreign Policy: Response to a Sense of Threat*. Homewood, Ill.: Dorsey, 1973.

Neal, Fred Warner. *War and Peace and Germany*. New York: Norton, 1962.

Nelson, Daniel J. *Wartime Origins of the Berlin Dilemma*. University, Alabama: University of Alabama Press, 1978.

Nettl, J. P. *The Eastern Zone and Soviet Policy in Germany, 1945–1950*. London: Oxford University Press, 1951.

Neumann, Franz. "Soviet Policy in Germany." *Annals of the American Academy of Political and Social Science*, Vol. 263 (May 1949).

Neustadt, Richard E. *Alliance Politics*. New York: Columbia University Press, 1970.

———. *Presidential Power: The Politics of Leadership*. New York: Wiley, 1960.

Nicholson, Michael. *Conflict Analysis*. London: English Universities Press, 1970.

Nicolson, Harold. *Diaries and Letters, 1945–1962*. Edited by Nigel Nicolson. London: Fontana, 1971.

Nolte, E. *Deutschland und der Kalte Krieg*. Munich: Riper, 1974.

North, Robert C. "Decision-Making in Crisis: An Introduction." *Journal of Conflict Resolution*, Vol. 6, No. 3 (1962).

Northedge, F. S. *Descent from Power: British Foreign Policy, 1945–1973*. London: Allen and Unwin, 1974.

Oneal, John R. *Creative Adaptation: Process and Potential for Foreign Policy Making in Times of Crisis*. Ph.D. dissertation, Stanford University, 1979.

Orion. "The Berlin Airlift." *Journal of the Royal United Service Institute*, Vol. 94, No. 573 (February 1949).

Paige, Glenn D. *The Korean Decision*. New York: The Free Press, 1968.

Paterson, Thomas G. *On Every Front: The Making of the Cold War*. New York: Norton, 1979.

———. *Soviet-American Confrontation: Postwar Reconstruction and the Origins of the Cold War*. Baltimore: Johns Hopkins University Press, 1973.

———, ed. *Cold War Critics: Alternatives to American Foreign Policy in the Truman Years*. Chicago: Quadrangle, 1971.

———, ed. *Containment and the Cold War: American Foreign Policy Since 1945*. Reading, Mass.: Addison-Wesley, 1973.

Payne, Robert. *The Marshall Story: A Biography of General George C. Marshall*. New York: Prentice-Hall, 1951.

Peterson, Edward N. *The American Occupation of Germany: Retreat to Victory*. Detroit: Wayne State University Press, 1977.

Phillips, Cabell. *The Truman Presidency: A History of Triumphant Succession*. New York: Macmillan, 1966.

Pierre, Andrew J. *Nuclear Politics: The British Experience with an Independent Strategic Force, 1939–1970*. London: Oxford University Press, 1972.

Plischke, Elmer. *Berlin: The Development of Its Government and Administration*. Westport, Conn.: Greenwood Press, 1970.

Pogue, Forrest C. *Education of a General*. New York: Viking, 1963.

———. *George C. Marshall: Ordeal and Hope*. New York: Viking, 1966.

———. *George C. Marshall: Organizer of Victory*. New York: Viking, 1973.

Potichnyj, Peter J., and Shapiro, Jane P., eds. *From Cold War to Detente*. New York: Praeger, 1976.

Powers, Richard J. "Who Fathered Containment?" *International Studies Quarterly*, Vol. 15, No. 4 (December 1971).

Price, Don K., ed. *The Secretary of State*. Englewood Cliffs, N.J.: Prentice-Hall, 1960.

Quester, George H. *Nuclear Diplomacy: The First Twenty-Five Years*. New York: Dunellen, 1970.

Ransom, Harry H. *Central Intelligence and Foreign Policy*. Cambridge, Mass.: Harvard University Press, 1958.

Rapoport, Anatol. *The Big Two: Soviet–American Perceptions of Foreign Policy*. New York: Pegasus, 1971.

Ratchford, B. U., and Ross, W. D. *Berlin Reparations Assignment*. Chapel Hill: University of North Carolina Press, 1947.

Reynolds, Charles. *Theory and Explanation in International Politics*. London: Martin Robertson, 1973.

Richardson, James L. *Germany and the Atlantic Alliance*. Cambridge, Mass.: Harvard University Press, 1966.

Riess, Curt. *The Berlin Story*. New York: Dial Press, 1952.

Robinson, James A. "The Concept of Crisis Decision-Making." In *Readings on the International Political System*, edited by Naomi Rosenbaum. Englewood Cliffs, N.J.: Prentice-Hall, 1970.

———. "Crisis Decision-Making: An Inventory and Appraisal of Concepts, Theories, Hypotheses, and Techniques of Analysis." *Political Science Annual*, Vol. 2 (1969).

Robson, Charles B., ed. *Berlin: Pivot of German Destiny*. Chapel Hill: University of North Carolina Press, 1960.

Rogow, Arnold A. *Victim of Duty: A Study of James Forrestal*. London: Rupert Hart-Davis, 1966.

Rosenau, James N., ed. *Domestic Sources of Foreign Policy*. New York: The Free Press, 1967.

———, ed. *International Politics and Foreign Policy: A Reader in Research and Theory*. New York: The Free Press, 1969.

Rosenberg, Jerry Philip. *Berlin and Israel 1948: Foreign Policy Decision-Making During the Truman Administration*. Ph.D. dissertation, University of Illinois, Urbana-Champaign, 1977.

Royal Institute of International Affairs. *Defence in the Cold War*. London: Oxford University Press, 1950.

Sander, Alfred D. "Truman and the National Security Council: 1945–1947." *Journal of American History*, Vol. 49, No. 2 (September 1972).

Sapin, Burton M. *The Making of United States Foreign Policy*. New York: Praeger, 1966.

Scheinman, Lawrence. "The Berlin Blockade." In *International Law and Political Crisis*, edited by Lawrence Scheinman and David Wilkinson. Boston: Little, Brown, 1968.

Schelling, Thomas C. *Arms and Influence*. New Haven: Yale University Press, 1966.

———. *The Strategy of Conflict*. London: Oxford University Press, 1961.

Schick, Jack. *The Berlin Crisis, 1958–1962*. Philadelphia: University of Pennsylvania Press, 1971.

Schilling, Warner R.; Hammond, Paul Y.; and Snyder, Glenn H. *Strategy, Politics and Defense Budgets*. New York: Columbia University Press, 1962.

Schlesinger, Arthur M., Jr. *The Imperial Presidency*. London: André Deutsch, 1974.

Schmitt, Hans A., ed. *U.S. Occupation in Europe After World War II*. Lawrence: Regents Press of Kansas, 1978.

Schnabel, James F. *The History of the Joint Chiefs of Staff*. Vol. 1: *1945–1947*. (Washington, D.C.: Historical Division, Joint Secretariat, Joint Chiefs of Staff, 1979). Record Group 218, Records of the United States Joint Chiefs of Staff, The National Archives.

Schnapper, M. B., ed. *The Truman Program: Addresses and Messages by President Harry S. Truman*. Washington, D.C.: Public Affairs Press, 1949.

Schwarz, Hans-Peter. *Vom Reich zur Bundesrepublik*. Berlin: Luchterhand, 1966.

Sharp, Tony. *The Wartime Alliance and the Zonal Division of Germany*. London: Oxford University Press, 1975.

Shlaim, Avi. "Crisis Decision-Making in Israel: The Lessons of October 1973." In *The International Yearbook of Foreign Policy Analysis*, Vol. 2, edited by Peter Jones. London: Croom Helm, 1975.

———. "Failures in National Intelligence Estimates: The Case of the Yom Kippur War." *World Politics*, Vol. 28, No. 3 (April 1976).

———; Jones, Peter; and Sainsbury, Keith. *British Foreign Secretaries Since 1945*. London: David and Charles, 1977.

———, and Tanter, Raymond. "Decision Process, Choice and Consequences: Israel's Deep-Penetration Bombing in Egypt, 1970." *World Politics*, Vol. 30, No. 4 (July 1978).

Simon, Herbert A. *Administrative Behavior: A Study of Decision-Making Processes in Administrative Organizations*. 2nd edition. New York: Macmillan, 1957.

Singer, J. David, ed. *Quantitative International Politics: Insights and Evidence*. New York: The Free Press, 1968.

Slusser, Robert, ed. *Soviet Economic Policy in Postwar Germany*. New York: Research Program on the U.S.S.R., 1953.

Smart, Carolyne, and Vertinsky, Ilan. "Designs for Crisis Decision Units." *Administrative Science Quarterly*, Vol. 22 (December 1977).

Smith, Gaddis. *Dean Acheson*. New York: Cooper Square, 1972.

Smith, Howard K. *The State of Europe*. London: Angus and Robertson, 1950.

Smith, Jean Edward. *The Defense of Berlin*. Baltimore: Johns Hopkins University Press, 1963.

———, ed. *The Papers of General Lucius D. Clay: Germany, 1945–1949*. 2 vols. Bloomington: Indiana University Press, 1974.

Smith, Walter Bedell. *Moscow Mission, 1946–1949*. London: Heinemann, 1950.

Snyder, Glenn H., and Diesing, Paul. *Conflict Among Nations: Bargaining, Decision-Making and System-Structure in International Crises*. Princeton: Princeton University Press, 1977.

Snyder, Richard C.; Bruck, W. H.; and Sapin, Burton. *Foreign Policy Decision-Making*. New York: The Free Press, 1962.

Sorenson, Theodore C. *Decision-Making in the White House*. New York: Columbia University Press, 1963.

Spanier, John W. *Games Nations Play*. London: Nelson, 1972.

Sparrow, John C. *History of Personnel Demobilization in the United States Army*. Washington, D.C.: Office of the Chief of Military History, Department of the Army, 1951.

Speier, Hans. *Divided Berlin: The Anatomy of Soviet Political Blackmail*. New York: Praeger, 1961.

Spencer, Robert. "Berlin, The Blockade, and the Cold War." *International Journal*, Vol. 29 (1967–1968).

Steinberg, Alfred. *The Man from Missouri: The Life and Times of Harry S. Truman*. New York: Putnam's, 1962.

Steinbruner, John D. *The Cybernetic Theory of Decision*. Princeton: Princeton University Press, 1974.

Stoessinger, John G. *Nations in Darkness*. New York: Random House, 1971.

Strategic Air Command. *The Development of Strategic Air Command, 1946–1973*. Offult Air Force Base, Nebraska: Headquarters of Strategic Air Command, 1974.

Tanter, Raymond. *Modelling and Managing International Conflicts: The Berlin Crises*. Beverly Hills, Calif.: Sage, 1974.

———, and Ullman, Richard, eds. *Theory and Policy in International Relations*. Princeton: Princeton University Press, 1972.

Trivers, Howard. *Three Crises in American Foreign Affairs and a Continuing Revolution*. Carbondale: Southern Illinois University Press, 1972.

Truman, Harry S. *Memoirs*. Vol. 1: *Year of Decisions, 1945*. London: Hodder and Stoughton, 1955.

———. *Memoirs*. Vol. 2: *Years of Trial and Hope, 1946–1953*. London: Hodder and Stoughton, 1956.

———. *Mr. Citizen*. New York: Bernard Geiss, 1960.

———. *Off the Record*. New York: Harper and Row, 1980.

Truman, Margaret. *Harry S. Truman*. New York: William Morrow, 1973.

Tucker, Robert W. *The Radical Left and American Foreign Policy*. Baltimore: Johns Hopkins University Press, 1971.

Tunner, Lt. Gen. William. *Over the Hump*. New York: Duell, Sloane and Pearce, 1964.

Ulam, Adam B. *Expansion and Coexistence: Soviet Foreign Policy, 1917–1973*. 2nd edition. New York: Praeger, 1974.

———. *The Rivals: America and Russia Since World War II*. London: Allen Lane, 1971.

Vagts, Alfred. *Defense and Diplomacy: The Soldier and the Conduct of Foreign Relations*. New York: King's Crown, 1956.

Vandenberg, Arthur H., Jr., ed. *The Private Papers of Senator Vandenberg*. London: Gollancz, 1952.

Wagner, R. Harrison. "The Decision to Divide Germany and the Origins of the Cold War." *International Studies Quarterly*, Vol. 24, No. 2 (June 1980).

Walker, J. Samuel. "'No More Cold War': American Foreign Policy and the 1948 Soviet Peace Offensive." *Diplomatic History*, Vol. 5, No. 1 (Winter 1981).

Walton, Richard J. *Henry Wallace, Harry Truman and the Cold War*. New York: Viking, 1976.

Waltz, Kenneth. "International Structure, National Force and the Balance of Power." *Journal of International Affairs*, Vol. 2, No. 2 (1967).

Warburg, James P. *Germany: Key to Peace*. Cambridge, Mass.: Harvard University Press, 1953.

Warner, Geoffrey. "The Division of Germany, 1946–1948." *International Affairs*, Vol. 51, No. 1 (January 1975).

Watt, D. C. *Britain Looks to Germany: A Study of British Opinion and Policy Towards Germany Since 1945*. London: Oswald Wolff, 1965.

Welch, William. *American Images of Soviet Foreign Policy*. New Haven: Yale University Press, 1970.

Wells, Samuel F., Jr. "America and the 'Mad' World." *The Wilson Quarterly*, Vol. 1, No. 5 (Autumn 1977).

Westerfield, H. Bradford. *Foreign Policy and Party Politics: Pearl Harbor to Korea*. New Haven: Yale University Press, 1955.

Wheeler, G. S. *Die Amerikanische Politik in Deutschland, 1945–1950*. Berlin: Kongress-Verlag, 1958.

Whyte, Anne. "Quadripartite Rule in Berlin." *International Affairs*, Vol. 23, No. 1 (January 1947).

Wiegle, Thomas C. "Decision-Making in International Crisis: Some Biological Factors." *International Studies Quarterly*, Vol. 17, No. 3 (September 1973).

Williams, Francis. *A Prime Minister Remembers: The War and Post-War Memoirs of the Rt. Hon. Earl Attlee*. London: Heinemann, 1961.

Williams, Phil. *Crisis Management: Confrontation and Diplomacy in the Nuclear Age*. London: Martin Robertson, 1976.

Willis, Roy F. *The French in Germany, 1945–1949*. Stanford: Stanford University Press, 1962.

Windsor, Philip. "Berlin." In *The Cold War: A Reappraisal*, edited by Evan Luard. London: Thames and Hudson, 1964.

———. *City on Leave: A History of Berlin, 1945–1962*. London: Chatto and Windus, 1963.

———. *German Reunification*. London: Elek Books, 1969.

Winter, Bernard. *Berlin: Enjeu et Symbole*. Paris: Calmann-Levy, 1959.

Wright, C. Ben. "Mr. 'X' and Containment." *Slavic Review*, Vol. 35, No. 1 (March 1976).

Yaniv, Avner. "Domestic Structure and External Flexibility: A Systemic Restatement of a Neglected Theme." *Millennium*, Vol. 8, No. 1 (Spring 1979).

Yergin, Daniel. *Shattered Peace: The Origins of the Cold War and the National Security State*. Boston: Houghton Mifflin, 1977.

Young, Oran R. *The Intermediaries: Third Parties in International Crises*. Princeton: Princeton University Press, 1967.

———. *The Politics of Force: Bargaining During International Crises.* Princeton: Princeton University Press, 1968.

Zink, Harold. "American Civil-Military Relations in the Occupation of Germany." In *Total War and Cold War: Problems in Civilian Control of the Military*, edited by Harry Coles. Columbus: Ohio State University Press, 1962.

———. *The United States in Germany, 1944–1955.* Princeton: Van Norstad, 1957.

Zinnes, D. A. "Hostility in International Decision-Making." *Journal of Conflict Resolution*, Vol. 6, No. 3 (1962).

Index

ACC. *See* Allied Control Council
Acheson, Dean, 51, 52, 61n, 70n, 71, 77, 377; airlift interpreted by, 266, 388; foreign policy guided by, 300–303, 379–381, 384, 385, 399; images of, 299–303; G. Marshall evaluated by, 86–87; opinion of the National Security Council, 398; in the post-crisis period, 283, 284–285, 299–303, 397; replacement of, 90; Riga axioms promoted by, 79, 287
Adenauer, Konrad, 344, 388
AEC. *See* Atomic Energy Commission
Airlift, 71, 196, 241, 301, 390; augmentation in the post-crisis period, 349, 350–360, 361–362, 364, 365–366; "baby airlift" instigated by Clay, 133, 135; British role in, 202, 206, 214–215, 226, 237, 248, 319; C-54 aircraft for, 332, 359–360, 365, 366; capacity of, 242, 243, 244, 258, 261, 320, 347–348; continuance of defended by Clay, 364–366; criticism of, 265–266; decision to expand, 171, 180, 204, 205–206, 208–211, 262–263, 268–269, 279, 417; evolution of, 202–204, 296; instigated by Clay, 133, 135, 204, 279, 416; potentiality for defeating the blockade, 211, 399; political significance of, 206, 210, 294, 296, 319, 377, 388; risks of, 224; Soviet attitudes and response to, 211, 226, 288, 310, 330, 332, 365; in strategic options at the height of the crisis, 244–246, 248, 261–263, 279; success of, 261, 296, 345, 366, 377, 417–418; symbolism of, 374, 377, 389; time pressure reduced by, 391–392
Allied Control Council (ACC): and American role in the establishment of Western Germany, 142–143; attitudes of the CIA on, 155; and centralized administration for Germany, 14, 113–114; and the currency reform, 151, 152; government of occupied Germany by, 14–15; and Soviet attitudes on the division of Germany, 33; Soviet exodus from, 34–35, 43, 101, 113–114, 116, 117, 121, 162–163
Allies: and the armed convoy plan, 309; and the creation of Western Germany, 33, 144; role in American strategy choices to resolve the Berlin crisis, 37, 137, 139–142, 146–147, 166, 184–185, 192, 193, 198, 202, 212–216, 224–227, 228–231, 244, 253, 413; role in the diplomatic approach to resolve the Berlin crisis, 228–231, 233, 253, 310–315, 317, 324, 328, 329, 333, 336, 338, 342–343, 349–351, 353, 387, 393–395, 406; rupture in relations over Germany, 32, 113; unanimous agreement required for rule of occupied Germany, 14–15; and the United Nations consideration of the Berlin crisis, 339, 355, 367, 368, 376. *See also* Britain; France
Allison, Graham T., 209
Alternatives, search for and evaluation of: for American strategies in the

Alternatives (*continued*)
  United Nations, 367–368; armed convoy plan, 130–131, 171, 189, 200–201, 202, 232, 234, 243, 244, 245, 258, 260, 262, 264, 269, 271, 272, 275, 280, 301, 305, 307, 309, 319, 383, 384, 400, 407, 417, 418, 421; by the Cabinet, 71–72, 117–118, 206–207; in the crisis period, 184–185, 200–203, 206–207, 212, 216–226, 242–246, 278–280, 416–418; by W. Draper, 216–217; effects of crisis-induced stress on, 8, 278–279, 400–401, 415–423; evacuation of Berlin, 217, 247; evaluated by Clay in the crisis period, 200–203; by the Joint Chiefs of Staff, 362–363, 399–400; long-term options in, 89, 285, 302, 316–317, 317n, 345, 369, 409; by G. Marshall, 184–185; by the National Security Council, 331–332, 339–340, 398; perceived range of, 418; by the Policy Planning Staff, 89, 320–322, 360–361, 369–370, 399, 417; in the post-crisis period, 285, 302, 316–317, 320–322, 332, 345–346, 362–363, 367, 369–370, 383, 399–401; in the pre-crisis period, 124–127, 130–131, 167–168, 415–416; for Soviet restrictions on train service to Berlin, 124–127, 130–131; to submit the Berlin dispute to the United Nations, 332, 333, 336, 338–339, 345–346, 350, 352, 353; withdrawal from Berlin, 212, 217, 218, 219, 223–224, 308, 346, 353, 364, 365, 383, 400, 421–422. *See also* Strategy choices

American decision-makers: advance planning by, 145, 195; attitudinal prism of, 47–69, 173–174, 287–292; bureaucratic institutions bypassed by, 209–210, 219–220, 222, 251–252, 267–268, 277, 278, 414; capacity for decision-making, 77–78, 98–100, 102, 118, 195, 206, 208–209; conflicting views of Soviet foreign policy, 49–50; cognitive performance of, 406–410, 422–423; evaluation of, 420–422; impact of the international system and military technology on, 36–38, 47, 68–69, 95, 107; influence of the American presidency on, 69–75; failure in policymaking, 416; foreign policy of, 65–69, 75–84, 94–95, 104–105, 117–119 (*see also* Foreign policy); and the "groupthink" hypothesis, 418–419; and results of the Berlin crisis, 388–389; response to the Soviet exodus from the Allied Control Council, 115–121, 162–163; response to Soviet restrictions on U.S. train service to Berlin, 122–125; on Russian views of American foreign policy goals, 64–65; sources of stress and conflict in the decision-making process, 49, 195–196, 198, 416; and the surprise factor in the Berlin crisis, 11, 31, 107, 110–115, 119–120, 154; time available to respond to the Soviet blockade, 12, 14. *See also* Clay, Lucius D.; Marshall, George; Truman, Harry

American presidency, 69–84; consultation used by, 249–251, 260–263, 274–275, 413; decision-making during crisis, 78–79, 171, 176–181, 208–210, 220–221, 251–252, 266, 268–269, 277, 278, 358, 414–415; deployment of atomic weapons by, 340; in diplomatic relations, 356–359; powers of during crisis, 76; reduced involvement in the post-crisis period, 396–397; relationship with the Secretary of State, 88, 300; role in the decision-making process, 69–75, 126, 176–181, 269, 283–284, 396–397. *See also* Truman, Harry

Appeasement. *See* Foreign policy

Armed convoy plan. *See* Alternatives

Atomic bomb: in American military policy, 228, 236–237, 245–246, 254–260; American public opinion on use of, 294, 339, 341; attitudes toward the use of, 294, 297, 337–338, 339, 341, 359; in B-29 bombers, 228, 238; in Britain, 238, 337; and the convoy plan, 421; custody of, 254–257, 278, 340–341; deterrent effects of, 240, 243–244, 359; NSC decision on use of, 339–340. *See also* Nuclear weapons

INDEX

Atomic Energy Commission (AEC), 117; and custody of the atomic bomb, 254–255, 256
Attitudinal prism: in the crisis period, 173–174; defined, 45; image of the adversary in, 46, 55, 58–63, 65–66, 80–81, 83, 91–92, 96–97, 173–174, 177–178, 181, 182, 183, 186, 271, 287–292, 293–294, 299–300, 300; in the post-crisis period, 287–292; in the pre-crisis period, 47–69; realism in, 44, 49, 55–56, 57, 64, 101, 109, 287; self-image in, 55, 63–65, 173; strategy preferences in, 55, 65–69; world-view in, 45, 55–58, 65, 66, 68, 81–83, 173, 287
Attlee, Clement, 341
Auriol, Vincent, 142, 198n, 368n, 377n
Austin, Warren, 353
Authority, decisional, 414

B-29 bombers, 228, 235–240, 243, 254, 263
Backer, John H., 23n
Bargaining style of the Soviet Union, 174, 181, 303
"Basic Assumption" plan, 119–120
Beam, Jacob, 100, 248
Belgium, U.S. military bases in, 121
Benelux countries, 33, 113, 142
Berlin: access to, 15, 35, 111, 112, 115, 122–135, 162, 165, 178; air corridors to, 115, 122, 135, 178, 226, 240, 330; Air Safety Center, 133, 134; American civilians in, 132–133, 136, 173 (see also Civilians in Berlin); currency reform for, 151–152, 156–157, 158–160 (see also Currency reform); division of, 373, 375, 376; food and coal in, 186–187; legal position of Western powers in, 178–179, 182–183, 207, 228, 297, 313, 318, 324, 335–336, 408; "Magistrat" in, 334, 335, 372–373; maintenance of the American position in, 135, 154–155, 176–179, 183, 187, 188, 196, 199, 200, 206, 210, 218–219, 220–221, 223, 227, 250, 251, 252–253, 263, 295, 347–349, 362, 363, 376, 408, 414, 416; quadripartite administration of, 113, 115, 324, 325, 344, 361; riots in, 332, 333, 334; Soviet recognition of an east Berlin government, 373; Soviet restrictions on U.S. train service to, 122–135, 162, 229
Berlin blockade: American anticipation of, 31, 107, 110–115, 119–120, 168, 195; and American experience with Nazi Germany, 66; American values threatened by, 389–390; commencement of, 101, 162, 197; end of, 118, 283, 293, 303, 387–388; international peace threatened by, 355; interpreted by Lucius Clay, 107–109, 187, 193; interpreted by G. Marshall, 96, 182, 183; interpreted by President Truman, 84, 178, 179; potentiality of the airlift to defeat, 211, 399; preparation by the American military for, 119–121; Soviet motivations for, 35–36, 64–65, 84, 96, 107–108, 113–114, 115, 197, 230, 373; stress in the decision-making process on, 195–196, 198, 199, 201, 278–280. See also Stress induced by crisis
Berlin crisis: catalysts of, 35–36, 43, 154, 162, 270; choice of an American strategy for, 138–141, 176–181, 184–186, 189–191, 195–198, 200–203, 206–207, 212, 216–226, 242–251, 260–263, 419–422; Churchill's advice on, 138; Clay's plans for resolution of, 137–138, 189–190, 200–206, 232, 234, 240–241, 243, 244, 258–259, 264, 421; and effect of stress on American decision-makers, 195–196, 198, 406–423 (see also Stress induced by crisis); end of, 269, 387; evaluation of American policies in, 420–422; interpreted by Dean Acheson, 301; interpreted by L. Clay, 107–109, 295; interpreted by Harry Truman, 83–84, 366; level of American military preparation for, 92, 93, 120–121, 183, 187, 214, 250, 267, 290; Marshall's approach to resolution of, 184–185; and nuclear weapons, 38 (see also Nuclear weapons); origins of, 14–39; symbolism of, 35–36, 179, 295, 390, 422

Berlin Group, 310; establishment and functions of, 246, 273, 317; head of, 353, 380, 393; information processing by, 393, 411; members of, 248
Bevan, Aneurin, 237
Bevin, Ernest, 32, 140, 142, 149, 150, 185, 319, 385; and the British response to the Berlin crisis, 198, 212–215, 226, 228, 235; and diplomatic efforts to resolve the Berlin crisis, 212–213, 311, 339, 342, 346, 349, 352, 380, 382, 384, 387, 395; on the political structure in Bizonia, 33; on relations with the Soviet Union, 141; and the UN consideration of the Berlin crisis, 339, 351, 355. *See also* Britain
Bidault, Georges, 33
Bipartisanship in American foreign policy, 247, 257, 275–276, 396, 412, 413; promoted by President Truman, 75–76, 247, 372; reasons for, 305–306
Bipolarity: advocated by Dean Acheson, 299; impact on American decision-makers, 36–37, 47–48, 57
Bizonia, 26, 29, 33, 151, 153
Bohlen, Charles, 90, 92n, 147, 198, 199; and American foreign policy, 144–145, 249; and B-29 bombers in Britain, 235; Berlin Group headed by, 246, 248, 273; in diplomatic efforts to resolve the Berlin crisis, 310, 311, 315, 316, 318, 380, 382, 393; in the post-crisis period, 285, 339, 347, 380, 382, 393; role in the United Nations consideration of the Berlin dispute, 353, 355, 367
Bradley, Omar, 43, 116, 134, 149; in the crisis period, 218, 223, 225, 226, 229, 234, 250, 258, 260; on maintenance of the American position in Berlin, 136, 137–138; in the post-crisis period, 332, 333, 337, 360, 386; and Soviet restrictions on American train service to Berlin, 122, 125, 127, 128, 129, 131; on strategies to resolve the Berlin crisis, 244–245
Bramuglia, Juan, 372
Brandt, Willy, 203
Brecher, Michael, xi, 5, 403; crisis behavior model developed by, 6–9, 403; crisis defined by, 5–6, 403
Britain: aircraft of destroyed by the Soviet Union, 133–135; and the airlift to Berlin, 202, 206, 214–215, 225, 226, 237, 248, 319; in American strategy choices to resolve the Berlin crisis, 37, 137, 139–141, 184–185, 198, 202, 203, 204, 205, 212–215, 224–226, 228–231, 235; and the armed convoy plan, 309; attitudes on use of the atomic bomb, 341; atomic bomb in, 238, 337; B-29 bombers in, 228, 234, 235–240, 243, 254, 263; and diplomatic efforts to resolve the Berlin crisis, 311, 324, 328, 329, 333, 336, 338, 339, 342–343, 349, 387, 394–395; first U.S. Strategic Air Command base in, 237; joint military planning with the U.S., 214–215, 224–226; policies for Germany, 18, 19, 24; position in American world-view, 57–58; response to Soviet restrictions of American train service to Berlin, 129, 131; train service to Berlin maintained by, 127; and Soviet departure from the Allied Control Council, 113–114; and the United Nations consideration of the Berlin dispute, 339, 355, 367, 376, 377
Brownjohn, N.C.D., 129
Bureaucratic institutions: bypassing of, 209–210, 219–220, 222, 251–252, 267–268, 277, 278, 414
Bureaucratic politics: challenged by military recommendations for caution, 267–268; in government decision-making, 209–210, 219–220
Byrnes, James, 80, 105, 338; and American postwar policy toward Germany, 23–26; political relationship with L. Clay, 102; replaced by G. Marshall, 85–86, 87, 93; and role of the State Department in occupied Germany, 100; "Stuttgart speech" of, 25–26

Cabinet, American, 372; decisions on the Berlin crisis, 44, 71–72, 206–207; and export controls to the Soviet Union, 117–118; minimal role

INDEX

in the crisis period, 277; passivity in the post-crisis period, 336, 338, 398; in the pre-crisis period, 167; restoration of the balance of power endorsed by, 95
Cadogan, Alexander, 387
Caffery, Jefferson, 347
Capitalism, 18; vs. communism, 48, 56–57; in Germany, 105, 142; vs. socialism, 105
Carr, Alfred Z., 356
Central Intelligence Agency (CIA), 12, 339, 410; on the American position in Berlin, 154–155; change in Soviet foreign policy noted by, 373; establishment of, 74; on the option of negotiating with Russia, 196; role in crisis situations, 220; on short-term vs. long-term results of diplomacy, 317n; Soviet capabilities estimated by, 165; Soviet motivations in Berlin analyzed by, 113; war possibility estimated by, 126, 131–132
Chamberlin, Stephen, 106, 107
Chataigneau, Yves, 311
Chauvel, Jean, 387
China, 205, 215, 320; G. Marshall's mission in, 86; and the Quemoy crisis, 420
Churchill, Winston, 17, 237; advice on the American position in Berlin, 138; on use of atomic weapons, 341
Civilians in Berlin: Clay's concern for, 132–133, 136, 187, 189, 201, 263; estimate of their resistance to Soviet control, 202–203, 261; evacuation of, 132–133, 136, 263; German, 187, 189, 201, 218; response to the Berlin blockade, 313; role in American strategy choices, 218; in Russian strategies, 173
Clay, Henry, 103
Clay, Lucius D., 11, 24, 27, 85, 114, 171, 186–190, 406; airlift augmentation advocated by, 364–366, 388; airlift decision of, 204, 205–206, 241, 277, 279, 416; airlift directed by, 215–216, 359–360; and American foreign policy in Germany, 25, 26, 97–109, 119, 128–134, 152, 159, 199–206, 284, 348, 365; and American preparation for war, 121,

187; approach to decision-making, 98–102, 118, 406–407, 409, 411–412; attitude toward atomic weapons, 341; attitudes on formation of West Germany, 297–299, 315, 318–319, 345, 392; authorized to send test trains to Berlin, 128, 416; "baby airlift" instigated by, 133, 135; Berlin blockade anticipated by, 31, 110, 112, 115, 119, 154; concern for civilians in Berlin, 132–133, 136, 187, 189, 201, 263; and currency reform, 151–152, 153–154, 156, 157, 158–160, 167, 188, 200–201, 219, 222, 233, 315, 328; and decision-making during the pre-crisis period, 43, 44, 97–109, 119, 134, 153; and diplomatic efforts to resolve the Berlin crisis, 279, 297, 324, 326–330, 333, 342; dual positions of, 97–98, 115–116; on economic recovery of Germany, 142; on free access to Berlin, 15; on French attitudes toward Germany, 58; images of, 97–109, 130, 295–299; information processing by, 411–412; impact of Nazi Germany on, 406–407; on maintenance of the American position in Berlin, 136–137, 176, 186, 188, 189, 200, 284, 347–348, 365; meetings with Truman, 258, 261, 262, 263–264, 275, 411; and the military role in American foreign policymaking, 97–103, 115–117, 200–206, 229, 277; perception of time pressure, 164, 186, 232, 272, 279, 296, 297, 416; plans for resolving the Berlin crisis, 130–131, 137–138, 139, 140–141, 189–191, 200–206, 214, 232, 234, 240–241, 243, 244, 258–259, 264, 269, 348, 383–384, 421; possibility of war doubted by, 106–107, 123, 124, 137, 167, 187, 188, 194, 232, 259, 271, 296, 297, 349, 391; in the post-crisis period, 283, 284, 295–299, 310, 319; response to Soviet restrictions on U.S. trains to Berlin, 122–131, 133; response to the trade embargo, 118–119; Russian foreign policy interpreted by, 103–104, 105–106, 174, 191–193, 194, 200,

Clay, Lucius D. (*continued*) 232, 233–234; stress experienced by, 186–187, 188, 327, 408, 409, 411; teleconferences evaluated by, 166; on threat to American values, 271; and the UN deliberations on the Berlin dispute, 365, 373

Clifford, Clark, 52, 139, 147; American foreign policy influenced by, 175, 176; and the influence of the American presidency on foreign policymaking, 69, 70–71; on public opinion in foreign policymaking, 76; Riga axioms promoted by, 79; Soviet foreign policy reviewed by, 53–54, 55, 60, 67

Cognitive performance, effect of stress on, 405–410, 422–423

Cold War, 18, 173; American foreign policy during, 52, 56–57; and American national security, 72–73; causes and origins of, 48, 50; democracy vs. totalitarianism in, 82; historiography of, 23n, 24–26, 48, 49, 238; impact of Lucius Clay on American foreign policy during, 102–103, 105; influence of G. Marshall on, 86, 92, 97; intensification of, 30, 31, 32; nuclear crisis in, 38; symbolism of Berlin in, 295; West Germany in American long-term strategies for, 409

Collins, J. Lawton, 125

Cominform, 31, 108

Communism, 18, 63; American containment of, 82–83, 94, 95; vs. capitalism, 48, 56–57; in China, 86; compared with German fascism, 62, 81; in Czechoslovakia; fear of, 56n; in Germany, 21–22, 24, 29, 104–105, 179, 189, 197, 200, 299; monolithic power structure in, 59–60, 92; opposed by L. Clay, 101, 103, 104–105; symbol of American resistance against, 295; in Western Europe, 365. *See also* Containment policy

Conally, Tom, 357, 396

Congress: appropriations for military defense by, 107; and the Berlin crisis, 165, 247, 250; relations with President Truman, 54–55, 75–76, 83, 88, 165, 247, 250; and the U.S. trade embargo with the Soviet Union, 117–118

Connelly, Matthew, 117

Consultation: and American decision on Soviet restrictions on American train service to Berlin, 127–128; bypassed by President Truman in the crisis period, 210; characteristics of, 7–8; effect of crisis-induced stress on, 396–397, 412–413; in the crisis period, 210, 246–251, 273–276, 412, 413; and inter-Allied conflicts, 342; expanded during stress, 125, 246–251, 274–277; institutional framework in, 396–397; in the post-crisis period, 339, 342, 347, 394–397, 412–413; for the pre-crisis period, 125–128, 165–166, 412

Containment policy: in American domestic politics, 175, 176; basis of, 67–68; defined, 55; generated by Truman's world-view, 82–83; military preparation for, 291; in Western Germany, 105

Convoy plan. *See* Alternatives

Copying mechanisms: ad hoc decisional forums, 278, 280; case findings relative to theoretical propositions on, 410–423; centralized decision-making in, 278; in crisis behavior theory, 7–8, 9, 10; in the crisis period, 272–280; in the post-crisis period, 393–401; in the pre-crisis period, 164–167

Council of Foreign Ministers, 23, 27, 28–30, 31, 33, 55, 80, 93, 231, 283, 286, 324, 354, 355, 369, 379, 380, 382, 385, 387

Counterblockade: decision-making process for, 117–119, 165, 206–207, 319; efficacy of, 118, 377, 378, 380, 392; lifting of, 385

"Creeping blockade," 112

Cripps, Stafford, 339, 341

Crisis, 171; American view of, 68; behavior model for, 6–9; case findings applied to theoretical propositions on, 402–423; components of, 162–164, 260–272, 389–393; decision-making approach to, 3–6, 11; definitions of, 3–6, 11, 37, 68, 162, 164; impact of the international structure

INDEX   451

on, 36–38, 47; stages of, 8–9, 162; systemic approach to, 3–4
Crisis-induced stress. *See* Stress induced by crisis
Crisis period, 171–280; assessment and search for alternatives during, 184–185, 200–203, 206–207, 212, 216–226, 242–246, 278–280, 416–418; beginning of, 171; bureaucratic procedures and structures bypassed during, 209–210, 219–220, 222, 251–252, 267–268, 277, 278, 414; caution in military recommendations for, 267–268; characteristics of, 8, 171; consultation during, 210, 246–251, 273–276, 412, 413; decisional forums during, 218–219, 221–222, 251, 276–278; decision-makers during, 171 (*see also* Clay; Marshall; Truman); decisions made during, 172, 204, 207, 208, 221, 224, 230, 236, 251, 256, 263, 414, 416; end of, 269, 283; information processing in, 232, 272–273; interdependence between Russia and the U.S. during, 193–194; psychological environment of, 173–194; threat to American values in, 181–182, 186–187, 189–190, 270–271; time pressure in, 171, 182, 186–187, 188, 232, 247, 269, 272, 279; war probability in, 171, 174, 175, 181, 200, 207, 243–244, 271
Currency reform, 151–162, 165, 167, 233, 380, 382, 388; in diplomatic efforts to resolve the Berlin crisis, 158, 314, 315, 316, 318, 319, 322, 323, 326, 380, 382; plans for negotiations on, 219, 222, 229; and possibility of war, 188, 189; and resolution of the Berlin crisis, 200–201, 233; and the United Nations considerations of the Berlin dispute, 367, 368, 372, 373, 374–376
Czechoslovakia, 108, 126; communist control of, 33–34, 83; U.S. trade with, 118

Decisional forums: in the crisis period, 218–219, 221–222, 235–236, 249–252, 260, 276–278; effect of stress on, 8, 414–415; in the post-crisis period, 397–398; in the pre-crisis period, 166–167
Decision-making: in approach to crisis, 4–6; authority in, 414; effects of indecision in, 139, 171, 195–196; flow in, 9–10; and the model of crisis behavior, 6–10
Decisions: in the crisis period, 172, 204, 207, 208, 221, 224, 230, 236, 251, 252, 256, 263, 414, 416; in the post-crisis period, 285–286, 316, 319, 332, 340, 350, 352, 355, 357, 366, 368, 375, 381, 383; in the pre-crisis period; 44, 115, 118, 127, 152, 159
De Murville, Couve, 143, 349n
Denfield, Louis E., 225
Destler, I. M., 210n
Deterrent strategies, 239–240, 244, 359; and American public opinion on the use of the atomic bomb, 294; evolution of, 254. *See also* Atomic bomb
Dewey, Thomas, 176, 247, 249, 259, 395; attitude on bipartisan foreign policy, 305–306
Diesing, Paul, 4, 47n, 55n, 68n, 173n, 196n
Diplomacy, 65–66; Acheson's views of, 303; *aide-mémoire* in, 342, 343, 344; American attitudes toward, 147, 180, 183, 279, 291, 303, 311; American avoidance of appeasement in, 292–293, 295, 297, 304, 346, 353, 407; American bargaining position in, 294–295, 316–317, 325–326, 335–336, 350; and attitudinal changes during the crisis period, 279; to avoid military confrontation, 128–129; and the Berlin Group, 246; Clay's response and role in, 279, 297, 324, 326–330, 333, 394; end of the Berlin crisis achieved by, 387; failure of, 336, 337, 351, 352, 392; inter-Allied conflicts in, 338, 342, 353, 386; G. Marshall's opinion and approach to, 93–94, 183, 184–185, 294–295; private and secret negotiations in, 381–383, 384–385, 386, 397; refusal to negotiate under duress, 373; to resolve the

Diplomacy (*continued*)
  Berlin crisis, 227–231, 233, 310–320, 322–331, 332–333, 335–336, 342–344, 349–351, 381–387, 397; role of the American presidency in, 356–359, 372, 386; in strategy choices to resolve the Berlin crisis, 184–185, 190, 196, 198, 202, 207, 211, 212–213, 222, 225, 226, 242, 250, 269, 279; stress caused by, 336, 337; threat of force in, 240, 254
Diplomacy, Soviet, 67, 174, 181, 303. *See also* Molotov, Vyacheslav; Sokolvsky, Vassily; Stalin, Joseph
Djilas, Milovan, 18
Domino theory, 108
Donovan, William, 240–241
Douglas, Lewis, 91, 96, 147; and American goals in the United Nations, 354; in the crisis period, 182, 183, 185, 212, 213, 219; and diplomatic efforts to resolve the Berlin crisis, 310, 311, 336, 349, 393–394, 395; information processed by, 411; on maintenance of the American position in Berlin, 138; and role of the allies in American strategy choices, 139–140, 149
Draper, William, 98, 152, 153, 156, 160, 377n; in the crisis period, 171, 201, 205, 206, 213, 214–215, 216, 222, 245, 246, 250, 252, 273; in the post-crisis period, 318, 333, 364, 396; role in negotiations to resolve the Berlin crisis, 327–328, 342, 344, 375; strategic options evaluated by, 216–217
Dratvin, Mikhail, 121–122, 124, 125, 126, 128, 164
Dulles, John Foster, 46n, 412; in the American delegation to the United Nations, 338, 346–347, 372, 395–396, 413; and bipartisan foreign policy, 247, 275, 305, 306; and the formation of West Germany, 27–28; on the potential consequences of a UN failure to resolve the Berlin crisis, 353–354; on strategies to resolve the Berlin crisis, 247–249; on use of the atomic bomb, 341, 359

Eden, Anthony, 227
Eisenhower, Dwight, 15, 70
Elsey, George, 71, 123
Environmental change: in the crisis period, 270, 279; in the post-crisis period, 389; in the pre-crisis period, 162–163
Europe: American commitment to the defense of, 108–109; avoidance of communism in, 179; economic recovery of, 94, 188, 319, 390; threat to the freedom of, 83, 86
Europe, Eastern, economic counterblockade of, 118. *See also* Counterblockade
European Command (EUCOM), 97
European Recovery Program, 30, 34, 83, 94, 142, 191; success of, 144, 149, 179, 348
Evatt, Herbert, 371, 372
Export controls, 165, 206. *See also* Counterblockade

Feis, Herbert, 23n
Finland, 179, 182, 249
Foreign Affairs, 55
Foreign policy: avoidance of appeasement in, 292–293, 295, 297, 304, 346, 353, 407; basic values of, 269; bipartisanship in, 75–76, 247, 257, 275–276, 305–306, 372, 396, 412, 413; conducted by Dean Acheson, 300–303, 379–381, 384, 385, 399; criticized by the Joint Chiefs of Staff, 362–364; current evaluation of, 420–422; influenced by domestic politics, 256–257, 305, 325–326, 340–341, 346–347, 355–359, 369; influenced by the military, 85, 90, 98–103, 115–117, 124–128, 159, 169, 173, 199–206, 225, 266–267, 275, 277–278, 290–291; interaction between the Secretary of State and the President in, 88, 356–358; psychological factors in formation of, 45–46; restoration of the balance of power in, 95; risk taking in, 83–84, 137, 148; role of G. Marshall in, 87–97 (*see also* Marshall, George C.); toward the Soviet Union in the post-crisis period, 288, 290–292, 305; of President Truman, 175–181, 220–222, 247, 292–293, 300, 305–308, 310, 356–359, 362–363, 371–372, 375, 396; of the Truman

INDEX

Administration, 75–84, 105, 147, 175–181, 275–276, 362–364, 369, 377, 378
Forrestal, James V., 31n, 43, 52, 55, 67, 71, 72, 74, 94, 125, 147, 149, 295; as adviser to President Truman, 249, 250, 252, 278; and the American commitment to remain in Berlin, 111–112; on American instigation of war, 341–342; and the armed convoy plan, 309; concern for American security, 56n; in the crisis period, 171, 181, 204, 206, 218, 219–220, 222, 225, 228, 229, 250, 258, 260; on defense budget increases, 359; information processing by, 411; on policy for use and custody of atomic bombs, 236, 254, 256, 337, 339, 340–341; in the post-crisis period, 285, 287–288, 327, 331, 333, 334, 336, 344, 364, 393, 396; on powers of the Secretary of Defense, 334; rearmament advocated by, 95; Riga axioms promoted by, 79; role in the negotiations to resolve the Berlin crisis, 344, 345; Soviet foreign policy viewed by, 62
France, 26, 37; acceptance of Western Germany, 147–150; in American world-view, 57–58; and the armed convoy plan, 309; attitudes toward the American role in reviving German power, 142, 143–144; attitudes toward the currency reform, 152–153, 155–156, 159; in Clay's plan to resolve the Berlin crisis, 137; and diplomatic efforts to resolve the Berlin crisis, 310, 311, 324, 328, 329, 333, 336, 338, 342–343, 349, 387, 394–395; position on the centralized administration of occupied Germany, 19, 21, 24, 29, 103; role in American policy toward the formation of West Germany, 28, 29, 33; role in American policy on the Berlin crisis, 198, 216, 222, 228, 229–231; and the Soviet departure from the Allied Control Council, 113–114; and the UN review of the Berlin dispute, 352, 353, 367, 368n, 376, 377; U.S. military bases in, 121
Frankfurter, Felix, 86
Franks, Oliver, 235

Gaddis, John Lewis, 24, 49n, 60n, 67n
Gailey, Charles, 154
Galbraith, John, 103
Gardner, Lloyd C., 26
George, Alexander L., xi, 46, 63n, 70n, 181n; on American view of the international system, 68–69; concept of consultation, 273–274, 413; literature reviewed by, 403, 405; on stress in decision-making, 195n, 414; on stress and information processing, 410; on "test of capabilities" strategy, 419–420
Gerhardt, General, 273
German Bank of Emission, 332–333, 393; quadripartite control of, 328, 329–330
Germany: and American anticipation of the Berlin blockade, 110–115; American foreign policy toward, 23–30, 55, 71, 95–96, 97–102, 115–117, 297–299, 301–303; American occupation of, 97–102, 299; centralized administration of, 19, 22, 24, 32, 113–114, 196; compared by Americans to the Soviet Union, 61–62, 66, 81, 113; critical role in the balance of power, 17–18, 30, 31, 84, 302, 303, 319; currency reform in, 151–152, 156, 188, 189, 196 (*see also* Currency reform); economic strength of, 27, 30, 101, 104, 105; evolution of the partition of, 20–36 *passim*, 114; Nazi Germany compared with the Berlin crisis, 66, 406–407; occupation of, 14–15, 18, 30, 71, 110–115, 196; Russian foreign policy toward after the Berlin blockade, 197; Social Democratic Party in, 203; Socialist Unity Party in, 189, 334; unification of, 12, 18, 24, 29, 32
Germany, Eastern, 96, 97
Germany, Western: American role in the formation of, 22–23, 27–28, 31, 34, 96, 101, 105, 106, 113, 141, 143, 148–150, 189, 284, 297–299, 315, 318–319, 345, 361, 387, 389, 390, 392, 409; French acceptance of, 147–148, 150; Russian attitudes toward formation of, 323, 324, 344, 385; Western Allies' attitudes toward, 144

Gimbel, John, 25
Glover, C. D., 225
Graham, Philip L., 339
Greece, 38, 84, 178, 182, 249
Gross, Ernest A., 124n
"Groupthink" hypothesis, 418–419

"Halfmoon" emergency plan, 239
Halle, Louis J., 48n, 51, 66n
Harriman, Averell, 52, 72, 147; advice on the Berlin crisis, 246, 250; and decision to restrict U.S. trade with Russia, 117–118; role in foreign policymaking, 79–80; on use of nuclear weapons, 246
Hays, George, 122
Herblock (cartoonist), 147
Hermann, Charles F., 4n, 5
Hickerson, John, 66n, 90; on policy options to resolve the Berlin crisis, 321
Hillenkoetter, Roscoe, 110, 113, 261, 317n; on changes in Soviet foreign policy, 373; on Soviet goals in negotiations, 196
Historians, 238; interpretation of the Cold War by, 23n, 24–26, 48, 49, 238; of diplomatic behavior, 402–403; G. Marshall's role in American foreign policy interpreted by, 85–88
History, role in foreign policymaking, 77, 81
Hitler, Adolf: and the Berlin crisis, 406–407; compared with Joseph Stalin, 61–62, 66n; totalitarianism of, 81
Holsti, Ole: on cognitive abilities and stress, 423; crisis literature reviewed by, 403, 405; on decision groups and stress, 414; on effect of stress on information processing, 410
Howley, Frank, 214n; American foreign policy influenced by, 199; on American military power in Berlin, 187; preparation for the Berlin blockade by, 119–120; role in U.S.-Soviet relations, 155
Hull, Arthur N., 260
Huntington, Samuel, 103, 267

Ideologies, conflict of, 48, 56, 82–83, 105
Images: of D. Acheson, 299–303; of L. Clay, 97–109, 191–193, 295–299; in the crisis period, 173–194; in decision-making, 45–46; of G. Marshall, 85–97, 181–186, 293–295; in the post-crisis period, 292–304; in the pre-crisis period, 69–109; self-image of the Truman Administration, 63–65, 180; of Harry Truman, 69–84, 174–181, 292–293; of the Soviet Union's bargaining style, 174, 181; of the United States, 63–65, 81, 178
Images of the adversary: in the crisis period, 173–174, 177–178, 181, 182, 183, 186, 271; in the post-crisis period, 287–292; in the pre-crisis period, 46, 58–63, 65, 80–81, 83, 91–92, 96–97, 103–104, 105–106; Truman's view of Russia, 81, 408
Information: acquisition of, 7; on Clay's plan for an armed convoy, 232; in the crisis period, 232, 272–273; for diplomatic purposes, 246; impact of crisis-induced stress on, 410–412, 413, 422; from past experience, 406–407, 409; in the post-crisis period, 393–394, 411; in the pre-crisis period, 123–124, 164–165, 167
"Inherent bad faith" model, 62–63
International Court of Justice, 234
International Crisis Behavior project (ICB), ix, 9; decision-making approach to conflict, 5; theoretical propositions and methodology in studies by, 404
International News Service, 380
International structure, influence on American decision-makers, 36–38, 47, 68–69
Iran, 38
Israel, recognition of, 167
Italy, 144, 182, 249

Janis, Irving, 418
Jervis, Robert, 60n
Jessup, Philip: and end of the Berlin crisis, 387; in the post-crisis period, 285, 347; private discussion with Soviet representative Malik, 381–383, 384–385, 386, 395, 397; role in the UN review of the Berlin dispute, 353, 354, 367, 381–382

INDEX   455

Johnson, Louis, 386
Joint Chiefs of Staff (JCS), 97, 123, 125, 132, 165; alternative options evaluated by, 244–245, 258, 259–260, 307–309, 362–363, 399–400, 417, 421; on the armed convoy plan, 307, 309, 400; caution advised by, 267–268; in the crisis period, 186, 213, 224–225, 226, 244–245, 259–260, 265, 266, 267–268, 277; and decisions on the airlift, 332, 333, 360, 361–362, 365–366; emergency plan of, 239, 307; foreign policy criticized by, 362–364, 400; legal standing of, 75; on the possibility of war, 174, 239, 271; in the post-crisis period, 307, 361–363, 396; role in the decision-making process, 277; on withdrawal from Berlin, 308, 400

Kennan, George, 22, 23, 147, 195–196, 378–379; airlift interpreted by, 399; American foreign policy influenced by, 144–145, 290, 370–371; in the Berlin Group, 248; on the communist takeover in Czechoslovakia, 33–34; on containment of Soviet power, 67–68; opinion of G. Marshall, 88–89; OMGUS criticized by, 101n–102n; on policy options to resolve the Berlin crisis, 320, 321, 322, 360–361, 370, 379–380; and the Policy Planning Staff, 89, 94, 285, 320, 321–322; relationship with G. Marshall, 89, 90; Soviet foreign policy interpreted by, 50–52, 59, 65, 66n, 290; on withdrawal of occupation forces from Germany, 298, 303
Kennedy, John F., 70
Kissinger, Henry, 62
Klimov, Gregory, 99n
Koenig, Pierre, 142, 152
Kommandatura, 14, 152, 157, 158, 160, 166; breakup of, 155; change of Soviet tactics in, 113
Korean War, 74
Kuklick, Bruce, 23n, 25n

Landry, Robert B., 243–244
Lange, Halvard, 293–294
League of Nations, 17
Leahy, William D., 75, 243; attitude toward use of atomic bombs, 239; Berlin crisis interpreted by, 176, 224, 225, 226, 234–235; Riga axioms promoted by, 79
Legalism in American foreign policy, 178–179, 182–183, 207, 228, 408; and juridical rights of Western powers in Berlin, 297, 313, 318, 324, 335–336
LeMay, Curtis, 135, 267, 310n–311n; and preparation for war, 120–121; role in the airlift, 204, 243
Lenin, N., 17, 62, 91
Lie, Trygve, 353, 368–369, 371
Lilienthal, David, 254, 255, 338, 391
Lippmann, Walter, 18, 67, 100n; on avoidance of war, 241–242
London conference, 33–34, 110, 143, 229–230; recommendations of, 149–150
London Program, 105, 190, 231; Acheson's commitment to, 379; avoidance of American compromise on, 148, 231, 294, 297–298, 318, 409; completion of, 149, 298; French attitude toward, 148, 156; implementation of, 148–149, 196, 216, 378, 409; role in negotiations to resolve the Berlin crisis, 231, 321, 325, 326, 409; in Stalin's proposals to resolve the Berlin crisis, 314, 316
Long Telegram, 51–53, 55, 103; significance of, 50–52, 54
Lovett, Robert, 43, 125, 147, 182; attitudes toward the ACC and the establishment of Western Germany, 142–143; and bipartisanship, 247, 305; in the crisis period, 171, 199, 206, 218, 219, 220, 222, 235, 247, 248, 249, 250, 260, 263, 273, 278; on diplomatic relations with the Soviet Union, 331; on policy options to resolve the Berlin crisis, 320, 322; in the post-crisis period, 285, 327, 338, 339, 346, 363, 368; replacement of, 377; role in foreign policy, 90, 126, 139, 140, 263, 320, 322; and Truman's decision to retain the American position in Berlin, 408

MacArthur, Douglas, 85, 100
McClelland, Charles, 3, 35n
McCloy, John, 98

"Magistrat" in Berlin, 334, 335, 372–373
Malik, Jacob: and end of the Berlin crisis, 387; private discussions with U.S. representative Jessup, 381–383, 384–385, 386, 395, 397
Marshall, George C., 30, 31, 71, 72, 77, 115, 116, 125, 140, 167; on American military preparation for the Berlin crisis, 182; and American policy in Germany, 95–96, 100; on American resolve to maintain its position in Berlin, 252–253; approach to decision-making, 396–397, 397–398, 407, 409; attitudes on use of the atomic bomb, 359; and the Berlin Group, 246, 273, 393; and the Cold War, 86, 92, 97; on communist-inspired attacks in Berlin, 334; in the crisis period, 171. 181–186, 213, 227, 228, 230, 236, 247, 249, 260, 265, 277; and decision-making in the pre-crisis period, 43, 44, 85–97; decision on the diplomatic approach to resolve the Berlin crisis, 230; diplomatic bargaining position of, 294–295, 316–317, 325–326, 335–336, 350; in diplomatic efforts to resolve the Berlin crisis, 93–94, 315, 316–317, 319, 322, 324–326, 329–330, 331, 335–336, 342, 349–350, 393, 395, 407; evaluated by historians, 85–88; and formation of NATO, 406; and formation of West Germany, 27–28; on French attitudes toward Germany, 58, 147–148, 149; images of, 85–97, 181–186, 293–295; and inter-Allied conflicts, 342; on juridical rights in Berlin, 335–336, 408; military background of, 85, 89–90, 93; opinion of the Soviet Union, 92, 97, 182, 293–294; policies to resolve the Berlin crisis, 184–186, 332, 335–336; on the possibility of war, 174, 391; in the post-crisis period, 283, 284, 293–295, 302, 309, 310; relationship with President Truman, 88, 89, 249–250, 356–359; retirement of, 287, 377; role in foreign policy, 87–97, 145, 182–183; on Russian policies in Germany, 29, 32; stress experienced by, 181–182, 358, 407–408, 409; and the UN treatment of the Berlin crisis, 338–339, 346, 347, 349, 353, 354, 355, 357, 359, 361, 368, 371, 372; and U.S. propaganda, 157; and U.S. universal military training, 95
Marshall Plan, 29, 31, 84, 179; and communist takeover of Czechoslovakia, 33; genesis of, 94; public opinion of, 30; success of, 144
Masaryk, Jan, 34
Massigli, René, 311
Military: and American B-29 bombers in Britain, 228, 234, 235–240, 243–244, 254, 263; caution in crisis advised by, 267–268, 290; custody of the atomic bomb by, 254–255, 256, 257; diplomatic negotiations of, 229–230, 273; joint planning with Britain, 214–215, 224–226; level of American strength during the Berlin crisis, 38, 183, 187, 214, 250, 267, 290; powers of the Secretary of Defense, 334; preparation for the Berlin crisis, 119–121; reasons to increase the strength of, 92, 93; recommendations on American strategy choices, 217–218, 223–224, 244–246, 266, 267–268, 275, 307–310; requests for increases in the defense budget, 107, 359, 363; role in policymaking and decision-making, 85, 90, 98–103, 115–117, 128–134 *passim*, 159, 169, 173, 199–206, 225, 266–267, 275, 277–278, 290–291; technology in, 36, 37–38; universal training for, 95. *See also* Clay, Lucius D.; National Military Establishment
Millis, Walter, 219–220, 238
"Mini-blockade," 163, 202, 416; defined, 43
Models: of American presidential choices in foreign policy, 70–71; of crisis behavior, 6–10, 402–423; of "inherent bad faith," 62–63; U-curve model, 403–404, 405, 410
Molotov, Viacheslav, 248, 249, 250, 311, 313; responses to Western diplomatic efforts, 312, 314, 322, 323, 326, 331, 333, 336, 343, 344–345; role in Soviet-American relations, 145, 146, 314, 317, 318; on Soviet

INDEX 457

postwar policies in Germany, 23–24, 26, 28, 32
Monde, Le, 145
Moore, Admiral, 225–226
Moscow conference, 28–30, 80, 93
Munich analogy, 66, 409
Murphy, Robert, 11, 21, 27, 29, 43, 260; airlift strategy criticized by, 264–266; and American anticipation of the Berlin blockade, 110, 112, 113; and American foreign policy, 101, 129, 212; Berlin crisis interpreted by, 270; on the Byrnes-Clay partnership, 102; in the crisis period, 171, 176, 200, 212, 258, 259–260; on the currency reform, 151, 157, 270; on the establishment of West Germany, 143; land convoy and the airlift compared by, 418–419; in the post-crisis period, 342, 347, 364, 366, 370, 382, 394; Soviet foreign policy interpreted by, 115, 161, 163, 174, 270; and U.S. diplomatic encounters with the Soviet Union, 93

National Military Establishment, 364; creation of, 74–75; and custody of the atomic bomb, 254–255, 256, 257, 278; use of atomic weapons by, 340
National Security Act: bypassing of, 220, 222, 280, 414; establishment and purposes of, 72–74
National Security Council (NSC), 147, 245, 254, 259, 276; and anticipation of the Berlin blockade, 110, 111; and augmentation of the airlift in the post-crisis period, 349, 360, 365, 366, 389, 398; bypassed in the crisis period, 277, 278; decision on the airlift, 260–263, 265–269, 280, 283; decision on B-29 bombers in Britain, 235–236; decision on use of atomic weapons, 339–340, 391; in the decision-making process during the crisis period, 199, 235–236, 251, 260–263, 265–266, 276, 277, 414; establishment and duties of, 73–74, 220; evaluation of, 398, 400, 417; information available to and processed by, 276, 411; options in the Berlin crisis reviewed by, 331–332, 417; on the possibility of war, 174; in the post-crisis period, 336, 339–340, 368, 374, 389, 397, 398, 400; relationship with the American president, 284; response to criticism by the JCS, 363–364; on U.S. policy toward the Soviet Union, 288, 305, 308
NATO, origins and formation of, 121, 378, 406
Negotiations. *See* Diplomacy
Noce, Daniel, 116, 125
Noiret, Roger, 327
Norstad, Lauris, 218
North Atlantic Treaty Organization. *See* NATO
Norway, 108
Noyes, David, 356
NSC. *See* National Security Council
Nuclear weapons: American deployment and stockpile of, 238–239; and American deterrent strategies, 239–240, 244; American monopoly of, 38, 359; custody of, 254–257; decision on use of, 339–341, 391; recommendations for use of, 245–246, 359; and threat of nuclear retaliation, 238, 359; and U.S. instigation of war, 341–342; and the U.S. Strategic Air Command, 237. *See also* Atomic bomb

Oder-Neisse line, 22, 28
Office of European Affairs, 321
Office of Military Government of the United States for Germany (OMGUS), 97, 157, 160, 205; criticism of, 101n–102n; information supplied by, 272–273; role in American policymaking, 101
Office of United Nations Affairs, 354
OMGUS. *See* Office of Military Government of the United States for Germany
"Operation Bird Dog," 151

Petersen, Maurice, 311
Policy Planning Staff (PPS), 94, 285; current evaluation of, 399, 417; establishment of, 89; opinion of the Soviet Union, 287, 291; on options to resolve the Berlin crisis, 320–322, 360–361, 369–370, 399, 417;

Policy Planning Staff (*continued*)
and Smith's analysis of the American position in Berlin, 348n
Politics, American attitudes toward power politics, 63–64
Politics, domestic: and bureaucratic influences on decision-making, 209–210; influence on foreign policy, 305, 325–326, 340–341, 346–347, 355–359, 369; influence on national security, 256–257. *See also* Truman, Harry, presidential campaign of
Post-crisis period, 283–401; attitudinal prism during, 287–292; assessment and search for alternatives in, 285, 302, 316–317, 320–322, 332, 345–346, 362–363, 367, 369–370, 383, 399–401; consultation in, 339, 342, 347, 394–397, 412–413; coping mechanisms in, 393–401; decisional forums in, 397–398; decisions made during, 285–286, 316, 319, 332, 340, 350, 352, 355, 357, 366, 368, 375, 381, 383; defined, 8; environmental change in, 389; images in, 292–304; information processing in, 393–394; probability of war in, 284, 289, 290, 292, 294, 296, 297, 310, 345, 348, 388, 389, 390–391, 392; psychological environment of, 287–304; threat to basic values in, 389–390, 392; time pressure in, 283, 294, 296, 304, 345, 354, 355, 359, 361, 388, 389, 391–393, 395
Potsdam conference, 14, 26, 30; agreements of, 19, 21–22, 24, 25, 81, 113, 156, 197, 354
Power: in American world-view, 56; balance-of-power after the Second World War, 17–18, 95; global struggle for, 31; in international communism, 59–60; Truman's images of, 82
Powers, Richard J., 54n
Pre-crisis period, 43–168; assessment and search for alternatives during, 124–127, 130–131, 167–168, 415–416; case findings applied to theories on, 162–168; consultation in, 125–128, 165–166, 412; decisional forums in, 166–167; decisions made during, 44, 115, 118, 127, 152, 159; defined, 8; duration of, 43; environmental change in, 162–163; information processing in, 123–124, 164–165, 167; perceived by President Truman, 83–84; probability of war in, 163–164; threat to basic American values in, 163, 165; time pressure in, 12, 14, 164
"Press leaks," and decision-making, 358, 386
Progressive Party, 176
Propaganda: American, 155, 157; Soviet, 112–113, 149
Psychological environment: in the crisis period, 173–194; effect of stress on cognitive performance, 405–410, 422–423; in the post-crisis period, 287–304; in the pre-crisis period, 45–109. *See also* Attitudinal prism; Images
Public opinion, American. *See* United States, public opinion in foreign policy of

Quemoy crisis, 420

Radford, Arthur W., 260
Realism, in American approach to foreign policy, 47, 49, 55–56, 57, 64, 101, 109, 287
Reber, Samuel, 248
Republicans, opinions of, 75–76, 88, 247, 287, 305, 306, 411
Reuter, Ernst, 203
Riga axioms, 55, 66n, 103, 371; advocated by Dean Acheson, 79, 287; American foreign policy dominated by, 173; ascendancy of, 52, 53, 87; described, 50–52; linked with national security, 56; proponents of, 79, 87, 287; viewed by G. Marshall, 87–88, 92
Risk in foreign policy, 210, 390; in American foreign policy, 179–180, 181; of the armed convoy plan vs. the airlift, 262–263, 271; evaluation of, 419; in Soviet foreign policy, 174, 182, 288
Roberts, Frank, 311
Robertson, Brian, 129, 131, 140, 142, 163, 386; and British aircraft destroyed by the Soviet Union, 133–134; in the crisis period, 188, 202, 204, 215, 222, 225; and the

currency reform, 152, 153, 157, 159; diplomatic relations with Sokolovsky, 228, 229; role in diplomatic efforts to resolve the Berlin crisis, 152, 153, 327, 349, 355
Roosevelt, Franklin D., 72, 77, 176; and presidential decision-making, 70; postwar strategies of, 17, 48, 49
Royall, Kenneth, 43, 98, 100, 108; and American commitment to remain in Berlin, 111; in the crisis period, 171, 187, 188, 199, 201, 202, 205, 206–207, 216, 218, 219, 220, 229, 250, 260, 278; and diplomatic negotiations to resolve the Berlin crisis, 327, 330, 342, 344–345, 374–375; and free access to Berlin, 123, 124, 125, 127–128, 129; on policy options to resolve the Berlin crisis, 383; on the possibility of war, 163; in the post-crisis period, 285, 318, 319, 327, 332, 333, 337, 363, 364, 374n, 396; Soviet motivations interpreted by, 64–65; strategy recommended by, 245–246
Ruhr district: British occupation of, 19; control of, 24, 27, 28, 32, 149, 150, 153
Rusk, Dean, 248, 249; and UN consideration of the Berlin dispute, 354
Russia. *See* Soviet Union

SAC. *See* Strategic Air Command
Saltzman, Charles, 90, 100, 101n, 364; in the Berlin Group, 248
Saxony, 207
Schlesinger, Arthur, 23n
Schnabel, James F., 57n, 58n
Schuman, Robert, 286, 349, 352, 382, 385, 395
Security, American, 56, 61, 72–74; in the "bureaucratic politics" paradigm, 209–210; influence of domestic politics on, 256–257; threat of the Berlin blockade to, 96, 97; threat of Russian totalitarianism to, 79–84, 177. *See also* Central Intelligence Agency; National Security Council
Security, Soviet, 49, 50–51, 64, 80
Self-image: of President Truman, 180; of the United States, 63–65, 81, 178–179

Shlaim, Avi, ix–x
Smith, Jean Edward, 102n; evaluation of George Marshall, 85–86, 87, 96
Smith, Kinsbury, 380
Smith, Walter Bedell, 22–23, 29n, 85, 91, 211n, 347, 382; on the American position in Berlin, 348; and American-Soviet relations, 145, 146, 289; on American strategy choices, 139; Berlin blockade anticipated by, 31; in diplomatic efforts to resolve the Berlin crisis, 297, 310, 311, 312, 313–315, 316, 318, 322, 323–325, 333, 334, 335, 342, 343, 344, 395; negotiations with Stalin, 297, 313–315, 322–325
Smoke, Richard, 68–69, 181n
Snyder, Glenn H., 4, 47n, 55n, 68n, 173n, 196n
Socialism, 105
Sokolovsky, Vassily Danilovitch, 161, 183, 216n, 219, 222, 279; and British aircraft destroyed by the Soviet Union, 133–134; and commencement of the Berlin blockade, 34, 43, 101, 116; in diplomatic efforts to resolve the Berlin crisis, 189, 229–230, 328, 329, 330, 331, 332–333, 336, 343, 344, 391, 394; diplomatic relations with Britain, 228; reaction to the currency reform proposal, 156–157, 158, 159; reasons for departure from the Allied Control Council, 113–114; meetings with Western leaders, 229–230
Souers, Sidney, 147
Soviet Union: agreement to end the Berlin blockade, 118, 364–365; attitude toward the formation of West Germany, 323, 324, 344, 385; and American anticipation of the Berlin blockade, 110–115; and American foreign policy in the post-crisis period, 288, 290–292; on centralized administration of Germany, 32, 113–114, 197; changes in foreign policy of, 373–374, 380; and communization of Germany, 21, 24, 29, 104–105, 197; compared with Nazi Germany, 61–62, 66, 81, 113, 406; and the currency reform in Germany, 156–157, 158, 159–161, 196, 233, 314, 315, 316, 318, 319, 322,

Soviet Union (*continued*)
323, 326, 375–376, 380, 382; departure from the Allied Control Council, 34–35, 43, 101, 113–114, 116, 117, 121, 162–163; diplomatic encounters with the United States and the Western powers, 28–30, 93–94, 229–231, 233, 322–325, 328–330, 343–344, 350–352, 381–382, 411 (*see also* Molotov; Sokolovsky; Stalin); East European satellites of, 30, 118–119; and end of the Berlin crisis, 364–365, 387–388, 392; and the "inherent bad faith" model, 62–63; interpretation of American foreign policy goals by, 64–65; foreign policy goals viewed by American decision-makers, 21, 49–55, 60–61, 66–67, 79–84, 91–94, 96–97, 103–104, 110–115, 138–139, 144, 157, 174, 179, 197, 287–288, 331, 373, 411; and the formation of Eastern and Western Germany, 34, 197; interaction with American policy toward postwar Germany, 23–30, 110–111, 144–145, 193–194, 373–374, 376; nuclear weapons of, 38; policy on unification vs. occupation of Germany, 18, 19–20, 21, 23–36, 110–111, 197, 233; possible response to an armed convoy, 421; reasons for the Berlin blockade, 35–36, 64–65, 84, 96, 107–108, 113–114, 115, 197, 230, 373; restrictions on American trains to Berlin, 122–135, 162, 229; and the United Nations consideration of the Berlin dispute, 352, 354, 355, 364, 367, 371; U.S. trade embargo of, 117–119, 206–207 (*see also* Counterblockade); viewed by the United States as an adversary, 58–63, 65–66, 80–83, 91–92, 96–97, 103–104, 173–174, 177–178, 287–292, 293, 408

Spanier, John, 36–37

Stalin, Joseph, 17, 23, 71, 80; American interest to negotiate with, 184, 248, 250, 253, 254, 263, 269, 310, 311, 356, 357, 371, 396; and American-Soviet relations, 29, 147; compared with Hitler, 61–62, 66n; on the division of Germany, 34; on imposition of social systems, 18; in negotiations to resolve the Berlin crisis, 297, 313–314, 322–325, 329, 330, 331, 342, 343, 344; proposals to end the Berlin crisis, 314, 315, 316, 317; and resolution of the Berlin crisis, 118, 380, 381; and U.S. access to Berlin, 124, 126; and Soviet power, 59–60

Stereotypes, use of, 405, 407

Stimson, Henry, 64

Strang, William, 140–141, 150, 163, 212, 273, 311; information processed by, 411

Strategic Air Command (SAC), 223; effect of the airlift on, 244; nuclear weapons of, 237

Strategy choices: American allies in, 139–142, 147–150, 153, 166, 184–185, 198, 214–216; by the American presidency, 207–211 (*see also* Truman, Harry); analyzed by Draper, 216–217; based on assessment of Soviet intentions, 138–139, 174, 181, 183–186, 191–193; based on testing of capabilities, 419–420; current evaluation of, 419–422; government decision-making process on, 206–207, 218–22, 235–236, 251–252; at the height of the crisis, 242–251, 260–266, 268–269; influences on, 65–69; recommended by G. Marshall, 184–186; recommended by L. Clay in the crisis period, 189–191, 200–206 (*see also* Clay, Lucius D.); stress caused by conflicting values in, 195–196. *See also* Alternatives

Stress induced by crisis: assessment of the level of, 404–405, 410; beneficial effects of, 422–423; case findings applied to theories on, 402–423; causes of in the decision-making process, 195–196, 198, 199, 269; coping mechanisms activated by, 164–165; in the crisis behavior model, 7–9, 402–423; defined, 7, 164; experienced by L. Clay, 186–187, 188, 327, 408, 409, 411; experienced by G. Marshall, 181–182, 358, 407–408, 409; experienced by President Truman, 209, 275, 338, 358, 408, 409; and failure in ne-

INDEX

gotiations, 336, 337; and the possibility of war, 338; in the pre-crisis period, 164–165, 166–167; reduction of, 269, 270, 345
Stress induced by crisis, effects on, 9, 402–423; assessment and search for alternatives, 278–279, 400–401, 415–423; cognitive performance, 405–410, 422–423; the consultative process, 246–251, 274–275, 276–277, 396–397, 412–413; decisional forums, 8, 414–415; information processing, 410–412, 422; presidential decision-making, 358
"Structured empiricism," 6–10
Sullivan, John L., 218, 260
Surprise element in crisis, 11, 110, 195; and American anticipation of the Berlin blockade, 37, 107, 110–115, 119–120, 154, 168, 195
Symington, Stuart, 204, 254, 255, 260; and the airlift, 319–320, 374; and the possibility of war, 338

"Task Force Truculent," 383
Teleconferences, 410; evaluated by L. Clay, 166
Thompson, Llewellyn, 382
Thorp, Willard, 347
Threat, 6; to the American position in Berlin, 115; to American security, 177; American sensitivity to, 56; increase of, 171; information processing influenced by, 410–412; to international peace, 355; of Russian totalitarianism, 79–83, 177; of Soviet restrictions on trains to Berlin, 124–126
Threat to basic American values: caused by the Berlin blockade, 12, 304; in the crisis period, 181–182, 186–187, 189–190, 270–271; in the definition of crisis, 5, 6, 7, 11–12; and effects of crisis-induced stress, 406; in the post-crisis period, 389–390, 392; in the pre-crisis period, 163, 165
Thuringia, 161, 207
Time pressure: in American decision to use the United Nations, 354, 361; in American response to the blockade, 11–12, 14; in the crisis period, 171, 182, 186–187, 188, 232, 247, 268, 269, 272, 279; in the definition of crisis, 5–6, 7; effects of crisis-induced stress on, 9, 409; in favor of the Russians, 345, 392; in the post-crisis period, 283, 294, 296, 304, 345, 354, 355, 359, 361, 388, 389, 391–393, 395; in the pre-crisis period, 12, 14, 164; reduction of, 283, 294, 296, 304
Totalitarianism, American perception of, 49, 79–83, 177, 406
Trade embargo: decision-making process on, 117–119, 165, 206–207, 319; efficacy of the counterblockade, 118, 377, 378, 380, 392; and retaliation against Soviet shipping, 130
Trizonia, 136
Truman Administration, 23; attitudinal prism of, 55–69; anticipation of the Berlin blockade, 110–115, 195; attitude toward Western Germany, 27, 105; Cold War strategy of, 26, 27, 82; containment strategy of, 67–68 (*see also* Containment policy); decisions in response to the Soviet exodus from the ACC, 115–119; foreign policy of, 75–84, 105, 147, 175–181, 275–276, 362–364, 369, 377, 378; options reviewed by, 242–251, 260–263, 278, 302; personnel changes in, 377; role of the Cabinet in, 44, 71–72, 95, 117–118, 206–207, 277, 336, 338, 398; self-image of, 63–65; Soviet foreign policy interpreted by, 49–55, 62, 79–84; stress in the decision-making process of, 195–196. See also Truman, Harry
Truman Doctrine, 30–31, 55, 64, 299; described, 82; G. Marshall's opinion of, 92
Truman, Harry, 12, 146, 147; airlift decisions of, 207–211, 262–263, 268–269, 275, 366, 415, 416; American-Soviet relations viewed by, 54–55, 79–84, 408; attitudes on the use of the atomic bomb, 255–257, 337–338, 340, 391; Berlin crisis interpreted by, 35, 83–84, 366; bipartisanship promoted by, 75–76, 247, 275–276, 305–306, 372, 396; and Cabinet influences on decision-making, 71–72, 208, 398 (*see also* Cabi-

462 INDEX

Truman, Harry (*continued*)
net, American); capacity and approach to decision-making, 77–79, 177, 180, 208–209, 221–222, 251–252, 268, 275, 278, 280, 358, 366, 396, 408, 409, 413, 414–415; consultation used by, 249–251, 260–263, 274–275, 413; decisions in the crisis period, 171, 175–181, 207–211, 220–222, 235, 236–237, 239, 250, 251–252, 255–256, 273, 277, 408, 414–415, 416–417; decision on the B-29 bombers, 235, 236–237, 239, 417; decision on custody and use of the atomic bomb, 255–257, 337; decision on maintenance of the American position in Berlin, 220–222, 224, 225, 227, 250, 251, 252, 277, 280, 408, 414; and decision-making during the pre-crisis period, 43, 44, 69–84; and end of the Berlin blockade, 388; foreign policy of, 175–181, 220–222, 247, 292–293, 300, 305–308, 310, 356–359, 362–363, 371–372, 375, 396; historical approach to policymaking, 77, 81, 406–407, 409; images of, 69–84, 174–181, 292–293, 408; information processing by, 410–411; institutional framework bypassed by, 210, 219–220, 221–222, 251–252, 268, 277, 278, 414; interest in negotiating with Stalin, 356, 357, 371, 396; meetings with Clay, 258, 261, 262, 263–264, 275, 366, 411; on the possibility of war, 12, 174, 179–180, 251, 338, 391; presidential campaign of, 174–176, 247, 256–257, 259, 283, 305–306, 340–341, 346–347, 355–359, 369, 393, 396, 406; in the post-crisis period, 283–284, 329, 331, 332, 338–339, 346, 356–359, 366, 371, 375, 381, 385–386, 393; relations with Congress, 54–55, 75–76, 83, 88, 165, 247, 250; relationship with G. Marshall, 88, 356–359; response to Soviet restrictions on American train service to Berlin, 126–127; self-image of, 180; stress experienced by, 209, 275, 338, 358, 408, 409; as the "ultimate decision-maker," 69, 277; world-view of, 81–83, 222. *See also* American presidency
Turkey, 38, 80, 84, 178

U-curve model, 403–404, 405, 410
United Nations, 83, 346–347, 352–355, 359, 371–372, 374–377, 397; alternatives for American strategies in, 367–368; American consideration of referring the Berlin dispute to, 332, 333, 336, 338–339, 345–346, 350, 353; American delegation to, 338, 346, 353, 372, 395–396, 413; and the currency reform, 367, 368, 372, 373, 374–376; goals of the U.S. in, 353–354, 359, 361, 368–369, 392; and resolution of the Berlin crisis, 185, 234, 245, 248; Security Council consideration of the Berlin dispute, 284, 351, 352–355, 359, 364, 366–367, 372, 376, 392; suspicion of U.S. motives in, 368–369, 374
United States: attitude toward allies of, 57–58, 96, 97, 108–109 (*see also* Allies); credibility of commitment to allies of, 12, 237, 339–340, 347; interaction with Russian policies in Germany, 23–27, 95–97; occupation of Germany by, 71; policies leading to the partition of Germany, 21–35 *passim*, 96 (*see also* Germany, Western); position on centralized administration of occupied Germany, 19, 23; propaganda of, 155, 157; public opinion in foreign policy of, 30, 63–64, 65, 76–77, 92, 107, 132, 147, 176, 241, 257, 294, 326, 339, 356; self-image of, 63–65, 81, 178–179; trade embargo with Soviet Union and satellites, 117–119, 130, 165, 206–207, 319 (*see also* Counterblockade); universal military training in, 95. *See also* American presidency; Foreign policy; National Security Act; National Security Council
United States Air Force in Europe (USAFE), 120–121

Vandenberg, Arthur, 249, 412; and bipartisan foreign policy, 75–76, 247, 275, 306; in the post-crisis period, 338, 342, 353, 357, 372, 395
Vandenberg, Hoyt, 225, 260; airlift strategy evaluated by, 244, 261–262, 263, 268, 269, 275, 319–320; emergency war plans of, 244; and use of the atomic bomb, 337, 338

INDEX

Vinson, Fred, 72, 356–358, 396
Vishinsky, Andrey, 331, 351, 385
Vyrianov, Colonel, 161, 207

Wallace, Henry, 147, 176, 177–178, 356
Walsh, Robert, 200
Waltz, Kenneth, 37
War: American avoidance of, 131, 176, 196, 201, 250, 262, 267, 269, 291, 292, 419; American public opinion of, 257–258; avoided by the Soviet Union, 288–289; British attitudes toward, 141; and the currency reform, 188, 207; and maintenance of the American position in Berlin, 179–181, 362, 363, 364; preparation for, 120–121, 244; preventive, 341, 353, 356; and Soviet restrictions on American access to Berlin, 123, 124, 125, 126, 131–132; U.S. instigation of, 341–342
War, probability of, 69, 83; in the definition of crisis, 5, 6, 7, 9, 37; doubt of, 106–107, 123, 124, 137, 187, 188, 194, 216, 217; during failure of diplomatic negotiations, 337, 338; increase during the crisis period, 171, 174, 175, 181, 200, 207, 243–244, 271; in the post-crisis period, 284, 289, 290, 292, 294, 296, 297, 310, 345, 348, 388, 389, 390–391, 392; in the pre-crisis period, 163–164
Warsaw declaration of the Soviet Union, 212, 230, 279; described 196–197
Washington Post, 147, 339
Webb, James, 377, 382
Wedemeyer, Albert, 125, 127, 130, 261, 333; and the airlift to Berlin, 205, 206; Berlin crisis interpreted by, 203–214, 217
Welles, Sumner, 241
Williams, Phil, 419n
World-view, 45; of American decision-makers, 55–58, 65, 66, 68, 287; of President Truman, 81–83

Yalta axioms, 79; defined, 50. *See also* Riga axioms
Yergin, Daniel: convoy plan evaluated by, 421; George Marshall evaluated by, 86–87; on the origins of the Cold War, 50
Young, Oran, 4
Yugoslavia, 60n, 179, 182, 249

Zarubin, Georgiy, 150
Zhukov, Georgiy, 123
Zorin, Valerian, 312

Designer: Eric Jungerman
Compositor: G & S Typesetters, Inc.
Text: 11/13 Caledonia
Display: Caledonia